ADVANCES
in FORENSIC
HUMAN
IDENTIFICATION

ADVANCES
IN FORENSIC
HUMAN
IDENTIFICATION

Edited by

Xanthé Mallett
Teri Blythe
Rachel Berry

CRC Press
Taylor & Francis Group
Boca Raton   London   New York

CRC Press is an imprint of the
Taylor & Francis Group, an **informa** business

BAHID
British Association for Human Identification

Cover image produced by Greg Mahoney.

CRC Press
Taylor & Francis Group
6000 Broken Sound Parkway NW, Suite 300
Boca Raton, FL 33487-2742

© 2014 by Taylor & Francis Group, LLC
CRC Press is an imprint of Taylor & Francis Group, an Informa business

No claim to original U.S. Government works

Printed on acid-free paper
Version Date: 20131114

International Standard Book Number-13: 978-1-4398-2514-3 (Hardback)

Visit the Taylor & Francis Web site at
http://www.taylorandfrancis.com

and the CRC Press Web site at
http://www.crcpress.com

Contents

Part III

DIGITAL AND BIOMETRIC EVIDENCE

Preface

This book is the second publication by the British Association for Human Identification (BAHID, www.BAHID.org). The primary aim of the association is to encourage productive interchange between various disciplines in human identification, promote the academic integration of individual subjects and, through the medium of a collective body, pursue standards of excellence and innovative developments. The membership includes, but is not limited to, professionals in the fields of policing, anthropology, odontology, archaeology, facial anthropology, podiatry, pathology and disaster victim identification. Having been in existence for over a decade, the association now boasts over 500 members from academia, law enforcement and private business, as well as those with institutional and legal backgrounds. Although entitled the British Association, there are members outside the United Kingdom from elsewhere in Europe, the United States and Australia.

Forensic human identification is receiving increased global attention, and an accurate and honest representation of the current methods and modalities that have shaped our current policies and protocols is essential. Consequently, this text was developed in response to the recognised need for suitable and appropriate information that can provide information for practitioners, policymakers and students of this subject by raising awareness of the available technologies and developing themes.

The inaugural text published by BAHID, *Forensic Human Identification: An Introduction* (2007), examined the variety of biological indicators that are available to investigators and illustrated the basic principles of each discipline. The second book is not a re-write of the first text, but instead acts as an addition to, and covers advances in, the most well-known scientific techniques as well as discusses new and developing subjects and modalities of human identification. *Advances in Forensic Human Identification* is a heavily referenced textbook, providing a detailed summary of methods and techniques in international practice either not covered in the original text or aspects that required updating or expansion.

Summary of This Text

This advanced text examines several areas pertinent in today's society in the context of human identification. While some would think of forensic human identification as the physical identification of human remains or identification of offenders, the discussion here looks at a broader definition, to include several additional aspects, for example, online, sexual and biometric identities. Problems associated with investigative practice are discussed, including the developing use of the Internet as a distribution and communication medium for criminal activities, as well as miscarriages of justice resultant from flawed applications or interpretations of forensic evidence and the future of forensic science provision. Dialogue is undertaken from an international perspective, as criminal activity is rarely limited by geographical or procedural boundaries. Where appropriate, case studies are provided to illustrate the use of techniques and the associated problems described in the text.

The book is divided into five parts: (I) Identifying the Unknown, (II) Identification from Soft and Hard Tissues, (III) Digital and Biometric Evidence, (IV) Legal Issues: An International Perspective and (V) Future Considerations and Conclusions.

Part I contains four chapters. Chapter 1 addresses the serious (but largely unacknowledged) issue of people who go missing, a situation that has far-reaching and enduring consequences. Included is a discussion of the emotional, social, legal, financial and practical impacts on families of missing people who are unable to gain closure as they experience the ambiguous loss of mourning someone whose fate is unknown. Chapter 2 clarifies the coroner's role in death investigations in the United Kingdom—important information for all involved in forensic investigations as the coroner has the ultimate responsibility under statute for identification of individuals. This chapter begins with a summary of the general laws and guidelines that influence a coroner's practice, followed by a summary of the coroner's role in mass fatality incidents, both at home and abroad. Chapter 3 looks at the identification process following a mass fatality event, facilitated by the comparison of antemortem and postmortem records. This chapter describes up-to-date standards, guidelines and procedures currently used for disaster victim identification, as proficient data management is pivotal to the success of the identification process in large-scale identification events. Further discussion highlights the human rights issues associated with mass fatality events. Chapter 4 addresses the challenging topic of the identification of child sex offenders. Accurate and reliable methods of identifying those who offend against children is becoming ever more pertinent, as almost daily, news agencies around the world cover new and historical cases of alleged child sexual abuse. In terms of forensic human identification, this is unfortunately set to be a key theme for many years to come. This chapter aims to offer some insight into offender demographics, with a view to improving our understanding of child sex offenders and therefore our ability to identify them and manage high-risk cases.

Part II comprises five chapters. It begins with Chapter 5. A key aspect of the forensic anthropologist's role, and the question often at the forefront of an inquiry when skeletal material is recovered, is 'are the remains human?' Intact elements are often fairly easily identified by an experienced forensic anthropologist; however, it is more difficult to make a diagnosis with fragmentary bones present, or those with adhering soft tissue. This chapter summarises some of the key differences and identifiers to help determine the origin of a bone or skeleton, with discussion limited to those areas most often discovered and most often confused with human remains. Chapters 6 and 7 together offer a comprehensive discussion of the identification of fire-damaged human remains, a topic not covered in the original text. In cases of fire-related deaths, there is generally a legal requirement for positive identification of any individuals fatally involved. However, fire is one of the most destructive forces encountered in the modern environment, and individuals in cases of extreme thermal disruption are particularly difficult to identify as a result of other primary identifiers often being lost. An understanding of the heat-induced alterations to bone is a necessary prerequisite for the subsequent identification of any remains (human or otherwise) encountered. Therefore, Chapter 6 details fire dynamics and the effects on human remains, as well as body recovery techniques, including methods of documentation and excavation in the field. Chapter 7 develops this through discussion of contemporary methods of identification and laboratory analysis. Chapter 8 reviews the use of stable isotope profiling (also known as 'human provenancing') in forensic casework, building on the chapter relating to this topic in the original text and evaluating advances in the field since 2007. Stable isotope profiling is a particularly useful tool for forensic investigators as it can distinguish between two seemingly 'identical' materials, thus making this science an invaluable means for providing comparative analysis of materials of interest in forensic casework. Chapter 9 details a case study that incorporated many aspects of forensic human identification, illustrating their usage in a complex case where the skull of a Caucasian male was recovered from the nets of a fishing trawler. The subsequent investigation demonstrates how a significant amount of information can be gathered from the sciences of forensic pathology, anthropology and odontology, as well as stable isotope profiling and craniofacial analysis.

Part III comprises five chapters. Chapter 10 raises concerns around the use of the term 'unique' in relation to the human face—a discussion that has become increasingly prominent in the forensic sphere, as the face is the most individually recognisable part of the human body, and this, taken together with the increase in crime levels, means that forensic facial recognition experts are more frequently called upon to express opinions in an attempt to identify victims or offenders. Chapter 11 details the complex procedure by which a witness and a composite operator arrive at a final image, which is demonstrated to be a multifaceted interplay of computer imaging and human cognitive function. Different types of facial composite generation are described.

One technique, in particular, is highlighted, that of EFIT-V, and the operational procedure employed is provided, in association with future directions of the technology. Chapter 12 discusses relatively new methods applied to the evaluation of human remains that were not covered in the original book. The text focuses on three-dimensional surface scanning technologies and their utility for forensic human identification. Discussion relates to the development of these technologies into the capacity to perform 'virtual autopsies', whereby noninvasive imaging techniques can be used as an alternative to postmortems. The process involves surface laser scans being taken prior to autopsy, which can be photomapped to document injuries or other markings. This is a noncontact method, and internal structures can be examined via medical imaging before they are irreversibly disturbed by more invasive examinations during the postmortem. The benefits of using anthropological techniques in virtual space that extend beyond the autopsy suite and into teaching and research are also illustrated. Chapter 13 addresses advances in genetic identification techniques. Here, the potential forensic uses of ribonucleic acid (any of a class of single-stranded nucleic acid molecules of ribose and uracil, important in protein synthesis and in the transmission of genetic information transcribed from DNA) are discussed. This is a significant development, as in forensic casework the 'remains' often occur in the form of body fluid stains such as blood, semen or saliva. Identification in these cases is usually performed via analysis of specific markers or polymorphisms in the human genetic material, the deoxyribonucleic acid (DNA). This chapter, however, focuses primarily on the fact that RNA pools are tissue specific, leading to the possibility of 'RNA fingerprinting' for the identification of unknown tissue types, for example, body fluids found in biological traces. If current predictions regarding the potential for RNA analysis in forensic casework prove correct, the use of RNA techniques may revolutionise forensic body fluid analysis. Chapter 14 also deals with a staple of forensic human identification, namely, advances in fingerprint techniques. This chapter discusses the progression of fingerprint retrieval and analytical techniques developed since the publication of *Forensic Human Identification: An Introduction* in 2007. Since then, there have been many advances in this field, with legislative and technological changes impacting the collection, retention and processing of fingerprints. Furthermore, as a result of mass disasters such as the 2004 Boxing Day tsunami, progression is particularly evident within the disaster victim identification context, and the collection of friction ridge detail from deceased individuals, including heavily decomposed human remains.

Part IV consists of five chapters. Chapter 15 details pertinent issues in the admissibility of expert evidence, both in the United Kingdom and the United States. As a result of the increased reliance of expert testimony, the significance of the practitioners involved in criminal proceedings having a solid grounding in this area cannot be overemphasised. Relevant sources are evaluated, and the discussion provides insight into the responsibilities of the expert witness in court. In addition, a summary of the most relevant subjects all practitioners engaged in forensic practice should be aware of is provided. Chapter 16 builds on the discussion of expert evidence testimony initiated in previous chapters, exploring some problematic areas for expert scientific evidence in the investigation and prosecution of cases of child sexual abuse, a topic of increased social importance. In particular, the text focuses on the difficulties of gathering sufficient evidence to justify a prosecution, as well as the challenges concerning trustworthiness presented by emerging science together with the significant obstacles facing the law and science relationship, especially the use of expert scientific evidence in court. Chapter 17 addresses the issue of sex tourism, as illustrated through the case study at the US–Mexico border. This has always been a region of shifting and contested boundaries, legal and illegal immigration, cross-border trade and illegal smuggling, and military, cultural, economic and legal struggles. However, the scale of sex tourism involving women and children, both at the border and in other parts of the world, goes largely unrecognised. Although seldom acknowledged, the international exploitation of women and children in the illicit sex trade is a burgeoning twenty-first-century problem, discussed here to emphasise the issues involved, including the problems associated with reducing child sex trafficking and exploitation. Chapters 18 and 19 review the various causes of miscarriages of justice in the United Kingdom and the United States respectively. Initially, Chapter 18 outlines the definitions and prime causes of 'miscarriage of justice', providing examples of cases where forensic identification methods have been at the heart of these incidents. The text then goes on to examine the mechanisms in England and Wales for remedying miscarriages of justice and evaluates their success. Chapter 19 continues this discussion, debating the weaknesses in seemingly reliable forensic evidence types, using the DNA 'gold standard' as an illustration of the difficulties that arise when evidence is misinterpreted or misrepresented. Dialogue relates to flawed evidence being admitted in legal proceedings and the resultant damage done to the justice system as a whole.

Part V concludes the book. It comprises one chapter that summarises the current position of forensic science in the United Kingdom and what the future may hold. Written by the United Kingdom's forensic regulator, Chapter 20 synopsises the recent changes to the structuring of forensic science provision, exploring recent events and the pressures for change as the context within which to assess the future for forensic science, ultimately asking what the future is for forensic science in the United Kingdom.

Taken together, the chapters illustrate a number of key themes in forensic human identification: the continued and increasing reliance on forensic techniques in court; the significance of suitable rules governing the admissibility of expert evidence, as well as the problems that can occur when forensic evidence is misinterpreted or misrepresented in judicial proceedings; changes in criminal behaviour as a result of technological advances and increased globalisation of resources and the requirement for subsequent associated changes to methods of crime investigation, including novel techniques to keep up with new illicit activities; and questions as to what the future of forensic science may be, given its recent turbulent history. The collection provides an important contribution to the ongoing practitioner and academic debates surrounding the application of forensic technologies and underlines the need to research, evaluate and apply techniques appropriately, as issues certainly arise when this does not happen. A CD featuring color images from the text is included.

Editors

Xanthé Mallett is a senior lecturer in forensic criminology and forensic science and is now based in Australia. She has worked on a collaborative facial recognition project with the FBI, undertaken casework in the area of child sex abuse and has coauthored expert witness reports. Her research relates to behaviour patterns of sex offenders, and societal, legal and political responses to cases of child sexual abuse on an international scale. Xanthé has been involved with BAHID for many years, fulfilling several roles including serving as student representative, conference convener and membership secretary. In her professional capacity, she has also presented and contributed to a number of television series, including *History Cold Case*, *The Decrypters*, *National Treasures Live*, *Coast Australia* and *Wanted*.

Teri Blythe is a specialist in forensic art and human identification with a background in human anatomy and forensic anthropology. She has spent many years working in the field of missing persons, including as head of identification while with the Missing People charity. Her expertise includes forensic artwork such as postmortem facial reconstructions and both child and adult age progressions. Teri has been a council member of BAHID for a number of years.

Rachel Berry is currently undertaking a PhD in biomedical engineering at the University of Auckland, New Zealand. She holds a BSc (hons) in forensic anthropology, an MSc in human identification and has over five years experience demonstrating gross human anatomy. Her previous research projects include the impact of scavenging on the recovery of human remains, evaluation of the potential of geometric morphometric techniques to identify offenders by the shape of their hand and human provenancing using stable isotope analysis of hair and bone. Rachel was previously a member of the Council for the British Association for Human Identification.

Contributors

Llian Alys is a lecturer in forensic psychology at the University of Bedfordshire. She is a British Psychological Society chartered psychologist, a full associate of the International Association of Investigative Psychology and a consultant for forensic psychological services (University of Middlesex). She has previously worked in the National Policing Improvement Agency's Serious Crime Analysis Section as a crime analyst and the UK Missing Persons Bureau as the policy and research officer. Her research relates to missing persons and sexual and violent offending.

Joe Apps is a retired police officer having worked for Hampshire Constabulary for 33 years, the last five of which were as basic command unit commander for North East Hampshire. On retirement, Joe worked as the head of criminal justice for the States of Jersey Police before taking on the manager's post with the Missing Persons Bureau in 2008. At the Missing Persons Bureau, Joe leads, develops and manages the national unit supporting missing person enquiries within the United Kingdom and is responsible for national policy regarding this area, requiring extensive consultation with the Association of Chief Police Officers (ACPO) leads, ministerial leads, NGOs and other key partners. He has a BA (honours) in policing studies from Portsmouth University and an MA in criminal justice from Reading University.

Eric Bartelink is an associate professor of anthropology at California State University–Chico and the director of the Human Identification Laboratory and co-coordinator of the Certificate in Forensic Identification. He has worked on domestic casework in the United States and previously assisted with the excavation of mass graves in Bosnia–Herzegovina and in the World Trade Center victim identification effort. His research interests include taphonomy, trauma analysis and the application of stable isotope analysis to human identification. He is a diplomate of the American Board of Forensic Anthropology and a fellow of the American Academy of Forensic Sciences.

Jan Bikker is a postdoctoral researcher at the Centre for Anatomy and Human Identification, University of Dundee, Scotland, United Kingdom. He obtained a doctorate from the University of Sheffield on the subject of disaster victim identification. He has participated in disasters in Thailand, Haiti and Peru and participates in forensic anthropology casework for national and international police forces. Jan currently works on the FASTID project with INTERPOL to assist in establishing the first centralised international database for the identification of unidentified bodies and missing persons, and in this capacity works with international disaster victim identification (DVI) teams and UK police forces on DVI-related training and guidance. Jan is the membership secretary and council member of the British Association for Human Identification (BAHID) and a committee member of the British Association for Forensic Anthropologists.

Laureen Buckley is a Consultant Forensic Anthropologist from County Louth in Ireland.

Michael J.C. Burgess was admitted as a solicitor in 1970. He served as HM Coroner for Surrey (1986–2011) and served as a deputy from 1979 to 1986. He has been serving as coroner of The Queen's Household from January 2002 (worked as a deputy from 1991 to 2002). He was honorary secretary of the Coroners' Society of England and Wales from 1993 to 2003 and served as an assistant secretary from 1991 to 1993. During this time, he was responsible for the day-to-day running of the society, including close liaison with various government departments. He has represented (and continues to represent) the society and coroners generally on a number of committees and working parties, covering mass fatalities and emergency planning (including the working party that wrote the original *'Dealing with Fatalities during Disasters'—1993)* (1990–1999, 1993–1994, 2002–present). This extends to the field of chemical, biological, radiological and nuclear (CBRN) defence (2005–2006 and 2007–present), considering methods of dealing with fatalities in no-notice CBRN situations. He is one of the coordinators of the UK DVI Cadre of Coroners. Michael was appointed OBE in June 2009 for services rendered to the administration of justice.

Marie Cassidy is the State Pathologist at the State Pathologist's Office in Dublin, Ireland.

Lesley Chesson is a research scientist with more than 10 years of experience conducting stable isotope analyses. Her interests lie primarily in the forensic applications of stable isotope analysis for various materials. She has investigated microbes, human hair, tap water and a variety of foods and beverages. Lesley has aided law enforcement in investigations via the stable isotope analysis of human remains and other evidence. One of her current areas of focus is answering questions of food adulteration, authentication and origin.

Stephen Clifford is a forensic scientist at the Forensic Science Laboratory, Garda, Dublin.

Patricia H. Davis is the director of research and training for the Frederick Douglass Family Foundation. She is also a consultant for the Department of Justice on human trafficking and works with NGOs and law enforcement agencies across the country to combat this problem. She was previously associate director of the Embrey Human Rights Program and director of the Pastoral Leadership Center at Southern Methodist University (SMU) in Dallas, Texas, where she taught human rights, theology, ethics and organisational behaviour for over 20 years. Patricia is the author of two books and multiple articles on gender issues, ethics and human trafficking, in addition to being a licensed attorney in the State of Texas since 2002. Patricia clerked for the Honorable Barefoot Sanders (Northern District of Texas) and practiced law with Jackson Walker LLP in Dallas in the area of corporate litigation. She received her PhD at Princeton Theological Seminary and her JD at Dedman School of Law at SMU.

Stephanie L. Davy-Jow works at Liverpool John Moores University, Liverpool, United Kingdom.

Summer J. Decker is an assistant professor of radiology, surgery and pathology at the University of South Florida Morsani College of Medicine, where she is also the director of imaging research and applied anatomy. Her research focuses on quantitative analyses of medical image data and three-dimensional computer models for medicine, biometrics and forensics. She has assisted in forensic casework for local, state and federal law enforcement agencies using virtual forensic methodologies for identification and incident reconstruction.

John Dixon is a fingerprint expert for West Yorkshire Police, with 24 years experience, including 16 years working in the Major Crime Team. He specialises and lectures on cadaver print recovery from damaged or decomposed bodies and is a member of the Police National Disaster Victim Identification Team, United Kingdom.

Ray Evans is a visiting lecturer to the Universities of Manchester, Dundee and Cranfield (United Kingdom), where he lectures on facial comparison and identification. Ray is the CEO of SRi Forensics Limited based within the University of Manchester Incubator Building. His company specialises in facial identification analysis, video footage analysis, evidence presentation to courts and installation of AV equipment into courts. SRi Forensics holds a number of contracts to supply expertise and services to government bodies such as the CPS, HMRC and SFO among others. Ray is one of only a handful of recognised facial photocomparison experts in the United Kingdom and is listed with the National Crime Agency as an expert. With more than 18 years experience in producing material and reports used in the production of facial identification statements for court, Ray has prepared a large number of photocomparison reports both for the prosecution and the defence and has given evidence in court as an expert witness on numerous occasions. Ray has also prepared affidavits and appeared in the same capacity in court in the United States.

Robin Foyle works at Wexford Dental Clinic, Ireland.

Diane L. France is the director of the Laboratory for Human Identification, Colorado State University Fort Collins, Colorado.

René Gapert holds a doctoral degree (PhD) in forensic anthropology and human anatomy from University College Dublin (UCD), National University of Ireland. He works in the Human Anatomy Laboratory at UCD, where he manages the Plastination Laboratory. He has undertaken casework and collaborative research in Ireland and Germany. René's doctoral research examined the expression of sexual dimorphism in the skull base and the development of population-specific discriminant functions and regression equations. His current postdoctoral collaborative research projects involve computerised craniometric discriminant analyses, postmortem computed tomography (PMCT) and virtual anthropology. René is the chair of the internationalisation committee of the British Association for Forensic Anthropologists (BAFA) and a council member of both the British Association for Human Identification (BAHID) and the European Anthropological Association (EAA).

Stuart Gibson received his BSc in physics in 1998 and his PhD in physics in 2007 from the University of Kent, Canterbury, United Kingdom. He was awarded the postgraduate certificate in higher education in 2011. He currently serves as a lecturer in forensic science in the School of Physical Sciences, University of Kent. He is a coinventor of the EFIT-V facial composite system, which utilises an interactive evolution strategy and is used to locate suspects in criminal investigations. The system is widely used by police services in the United Kingdom and many law enforcement agencies worldwide. His research interests include interactive evolutionary computation, face perception, image processing and computer vision.

Melanie Hargreaves-O'Kane is an identification expert with West Yorkshire Police, United Kingdom, producing expert witness statements in the area of fingerprint identification and on first reserve for the National UK DVI team. She has an MSc in forensic anthropology and a BSc (honours) in archaeology. Her research areas include the estimation of postmortem interval in suspicious and non-suspicious deaths and the effects that location and predisposal storage have on the condition and recovery of human remains.

Antje Huth is a DNA expert at Eurofins Medigenomix. She has experience in forensic molecular genetics both as a reporting scientist and as a researcher. At the Institute of Legal Medicine in Freiburg, Antje investigated the possibilities and limitations of gene expression studies in postmortem human tissue from donors with prolonged postmortem interval. Antje also examined several parameters influencing the reliability of reverse transcription quantitative polymerase chain reaction (PCR), the long-term objective of which is the implementation of postmortem gene expression analyses as an additional tool in the determination of the pathophysiology of death.

Jann Karp is a lecturer in criminology and holds a PhD in social policy. Having spent 23 years as a serving police officer in New South Wales, Jann's research interests consist of monitoring criminal and deviant behaviour within discreet groups. She has published two books: the first addresses police corruption and the second centres on the professional activities of interstate truck drivers. Jann's current research relates to the evaluation of increasing regulatory oversight and consideration of its effectiveness in crime prevention.

Gerard Kealy retired in 2011 after 34 years as a detective and member in charge of Wexford Crime Scene Investigation Unit. He is a veteran of several thousand crime scenes, both as an investigating officer and as a crime scene investigator (CSI). In his professional capacity, Gerard has lectured in academic institutions and has given many presentations at conferences. He is the author of *The Forensic Recovery of Decomposed and Skeletal Human Remains*, adopted by the Commissioner of An Garda Siochana and the State Pathologist (Ireland) as the procedure and protocol for dealing with fatal scenes. Gerard holds a postgraduate diploma and an MSc in forensic science.

Helen Kemp is a senior research fellow, specialising in the field of stable isotope forensics. She works at the James Hutton Institute (Dundee, United Kingdom). Her research interests include stable isotope profiling of controlled drugs, explosives and human tissue(s). Helen is a forensic isotope ratio mass spectrometry (FIRMS)-approved lead forensic practitioner and a registered expert advisor to the National Policing Improvement Agency (NPIA), where she assists law enforcement agencies in the United Kingdom and the United States with cold-case investigations, victim recovery and human provenancing.

Carole McCartney is a reader in law at Northumbria University and has written widely on forensic science and criminal justice issues, in particular miscarriages of justice. She was an EU Marie Curie international research fellow on a project entitled 'Forensic Identification Frontiers' from 2009 to 2012. She continues as adjunct research fellow at the Australian Centre of

Excellence in Policing and Security. She also works on projects to improve the cross-disciplinary education of law and forensic science students.

Jonathan McNulty is head of teaching and learning for diagnostic imaging programmes at the University College Dublin (UCD) School of Medicine and Medical Science, where he introduced a graduate programme in forensic imaging. He is the founder and chair of the Irish Forensic Imaging Group and was editor of the *Irish Institute of Radiography and Radiation Therapy Guidelines on Best Practice in Forensic Imaging.* Jonathan is a founding member of the International Society for Forensic Radiology and Imaging, has been involved in a number of international collaborative cases and has given many presentations on forensic imaging as an invited speaker.

Wolfram Meier-Augenstein is a visiting professor at the Robert Gordon University (Aberdeen, United Kingdom) and the principal scientist (stable isotopes) at the James Hutton Institute (Dundee, United Kingdom). Professor Meier-Augenstein is one of the three directors of the Forensic Isotope Ratio Mass Spectrometry (FIRMS) Network Ltd, a council member of the British Association for Human Identification and a registered expert forensic advisor with the United Kingdom's National Policing Improvement Agency (NPIA). He is an approved forensic lead practitioner and has assisted police forces in the United Kingdom and other countries in drugs and murder-related investigations with provision of forensic intelligence based on stable isotope 'signatures'. His work has resulted in over 150 publications, book chapters and conference presentations, including the first textbook dedicated to the forensic application of stable isotope analytical techniques entitled *Stable Isotope Forensics.*

Fiona E. Raitt is a solicitor and professor of evidence and social justice at the University of Dundee. She has published primarily in the area of the law of evidence and criminal justice but also in family law, access to justice and gender. She has held a number of public appointments within Scotland, including at the Criminal Courts Rules Council (2006–2011) and the Advisory Group for the Scottish Law Commission Project on Similar Fact Evidence and the Moorov Doctrine (2011). She has contributed seminars for the Judicial Studies Committee in Scotland on Vulnerable Witnesses and on Scientific Evidence (2010–2012). She was also a programme leader in the recent law reform programme funded by the Scottish Universities Insight Institute's Scots Law of Evidence: Fit for Purpose in the Digital Age? (2011), which concerned emerging expert scientific evidence and miscarriages of justice.

Patrick Randolph-Quinney is a lecturer in the School of Anatomical Sciences at the University of the Witwatersrand, Johannesburg. Patrick is an experienced researcher and fieldworker with interests in the application of biological anthropology across differing historical time scales, from the Middle Pleistocene to the present. His areas of interest include forensic anthropology and archaeology; palaeoanthropology; prehistoric archaeology and bioarchaeology; geometric morphometric methods; and the application of statistics in the life sciences, forensic sciences and evolutionary biology. Patrick has over 20 years experience in the archaeological field, much at directorial or specialist level, in the recovery, identification and analysis of human skeletal remains and archaeological faunas. He is an experienced forensic caseworker in areas of forensic human identification and forensic anthropology, human/non-human bone identification, forensic cremain analysis, and forensic archaeology and body recovery, including archaeological search strategies for discovery and recovery of clandestine burials and recovery from fatal fires.

Andrew Rennison is a Home Office public appointee serving in dual roles as the forensic science regulator and the surveillance camera commissioner. As a public appointee, he is independent of government and is expected to set and monitor the quality standards that apply to forensic science and to encourage adoption of codes of practice for surveillance cameras (Surveillance Camera Code of Practice Pursuant to Section 29 of the Protection of Freedoms Act 2012). He previously completed a career in policing. He holds a master of science degree in psychology and an honorary doctor of science degree from Bournemouth University, where he lectures on forensic science quality standards.

Christopher Rynn works at the Centre for Anatomy and Human Identification at the University of Dundee, Scotland.

Donald E. Shelton is an active jurist scholar, writer and academic. He is the chief judge of the court system in Ann Arbor, Michigan, and an adjunct professor at Eastern Michigan University and Cooley Law School. Judge Shelton's active research focuses on the impact of science and technology on the judicial system. He is the author of several texts, including his latest book *Forensic Science Evidence: Can the Law Keep Up with Science?*

Dr. Chris Solomon is a reader in physics at the University of Kent. He graduated in theoretical physics from Durham University in 1983 and gained a PhD in medical image processing from the Institute of Cancer Research, London, in 1989. After postdoctoral research at the Blackett Laboratory, Imperial College, he moved to Kent University, where he is now a reader in physics and leads the forensic image analysis group. The group currently has active research projects in digital image watermarking, evolutionary image processing, digital camera identification, automated age progression and facial composite construction. He has published more than 50 peer-reviewed research papers and four book chapters and is also the author of the textbook *Fundamentals of Digital Image Processing—A Practical Approach* published by Wiley-Blackwell in 2011. In 1998, Chris founded Visionmetric Ltd. He has since built an outstanding record in technology innovation and the commercialisation of university research. Visionmetric is now the leading provider of facial composite software and services in the United Kingdom, providing systems, training and support services in 34 countries worldwide.

Marielle Vennemann is a scientist at the Institute of Legal Medicine, Medical School Hannover, and honorary lecturer at the Centre for Forensic Science, University of Strathclyde, Glasgow. She is a forensic DNA expert with many years of experience as expert witness and scientist. Her main research interest is the methodological validation of postmortem RNA profiling as a new tool to complement current methods of determining the cause of death. Furthermore, she works on new and innovative techniques to improve forensic DNA testing in general.

Louise Vesely is the police liaison and support officer for the UK Missing Persons Bureau, where her work has included managing a review of outstanding unidentified bodies across the United Kingdom and implementation of procedures regarding collation of DNA and fingerprints for missing and unidentified persons. Louise has previously worked as a tactical analyst for the bureau and as a crime analyst for the Serious Crime Analysis Section. She holds a BSc in psychology and an MSc in forensic psychology, undertaking a dissertation in predicting outcomes in missing person reports involving older individuals.

Clive Walker His books, which include *Justice in Error* (Blackstone Press, 1993), *Miscarriages of Justice* (Oxford University Press, 1999) and *Terrorism and the Law* (Oxford University Press, 2011), have focused on miscarriages of justice especially those arising from forensic processes and terrorism.

Jim Walters is the assistant chief of police at Southern Methodist University (SMU) in Dallas, Texas, and the director of the SMU Center for Public Safety Training, an accredited law enforcement training academy which develops and conducts advanced training for public safety professionals. Walters is also a consultant to the US Department of Justice and is responsible for the US Department of Justice Southern Border Initiative. This joint programme with the Mexican government has developed a comprehensive child abduction recovery programme in Mexico, which works with programmes in the United States to assist in the rapid recovery of trafficked, exploited and abducted children from both countries. Jim is the director of the Border Resource Group, a non-profit group made up of law enforcement and military personnel who donate time, expertise and resources to assist communities in developing counties and rural areas of the United States in developing safe havens for abused, exploited and trafficked women and children. The group provides investigative assistance and logistical support to government officials in kidnapping and abduction investigations upon request.

Caroline Wilkinson is a professor of craniofacial Identification in the Centre for Anatomy and Human Identification at the University of Dundee, Scotland. She is an expert in facial anthropology and anatomy and her forensic casework includes skeletal interpretation, facial identification, facial depiction from skeletal remains and craniofacial superimposition. Caroline is the author of *Forensic Facial Reconstruction* and *Craniofacial Identification* and was the first woman president of the International Association of Craniofacial identification in 2008. She has also been involved in many archaeological investigations, and her work is exhibited in museums around the world. Caroline has also appeared in popular science TV programmes such as *History Cold Case, Meet the Ancestors, Secrets of the Dead* and *Mummies Unwrapped*.

Richard Wright is emeritus professor of anthropology at the University of Sydney, Australia. In 1990 and 1991, he worked as archaeologist for the Australian Government in the context of war crimes trials. In Ukraine, he directed excavation of three mass graves dating from the Holocaust of 1942—at Serniki, Ustinovka and Gnivan. From 1997 to 2000, he was chief archaeologist for the International Criminal Tribunal for the Former Yugoslavia and has given testimony in The Hague in the cases of ten accused. In 2009, he was appointed senior forensic adviser to Oxford Archaeology during their exhumation of World War I soldiers from mass graves at Fromelles in Northeast France. His anthropological interests include estimating ancestry from cranial attributes. He has written the freeware package CRANID.

Identifying the Unknown

I

Two Sides of the Same Coin
Missing and Unidentified People

1

JOE APPS, LOUISE VESELY, LLIAN ALYS,
AND TERI BLYTHE

Contents

Introduction

'The impact of going missing has never been higher in the national consciousness' (Richard Bryan, previous Association of Chief Police Officers [ACPO] lead for missing persons, in ACPO, 2010, p.5). Thanks to media interest in a number of high-profile cases and the lobbying of charities and other agencies, going missing is now recognised as a serious issue with far-reaching and enduring (even fatal) consequences. The charity, Missing People*, published a report on the emotional, social, legal, financial, and practical impacts

---

* Formerly known as the National Missing Persons Helpline.

on families (Holmes, 2009). It describes how these people who 'live in limbo' are unable to gain closure and vacillate between hope and despair as they experience the ambiguous loss of mourning someone whose fate is unknown. Increased understanding and awareness has culminated in the appointment of a 'Minister for Missing', a government minister to represent the interests of missing people and their families and the Home Office (2011).

Despite this emerging recognition of the problem, the issue of unidentified bodies and people is still largely unacknowledged. As explained by Blythe and Woodforde (2007), many of the unidentified alive and deceased are likely to be considered as missing people, even if not reported. Whilst many are identified relatively quickly, there are a small number that will not be identified for a long time, if ever. As a virtue of their lack of identity, they are easily forgotten; they do not have family and friends to champion for them, to raise awareness of their case, and to bring it to resolution.

Missing Persons

The Association of Chief Police Officers (ACPO) defines a missing person as 'anyone whose whereabouts cannot be established and where the circumstances are out of character or the context suggests the person may be a subject of crime or at risk of harm to themselves or another' (ACPO, 2013, p.5). This captures a range of vulnerable individuals who go missing in diverse circumstances, from the abducted child or teenage runaway to the depressed adult or confused and lost elderly person.

From a police perspective, there is a difference between missing persons and individuals whose whereabouts are unknown because they are evading the police or have absconded from custody ('wanted' people)—there will not be the same concern for the welfare of a wanted individual. An individual can, however, be both wanted and missing, if, for example, they have absconded from custody but there are also concerns that they may be at risk of harm from others or may harm themselves. A risk assessment (discussed in more detail later) will help to determine how to deal with such cases.

The scale of the problem is often not recognised. The National Policing Improvement Agency (NPIA, 2012) estimated that police forces in Britain recorded approximately 327,000 missing person reports in 2010/2011. This equated to 900 missing reports a day. It was further estimated that 200,000 individuals were the subject of these reports. The true number is likely to be higher, however, as not all missing people are reported to the police. In their 2011 publication (Newiss, 2011), the charity Missing People reported that of the 250 disappearances closed by the charity during 2006 and 2007 in which the missing person had died, 64 (26%) had not been reported to the police or had not been regarded as missing person cases by the police. Many of these individuals were considered 'lost contact' cases, where someone has simply drifted away from his or her family and friends.

Who Goes Missing and Why?

Individuals go missing for a variety of reasons. Some choose to leave and do not wish to be found; others unconsciously go missing (e.g. they are unaware that people are looking for them); some are missing due to the actions of others (e.g. abduction or homicide) or by virtue of circumstance (e.g. they have drowned and their body has not been found). It is not known whether the people who are missing would recognise themselves as missing people. A wide variety of reasons and explanations for going missing include financial problems, abuse and violence within relationships, abduction, forced marriage and 'honour'-based violence, people trafficking, murder, suicide, accidents, lost contact, as well as mental health issues (Blythe and Woodforde, 2007).

The NPIA (2012) found that, overall, an approximately equal number of males and females were reported missing in 2010/2011. However, in the 12- to 17-year-old age group, more females were recorded missing by the police than males. In every other age group, more males than females were reported missing. Previous research supports this observation (e.g. Biehal et al., 2003) and has shown that as the duration of missing episode increases, the more likely the missing person is to be male (Newiss, 2005). The NPIA (2012) also reported that children and young people under 18 years were the subject of 66% of the reports (2010/2011), with the 15- to 17-year-olds accounting for 36%. Children's care homes often have protocols regarding notifying the police when a child goes missing, as legally a child under 16 years cannot choose to go missing. An adult, however, can choose to go missing and remain so (unless they are the subject of some manner of detention order, or there is sufficient concern that they are a danger to themselves or others). When found, if an adult does not want their family to be notified of their location, the police must respect this.

Consequences of Going Missing

The majority of missing people return relatively quickly: NPIA's data (2012) indicated that 77% of missing people returned within 16 h in 2010/2011, with only 3% missing for more than 7 days. Vulnerable individuals, such as children or adults with mental health difficulties, are more likely to be reported missing rapidly by their families and the people who care for them. Tarling and Burrows (2004) stated that, in a random sample of over 1000 cases reported to the Metropolitan Police Service, 92% were resolved within 1 week and 99% within a year.

The majority of missing people are also found safe and well. Some, however, may have been harmed when missing and an even smaller proportion will have died. NPIA (2012) estimated that around 800 people reported as missing may be found dead in the United Kingdom each year.

Police Procedures and Inter-Agency Co-Operation

An investigation begins when the police are first notified that a person is missing (ACPO, 2010). The first report should contain as much information as possible in order to inform a risk assessment and allocate resources accordingly. This will be reviewed regularly and revised as appropriate, whilst information gathered also provides the basis for lines of enquiry. The police use a three-tiered model of risk to classify missing persons: high, medium and low (see Table 1.1). These stages take into account factors such as age and

Table 1.1   Police Classification of Risk and Response

Level of Risk	Description	Response
High risk	The risk posed is immediate: Substantial grounds for believing subject is in danger through their own vulnerability or may have been the victim of a serious crime and/or substantial grounds for believing that the public is in danger	• Immediate deployment of police resources • Senior police officer involved in examining initial lines of enquiry and approving staffing levels • Appointment of investigating officer and possibly senior investigation officer and Police Search Adviser (PolSA) • Press/media strategy and/or close contact with outside agencies • Support to the family in place • UK Missing Persons Bureau to be notified • Child Exploitation & Online Protection Centre (CEOP) and Children's Services to be notified if missing person is under 18
Medium risk	The risk posed is likely to place the subject in danger and/or the missing person is a threat to themselves or others	• Active and measured response by police and other agencies to trace the missing person and support the person reporting
Low risk	No apparent threat of danger to either the subject or the public. Children and young people under 18 years of age should not be included in this classification.	• Information recorded on the PNC • Once all active enquiries are exhausted, the case is deferred to a regular review pending any further information coming to notice.

Source: Association of Chief Police Officers, *Guidance on the Management, Recording and Investigation of Missing Persons*, 2nd Edn., National Policing Improvement Agency, London, U.K., 2010.

whether the individual is considered a risk to himself or herself or the public. It must also consider personal risk factors, both psychological and physical (e.g. whether suicidal, medication needs); environmental factors (e.g. the weather, the terrain); and social factors (e.g. exploitative individuals). Risk is not static; moreover, a classification of low risk does not mean that a person is not at risk. A number of homicide investigations started as low-risk missing person investigations (ACPO, 2010).

An initial investigation may include searching the place from which the person went missing and collecting physical evidence such as photographs and objects from which fingerprints and DNA samples can be captured. Lines of enquiry will be dictated by the evidence and information gathered from the missing person's family, friends, colleagues and personal property (including, for instance, diaries and data from telephones, and computers). When a person is found or returns home, a safe and well check is completed and the ACPO guidance (2010, 2013) recommends conducting a fuller return interview to identify the reasons for the missing episode in order to reduce any remaining risk of harm or the risk of going missing again.

A number of statutory and non-governmental organisations (NGOs) are involved in assisting the police to search for missing people and in supporting the missing person's family and friends. This includes the UK Missing Persons Bureau*, part of the National Crime Agency (NCA), a crime-fighting agency dedicated to tackling serious and organised crime and protecting the public. The Bureau is the United Kingdom's national and international point of contact for all missing persons and unidentified body cases and the centre for information exchange and expertise on missing person issues. It is the only UK public body focussed exclusively on missing people.

The Bureau launched the Code of Practice on the Collection of Missing Persons Data in 2009. This requires police forces in England and Wales to submit information on missing persons and unidentified people, bodies, and remains to the Bureau (it is also open to adoption by forces in Scotland and Northern Ireland). The Bureau collects data for operational purposes, to provide support to police investigations and share information with partners such as the NCA's Child Exploitation & Online Protection Centre (CEOP) Command, and for strategic purposes in order to gain an understanding of the extent and nature of the 'missing' issue. The Bureau's services include national and international reconciliation of missing and found people through its national database and provision of tactical advice and support to police investigations. The Bureau also provides specialist access to critical national services such as the National DNA Database and National Missing Persons DNA Database (MPDD).

* Located within NPIA from 2008 to 2012, and the Serious Organised Crime Agency (SOCA) 2012 to 2013.

NCA CEOP Command is also involved in missing person cases, providing a multi-agency service to combat the exploitation of children. Its work includes targeting sex offenders who groom children online and sex tourists, as well as identifying victims and perpetrators from child abuse images. NCA CEOP Command has the policy lead for missing children and provides key services for safeguarding missing and runaway children. These include online resources for children, parents, and teachers; training for professionals; managing Child Rescue Alert on behalf of police forces; and managing the UK Missing Kids website which provides publicity for missing children.

The Foreign and Commonwealth Office (FCO), a department of the British Government, is also able to assist in some missing person cases. If it is suspected that someone may have gone missing abroad, the Consular Directorate may be able to assist. The FCO can provide information about appropriate local authorities and relevant local charitable and voluntary organisations specialising in tracing missing people, or can also assist when a deceased or live individual is found outside the United Kingdom but is believed to be British.

A number of charities also play a part in finding missing people. Missing People is the largest UK charity dealing with both missing children and adults. It offers support and services for the family and friends of missing people and provides helplines that offer assistance to missing adults and children. Missing People provides publicity for missing person cases, raises awareness of issues associated with going missing, and actively lobbies for improved services for families. Missing Abroad is a charity run by the Lucie Blackman Trust, which provides advice and support for the families of children or adults missing abroad and can provide practical assistance and advice to individuals missing and stranded abroad. It works closely with the FCO.

There are also a number of other NGOs or charities providing assistance to specific groups of missing people or focussing upon issues associated with going missing; for example, the Salvation Army provides a service for tracing adult relatives with whom contact has been lost. A number of charities focus upon children and young people in particular. The Children's Society, Barnardo's, and the Railway Children all assist children who run away and go missing, whilst the reunite International Child Abduction Centre and Parents and Abducted Children Together (PACT) raise awareness and provide advice regarding international parental child abduction.

Unidentified Bodies and Remains

Whilst dealing with the deceased is a relatively common occurrence for police, in a small proportion of cases, the identity of an individual may initially be unknown. These unidentified cases may involve people who have died naturally, accidentally, purposefully or due to the actions of a third party.

Newiss (2003) estimated, however, that only 1 in 7400 missing people is the victim of homicide. The remains may be found immediately, such as at the site of an accident, or many years later due to the remoteness of the location or attempts to conceal the death. The extent of the remains found varies considerably from only a few fragmented bones to entire bodies. Each case therefore presents various challenges to the police, but more crucially may also represent a family waiting for news of the whereabouts of their missing loved one.

Cases that pose significant challenges include unidentified babies that may be found abandoned, murder victims and individuals found in circumstances suggesting an itinerant or homeless lifestyle. A possible key problem for such cases is the probable lack of a missing person report and thus no corresponding list to suggest a possible identity. Creative investigation, publicity, and the use of forensic techniques can be crucial, as without an identity, it can be extremely difficult for any investigation to progress.

The challenges facing investigators when a single unidentified body is found can be quite different to the difficulties confronted in the face of a mass disaster such as a plane crash or boat incident. Disaster victim identification (DVI) often involves the identification of individuals where the possible identity is known (e.g. due to passenger lists) but requires confirmation. In single victim identification, however, there is often little evidence suggesting a possible identity for the individual.

It is not clear exactly how many of these unidentified remains are found each year. In 2010/2011, British police recorded 154 newly found unidentified remains, and the Missing Persons Bureau was notified of an additional 26 remains found abroad (NPIA, 2012). However, this is considered to be an underestimate due to under-reporting. Whilst many of these will eventually be identified, every year, a number of cases remain unresolved. To date, the Bureau has records of nearly 1100 bodies or body parts that remain unidentified a year or more after they were found, with some dating back to the 1950s.

The majority of long-term unidentified individuals are male (see Figure 1.1), although this sex discrepancy is more marked in those found deceased than those found alive. A relatively high proportion (10%) of these long-term unidentified deceased cases are newborn babies (see Figure 1.2), the only age range to demonstrate a female bias. The majority of cases involve adults, with less than 1% involving individuals aged 2–17 years, which is similar to the pattern found in long-term missing person cases (Newiss, 2005). Due to the condition of the remains, approximately 6% do not have a specific age range, and it is not possible to determine the ancestral origin in nearly a third of these cases, although the majority are classified as White Europeans (see Figure 1.3). Furthermore, just over 10% of cases involve partial remains rather than full bodies.

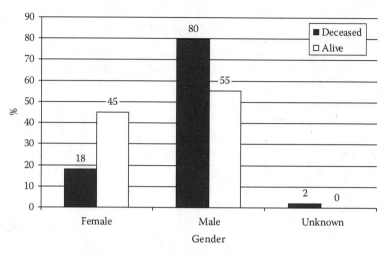

Figure 1.1 Gender distribution of unidentified cases.

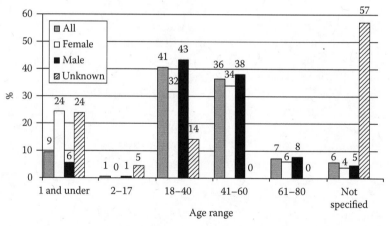

Figure 1.2 Age distribution of unidentified cases, separated by gender.

Unidentified Living Individuals

In general, unidentified alive people fall into one of three categories: people who have genuinely lost their memory or who are confused, people who seek the attention of authorities for a variety of reasons and who do not want to disclose their true identities, and found babies. Relatively few of those found fall within the first category. Most of these cases do not achieve significant media coverage; however, many will remember the story of 'piano man',—an Eastern European man suffering memory loss, found in Kent, United Kingdom, in 2005. Those in the second category are known by

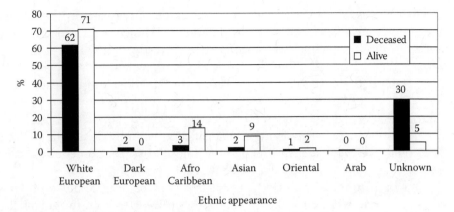

Figure 1.3 Ethnicity of unidentified cases.

the Bureau as 'come to notice' individuals. The Bureau has physical descriptions and details of the modus operandi of just over 130 such people and keeps records to provide assistance to police forces seeking to identify them. Often, these people present with the same or a similar medical condition or make the same or similar allegations to the police, of sexual assault, for instance. A good example is of a man who often presents with a cut arm to hospital emergency rooms across the north and central England. Police investigations can prove fruitless without the assistance of the Bureau and its database of 'come to notice' individuals.

The last category is found babies. In these cases, locating the mother takes priority to ensure that the correct medical treatment is provided following the birth of the child and to reunite the mother and child and ensure their future welfare. If the mother cannot be located, the babies are offered for adoption through local children's services. Once adopted, police force and Bureau records on the found child are closed, although these should be retained indefinitely in order to provide a record for the individual when they are older should they wish to know more about their background.

Police Procedures

When an unidentified person or remains are found, the police are usually the first point of contact. The police have a duty to treat unidentified deceased cases as suspicious until it can be proven otherwise. The police will contact the local coroner to inform them that a body has been found; however, it remains the primary responsibility of the police to investigate the death to conclude whether it is suspicious or not. Where murder is deemed likely, experts from relevant forensic fields may attend the scene and provide advice prior to recovery. Should it be shown that the death was not a murder, the primary responsibility for investigation will shift to the coroner (see Chapter 2). The coroner will then have a duty to investigate and establish the identity of the deceased, the time/location of death and the cause of death. Initial police and forensic enquiries will involve undertaking a survey of the scene and collecting relevant samples for further examination. In cases involving unidentified alive individuals, the police will contact relevant agencies such as local hospitals, care homes and local authority services in an attempt to identify the person.

When an unidentified alive person or a full (or near complete) body has been recovered, police should enter descriptive details on to the Police National Computer (PNC) as soon as possible, enabling other forces across the country to search for details of these cases for comparison with their outstanding missing persons. In practice, this often does not occur and consideration is being given to the development of the recently launched Police National Database (which was developed as a result of the Bichard enquiry following the murder of Holly Wells and Jessica Chapman in 2002; see Bichard, 2005) to better accommodate details of these unidentified individuals.

If the individual remains unidentified, details should be notified to the UK Missing Persons Bureau within 48 h. The Bureau can then cross-match the description of the person with the outstanding missing persons recorded on the national database. However, consideration is also given to cross-matching details of these unidentified individuals with those recorded as missing by the Missing People charity, as some cases may not have been reported to the police. Due to the confidential nature of the information held by the charity, this tends to be considered after other lines of enquiry and cases from the Bureau have been exhausted.

Forensic Samples

A post-mortem (PM) DNA sample should be taken from all unidentified bodies or remains, for profiling by an accredited forensic service provider (FSP), in order for it to be compared against profiles on the National DNA Database and the MPDD. Where no match is found, the profile will be retained on the MPDD for comparison against any future submissions.

Case example: In 2010, a man's body was found off the coast in Kent, but only minimal descriptive details could be determined. Only his clothing could be used to compare to possible matches—a huge and unreliable task. A search of the MPDD, however, immediately hit against the profile of a man reported missing in Sussex 6 weeks prior to being found.

A DNA sample may also be taken from an unidentified alive person to assist identification if other investigative avenues have failed. In these cases, the person's consent is required, although a medical professional may provide this on their behalf if they are considered incapable of consenting.

The MPDD was formally recognised in May 2010 and is now managed by the UK Missing Persons Bureau. The database holds direct reference profiles from missing persons, as well as some kinship profiles from the biological relatives of those missing where a reference profile from the missing person is not available, in the hope of establishing a full or partial match to a body. Also held are profiles from human remains and crime scenes (e.g. if blood, but no body, is found), as are profiles found on items in the possession of known serial killers (such as the jewellery found in the residences of Peter Tobin, who murdered three women and hid each of their bodies [Evans, 2009]). It can be extremely costly to obtain profiles in those circumstances, especially as all samples have to be processed by an FSP that has been accredited by the National DNA Strategy Board in order to quality assure the profile obtained. Only profiles from those suppliers will be searched and retained on the MPDD.

Where possible, fingerprints (see Chapter 14) should be obtained from the unidentified alive person or body and checked against the national fingerprint database, IDENT1. This database holds details of all suspects'/offenders' fingerprints, as well as fingerprint, palm or plantar (foot) print marks found at crime scenes that cannot be attributed to a known individual. This process can be done locally by police, often with a mobile scanning device, which will provide details of any matches within minutes, thus reducing the need to notify the Bureau. The Bureau has established a process for storing the prints from unidentified remains within an ad hoc collection on IDENT1. This means that any cases that are not immediately identified due to the person previously being known to police can be retained and checked against prints that may not have been entered onto IDENT1. This can be extremely useful for international cases as many foreign nationals may have prints taken in their home country. This means of identification is often cheaper than trying to obtain DNA for the body or the missing person.

> Case example: Following a delay in obtaining viable DNA in 2011 a fingerprint match was made between a deceased man in London and a Swedish national reported missing in Norway—an unlikely match by other means—thus saving time and other expense.

Another key means of identifying a found individual is the use of dental records, often less resource intensive than DNA collection. The Bureau maintains a missing person's dental index, which holds copies of ante- and postmortem records for comparison. These records are used to eliminate missing persons who are known to have fewer teeth than the found body. When a reasonable match is found, a forensic odontologist may be consulted for a professional opinion. It is therefore recommended that for all remains where an intact jaw is found, a dental record be submitted to the Bureau.

Media and Publicity

A particularly effective tool available to the police is the use of the media as not all people will be reported missing. If initial attempts to identify the individual (alive or dead) are unsuccessful, the police will often release details to the media in the hope that someone may recognise them. It is the most effective method of identifying living people. The police are always mindful of the need to respect the privacy of the individual even if they are deceased, and only details that may enable others to identify the person are published.

In some cases, the initial local appeals receive national attention. An example is the 'jigsaw man' case, where body parts from the same individual were found 100 miles apart in different counties (Pidd, 2010). This multiforce murder enquiry captured the interest of the national press, and his story made headlines across the United Kingdom. He was eventually identified after his brother contacted the investigating team. However, such high profile media interest is rare and is often reserved for those that attract macabre fascination, such as murder enquiries.

It can be difficult to judge which cases will capture the imagination of the press and it is therefore crucial to have other means to publicise these unidentified cases. The Bureau has recently developed a website where details of these cases can be displayed to allow members of the public, police, or other relevant agencies to review them and suggest possible identities.

Forensic Artwork and Facial Reconstructions

An image of an individual can increase the effectiveness of publicity. Such images may be of the person or of some distinctive feature such as a tattoo or clothing that those who knew the individual would recognise. In cases of long-term missing persons an age progression may be produced to illustrate how an individual may look many years after they were last seen, thus aiding in potential recognition and location of that person (see Figure 1.4).

In cases of unidentified bodies, the extent of decomposition or the nature of the injury suffered may make a photograph of the individual/feature unsuitable for publication. Specialist techniques can instead be used either to manipulate post-mortem photographs to produce an image or to produce a 3D facial reconstruction from the skull, both of which can realistically depict how that person may have looked in life. A list of forensic artists with this expertise is maintained by the NCA Specialist Operations Centre, a dedicated police 'helpline' that forces can contact to obtain specialist advice.

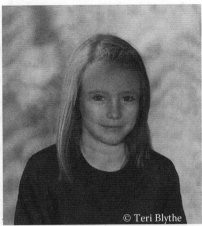

Figure 1.4 (See companion CD for colour figure.) Madeline McCann at 3.5 years and age progressed to 9 years. (Photo courtesy of the McCann family; age progression produced by Teri Blythe©.)

Further information on these techniques can be found in 'Forensic Human Identification: An Introduction' (Thompson and Black, 2007).

International Perspective

Missing persons is an area that has received attention on an international scale, with the European Union, in particular, seeking greater harmonisation of procedures and exchange of information between member states. For example, the need for national missing persons bureaux has been highlighted with governments across the world. There is also a significant political will to maintain databases of missing and found people. The landscape in other countries is similar to that in the United Kingdom; work is often shared by official organisations and the voluntary sector. The Bureau and NCA CEOP Command are part of a strong network of government departments, law enforcement agencies and third-sector organisations across Europe and the wider world. They are members of the Global Missing Children's Network, closely associated with Missing Children Europe and the International Centre for Missing and Exploited Children in Washington, DC.

In existence since 1923, Interpol is an international police organisation with 190 member countries at the time of writing, and, as such, is the largest organisation of its kind in the world. It facilitates cross-border and international police co-operation and provides support and assistance to agencies involved in the fight against international crime. To facilitate international communication, standard form templates (DVI forms) are used by Interpol for the collection of ante-mortem (AM) and PM data, both in major disasters and in day-to-day policing including missing and found person cases. These forms can be shared directly, and information is collated on the Interpol i24/7 system, which law enforcement agencies are able to search directly. The UK Missing Persons Bureau acts as the main point of contact for all cases where there is no specified UK police force involved, and receives details of all Interpol disseminations relating to missing or unidentified persons that are issued to the United Kingdom. The Bureau also facilitates communication with Interpol, ensuring that forces issue the relevant black (deceased) or yellow (missing) notice and utilise the available international DNA and fingerprint databases maintained by Interpol Secretariat General in Lyon.

One of the most useful and successful networks for identification from the UK perspective is the North Sea Convention. This group, which started as a group of maritime police forces concerned in the exchange of data about bodies found in the North Sea, now has an expanded remit and membership and shares data on missing and found people and bodies. Successful, closed cases include a training shoe, complete with a well-preserved foot found on a Humberside beach, matched to the opposite shoe and foot found on an island beach north of the Netherlands and subsequently linked to a missing person from the Yorkshire area.

Although there are various initiatives to improve the ease with which this information can be exchanged, there are a number of associated problems. For example, the variation in data protection laws between countries can cause problems when considering international data exchanges. The knowledge of procedural, legal and ethical issues on the international exchange of missing person and identification data is essential for professionals contemplating either single operational exchanges of forensic data or bulk exchanges. Differences in national standards, for example, on the production of DNA profiles, can also lead to difficulties when considering DNA comparisons across borders. No international standard has yet been defined.

Challenges and Future Developments

Despite the growing recognition of the importance of an improved police response to *missing* person cases and the clear link between them and unidentified cases, the needs of *unidentified* persons, bodies, and their families' cases (the other side of the coin) remain unacknowledged. At present, no common minimum standards on the investigation of unidentified bodies/people exist within the United Kingdom. The Bureau has produced good practice advice around this (NPIA, 2010) and is currently working with the College of Policing to produce formal authorised professional practice in this area. It is anticipated that this would improve the level of information routinely collected, which would assist with matching these cases against reports of missing people.

Additionally, despite the introduction within the 2009 Code of Practice of a requirement for relevant identification samples (such as DNA, fingerprints, and dental records) to be obtained for all cases, this statutory instrument only governs the police service and does not apply to coroner's investigations. Given that the majority of unidentified cases do not relate to murders (where samples are routinely collected), the collection of such materials is reliant on the coroner's judgment. The Bureau is working with the Ministry of Justice and the Chief Coroner, who has responsibility for regulating the work of the coroners, to improve practices; however, it is acknowledged that DNA, for example, is not currently being collected in all cases.

The importance of the international data exchange has been highlighted but is hindered by the practical and legal complexities of sharing such sensitive personal information. To enable international comparison of DNA profiles and to harmonise profiling arrangements, the United Kingdom is changing its current profiling process to be more compatible with other nations. Another initiative underway, known as the FASTID project, is the creation of a single international database for missing and unidentified persons/bodies and to standardise terminology and understanding across the member countries. This database is a development of the existing DVI International software (previously known as 'Plass data'), which in 2011 became the UK solution to be used in the event of a mass fatality/DVI situation.

In 2010 the coalition government announced major changes which resulted in the establishment of the new National Crime Agency (NCA) in October 2013. The NCA combines SOCA and its concentration on organised crime, including trafficking ('missing' is an indicator of trafficking), kidnap and extortion (with the associated crime of abduction), and its specialist operational and intelligence analysis services; UK Human Trafficking Centre (UKHTC) providing specialist services on human trafficking; some former UK Border Agency (UKBA) border security and protection services, including trafficking and asylum issues; SOCA International (Interpol Manchester); CEOP providing child sexual exploitation expertise, Internet safety knowledge and other child protection services; and specialist operational services including the UK Missing Persons Bureau.

However, the real implications of this are yet to be realised. It is anticipated that this will align the Bureau more closely with CEOP, Interpol Manchester, UKHTC and other relevant support functions, facilitating the sharing of intelligence to bring greater expertise to bear on cases as a matter of routine. The national databases relating to DNA and fingerprints for missing/unidentified cases are now managed by the Home Office, and it is hoped that provisions will be continued for effective and efficient access by units within the NCA (e.g. the Bureau).

Conclusion

As awareness of 'missing' and its profound effects on the individual, their family and friends increases, the opportunity should be taken to highlight the association between the 'lost' and the 'found'. On a local level, police forces and other agencies need an oversight of both areas, and ideally, the responsibility for both types of enquiry would rest with the same teams (or in co-located teams). Moreover, effective joint working is required between police officers and coroners along with increased awareness and adoption of the identification techniques available. On a national and international level, the recent improvements in co-operation need to be bolstered by improved data sharing and harmonised data standards. Improvements such as these will lead to greater resolution of cases, laying to rest the dead and helping the living to achieve peace.

References

Association of Chief Police Officers. (2005). *Guidance on the Management, Recording and Investigation of Missing Persons*. London, U.K.: National Centre for Policing Excellence.

Association of Chief Police Officers. (2010). *Guidance on the Management, Recording and Investigation of Missing Persons* (2nd Edn.). London, U.K.: National Policing Improvement Agency.

Association of Chief Police Officers. (2013). *Interim Guidance on the Management, Recording and Investigation of Missing Persons 2013*. London, UK.: Serious Organised Crime Agency.

Bichard, M. (2005). *The Bichard Inquiry: Final report*. London, U.K.: Cabinet office.

Biehal, N., Mitchell, F., and Wade, J. (2003). *Lost From View: Missing Persons in the UK*. Bristol, England: The Policy Press.

Blythe, T. and Woodforde, S. (2007). Missing persons in the United Kingdom. In T. Thompson and S. Black (eds.), *Forensic Human Identification: An introduction*. Boca Raton, FL: Taylor & Francis Group, pp. 425–443.

Boss, P.G. (1999). *Ambiguous Loss: Learning to Live with Unresolved Grief*. Cambridge, MA: Harvard University Press.

Boss, P.G. (2002). Ambiguous loss: Working with families of the missing. *Family Process*, 41, 14–17.

Boss, P.G. (2007). Ambiguous loss theory: Challenges for scholars and practitioners. *Family Relations*, 56, 105–111.

Holmes, L. (2008). *Living in Limbo: The Experiences of, and Impacts on, Families of Missing People*. London, U.K.: Missing People.

Home Office. (2011). *Missing Children and Adults: A Cross Government Strategy*. London, U.K.: Home Office.

National Policing Improvement Agency. (2010). *Identification Process—Good Practice*. London, U.K.: NPIA.

National Policing Improvement Agency. (2012). *Missing Persons: Data and Analysis 2010/2011*. London, U.K.: NPIA.

Newiss, G. (1999). Missing presumed...? The police response to missing persons. Police Research Series Paper 114. London, U.K.: Home Office, Policing and Reducing Crime Unit.

Newiss, G. (2003). *Homicides Which Begin as Missing Person Enquiries: A Study of Victims and Offences*. London, U.K.: Home Office.

Newiss, G. (2005). A study of the characteristics of outstanding missing persons: Implications for the development of police risk assessment. *Policing & Society*, 15(2), 212–225.

Newiss, G. (2011). *Learning from Fatal Disappearances: A Report by Missing People*. London, U.K.: Missing People.

Payne, M. (1995). Understanding "Going Missing": Issues for social work and social services. *British Journal of Social Work*, 25, 333–348.

Rees, G. (2011). *Still Running III: Early Findings from Our Third National Survey of Young Runaways*. London, U.K.: The Children's Society.

Rutty, G. (2009). *Body Identification: Briefing Guide to Assist in Body Identification*. London, U.K.: NPIA.

Tarling, R. and Burrows, J. (2004). The nature and outcome of going missing: The challenge of developing effective risk assessment procedures. *International Journal of Police Science and Management*, 6(1), 16–26.

Thompson, T. and Black, S. (Eds.) (2007). *Forensic Human Identification: An Introduction*. Boca Raton, FL: Taylor & Francis Group.

Further Information

UK Missing Persons Bureau: http://missingpersons.police.uk
Child Exploitation and Online Protection Centre (CEOP): http://www.ceop.police.uk/
Missing People: https://www.missingpeople.org.uk/
Missing Abroad: http://missingabroad.org/
Salvation Army: http://www.salvationarmy.org.uk/uki/familytracing
The Children's Society: http://www.childrenssociety.org.uk/
Barnardo's: http://www.barnardos.org.uk/
Railway Children: http://www.railwaychildren.org.uk/
Parents and Abducted Children Together (PACT): http://www.pact-online.org/
Reunite International Child Abduction Centre: http://www.reunite.org/

Identification
The Coroner's Perspective

2

MICHAEL J.C. BURGESS

Contents

Introduction

There are many individuals involved in death investigations, each with their own role to play to ensure that any victims (if deceased) are identified and returned to their families. Coroners have a crucial function within forensic investigations as the coroner has the ultimate responsibility under statute for identification of individuals (UK Government, 2009). Thus, the correct identification of those who have died is a major concern and interest for coroners, both in single-death cases and mass fatality incidents (MFIs).

This chapter will focus on clarifying the coroner's role in death investigations from a coroner's perspective, which may be very different to other investigators and the general public, many of whom do not understand the difference between a coroner and a pathologist, for example (Black et al., 2010a). When reviewing the role of the coroner, it must be recognised that while the law remains exactly the same in any given scenario, there are differences in the way in which cases are managed. For example, there are inevitable variations between the procedures in a mass fatality situation when compared to the more common unnatural or sudden deaths over which a coroner has jurisdiction (Black et al., 2010a). This chapter will therefore begin with a summary of the general laws and guidelines that influence a coroner's practice, followed by a summary of the coroner's role in MFIs, both at home and abroad.

The Coroner's Role

The coroner's function is to act as an 'independent judicial officer'. Each is appointed and resourced by 'relevant authority' (normally metropolitan/county/unitary authority council) for the district or territorial area for which he or she is responsible. Though the relevant authority appoints each senior coroner, he or she is not an employee of the authority. The appointment is held personally, and he or she remains personally responsible for any judicial decisions made.

In addition, all senior coroners will have the support of 'assistant coroners' (who have to have the same professional qualification as a senior coroner). Assistant coroners act in all material respects as the senior coroner for the area in the senior coroner's absence or at his or her direction. All appointments of assistant coroners are made by the relevant authority.

All references to 'coroner' apply equally to a senior coroner or assistant coroner.

In terms of professional qualification, to be appointed as a coroner, the individual must either be a lawyer (solicitor or barrister) at least 5 years' standing. However, those coroners appointed before July 25, 2013 and who were qualified only because they were a registered medical practitioner of 5 years' standing will be allowed to continue their appointments but will not qualify, on their medical qualification alone, to change their appointments or be appointed elsewhere.

A key aspect of a coroner's position is his or her territorial responsibility: each coroner has exclusive responsibility for carrying out his or her statutory duties in his or her own area. The restriction on a coroner only holding inquests in his or her own area has been repealed, but they are expected to carry out all their various judicial functions in their area. Coroners' courts where coroners hold inquests are recognised as 'inferior courts of record' and open to the public.

The coroner has various support staff, being both 'coroner's officers', who normally will be police civilian employees, and clerical and support staff normally employed by the relevant authority. Coroners' officers will make inquiries on the direction of the coroner.

There are numerous legal principles that govern the way coroners work, the principle law that empowers coroners and determines their function being the Coroners and Justice Act 2009 (UK Government, 2009). This act largely replaced the Coroners Act 1988, when it came into force (July 25, 2013) although many of the general principles governing the way in which coroners work remain broadly unchanged. In addition, there are various procedural rules, viz., the Coroners (Investigation) Regulations 2013, the Coroners (Inquest) Rules 2013, and the Coroners Allowances, Fees and Expenses Regulations 2013 (UK Government, 2013), which lay down the processes that are used by the coroner and those working for him or her.

The 2009 Act (UK Government, 2009) created a new post of chief coroner of England and Wales. He or she is to provide guidance and leadership for individual coroners and also has a number of executive powers and functions required of him under that act.

There are a number of obvious fundamental principles—the first is that the coroner must be available at all times to '… to address matters relating to an investigation into a death which must be dealt with immediately and cannot wait until the next working day' (as required by regulation 4 of the Coroners (Investigation) Regulations 2013 (UK Government, 2013). These duties may be undertaken either by the coroner in isolation or by his or her assistant coroner. The next principle determines which coroner should become involved in a death investigation and at what stage. This is synonymous with the basic function of the coroner and is to be found in Section 1(1) of the 2009 Act (UK Government, 2009), which provides that 'A senior coroner who is made aware that the body of a deceased person is within that coroner's area must as soon as practicable conduct an investigation into the person's death …. if the coroner has reason to suspect that—(a) the deceased died a violent or unnatural death, (b) the cause of death is unknown, or (c) the deceased died while in custody or otherwise in state detention'.

This sets out the coroner's responsibilities and also empowers him or her to conduct an investigation into a death. If the coroner has reason '… to suspect that the deceased—(a) died a violent or unnatural death, or (b) died while in custody or otherwise in state detention' then, in the course of his investigation, he must conduct an inquest into the death.

The chief coroner may direct a coroner to undertake a specific investigation and inquest, even if the body is lying other than in the coroner's own area. He or she may also appoint a judge or retired senior coroner to undertake a specific investigation and inquest, in place of the senior coroner (or one of the assistant coroners) for that particular area.

The inquest is conducted in public. Witnesses attend and give sworn evidence, although, in some instances, the evidence may be taken in the form of a statement, report or document without the personal attendance of the maker of the document. The choice of the witnesses is the coroner's.

The result of an inquest is 'a finding and determination', a formal document required under Section 10(1) of the 2009 Act (UK Government, 2009) and will detail those matters required to be found from the evidence by Section 5(3) of the 2009 Act (UK Government, 2009)—'(a) who the deceased was; (b) how, when and where the deceased came by his or her death; (c) the [personal] particulars (if any) required … to be registered concerning the death'.

However, Section 10(2) of the 2009 Act (UK Government, 2009) makes it clear 'that a determination ….. may not be framed in such a way as to appear to determine any question of—(a) criminal liability on the part of a named person, or (b) civil liability'.

The coroner is responsible for each individual dead body throughout the process. If more than one person has died (if there is more than one body lying in the coroner's area), then each body will form and be subject to a separate investigation and inquest, even if all the deaths occurred at the same time and in the same incident and all the inquests are held at the same time. In terms of what constitutes a 'body'—in cases, for example, where remains are highly fragmented—over which a coroner has jurisdiction, it is generally considered that the material recovered must be incompatible with life, that is to say that there is no prospect that an individual thought to be dead could be alive (Black et al., 2010a).

Section 5(3) of the 2009 Act (UK Government, 2009) also limits the scope of the coroner's inquest by providing that 'Neither the … coroner conducting an investigation …. into a person's death nor the jury (if there is one) may express any opinion on any matter …'

Consequently, it is clear that a coroner's investigation and inquest is a limited inquiry and that the evidence marshalled by the coroner can only be for the limited function of that investigation and inquest and he or she may not to conduct a wide-ranging fault-finding inquiry. The coroner has the authority to order post-mortem examinations (PMs) to be made to gather evidence for the inquest and for special examinations, including neuropathology or toxicology. This does not require familial consent; however, a number of obligations fall upon the coroner, particularly in relation to tissue retention. For example, although the majority of provisions of the Human Tissue Act (2004) do not apply to a coroner's autopsy, there is an expectation that coroners will adhere to the related Code of Practice (UK Government, 2004).

Under the Coroners (Investigation) Regulations 2013 (UK Government, 2013), the coroner has to inform a number of persons (including the next of kin) that a PM is going to take place, the reason for the examination, the time and place at which the PM will take occur, and the complete disclosure of all tissue retained. Under these same provisions, they may have disclosed to them, on application, a copy of the PM report.

By the Coroners (Investigation) Regulations 2013 and the Coroners (Inquest) Rules 2013 (UK Government, 2013), those who have recognised 'proper interests' are able to apply to the coroner to have disclosed to them documents and information obtained by the coroner in the course of the investigation and inquest. There may be restrictions imposed on the material disclosed and/or the use to which it may be put (see rules 12–16, the Coroners (Inquest) Rules 2013 [UK Government, 2013]).

In addition to the statutory laws (the Acts of Parliament and the various rules of procedure and regulations made under them), coroner law and practice is also shaped by the various court decisions of the Administrative Court (part of the High Court), the Court of Appeal and Supreme Court, as well as the European Court of Human Rights. These court decisions will determine the way that the coroner will be able to interpret and apply the law.

Mass Fatalities

MFIs are often some of the most complex scenes to investigate, and this complexity extends to the identification of victims of these events—a process known as disaster victim identification (DVI). In any MFI, an early, rapid deployment of specially trained DVI reconnaissance team is essential, if the requirements of victim recovery and identification are to be met to the standard of excellence required (Mallett et al., 2011).

When things have not gone entirely as would be hoped and problems have arisen with the identification process, lessons have been learned, often as a result of official investigations. From time to time, these have consisted of judge-led public inquiries that have resulted in reports, for example, those concerning MFIs in football grounds or on the transport system (Barron and Mallett, 2011; Bracken and Black, 2011; Galloway and Mallett, 2011; Hiley and Black, 2011; Hon Lord Cullen, 1996; Justice Popplewell, 1986; Mowat, 1991; Rt Hon Lord Justice Taylor, 1990; Walker and Mallett, 2011a–c; Walsh et al., 2011). These have had an impact on coroner practice. In particular, in the context of mass fatalities, the Marchioness non-statutory inquiry in 2000 (Lord Justice Clarke, 2001; Walker and Mallett, 2011b), reporting in early 2001, examined the processes of body retrieval and identification of individual victims and the need to secure clear unequivocal identification in respect of each body recovered in the event of a mass fatality occurrence.* The report (entitled *Report of the Public Inquiry into the Identification of Victims Following Major Transport Accidents—Report of Lord Justice Clarke*, but informally known as the Clarke Report [Lord Justice Clarke, 2001]) highlighted the importance of mutual understanding between those involved in DVI:

> It is vital that each agency knows not only what its role will be in the event of a disaster producing numerous fatalities but also the role of each of the other organisations involved (Lord Justice Clarke, 2001).

Lord Justice Clarke (2001), who led that inquiry, made it clear a number of general principles should be kept in mind throughout the identification process after a major disaster. These are:

- Provision of honest and, as far as possible, accurate information at all times and at every stage
- Respect for the deceased and the bereaved

* The inquiry sprang from the river Thames Marchioness disaster in August 1989 when 51 people died. (For an account of this event, see Walker and Mallett, 2011b.)

- A sympathetic and caring approach throughout
- The avoidance of mistaken identification

Further recommendations in the final report included the following:

Recommendation 5: It should be made clear that the methods used for establishing the identity of the deceased should, wherever possible, avoid any unnecessary invasive procedures or disfigurement or mutilation and that body parts should not be removed for the purposes of identification except where it is necessary to do so as a last resort. The position is somewhat different in the case of samples taken for DNA purposes

Recommendation 6: Consideration should be given to requiring coroners to undergo extensive training, both before appointment and from time to time thereafter. Such training should be uniformed across the country and should include:

- The identification of unknown bodies in multiple fatality incidents
- Dealing with bereaved relatives in major disasters
- The management of and contingency planning for multiple death disasters
- The likely ethnic, cultural and religious interests of minority and religious groups in case of death

Recommendation 7: I endorse the recommendations made by Michael Burgess, secretary to the Coroners' Society, that:

- While the actual methods for establishing the identity of the deceased person should in any particular case be left to the coroner, the Home Office should issue guidance on the criteria and suitable methods which might be used.
- Such guidance should be kept under regular review, and there should be consultation with such persons or organisations as the Home Office may from time to time determine.
- The guidance should take account of advances in scientific knowledge and available techniques.

Recommendation 8: Coroners and coroners' staff should meet with families or family groups to explain the identification and other procedures to be followed. They should also keep relatives informed of the progress of the identification process.

(Lord Justice Clarke, 2001)

It is a combination of all these principles that coroners apply when engaged in the identification of the dead, whether of a single person or where there are a number of dead as might arise in a mass fatality event. When looking at the role of coroner in an MFI, although the law remains basically the same, there are inevitable differences (Black et al., 2010a). One aspect of which that may have to be re-evaluated in an MFI is the concept of what constitutes a 'body', as the context in which the 'body' (and associated idea that a 'body' comprises elements without which life is not viable) is found is key. For example, a collection of body parts from one individual, which of themselves are not incompatible with life, if found in the majority of scenarios would not provide proof of death. However, if they have been found as a result of a plane crash, then the context of their recovery would be highly influential in determining if those elements may be regarded as a 'body', as in this example those elements may be all that will be recovered of that person (Black et al., 2010a). Much would of course depend on whether the individual was known to have been involved in that incident, in this example named on a passenger manifest.

There may also be limitations on what might be achieved. For example, what is the procedure when, because of the sheer scale of the occurrence, there are bodies arising from the same event lying in the districts of more than one coroner? Or what if no body exists, as in the case when it is argued that the body has been completely destroyed in the event? An example of this second scenario would be the Lockerbie plane bombing, which occurred on December 21, 1988, when 8 of the 270 victims were classified as missing, presumed dead through multiple injuries caused by the plane crash, and in all likelihood vaporised as a result of the extreme temperatures caused by the ignition of the aviation fuel (Galloway and Mallett, 2011) when the plane crashed onto the town of Lockerbie and surrounding area. (It should be noted that although the Lockerbie plane bombing was an MFI, no inquest was held as the incident occurred in Scotland, and Scottish law does not have coroners. The coroner's function, so far as necessary, is undertaken by 'procurators fiscal'.)

Within reason, the law can and does provide for both these instances. Included under Section 2 of the 2009 Act (UK Government, 2009), coroners may (subject to conditions) agree between themselves to transfer of jurisdiction from one coroner to another, so using this provision, it is possible for all the fatalities from a single event to be or become the responsibility of a single coroner; the chief coroner may direct that a transfer be made and/or for another coroner to undertake an investigation and inquest. In addition, Section 1(4) of the 2009 Act (UK Government, 2009), if a coroner receives evidence suggesting that there was a person who has died but whose body was destroyed, then he or she may apply to the chief coroner who, on the basis of the information supplied, may then direct a coroner, under Section 1(5) of the 2009 Act (UK Government, 2009), to undertake an investigation and inquest into the death of such person in the absence of a body. The coroner so directed does not have to be the coroner who made the report. The reporting coroner would have to satisfy the chief coroner that the death occurred in or near his or her area and that the body has been destroyed or cannot be recovered. For this to take place, there would have to be a high level of proof that the missing person was actually dead—as in the Lockerbie bombing example (Galloway and Mallett, 2011). Using all these statutory and other provisions and the proper exercise of the judicial authority of the coroner, the legal framework exists for coroners to undertake the necessary inquiry processes to establish the identity of the victims of a mass fatality event.

What Are the Coroner's Responsibilities?

In the event of mass fatality event, a number of decisions need to be undertaken and fall to the relevant coroner to make and/or facilitate because he or she is the only person with the legal responsibility and authority to undertake them.

Thus, the coroner for the area where the bodies are lying will, in consultation with his or her relevant authority and chief officer of police,

- Initiate the establishment of the emergency mortuary if the agreed criteria are satisfied and the capacity of the normal mortuary facility is not sufficient
- Authorise the removal of bodies of victims
- Authorise the examination of bodies to find a cause of the death

The coroner has the duty to consult with other relevant individuals and organisations, including the police, and it is he or she who selects a forensic pathologist to undertake any required examination of the bodies. If the bodies lie across the district of more than one coroner, then the coroners concerned should consult early on and agree which of them is to become responsible for the incident (and become the incident coroner), and then transfers of jurisdiction can be made under the provisions of Section 2 of the 2009 Act (UK Government, 2009) between the coroners in whose districts the bodies actually lie.

Under the UK law, the coroner is responsible for each body, including:

- Examination (if the family/next of kin object to an autopsy, the coroner can override their objections)
- Retention
- Transfer and eventually handing back to the family/next of kin
- Exhumation (should the need arise)

The coroner is ultimately responsible for the correct identification of an individual. The rules associated with the identification of individuals, whether in an individual case or an MFI, are so tightly controlled to ensure that the bodies are correctly identified, and coroners seek to establish unequivocal identification in every case. There are a number of reasons why the identification of the individual bodies remains an essential aspect of death investigations, including the following:

- Family members are entitled to and require some certainty if they are going to be able to grieve properly; further, they should have the body or human remains returned to them for whatever funeral 'rites' they require.
- As with a family, there are also wider social/religious reasons for ensuring that the identification of those who have died is known and properly recorded.
- The dead person's 'public' record requires updating, including the electoral and jury rolls, personal entitlement to medical services, driving licence, passport and any court, police or criminal record.
- If the person who died was married or in a civil partnership, then without the identification being confirmed, the surviving spouse or partner would be unable to remarry unless he or she is prepared to wait 7 years after which he or she may apply to the Divorce Court for a declaration of presumption of death.
- Various property and financial matters (including banking, inheritance, life insurance, and taxation) all require that the deaths of individuals are properly noted and that the necessary resulting action following such events is undertaken.
- Knowing the identification of deceased persons may be critical evidence for any criminal prosecution.

Did someone die? If so, who? Did the accused cause the death? If so, how? How is the identification achieved to the satisfaction of the coroner? In the simplest terms, various information, relating to the identification of PM data, is collected from the deceased and compared with the relevant personal information that has been collected from or about possible victim's antemortem (AM) data. The AM data will be collected by specially trained police family liaison officers from the family, homes and places of work of the persons who are believed to be possible victims. The PM data will be collected by the pathologist and other specialist examiners and police officers from the remains of the victim. If during the process of AM and PM data comparison a match is found, the identification has been achieved.

The complexity of this matching process varies depending on the incident, one variable of which is the incident 'classification'. Mass fatal events are categorised into one of the three groups:

- 'Closed event'—when all the victims arise from a recognised class of people, for example, the ticketed passengers on an aeroplane (e.g. the Manchester International Airport fire[*] [Goodwin et al., 2011]).
- 'Open event'—when the victims are apparently random members of the public who just happen to be victims because of the presence in the mass fatality event (e.g. the victims of the Kings' Cross fire[†]).
- There may also be a 'hybrid' or 'mixed' event when some victims are from a limited group or class and other random members of the public, for example, an aeroplane crash landing on a housing estate (e.g. the Lockerbie plane bombing [Galloway and Mallett, 2011] or the Brighton hotel bombing in 1984[‡] for which a hotel manifest was available, but there could have been additional unregistered individuals in the hotel at the time of the explosion [Buchan, 2011]).

Difficulties in obtaining unequivocal identification may arise from the gross disruption and/or decomposition of the bodies of victims in these cases. For example, the 52 victims and 4 bombers in the London bus and underground terrorist bombings, which took place on July 7 in London, were highly disrupted, and the identification of the individuals was complicated by the fact that it was also a known terrorist event from the beginning. Thus, terrorism investigators were also involved in scene examination (Walker and Mallett, 2011a), which can conflict with priorities of victim recovery and identification. In the Hillsborough football stadium disaster, 96 men, women, and children died as a result of crush injuries. However, although there were a large number of deceased victims, none suffered any significant disruption, thus facilitating expedited identification as part matching was not a requirement in this incident (Barron and Mallett, 2011).

---

[*] MFI in which 53 passengers and two crew members died aboard flight KT28M, as a result of smoke and toxic gas inhalation. This disaster was pivotal to bringing about changes in evacuation procedures and legislative control over materials utilised in plane interiors.
[†] Thirty-one people died as the result of a fire that ravaged London's underground network on the evening of November 18, 1987. This event had significant influence on future multiagency cooperation, as well as leading to amendments to safety guidelines and requirements for public transport providers (Bracken and Black, 2011). Another example would be the London bombings on July 7, 2005 (Walker and Mallett, 2011a). Commonly referred to as 7/7, this was a coordinated suicide terrorist attack carried out in the heart of London's transport system during the morning rush hour on July 7, 2005, in which 52 innocent people died in addition to the 4 bombers.
[‡] Bombing of the Grand Hotel, Brighton, where the Prime Minister and her cabinet were staying as part of the annual Conservative Party Conference. Five people were killed, and many more were seriously injured.

The material that is used to achieve an indisputable identification may take a number of different forms, although 'primary' criteria should wherever possible be used. The selection of what criteria will constitute an identification in any situation is at the discretion of the coroner, as they remain responsible for the remains at all times, as the sole judicial officer with the authority to remove, retain and examine dead bodies to achieve the necessary demands of the coroner's duties. It is under his or her authority that the police, pathologists and other professionals may each undertake their duties and examinations in relation to each body.

There are four accepted primary identification criteria, those that are considered 'unique' to the victim; these are as follows:

- DNA: The comparison of DNA from tissue recovered from victims' remains during examination with DNA either from artefacts used by potential victims (hairbrushes or toothbrushes) or the DNA profiles of family members of potential victims.
- Fingerprints: The comparison of fingerprints taken from the bodies of victims compared with prints collected from either criminal or official records or from personal items known to have been used by potential victims (as applied following the Asian tsunami in 2004) (see Chapter 14).
- Odontology: Original records from dentists can be compared against information collected by the odontologist during examination of the deceased in the mortuary.
- Medical information/prostheses: For example, an x-ray of the frontal sinuses (Black et al., 2010b), as this region is considered hypervariable between individuals.

Secondary criteria may be relevant. This may include

- Clothing
- Tattoos
- Jewellery
- Other medical conditions/scars
- Possessions, including personal identification that may have been carried and other documentation

Visual identification is not normally considered a safe method of achieving an accurate and reliable identification, as there are many cases where victims have been misidentified through visual means (e.g. as is known to have occurred following the 2004 Asian tsunami). Therefore, 'tertiary' criteria may be relevant in establishing or eliminating possible victims. This may include, among others, the location where the event took place.

In each case, of course, the successful identification depends upon the two distinct parts:

- The collection of AM data from possible victims (undertaken by the police under the overall direction of a senior investigating officer working with a casualty bureau)
- The collection of equivalent PM data/material from the victims (undertaken by the police and other specialists under the direction and authority of the coroner)

The comparison of these two data sets has to be undertaken in a controlled, disciplined, and rigorous environment, represented by the Identification Commission. The commission will be chaired by the relevant incident coroner and have as its members representatives of those responsible for collecting the two data sets—the pathologists and forensic odontologists for the PM data and the police specialists who collect the AM material, as well as any other independent experts that the coroner believes may assist. The commission will meet, firstly, to agree the criteria to be collected from which the identification is to be made. Subsequently, it will meet periodically to supervise the actual comparison of individual cases and sign each case off as the necessary agreed identification criteria have been satisfied. The results of the commission's deliberations will then be passed to the coroner's inquest.

In the context of mass fatality events, a coroner's inquest will be conducted into each body recovered. Each separate body will result in a separate inquest, which will be 'opened' following which the body will be handed over to the family for burial, cremation or removal from England and Wales for burial or cremation elsewhere. The individual separate inquests will then be 'consolidated' into a single inquest process after the MFI investigation has been completed. If serious criminal charges (of causing the death) are brought, the inquests will be adjourned, while the criminal court process proceeds and may never be resumed because the coroner inquest process will be subsumed into the criminal proceedings. Similarly, any overall judicial inquiry that has been ordered into the incident may replace the inquest process.

The chief coroner is likely to issue guidance to ensure consistency in the approach that individual coroners may take in dealing with these cases, and the chief coroner may personally become directly involved.

If a mass fatality event occurs abroad, a (English) coroner will only be involved if individual bodies are repatriated to England and Wales. Because of the wording of Section1(1) of the 2009 Act (UK Government, 2009), the (English/Welsh) coroner will take jurisdiction and carry through the coroner's investigation and inquest process, but he or she is legally only able to take jurisdiction and start once the body arrives in his or her district but, of course, then only in respect of that body or those bodies repatriated.

The question of the identification of each repatriated victim will remain critical, and the same criteria will be applied by the English coroner as far as he or she can as though the incident had occurred in England and Wales.

Under a direction from the Home Office (then responsible for coroner's law and practice)—Home Office Circular No 79 of 1983—it will normally be the coroner for the district where the funeral or cremation is to take place that should take jurisdiction (UK Government, 1983). In the event that more than one body is repatriated from the same event, either it will be the coroner for the port of arrival or it will be a matter that is agreed between individual coroners who will take jurisdiction. The general principle is that just one coroner will assume overall responsibility to ensure consistency of process.

The conduct of any coroner's investigation and inquest, when the death occurred outside England and Wales, will always be dependent upon receiving all the necessary evidence in an acceptable form. This is by no means easy and may require assistance from both the Foreign and Commonwealth Office and police forces in both the United Kingdom and overseas.

The identification of bodies where the primary process has been undertaken abroad, for example, can be far more difficult than starting the process again on repatriation to the United Kingdom. This occurs for a number of reasons, including the following: foreign staff practices and PMs may not be to the same standards, sites may be expeditiously cleared as the result of political and social pressures, and, importantly, the (English/Welsh) coroner does not have any legal status until the 'body' has actually been returned, when Section 1(1) of the 2009 Act (UK Government, 2009) becomes engaged.

Conclusion

In conclusion, a coroner has the sole responsibility for confirming a deceased person's identity in England and Wales, and although strict guidelines, as laid down by various acts, exist to ensure this process that is undertaken to exacting standards, in reality, it is complicated by the nature and location of the death event. This can be seen most obviously in mass fatality events that occur abroad, where the coroner has no status over the bodies until they are repatriated. Varying world standards of DVI, together with the pressure levied by politicians, the press and families for expedient identification, can further cloud this picture.

Lessons learned from previous events when mistakes have been made, either in identification or other parts of the repatriation process, have led to new rules governing the identification process. Each death and mass fatality event is individual, with its own challenges.

Thus, lessons remain to be learned, but it is hoped that the exacting standards coroners insist upon will prevent as many misidentifications as is feasibly possible given the recognised and considerable challenges in today's unstable world. If the reader would like further information, it can be obtained from the Cabinet Office (UK Government, ND) and the Home Office's publication 'Dealing with Fatalities during Disasters' (UK Government, 2003, soon to be revised and reissued).

References

Barron, D. and Mallett, X. 2011. The Hillsborough Football Stadium disaster, April 15, 1989. In: Black, S., Sunderland, G., Hackman, L., and Mallett, X. (eds.) *The DVI Casebook: Experience and Practice*. Boca Raton, FL: CRC Press, pp. 109–125.

Black, S., Walker, G., Hackman, L., and Brooks, C. 2010a. The coroner. In: Black, S., Walker, G., Hackman, L., and Brooks, C. (eds.) *Disaster Victim Identification: The Practitioner's Guide*. Dundee, U.K.: Dundee University Press, Ltd., pp. 43–58.

Black, S., Walker, G., Hackman, L., and Brooks, C. 2010b. Exhibits and personal effects. In: *Disaster Victim Identification: The Practitioner's Guide*. Dundee, U.K.: Dundee University Press, Ltd., pp. 205–212.

Bracken, N. and Black, S. 2011. King's cross underground fire, November 18, 1987. In: Black, S., Sunderland, G., Hackman, L., and Mallett, X. (eds.) *The DVI Casebook: Experience and Practice*. Boca Raton, FL: CRC Press, pp. 61–76.

Buchan, A. 2011. The Brighton hotel bombing. In: Black, S., Sunderland, G., Hackman, L., and Mallett, X. (eds.) *The DVI Casebook: Experience and Practice*. Boca Raton, FL: CRC Press, pp. 19–29.

Galloway, G. and Mallett, X. 2011. The Lockerbie bombing, December 21, 1988. In: Black, S., Sunderland, G., Hackman, L., and Mallett, X. (eds.) *The DVI Casebook: Experience and Practice*. Boca Raton, FL: CRC Press, pp. 89–107.

Goodwin, S., Wood, D., and Black, S. 2011. Manchester International Airport fire: Flight KT28M, August 22, 1985. In: Black, S., Sunderland, G., Hackman, L., and Mallett, X. (eds.) *The DVI Casebook: Experience and Practice*. Boca Raton, FL: CRC Press, pp. 51–60.

Hiley, D. and Black, S. 2011. Piper Alpha oil and gas platform disaster, July 6, 1988. In: Black, S., Sunderland, G., Hackman, L., and Mallett, X. (eds.) *The DVI Casebook: Experience and Practice*. Boca Raton, FL: CRC Press, pp. 77–87.

Hon Lord Cullen. 1996. *The Public Inquiry into the Shootings at Dunblane Primary School on 13 March 1996*. Available from: http://www.archive.official-documents.co.uk/document/scottish/dunblane/duncntnt.htm (accessed March 3, 2010).

Justice Popplewell. 1986. *The Papers of the Popplewell Inquiry into Crowd Safety at Sports Grounds*. Available from: http://www.brad.ac.uk/library/special/documents/popplecldtempl.pdf. (accessed May 3, 2010).

Lord Justice Clarke. 2001. *Report of the Public Inquiry into the Identification of Victims Following Major Transport Accidents—Report of Lord Justice Clarke*, London, U.K., Stationary Office.

Mallett, X., Hackman, L., and Black, S. 2011. Introduction: The DVI casebook, UK incidents. In: Black, S., Sunderland, G., Hackman, L., and Mallett, X. (eds.) *The DVI Casebook: Experience and Practice*. Boca Raton, FL: CRC Press, pp. 1–17.

Mowat, Q.C. 1991. Sheriffdom of South Strathclyde, Dumfries and Galloway determination by Sheriff Principal John S Mowat QC in the fatal accident inquiry relating to the Lockerbie air disaster. Available from: http://www.gla.ac.uk:443/lockerbie/leg/Fai_1.rtf. (accessed May 3, 2010).

Rt Hon Lord Justice Taylor. 1990. Final report—The Hillsborough stadium disaster: 15th April 1989. Inquiry by the Rt Hon Lord Justice Taylor. Available from: http://www.fsf.org.uk/uploaded/publications/pdfs/hillsboroughstadiumdisasterfinalreport.pdf. (accessed November 19, 2009).

UK Government. 1984. The Coroners Rules [1984]. Available from: http://www.legislation.gov.uk/uksi/1984/552/made. (accessed October 25, 2012).

UK Government. 1988. Coroners Act [1988]. Available from: http://www.legislation.gov.uk/ukpga/1988/13/contents. (accessed October 25, 2012).

UK Government. 2003. Dealing with Fatalities during Disasters. York, U.K.: Home Office, Emergency Planning College.

UK Government. 2004. Human Tissue Act [2004]. Available from: http://www.legislation.gov.uk/ukpga/2004/30/contents (accessed November 12, 2012).

UK Government. 2009. Coroners and Justice Act 2009. Available from: http://www.justice.gov.uk/publications/coroners-justice-bill.htm (accessed April 29, 2010).

UK Government. ND. Coroner. Cabinet Office. Available from: http://www.cabinetoffice.gov.uk/search/apachesolr_search/coroner. (accessed November 12, 2012).

Walker, G. and Mallett, X. 2011a. London bus and underground bombings, July 7, 2005. In: Black, S., Sunderland, G., Hackman, L., and Mallett, X. (eds.) The DVI Casebook: Experience and Practice. Boca Raton, FL: CRC Press, pp. 223–237.

Walker, G. and Mallett, X. 2011b. The Marchioness river boat disaster, August 20, 1989. In: Black, S., Sunderland, G., Hackman, L., and Mallett, X. (eds.) The DVI Casebook: Experience and Practice. Boca Raton, FL: CRC Press, pp. 127–141.

Walker, G. and Mallett, X. 2011c. Rail incidents. In: Black, S., Sunderland, G., Hackman, L., and Mallett, X. (eds.) The DVI Casebook: Experience and Practice. Boca Raton, FL: CRC Press, pp. 173–188.

Walsh, T., Rylatt, N., and Hackman, L. 2011. Bradford City football stadium fire, May 11, 1985. In: Black, S., Sunderland, G., Hackman, L., and Mallett, X. (eds.) The DVI Casebook: Experience and Practice. Boca Raton, FL: CRC Press, pp. 31–49.

Identification of Missing Persons and Unidentified Remains in Disaster Victim Identification

3

Recommendations and Best Practice

JAN BIKKER

Contents

Introduction

It is recognised that each disaster is unique in scale, causation and long-term effects, and as such different definitions have been published. The World Health Organization's (WHO) classification of a disaster is focused on the humanitarian effort by declaring it 'a sudden ecological phenomenon of sufficient magnitude to require external assistance' (Noji, 1997). The 'ologists' literature adopts a flexible definition in terms of the number of individuals killed and commonly refers to a disaster as an episode in which the number of fatalities is in excess of that which can be dealt with using the normal mortuary facilities (Royal College of Pathologists, 2000). Another distinction is made between the causation of a large-scale incident, either man-made or natural, the latter being further divided in mitigable and unmitigable events (Udayakumar, 2009). Indeed, a disaster creates many challenges whether it is man-made or natural, including the identification of potentially large numbers of deceased and the humanitarian response to identify the deceased and restore family links and social interactions within local communities.

In the aftermath of a disaster, all too often human rights of persons affected are insufficiently taken into account: identification is frequently seen as a small part of the humanitarian process. It can be argued, however, that the implementation of proper procedures may not only assist in the return of human remains to the next of kin but may also form an important part in addressing the psychosocial needs of the surviving relatives or local communities and thus aid in traumatic recovery following the following a mass fatality event (MFI). Consequently, providing relatives with psychosocial assistance and education about the identification process is an essential part of all forensic investigations involving recovery of human remains and the identification of deceased victims (Keough and Samuels, 2004).

Disaster victim identification (DVI), the identification process of missing persons and human remains following a MFI, is facilitated by the comparison of ante-mortem (AM) and post-mortem (PM) records. AM information is in the first instance obtained from relatives, which, depending on national law, are comprised of children born in and out of wedlock, adopted or stepchildren, lawfully wedded or unwedded partner, parents (including stepmother, stepfather, adopter) and full or half or adopted brothers and sisters (ICRC, 2009). Work colleagues, friends and neighbours are often also included within this definition in relation to missing person investigations. AM records are pivotal to collaborate a positive identification (Blau et al., 2006; Rai and Anand, 2007), and the availability and accuracy of these records determine the success of the identification process (Avon, 2004; Budowle et al., 2005; Calacal et al., 2005; Gonzales-Andrade and Sanchez, 2005. LeClair et al., 2004) The collection of AM and PM data is initially collected blindly, without prior knowledge as to which particular identification feature will be reported in the other set. In disasters and missing person investigations, it is therefore pivotal that both the AM and PM data collected are as comprehensive, detailed and as accurate as feasibly possible.

Proficient data management is pivotal to the success of the identification process in large-scale identification events. A number of different documents can be found detailing what and how data should be recorded, in the form of standards, guidelines and procedures. Those terms may be confusing. A *standard* (also *standard operation procedure* or SOP) is a written—mandatory—control, in accordance with agreed-upon specifications aimed at obtaining a desired outcome. *Guidelines* are recommended, non-mandatory sets of best practices that are supported by consensus that help support standards or serve as a reference when no applicable standard is in place. *Procedures* are step-to-step instructions that may assist in implementing the various policies, standards, and guidelines. This chapter describes current standards, guidelines, and procedures currently used for DVI.

Developments in Disaster Victim Identification

DVI is a complex process, which in many cases involves legal, political, ethical, cultural and psychosocial aspects, both on a national and international level. The 2004 tsunami in Southeast Asia demonstrated many new DVI challenges, and valuable lessons were learned (Interpol, 2010). The tsunami affected the coast of many countries around the Indian Ocean and the Andaman Sea, including Indonesia, Sri Lanka, Thailand, India and the island communities of the Maldives and the Seychelles, claiming the lives of 300,000 victims. While procedures were initially in place to identify the deceased, the Sri Lankan authorities were overwhelmed by the process and elected to limit the data collection to recording fingerprints and taking photographs of the deceased, after which the victims were buried in mass graves (Morgan et al., 2006; Perera 2005; Yamada et al., 2006). In some more remote areas, there were burials by villagers and family members without any records being made (Cordner, 2005; Fitrasanti and Syukriani, 2009).

It must be kept in mind that a sudden disaster may be so overwhelming that protocols cannot be followed (Sirisup and Kanluen, 2005), despite good preparation from national authorities and DVI teams (Kvaal, 2006). Inaccessibility of the disaster site(s) and destruction of basic services and facilities are further complicating factors in large natural disasters (Kubo, 2012), while the developing countries may be ill-equipped to tackle the problem (Olumbe and Yakub, 2001). In Thailand, Sirisup and Kanluen (2005) noted that initially, various protocols were used for the recording of unidentified bodies and missing persons, such as the dental report forms of the Thai National Police Office and AM and PM forms of the Federal Bureau of Investigation (FBI). In Indonesia, the pink Interpol DVI forms were completed for 'foreign' victims, while photographs were the only identification method employed for the Indonesian victims for visual identification by relatives (Fitrasanti and Syukriani, 2009). By using different reporting protocols, additional problems were caused in transferring data into the DVI database for matching and comparison, which is based on the Interpol forms (Interpol, 2008b,c). This problem has been subsequently addressed by the Interpol Tsunami Evaluation Working Group (Interpol, 2010).

Following the 2004 tsunami, the number of national DVI teams has increased, but they often follow local DVI standards normally practiced in the team's respective country, which may cause problems in international co-operation (Lessig and Rothschild, 2012). After that disaster it was reported, for example, that some international DVI groups refused to follow agreed procedures (De Valck, 2006; James, 2005; Scanlon, 2006; Sirisup and Kanluen, 2005; Tun et al., 2005) and did not respect the jurisdiction of the police services or local customs. Central co-ordination of the recovery and identification effort is essential (Huckenbeck et al., 2008), although this often does occur in the immediate aftermath of a disaster, nor is a framework of international agreement in place to streamline co-operation or delegation of responsibility for DVI (Kvaal, 2006). Countries with limited resources are still lacking functional disaster management mechanisms in legislation, at national and regional levels, to co-ordinate the relief missions and mitigate the after-effects of the disaster (Perera, 2006).

In 2006, the Pan American Health Organization (PAHO) and the International Committee of the Red Cross (ICRC), together with the WHO and the International Federation of Red Cross and Red Crescent Societies (IFRC), published guidelines to help improve the management of the dead after a disaster.* It was recognised that existing guidelines and manuals for forensic DVI specialists, including the Interpol DVI guidelines (Interpol, 2008b), are of little or no practical use for non-specialists, particularly in the early aftermath of a disaster when trained specialists are often not immediately available. Although the use of the Interpol DVI forms for *specialists* is recommended, *non-specialists* are encouraged to collect basic, albeit essential, information using different AM and PM forms, for example, those of the ICRC (Tidball-Binz, 2007). Guidelines have been prepared by the ICRC for data collation by non-specialists in *Operational Best Practices Regarding the Management of Human Remains and Information on the Dead by Non-Specialists* (ICRC, 2004), a manual aimed at humanitarian organisations and armed forces. The Interpol DVI guidelines do not explore the problematic issue of recovery of fatalities during active conflicts or peacekeeping operations in hostile environments (Thomson and Black, 2012), nor does guidance exist for DVI missions and deployment of DVI teams in failed states (Kirsch, 2010) or in post-conflict areas.

Many of the SOPs and protocols are based on western values, and those do not take into account local, religious, cultural and ethnic beliefs that may be relevant in certain communities (Hunter and Cox, 2005). DVI teams may need to operate in a host country with specific language and cultural and societal norms (Sweet, 2010), which must be taken into consideration (ICRC, 2010). Navarro-Garc'a et al. ([2010], citing [Carrillo, 2007]) mentioned that in Venezuela, for example, relatives will have an active role in AM data collection procedures, registration systems and the excavation process. While this may form part of the reparation process of relatives who lost family members, it may also evolve from the inherent lack of trust in experts appointed by the state, particularly in political post-conflict situations. Secondly, if the burial location of a relative is known or remains thought to be from the missing person are exhumed and interred by the relatives in a private grave, they may

---

* ICRC field manual for first responders on Management of Dead Bodies after Disasters. Available from http://www.icrc.org/eng/resources/documents/publication/p0880.htm

not request or report a missing person (Huffine et al., 2001). Displacement of relatives of missing persons to neighbouring countries is an additional complicating factor in establishing a consolidated list. Initiatives for restoring links between displaced family members are encouraged (ICRC, 2012). Mistrust or fear for the transitional government may prevent relatives returning to their country or report those missing (Clark, 2010). A notable example is the situation of the families of missing Burmese migrant workers in Thailand following the 2004 tsunami, who were hesitant to report their missing relatives and friends for fear of arrest and deportation (Hakoda, 2005). Since then, most notably non-government organisations (NGOs) such as the ICRC have made recommendations that governments adopt guidelines for the protection and management of personal data in humanitarian law and in particular DNA (ICRC, 2003).

Although often overlooked, a properly conducted DVI process (e.g. effective communication, respect for cultural and religious practices, and explanation of the DVI process) may assist in the psychological recovery of the surviving relatives following their traumatic experiences; if the process is not conducted properly, it may result in an additional 'disaster' for the families. Indeed, the lack of information on the identification process is often cited by relatives as a traumatic experience (Eyre, 2002), and a psychosocial approach to AM data collection is therefore recommended. Many of the manuals and guidelines for DVI have been developed from the perspective of responders' operational needs in terms of plans, procedures and protocols rather than the needs and interests of the bereaved (Eyre, 2002) or psychological assistance for responders themselves (Jones, 1985). Particularly, the right of families to conduct religious and cultural funeral rites should be respected (Pan American Health Organization, 2004). In some cultures or areas, communication with relatives will be guided by group elders in that community, while in other cultures, the expected cultural norm is for males only to act as the family spokesperson (Keough and Samuels, 2004). To avoid language barriers, it is recommended to find assistance from a local interpreter or professional with a thorough understanding of the language and cultural customs (Berketa et al., 2012). In the 2011 east Japan earthquake and tsunami, for example, language issues caused problems between international DVI and search and rescue teams (Kubo, 2012). The collection of AM data may be hampered if those local cultural customs are not addressed (Keough and Samuels, 2004). Communication with family associations is pivotal in this respect to establishing trust and credibility about the identification process, as detailed in an integrated psychosocial and scientific framework reported by Keough and Samuels (2004). In this case, providing relatives with psychosocial assistance and education about the identification process was an essential part of all forensic investigations involving recovery of human remains and identification of bodies (Keough et al., 2004). By convening small groups of five to ten families, usually in a family's home, Bosnian field staff could explain through discussion, question and answer, written and illustrative brochures, and use of a video presentation what the exhumation and identification process entailed leading to increased collaboration of families with the collection of AM data.

Prior to the 2004 tsunami, psychosocial aspects of disasters were hardly considered (Eyre, 2002); however, since that time, there have been increasing interest and research in the psychosocial dynamics of both natural and man-made disasters (Carballo et al., 2005). The implementation of the family liaison framework may contribute in addressing this (NPIA, 2008). In the United Kingdom, members of Disaster Action,* all of whom are survivors and bereaved people from disasters, have written and published documents with guidance for families, police family liaison officers (FLOs), and coroner's officers. Guidelines for integrating a psychosocial approach in the identification process have been widely accepted and implemented in cases of grave human rights violations such as enforced disappearances; those recommendations may form a basis for disasters (see Ecap et al., 2009; Equitas, 2010).

SOPs and Recording Protocols

The need for guidelines and procedural documentation is commonly reiterated in the literature (De Valck, 2006; Kvaal, 2006; Lessig et al., 2006; Nuzzolese and DiVella, 2007). Best-practice guidelines and protocols are intended to help forensic scientists to act within ethical and professional boundaries (Tidball-Binz, 2006), as well as enhancing commonality of data recording of missing person information and unidentified remains. However, detailed guidelines are only occasionally published, while further difficulty of both developing and obtaining agreement for international guidelines is often a complicating factor in establishing definitive protocols (Vermylen, 2006), specifically for dealing with large numbers of dead bodies following natural disasters (Morgan et al., 2006) including multiple nationalities.

Requirements for Harmonisation and Standardisation of Recording

Harmonisation and standardisation contained in an internationally acceptable legal instrument could be of great use for many reasons at international as well as at national level. An internationally recognised format would promulgate good practice and facilitate the exchange of identification data between countries, although Ferllini (2007) noted that standard operating

---

* http://www.disastcraction.org

procedures and protocols are merely idealised statements of how things should be done. Webb (2006) suggested that less attention is given by practitioners to codes of ethics in international settings, probably because many of the published codes are written for practicing experts on a local or regional level. Vermylen (2006) concluded that any international guidelines can only be broadly descriptive and outline general principles; local jurisdictions and parties involved in missing person investigations should use the general guidelines to develop procedures and protocols directly relevant to their own national laws or forensically accepted standards for data recording. Indeed, the circumstances surrounding each disaster, atrocity or missing person case are different, while Blau (2006) noted that practitioners (or teams) working in international settings may have a responsibility to different organisations, such as courts, relatives, local communities or governmental agencies, each with their own information requirements. Importantly, if standardised procedures are not followed, any subsequent judicial process may be jeopardised (Ferllini, 2007) or the identification process delayed.

Indeed, the lack of a general agreement on an internationally accepted system for recording may lead to errors in comparability, exchange, and translation of identification data. This is particularly true for dental data (Keiser-Nielsen, 1969). Moreover, Ferllini (2007) argued that guidelines must be clear and simple, separating what is essential and desirable, to achieve the required outcome. The need for forensic specialists to take language issues into account has also been acknowledged in both human rights situations (ICRC, 2004) and DVI (Lessig and Rothshield, 2011). Indeed, when multiple nationalities are involved, information exchange between countries can be challenging, and a standardised approach is therefore recommended (Lessig and Rothshield, 2011). Tidball-Binz (2006) noted that development and implementation of *ad hoc* forms for each particular context will slow down the overall process of identification; this is why existing protocols are often used, even though they may not suit a particular context.

International Guidelines and Recommendations for DVI

Various documents have been published detailing best-practice guidelines for the identification process or management of bodies in disasters. International recording formats for DVI include the Interpol Disaster Victim Identification protocol* and the *Disaster Mortuary Operational Response Team* (DMORT) VIP forms,† which are commonly used in the United States. Some countries and organisations have developed their own recording protocols. Interpol

---

* Available from http://www.interpol.int/INTERPOL-expertise/Forensics/DVI-Pages/Forms
† Available from http://www.dmort.org/forms/index.html

utilises separate mechanisms for the exchange of data relating to missing persons and unidentified bodies between member countries. The guidelines published by Interpol are currently the only internationally accepted standard for disaster DVI and recognised as the best-practice method for data collection in multiple fatality incidents to facilitate identification of victims (Vermylen, 2006), although it has been argued that the guidelines should be simplified (Syukriani, 2007). The Interpol DVI guide details the AM and PM collation processes, identification procedures and management principles; however, it does not provide specific operating procedures for each of the activities of the response (Taylor, 2009) as this is largely dependent on the local infrastructure, cultural processes, and legislation in individual countries. Interpol's DVI protocol should therefore be used in conjunction with local SOPs and memorandums of understanding. The Interpol DVI forms have been increasingly recognised as the standard identification protocol for disasters (De Valck, 2006; Petju et al., 2007), although it is noted that the use of the Interpol DVI forms is recommended rather than compulsory as Interpol does not have formal regulatory powers to enforce the use of the forms in internal law and practice. The Parliamentary Assembly of the Council of Europe in the Memorandum of Recommendation R(99)3 on the harmonisation of medicolegal autopsy rules recommends that all the member states apply the Interpol guidelines on DVI, at the time of writing 190 countries. Recently, alternative procedures for identifying remains believed to be from victims of human trafficking have been proposed in the Caribbean utilising standard DVI protocols (Winskog, 2012). An important consideration here is that no central organisation has authority of investigating deaths occurring in international waters and is frequently left to the country geographically closest to where the incident occurred.

While the Interpol DVI forms are internationally recognised for the exchange of data in disaster situations, the ICRC expressed the need to adopt a separate standardised form for the recording of data on missing persons and unidentified bodies relating to armed conflicts or internal violence (ICRC, 2004). The current Interpol DVI forms are to a large extent focused on the recording of the external and internal soft tissues and do not allow detailed recording of skeletal findings, anthropological methods, or archaeological exhumation and recovery protocols. Another important consideration is that the AM Interpol DVI forms do not permit the systematic documentation of the case history, circumstances or time of disappearance, or options to document details of alleged perpetrators (Tidball-Binz, 2006). It is therefore not surprising that human rights organisations have expressed the need to design their own recording protocols more suited for their investigations, such as the protocols used by the ICRC, forensic database of the International Commission of Missing Persons (ICMP), and those used by the Peruvian Forensic Anthropology Team (EPAF, 2002). On the other hand, it is important to note that guidelines produced for the exhumation, handling, and identification of remains in the aftermath of human rights violations (such as those produced by the ICRC) have been adapted for disaster management (Perera and Briggs, 2008). Indeed, many of the principles applied in mass grave investigations can equally be applied to DVI, albeit modified.

Further guidelines for DVI have been published by the National Institute of Justice (2005)* and DMORT (Standard Operating Procedures for NTSB[†] Activations, 2006) detailing the general identification procedures when activated under an interagency agreement with the NTSB following an aviation accident. The Australasian Disaster Victim Identification Committee (ADVIC) published the Australasian Disaster Victim Identification Standards Manual in 2004. The Scientific Working Group on Disaster Victim Identification (SWGDVI[‡]) has an aim to 'develop, disseminate, and advance consensus guidelines and best practices, studies, and other recommendations and/or findings for DVI; with an emphasis on quality assurance and quality control processes and methods' (SWGDVI, 2012). Another initiative by Physicians for Human Rights (PHR) resulted in the Forensic Training Programme.[§] 'The Missing' initiative of the ICRC has led to recommendations and 'minimal' data requirements for the identification process (e.g. see Rothschild, 2002).

Guidelines and Recommendations for Specific Identification Methods

In many countries, the identification standards are not in accordance with the Interpol DVI guidelines, and accepted methods for identification differ from country to country (Lessig and Rothschild, 2012). Visual identification is still an accepted method in many underdeveloped countries; however, it is recognised as inherently unreliable (Zugibe et al., 1996): As illustrated by the Bali bombing in 2002, where of the 18 victims who had been 'identified' visually by families, nine (50%) were shown to have been identified incorrectly (Lain et al., 2003), while the first two bodies shipped back to England after the 2004 tsunami had both been wrongly visually identified by relatives (Scanlon et al., 2007). Looting of personal effects from bodies is not uncommon in less developed and poorer countries (Rohan et al., 2009), resulting in loss of identification evidence. Further problems arise as a result of social pressures, as in some cultures and religions, burial within 24 h is required. In the 2004 tsunami, for example, visually identified bodies were almost immediately cremated, and further examination of the bodies to verify the identity was impossible. Many victims were buried without keeping proper forensic

---

* Mass Fatality Incidents: A Guide for Human Forensic Identification (NIJ, 2005).
† National Transportation Safety Board.
‡ http://www.swgdvi.org/
§ See http://www.phr.org

records other than counting the number of victims. Mass burial of unidentified and unrecognisable remains in the immediate aftermath of a disaster is still commonly initiated by local authorities, as recently seen after the 2010 Haiti earthquake (Gupta and Sadiq, 2010), often the result of the misguided beliefs that dead bodies pose a significant risk for the spread of infectious diseases (Morgan, 2004; Ville de Goyet, 2004). The cremation of deceased victims was witnessed in many of the countries affected by the 2004 tsunami, mainly in India and Thailand during the acute phase of the post-tsunami (Perera and Briggs, 2008) and recently following the earthquake and tsunami in Japan in accordance with Buddhist practices. Three days after Japan's 2011 earthquake and tsunami, for example, Japan's health ministry issued an emergency measure exempting families of tsunami and quake victims from having to obtain burial and cremation permits to expedite processing of bodies (Oh, 2012). As such, relatives may be denied the opportunity of knowing the fate of their loved one potentially resulting in a 'Zeigarnik effect', a failure to find closure or perform appropriate cultural death rituals (Zeigarnik, 1967; cited in Gupta and Sadiq, 2010). It is therefore that both NGOs (Morgan et al., 2006) and responders (Sumathipala et al., 2006) have been urged to adopt guidelines for the management of bodies into their contingency plans following a disaster, although they should allow for rational modifications of usual practices (Rohan et al., 2009). Those modifications may include light embalming of bodies (e.g. see Rohan et al., 2009) and (radio-frequency identification or RFID) tagging of bodies such as after the Hurricane Katrina disaster. Since then, some countries and local authorities have exercised caution in conducting mass burials (e.g. see the 2011 typhoon Washi disaster in the Philippines* and DANA crash in Nigeria†), and guidelines for the proper conduct of mass burials have been proposed (Perera and Briggs, 2008).

The standardisation of identification data has been particularly relevant to forensic odontology and genetic identification. As early as 1969, the subcommittee of the Federation Dentaire Internationale (FDI) urged the adoption of one uniform and universally acceptable system of dental recording (Keiser-Nielsen, 1969), ahead of the technological revolution of computerised data processing and retrieval facilities. Various tooth coding systems have been

---

* Today (December 20, 2011), *Philippines digs graves after floods caused by typhoon kill hundreds.* http://imcmsimages.mediacorp.sg/CMSFileserver/documents/006/PDF/20111220/2012HNP008.pdf. In this disaster, the argument of violations of International Humanitarian Law has been used by relatives to prevent the 'unlawful' burial of unidentified remains in a mass grave by the local authorities.
† Following the release of the bodies of the plane crash victims, the chief medical director of Lagos State University Teaching Hospital (Nigeria) was quoted as saying that 'it was agreed that the victims be buried separately as against mass burial, which is outdated in modern societies'. August 10, 2012; http://sunnewsonline.com/new/national/dana-plane-crash-families-bury-human-parts/

devised over the years to facilitate the exchange of dental data between countries (Solheim, 1997), and it has been estimated that approximately 30 dental notation systems are in use globally (Rötzscher, 1992). Forensic odontologists communicate internationally using the two-digit tooth notation of the FDI notation even in instances when other dental notation systems are commonly used in their respective countries (Clark and Dykes, 1985). The FDI notation is integrated within the Interpol DVI forms as the initial method of dental recording. While tooth notations are more or less standardised, Dumancic et al. (2001) noted that no internationally recognised list of abbreviations for the recording of dental findings is available, and this has led to incorrect identifications in the past (Cecchi et al., 1997). The use of professional abbreviations in various countries is justified but must leave no doubt about their meaning (Prieels, 2000, p. 136). Gustafson (1958) argued that it may be better to use straightforward description in the language of the country of origin and to rely upon accurate translation where necessary. The International Organisation for Forensic Odonto-Stomatology (IOFOS) published quality assurance recommendations for DVI* (IOFOS, 2008), and case studies using the recommendations have subsequently been published (Pereira and Santos, 2012). The American Board of Forensic Odontology (ABFO) adopted guidelines and standards for body identification† (ABFO, 1995), while a Disaster Victim Identification Forensic Odontology Guide has been published for the Australian Society of Forensic Odontology (ASFO) by Taylor (2009).

Following the 2004 tsunami, the need was recognised to draft acceptable scientific standards for the use of DNA-based methods in DVI (Prinz et al., 2007). These recommendations are intended to provide guidance on collecting and storing AM and PM samples, DNA extraction and processing strategies, data management and biostatistical interpretation and reporting of results. Recommendations have been published for the use of DNA in DVI (Huckenbeck et al., 2008; Prinz et al., 2007), while further guidelines have been set out by the DNA Commission of the International Society for Forensic Genetics (ISFG) for short tandem repeat (STR) (Bär et al., 1997), mitochondrial DNA (mtDNA) (Carracedo et al., 2000) and short tandem repeat on the Y-chromosome (Y-STR) (Gill et al., 2001; Gusmao et al., 2006). The ISFG guidelines have subsequently been adopted for DVI in Australia and New Zealand (Lee et al., 2008), Germany (Lessig et al., 2009) and Taiwan (Lin et al., 2011). The ICRC has written specific best-practice guidelines for the use of DNA for the identification of missing persons and unidentified remains in armed conflicts and other situations of armed violence‡ (ICRC, 2009).

---

* Available from http://www.iofos.eu
† Available from http://www.abfo.org
‡ Missing People, DNA Analysis and Identification of Human Remains: A Guide to Best Practice in Armed Conflicts and Other Situations of Armed Violence (ICRC, 2009).

The most common third-party accreditation system adopted by DNA testing laboratories is ISO/IEC 17025.1. In this respect, the number of core loci used internationally may differ; however, missing person investigations and mass DVI typically involve the same STR markers and kits (see the following for comprehensive reviews: Butler, 2006; Thompson et al., 2012).

Fingerprints are a primary method of identification and as such are used in many disasters (Morgan, 2004; Shribanditmongkol et al., 2005) (see Chapter 14). An internationally agreed standard for the examination of fingerprints is currently not in place, and various countries throughout the world apply different numbers of points in agreement (Evett and Williams, 1996). In England and Wales, a non-numerical qualitative approach was introduced in 2001, removing the requirement for a minimum number of matching points (Leadbetter, 2005). Few procedural guidelines are published with regard to fingerprinting process in DVI, rather focusing on methodology. The Scientific Working Group on Friction Ridge Analysis, Study and Technology (SWGFAST) published *The Fingerprint Sourcebook*, which provides a detailed review of current methodologies (SWGFAST, 2011).

The forensic pathologist has a central role in the identification process (Robertsen, 2011; Schuliar and Knudsen, 2012). A detailed review of the pathologists' role in major disasters has been published by the Royal College of Pathologists (Busuttil et al., 2000).

The involvement of forensic anthropology in DVI has extended over the past decade well beyond the traditional role to include increasingly diverse tasks and responsibilities (Mundorff, 2012). The diverse function of anthropology in DVI is well documented (Blau and Briggs, 2011; Kahana and Hiss, 2009; Mundorff, 2012, 2008). Moreover, methods used in forensic anthropology are increasingly guided by the need for objectivity and standardised methodologies in the forensic sciences following the *Daubert* ruling in 1993 (Christensen, 2004). It is now recognised that the application of incorrect population data is a likely source of error (Komar, 2003), and the need for age, sex and stature standards derived from local populations has stimulated population-based research in forensic anthropology (Steadman and Haglund, 2005).[*] In 2008, the Scientific Working Group for Forensic Anthropology (SWGANTH[†]) was set up to develop consensus best-practice guidelines and establish minimum standards for the forensic anthropology discipline. On a European level, the Forensic Anthropology Society of Europe (FASE) 'encourage and promote adherence to high standards of ethics, conduct and professional practice in forensic anthropology' and 'harmonize techniques and diagnostic procedures across Europe' (Baccino, 2004). This example

---

[*] For a summary of methods, see Black and Ferguson (2010).
[†] http://www.swganth.org/

was followed in the United Kingdom by the British Association for Forensic Anthropologists (BAFA).

Conclusion

The rights of relatives to know the fate of their missing family member(s) in armed conflicts are protected in international humanitarian law, while disaster response laws are slowly gaining recognition (Gavshon, 2009). The four Geneva Conventions (1949) and additional protocols (1977) not only recognise the right to know the fate of a missing relative but also acknowledge the right to have an identity. The Geneva Convention states that 'each party of the conflict must take measures to identify the dead before disposing of their remains' (GC, Articles 16–17). One may argue that the Geneva Conventions only relate to victims of armed conflict and the right to identity in disasters may not be protected. When a disaster occurs on the territory of a party to an armed conflict, it has been proclaimed that international humanitarian law shall be the prevailing body of law (IFRC, 2007). We can draw a parallel here with the importance of returning the remains of those killed in armed conflict and human rights abuses. The identification of those missing may not only aid in the grieving process of relatives but may also contribute in reducing hostility, mistrust, intolerance and inter-ethnic reconciliation processes within communities in regions affected by armed conflict and may thus aid in rebuilding society (Huffine et al., 2001) and restore the health and well-being of citizens (Stover et al., 2003).

A model protocol for DVI cannot be exhaustive due to legal and political arrangements (Rothschild, 2002). Despite the increase in general awareness and lessons gained from recent major disasters, the relative infrequency of major catastrophes leads to a certain degree of complacency and underestimation of the impact of such an event (Goolsby and Mothershead, 2011). This may explain in part why the standardisation of procedural, ethical, psychosocial, and organisational approaches to investigations into serious human rights violations has so far advanced to a greater extent than those in mass disasters. Nevertheless, important lessons can be learned from guidance produced to investigate those violations, which may potentially be integrated into existing DVI processes, particularly in disasters occurring in failed states or post-conflict areas. Natural disasters often occur in remote areas of the world or in countries that do not necessarily have the resources or facilities to deal with a large number of fatalities; only a small proportion of the people who lose their lives in large natural disasters may be subject to formal identification processes (Morgan et al., 2006).

Standards and guidelines not only need to be updated periodically to reflect advances in identification sciences but also need to be reviewed *throughout* the process in large disasters (Kieser et al., 2006). Goolsby and Mothershead (2011) noted that the best time to propose major changes for disaster preparedness, including its funding, is immediately following a major disaster, even if the event has occurred in a remote location. A further important point is knowledge transfer. Indeed, SOPs are often general descriptions of procedures to be followed in an investigation (Winskog et al., 2012). Those working in DVI not only need to understand the theoretical basis but must also acquire the practical skills which can only be obtained from training and exercises (Byard and Winskog, 2010) or working in actual DVI situations. Zohn et al. (2010) proposed the introduction of an odontology victim identification skill assessment system (OVID-SAS) to be able to optimally utilise the skills of forensic odontologists in DVI. The DVI process cannot rely solely on standardised protocols (Perrier et al., 2006). The circumstances for each disaster are unique, and the practical experiences of senior officers may assist those less experienced to adapt to the complexities of each identification effort. In conclusion, we can only agree with Interpol DVI Standing Committee's recommendations (De Valck, 2006) that forward planning, adequate funding, international co-operation, and standardisation are essential to guarantee an effective response albeit respecting local, cultural, social and religious customs. This requires knowledge transfer and publication of 'lessons learned' of disaster experiences and periodic review of existing standards to reflect those learning points.

References

ABFO (1995) Guidelines and standards. In: *Manual of Forensic Odontology,* Bowers, C.M. and G.L. Beli (Eds.). 3rd edn., Colorado Springs, CO: American Society of Forensic Odontology, pp. 334–353.

Avon, S.L. (2004) Forensic odontology: The roles and responsibilities of the dentist. *J Can Dent Assoc* 70(7):453–458.

Bär, W., Brinkmann, B., Budowle, B., Carracedo, A., Gill, P., Lincoln, P., Mayr, W., and Olaisen, B. (1997) DNA recommendations. Further report of the DNA Commission of the ISFG regarding the use of short tandem repeat systems. *Forensic Sci Int* 87(3):179–184.

Baccino, E. (2004) Forensic Anthropology Society of Europe: A section of the International Academy of Legal Medicine. *Int J Legal Med* 118:N1.

Berketa, J.W., James, H., and Lake, A.W. (2012) Forensic odontology involvement in disaster victim identification. *Forensic Sci Med Pathol* 8(2):148–156.

Black, S.M. and Ferguson, E. (2010) *Forensic Anthropology: 2000 to 2010.* Boca Raton, FL: CRC Press.

Blau, S. (2006) The powerful evidence of the bodies: Ethical considerations for the forensic anthropologist involved in the investigation of mass graves. *VIFM Review* 61:2–7.

Blau, S. and Briggs, C.A. (2011) The role of forensic anthropology in Disaster Victim Identification (DVI). *Forensic Sci Int* 205(1–3):29–35.

Blau, S., Hill, A., and Briggs, C.A. (2006) Missing persons–missing data: The need to collect antemortem dental records of missing persons. *J Forensic Sci* 51(2):386–389.

Byard, R.W. and Winskog, C. (2010) Potential problems arising during international disaster victim identification (DVI) exercises. *Forensic Sci Med Pathol* 6:1–2.

Budowle, B., Bieber, F.R., and Eisenberg, A.J. (2005) Forensic aspects of mass disasters: Strategic considerations for DNA-based human identification. *Leg Med (Tokyo)* 7(4):230–243.

Busuttil, A., Jones, J.S.P., and Green, M.A. (2000) *Deaths in Major Disasters: The Pathologist's Role*. 2nd edn., London, U.K.: Royal College of Pathologists.

Butler, J.M. (2006) Genetics and genomics of core short tandem repeat loci used in human identity testing. *J Forensic Sci* 51(2):256–265.

Calacal, G.C., Delfin, F.C., Tan, M.M., Roewer, L., Magtanong, D.L., Lara, M.C., Fortun, R., and De Ungria, M.C. (2005) Identification of exhumed remains of fire tragedy victims using conventional methods and autosomal/Y-chromosomal short tandem repeat DNA profiling. *Am J Forensic Med Pathol* 26(3):285–291.

Carballo, M., Heal, B., and Hernandez, M. (2005) Psychosocial aspects of the tsunami. *J R Soc Med* 98:396–399.

Carracedo, A., Bär, W., Lincoln, P., Mayr, W., Morling, N., Olaisen, B., Schneider, P. et al. (2000) DNA commission of the international society for forensic genetics: Guidelines for mitochondrial DNA typing. *Forensic Sci Int* 110(2):79–85.

Carrillo, C. (2007) El Caracazo: Exhumacion y lucha por la búsquyeda de la justicia. In *Resistencias Contra el Olvido: Trabajo Psicosocial en Procesos de Exhumaciones*, P. Pérez Sales and S. Navarro Garc'a (Eds.). Barcelona, Spain: Gedisa, pp. 247–266.

Cecchi, R., Cipolloni, and L., Nobile, M. (1997) Incorrect identification of a military pilot with international implications. *Int J Legal Med* 110(3):167–169.

Chatterji, A.P., Imroz, P., Navlakha, G., Ud-Din, Z., Desai, M., and Parvez, K. (2009) Buried evidence: Unknown, unmarked, and mass graves in Indian-administered Kashmir. International People's Tribunal on Human Rights and Justice in Kashmir (IPTK). http://www.kashmirprocess.org/reports/graves/ (Accessed May 10, 2012).

Christensen, A.M. (2004) The impact of Daubert: Implications for testimony and research in forensic anthropology (and the use of frontal sinuses in personal identification). *J Forensic Sci* 49(3):427–430.

Clark, P. (2010) *The Gacaca Courts, Post-genocide Justice and Reconciliation in Rwanda*. Cambridge, U.K.: Cambridge University Press.

Clark, D.H. and Dykes, E. (1985) The use of a microcomputer system for worldwide dental charting comparison. *Acta Med Leg Soc (Liege)* 35(1):285–299.

Cordner, S. (2005) The missing: Action to resolve the problem of those unaccounted for as a result of armed conflict or internal violence, and to assist their families. *Vic Inst Forensic Medi Rev* 3(1):2–6.

De Valck, E. (2006) Major incident response: Collecting ante-mortem data. *Forensic Sci Int* 159S:S15–S19.

Dumancić, J., Kaić, Z., Njemirovskij, V., Brkić, H., and Zecević, D. (2001) Dental identification after two mass disasters in Croatia. *Croat Med J* 42(6):657–662.

Ecap, Gac and Geza (2009) Working paper on international consensus on minimum standards for psychosocial work in exhumation processes for the search of the disappeared persons. Joint document by Comunitarios y

Acción Psicosocial (ECAP), Grupo de Acción Comunitaria (GAC) and Gemeinnützige Entwicklungszusammenarbeit GMBH (GEZA), Guatemala: F&G Editores. http://www.ecapguatemala.org/img/pdf/trabajopsicosocial/consensomundialdetrabajopsicosocial.pdf (Accessed July 5, 2012).

EPAF (2002). Manual para la investigación eficaz ante el hallazgo de fosas con restos humanos en el Perú. Defensoría del Pueblo y Equipo Peruano de Antropología Forense-Epaf. Lima, Peru, Mayo. http://www.derechos.org/nizkor/peru/libros/fosas/ (Accessed July 2, 2012).

Evett, I.W. and Williams, R.L. (1996) Review of the sixteen points fingerprint standard in England and Wales. *J Forensic Identif* 46(1):49–73.

Eyre, A. (2002) Improving procedures and minimising distress: Issues in the identification of victims following disasters. *Aust J Emerg Manage* 17(1):9–14.

EQUITAS (2008) Recommendations for work with a psychosocial approach in forced disappearance and other grave human rights violations. Prepared for the *2nd World Congress on Psychosocial Work in Exhumation Processes, Forced Disappearance, Justice and Truth*, Columbia, Bogotá, April 2010.

Ferllini, R. (2007) *Forensic Archaeology and Human Rights Violations*. Springfield, IL: Charles C Thomas.

Fitrasanti, B.I. and Syukriani, Y.F. (2009) Social problems in disaster victim identification following the 2006 Pangandaran tsunami. *Leg Med (Tokyo)* 11(Suppl1):S89–S91.

Gavshon, D. (2009) The applicability of IHL in mixed situations of disaster and conflict. *J Conflict Security Law* 14(2):243–263.

Gill, P., Brenner, C., Brinkmann, B., Budowle, B., Carracedo, A., Jobling, M.A., De K. et al. (2001) DNA Commission of the International Society of Forensic Genetics: Recommendations on forensic analysis using Y-chromosome STRs. *Forensic Sci Int* 124:5–10.

González-Andrade, F. and Sánchez, D. (2005) DNA typing from skeletal remains following an explosion in a military fort: First experience in Ecuador (South-America). *Leg Med (Tokyo)* 7(5):314–318.

Goolsby, C.A. and Mothershead, J.L. (2011) Disaster planning. Downloaded from: Disaster Planning—eMedicine Emergency Medicine http://emedicine.medscape.com/article/765495-overview (Accessed December 1, 2011).

Gupta, K. and Sadiq, A-A. (2010) Responses to mass-fatalities in the aftermath of 2010 haiti earthquake. Quick Response Reports, Natural Hazards Center, University of Colorado, Boulder, CO. http://www.colorado.edu/hazards/research/qr/submitted/gupta_2010.pdf (Accessed June 1, 2012).

Gusmao, L., Butler, J.M., Carracedo, A., Gill, P., Kayser, M., Mayr, W.R., Morling, N. et al. (2006) DNA Commission of the International Society of Forensic Genetics. DNA Commission of the International Society of Forensic Genetics (ISFG): An update of the recommendations on the use of Y-STRs in forensic analysis. *Forensic Sci Int* 157(2–3):187–197.

Gustafson, G. (1958) Research, organization and teaching in forensic odontology. *Proc R Soc Med* 51(12):1055–1057.

Hakoda, T. (2005) Invisible victims of the tsunami- Burmese migrant workers in Thailand. Focus number 39, March 2005, http://www.hurights.or.jp/archives/focus/section2/2005/03/invisible-victims-of-the-tsunami—burmese-migrant-workers-in-thailand.html (Accessed June 30, 2012).

Huckenbeck, W., Thiel, W., Krause, D., Lessig, R., and Szibor, R. (2008) Thoughts for the organisation of an early phase response to preserve victim identification information after mass disasters. A contribution to: ISFG: Recommendations regarding the role of forensic genetics for disaster victim identification (DVI by M. Prinz, A. Carracedo, W.R. Mayr, N. Morling, T.J. Parsons, A. Sajantila, R. Scheithauer, H. Schmitter, P.M. Schneider). *Forensic Sci Int* 177(2–3):e39–e42.

Huffine, E., Crews, J, Kennedy, B. et al. (2001) Mass identification of persons missing from the break-up of the Former Yugoslavia: Structure, function, and role of the international commission on missing persons. *Croat Med J* 42(3):271–275.

Hunter, J. and Cox, M. (2005) Social and intellectual frameworks. In: *Forensic Archaeology: Advances in Theory and Practice,* Hunter, J. and M. Cox (Eds.). London, U.K.: Routledge, pp. 204–225.

ICRC (2003) ICRC report: The missing and their families: Summary of the conclusions arising from events held prior to the International Conference of Governmental and Non-Governmental Experts (February 19–21, 2003). ICRC/TheMissing/01.2003/EN/10 (Accessed May 8, 2012).

ICRC (2004) Operational best practices regarding the management of human remains and information on the dead by non-specialists. Geneva, Switzerland: International Committee of the Red Cross, 2004, http://www.icrc.org/eng/resources/documents/publication/p0858.htm (Accessed May 8, 2012).

ICRC (2010) First Aid in armed conflicts and other situations of violence. Geneva, Switzerland: International Committee of the Red Cross, 2nd edn., 2010, http://www.icrc.org/eng/resources/documents/publication/p0870.htm (Accessed May 8, 2012).

ICRC (2009) Missing people, DNA analysis and identification of human remains: A guide to best practice in armed conflicts and other situations of armed violence. 2nd edn. Downloaded from: http://www.icrc.org/eng/assets/files/other/icrc_002_4010.pdf (Accessed December 1, 2011).

ICRC (2012) Restoring links between dispersed family members. Geneva, Switzerland: International Committee of the Red Cross, 2012, http://www.icrc.org/eng/resources/documents/publication/t099.htm

IFRC (2007) *Law and Legal Issues in International Disaster Response: A Desk Study.* Geneva, Switzerland: International Federation of the Red Cross and Red Crescent Societies (IFRC).

IOFOS (2008) Identification in single cases: Quality assurance. International Organisation for Forensic Odonto-Stomatology. http://www.iofos.eu/Quality-Ass/Identification-IOFOS.htm (Accessed May 10, 2012).

INTERPOL (2008a) Ante-mortem (yellow) victim identification: Missing person. Available from: http://www.interpol.int/content/download/10804/76858/version/6/file/AMFormEng.pdf (Accessed December 12, 2011).

INTERPOL (2008b) Disaster victim identification guide. Downloaded from: http://www.interpol.int/Public/DisasterVictim/guide/guide.pdf (Accessed December 26, 2011).

INTERPOL (2008c) Post-mortem (pink) Victim Identification: Dead body. Available from: http://www.interpol.int/content/download/10801/76833/version/5/file/PMForm.pdf (Accessed December 12, 2011).

INTERPOL Tsunami Evaluation Working Group (2010) The DVI Response to the South East Asian Tsunami between December 2004 and February 2006. Downloaded from: https://www.interpol.int/Public/.../TsunamiEvaluation20100330.pdz December 24, 2011).

James, H. (2005) Thai tsunami victim identification: Overview to date. *J Forensic Odontostomatol* 23(1):1–18.

Jones, D.R. (1985) Secondary disaster victims: The emotional effects of recovering and identifying human remains. *Am J Psychiatry* 142(3):303–307.

Kahana, T. and Hiss, J. (2009) The role of forensic anthropology in mass fatality incidents management. *Forensic Sci Policy Manage: Intern J* 1(3):144–149.

Keough, M. and Samuels, M. (2004) The Kosovo family support project: Offering psychosocial support for families with missing persons. *Social Work* 49(4): 587–594.

Keough, M.E., Simmons, T., and Samuels, M. (2004) Missing persons in post-conflict settings: best practices for integrating psychosocial and scientific approaches. *J R Soc Promot Health* 124(6):271–275.

Keiser-Nielsen, S. (1969) Forensic odontology. *U Toledo L Rev* 1:633–639.

Kieser, J.A., Laing, W., and Herbison, P. (2006) Lessons learned from large-scale comparative dental analysis following the south Asian tsunami of 2004. *J Forensic Sci* 51(1):109–112.

Kirsch, H. (2010) Problems of disaster victim identification (DVI) missions in failed states. http://hanskirsch.typepad.com/blog/2010/05/problems-of-disaster-victim-identification-dvi-missions-in-failed-states.html (Accessed 6 May 2012).

Komar, D.A. (2003) Lessons from Srebrenica: The contributions and limitations of physical anthropology in identifying victims of war crimes. *J Forensic Sci* 48(4):713–716.

Kubo, S.I. (2012) Great East Japan Earthquake: Postmortem examinations and personal identifications of victims. *Rechtsmedizin* 22:12–16

Kvaal, S.I. (2006) Collection of post mortem data: DVI protocols and quality assurance. *Forensic Sci Int* 159S:S12–S14.

Lain, R., Griffiths, C., and Hilton, J.M. (2003) Forensic dental and medical response to the Bali bombing: A personal perspective. *Med J Aus* 179:362–365.

Leadbetter, M.J. (2005) Fingerprint evidence in England and Wales: The revised standard. *Med Sci Law* 45(1):1–6.

Leclair, B., Frégeau, C.J., Bowen, K.L., and Fourney, R.M. (2004) Enhanced kinship analysis and STR-based DNA typing for human identification in mass fatality incidents: The Swissair flight 111 disaster. *J Forensic Sci* 49(5):939–953.

Lee, J., Scott, P., Carroll, D., Eckhoff, C., Harbison, S.A., Lentile, V., Goetz, R., Scheffer, J.W., Stringer, P., and Turbett, G. (2008) Recommendations for DNA laboratories supporting Disaster Victim Identification (DVI) operations: Australian and New Zealand consensus on ISFG recommendations. *Forensic Sci Int Genet* 3:54–56.

Lessig, R., Aspinall, l., and Bratzke, H. (2009) Identifizierungstatigkeit bei Massenunfallen und Katastrophen—Aktuelle Standards. *Rechtsmedizin* 19:209–211.

Lessig, R. and Rothschild, M. (2012) International standards in cases of mass disaster victim identification (DVI). *Forensic Sci Med Pathol* 8(2):197–199.

Lessig, R., Thiele, K., and Edelmann, J. (2006) Tsunami 2004: Experiences, challenges and strategies. *Int Congress Series* 1288:747–749.

Lin, C.Y., Huang, T.Y., Shih, H.C., Yuan, C.H., Chen, L.J., Tsai, H.S., Pan, C.H. et al. (2011) The strategies to DVI challenges in Typhoon Morakot. *Int J Legal Med* 125(5):637–641.

Morgan, O. (2004) Infectious disease risk from dead bodies after natural disasters. *Rev Panam Salud Pública* 15(5):307–312.

Morgan, O.W., Sribanditmongkol, P., Perera, C., Sulasmi, Y., Van Alphen, D. et al. (2006) Mass fatality management following the South Asian tsunami disaster: Case Studies in Thailand, Indonesia, and Sri Lanka. *PLoS Med* 3(6):809–815.

Mundorff, A.Z. (2008) Anthropologist-directed triage: Three distinct mass fatality events involving fragmentation of human remains. In: *Recovery, Analysis, and Identification of Commingled Human Remains*, pp. 123–144. Totowa, NJ: Humana Press.

Mundorff, A.Z. (2012) Integrating forensic anthropology into disaster victim identification. *Forensic Sci Med Pathol* 8(2):131–139.

Navarro-García, S., Perez-Salas, P., and Fernandez-Liria, A. (2010) Exhumations in Latin-America: Current status and pending challenges: A psychosocial view. *Peace Confl Rev* 4(2):1–16.

Noji, E.K. (1997) *The Public Health Consequences of Disasters*. New York: Oxford University Press.

NPIA (2008) Family liaison officer guidance. National Policing Improvement Agency. Wyboston. http://www.acpo.police.uk/documents/criminaljustice/2009/200909CJUFLO01.pdf (Accessed June 1, 2012).

Nuzzolese, E. and Di Vella, G. (2007) Future project concerning mass disaster management: A forensic odontology perspective. *Int Dent J* 57(4):261–266.

Oh, J.H. (2012) A consideration for the better preparedness against mega-disaster: Lessons from the 2011 Great Eastern Japan Earthquake and Tsunami. Available from: http://www.kf.or.kr/file/kor_1/Panel_1_Jai-Ho_Oh_%EB%B0%9C%ED%91%9C%EC%9A%94%EC%95%BD%EB%AC%B8.pdf (Accessed July 11, 2012)

Olumbe, A.K. and Yakub, A.K. (2002) Management, exhumation and identification of human remains: A viewpoint of the developing world. *IRRC* 84(848):893–902.

Pan American Health Organization (2004) *Management of Dead Bodies in Disaster Situations*. Washington, DC: Pan American Health Organization (PAHO).

Pereira, C.P. and Santos, J.C. (2013) How to do identify single cases according to the quality assurance from IOFOS. The positive identification of an unidentified body by dental parameters: A case of homicide. *J Forensic Leg Med*, 20(3):169–73.

Perera, C. (2005) After the tsunami: Legal implications of mass burials of unidentified victims in Sri Lanka. *PLoS Med* 2(6):e185.

Perera, C. (2006) Tsunami disaster victim identification in Sri Lanka: Legal aspects. *Med Sci Law.* 46(4):282–286.

Perera, C. and Briggs, C. (2008) Guidelines for the effective conduct of mass burials following mass disasters: Post-Asian tsunami disaster experience in retrospect. *Forensic Sci Med Pathol* 4(1):1–8.

Perrier, M., Bollmann, M., Girod, A., and Mangin, P. (2006) Swiss DVI at the tsunami disaster: Expect the unexpected. *Forensic Sci Int* 159(Suppl 1):S30–S32.

Petju, M., Suteerayongprasert, A., Thongpud, R., and Hassiri, K. (2007) Importance of dental records for victim identification following the Indian Ocean tsunami disaster in Thailand. *Public Health* 121:251–257.

Prieels, F. (2000) DVI Interpol procedures. The forensic odontologist. In: Willems, G. (ed.). *Forensic Odontology: Proceedings of the European IOFOS Millennium Meeting: Leuven, Belgium, August 23–26, 2000.* Leuven, Belgium: Leuven University Press, p. 136.

Prinz, M., Carracedo, A., Mayr, W.R., Morling, N., Parsons, T.J., Sajantila, A., Scheithauer, R., Schmitter, H., and Schneider, P.M. (2007) DNA Commission of the International Society for Forensic Genetics (ISFG): Recommendations regarding the role of forensic genetics for disaster victim identification (DVI). *Forensic Sci Int Genet* 1(1):3–12.

Rai, B. and Anand, S.C. (2007) Role of forensic odontology in tsunami disasters. The Internet Journal of Forensic Science (2)1. Downloaded from: http://www.ispub.com/journal/the-internet-journal-of-forensic-science/volume-2-number-1/role-of-forensic-odontology-in-tsunami-disasters.html (Accessed December 1, 2011).

Robertson, A.G. (2011) Aviation disasters: The role of the forensic pathologist. In: *Current Practice in Forensic Medicine,* Gall, J. and J. Payne-James (Eds.). Chichester, U.K.: John Wiley & Sons, Ltd.

Rohan, R.P., Hettiarachchi, M., Vidanapathirana, M., and Perera, S. (2009) Management of dead and missing: Aftermath tsunami in Galle. *Leg Med (Tokyo)* 11(Suppl 1):S86–S88.

Rothschild, M.A. (2002) Standard autopsy protocol and standardised collection of post mortem data and material. ICRC The missing 10/2002/EN/3; pp. 99–100. Downloaded from http://www.icrc.org/eng/assets_files/other/icrc_themissing_012003_en_10.pdf (Accessed June 3, 2012).

Rötzscher, K. (1992) The origins and development of FDI, INTERPOL and IOFOS: International co-operation in identification. *J Forensic Odontostomatol* 10(2):58–63.

Royal College of Pathologists (2000) *Deaths in Major Disasters: The Pathologists Role.* 2nd edn., London, U.K.: Royal College of Pathologists.

Sumathipala, A., Siribaddana, S., and Perera, U.C.P. (2006) Management of dead bodies as a component of psychosocial interventions after the tsunami: A view from Sri Lanka. *Int Rev Psychiatry* 18(3):249–257.

Scanlon, J. (2006) Dealing with the tsunami dead: Unprecedented international co-operation. *Aust J Emerg Manage* 21(2):57–61.

Scanlon, J., McMahon, T., and Haastert, C. van. (2007) Handling mass death by integrating the management of disasters and pandemics: Lessons from the Indian Ocean tsunami, the Spanish Flu and other incidents. *J Contingencies Crisis Manage* 15(2):80–94.

Schuliar, Y. and Knudsen, P.J. (2012) Role of forensic pathologists in mass disasters. *Forensic Sci Med Pathol* 8(2):164–173.

Shribanditmongkol, P., Pongpanitanont, P., Porntrakulseree, N., Petju, M., and Kunaratanapruk, S. (2005) Forensic aspect of disaster casualty management. WHO conference on the health aspects of tsunami disaster in Asia; Phuket, Thailand; May 4–6, 2005. Geneva, Switzerland: World Health Organization. Available: http://www.who.int/hc/events/tsunamiconf/presentations/en/index.html (Accessed May 11, 2012).

Sirisup N. and Kanluen, S. (2005) Role of forensic doctors in Thailand's tsunami: Experiences from Chulalongkorn Medical School. *J Med Assoc Thai* 88(Suppl 4):S335–S338.

Solheim T. (1997) A hierarchical system for the coding of dental information in reports and computer-assisted identifications. *J Forensic Odontostomatol* 15(1):5–8.

Steadman, D.W. and Haglund, W.D. (2005) The scope of anthropological contributions to human rights investigations. *J Forensic Sci* 50:1–8.

Stover, E., Haglund, W.D., and Samuels, M. (2003) Exhumation of mass graves in Iraq: Considerations for forensic investigations, humanitarian needs, and the demands of justice. *J Am Med Assoc* 290(5):663–666.

Syukriani, Y.F. (2007) Disaster victim identification from a cultural and religious perspective. 10th Seminar on the Indonesia–Malaysia, May 25–30, 2007, Kuala Lumpur, Malaysia.

Sweet, D. (2010) INTERPOL DVI best-practice standards: An overview. *Forensic Sci Int* 201(1–3):18–21.

SWGDVI (2012) The Scientific Working Group on Disaster Victim Identification (SWGDVI). http://www.swgdvi.org/ (Accessed May 3, 2012).

SWGFAST (2011) The fingerprint sourcebook. Scientific Working Group on Friction Ridge Analysis, Study and Technology, National Institute of Justice (NIJ). Available: http://www.nij.gov/pubs-sum/225320.htm

Taylor, J. (2009) Development of the Australian Society of Forensic Odontology disaster victim identification forensic odontology guide. *J Forensic Odontostomatol* 27(2):56–63.

Tidball-Binz, M. (2006) Forensic investigations into the missing. In: *Forensic Anthropology and Medicine: Complementary Sciences from Recovery to Cause of Death*, Schmitt, A. Cunha, E. and J. Pinheiro, (Eds.) Totowa, NJ: Humana Press.

Tidball-Binz, M. (2007) Managing the dead in catastrophes: Guiding principles and practical recommendations for first responders. *Int Rev of the Red Cross* 89(866): June 2007, Downloaded from: http://www.icrc.org/eng/assets/files/other/irrc_866_tidball-binz.pdf (Accessed January 2, 2012).

Thomson, G.S. and Black, S.M. (2012) Body recovery from hostile environments—A test of three kits. *Forensic Sci Int* 220(1–3):147–153.

Thompson, R., Zoppis, S., and McCord, B. (2012) An overview of DNA typing methods for human identification: Past, present, and future. In *DNA Electrophoresis Protocols for Forensic Genetics*, ed. A. Alonso. Totowa, NJ: Humana Press, pp. 3–16.

Tun, K., Butcher, B., Sribanditmongkol, P., Brondolo, T., Caragine, T., Perera, C., and Kent, K. (2005) Panel 2.16: Forensic aspects of disaster fatality management. *Prehosp Disaster Med* 20(6):455–458.

Udayakumar, S.P. (2009) Reading 'Development' as a disaster. Kirwan Institute for the Study of Race and Ethnicity. Kirwaninstitute.osu.edu/wp.../reading_development_as_disaster.pdf, (Accessed June 10, 2012).

Vermylen, Y. (2006) Guidelines in forensic odontology: Legal aspects. *Forensic Sci Int* 159S:S6–S8.

Ville de Goyet, C de. (2004) Epidemics caused by dead bodies: A disaster myth that does not want to die. *Pan Am J Public Health* 15(5):297–299.

Webb, J. (2006) Professional ethics: Forensic anthropology and human rights work. Unpublished Thesis for Syracuse University. http://honors.syr.edu/ThesisPresentations/06/JanaWebb.htm

Winskog, C. (2012) DVI missions in the Caribbean: The practical aspects of disaster victim identification. *Forensic Sci Med Pathol* 8(2):109–113.

Winskog, C., Tonkin, A., and Byard, R.W. (2012) The educational value of disaster victim identification (DVI) missions: Transfer of knowledge. *Forensic Sci Med Pathol* 8(2):84–87.

Yamada, S., Gunatilake, R.P., Roytman, T.M., Gunatilake, S., Fernando, T., and Fernando, L. (2006) The Sri Lanka tsunami experience. *Disaster Manag Response* 4(2):38–48.

Zeigarnik, B.V. (1967) On finished and unfinished tasks. In Ellis, W.D. (Ed.), *A Sourcebook of Gestalt Psychology*. New York: Humanities Press.

Zohn, H.K., Dashkow, S., Aschheim, K.W. et al. (2010) The odontology victim identification skill assessment system. *J Forensic Sci* 55(3):788–791.

Zugibe, F.T., Constello, J., and Segelbacher, J. (1996) The horrors of visual identification. *J Forensic Identif* 46:403–406.

Child Sex Offender Demographics
Towards an Improved Understanding

4

XANTHÉ MALLETT AND JANN KARP

Contents

Introduction

Since the 1990s, child sex offenders have been considered one of the ultimate dangerous criminal classes (Lynch, 2002), and given the complex nature of these crimes, society regularly asks how best to protect children from sexual abuse. This question is becoming ever more pertinent, as almost daily news agencies around the world cover new and historical cases of alleged child sexual abuse (CSA). This indicates that reporting rates may be improving, possibly as a result of campaigns fighting CSA, but proving abuse has taken place, sometimes decades after the event, is extremely challenging.

Mechanisms to reliably identify offenders could not be more important socially. As the number of reported cases is set to increase far into the future, the identification of child sex offenders will be a key investigative priority for many years to come.

An essential aspect of successful prosecution is, of course, how to identify those most at risk of offending, as well as those who have offended; prevention is ultimately preferable as there is no cure in this situation, many victims never recover from the abuse, and the events can haunt them into adulthood. This chapter will review the information currently available for offender demographics, with a view to aiding our ability to identify and manage high-risk offenders.

You will hear parents saying to their children not to go off with strangers, but do offender demographics support the notion of 'stranger danger'? The available evidence suggests not (U.K. Government, 2012), with statistics indicating that the majority of sexually abused children in the United Kingdom and the United States are abused by someone they know. A further fallacy that needs to be addressed is the common perception of who we 'expect' a paedophile to be, our innate prejudices which may impact on our judgement when determining aspects of our children's safety.

Part of the difficulty of getting to the facts around child abuse, and even more so with CSA, is that it is a highly emotive topic that many would rather avoid. The subject is discomforting, and child abuse in all forms causes a significant degree of alarm for a number of reasons. Part of the panic around CSA relates to the broad range of social identities of those found guilty—generally, offenders cover a wide demographic, and they cannot easily be differentiated from you or I. We would, as a society, be much more comfortable if we felt that something singled sexual predators out, that their sexual deviancy was matched to a physical variation that could be recognised easily.

Another aspect of the fear is the lack of power parents, and society in general, feels when trying to protect children, which is a strong societal and familial response: Without being able to readily identify the enemy, how can the vulnerable be protected? Fear is the driving force.

Society therefore demands the police and politicians protect us from sexual predators, usually in the form of increased sanctions. Problems exist, however, as although improvements have been made to policing procedures aimed at identifying offenders (Black et al., In Press-a,b, 2009) and prosecuting cases of CSA (see Chapter 16), for a complex set of reasons, there remains a lack of willing on the part of some victims and witnesses to report these offences. Police, therefore, are investigating intimate situations in which some parties are disinclined to give evidence against offenders, making successful prosecution of offenders difficult.

However, with a view to increasing child safely, we must achieve an improved understanding of who is actually perpetrating the abuse; otherwise, the impact of any sanctions may be limited. A review of the literature indicates that there are many types of CSA, including those who undertake the actual physical abuse at home, to those who download indecent images of children from the Internet. As the range of activity is so broad, this chapter will focus on local CSA (i.e. abuse perpetrated by individuals who are not travelling abroad to access children or downloading abusive material) (for a full discussion of the problems of sex tourism, see Chapter 17). The transnational nature of CSA-associated organised criminal activity (including sex tourism) is discussed elsewhere (Black et al., 2009; Fichtelberg, 2008;

Hart et al., 2011; Healy, 2004; Howitt, 2011; Interpol, n.d.-b; Mallett and Karp, 2013; Martellozzo et al., 2010; Obergfell-Fuchs, 2010; Rettinger, 2000; Rufo, 2012; United Nations, 2001; Winslow and Zhang, 2008a).

Problems with Terminology

Further issues arise as variations in terminology abound. For example, often the word 'juvenile' is used interchangeably with the word 'child', although legally the two are defined differently. Here we will use the definition of 'juvenile' as applied in UK law: a juvenile is a person under the age of 17 years. A distinction is made between 'children' (under 14 years) and 'young persons' (14–16 years).

Furthermore, although the word 'paedophile' is a term generically applied to a person who is sexually attracted to children, this is not accurate, as the developmental stage (not the age in years) of the child determines which of three definitions will be applied:

Paedophile = sexual interest in prepubescent children (approximately
    10 years)
Hebephile = sexual interest in pubescent children (approximately
    11–14 years)
Ephebophile = sexual interest in children in mid-to-late adolescence
    (approximately 15–19 years)

Perhaps the most appropriate definition of a paedophile comprises that earlier definition but with additional explanatory text to give context. Therefore, paedophilia is a condition linked with sexual offending against children: Child sex offenders are more likely to be paedophiles based on self-report or objective measures of sexual interests. At the same time, however, some paedophiles have not had any sexual contact with children, and perhaps half of sex offenders against children would not meet diagnostic criteria for paedophilia (Seto, 2009).

Other variations exist when talking about the crime itself. Is an offender, in the eyes of the public and media, accused of rape or sexual assault? Many people would not recognise the distinction, but the law is quite clear on the difference:

Rape being

Rape (1)
A person (A) commits an offence if –
(a) he intentionally penetrates the vagina, anus or mouth of another person
(B) with his penis,
(b) B does not consent to the penetration, and

(c) A does not reasonably believe that B consents.

(2) Whether a belief is reasonable is to be determined having regard to all the circumstances, including any steps A has taken to ascertain whether B consents.

(3) Sections 75 and 76 apply to an offence under this section.

(4) A person guilty of an offence under this section is liable, on conviction on indictment, to imprisonment for life.

(U.K. Government, 2003a: Sexual Offences Act: Rape)

Whereas sexual assault is

Sexual assault (1) A person (A) commits an offence if –

(a) he intentionally touches another person (B),

(b) the touching is sexual,

(c) B does not consent to the touching, and

(d) A does not reasonably believe that B consents.

(2) Whether a belief is reasonable is to be determined having regard to all the circumstances, including any steps A has taken to ascertain whether B consents.

(3) Sections 75 and 76 apply to an offence under this section.

(4) A person guilty of an offence under this section is liable—

(a) on summary conviction, to imprisonment for a term not exceeding 6 months or a fine not exceeding the statutory maximum or both;

(b) on conviction on indictment, to imprisonment for a term not exceeding 10 years.

(U.K. Government, 2003c: Sexual Offences Act: Sexual assault)

Furthermore, rape and other offences against children under 13 years are described separately under UK legislation:

Rape of a child under 13(1) A person commits an offence if –

(a) he intentionally penetrates the vagina, anus or mouth of another person with his penis, and

(b) the other person is under 13.

(2) A person guilty of an offence under this section is liable, on conviction on indictment, to imprisonment for life.

6 Assault of a child under 13 by penetration (1) A person commits an offence if—

(a) he intentionally penetrates the vagina or anus of another person with a part of his body or anything else,

(b) the penetration is sexual, and

(c) the other person is under 13.

(2) A person guilty of an offence under this section is liable, on conviction on indictment, to imprisonment for life.

7 Sexual assault of a child under 13(1) A person commits an offence if—

(a) he intentionally touches another person,

(b) the touching is sexual, and

(c) the other person is under 13.

(2) A person guilty of an offence under this section is liable—

(a) on summary conviction, to imprisonment for a term not exceeding 6 months or a fine not exceeding the statutory maximum or both;

(b) on conviction on indictment, to imprisonment for a term not exceeding 14 years.

8 Causing or inciting a child under 13 to engage in sexual activity (1) A person commits an offence if—

(a) he intentionally causes or incites another person (B) to engage in an activity,

(b) the activity is sexual, and

(c) B is under 13.

(2) A person guilty of an offence under this section, if the activity caused or incited involved—

(a) penetration of B's anus or vagina,

(b) penetration of B's mouth with a person's penis,

(c) penetration of a person's anus or vagina with a part of B's body or by B with anything else, or

(d) penetration of a person's mouth with B's penis,

is liable, on conviction on indictment, to imprisonment for life.

(3) Unless subsection (2) applies, a person guilty of an offence under this section is liable—

(a) on summary conviction, to imprisonment for a term not exceeding 6 months or to a fine not exceeding the statutory maximum or both;

(b) on conviction on indictment, to imprisonment for a term not exceeding 14 years.

(U.K. Government, 2003b: Rape and other offences against children under 13)

Victims of Child Sexual Abuse: Demographics

Applying suitable terminology to the victims of this type of abuse is essential, not just legally but also culturally. CSA can be defined as sexual contact between a child and an adult (or other persons significantly older than the child), who is in a position of power or control over the child (Hersen and Gross, 2008). CSA is therefore non-consensual by definition (Frank et al., 2010). In terms of the images produced as part of the abuse, Interpol suggests that indecent images of a child should not be referred to as 'pornography', as this term refers to adults engaged in consensual sexual acts largely distributed legally to the general public (Interpol, n.d.-a).

Victims of all types of crimes appear to be taking a more prominent position in criminal justice policy (rhetorically at least), with a view to defining victims by their suffering rather than more exclusionary legal definitions (Frank et al., 2010; U.K. Government, 2003). However, this is only of relevance in a criminal justice system in which the victims can be identified and when victims elect to disclose the incident. It is widely acknowledged that the reported incidence* of sexual assaults and rape does not reflect the true levels—which is reflected as disclosure rates following CSA—and reporting numbers may be declining in some countries for a number of social and cultural reasons (Milivojevic and Ćopić, 2010).

Accessing accurate and reliable data on the prevalence[†] and incidence of children affected by CSA is very difficult for a number of reasons. The first is that this is essentially a 'secret' crime, which many of the victims will choose not to disclose for many years post-event, if at all. The rate and timing of the disclosure rate are also affected by the victim's sex and age, as well as environmental and cultural factors such as religion and ethnicity. The response of the victim's family is equally affected by cultural norms, which influence whether the child's family will report the abuse to the authorities (Fontes and Plummer, 2010) (this further reduces the opportunities for identification of offenders). Consequently, determining the size and distribution of the problem is extremely challenging; however, from the information available it is widely accepted that this is a very significant, international problem across all cultural and socio-economic groups (Chapter 17).

The sexual abuse of children happens in a number of ways. The first is CSA that occurs at a 'local' level, usually taking place in the home or within the circle of family and close friends. The second is sex trafficking, where children are sold into the sex trade, also known as 'sex slavery' (Milivojevic and Ćopić, 2010) (see Chapter 17). The third is online CSA (Interpol, N.D.-c). Each type of offending behaviour has a set of characteristic traits associated with it, for example, those who offend in person have different psychological attributes to those that download indecent images of children from the Internet—an important distinction as this means that there are individuals who can access thousands of potential victims without leaving the security of their home[‡] (Howitt, 2011).

The profile of the victim in local CSA is broad, as this includes the intra-familial category (i.e. abuse perpetrated by close family and friends) as well as the extrafamilial assault (including offenders who use their hobby as a means of accessing juveniles for sexual gratification); schools and youth clubs are common contact points, as are day-care centres (Colton et al., 2010; JSOnline, 2012). Church groups (Parkinson et al., 2009) are infamous with paedophilic activity, with data published by the John Jay College of Criminal Justice which demonstrate that approximately 4,392 Roman

---

* Number of new cases per annum.
† Proportion of people affected in a population.
‡ Evidence suggests that up to 97% of UK Internet paedophiles have no previous convictions and have not previously come to the police's attention (Brookes, 2003).

Catholic priests were accused of sexually assaulting 11,000 children in the United States between 1950 and 2002 (John Jay College of Criminal Justice, 2004). This illustrates the problem of variations in terminology, as from the information available it is not possible to determine if any of the children had been raped or assaulted by penetration.

Teaching is another profession which gives child abusers ready access to children of all ages, and data suggest that potentially 20% of female students in the United States have been sexually harassed by their teachers (Winslow and Zhang, 2008b). The problem appears to be even wider in developing nations, particularly Africa, where a recent survey (South Africa) indicated that school teachers were responsible for 32% of reported cases of child sexual assault (Krug et al., 2002). The definitions for this are not available, and given that under UK legislation sexual assault occurs when a child under 13 years is 'intentionally touched' in a 'sexual manner,' the resultant ambiguity is evident. What one person may consider innocent may to another be sexual touching. Determining that the intent behind the touch was sexual is very difficult and extremely hard to prove to a standard required in court.

CSA as a criminal activity necessitates a high level of covert practice: the elements of *mens rea** and *actus reus*† are carried out in private. Sex offenders have been shown to behave in an objective manner while participating within the communities in which they live, often only becoming active offenders when they notice a personal advantage (Richards, 2011), that is, solitary and safe access to children. Rarely do perpetrators see their behaviour as gratuitous or unjustified; instead they often view their acts as reasonable and justifiable (Baumeister, 1997; Martellozzo et al., 2010; Walters, 2012). Consequently, guilt of harm caused to the victim is not a significant aspect of the offender's response. Therefore, any child can be a victim to this type of offender, and cases have occurred where adults have only relayed the abuse many years after the event; the investigative agencies then determine if sufficient evidence is available to pursue a historical case against the accused. As a result of this plethora of problems, we do not know how many children around the world are subject to this type of activity per annum.

Some offenders are specific in the types of victims they will target, for example, sex offenders will often victimise vulnerable children, including those with low self-esteem, or may select a juvenile known to be a habitual liar, as they are less likely to be believed should they disclose the abuse (Rufo, 2012). Other sex offenders will offend against only males, or only

* Guilty thought.
† Guilty act.

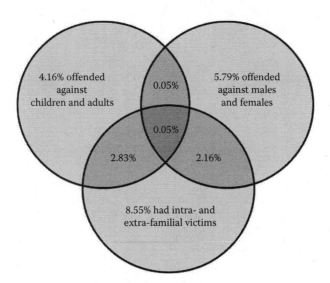

Figure 4.1 (See companion CD for colour figure.) Crossover among sexual offenders in terms of victim selection, in the following dimensions: victim age, sex and relationship to the offender (intra-familial vs. extrafamilial). (After Howitt, D., *Introduction to Forensic and Criminal Psychology*, 4th edn., Pearson Education Limited, England, U.K., 2011, p. 148.)

females, or may simply victimise as a result of opportunity. Victim selection can be useful when attempting to identify offenders. A recent study (Cann et al., 2007) looked at crossover* among sexual offenders in terms of victim selection, in the following dimensions: victim age, gender, and relationship to the offender (intra-familial vs. extrafamilial) (Figure 4.1). The results indicated that 25% of the offenders showed evidence of crossover in at least one dimension, with some showing multidimensional crossover. However, only 0.05% showed crossover between all victim dimensions. Another study, comprising data from a large number of sex offender programmes in the United States, suggests that approximately 40% of victims were related to the offender and live in the same household, while only 6% were victimised by strangers (Ruan et al., 1996), but crossover can also occur in this category.

In terms of crossover, there is a paucity of information available as to whether the categories of child sex offender (paedophile, hebephile, ephebophile) offend across categories, although in its clearest expression, it is recognised that some individuals with sexual interest in children have no sexual interest in adults (Seto, 2009).

---

* The extent to which a sex offender offends against victims in a variety of categories: adults and juveniles, for example Howitt (2011).

Offenders of Child Sexual Abuse: Demographics and Behaviours

In adults, there exist two conceptually distinct models of sex offenders—although it must be noted that the majority of this research has been undertaken on male offenders. The first is based on a general deviancy model; this suggests that sex offenders offend sexually as only one aspect of a general tendency to engage in various aspects of criminal activity. The second, or 'specialist' model, indicates that sex offenders largely specialise in sex crimes and do not engage in other types of criminal activity (Howitt, 2011). Put simply, those who commit sexual offences are not the same as non-sexual offenders (Harris et al., 2009).

Globally, categorisations such as 'sex offender' often subsume a variety of different types of offences, potentially masking the degree to which various categories of sex offenders specialise. For example, the failure to differentiate rapists from child molesters may result in important variation between the two not being recognised. However, the differences between the two types of offenders are key, for example, it has been suggested that rapists represent 'generalist' offenders, showing signs of criminal versatility not seen in child sexual abusers who are argued to be more 'specialist' (Knight and Prentky, 1990).

The specialist child sex offender can be further subdivided into two categories: (1) versatile child molesters are more likely to abuse alcohol or other substances, may have had difficulties in their formative years at school, and show behavioural problems during adolescence, and (2) specialist child molesters who are more likely to be sexually preoccupied, to have an emotional congruence with children, and to offend against male victims (Howitt, 2011).

The local abuser category also includes those who use their profession or hobby as a means of accessing minors. Although these are extrafamilial offenders, their work environments often place them in the position of *in loco parentis*; consequently, the grooming methods employed are more similar in nature to those of intra-familial abuse than those who engage in other forms of extrafamilial abuse (Colton et al., 2010). The specialist model of predatory sexual behaviour would fit with this type of local child sexual offender (Harris et al., 2009): To be successful and gain access to children, the offenders must be socially competent to some extent and capable of 'normal' interactions. If child abusers were not capable of gaining people's trust, they would not have the opportunity to access children as readily to undertake the abuse.

Males as Offenders

Currently it is believed that the majority of those who undertake CSA are men, as it is an act commonly associated with male sexual aggression (Martellozzo et al., 2010). Research conducted with online sexual offenders indicates that they represent a mixed and broad demographic (as with other sex offenders) (Sheehan and Sullivan, 2010) and therefore cannot be easily differentiated from other members of society (Howitt, 2011; Martellozzo et al., 2010). As a result, researchers focus on taxonomic variations (Howitt, 2011) and distinctive behaviours (Grubin, 1998).

There are two common taxonomies of child sexual offenders, with dichotomy noted between 'fixated'* and 'regressed'† types. The distinction is important when attempting to identify offenders, as significant differences are found in the relationship histories of the two types. Fixated offenders are rarely or have ever been married—approximately 12.5% have been married as compared to 75% of regressed offenders. Perhaps the most significant distinction, however, is that fixated-type offenders offend most often against strangers or acquaintances, whereas the regressed offender typically offends within their network of friends and relatives (Howitt, 2011). This simplistic taxonomy, although useful, should not be rigidly applied when investigative agencies are attempting to locate a child sex offender, as there are many examples where this system would not apply; for example, fathers who sexually abuse their children also offend against children outside of the family or rape adult women (Howitt, 2011; Miner and Dwyer, 1997).

In terms of strategy, there are a number of common mechanisms when considering local access child sex offenders that do not occur with other forms of CSA—abuse that is being perpetrated as part of an illicit sex trade (e.g. sex tourism) does not require the same level of relationship development in order to gain the sexual gratification. As a generalisation, males often use manipulation to isolate the victim (psychologically and/or physically) for a sexual relationship, in concurrence with coercive approaches to ensure the victim does not reveal the true nature of the relationship to others (Campbell, 2009). One study provided information on child sex abusers brought before the court in an area in London over a 2 year period, 40% used bribery to encourage victim participation (known as grooming), 24% used verbal threats and 16% used physical threats (Craissati and McClurg, 1997).

The public perception is that sex offenders are persistent and repetitive offenders and consequently remain a threat post-release from prison. However, research demonstrates that there are professionally dichotomous

---

* Fixated offenders are thought to be developmentally fixated, on either a temporary or permanent basis, so that their sexual interest is focussed on juveniles as opposed to adults. Although they may have sexual contact with adults, this is more coincidental as peer relationships are not psychologically integral to their sexuality (Howitt, 2011).

† Regressed offenders are men who have matured in their sexuality but have demonstrated a return to a previous phase of psychosexual development. Their psychosexual history would demonstrate primary interest in peer-age or adult individuals, rather than younger ones; interest in the latter appears to reflect almost a reversal to a more immature sexuality (Howitt, 2011).

views on recidivism rates. The first perspective suggests that sex offenders convicted appear in court only once (West, 1987) (although it should be noted that being caught only once does not equate to offending only once). The opposing view to this is that sex offenders are habitual sexual abusers (Abel et al., 1987). It would seem logical to assume that neither extreme is the case (Fisher and Thornton, 1993) and rather some offenders who reoffend do so at a high rate, while others offend on a single occasion (Hanson and Bussière, 1998). Thus, it is very difficult to reliably or accurately predict future offending behaviour on the basis of past occurrence.

Females as Offenders

Cases of CSA perpetrated by females have been documented since the 1930s (Bender and Blau, 1937). However, cultural resistance has hindered the recognition of sexual crimes committed by women, as only since the 1990s this group of offences has been researched more systematically (Hislop, 2001; Hunter and Matthews, 1997). As a consequence, women sexual predators have remained well hidden (Strickland, 2008), in society as well as the scientific literature. Although it remains a taboo subject (Elliot, 1993), the myth that females do not commit sexual abuse against children is slowly dissipating. It is now recognised that although the majority of CSA is carried out by males, the number of reports of offences to police has been gradually increasing (Rufo, 2012).

In terms of *modus operandi*, some women act alone, while others undertake the abuse with their male partner (Rufo, 2012). Some groom children for sale, while other women are passively involved in the abuse through lying to authorities for their partners: When males are accused of abusing children or holding indecent images of children, some female partners will offer the male an alibi or claim that they are represented in the images, and not a child.

When attempting to identify female child sex offenders and prosecute resultant cases, recent studies indicate that they possess specific traits that may be of assistance. For example, women sexual predators are likely to be aged between 21 and 35 years and have come from an abusive home and have suffered sexual abuse themselves as children (Glasser et al., 2001; Strickland, 2008). This difference includes the generalisation that females are more likely to be the victim of abuse than men, have a history of alcohol and/ or drug dependency, have (potentially) experienced periods of depression or anxiety and suffer from a personality disorder, are employed in professional or skilled occupations, struggle with intimate relationships and have a neglected, or have withdrawn entirely from, a relationship with one or both parents (Rufo, 2012).

Although little research has been undertaken to compare adult male and female child sex offenders, it is generally accepted that the two groups differ significantly (Sandler and Freeman, 2008), including the fact that females are more likely to admit the abuse to the authorities, are less predatory in their grooming behaviours, tend to take fewer risks in soliciting their victims, victimise children in their care, and victimise male children (Rufo, 2012). Female child sexual abusers normally fit into one of five categories (Rufo, 2012):

- A mother victimising her children
- A sibling or relative who abuses someone in her family
- A female who is abusing with a dominant male partner
- A female who holds a position of authority over the victim
- A female who is curious and has risk-taking tendencies

Estimates of the scale of females' sexual predation on juveniles vary, with Corby (1998) suggesting that women account for around 4% of offenders; another study postulates 5% (Grubin, 1998). A more recent study, however, proposes that females now perpetrate up to 25% of all CSA (Rufo, 2012). What authors do agree on is that the majority of female sex offenders will take advantage of any situation and many have a history of incestuous sexual victimisation (Rufo, 2012).

Although more contemporaneous data are difficult to obtain, one study suggests mothers may account for approximately 2% of the total (Grubin, 1998), exploiting either their own children or other children in their family, with daughters being the primary victims in this category. Studies have shown that in cases of mother–daughter incestuous relationships, there is a greater acceptance of the intimacy by the child, who is less willing to reveal the abuse to others. Male children can be targeted for incestuous relationships by their mothers as replacement sexual partners following the deterioration of an adult relationship; this type of abuse is also under-reported and difficult to detect and subsequently prosecute. Exposure, disclosure, and prosecution rates in incestuous mother–child relationships are particularly low, as, regardless of the abuse taking place, the child wants to remain with their birth parent and fears the further breakdown of the familial relationships (Rufo, 2012; Summit, 1983).

The acknowledgment that women groom children for sexual activity is also taboo, even within academic circles, which may reduce the reporting rate (Elliott, 1993). Grooming by both males and females in schools is one significant problem, the scale of which is again difficult to determine as some researchers suggest disclosure rate to be as low as 6% (Knoll, 2010). Add to this the stigma associated with reporting women for sexual assault and disclosure against female teachers may be further reduced.

The low conviction rate of females for CSA is also exacerbated by the fact that many victims of female sex abusers are not believed (Strickland, 2008) and female child sex offenders is not of high public concern (Rufo, 2012). While it remains unclear why relatively little attention has been paid to the female child sex offender, what is recognised is that the picture is complicated by the fact that evidence suggests (Denov, 2004) that female sex offenders are treated less seriously than males by all professionals with which they came into contact, including the therapists and those within the criminal justice system (Mallett and Karp, 2013). Together these factors contribute to the problems of investigating and prosecuting women for child sexual offences. This can be demonstrated by the fact that under UK law women cannot be prosecuted for rape, as the definition includes penile penetration (U.K. Government, 2003a).

Juveniles as Offenders

Childhood is the starting point for many types of criminal activity, and this general trend can be demonstrated in young child sex offenders; a high proportion of sex offenders are in their late teens or younger. The pattern of abusive behaviour is often similar to that of violent offences that are most commonly a youthful offence that declines sharply in middle age and beyond. However, a number of adults found guilty of CSA have been shown to have begun molesting children in their teens (Grubin, 1998; Vielmetti, 2010).

Juvenile (those under the age of 17 years) sex offenders (although largely ignored by researchers) appear to be as heterogeneous as the adult group. From the information that is available, statistics indicate that young offenders are responsible for a moderate–high proportion of sex offences (Langstrom, 1990). For example, juvenile sex offenders are thought to account for around 33% of all sex crimes (including a third of rapes of adult women) (Howitt, 2011), with 20% of those convicted for a sexual crime being under 18 years of age (Home Office, 2003).

In terms of juveniles sexually offending against other juveniles or children, it has been estimated that up to 50% of CSA in the United States (Graves et al., 1996) and United Kingdom (Home Office, 2003) is perpetrated by offenders under the age of 21 years (although a significant proportion of this is related to the fact that the age of the victim will be similar to the age of the offender, that is, their sexual interest is 'age appropriate'). One study looking at juvenile sex offenders differentiated specifically between those who offended against adults and those who victimised children (Worling, 1995). In terms of causation for the offence, the results indicated that those offending against an adult had experienced greater levels of physical punishment, and interestingly, sexual abuse by men appeared to lead to abuse against younger children by the victims. Another study supported these results and indicated that sex offenders who victimised children are more likely to have been sexually abused in childhood than those who offend against adults (Jespersen et al., 2009).

Little information is available regarding the age at which individuals begin to sexually offend, and the patterns of CSA by children may differ to patterns of sexual abuse by juveniles. Again here we encounter the problem of terminology—some studies will use the term adolescent, which is defined as 'the period of time in a person's life when they are developing into an adult' (Cambridge Dictionaries Online, n.d.), others child and still others juvenile, often interchangeably, making evaluation of the results and further inference difficult.

Conclusion

Denouncing those who commit sexual crimes against children is easy; understanding the behaviour and motivation of the perpetrators with a view to increasing the safety of children is not. As a result, identifying child sexual offenders is a challenging task, with offenders demonstrating significant variation in demographics, behaviours and offending patterns. The requirement for increased identification and successful prosecution of offenders could not be more relevant than in today's society, where we are almost daily faced with new cases of alleged abuse and, in terms of forensic human identification, is unfortunately set to be a key theme for many years to come.

There is also the added complication that much of the abuse is taking place on a global scale, with images being distributed across the Internet, and sex tourism. Any attempt at controlling and reducing the abuse of children must therefore occur within international legislative frameworks (Tagwireyi, 2011) and must address the current paucity in reliable, evidence-based information available regarding women and juveniles who undertake CSA.

The contemporary situation for victims of CSA appears to be comparable to that of adult rape victims prior to 1974 (Summit, 1983), when women felt guilt and shame and were not reporting incidents of sexual assault. Although the situation may be improving (as indicated by the increased levels of reporting), further improvements in disclosure rates are still required, as are mechanisms for helping victims.

While much work has been done in understanding the psychological climate and policing procedures involved in identifying offenders and prosecuting cases of sexual abuse, there is still a lack of willing on the part of some victims and witnesses to report these offences. The police can therefore undertake due process, but moving the case forward to prosecution is extremely challenging. As always, these offences involve intimate disclosure, and making them public through reporting can be damaging to victims, their family, and their community. Going forward, to further increase disclosure rates, these issues need to be addressed, so that recidivists can be more readily identified and successfully prosecuted, without detriment to the victims.

Here we have reviewed the information available for offender demographics, with a view to aiding in the identification of offenders as well as breaking down some of the myths surrounding abuse of this nature. Strangers are not the only ones we need to protect our children from; rather the majority of offenders, especially adults, are in positions of trust and/or authority in our communities. It would appear that the most efficient and effective way to identify child sex offenders is to reduce the fear of reporting, as this would prevent offenders from silencing their victims due to the stigma of coming forward. It is hoped that by addressing this issue more openly and directly, we can increase the identification and successful prosecution rate and in that way protect children.

References

Abel, G. G., Becker, J. V., Mittleman, M. S., Cunningham-Rathner, J., Rouleau, J. L., and Murphy, W. D. 1987. Self-reported sex crimes on non-incarcerated paraphiliacs. *Journal of Interpersonal Violence,* 2, 3–25.

Baumeister, R. F. 1997. *Evil: Inside Human Violence and Cruelty.* New York: Freeman.

Bender, L. and Blau, A. 1937. The reaction of children to sexual relations with adults. *American Journal of Orthopsychiatry,* 7, 500–518.

Black, S., Macdonald-Mcmillan, B., and Mallett, X. 2013a. The incidence of scarring on the dorsum of the hand. *International Journal of Legal Medicine.*

Black, S., Macdonald-Mcmillan, B., Mallett, X., Rynn, C., and Jackson, G. 2013b. The incidence and position of melanocytic nevi for the purposes of forensic image comparison. *International Journal of Legal Medicine.*

Black, S. M., Mallett, X., Rynn, C., and Duffield, N. 2009. Case history: Forensic hand image comparison as an aide for paedophile investigations. *Police Professional,* 184, 21–24.

Brookes, D. 2003. Investigating child sexual abuse on-line: The interactive approach. In: Macvean, A. and Spindler, P. (eds.) *Policing Paedophiles on the Internet.* Bristol, England: New Police Bookshop. pp. 49–60.

Cambridge Dictionaries Online. n.d. Adolescence. Available from: http://dictionary. cambridge.org/dictionary/british/adolescence, accessed January 18, 2013.

Campbell, A. M. 2009. False faces and broken lives: An exploratory study of the interaction behaviors used by male sex offenders in relating to victims. *Journal of Language and Social Psychology,* 28, 428–440.

Cann, J., Friendship, C., and Gozna, L. 2007. Assessing crossover in a sample of sexual offenders with multiple victims. *Legal and Criminological Psychology,* 12, 149–163.

Colton, M., Roberts, S., and Vanstone, M. 2010. Sexual abuse by men who work with children. *Journal of Child Sexual Abuse,* 19, 345–364.

Corby, B. 1998. *Managing Child Sexual Abuse Cases.* London, U.K.: Jessica Kingsley Publishers.

Craissati, J. and McClurg, G. 1997. The challenge project: A treatment program evaluation for perpetrators of child sexual abuse. *Child Abuse and Neglect*, 21, 637–648.

Denov, M. 2004. *Perspectives on Female Sex Offending: A Culture of Denial*. Aldershot, U.K.: Ashgate.

Elliot, M. (ed.) 1993. *Female Sexual Abuse of Children: The Ultimate Taboo*. Essex, U.K.: Longman.

Elliott, M. 1993. *Female Sexual Abuse of Children*. New York: The Guildford Press.

Fichtelberg, A. 2008. *Crime Without Borders: An Introduction to International Criminal Justice*. Upper Saddle River, NJ: Pearson.

Fisher, D. and Thornton, D. 1993. Assessing risk of reoffending in sexual offenders. *Journal of Mental Health*, 25, 105–117.

Fontes, L. A. and Plummer, C. 2010. Cultural issues in disclosures of child sexual abuse. *Journal of Child Sexual Abuse*, 19, 491–518.

Frank, D. J., Camp, B. J., and Boutcherc, S. A. 2010. Worldwide trends in the criminal regulation of sex, 1945 to 2005. *American Sociological Review*, 75, 867–893.

Glasser, M., Campbell, D., Glasser, A., Leitch, I., and Farrelly, S. 2001. Cycle of child sexual abuse: Links between being a victim and becoming a perpetrator. *The British Journal of Psychiatry*, 179, 482–494.

Graves, R. B., Openshaw, D. K., Ascione, F. R., and Ericksen, S. L. 1996. Demographic and parental characteristics of youthful sexual offenders. *International Journal of Offender Therapy and Comparative Criminology*, 40, 300–317.

Grubin, D. 1998. Sex offending against children: Understanding the risk. *Police Research Series*. Available from: http://library.npia.police.uk/docs/hopolicers/fprs99.pdf, accessed May 02, 2012.

Hanson, R. K. and Bussière, M. T. 1998. Predicting relapse: A meta-analysis of sexual offender recidivism studies. *Journal of Consulting and Clinical Psychology*, 66, 348–362.

Harris, D. A., Mazerolle, P., and Knight, R. A. 2009. Understanding male sexual offending: A comparison of general and specialist theories. *Criminal Justice and Behavior*, 36, 463–486.

Hart, S. N., Lee, Y., and Wernham, M. 2011. A new age for child protection—General comment 13: Why it is important, how it was constructed, and what it intends? *Child Abuse & Neglect: Convention on the Rights of the Child Special Issue*, 35, 970–978.

Healy, M. A. 2004. Child pornography: An international perspective. Prepared as a working document for the World Congress against Commercial Sexual Exploitation. Available from: http://www.crime-research.org/articles/536/, accessed May 16, 2012.

Hersen, M. and Gross, A. M. 2008. *Handbook of Clinical Psychology, Volume 2—Children and Adolescents*. New York: John Wiley & Sons.

Hislop, J. 2001. *Female Sex Offenders: What Therapists, Law Enforcement and Child Protective Services Need to Know*. Ravensdale, WA: Issue Press.

Home Office. 2003. *Criminal Statistics: England and Wales 2002. Statistics Relating to Criminal Proceedings for the Year 2002*. London, U.K.: The Stationary Office.

Howitt, D. 2011. *Introduction to Forensic and Criminal Psychology*, 4th edn. England, U.K.: Pearson Education Limited.

Hunter, J. A. and Matthews, R. 1997. Sexual deviance in females. In: Laws, D. R. and O'Donohue, W. (eds.) *Sexual Deviance: Theory, Assessment and Treatment.* New York: Guildford. pp. 465–480.

Interpol. n.d.-a. Appropriate terminology. Available from: http://www.interpol.int/ Crime-areas/Crimes-against-children/Appropriate-terminology, accessed April 29, 2012.

Interpol. n.d.-b. Combating sexual exploitation of children on the internet using all available technical solutions, including access-blocking by INTERPOL member countries. Interpol General Assembly Resolution AG-2009-RES-05. Available from: http://www.interpol.int/contentinterpol/search?SearchText=AG-2009-RES-05&x=0&y=0, accessed January 20, 2012.

Interpol. n.d.-c. Crimes against children. Available from: http://www.interpol.int/ Crime-areas/Crimes-against-children/Crimes-against-children, accessed April 29, 2012.

Jespersen, A. F., Lalumière, M. L., and Seto, M. C. 2009. Sexual abuse history among adult sex offenders and non-sex offenders: A meta-analysis. *Child Abuse and Neglect,* 33, 179–192.

John Jay College of Criminal Justice. 2004. The nature and scope of the problem of sexual abuse of minors by catholic priests and deacons in the United States. Available from: http://www.usccb.org/nrb/johnjaystudy/, accessed August 06, 2012.

JSOnline. 2012. Dutch prosecutors demand 20-year sentence for man accused of molesting dozens of minors. *Journal Sentinel* Online. Available from: http:// hosted.ap.org/fynamic/stories/E/EU_NETHERLANDS_PEDOPHILE_ TRIAL?SITE=WIMIL%SECTION=HOME&TEMPLATE+DEFAULT, accessed April 16, 2012.

Knight, R. A. and Prentky, R. A. 1990. Classifying sexual offenders: The development and corroboration of taxonomic models. In: Marshall, W. L., Law, D. R., and Barbaree, H. E. (eds.) *Handbook of Sexual Assault: Issues, Theories, and Treatment of the Offender.* New York: Plenum. pp. 23–52.

Knoll, J. 2010. Teacher sexual misconduct: Grooming patterns and female offenders. *Journal of Child Sexual Abuse,* 19, 371–386.

Krug, E. G., Dahlberg, L. L., Mercy, J. A., Zwi, A. B., and Lozana, R. 2002. *World Report on Violence and Health.* Geneva, Switzerland: World Health Organization.

Langstrom, N. 1990. *Young Sex Offenders: Individual Characteristics, Agency Reactions and Criminal Recidivism,* Stockholm, Sweden: Karolinka Institutet, Department of Public Health, Division of Psychosocial Factors and Health, Division of Forensic Psychiatry.

Lynch, M. 2002. Pedophiles and cyber-predators as contaminating forces: The language of disgust, pollution, and boundary invasions in Federal debates on sex offender legislation. *Law & Social Inquiry,* 27, 529–566.

Mallett, X. and Karp, J. 2013. Hell is other people: The importance of controlling paedophilic activity. In: Harrison, K. and Rainey, B. (eds.) *The Wiley-Blackwell Handbook of Legal and Ethical Aspects of Sex Offender Treatment and Management.* Chichester, U.K.: Wiley-Blackwell. pp. 462–478.

Martellozzo, E., Nehring, D., and Taylor, H. 2010. Online child sexual abuse by female offenders: An exploratory study. *International Journal of Cyber Criminology,* 4, 592–609.

Milivojevic, S. and Ćopić, S. 2010. Victims of sex trafficking: Gender, myths, and consequences. In: Shoham, S. G., Knepper, P., and Kett, M. (eds.) *International Handbook of Victimology*. Boca Raton, FL: CRC Press.

Miner, M. H. and Dwyer, S. M. 1997. The psychological development of sex offenders: Differences between exhibitionists, child molesters and incest offenders. *International Journal of Offender Therapy and Comparative Criminology*, 41, 36–44.

Obergfell-Fuchs, J. 2010. Perpetrators and victims of sex crimes. In: Shoham, S. G., Knepper, P., and Kett, M. (eds.) *International Handbook of Criminology*. Boca Raton, FL: CRC Press. pp. 259–307.

Parkinson, P., Oates, K., and Jayakody, A. 2009. Study of reported child sexual abuse in the Anglican Church. Available from: http://www.archive.anglican.org.au/docs/StudyofReportedChildSexualAbuseintheAnglicanChurchMay2009Full Report.pdf, accessed April 30, 2012.

Rettinger, L. J. 2000. Relationship between child pornography and the commission of sexual offences against children: A review of the literature. National Criminal Justice Reference Service Library Collection. U.S. Department of Justice. Available from: https://http://www.ncjrs.gov/App/Publications/abstract.aspx?ID=206309, accessed August 05, 2012.

Richards, K. 2011. Misperceptions about child sex offenders. *Trends & Issues in Crime and Criminal Justice*, 429, 421–440. Australian Institute of Criminology, Canberra, New South Wales, Australia. Available from: http://www.aic.gov.au/publications/currentseries/tandi/421-440/tandi429.aspx, accessed August 05, 2012.

Ruan, G., Miyoshi, T. J., Metzner, J. L., Frugman, R. D., and Fryer, G. E. 1996. Trends in a national sample of sexually abusive youths. *Journal of the American Academy of Child and Adolescent Psychiatry*, 35, 17–25.

Rufo, R. A. 2012. *Sexual Predators amongst Us*. Boca Raton, FL: CRC Press.

Sandler, J. and Freeman, N. 2008. Female and male sex offenders: A comparison of recidivism patterns and risk factors. *Journal of Interpersonal Violence*, 23, 1294–1413.

Seto, M. C. 2009. Pedophilia. *Annual Review of Clinical Psychology*, 5, 391–407.

Sheehan, V. and Sullivan, J. 2010. A qualitative analysis of child sex offenders involved in the manufacture of indecent images of children. *Journal of Sexual Aggression*, 16, 143–167.

Strickland, S. M. 2008. Female sex offenders: Exploring issues of personality, trauma, and cognitive distortions. *Journal of Interpersonal Violence*, 23, 474–490.

Summit, R. C. 1983. The child abuse accommodation syndrome. *Child Abuse & Neglect*, 7, 177–193.

Tagwireyi, G. 2011. Comprehensive legal approaches to combat child pornography: An international and regional perspective. *Conference paper*. Available from: http://www.commonwealthigf.org/wp-content/uploads/2011/03/ICIA-Conference-Paper-ICMEC-FINAL.pdf, accessed August 11, 2013.

U.K. Government Sexual Offences Act. 2003. Available from: http://www.legislation.gov.uk/ukpga/2003/42/contents, accessed May 16, 2012.

U.K. Government. 2003a. Sexual Offences Act: Rape. Available from: http://www.legislation.gov.uk/ukpga/2003/42/section/1, accessed January 18, 2013.

U.K. Government. 2003b. Sexual Offences Act: Rape and other offences against children under 13. Available from: http://www.legislation.gov.uk/ukpga/2003/42/part/1/crossheading/rape-and-other-offences-against-children-under-13, accessed January 18, 2013.

U.K. Government. 2003c. Sexual Offences Act: Sexual assault. Available from: http://www.legislation.gov.uk/ukpga/2003/42/section/3, accessed January 18, 2013.

U.K. Government. 2012. Formal memorandum—Child sexual abuse cases. Available from: http://www.justice.gov.uk/search?collection=moj-matrix-dev-web&form=simple&profile=_default&query=child+sexual+abuse, accessed August 05, 2012.

United Nations. 2001. Optional protocol to the UN convention on the rights of the child on the sale of children, child prostitution and child pornography. Available from: http://www.undemocracy.com/A-RES-54-263.pdf, accessed April 30, 2012.

Vielmetti, B. 2010. Jury to decide fate of pedophile held at a mental health facility. *Journal Sentinel*. Available from: http://www.jsonline.com/news/crime/80762252.html accessed April 16, 2012.

Walters, G. D. 2012. *Crime in a Psychological Context: From Career Criminals to Criminal Careers*. London, U.K.: Sage.

West, D. J. 1987. *Sexual Crimes and Confrontations: A Study of Victims and Offenders*. Aldershot, U.K.: Gower.

Winslow, R. W. and Zhang, S. X. 2008a. *Criminology: A Global Perspective*. Upper Saddle River, NJ: Pearson.

Winslow, R. W. and Zhang, S. X. 2008b. *Forcible Rape*. Upper Saddle River, NJ: Pearson.

Worling, J. R. 1995. Sexual abuse histories of adolescent male sex offenders: Differences on the basis of the age and gender of the victims. *Journal of Abnormal Psychology*, 104, 610–613.

Identification from Soft and Hard Tissues

II

Distinguishing Human from Non-Human Bone*

5

DIANE L. FRANCE

Contents

Hints

'Form follows function' and the morphology of skeletal elements may give important clues about how that element was used in the animal's life.

More sculpted articular surfaces have decreased range of motion, while less sculpted articular surfaces may have greater range of motion. In mammals, more sculpted bones are usually non-human (even in immature bones). Bird appendicular skeletal elements are more sculpted, but reptiles (such as alligators) may have a relatively smooth articular surface.

Introduction

Experienced forensic anthropologists recognise human bones so well that when handed an intact bone or intact skeleton, we are pretty adept at stating whether or not the bone is human. It is more difficult to diagnose the species (or genus or even family) represented by the bone, and it is more difficult yet to make that diagnosis with fragmentary bones or bones still covered with soft tissue. Luckily, there are a few clues that go beyond the 'hints' previously listed that

* All figures in this chapter are copyright Diane France.

assist in identifying the bones that are from a non-human animal (particularly mammals). These clues largely relate to the basic biomechanics (form follows function) of the axial and appendicular skeleton of quadrupeds and birds, and the way that they evolved in different species (see Figures 5.1 through 5.4).

Although all skeletons are interesting, this chapter will be limited to clues for distinguishing between humans and other mammals, with bits about a few birds and some reptiles. These gross morphological differences will not include non-human primates, which are, of course, more similar to the human form than are other mammals. Also, it is unlikely that someone will be unable to determine that a frog or salamander skeleton is not human, so amphibians will not be included. One should remember that there is great variation among mammals, birds and reptiles, so to talk about a bird skeleton, for example, should not imply that we know everything about all bird skeletons. Also, because this is a chapter and not an entire book, the discussion will be limited to those areas most often discovered and most often confused with human remains.

Skull, Vertebral Column and Ribs

Complete skulls are not usually a problem in the assessment of forensic significance. In fact, intact skulls are not usually presented to the forensic anthropologist because the medical examiner, law enforcement and even the general public cannot only determine that it is not human, they will often keep it for themselves without engaging the expert. Sometimes, however, a pathological human cranium (Figure 5.5, showing a human infant with anencephaly, a congenital defect resultant from a neural tube defect, in which a large portion of the brain fails to form) will be mistaken for non-human, or a partial pathological non-human cranium (Figure 5.6, showing a cow with hydrocephalus, more commonly known as 'water on the brain') may be mistaken for human.

We know that the shape of a skull reflects the extent to which an animal relies on vision, smell, hearing, the size of the brain, diet, and, in some animals, aerodynamic or aquadynamic qualities (e.g. in flying or swimming birds). In addition, it is important to remember that the centre of gravity in quadrupeds is near the forelimbs, and the cranium is not balanced on the vertebral column as it is in humans. Instead, it projects far forward of the scapula, so the foramen magnum is located on the posterior aspect of the occipital. Because the cranium and mandible must be held up against gravity, the muscles inserting on the posterior occiput and on the spinous processes are large and require larger areas of muscle insertion on the posterior occiput and on the spinous processes of the thoracic vertebrae. The larger the head, the larger the areas of muscle insertion and the greater area of bone devoted to the areas of insertion. Therefore, those areas are very large (Figures 5.7 and 5.8) in grazers and browsers with heavy dentition (deer, elk, cows, horses, etc.).

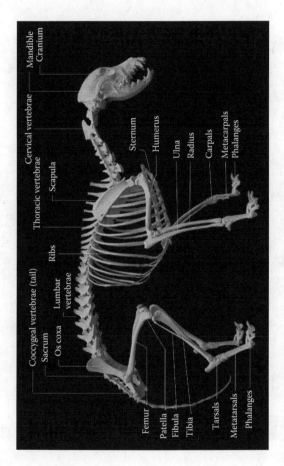

Figure 5.1 (See companion CD for colour figure.) Dog (*Canis familiaris*) skeleton.

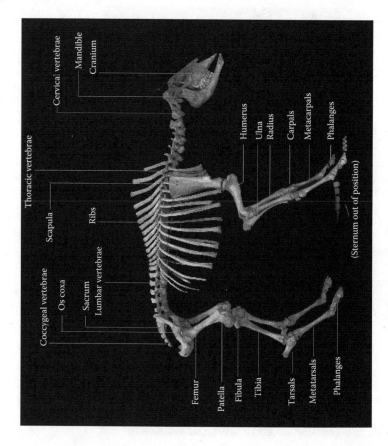

Figure 5.2 (See companion CD for colour figure.) Bison (*Bison bison*) skeleton.

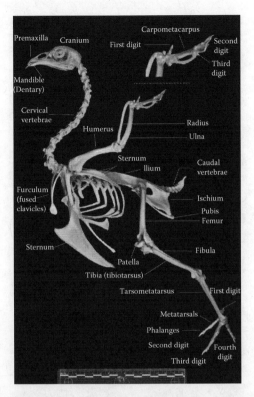

Figure 5.3 (See companion CD for colour figure.) Chicken (*Gallus* sp.) skeleton.

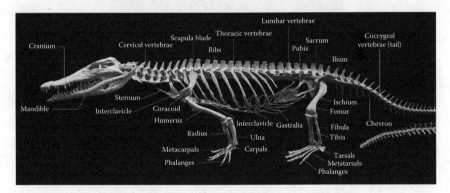

Figure 5.4 (See companion CD for colour figure.) Crocodile (*Crocodylus niloticus*) skeleton.

In smaller quadrupedal mammals with the dentition of a carnivore (dogs, cats, etc.), those muscles are not as large and the areas for insertion are not as pronounced (Figures 5.9 and 5.10), but they are still larger than those of a human relative to vertebral body size (Figures 5.11 and 5.12). In humans, of course, gravity is pushing the head onto the vertebral column. Instead of the

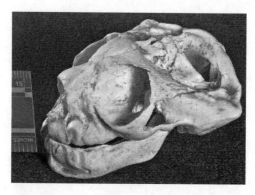

Figure 5.5 (See companion CD for colour figure.) Anencephalic human infant.

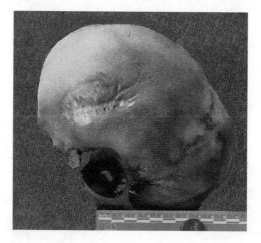

Figure 5.6 (See companion CD for colour figure.) Hydrocephalic calf without the diagnostic facial features.

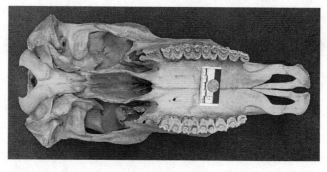

Figure 5.7 (See companion CD for colour figure.) Cow (*Bos taurus*) cranium (inferior view). Note position of foramen magnum.

Figure 5.8 (See companion CD for colour figure.) Bison (*Bison bison*) spinous process.

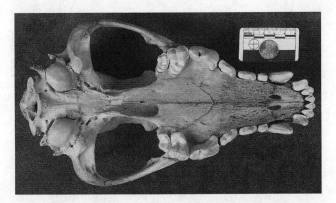

Figure 5.9 (See companion CD for colour figure.) Wolf (*Canis lupus*) cranium (inferior view).

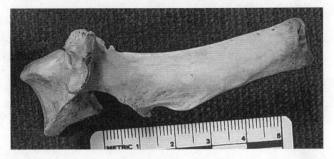

Figure 5.10 (See companion CD for colour figure.) Wolf (*Canis lupus*) spinous process.

large nuchal muscles (and resulting large spinous processes) to pull the head to a more dorsal position, humans have relatively large sternocleidomastoid muscles, which act on both sides to pull the head forward from a dorsal position (and act separately to turn the head). Therefore, if a significant mastoid process is discovered, it is human (Figures 5.13 and 5.14).

Even in the small mammals (e.g. rodents), the occiput shows relatively rugged areas for muscle insertion and the spinous processes are large

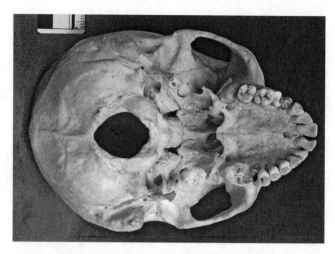

Figure 5.11 (See companion CD for colour figure.) Human cranium (inferior view).

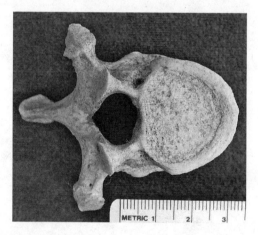

Figure 5.12 (See companion CD for colour figure.) Human thoracic vertebra (superior view).

relative to the size of the vertebral body. One might ask why a rodent would be brought into this discussion, because 'who would ever mistake a rodent skeleton for human?' In fact, small bones are sometimes mistaken for human infants. Several years ago a professional anthropologist who should have known the difference (not a forensic anthropologist, however) caused quite a stir when a county coroner, the sheriff and this author (DLF) responded to a very remote location in Colorado because the informant found the skeletal remains of a human infant in a cave. The infant turned out to be a porcupine skeleton.

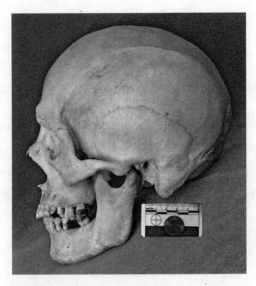

Figure 5.13 (See companion CD for colour figure.) Human cranium showing mastoid process (lateral view).

Figure 5.14 (See companion CD for colour figure.) Wolf (*Canis lupus*) cranium (lateral view). Arrow indicates small mastoid process.

Although it is unlikely to mistake even a partial bird cranium as human, the foramen magnum in some birds is near the base of the cranium, a more human-like position. Bird skulls (even from large birds) are thinner than any, even in a young human infant, and they only have one occipital condyle in the midline of the foramen magnum (Figure 5.15), although a few birds have an accessory condyle.

Reptiles, too, have only one occipital condyle, and the birds and reptiles share the additional cranial trait of sclerotic rings (Figure 5.16). These rings help support the eyes and consist of many bony plates different enough in

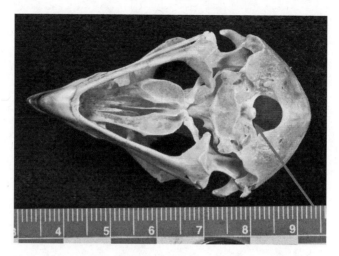

Figure 5.15 (See companion CD for colour figure.) Cooper's hawk (*Accipiter cooperii*) cranium (inferior view). Arrow indicates single occipital condyle in the middle of the foramen magnum.

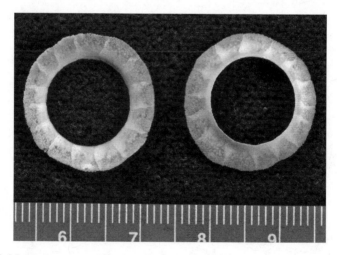

Figure 5.16 (See companion CD for colour figure.) Cooper's hawk (*Accipiter cooperii*) sclerotic rings.

size and shape that they can sometimes be used for species identification (Kaiser, 2007), although because they are so small and fragile, they are unlikely to be found in a forensic situation.

The vertebrae in all vertebrates are divided into cervical, thoracic, lumbar, sacral, and caudal, although the number of vertebrae in each section is reduced and expanded, or the sections are even combined, depending upon the species. In addition to long spinous processes in quadrupedal mammals, the morphology of the individual vertebrae differs. In quadrupedal mammals the vertebral

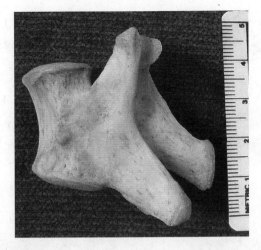

Figure 5.17 (See companion CD for colour figure.) High vertebral body seen in non-human mammals (lateral view).

Figure 5.18 (See companion CD for colour figure.) Human thoracic vertebra (lateral view).

body is usually longer (or higher, depending upon your plane of reference) relative to the diameter than in humans (Figures 5.17 and 5.18), and some, but not all, have a ventral ridge running cranio-caudally in the centre of the vertebral body (Figure 5.19). Of course, if you see this ridge (and it can be seen in radiographs as well), it is obviously not human. The caudal vertebrae of some small mammals (Figure 5.20) may be mistaken for a human phalanx. Human vertebral bodies are more wedge-shaped and the diameter is often equal to or larger than the height. The superior and inferior surfaces are usually relatively flat or slightly concave in humans. The concavity or convexity of quadrupedal mammalian vertebrae may be somewhat exaggerated but may be pronounced

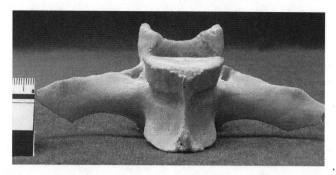

Figure 5.19 (See companion CD for colour figure.) Pig (*Sus scrofa*) vertebra (frontal view).

Figure 5.20 (See companion CD for colour figure.) Bobcat (*Lynx rufus*) caudal (tail) vertebrae. The cylindrical vertebrae on the left of the image are sometimes mistaken for human phalanges.

in birds and reptiles (Figure 5.21). Mammals have a single neural arch supporting the spinal cord, but birds and reptiles often have a second neural arch on the ventral side of the body, called a chevron (see Figure 5.21), in most of the caudal vertebrae (Romer, 1997). The synsacrum of the bird contains not only the sacral vertebrae but also three lumbar and the first six caudal vertebrae (Figure 5.22). The sacrum in many reptiles consists of only two fused vertebrae.

The thorax of quadrupedal mammals is long and narrow in the dorsoventral plane, and the ribs are long and relatively straight (Figure 5.23), while human ribs are more curved (Figure 5.24) to reflect the short distance between the vertebrae and sternum. In addition to the curvature of the rib, the position, size and shape of the vertebral articular facets can assist in distinguishing between human and non-human mammals (Figure 5.25). If an entire rib is present, the differences are relatively easy to see, but segments of ribs that turn out to be from barbecued pork or beef are frequently discovered, and these can be a bit tricky.

In mammals, part of the definition of thoracic vertebrae is that they carry ribs, and most of the ribs connect with the sternum (except the 'floating ribs'). Mammals have neither cervical nor lumbar ribs, but many species of reptiles and birds have cervical, thoracic, lumbar and even sometimes caudal

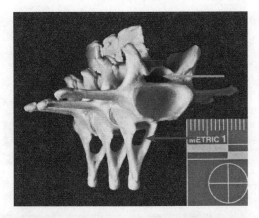

Figure 5.21 (See companion CD for colour figure.) Monitor lizard (*Varanus salvadorii*) caudal vertebrae showing a dorsal neural arch and a chevron. Top arrow indicates the dorsal neural arch and the bottom arrow indicates a chevron.

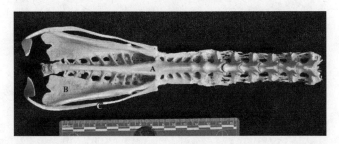

Figure 5.22 (See companion CD for colour figure.) Swan (*Coscoroba coscoroba*) pelvic girdle, including synsacrum (A), ischium (B) and pubis (C).

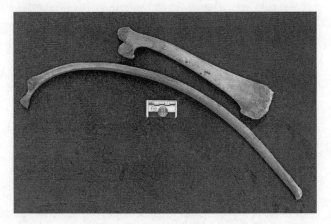

Figure 5.23 (See companion CD for colour figure.) Cow (*Bos taurus*) ribs (inferior view).

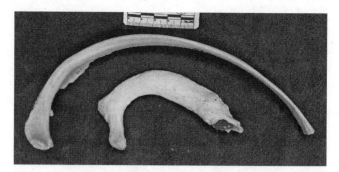

Figure 5.24 (See companion CD for colour figure.) Human ribs (superior view).

Figure 5.25 (See companion CD for colour figure.) Dog (*Canis familiaris*) rib (superior view).

ribs (Kaiser, 2007; Romer, 1997). Bird ribs are actually in two parts: the dorsal rib and a ventral rib that meet about halfway. The dorsal ribs articulate with the vertebrae and have an extra process called the uncinate process (Figure 5.26), which overlaps the next rib in the caudal direction (Kaiser, 2007). The ventral ribs articulate with the sternum. Most reptiles have simple ribs with one 'head' that articulate with the vertebra, and these could be mistaken for human (Figure 5.27). Crocodilians (crocodiles and alligators) have ribs (Figure 5.28) with two articular processes (Vitt and Caldwell, 2009; Zug et al., 2001). These reptiles also have gastralia, sometimes called abdominal ribs (see Figure 5.4).

Pectoral Girdle

The scapulae of mammals are similar enough in all species to be readily recognised as scapulae, and they are very dissimilar to reptiles and birds. In fact, the scapula is a fairly good diagnostic tool for diagnosing mammalian species. Most mammalian scapulae are triangular in shape (particularly the large grazers and browsers such as elk, cow and sheep, although the horse is

Figure 5.26 (See companion CD for colour figure.) Uncinate process of a swan (*Coscoroba coscoroba*) dorsal rib.

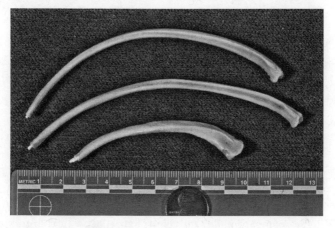

Figure 5.27 (See companion CD for colour figure.) Monitor lizard (*Varanus salvadorii*) ribs.

more elongated), and they usually have a small or absent acromion process (Figure 5.29). The bear is distinctive as it is almost a square with rounded edges and has a prominent acromion process (Figure 5.30). The smaller carnivore (the wild and domestic dogs and cats) scapulae are more paddle-shaped with a significant (but thinner than human) acromion process (Figure 5.31), while the seal scapula is more comma-shaped with a very short acromion process (Figure 5.32). Fortunately the human scapula is readily recognisable by the triangular shape with the scapular spine and glenoid fossa at an upward angle to the vertebral border and a prominent scapular spine that ends in the bulky, roughened acromion process (Figure 5.33).

Note that the bird scapula (Figure 5.34) is actually two bones: the scapula blade and the coracoid. It is easy to mistake the scapula blade as a rib

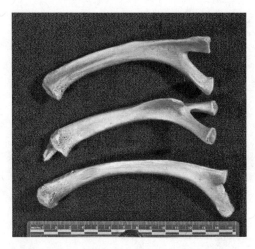

Figure 5.28 (See companion CD for colour figure.) Alligator (*Alligator* sp.) ribs.

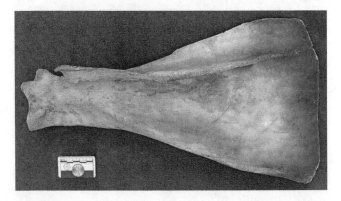

Figure 5.29 (See companion CD for colour figure.) Cow (*Bos taurus*) scapula.

and mistake the glenoid fossa on that blade as a point for vertebral articulation. The alligator scapula also consists of a scapula and a separate coracoid process (Figures 5.35 and 5.36).

The clavicle maintains the distance between the sternum and scapula and is present in humans, a few other mammals (such as beaver), and birds (the furculum, often called the wishbone). The furculum of large birds (Figure 5.37) might be mistaken for an edentulous human mandible. Many reptiles have a clavicle, but it is absent in the crocodilians.

The sternum is present in mammals and reptiles, but it is particularly prominent in birds. Birds that fly (see Figure 5.3) and birds such as the penguin that use their wings for swimming have a sternum with a prominent keel for attachment of the pectoral muscles, while flightless birds such as the ostrich and cassowary have a prominent sternum without a keel (Figure 5.38).

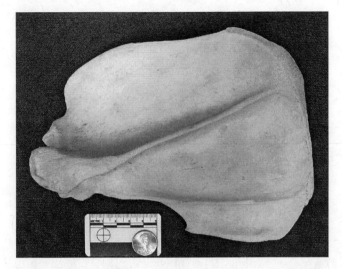

Figure 5.30 (See companion CD for colour figure.) Bear *(Ursus americanus)* scapula.

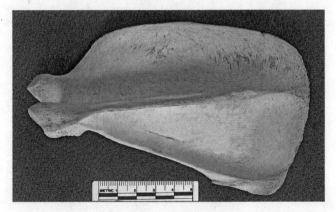

Figure 5.31 (See companion CD for colour figure.) Wolf *(Canis lupus)* scapula.

Pelvic Girdle

The pelvic girdle consisting of the ilium, ischium and pubis is easily recognisable in mammals but has a very different morphology in birds and reptiles. The pelvic girdle in quadrupedal mammals is long and narrow (primarily because of the long, narrow ilium) and reflects the function of the leg muscles that attach to the pelvis (Figure 5.39). The lower limbs in the large quadrupeds move antero-posteriorly with very little lateral motion, so the strength of the muscles of the leg that makes this movement possible is benefited by a long pelvis (particularly the ilium, which acts as

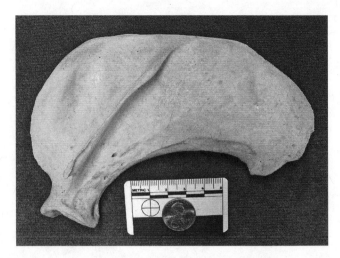

Figure 5.32 (See companion CD for colour figure.) Seal *(Phoca vitulina)* scapula.

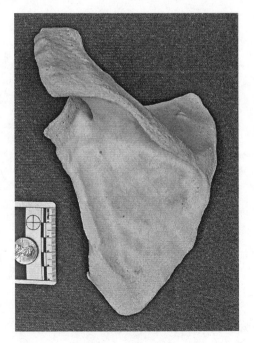

Figure 5.33 (See companion CD for colour figure.) Human scapula.

a long lever arm). The sacrum in the large grazers and browsers is long relative to its width. Some of the smaller quadrupedal mammals (wild and domestic dogs and cats and raccoons, otters, etc.) have somewhat wider sacrum relative to its width (Figure 5.40), but not as wide as in humans (Figure 5.41).

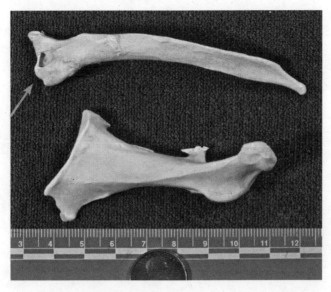

Figure 5.34 (See companion CD for colour figure.) Goose (*Cereopsis* sp.) scapula. The upper bone is the scapular blade with arrow pointing to the glenoid fossa. The lower bone is the coracoid process.

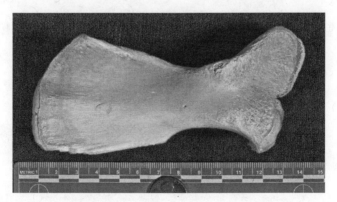

Figure 5.35 (See companion CD for colour figure.) Alligator (*Alligator* sp.) scapula (left side).

The pelvic girdle in humans has, of course, become shorter and wider, reflecting the different locomotion patterns (balancing the weight over each leg independently as forward movement occurs) as well as the difference in support of the abdominal contents and the need for a large pelvic outlet for childbirth in females. The elements of the reptile pelvic girdle are not as easily recognised, unless they are discovered as a pelvic girdle unit with the

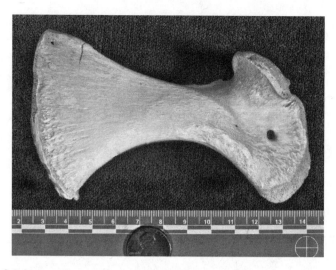

Figure 5.36 (See companion CD for colour figure.) Alligator (*Alligator* sp.) coracoid (left side).

Figure 5.37 (See companion CD for colour figure.) Goose (*Cereopsis* sp.) furculum.

sacrum (two sacral vertebrae) attached. Even then, it is easy to mistake the individual bones (Figures 5.42 and 5.43).

The pelvic girdle of birds is also very distinctive (Figure 5.44) but might be mistaken for the skull of a strange animal (by someone with an active imagination). As previously mentioned, the sacrum consists of a few lumbar and caudal vertebrae fused to the sacral vertebrae.

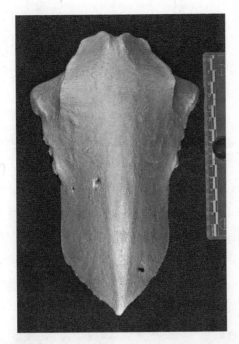

Figure 5.38 (See companion CD for colour figure.) Cassowary (*Casuarius* sp.) sternum (anterior view).

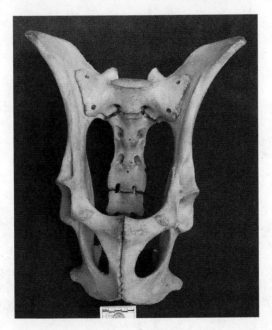

Figure 5.39 (See companion CD for colour figure.) Elk (*Cervus elaphus*) pelvic girdle (anterior view).

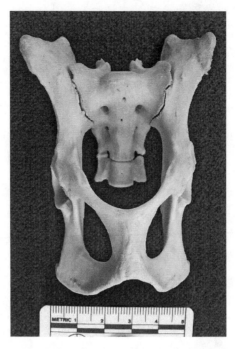

Figure 5.40 (See companion CD for colour figure.) Raccoon (*Procyon lotor*) pelvic girdle (anterior view).

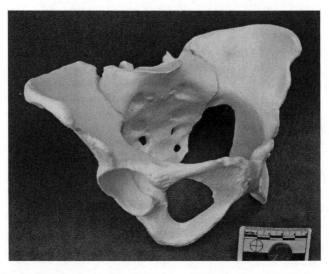

Figure 5.41 (See companion CD for colour figure.) Human pelvic girdle.

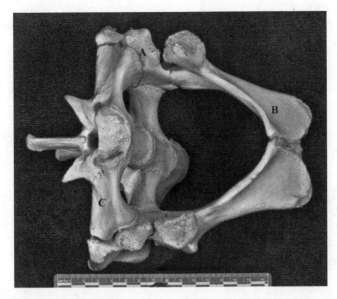

Figure 5.42 (See companion CD for colour figure.) Alligator (*Alligator* sp.) pelvic girdle without pubis, including ischium (A), ilium (B) and sacrum (C).

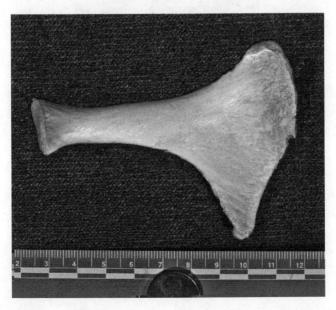

Figure 5.43 (See companion CD for colour figure.) Alligator (*Alligator* sp.) pubis (left side).

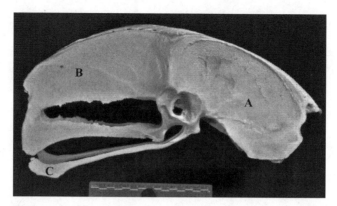

Figure 5.44 (See companion CD for colour figure.) Bird pelvic girdle (cassowary) including ilium (A), ischium (B) and pubis (C).

Forelimbs and Hind Limbs

Postcranial material is very often a problem for the medico-legal community, particularly if soft tissue remains on the specimen, if it is from an immature individual, or if the specimen is fragmentary. Food animals are quite often on the forensic 'menu'. The remains of fried chicken look somewhat like an immature human (Figure 5.45). The cut bone from a roast frequently turns

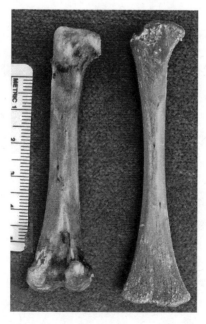

Figure 5.45 (See companion CD for colour figure.) Chicken (*Gallus* sp.) (left) and human infant (right) left femur (posterior view).

Figure 5.46 (**See companion CD for colour figure.**) Bone from a beef roast.

up as a suspected dismemberment case (Figure 5.46). While it is true that a homicide victim could be dismembered with a band saw, creating the fine, even striations seen in processed meat, the bone section in a human will not have thick cortical bone relative to the bone's diameter. Cut pork and beef ribs look very much like an adult human and provide only a small number of clues that they are not from a human. The good news is that if there is an articular surface of the humerus, femur, radius, ulna or tibia, they are similar enough to human that you can at least determine what bone you are holding and get closer to determining what species it represents. There are actually a couple of 'slam-dunk' clues on the long bones (particularly on the metatarsals, metacarpals, and phalanges) that will indicate that the bone is not human. These will be described later.

Among the quadrupedal mammals covered in this chapter, the differences in locomotor patterns are reflected in the morphology of the appendicular skeleton. The skeleton of a pronghorn reflects the need for an animal of moderate size to move quickly (Figure 5.47). The buffalo and cow are massive animals that do not move as quickly, so their skeletons must support much more weight without the need for great speed (Figure 5.48). Dogs and cats are fast runners that do not carry much weight (Figure 5.49). Badgers are digging animals and their forearms demonstrate that pattern of areas of muscle attachment (Figure 5.50).

Certain bones of the forelimbs and hind limbs of many quadrupeds are modified so as to increase the power to the legs. The concept of lengthening certain bones (and therefore muscle attachment areas) to increase the power of the muscle is easy to understand if we liken it to jacking up a car to change

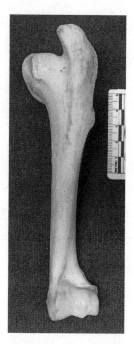

Figure 5.47 (See companion CD for colour figure.) Pronghorn (*Antilocapra americana*) humerus (anterior view).

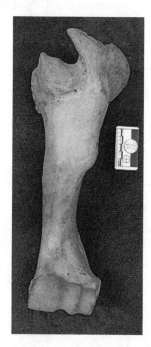

Figure 5.48 (See companion CD for colour figure.) Cow (*Bos taurus*) humerus (anterior view).

Figure 5.49 (See companion CD for colour figure.) Coyote (*Canis latrans*) humerus (anterior view).

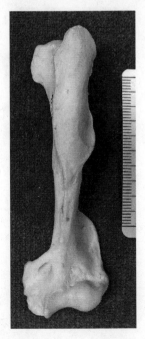

Figure 5.50 (See companion CD for colour figure.) Badger (*Taxidea taxus*) humerus (anterior view).

a tyre. If you were trying to use a jack to lift a car, would you use more energy if you used a short handle or a long one? Naturally a long handle would use less of your energy, and it would move through a greater distance to get the car the same distance off of the ground. The biomechanics of a long lever arm in animal locomotion works the same way. The animal uses less energy to move what is on the end of the long lever arm. In addition (and this is particularly important in animals that run at high speed), that lever (or leg) moves through a greater range of motion than does a leg that is shorter or that has a shorter lever arm. Therefore, if you have an ulna with a very long olecranon process (compare Figures 5.1, 5.2, 5.51 and 5.52) or a calcaneus with a long attachment area for the Achilles tendon (compare Figures 5.1, 5.2, 5.53 and 5.54), you can be sure that the bone is not human. Size matters, of course, in narrowing the species list.

The radius and ulna and tibia and fibula allow rotary (pronation and supination) motion in humans and, to some extent, in most smaller mammals. In humans, the radius and ulna are roughly equal in size and allow great flexibility in pronation and supination. The tibia and fibula in humans still allow at least a little rotary motion in the foot (though it is greatly reduced when compared to other primates). In many quadrupeds, the radius and ulna (Figures 5.55 and 5.56) and the tibia and fibula (Figures 5.57 and 5.58)

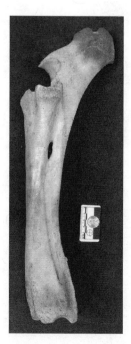

Figure 5.51 (See companion CD for colour figure.) Cow (*Bos taurus*) radius and ulna with long olecranon process (lateral view).

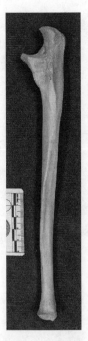

Figure 5.52 (See companion CD for colour figure.) Human ulna with short olecranon process.

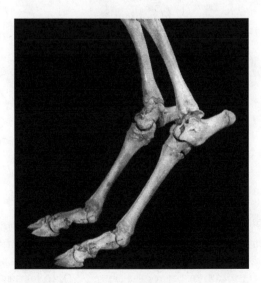

Figure 5.53 Bison *(Bison bison)* calcaneus.

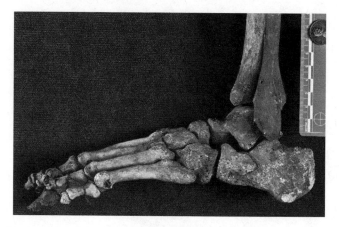

Figure 5.54 (See companion CD for colour figure.) Human calcaneus (lateral view).

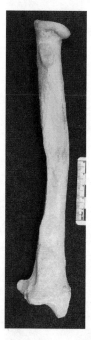

Figure 5.55 (See companion CD for colour figure.) Bear *(Ursus americanus)* radius.

are still separate bones and allow some rotary motion, but in the large grazing and browsing quadrupeds (the hoofed animals), the ulna and fibula are greatly reduced and often fused to the radius and tibia, respectively, so that there is no rotary motion of the foot (Figure 5.51). In fact, the fibula may be only vestigial or even absent (Figure 5.59).

Figure 5.56 **(See companion CD for colour figure.)** Bear (*Ursus americanus*) ulna.

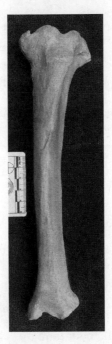

Figure 5.57 **(See companion CD for colour figure.)** Bear (*Ursus americanus*) tibia.

Figure 5.58 (See companion CD for colour figure.) Bear (*Ursus americanus*) fibula.

Most of the hoofed mammals have reduced numbers of metacarpals and metatarsals. Artiodactyls (two-hoofed animals such as deer, elk, sheep) have reduced the metacarpals and metatarsals to two (the third and fourth) that are fused into a single bone (Figure 5.60), while the single-hoofed horse has reduced the number of metacarpals and metatarsals to a single one (the third). There may be vestigial metacarpals (Figures 5.60 and 5.61) or metatarsals, but they are not weight bearing. Therefore, if you have what looks like two bones fused into one, with a groove along the anterior and posterior aspects of the shaft, the bone is from an artiodactyl. The union of the two bones can often be seen even in fragmentary bones (Figure 5.62).

In general, the articular surfaces of the limbs of quadrupeds such as artiodactyls, horses, bears, horses, dogs and cats are more sculpted than those of humans. Observe the articular surface of the distal femur of a prong-horn (Figure 5.63) and compare it to the human distal femur (Figure 5.64). The smaller mammals have somewhat less sculpted articular surfaces, but they are usually still more sculpted than in humans, although the bear (Figure 5.65) is closer to the human condition. In fact, smaller bear skeletal elements are frequently mistaken for human, particularly if a hunter removes the head and claws with the pelt.

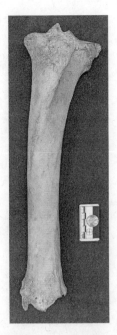

Figure 5.59 (See companion CD for colour figure.) Cow (*Bos taurus*) tibia (fibula is absent).

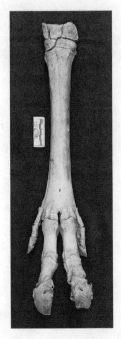

Figure 5.60 (See companion CD for colour figure.) Moose (*Alces alces*) forelimb. Note the two metacarpals fused into one bone and the two vestigial metacarpals.

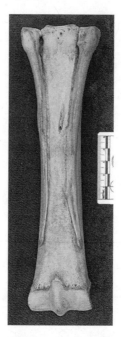

Figure 5.61 (See companion CD for colour figure.) Horse *(Equus)* metacarpals. Note the two lateral 'splint' bones (vestigial metacarpals) (left, posterior view).

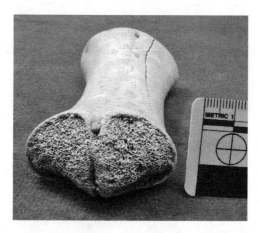

Figure 5.62 (See companion CD for colour figure.) Distal aspect of artiodactyl metapodial (metacarpals).

Of particular interest, however, are the articular surfaces of the metacarpals, metatarsals, and phalanges. Non-human mammals tend to have a ridge running in the antero-posterior direction on the distal aspect of the metacarpals and metatarsals (Figures 5.60, 5.61, 5.66 and 5.67). This is one of those 'slam-dunk' rules. If you see that ridge, it is not human. That ridge fits into a groove on the proximal aspect of the proximal phalanx, creating a very strong

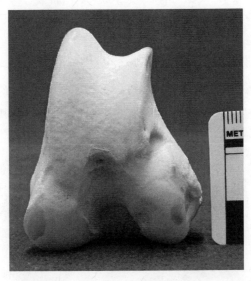

Figure 5.63 (See companion CD for colour figure.) Pronghorn (*Antilocapra americana*) distal femur.

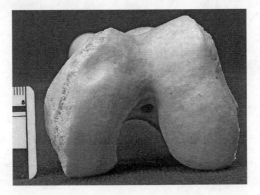

Figure 5.64 (See companion CD for colour figure.) Human distal femur.

joint, but not a very flexible joint, when compared to the smooth, somewhat flexible joint of the human hand and foot. These features can be seen in radiographs as well as in dry bone. The fused metacarpals and metatarsals of the artiodactyls (Figure 5.68) and horse (Figure 5.69) show a ridge on each of the metacarpals and metatarsals: two for the artiodactyl and one for the horse. Figure 5.70 shows the grooves on the proximal aspect of pig phalanges. These grooves can be seen on dogs, cats, deer and many other animals.

Birds also have more sculpted joint surfaces in the leg elements, but not as much in the wing elements. The femur of an adult bird is clearly a femur (although the orientation of the femoral head is different relative to the shaft)

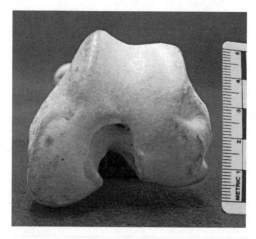

Figure 5.65 (**See companion CD for colour figure.**) Bear (*Ursus americanus*) distal femur.

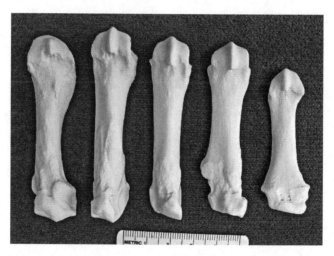

Figure 5.66 (**See companion CD for colour figure.**) Bear (*Ursus americanus*) metacarpals (inferior view).

(Figure 5.71). The tibia and fibula can be identified, as well, but the humerus, radius, and, to a lesser extent, the ulna are a bit more difficult to identify as humerus, radius, etc. (Figure 5.72).

Crocodiles and alligators are even more difficult to diagnose, as the articular surfaces are usually not as sculpted as in non-human mammals (Figures 5.73 and 5.74). In addition, the articular surfaces of the metacarpals and metatarsals do not have the central ridge (Figure 5.75), and the proximal aspect of the phalanges is not as grooved. In crocodiles and alligators, a femur

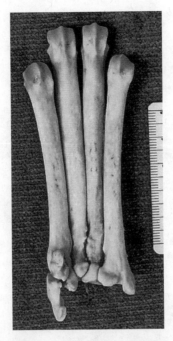

Figure 5.67 (See companion CD for colour figure.) Wolf (*Canis lupus*) metacarpals (inferior view).

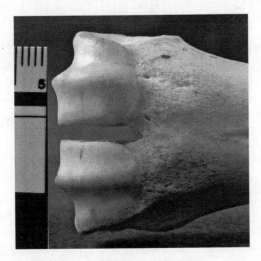

Figure 5.68 (See companion CD for colour figure.) Deer (*Odocoileus* sp.) distal metacarpals (anterior view).

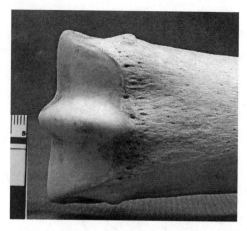

Figure 5.69 (See companion CD for colour figure.) Horse (*Equus*) distal metacarpal (anterior view).

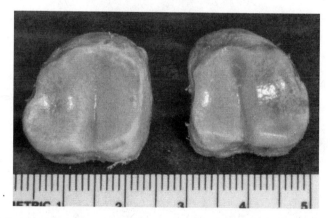

Figure 5.70 (See companion CD for colour figure.) Pig (*Sus scrofa*) proximal phalanges showing groove that accepts the ridge on the metacarpals (proximal view).

or humerus does not look like a mammalian femur or humerus, for example, so it is more difficult to determine even what bone you are holding, although in some other reptiles the specific bone (e.g. femur) is more easily identifiable.

Growth Centres

Some of the reason why reptilian bones do not look like mammalian long bones is that they grow and develop differently. Mammals have primary (diaphyses) growth centres and secondary (epiphyses) growth centres that determine how large the animal will be when the growth centres unite. Even elephants, which seem to continue to grow throughout their lives, have

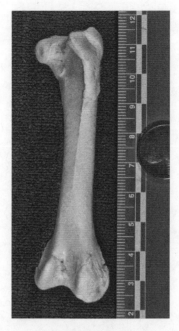

Figure 5.71 (See companion CD for colour figure.) Goose (*Cereopsis* sp.) femur (left, anterior view).

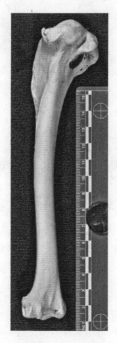

Figure 5.72 (See companion CD for colour figure.) Goose (*Cereopsis* sp.) humerus (left, anterior view).

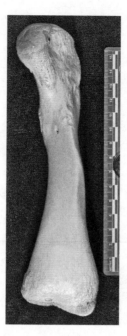

Figure 5.73 (See companion CD for colour figure.) Alligator (*Alligator* sp.) femur (anterior view).

Figure 5.74 (See companion CD for colour figure.) Alligator (*Alligator* sp.) femur distal. Some trabecular bone is showing, but note the general outline of the articular surface.

epiphyses that eventually unite and cease growth in that area (although this may take many decades to occur) (Haynes, 1991). This 'determinate growth' results in an articular surface that is initially formed in cartilage but is, of course, turned in to a bony articular surface. Birds have a determinate growth pattern, although most of the long bones lack a true epiphysis (Carter, 1998).

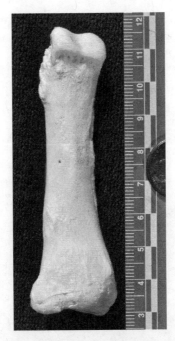

Figure 5.75 (See companion CD for colour figure.) Alligator (*Alligator* sp.) fifth metatarsal (inferior view).

Most reptiles however maintain an epiphysis that remains cartilaginous (see Reno et al., 2007, for discussion of alligator metapodials). This makes a more flexible joint, but it is not as stable as a bony articular surface. Also, a reptile (with few exceptions) has an 'indeterminate growth' pattern, in which the animal can continue to grow in size throughout its lifetime. The morphology of a long bone such as the femur (Figure 5.76) does not change much from a very young to an old alligator. Bone in many reptiles is deposited in concentric annular rings (Hall, 2005; Romer, 1997).

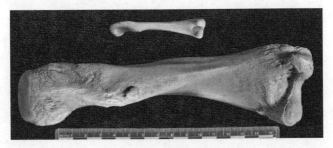

Figure 5.76 (See companion CD for colour figure.) Young alligator (*Alligator* sp.) and older alligator showing no real change in morphology.

The morphology of the diaphyseal and epiphyseal surfaces of large quadrupedal mammals differs from that of humans. Just as the articular surfaces are more sculpted in non-human quadrupeds, the diaphyseal and epiphyseal surfaces are also often more sculpted (Figures 5.77 and 5.78). If you see a diaphyseal or epiphyseal surface that has this 'crown' effect, it is not human (another 'slam dunk'). The reverse is not necessarily true, however, as some (particularly small) non-human mammals have an epiphyseal surface in some bones that is not highly sculpted.

Figure 5.77 (See companion CD for colour figure.) Human proximal tibia diaphysis.

Figure 5.78 (See companion CD for colour figure.) Quadrupedal mammal diaphysis. Note 'crown' effect.

Figure 5.79 (See companion CD for colour figure.) Non-human 'crown' effect. Arrows outline the epiphyseal line.

This 'crown' effect on the diaphysis and epiphysis is a very useful clue even when you cannot see the surface itself, as in Figure 5.79. Even though there is a great deal of soft tissue on the remains, the 'crown' effect is visible. It can also be seen on radiographs.

Other Methods of Identification

Determining human from non-human bone using morphological differences saves money and time, but in those cases in which the gross morphology just does not offer the clues necessary for a diagnosis, the investigator can turn to metric, histological, antigen or DNA evidence to determine species. A few of these studies are detailed later. This is usually more expensive and time consuming, although for a couple hundred dollars, it is now possible to submit a blood sample of a dog or cat for DNA analysis to determine the breed. Genetic tests have been used to determine the species of food animals, particularly when someone suspects that less expensive meat is being sold as more expensive meat in restaurants and in forensic situations such as illegal hunting of protected species.

Simple measurements of long bones may yield clues about species. Saulsman et al. (2010) measured long bones of animals commonly found in Australia and compared them to human long bone measurements and found that they could reliably distinguish between human and non-human bone with metrics alone.

Various histological techniques have been used to distinguish between human and non-human bone. It has long been understood that while humans have circular osteons (Figure 5.80), artiodactyls have plexiform bone, in which the osteons are arranged in a curved, flattened brick-like arrangement (Figure 5.81). Plexiform bone is not seen in humans, except perhaps for immature individuals going through a rapid growth spurt (Mulhern and Ubelaker, 2012). Mulhern and Ubelaker (2012) also found that non-human

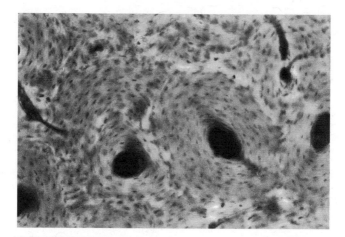

Figure 5.80 Human osteons.

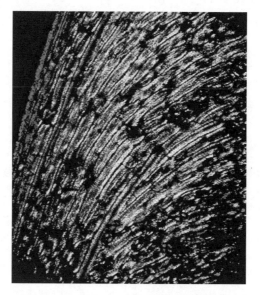

Figure 5.81 Deer (*Odocoileus* sp.) osteons with plexiform structure.

bones have small secondary osteons and Haversian canals. Cattaneo et al. (2009) measured Haversian canals and found some success in identifying non-human and human bone, but the technique is not foolproof, particularly in human flat bones and subadults. They recommend using the technique with other techniques such as osteon morphology and distribution.

In an earlier study, Mulhern and Ubelaker (2001) used histological methods to see differences in osteon banding in human and non-human samples. Osteon banding is the organisation of osteons into distinct layers or bands, and they found that humans generally do not form osteons in distinct layers. In addition, Crescimanno and Stout (2012) found that non-human osteons are more likely to be more completely round than in humans.

Immunoassay Techniques

Many researchers have used immunoassay techniques (basically measuring the interspecies interactions of antigens and antibodies) in determining human from non-human bone and even in diagnosing species. Ubelaker et al. (1991) successfully used immunological techniques to identify calvaria as having come from bovids, and he and others (Ubelaker et al., 2004) successfully used protein radioimmunoassay techniques (using antibody reactions combined with radioactive iodine) to distinguish between human and non-human bone fragments.

Studies such as Pavelka et al. (2011) even used immunoassay techniques to isolate non-human species in bones thousands of years old in Czech Republic. They used the Enzyme-Linked Immunosorbent Assay (ELISA) in fragmentary materials in archaeological contexts. Potter et al. (2010) applied a radioimmunoassay technique to study faunal remains from archaeological sites but found that they are more useful in recent forensic cases than in remains that may have undergone diagenetic change.

Conclusion

While this chapter explores some of the biomechanical, developmental, and evolutionary differences between human and non-human skeletal elements, it is not a comprehensive guide (and cannot be in the allotted space). It is intended to demonstrate that by understanding some of the basic principles underlying morphological variations, it is possible to go beyond merely identifying whether or not a bone is human. Without having to memorise the differences between each species, it is relatively simple to determine whether the non-human bones are from two-hoofed animals (artiodactyls), single-hoofed animals (horses, donkeys, etc.), birds or reptiles. This is particularly true in those bones (such as limb bones) that are most often confused with human bones by the medico-legal community and by the general public.

References

Carter DR. 1998. Epigenetic mechanical factors in the evolution of long bone epiphyses. *Zoological Journal of the Linnean Society* 123:163–178.

Cattaneo C, Porta D, Gibelli D, and Gamba C. 2009. Histological determination of the human origin of bone fragments. *Journal of Forensic Sciences* 54:531–533.

Crescimanno A and Stout SD. 2012. Differentiating fragmented human and nonhuman long bone using osteon circularity. *Journal of Forensic Sciences* 57:287–294.

Hall B. 2005. *Bones and Cartilage: Developmental and Evolutionary Skeletal Biology*, 1st edn. London, U.K.: Elsevier Academic Press.

Haynes G. 1991. *Mammoths, Mastodons, and Elephants: Biology, Behavior, and the Fossil Record*. Cambridge, U.K.: Cambridge University Press.

Kaiser GW. 2007. *The Inner Bird: Anatomy and Evolution*. Vancouver, British Columbia, Canada: UBC Press.

Mulhern DM and Ubelaker DH. 2001. Differences in osteon banding between human and nonhuman bone. *Journal of Forensic Sciences* 46:220–222.

Mulhern DM and Ubelaker DH. 2012. Differentiating human from nonhuman bone microstructure. In: Crowder C and Stout SD, eds. *Bone Histology: An Anthropological Perspective*. Boca Raton, FL: CRC Press. pp. 109–134.

Pavelka J, Kovačiková L, and Šmejda L. 2011. The determination of domesticated animal species from a Neolithic sample using the ELISA test. *Comptes Rendus Palevol* 10:61–70.

Potter BA, Reuther JD, Lowenstein JM, and Scheuenstuhl G. 2010. Assessing the reliability of pRIA for identifying ancient proteins from archaeological contexts. *Journal of Archaeological Science* 37:910–918.

Reno PL, Horton WEJ, Elsey RM, and Lovejoy CO. 2007. Growth plate formation and development in alligator and mouse metapodials: Evolutionary and functional implications. *Journal of Experimental Zoology, Part B: Molecular and Developmental Evolution* 308B:283–296.

Romer AS. 1997. *Osteology of the Reptiles*. Boca Raton, FL: Krieger Publishing Company.

Saulsman B, Oxnard CE, and Franklin D. 2010. Long bone morphometrics for human from nonhuman discrimination. *Forensic Science International* 202:110. e111–110.e115.

Ubelaker DH, Berryman HE, Sutton TP, and Ray CE. 1991. Differentiation of hydrocephalic calf and human calvariae. *Journal of Forensic Sciences* 36:801–812.

Ubelaker DH, Lowenstein JM, and Hood DG. 2004. Use of solid-phase double-antibody radioimmunoassay to identify species from small skeletal fragments. *Journal of Forensic Sciences* 49:924–929.

Vitt LJ and Caldwell JP. 2009. *Herpetology: An Introductory Biology of Amphibians and Reptiles*, 3rd edn. London, U.K.: Elsevier Academic Press.

Zug GR, Vitt LJ, and Caldwell JP. 2001. *Herpetology: An Introductory Biology of Amphibians and Reptiles*, 2nd edn. London, U.K.: Elsevier Academic Press.

Burnt Human Remains Part I

6

Fire Dynamics and Body Recovery

PATRICK RANDOLPH-QUINNEY

Contents

Introduction

Fire is one of the most destructive forces encountered in the modern environment. Fires can occur in residential dwellings, non-residential structures, motor vehicles, ships and aircraft, industrial plants, underground mines and open spaces, all of which can lead to significant loss of human life. Fires can arise through natural causes or result from accidents or negligence. They can be used legitimately and legally to dispose of the dead, and can also be employed in an attempt to destroy forensic evidence in criminal cases (often in an attempt to prevent identification of a victim), to cover up a homicide, or to prevent recovery of human remains and any associated forensic trace evidence (Fanton et al., 2006).

The global incidence of fires and fire fatalities is currently unquantifiable, but data from the United Kingdom and United States alone (with a well-reported system of fire statistics) indicate an average incidence of some 370,000 and 1.5 million reported fires, respectively, from 2004 to 2010 (Table 6.1) with significant injuries and loss of human life. In the United Kingdom and United States, the majority of fatalities tend to occur in residential dwelling fires, followed by (in order of absolute and relative occurrence) vehicular fires, non-residential buildings and fires occurring outside built structures or in open spaces. Catastrophic multiple deaths from fires (defined as fires that kill five or more people in a residential property or

Table 6.1 Number of Fires, Injuries and Fire-Related Deaths Divided by Major Category Type for the United Kingdom and United States from 2004 to 2010

Country	Year	Total Fires	Total Injuries	Total Deaths	Residential	Non-Residential	Vehicle Fire	Outside or Other	Catastrophic[a]
United Kingdom	2004	442,700	14,600	508	375	55	50	28	19
	2005	430,300	14,100	491	376	27	62	26	5
	2006	426,200	13,800	491	373	37	66	25	6
	2007	384,600	13,200	443	331	36	48	28	7
	2008	328,000	12,200	404	324	17	38	29	0
	2009	299,000	11,655	416	319	17	38	25	N/A
	2010	287,000	11,100	388	306	19	44	19	N/A
United States	2004	1,550,500	17,875	3,900	3,050	70	550	45	152
	2005	1,602,000	17,925	3,675	2,895	40	520	50	134
	2006	1,642,500	16,400	3,245	2,495	75	490	50	223
	2007	1,557,500	17,675	3,430	2,770	90	385	45	190
	2008	1,451,000	16,705	3,320	2,780	120	365	55	114
	2009	1,348,500	17,050	3,010	2,590	105	260	35	103
	2010	1,331,500	17,720	3,120	2,640	90	285	55	175

Source: United Kingdom: Fire Statistics United Kingdom, 2004 to 2010 editions; U.S. Fire in the United States 2003–2007 (FEMA); Fire Loss in the United States (National Fire Protection Association Fire Analysis and Research Division) 2008 to 2010 editions; Catastrophic Multiple-Fire Deaths (National Fire Protection Association Fire Analysis and Research Division) 2004 to 2010 editions.

[a] Catastrophic multiple-death fires are defined as fires that kill five or more people in a residential property or three or more in a non-residential or non-structural property. N/A indicates published data not available.

three or more in a non-residential or non-structural property) are rare in the United Kingdom and United States, accounting for between 2% and 5% of fire fatalities, respectively. However, depending on the geographical location, the nature of local emergency service provision, or the ability for rescue services to access the fire scene, such incidents can have a much greater impact in terms of the number of fatalities and the consequent impact on local communities. This can include multiple deaths in shared dwellings such as apartment blocks or hotels, commercial centres, factory fires or industrial accidents, forest and bush fires or fires following bombings, accidental and deliberate explosions, aircraft crashes and earthquakes.

In cases of fire-related deaths, there is generally a legal requirement for positive identification of any individuals fatally involved in such conflagrations. While authorities may be able to positively identify the majority of fire fatalities by conventional means, fire or any form of combustion, has the capability to alter, damage or destroy evidence that is vital to the identification process. This often means that fingerprints, DNA and dental evidence will not survive incineration to the degree or quality needed to achieve a positive identification; as such, situations that deal with the accidental or intentional burning of human remains are among the most difficult for law enforcement and medico-legal investigators to analyse, and in cases of extreme thermal disruption, an understanding of the heat-induced alterations to bones is a necessary prerequisite for the subsequent identification of any remains (human or otherwise) encountered.

This chapter will detail fire dynamics and the effects on human remains, as well as body recovery techniques including methods of documentation and excavation in the field. The second part of the discussion relating to burnt human remains will address methods of identification and laboratory analysis (see Chapter 7).

Dynamics of Fire-Related Deaths

At its most simple level, fire is an oxidative chemical reaction of a solid, liquid or gaseous fuel by atmospheric oxygen, which generates energy in the form of heat and light; this process is generally referred to as combustion, which releases visible energy in the form of flames in cases where there is sufficient oxygen availability. The chemistry and physics of fire and the role of other investigative agencies in fire recovery and analysis are outside the scope of this chapter, but the interested reader is directed to two seminal volumes *Kirk's Fire Investigation* (DeHaan and Icove, 2012) and *Forensic Cremation: Recovery and Analysis* (Fairgrieve, 2008); the former, in particular, is indispensable for anyone wishing to know about the fundamentals of fire behaviour; combustion properties of liquid, gaseous and solid fuels; sources of ignition; the investigation of fire residues; and the causes of fire-related deaths.*

A number of dynamic factors will determine how much energy is released during combustion, which together will influence the degree of damage done to the human body. The first of these is the heat of combustion which will differ depending on the fuel source; for instance, wood burns at a maximum flame temperature of 1027°C, kerosene at 990°C, animal fat at 800°C–900°C and charcoal at 1390°C (DeHaan and Icove, 2012). The second factor is the heat-release rate (HRR), which is a measure of the amount of heat released per unit time (often expressed in kilowatts [kW] or kilojoules per second [kJ/s]) by a fire or other heat sources, and is a good measure of the size and power of a fire; it can be considered the product of the amount of fuel consumed per second and the heat of combustion. Typical HRRs include 50–80 W for a burning candle, 50–150 kW for a burning wastebasket of paper, 1–3 MW for a burning synthetic sofa and 3–10 MW for full involvement of a living room or bedroom (DeHaan and Icove, 2012). The third factor is the heat flux, which is the rate at which heat strikes a surface or passes through an area, expressed as kilowatts per square metre (kW/m^2); the heat flux, together with duration of exposure, will influence the extent of heat-induced injuries in human tissues. Second-degree burns to human skin can be generated with a radiant heat flux of only 4–6 kW/m^2 in 20–30 s of exposure, whereas 50 kW/m^2 (equivalent to being immediately adjacent to an open fire)

---

* Deaths caused by fire can be immediate or delayed in nature. Delayed deaths that occur within the first 2 or 3 days after fire exposure (the proximate cause) are generally brought about by shock, fluid loss following burning of the dermis or acute respiratory failure due to gas inhalation. Deaths occurring outside this period are generally caused by sepsis or chronic respiratory insufficiency (DiMaio and DiMaio, 2001). Immediate deaths are generally caused either by direct thermal burning of tissues or, more frequently, by smoke inhalation with accompanying toxicity and/or asphyxia; individuals whose death may be caused by smoke inhalation (as evidenced by deposits of soot in the nostrils and mouth, and the larynx, trachea and bronchi) may continue to express thermal injuries and progressive stages of tissue burning, but the burning process is not casual to cessation of life. The most commonly reported cause of fire death is asphyxiation, with carbon monoxide poisoning (CO intoxication brought about by the incomplete combustion of carbon compounds) the principal culprit, although it may also include the inhalation of toxic or irritant gases such as hydrogen cyanide, nitrous oxide, nitric oxide, hydrochloric or hydrofluoric acid, sulphur dioxide, hydrogen sulphide and carbonyl sulphide. Chemical tests on blood drawn from the major blood vessels and the chambers of the heart and tissue biopsy of the internal organs (particularly brain, kidney, liver, and lung) will generally be required to evaluate the presence and interaction of gaseous toxins and volatile hydrocarbons absorbed during the peri-mortem period. Transection of the airways from the oral cavity to the lungs during autopsy will be required to ascertain evidence of heat- or gas-induced trauma, such as oedema, scorching, dehydration and soot deposition in the airway and lungs. It should be noted that an absence of soot in the airway does not necessarily mean that the individual was dead prior to the start of the fire; cases are reported in which there was no soot in the larynx or trachea, yet blood chemistry revealed lethal levels of carbon dioxide (DiMaio and DiMaio, 2001, p. 394).

will cause auto-ignition of wood, plastic and human tissue in less than 5 s. The maximum heat flux measured in post-flashover fires is 150 kW/m^2— the near-simultaneous ignition of most of the directly exposed combustible material in an enclosed area (Bass, 1984; DeHaan and Icove, 2012; DiMaio and DiMaio, 2001; Eckert et al., 1988).

As such, and taking these factors into account, the burning of the human body progresses in a relatively well-understood fashion. It is fair to say, however, that the generality of the destructive process is recognised and articulated, whereas the specific mechanisms of change (particularly at the microstructural level) are less clearly understood. At its most basic level, the general process of burning is exemplified by the Crow–Glassman scale* (Crow and Glassman, 1996) detailed in Table 6.2. This five-part scale highlights the progressive destruction of the body from singeing, blistering and superficial burning of the epidermis and dermis (Stage 1) with only limited exposure to heat, through to complete rendering of the body (Stage 5) into a highly fragmented, distorted and incomplete state where only cremated bone remains; the recovery and identification of bodies in Stages 3–5 will generally require the assistance of a forensic anthropologist working with the forensic pathologist to achieve identification.

In forensic practice, we start from the assumption of situational 'normality' in burn-pattern expression. As Symes et al., (2008, p. 29) suggest,

> ... if expectable burning patterns under normal circumstances (totally engulfed) can be defined and recognized, abnormal burning due to perimortem trauma, criminal behaviour, or other factors should become evident as departure from this normal patterning.

So, the question remains—what is 'normal'? As most bodies do not burn evenly due to the nature of the fire environment, it is possible to see different manifestations and stages of the burning process when a body is recovered, which can include heat-related injuries to both the remaining hard and soft tissues. Put most simply, a normal burn pattern (due to an engulfing or multidirectional heat source) will tend to progress from the outside of the body (dermis) inward toward the tissues of the centre of an anatomical unit (head, upper limb, torso, etc.) and from the extremities toward the core—in this way, heat is transferred from the exposed surfaces to the inner tissues by conduction, causing them to denature and thermally decompose, acting

---

* The use of the Crow–Glassman scale is preferred here to the commonly used scale of Eckert et al. (1988) that divides the process into four general stages of charred (internal organs survive intact), partial (some soft tissues survive), incomplete (body recovered as bone fragments) or complete (body survives as ashes only). As will be discussed in Chapter 7, complete cremation (i.e. the rendering of the body to ashes) is extremely rare in forensic contexts, and such a level of destruction generally requires further mechanical application of force to the cremains (grinding or pulverisation) to render them into a dustlike state (Bass, 1984; DeHaan and Icove, 2012; Symes et al., 2008).

Table 6.2   Crow–Glassman Scale for Burn Injury to Human Remains

CGS	Description
1	Constitutes burn injury characteristic of typical smoke death. The body may exhibit blistering of the epidermis and singeing of the head and facial hair. Recovery of the body is similar to that for other victims not involving burn injury. The body is recognisable for identification at this level.
2	Defines a body that may be recognisable but most often exhibiting varying degrees of chafing. Further destruction of the body is limited to the absence of elements of the hands and/or feet and, possibly, the genitalia and ears. Additional searching near the body is warranted for the recovery of disarticulated elements. Identification is made, most often, by the collaboration of medical examiner and forensic odontologist.
3	Shows further destruction of the body, with major portions of the arms and/or legs missing. The head is present at this level although identity is non-recognisable. The search area for associated disarticulated remains should be widened. A forensic anthropologist should be included to facilitate successful search and recovery procedures at the death scene. Identification is coordinated by a medical examiner that may require the aid of a forensic odontologist. If needed, a forensic anthropologist may be called on to determine gender, age, race, etc., from the skeleton.
4	Corresponds to a degree of extensive burn destruction whereby the skull has fragmented and is absent from the body. Some portions of the arms and/or legs may still remain articulated to the charred body. Search and recovery should be aided by a forensic anthropologist using systematic bioarchaeological methods including screening procedures to locate small body fragments and dental elements. Identification is coordinated by a medical examiner using forensic anthropologist and odontologist consultants as needed.
5	Represents the final level of the proposed scale. At this level, the body has been cremated, and little or no tissue is present. The remains are highly fragmentary, scattered and incomplete. A forensic anthropologist should be an on-site consultant for the identification and recovery of the cremains. Personal identification is most difficult at this level, and a forensic anthropologist may be best trained to interpret cremains for identifying physical attributes of the deceased. Recovery of dental elements will require the expertise of a forensic odontologist.

Source: Crow, D.M. and Glassman, R.M., *J. Forensic Sci.*, 41, 152, 1996.

in a similar way to that of a joint of meat cooking in a hot oven.* The two most obvious components that make up the 'normal' burning scenario are the adoption of the so-called pugilistic posture and the directional pattern of thermal destruction of tissues.

---

* In keeping with that analogy, the reader may recognise that such tissues do not 'cook' evenly but instead, while the outer surface may char and distort under the effects of heat, that inner tissues (particularly those situated deepest or adjacent to bone) will exhibit progressively less thermal damage (at least from visual inspection). Similarly, the soft tissue and muscle closest to the ends of a long bone will retract or regress away from the joint, progressively exposing skeletal tissue. This analogy reflects the importance of overlying soft tissues and muscles in influencing and determining the pattern and expression of thermal destruction of the body (Symes et al., 2008).

Pugilistic posture refers to the pose seen in charred and moderately burnt bodies that have been compared to that of a boxer, with the upper extremities assuming a facsimile of a defensive posture and varying degrees of flexion of both the upper and lower limbs. The process is a purely physiological one and is caused by heat-induced contraction (shortening) of muscle fibres, ligaments and tendons brought about by dehydration and protein denaturation. The flexor muscles of the human body are generally bulkier (i.e. have greater muscle mass) and are proportionally stronger and capable of greater loading than the opposing extensor muscles. It is reported that bodies exposed to temperatures of between 670°C and 810°C will begin to adopt a pugilistic pose within as little as 10 min of starting to burn (Bohnert et al., 1998) with the flexors contracting more than the extensors under the effects of heat. Thus, bodies that are burning will tend to rapidly adduct at the shoulder and hip, with varying degrees of flexion at all the major joints (such as the knee, elbow and wrist). The digits of the hands and feet will generally curl inward toward the palmar and plantar surfaces, respectively, often simulating a boxing or defensive pose in the process. Muscle contraction can dislocate and fracture heat-compromised bones and joints, assisting in the rapid dissociation and fragmentation of the burning body. The assumption of the pugilistic posture does not (as was once thought) indicate that the individual was alive at the time of the fire and is solely a post-mortem taphonomic process induced by high temperatures. The muscle reaction forces can be sufficiently great to cause the body to move or shift position, which may confuse attempts at scene reconstruction or provide misleading evidence that a body was moved post-mortem. The lack of a pugilistic posture is also significant and suggests that the body was restrained in some way during the burning process and may thus indicate foul play.

Directional patterning of thermal destruction goes hand in hand with the physical and physiological processes that produced the pugilistic posture. In general, the skeletal regions of the body and anatomical elements most exposed to the fire and least protected by overlying muscle mass, viscera or internal organs will tend to burn and be destroyed first. Exposed surfaces and distal extremities will burn rapidly, with heat conducted from the outer tissues to the inner and from the distal ends of bones proximally toward the core. As such, an unrestrained body lying on its back with the face uppermost will tend to burn most rapidly at the distal ends of the toes, the ankle, the knee, the dorsum of the hand, the elbow, the clavicular–humeral junction, the anterior sternum, the medial ends of the ribs and the face and forehead. The regions in contact with the underlying substrate such as the calves, buttocks, vertebral column, shoulder blades, neck region and cranial base will tend to burn last. Regions protected by the insulating effects of overlying masses of muscle tissue (such as the mid-thigh, calf, forearm, shoulder blade and thorax) or shielded by context (such as teeth inside the oral cavity or palmar surface of the hand in a pugilistic posture) will be some of the last elements to burn.

Postural and patterned changes are dynamic and are influenced most strongly by the structural anatomy and underlying physiology of the tissues being affected by levels of heat, as well as the nature of the chemical atmosphere in which thermal alteration takes place (oxidative or reducing) and the duration over which the process occurs. As Symes et al., (2008) note, rarely do anthropologists consider all three variables in their analyses, highlighting the fact that much past research has dealt solely with the effect of temperature on tissues and often in a defleshed (and thus highly artificial) state. However, while Symes and colleagues (*ibid.*) are ostensibly correct, they adopt a rather simplistic assessment of both the number and relative impact of intrinsic and extrinsic environmental factors on the patterning of thermal destruction. In interpreting the specific progression of damage and burning pattern on a body, a large number of covarying factors will affect the degree to which that body is modified by fire, the progressive burning of which will render some or all of the standard methods of identification (i.e. DNA, odontology, fingerprints and anthropological assessment) untenable to a greater or lesser extent. The fire environment is a complex dynamic one, and the specific taphonomic* or site-formation processes that generate a fatal fire environment will be unique to every fire scene. As such, the HRR, the heat of combustion, the heat flux, the atmospheric composition, the type of heating (e.g. conduction, radiation, convection), the location of the fuel in relation to the body, the duration of burning, the nature of fire progression, and any subsequent modifications to the environment (such as those caused by fire and rescue services) will influence the degree of damage done to human tissues and have an effect on burning patterns observed. Furthermore, the body itself represents a fuel package and will continue to undergo post-mortem changes as long as it is exposed to the fire, with the body itself often contributing to the fuel load for that fire, most notably through the rendering of volatile organic components, fats and marrow. Where possible, these factors must be taken into account in interpreting the extent and pattern of fire-related injuries expressed by a body, though in reality it may be impossible to arrive at a precise narrative due to the multiplicity of covarying factors and their interactions (DeHaan, 2008); in many cases, bodies from very different fire scenes may reach the same final state from different initial conditions—a

---

* Forensic taphonomy represents '... the analysis of the spatial distribution of remains at their location of discovery, a careful consideration of the environmental setting after death, analysis of the soft tissue remaining...and a thorough analysis of bone modification from staining to trauma.' (Dirkmaat et al., 2008, p. 46)

situation referred to as equifinality—which may present a significant limitation in attempting to understand the interaction of individual processes on the expression of the final fire environment.*

Anthropological Recovery from Fire Scenes

A fire scene can be a stratigraphically complex environment, which may contain the collapsed burnt remnants of a building structure (such as brick and mortar, asbestos, wood, plastic, electrical wiring, glass and metal), electrical appliances, fabrics and soft furnishings, organic tissues (human remains and/or the remains of animals trapped in the fire) and the residues deposited by the fire and rescue services in controlling the blaze. The context within which remains can be deposited can be highly variable, and charred and cremated remains may be found on the surface, partially buried, completely buried, in standing water, inside a structure, motor vehicle or aircraft. As such, special care and attention is required in the recovery of any potential human remains, the recognition, excavation and removal of which need to be balanced against the evidential needs of other investigative agencies at the fire scene. The roles and requirements of the respective specialists are detailed in DeHaan and Icove (2012) and Fairgrieve (2008) and are only summarised here with respect to the responsibilities of the forensic archaeologist and the forensic anthropologist—obviously, in the case of a multi-agency and multidisciplinary fatal fire investigation, many other specialists may be involved in on-site analyses and recovery of evidence. Ideally, a forensic anthropologist should participate in the recovery process since they are (usually) trained to recognise fragmented human remains. This capacity may be further enhanced if the anthropologist is trained in the recognition and analysis of anthropological evidence from the soft as well as the hard tissues (Bristow et al., 2011; Lyman, 2004; Randolph-Quinney et al., 2009).

On-Site Role of the Forensic Archaeologist

The role of the archaeologist is primarily to assist in the recording, excavation and recovery of any possible human tissues that may be present at

---

* Lyman (2004) highlights the issues that equifinality raises, and whether two alternate taphonomic models can be distinguished is due to equifinality or as a problem of statistical indistinguishability. This is one of the great problems with taphonomic interpretation, in that while there is only one physical past, there may be multicausative agents that produce that past and as such can affect our reconstruction of an event (Bristow et al., 2011).

the fire scene. Although there are a number of authoritative texts that deal with the application of archaeological excavation methods to the forensic recovery process (e.g. Adams and Byrd, 2008; Bass, 1995; Hunter and Cox, 2005; Skinner and Lazenby, 1983; Ubelaker, 1989b), there are none that deal specifically and in depth with the recovery of burnt and cremated remains from forensic fire scenes.* It is important to stress that the archaeologist may transfer conventional forensic archaeological recording and recovery methods to the fire scene in partnership with the fire investigation team; with careful planning and implementation, suitable strategies may be applied which maximise the potential for recognition and recovery of any human remains and any additional classes of forensic and trace evidence required by other investigative agencies. As such, the archaeologist can assist other agencies in

- Development of search strategies and methods (these may be a systematic, grid-based or random sampling in nature)
- Delineation of site boundaries and limits of excavation
- Detailed photographic documentation of the scene
- Spatial recording of the scene before, during and after excavation, ideally undertaken through the use of 3D recording equipment such as a total station, supplemented by precise and detailed hand-drawn scale plans and stratigraphic sections
- Systematic excavation of stratigraphic deposits within the scene and can assist in the recording and retrieval of forensic trace evidence as directed by other specialists
- Recognition of charred and burnt skeletal remains (in conjunction with the forensic anthropologist)
- The fully documented and contextualised recovery of burnt remains
- Packing and stabilisation of remains prior to transport for laboratory analysis
- Assistance in maximising tissue retrieval through sieving and other sorting methods

The process of documentation, scene photography and spatial recording will generally also be undertaken by the police, rescue services and other investigative agencies. It is important to note that the archaeologist may have very different evidential requirements from other agencies, and as such some duplication of tasks may occur.

---

* Fairgrieve (2008, pp. 61–90) provides a good overview of fatal fire recovery strategies and a summary of the role of the forensic archaeologist in the investigative process.

Role of the Forensic Anthropologist

The role of the anthropologist* is primarily to assist in the identification, recovery (and ideally) and postexcavation analysis of any possible human tissues that may be present at the fire scene. The on-site assistance of the anthropologist will generally lend itself to three principal areas of enquiry to (1) assist in the recognition of any encountered remains, however badly fragmented, if possible to classify them as human or animal, and determine how many individuals may be present; (2) provide an *in situ* assessment of morphological and metric parameters of identity which may not survive the retrieval process and subsequent transportation to the laboratory; and (3) understand patterned thermal destruction of the body in relation to the context of the fire scene and to help in the differential recognition of damage caused by the burning process from other classes of trauma.

From an identification standpoint, the anthropologist is interested in four basic biological criteria that can help narrow the range of identifying criteria of a fire victim from skeletonised cremains—age at death, biological sex, living stature and ancestry or racial affiliation (Randolph-Quinney et al., 2009). At present, both metric and morphological techniques employed to analyse human skeletal remains for the purpose of establishing biological identity are generally applied to complete or near-complete skeletal elements; with fragmentation and disruption, the amount of useful biological data such remains yield is reduced. Since bone undergoes extensive alterations when exposed to heat, the accuracy of standard identification methods will therefore be detrimentally affected. Thermal alterations to bones are substantial, primarily involving cracking, splitting, shrinkage and fragmentation, and subsequently the accuracy of almost every anthropological technique is dramatically affected. However, the effect of fire-related damage may be mitigated if the anthropologist is on hand and able to record any obvious

---

* Ideally, the senior archaeologist and the senior anthropologist should be one and the same person with dual competency. Depending on where the respective anthropologist has been trained and their level of field craft, they should have significant experience in archaeological recording and excavation and the understanding of complex archaeological stratigraphy. Ideally, the anthropologist (if so trained) should be able to provide direction in the formulation of search protocols and strategy for the scene and be able to direct archaeological recovery methods in order to maximise the retrieval of both archaeological (stratigraphical and contextual) data and anthropological data that may assist the identification process. They should have a detailed understanding of both human skeletal anatomy and non-human comparative anatomy and be cognizant of the differences between ante- and peri-mortem traumas and trauma induced by the burning process. It is obvious that archaeological recovery is a destructive process, and once deposits have been dug up, the contextual information is lost unless the recording and recovery process has been carried out competently and fully. The fire scene is one of the most complex burial environments that an anthropologist is likely to encounter, and as such we owe it to the investigative and medico-legal process not to stray beyond the bounds of our professional competency.

characteristics of biological identity *in situ* before the tissues are disturbed by lifting and transportation; the anthropologist may be able to record characteristics at the fire scene, which, while presumptive ahead of laboratory analysis, may be able to expedite the identification process. The characteristics which the anthropologist may be able to recognise and record on burnt tissues comprise the following:

- *Assessment of age at death*: Evidence for stages of crown and root formation and eruption and dehiscence of the dentition (Haaviko, 1970a,b; Liversidge et al., 1998, 2003; Liversidge and Molleson, 1999, 2004; Lysell et al., 1962; Moorrees et al., 1963a,b; Smith, 1991), appearance of primary and secondary ossification centres of the cranial and post-cranial skeleton (Fazekas and Kosa, 1978; Scheuer and Black, 2000), patterns of unification or fusion of the bones of the post-cranial skeleton (Albert et al., 2007; Albert and Maples, 1995; Johnston and Zimmer, 1989; Schaefer and Black, 2005; Ubelaker, 1989a), age-related changes affecting the face of the pubic symphysis (Brooks and Suchey, 1990; Gilbert and McKern, 1973; Katz and Suchey, 1986; McKern and Stewart, 1957; Suchey, 1979), degeneration of the auricular surface (Buckberry and Chamberlain, 2002; Lovejoy et al., 1985; Mulhern and Jones, 2005), degenerative change in the sternal end of the ribs (İşcan et al., 1984, 1985; Yoder et al., 2001) or the degree of closure and obliteration of the cranial sutures (Meindl and Lovejoy, 1985).
- *Assessment of biological sex*: Recording of cranial characters such as the expression of the nuchal crest, size of the mastoid process, shape of glabella and supraorbital margin and the chin (Wilkinson, 2004); pelvic morphology such as the shape of the greater sciatic notch, pubis morphology and the sacroiliac articulation (St. Hoyme and İşcan, 1989); diameters of the radial, humeral and femoral head (Berrizbeeitia, 1989; Stewart, 1979); or patterns of the ossification of the costal cartilages (McCormick, 1983; McCormick et al., 1985).
- *Assessment of living stature*: Metric measurements of long bone length can be used to predict an individual's stature by regressing the lengths of individual limb segments. A range of regression equations have been developed and are generally element- and population-specific (Feldesman and Fountain, 1996; Genovés, 1967; Jantz, 1992; Jantz et al., 1995; Trotter, 1970; Trotter and Gleser, 1952, 1958). Stature estimation usually requires a complete long bone to measure, which may not be easily recoverable from burnt tissues, though maximum length may be estimated with an unknown level of certainty; it should be noted that estimation of living stature from fragmentary remains is generally considered too inaccurate and statistically inappropriate for forensic applications (Badkur and Nath, 1990).

- *Assessment of ancestry*: Ancestry is often expressed in morphological cranial characters such as the frontal profile, shape of the supraorbital ridges, the inter-orbital breadth, cheek form, orbital shape, nasal aperture shape, lower nasal margin and nasal root morphology (Randolph-Quinney et al., 2009; Wilkinson, 2004); variable evidence of these features may survive the burning process, whereas metric assessment of ancestry generally requires cranial multiple metric measurements applied to multivariate discriminant function analyses (Craig, 1995; Edgar, 2005; Feldesman and Fountain, 1996; Gilbert, 1976; Giles and Elliot, 1962; Gill and Rhine ,1990; İşcan and Steyn, 1999; Snow et al., 1979) and as such is unlikely to be useful in a cremated context.

The anthropologist may also assist in recognising evidence of individuating surgical prosthetics (Clarkson and Schaefer, 2007), evidence of healed ante-mortem trauma or chronic hard and soft tissue diseases that may leave characteristic macroscopic lesions on surviving tissue (Cunha, 2006). Furthermore, the anthropologist may aid in the recognition of, and differentiation between, ante-, peri- and post-mortem traumatic effects and, in particular, to differentiate traumatic lesions which may be attributable to manner and cause of death, such as gunshot wounds, stab wounds, bludgeoning or trips and falls, from the traumatic effects of the burning process. Such analyses are generally conducted as part of the postexcavation process, though any lesions directly observed during the excavation and recovery process (such as radiating fractures from ballistic trauma or cut marks from a knife wound) should be carefully and systematically documented and photographed prior to lifting and transportation of the remains.

Cautious lifting of burnt tissues encountered in the field may necessitate consolidation using bandages, plastic film, plaster of Paris encapsulation or other reversible means (Watkinson, 1987). Upon delivery to the laboratory, the remains will require meticulous documentation and de-consolidation from surrounding matrix and fire debris. At this point, it may be appropriate to clean and sort the material. The processing of fire-scene debris is neither simple nor clean, and any analysis of possible cremains requires that skeletal tissue be separated from the rest of the fire debris (McKinley, 2000; McKinley, and Roberts, 1993). This can be undertaken with careful water processing of any individually bagged bone specimens or sieving of bulk samples of fire debris (Byard et al., 2001). The preferred method is to sieve samples of debris through a stack of wire laboratory sieves with 10, 5, 2 and 1 mm mesh sizes. Water is run at very low pressure over the topmost sieve, and the residues are gradually and gently graded as they pass through the stack. The finest fraction (<1 mm diameter) should be saved in a collection tray after passing through the sieves. Evidence numbers should be assigned to all material produced from initial processing; this should include contextual information (such as excavation square and level of recovery), the sieve fraction from which it was derived, and the pre- and postprocessing weight of material. A basic inventory should then be compiled before any further analysis takes place (Fairgrieve, 2008).

Conclusion

Reconstruction is generally a necessary and useful process at this point, and this will be covered in Chapter 7. This will require the painstaking matching of fragments and photography of individual pieces both before and after reassembly in the laboratory. The reconstruction of burnt elements provides an opportunity for morphological interpretation and can greatly facilitate the assessment of human vs. non-human bone in commingled assemblages, and the recognition and correct siding of skeletal elements. Furthermore it increases the probability of correct morphological assessment of age, sex or ancestry markers (as these larger require complete or near-complete specimens for successful assessment). Finally, it is a necessary prerequisite in the correct three-dimensional analysis of trauma; this can include evidence of the burning process itself through the analysis of patterned thermal destruction, the evaluation of ante-mortem individuating trauma and evidence of peri-mortem trauma such as blunt-force fractures, sharp-force or hacking trauma (stabbing or cutting) and ballistic or projectile trauma—given that fire is often used in an attempt to mask the manner or mechanism of criminal injury, the successful reconstruction of non-fire-related trauma is a critical activity in cremain analysis.

References

Adams BJ and Byrd JE, eds. 2008. *Recovery, Analysis and Identification of Commingled Human Remains*. New York: Humana Press.

Albert AM and Maples WR. 1995. Stages of epiphyseal union for thoracic and lumbar vertebral centra as a method of age determination for teenage and young adult skeletons. *Journal of Forensic Sciences* 40:623–633.

Albert AM, Ricanek Jr K, and Patterson E. 2007. A review of the literature on the aging adult skull and face: Implications for forensic science research and applications. *Forensic Science International* 172:1–9.

Badkur P and Nath S. 1990. Use of regression analysis in reconstruction of maximum bone length and living stature from fragmentary measures of the ulna. *Forensic Science International* 45:15–25.

Bass WM. 1984. Is it possible to consume a body completely in a fire? In: Rathburn T and Buikstra JE, eds. *Human Identification: Case Studies in Forensic Anthropology*. Springfield, IL.: Charles C. Thomas, pp. 159–167.

Bass WM. 1995. *Human Osteology: A Laboratory and Field Manual*. Columbia, MO: Missouri Archaeological Society.

Berrizbeeitia EL. 1989. Sex determination with the head of the radius. *Journal of Forensic Sciences* 34:1206–1213.

Bohnert MT, Rost T, and Pollack S. 1998. The degree of destruction of human bodies in relation to the duration of the fire. *Forensic Science International* 95:11–21.

Bristow J, Simss Z, and Randolph-Quinney P. 2011. Taphonomy. In: Black S and Ferguson E, eds. *Forensic Anthropology: 2000 to 2010*. Boca Raton, FL: CRC Press, pp. 279–317.

Brooks S and Suchey JM. 1990. Skeletal age determination based on the Os pubis: Comparison of the Acsádi-Nemeskéri and Suchey-Brooks methods. *Human Evolution* 5:227–238.

Buckberry J and Chamberlain A. 2002. Age estimation from the auricular surface of the ilium: A revised method. *American Journal of Physical Anthropology* 119:231–239.

Byard RW, James RA, and Zuccollo J. 2001. Potential confusion arising from materials presenting as possible human remains. *American Journal of Forensic Medicine and Pathology* 22(4):391–394.

Clarkson J and Schaefer M. 2007. Surgical intervention. In: Thompson T and Black S, eds. *Forensic Human Identification*. Boca Raton, FL: CRC Press, pp. 127–146.

Craig EA. 1995. Intercondylar shelf angle: A new method to determine race from the distal femur. *Journal of Forensic Sciences* 40:777–782.

Crow DM and Glassman RM. 1996. Standardization model for describing the extent of burn injury to human remains. *Journal of Forensic Sciences* 41:152–154.

Cunha E. 2006. Pathology as a factor of personal identity in forensic anthropology. In: Schmitt A, Cunha E, and Pinheiro J, eds. *Forensic Anthropology and Medicine: Complementary Sciences from Recovery to Cause of Death*. Totowa, NJ: Humana Press, pp. 333–358.

DeHaan JD. 2008. Fire and bodies. In: Schmidt CW and Symes SA, eds. *The Analysis of Burned Human Remains*. London, U.K.: Academic Press, pp. 1–13.

DeHaan JD and Icove DJ. 2012. *Kirk's Fire Investigation*. Boston, MA: Pearson.

DiMaio VJ and DiMaio D. 2001. *Forensic Pathology*, 2nd edn. Boca Raton, FL: CRC Press.

Dirkmaat DC, Cabo LL, Ousley SD, and Symes SA. 2008. New perspectives in forensic anthropology. *Yearbook of Physical Anthropology* 43:211–214.

Eckert WE, James S, and Kathis S. 1988. Investigation of cremations and severely burned bodies. *American Journal of Forensic Medicine and Pathology* 9:188–200.

Edgar HJH. 2005. Prediction of race using characteristics of dental morphology. *Journal of Forensic Sciences* 50:1–5.

Fairgrieve SI. 2008. *Forensic Cremation: Recovery and Analysis*. Boca Raton, FL: CRC Press. 206p.

Fanton L, Jdeed K, Tilhet-Coartet S, and Malicier D. 2006. Criminal burning. *Forensic Science International* 158:87–93.

Fazekas IG and Kosa F. 1978. *Forensic Fetal Osteology*. Budapest, Hungary: Akedemiai Kiado.

Feldesman MR and Fountain RL. 1996. 'Race' specificity and the femur/stature ratio. *American Journal of Physical Anthropology* 100:207–224.

Genovés S. 1967. Proportionality of the long bones and their relation to stature among Mesoamericans. *American Journal of Physical Anthropology* 26:67–78.

142   Advances in Forensic Human Identification

Gilbert BM. 1976. Anterior femoral curvature: Its probable basis and utility as a criterion of racial assessment. *American Journal of Physical Anthropology* 45(3):601–604.

Gilbert BM and McKern TW. 1973. A method for aging the female Os pubis. *American Journal of Physical Anthropology* 38:31–38.

Giles E and Elliot O. 1962. Race identification from cranial measurements. *Journal of Forensic Sciences* 7:147–157.

Gill GW and Rhine S, eds. 1990. *Skeletal Attribution of Race: Methods for Forensic Anthropology.* Albuquerque, NM: Maxwell Museum of Anthropology.

Haavikko K. 1970a. The formation and the alveolar and clinical eruption of the permanent teeth. An orthopantographic study. *Proceedings of the Finnish Dental Society* 66:101–170.

Haavikko K. 1970b. The formation of the alveolar and clinical eruption of the permanent teeth. *Proceedings of the Finnish Dental Society* 61:101–170.

Hunter J and Cox M. 2005. *Forensic Archaeology: Advances in Theory and Practice.* London, U.K.: Routledge.

İşcan MY, Loth S, and Wright R. 1984. Age estimation from the ribs by phase analysis: White males. *Journal of Forensic Sciences* 29:1094–1104.

İşcan MY, Loth SR, and Wright RK. 1985. Age estimation from the rib by phase analysis: White females. *Journal of Forensic Sciences* 30:853–863.

İşcan MY and Steyn M. 1999. Craniometric assessment of population affinity in South Africans. *International Journal of Legal Medicine* 112:91–97.

Jantz RL. 1992. Modification of the Trotter and Gleser female stature estimation formulae. *Journal of Forensic Sciences* 37(5):1230–1235.

Jantz RL, Hunt DR, and Meadows L. 1995. The measure and mismeasure of the tibia: Implications for stature estimation. *Journal of Forensic Sciences* 40(5):758–761.

Johnston FE and Zimmer LO. 1989. Assessment of growth and age in the immature skeleton. In: İşcan MY and Kennedy KAR, eds. *Reconstruction of Life from the Skeleton.* New York: Alan R. Liss, Inc, pp. 11–21.

Katz D and Suchey JM. 1986. Age determination of the male Os pubis. *American Journal of Physical Anthropology* 69:435–436.

Liversidge HM, Herdeg B, and Rosing FW. 1998. Dental age-estimation of non-adults. A review of methods and principles. In: Alt KW, Rosing FW, and Teschler-Nicola M, eds. *Dental Anthropology, Fundamentals, Limits and Prospects.* Vienna, Austria: Springer, pp. 419–442.

Liversidge HM, Lyons F, and Hector MP. 2003. The accuracy of three methods of age estimation using radiographic measurements of developing teeth. *Forensic Science International* 131:22–29.

Liversidge HM and Molleson TI. 1999. Developing permanent tooth length as an estimate of age. *Journal of Forensic Sciences* 44(5):917–920.

Liversidge HM and Molleson T. 2004. Variation in crown and root formation and eruption of human deciduous teeth. *American Journal of Physical Anthropology* 123:172–180.

Lovejoy CO, Meindl RS, Mensforth RP, and Barton TJ. 1985. Chronological metamorphosis of the auricular surface of the ilium: A new method for the determination of adult skeletal age at death. *American Journal of Physical Anthropology* 68:15–28.

Lyman RL. 2004. The concept of equifinality in taphonomy. *Journal of Taphonomy* 2:15–26.

Lysell L, Magnusson B, and Thilander B. 1962. Time and order of eruption of the primary teeth: A longitudinal study. *Odontologisk Revy* 13:217–234.

McCormick WF. 1983. Ossification patterns of costal cartilages as an indicator of sex. *Archives of Pathology & Laboratory Medicine* 107:206–210.

McCormick WF, Stewart JH, and Langford LA. 1985. Sex determination from chest plate roentgenograms. *American Journal of Physical Anthropology* 68:173–195.

McKern TW and Stewart TD. 1957. Skeletal age changes in young American males analysed from the standpoint of age identification. Headquarters Quartermaster Research and Development Command, Technical Report EP-45, Natick, MA.

McKinley JI and Roberts CA. 1993. Excavation and post-excavation treatment of cremated and inhumed human remains. Institute of Field Archaeologists Technical Paper No. 13, pp. 1–11.

McKinley JL. 2000. The analysis of cremated bone. In: Cox A and Mays S, eds. *Human Osteology in Archaeology and Forensic Science*. London, U.K.: Greenwich Medical Media Ltd, pp. 403–421.

Meindl RS and Lovejoy CO. 1985. Ectocranial suture closure: A revised method for the determination of skeletal age at death based on the lateral-anterior sutures. *American Journal of Physical Anthropology* 68:57–66.

Moorrees CF, Fanning EA, and Hunt EE. 1963a. Age variation of formation stages for ten permanent teeth. *Journal of Dental Research* 42:1490–1502.

Moorrees CF, Fanning EA, and Hunt EE. 1963b. Formation and resorption of three deciduous teeth in children. *American Journal of Physical Anthropology* 21:205–213.

Mulhern DM and Jones EB. 2005. Test of revised method of age estimation from the auricular surface of the ilium. *American Journal of Physical Anthropology* 126:61–65.

Randolph-Quinney P, Mallett X, and Black SM. 2009. Forensic anthropology. In: Jamieson A and Moenssens A, eds. *Wiley Encyclopedia of Forensic Science*. London, U.K.: John Wiley & Sons Ltd, pp. 152–178.

Schaefer M and Black SM. 2005. Comparison of ages of epiphyseal union in North American and Bosnian skeletal material. *Journal of Forensic Sciences* 50:777–784.

Scheuer L and Black S. 2000. *Developmental Juvenile Osteology*. San Diego, CA: Academic Press.

Skinner M and Lazenby RA. 1983. *Found! Human Remains*. Burnaby, British Columbia, Canada: Archaeology Press, Simon Fraser University.

Smith BH. 1991. Standards of human tooth formation and dental age assessment. In: Kelley MA and Larsen CS, eds. *Advances in Dental Anthropology*. New York: Wiley-Liss, pp. 143–168.

Snow CC, Hartman SE, Giles E, and Young FA. 1979. Sex and race determination of crania by calipers and computer: A test of the Giles and Elliot discriminant functions in 52 forensic science cases. *Journal of Forensic Sciences* 24:448–460.

St. Hoyme LE and İşcan MY. 1989. Determination of sex and race: Accuracy and assumptions. In: İşcan MY and Kennedy KAR, eds. *Reconstruction of Life from the Skeleton*. New York: Alan R. Liss Inc, pp. 53–93.

Stewart TD. 1979. *Essentials of Forensic Anthropology*. Springfield, IL: Charles C. Thomas.

Suchey JM. 1979. Problems in the aging of females using the Os pubis. *American Journal of Physical Anthropology* 51:467–471.

Symes SA, Rainwater CW, Chapman EN, Gipson DR, and Piper AL. 2008. Destruction of human remains in a forensic setting. In: Schmidt CW and Symes SA, eds. *The Analysis of Burned Human Remains*. London, U.K.: Academic Press, pp. 15–54.

Trotter M. 1970. Estimation of stature from intact long limb bones. In: Stewart TD, ed. *Personal Identification in Mass Disasters*. Washington, DC: Smithsonian Institute Press, pp. 71–83.

Trotter M and Gleser GC. 1952. Estimation of stature from long bones of American Whites and Negroes. *American Journal of Physical Anthropology* 10:463–514.

Trotter M and Gleser GC. 1958. A re-evaluation of estimation of stature based on measurements of stature taken during life and of long bones after death. *American Journal of Physical Anthropology* 16:79–123.

Ubelaker DH. 1989a. The estimation of age at death from immature human bone. In: İşcan MY, ed. *Age Markers in the Human Skeleton*. Springfield, IL: Charles C. Thomas, pp. 55–70.

Ubelaker DH. 1989b. *Human Skeletal Remains: Excavation, Analysis, Interpretation*. Washington, DC: Taraxacum.

Watkinson D, ed. 1987. *First Aid for Finds*, 2nd edn. London, U.K.: Rescue.

Wilkinson C. 2004. *Forensic Facial Reconstruction*. Cambridge, U.K.: Cambridge University Press.

Yoder C, Ubelaker DH, and Powell JF. 2001. Examination of variation in sternal rib end morphology relevant to age assessment. *Journal of Forensic Sciences* 46(2):223–227.

Burnt Human Remains Part II
Identification and Laboratory Analysis

7

PATRICK RANDOLPH-QUINNEY

Contents

Introduction

Part I of *Burnt Human Remains* (see Chapter 6) detailed how to properly document, excavate and package elements found in the field. The second part presented here, will describe the subsequent methods of laboratory analysis and identification techniques.

While fire scene investigation and any recovered fire debris may provide strong evidence with regard to the cause, mechanism and development of the fire (electrical, chemically accelerated, accidental, arson, etc.), burnt remains also have the potential to provide information concerning the temperature, duration and procession of the fire from the analysis of macro- and microstructural changes in skeletal tissue. They may also provide biochemical evidence for the use of ignitable liquids such as accelerants, or yield heat-transformed chemical markers from the destruction of soft tissues, clothing, and other components of the fire environment (DeHaan et al., 2004; DeHaan, 2008; DeHaan and Icove, 2012; DeHaan and Nurbakhsh, 2001).

Depending on the nature of the fire, the circumstances (non-suspicious, suspicious, arson, confirmed homicide, etc.) and condition and level of preservation, the tissues may undergo differing laboratory analyses by a variety of specialists; this may include the forensic pathologist or medical examiner, forensic odontologist, forensic entomologist, toxicologist, forensic botanist, fire investigator and forensic anthropologist. Each specialist will bring their own expertise in addressing medico-legal questions relating to the identity of the deceased, time since death, physiological and chemical status, and manner and cause of death. Here we will focus on the avenues of enquiry available when remains are severely burnt, skeletonised, and disrupted; such analyses are primarily the purview of the forensic anthropologist.

Process of Identification

The forensic anthropologist will generally address a series of issues relating to the identity of the deceased, the number of individuals involved, and the nature of any trauma recorded on the preserved tissues. These can be summarised as a series of questions posed by the anthropologist.

Differentiating between Burnt Human and Non-Human Remains

The first and most obvious task of the forensic anthropologist is to identify whether any remains encountered are human or not (see Chapter 5); this will ensure that valuable resources are not wasted investigating non-human remains. In dealing with un-burnt dry bone, the forensic anthropologist should be able to determine whether bones are human or animal. However, when skeletal tissues are charred or burnt, identification of their human or non-human origin may be impossible by gross morphology alone, as the burning process will cause morphological changes (such as warping, fracturing and patination) that may remove or obliterate the markers used for taxonomic identification (Whyte, 2001). In such instances, other analytical techniques need to be adopted.

The microscopic evaluation of bone histology (Cuijpers, 2006) may be useful, although this is not without its own set of problems depending on the temperature at which bone is burnt. At its most basic level, histological identification is predicated on the fact that different species both lay down bone and remodel it during life in different ways (Randolph-Quinney et al., 2009). Human non-foetal bone is made up of tubular cellular structures, known as Haversian osteonic systems, that appear circular in cross section. Many animals, herbivores in particular, present a plexiform osteon pattern, made up of rectangular laminar plates, which are only replaced and overprinted by

Haversian osteons in mature adult animals. The banding of osteonic units may also be used to differentiate human from non-human. While the presence of plexiform bone is a ready indication of non-human origin, it should be borne in mind that some animals present a combination of histological types, which may make microscopic evaluation difficult (see Chapter 5). In such instances the application of both morphological (qualitative assessment of osteon patterning) and metrical analyses of osteon parameters (based on measurement of osteon diameters, perimeters and areas) in the formulation of multivariate discriminant function models has been shown to be highly effective (reported 79% classification accuracy) in separating between burnt bones of humans and other commonly occurring species (Cattaneo et al., 1999).

In dealing with very small fragments, the use of serological or immunological studies (Lowenstein et al., 2005) or DNA analyses may be useful (Guglich et al., 1994), and specific coding regions (such as the MtDNA cyt-b gene) may be used to distinguish between taxa (Linacre and Lee, 2005; Matsuda et al., 2005). Some success has been noted in the recovery of recognisable and amplifiable DNA from burnt remains (Xu et al., 2007; Ye et al., 2004), including forensic cases with extreme charring (Sajantila et al., 1991) and archaeological cremains (Brown, 2000), although the quantity of DNA is unlikely to be sufficient to assist in anything other than specific identification. However, DNA has been successfully recovered from dental pulp after the teeth had been exposed to temperatures up to 300°C (Duffy et al., 1991), though attempts were not successful using teeth exposed to temperatures above this range which may limit the forensic utility of the technique (Tsuchimochi et al., 2002). However, the oral cavity may provide a protected environment for DNA survival (at least until such time as the soft tissues of the cheeks are destroyed; temperatures within the oral cavity have been reported to be as low as 75°C within a fire environment of 500°C–700°C (Duffy et al., 1991).

The Gross Effects of Heat on Skeletal Tissue

We have discussed in Chapter 6 the nature of the burning process as it affects the human body; this procedure is a complex one, made all the more so by the disparate physical, physiological and biochemical makeup of the human body. The body itself represents a fuel package and will contribute to the fuel load for the fire; subcutaneous body fat, organ fat, volatile organic components and clothing all contribute to the overall fuel load (DeHaan, 2008; DeHaan and Icove, 2012; DeHaan and Nurbakhsh, 2001). However, the chemistry of combustion of soft tissues and other non-skeletal elements is fundamentally different from that of the hard tissues (Fairgrieve, 2008) and is predicated upon the multiphasic nature of bone, being composed of physiologically bound organic materials that exhibit both a crystalline and amorphous phase (primarily type I collagen, with glycoaminoglycins [GAGs] and other protein constituents); an inorganic matrix of hydroxyl or bioapatite (inorganic salts largely made up of calcium and phosphorous), which again exhibit both a crystalline and amorphous phase; and water (Currey, 2002). As such, bone burns in a very different manner from other tissues, due to the extremely high content of inorganic matrix (Fairgrieve, 2008). The tough inorganic matrix means that bone does not burn easily and thus exhibits a relatively high thermal inertia when exposed to high levels of heat (DeHaan et al., 2004; DeHaan, 2008; DeHaan and Icove, 2012).

Put simply, the burning of skeletal tissue is essentially a process of dehydration and recrystallisation as a direct function of both increasing temperature and duration of burning. Specifically this leads to the elimi-nation of physisorbed and chemisorbed water, the thermal decomposition of organic components such as collagen and GAGs, the conversion (inver-sion) of hydroxyapatite to β-tricalcium phosphate, and eventually the fusion and recrystallisation of the remaining inorganic components (Correia, 1997; Hiller and Wess, 2006; Rogers and Daniels, 2002; Stiner et al., 1995). This four-stage process leads to a series of recognisable gross morphological, macrostructural and microstructural changes.

Approximately 90% of bones' organic matrix is composed of collagen, produced by osteoblast cells (White, 2000). In bone, collagen molecules intertwine to form slightly elastic, flexible fibres (fibrils) via a number of cross-link bonds (Hiller and Wess, 2006), which provide ductility and a degree of mechanical flexibility to bone, allowing it to resist tensile stress and strain to an extent. During the burning process, collagen fibrils are destroyed by heating at around 600°C (Thompson, 2005), and attendant hydrogen bonds are removed by dehydration (Nordin and Frankel, 1989); these factors induce bone to become brittle and more vulnerable to frac-ture. This brittleness is ultimately offset by the processes of recrystallisation and fusion of bioapatite crystals. This begins with the chemical conversion (inversion) of the inorganic matrix (hydroxyapatite) to β-tricalcium phos-phate (Grupe and Hummel, 1991). This change results in recrystallisation of apatite at temperatures up to 1000°C where they change from spherical in morphology to spherical and hexagonal; as part of this process, the lamellar structure of bone is destroyed. Some crystal fusion occurs above 1000°C, with melting of the bone mineral by 1600°C and above, leading to complete obliteration of any internal structural features. Recrystallisation and fusion generate structure up to 30% smaller than the original crystal, but one which is more stable, stronger, and less prone to fracturing and mechanical damage.

Dental tissue (comprising enamel, dentine and cementum) presents a similar resistance to burning to bone, but begins to degrade at a somewhat lower temperature (185°C–200°C) if directly exposed to heat (Harsányi, 1976; Shipman, 1984). This leads to a variety of morphological changes, particularly affecting the enamel of the tooth crown, which by 700°C (based on 1 h exposure) is usually pitted and fissured, or broken into fragments, and is rendered into minute smooth white glass-like fragments by 1300°C. Dentine and cementum fare somewhat better and will preserve recognisable (but fragmented) morphology to 900°C (Harsányi, 1976). An excellent guide to the recovery and analysis of burnt dental remains can be found in Schmidt (2008).

Dehydration and Mass Loss

Significant research has been conducted dealing with the compositional and mass changes in burnt bone following increases in temperature. These changes are due to the loss of both physisorbed and chemisorbed water and other volatile components, and primarily occurs in three phases—the pyrolysis of organic components, the loss of carbonates, and crystal fusion. Pyrolysis begins at around 100°C and is primarily the loss of adsorbed or physisorbed water. The second phase (decomposition of organic components) involves the evulsion of collagen, amino acids, mucopolysaccharides and GAGs, and is complete at around 600°C (Correia, 1997). The final phase concerns the ultrastructural change of hydroxyapatite to β-tricalcium phosphate, with concomitant increase in crystal size, and reduction in density. All three phases lead to a progressive loss of mass from the burning skeletal tissues.

This mass loss has been exploited by anthropologists to assess the likely post-cremation weight of remains in order to estimate the minimum number of individuals in large commingled samples, and to examine the possibility of commingling in civil cases relating to commercial cremations. Published cremation weights on 100 bodies taken before and after burning indicate a loss of some 96.3% of body mass on average (96.5% in adults, 96.0% in adolescents, and 97.60% in infants and children), with retained weights for adult individuals ranging from 876 to 3784 g with a mean of 2430 g. All males presented post-cremation values above 1798 g (value including pathological specimens), and all females had values below 1887 g (Warren and Maples, 1997). These figures are largely corroborated by cremation weights from adults in East Tennessee, United States, where male values ranged from 1865 to 5379 g with a mean of 3380 g and female values ranged from 1050 to 4000 g with a mean of 2350 g (Bass and Jantz, 2004), and further studies published by Sonek (1992) and Trotter and Hixon (1973). When comparing the results of published cases it is clear that variability in surviving cremation weight compared to pre-cremation body weight is highly variable, and the use of surviving weight to calculate the minimum number of individuals present in a cremation sample should not be advocated for forensic samples.

Colour Changes

Burnt bone displays a wide variety of colours ranging from brown to grey–blue, black, grey, grey–white and chalk white. Traditionally, colour change has been cited as evidence of firing temperatures ranging from brown/orange (unburnt) to black, to hues of blue and grey, to the fully oxidised china white of fully cremated and calcined bone. Colour is also seen as a reflection of organic and inorganic materials associated with the bone or body as it responds to increased temperatures; brown is associated with haemoglobin and/or soil discolouration, black with carbonization of bone in an oxygen-starved state, grey with organic pyrolisation, and china white with the final stage of organic degradation and fusion of bone salts.

It should be noted that much of the early literature regarding burnt bone analysis did not originate from the forensic sphere, instead often coming from specialists looking at archaeological cremations or paleoanthropological burnt bone (Binford, 1963; Brain, 1993; Curtin, 2008; Gejvall, 1969; Gilchrist and Mytum, 1986; Herrmann, 1976, 1977; Hiller and Wess, 2006; Kaczmarek and Piontek, 1982; Lisowski, 1968; McKinley, 1989, 1994; 2000; McKinley Roberts, 1993; Merbs, 1967; Rossi et al., 2004; Shahack-Gross et al., 1997; Sillen and Hoering, 1993; Spennemann and Colley, 1989; Thurman and Wilmore, 1980, 1981; Wells, 1960; Whyte, 2001). As such, many early studies relate to attempts to characterise a number of discrete covariables which are encountered as part of the burning process: temperature of burning, duration of burning, the atmosphere (whether oxidative or reducing), whether the tissues were fleshed or defleshed, human or non-human, and the presence of artefacts in the burning environment (Bennett and Benedix, 1999; Brain, 1993; Cattaneo et al., 1999; Grevin et al., 1998; Herrmann and Bennett, 1999; Huxley, 1994; Huxley and Kosa, 1999; Kennedy, 1996; Murray and Rose, 1993; Owsley, 1993; Sillen and Hoering, 1993; Stiner et al., 1995; Warren et al., 1999; Warren and Maples, 1997; Warren and Schultz, 2002).

Historically, the range and pattern of bone colour exhibited following burning has perhaps been of greatest interest to archaeological and forensic researchers (Gejvall, 1969; Gilchrist and Mytum, 1986; Lisowski, 1968; McKinley, 1989, 2000; Shipman et al., 1984; Walker et al., 2008), and it is generally considered an immutable fact in cremation analysis that temperature can provide quantifiable information about burning temperatures, duration of burn, combustion environment, and materials in contact with the burning tissues. However, the simple fact remains that all possible colours can be (and often are) exhibited by a single piece of bone when recovered from archaeological or forensic contexts, a process that can readily be demonstrated when one conducts actualistic burning experiments on bone samples (something interested readers are strongly encouraged to attempt), and this is especially evident in cases of the burning of fleshed remains. Recently, Symes et al. (2008) highlighted the protective role played by soft tissue in thermal colour changes and note that within a relatively short distance, soft tissue–protected bone can display a sequence of calcined (white), charred (black) and border and heat line (yellow) zones that define the area of bone exposure to heat and help to differentiate bones burnt in the flesh compared to those burnt as dry bone. Thus, it is fair to stress that a general pattern can be elucidated from bone colour with regard to a small number of variables but that accurate and precise quantification of the causal relationships is currently beyond the state of the science to date. These variables comprise

- General temperature of burning
- Direction of heat flow
- Fleshed versus defleshed bone

Heat-related colour change is one of the primary methods by which archaeologists and anthropologists have historically identified whether bone has been subjected to heat or not—this can be subjective where bone is highly fragmented. In the light of the many reported uses of controlled fire by early human ancestors (Bellomo, 1994; Brain, 1993; James, 1989; Straus, 1989), considerable experimental work and debate has ensued (Beach et al., 2008; Delvin and Herrmann, 2008; Shahack-Gross et al., 1997; Shipman et al., 1984; Walker et al., 2008) in order to differentiate heat-related colour change from depositional factors such as chemical impregnation from the burial environment or the effects of diagenesis (Brain, 1993; Delvin and Herrmann, 2008; Gilchrist and Mytum, 1986; Shahack-Gross et al., 1997; Shipman et al., 1984; Sillen and Hoering 1993). From a forensic perspective, current best practice would indicate that in cases where the presence of burning through colour change cannot unequivocally be differentiated from environmental or diagenetic processes, then destructive physical analyses which identify heat-related changes to bone mineral structure should be used. These include the use of inductively coupled plasma optical emission spectroscopy (ICP-OES) to determine concentrations of elements (Brooks et al., 2006), Fourier transform infrared spectroscopy (FTIR), or x-ray diffraction (Bergslien et al., 2008; Bush et al., 2007; Enzo et al., 2007; Hiller et al., 2003; Hiller and Wess, 2006; Lebon et al., 2008; Rogers and Daniels, 2002; Thompson et al., 2009) or histological (Brain, 1993; Cattaneo et al., 1999; Hanson and Cain, 2007) and histochemical methods (Grupe and Hummel, 1991; Schultz et al., 2005; Sillen and Hoering, 1993).

Dimensional and Shape Changes

While heat-induced colour change is one of the most obvious (and most often discussed) physical changes affecting burnt bone, perhaps the most disruptive changes (from an identification perspective) are presented as multivariate 3D changes associated with shrinkage, warping, changes to the bone surface (including ablation of surface tissues and bone cortex, spalling, and increased porosity) and heat-induced fracturing. As such, with fragmentation and disruption, the amount of useful biological data human remains may yield for morphological identification is reduced, and subsequently the accuracy of almost every anthropological identification technique is dramatically affected.

Of these macroscopic changes, dimensional alterations are perhaps the most extensively documented in terms of recent literature (McKinley, 2000; Thompson, 2005). This is due to their highly adverse effect on anthropological identification techniques, although the exact mechanism behind this response and the influencing factors are much debated. This is in part due to the large variation in experimental models used by investigators; different temperature intervals, recorded measurements, and statistical analyses have led to confusion in the literature regarding the typical mechanism and expression of this alteration (Correia, 1997; Mayne-Correia and Beattie, 2002). However, it is generally agreed that peak dimensional alterations occur between inversion and fusion, when carbonates are completely removed and hydroxyapatite crystals begin to coalesce and fuse, at approximately 800°C (Thompson, 2005). As noted previously, bone loses water as it is heated, first from the external organic matrix, then the hydration shell of the hydroxyapatite crystals, in the process of dehydration (Correia, 1997). Decomposition of the organic matter ensues, followed by a significant change in the crystallite structure. Although McKinley (2000) only noted the first two processes as possible mechanisms for dimensional change, Thompson (2005) subsequently suggested that alterations related to the crystallite structure may be equally influential in the degree of shrinkage observed.

A growing literature of experimental studies documents the range of bone shrinkage related to burning. Experiments involving combustion of fragments of differing skeletal elements (including cranial, axial and appendicular) burnt at temperatures ranging from 200°C to 1500°C indicate shrinkage to initiate at 700°C, with augmentation at 800°C, and with no further shrinkage at higher temperatures. Subsequent research has suggested considerable variation in shrinkage, which correlated with temperature, duration of heat exposure, and bone type (Fairgrieve, 2008). When only minimal heat has been applied, the effects of and evidence for burning can be difficult to detect, with most dimensional change not evidenced until temperatures exceed 800°C for at least a 20 min duration (Fairgrieve, 2008;

Thompson, 2005). The ultimate effects on bone are determined not just by the temperature of the heat applied but also by the duration of the heat event, oxygen supply and the extent of flesh or other protective materials in contact with the skeletal remains (Symes et al., 2008). The extent of protective materials present represents an important factor since they maximise differences in temperature between that of the heat source and the temperature of the affected skeletal remains, and since temperature of the heat source can differ extensively from bone temperature due to conductivity and thermal inertia (DeHaan and Icove, 2012), the duration of the heating process becomes important.

It should be noted that burning does not solely precipitate shrinkage in bone dimensions. In an experimentally robust study, Thompson (2005) burnt 60 sheep long bones to explore the bi-variable impact of heating temperatures and duration on heat-induced dimensional changes in bone. Eleven dimensions were measured across each of the long bones, before and after subjecting the bones to one of six different burning regimes, in order to assess the structural alterations in numerous aspects of the hard tissue. Ten bones were heated per burning duration (15 or 45 min) and temperature (500°C, 700°C, or 900°C), and after removal from the furnace were remeasured at 5, 15 and 30 min to observe further changes while cooling. Most interestingly, by measuring the bones at different stages of cooling, Thompson noted that 8.6% of the samples presented an overall expansion in bone dimensions in contrast to the expected shrinkage. He makes a number of significant assertions:

- Warping is the primary process in heat-induced shape change.
- Heat-induced warping is more apparent in bone that was fleshed at the time of burning and implies that the heat-induced contraction of muscle fibres pulls and twists the bone away from its natural shape.
- Heat-induced expansion of air within the medullary cavity also causes dimensional change, which leads to an increase in size of the diaphysis and particularly the epiphyses of long bones.
- In areas of dense bone with little porosity or trabecular influence, heat-induced warping is limited.
- Greatest percentage changes in overall dimensions were observed along the principal axis of loading (the axial length), followed by transverse diameters; this makes it likely that intrinsic properties of bone geometry and biomechanical stress resistance play a significant part in determining how bone distorts.

Changes to the surface quality of bone are also significant in altering the viability of identification protocols, as well as helping initiate further mechanical breakdown and disaggregation of the bone itself. Again, as with the expression of colour changes, a single element can express multiple patterns of bone patina, surface modification and fracture patterning. It is likely that much of this comes down to the inherent mechanical properties of skeletal tissue in presenting anisotropic (transversely isotropic) adaptive properties (Currey, 2002; Randolph-Quinney, 2010; Thompson, 2005). This has been practically applied for some time, and the intrinsic mechanical properties of bone are such that we can utilise heat-related structural modifications to help differentially diagnose between heat-induced fractures and those caused by other traumatic agents (see below). Fracture and surface analysis also allows us to define differences between bones burnt in the flesh versus those burnt without flesh. Studies have documented that dry bones exhibited longitudinal splitting and superficial ablation of the external surfaces and less evidence of warping (Nelson, 1992; Shipman et al., 1984; Symes et al., 2008; Ubelaker, 2009). In contrast, those burnt with flesh displayed considerable warping, transverse fractures, frequently in a curvilinear pattern and more irregular longitudinal splitting.

Differential Diagnosis of Trauma: Separating Burning Trauma from Other Classes

Skeletal trauma is caused by the application of energy to the human body and can be considered as an energy continuum from low to high levels of energy input which can be arbitrarily divided into a number of manners of application: blunt force (including asphyxia), sharp force, and ballistic trauma. Burning trauma is the direct application of thermal energy through heat induction, convection, or radiation, though this may also be concomitant with other primary traumatic types. In recent decades anthropologists have been of great assistance in documenting and explaining traumatic patterning in relation to violent death through analyses of the effects of applied loading or energy to bone, including differential diagnosis of burning from other classes of trauma (Berryman and Symes, 1998; Black, 2005; Bontrager and Nawrocki, 2008; Galloway, 1999; Kimmerle and Baraybar, 2008; Pope and Smith, 2004). Skeletal trauma is highly variable, and each case presents its own set of unique characteristics and challenges to the interpretation and reconstruction of the causative events.

The aim of the forensic practitioner in regard to the assessment of trauma is to attempt to answer three primary questions: (1) When did the trauma occur? Did it occur ante-, peri-, or post-mortem? (2) How was it induced? Was it accidentally, deliberately self-induced, or deliberately by a second party? And (3) how much force or energy (including thermal) was applied in order to cause the observed injury (Komar and Buikstra, 2008)? The forensic anthropologist must first isolate evidence of skeletal trauma from natural variations and subsequently determine the nature of the trauma, that is, blunt, sharp, ballistic, burning, or explosive. Secondly, determination of the number of insults and the order in which these occurred is required, in conjunction with a determination of the time at which the injuries were sustained, that is, ante-, peri-, or post-mortem. As injuries sustained at each of these stages exhibit individual morphological characteristics, the forensic practitioner is able to distinguish between those injuries which occurred prior to, at the time of, or subsequent to death (Byers, 2009; Kimmerle and Baraybar, 2008; Komar and Buikstra, 2008). However, trauma interpretation for skeletal remains in cases involving burning can be extremely difficult due to heat-related fractures and skeletal fragmentation, and careful reconstruction of affected remains is a prerequisite for effective trauma analysis. Issues are compounded by the trauma often induced in burnt skeletal remains by the post-fire recovery process.

Both experimental studies and casework experience indicate that diagnostic evidence of trauma can survive the burning event. In a 2004 experimental approach working with cranial bone, Pope and Smith documented the post-burning survival of pre-existing trauma. Conducting similar research in 2002, de Gruchy and Rogers were able to identify chop marks in cremated bone, but found that their appearance could be influenced by burning-related fragmentation (de Gruchy and Rogers, 2002). Herrmann and Bennett, (1999) also found that signatures of sharp force trauma survived incineration but argued that an analysis of fracture patterns and surface morphology was required. They suggested that blunt force trauma was difficult to distinguish from heat-related fractures (Herrmann and Bennett, 1999), though subsequent work has indicated that sufficient diagnostic criteria exist to differentiate the respective classes of trauma if careful macroscopic and microscopic analyses are adopted (Pope and Smith, 2004; Symes et al., 2008). In a major case application, the study of the fatalities from the Branch Davidian incident in Waco, Texas (Owsley et al., 1995; Ubelaker et al., 1995) demonstrated that various kinds of peri-mortem trauma could survive the burning process. Since heat exposure can lead to extensive bone fracturing, differentiating peri-mortem trauma from post-mortem thermal-related alterations can be challenging, though Symes et al., (2008) provide useful discussion of this issue, noting that observations of the pattern of fractures can enhance effective diagnosis (Symes et al., 2008).

Summary and Conclusions

In spite of many years of published research and (intermittently) reported forensic casework, there is still a great deal that is not fully understood regarding the transformative process that heat causes to bone and the most appropriate method for studying such material. It is sadly fair to say that much of the published research dealing with burnt bone and tissues has had little *direct* application to the human identification process to date or made a significant impact in real-world forensic fire investigation. There are a number of potential reasons for this:

1. Models established for thermal alteration have invariably been developed using non-human analogues (usually pig or sheep), which present significant structural (gross morphological and micro-histological) and biochemical differences when compared to human bone.
2. There has been substantial variation in experimental models used by investigators. Different methods of heating and cooling, temperature intervals, the range of recorded measurements and statistical analyses have led to confusion in the literature regarding the typical mechanism and expression of heat alteration.
3. Many of the published studies are based on experiential approaches from bioarchaeology and/or actualistic burning experiments using qualitative features based on absolutely or relatively small sample sizes or anecdotal evidence. Many of these studies are neither statistically robust nor repeatable and thus of limited utility in current medico-legal practice.

All is not doom and gloom, however. Innovative work in recent years of direct forensic relevance has finally begun to address some of the core questions surrounding burnt human tissues in a systematic fashion, dealing with new imaging modalities (Thompson and Chudek, 2007); quantification of changes to trabecular morphology and cortical thickness (Randolph-Quinney, 2010); differentiation of burning from other trauma types (de Gruchy and Rogers 2002; Pope and Smith 2004) the effects of contamination, commingling, or diagenesis (Bass and Jantz, 2004; Bergslien et al., 2008; Brooks et al., 2006; Enzo et al., 2007; Mayne-Correia and Beattie, 2002; Warren and Schultz, 2002; Worley, 2005); or case-based or review studies (Almirall and Furton, 2004; Bohnert and Rothschild, 2003; Byard et al., 2001; Calacal et al., 2005; Daeid, 2003; DeHaan et al., 2004; Delattre, 2000; Hanson and Cain, 2007; Hillier and Bell, 2007; Hiller et al., 2003; Koon et al., 2003; Kosanke et al., 2003; Lain et al., 2003; Pai et al., 2007; Panaitescu and Rosu, 2007; Phillips, 2001; Rothschild et al., 2001; Stauffer, 2003; Thali et al., 2002; Thompson, 2004; Thompson et al., 2009; Ubelaker, 2009; Valenzuela et al., 2000; Ye et al., 2004; Zavoi et al., 2007) dealing with issues such as detection and recognition of remains in fire contexts, archaeological recovery methods and recovery biases, reconstruction of biological identification parameters, differentiation of fire damage from other trauma classes and taphonomic effects on tissue loss and survival. While forensic cremation analysis may still shed light on the burning of human and animal tissues in the archaeological past, it is encouraging to note that a coherent focus on forensic relevance, quantification and reproducibility is now developing; the future is bright, at least for now.

References

Almirall JR and Furton KG. 2004. Characterization of background and pyrolysis products that may interfere with the forensic analysis of fire debris. *Journal of Analytical and Applied Pyrolysis* 71:51–67.

Bass WM and Jantz RL. 2004. Cremation weights in East Tennessee. *Journal of Forensic Sciences* 49:901–904.

Beach JJ, Passalacqua NV, and Chapman EM. 2008. Heat-related changes in tooth color: Temperature versus duration of exposure. In: Schmidt CW and Symes SA, eds. *The Analysis of Burned Human Remains*. London, U.K.: Academic Press. pp. 137–144.

Bellomo RV. 1994. Methods of determining early hominid behavioural activities associated with the controlled use of fire at FxJj 20 Main, Koobi Fora, Kenya. *Journal of Human Evolution* 27:173–195.

Bennett JL and Benedix DC. 1999. Positive identification of cremains recovered from an automobile based on presence of an internal fixation device. *Journal of Forensic Sciences* 44:1296–1298.

Bergslien ET, Bush M, and Bush PJ. 2008. Identification of cremains using x-ray diffraction spectroscopy and a comparison to trace element analysis. *Forensic Science International* 175:218–226.

Berryman HE and Symes SA. 1998. Recognizing gunshot and blunt cranial trauma through fracture interpretation. In Reichs, K. J. (Ed.), *Forensic Osteology: Advances in the identification of human remains*. Springfield, Il: Thomas, 333–352.

Binford LR. 1963. An analysis of cremations from three Michigan sites. *Wisconsin Archaeology* 44:98–110.

Black S. 2005. Bone pathology and ante-mortem trauma in forensic cases. In Payne-James, J. (Ed.), *Encyclopedia of forensic and legal medicine*. London: Elsevier, 105–113.

Bohnert M and Rothschild MA. 2003. Complex suicides by self-incineration. *Forensic Science International* 131:197–201.

Bontrager AB and Nawrocki SP. 2008. A taphonomic analysis of human cremains from the Fox Hollow Farm serial homicide site. In Schmidt, C. W. and Symes, S. A. (Eds.), *The analysis of burned human remains*. London: Academic Press, pp. 211–226.

Brain CK. 1993. The occurrence of burnt bones at Swartkrans and their implications for the control of fire by early hominids. In: Brain CK, ed. *Swartkrans: A Cave's Chronicle of Early Man*. Pretoria, South Africa: Transvaal Museum Monograph 8. pp. 229–242.

Brooks TR, Bodkin TE, Potts GE, and Smullen SA. 2006. Elemental analysis of human cremains using ICP-OES to classify legitimate and contaminated cremains. *Journal of Forensic Sciences* 51:967–973.

Brown K. 2000. Ancient DNA applications in human osteoarchaeology. In: Cox M and Mays S, eds. *Human Osteology in Archaeology and Forensic Science*. London, U.K.: Greenwich Medical Media Ltd. pp. 455–473.

Bush MA, Miller RG, Prutsman-Pfeiffer J, and Bush PJ. 2007. Identification through x-ray fluorescence analysis of dental restorative resin materials: A comprehensive study of noncremated, cremated, and processed-cremated individuals. *Journal of Forensic Sciences* 52:157–165.

Byard RW, James RA, and Zuccollo J. 2001. Potential confusion arising from materials presenting as possible human remains. *American Journal of Forensic Medicine and Pathology* 22(4):391–394.

Byers SN. 2009. *Introduction to Forensic Anthropology*. Boston, MA: Pearson Education.

Calacal GC, Delfin FC, Tan MMM, Roewer L, Magtanong DL, Lara MC, Fortun RD, and De Ungria MCA. 2005. Identification of exhumed remains of fire tragedy victims using conventional methods and autosomal/Y-chromosomal short tandem repeat DNA profiling. *American Journal of Forensic Medicine and Pathology* 26:285–291.

Cattaneo C, Di Martino S, Scali S, Craig OE, Grandi M, and Sokol RJ. 1999. Determining the human origin of burnt bone: A comparative study of histological, immunological and DNA techniques. *Journal of Forensic Sciences* 102:181–191.

Correia PMM. 1997. Fire modification of bone: A review of the literature. In: Haglund WD and Sorg MH, eds. *Forensic Taphonomy: The Postmortem Fate of Human Remains*. Boca Raton, FL: CRC Press LLC. pp. 275–294.

Cuijpers AGFM. 2006. Histological identification of bone fragments in archaeology: Telling humans apart from horses and cattle. *International Journal of Osteoarchaeology* 16:465–480.

Currey JD. 2002. The structure of bone tissue. In: *Bones: Structure and mechanics*. Princeton, NJ: Princeton University Press. pp. 3–25.

Curtin AJ. 2008. Putting together the pieces: Reconstructing mortuary practices from commingled ossuary cremains. In Schmidt, C, W. and Symes, S. A. (Eds.), *The analysis of burned human remains*. London: Academic Press, pp. 201–209.

Daeid NN. 2003. The ENFSI fire and explosion investigation working group and the European live burn tests at Cardington. *Science & Justice* 43:49–54.

DeHaan JD. 2008. Fire and bodies. In: Schmidt CW and Symes SA, eds. *The Analysis of Burned Human Remains*. London, U.K.: Academic Press. pp. 1–13.

DeHaan JD, Brien DJ, and Large R. 2004. Volatile organic compounds from the combustion of human and animal tissue. *Science & Justice* 44:223–236.

DeHaan JD and Icove DJ. 2012. *Kirk's Fire Investigation*. Boston, MA: Pearson Education.

DeHaan JD and Nurbakhsh S. 2001. Sustained combustion of an animal carcass and its implications for the consumption of human bodies in fires. *Journal of Forensic Sciences* 46:1076–1081.

Delattre VF. 2000. Burned beyond recognition: Systematic approach to the dental identification of charred human remains. *Journal of Forensic Sciences* 45:589–596.

Delvin JB and Herrmann NP. 2008. Bone color as an interpretive tool of the depositional history of archaeological cremains. In: Schmidt CW and Symes SA, eds. *The Analysis of Burned Human Remains*. London, U.K.: Academic Press. pp. 109–128.

Duffy JB, Waterfield JD, and Skinner MF. 1991. Isolation of tooth-pulp cells for sex-chromatin studies in experimental dehydrated and cremated remains. *Forensic Science International* 49:127–141.

Enzo S, Bazzoni M, Mazzarello V, Piga G, Bandiera P, and Melis P. 2007. A study by thermal treatment and x-ray powder diffraction on burnt fragmented bones from Tombs II, IV and IX belonging to the hypogeic necropolis of "Sa Figu" near Ittiri, Sassari (Sardinia, Italy). *Journal of Archaeological Science* 34:1731–1737.

Fairgrieve SI. 2008. *Forensic Cremation: Recovery and Analysis.* Boca Raton, FL: CRC Press. 206p.

Gejvall N. 1969. Cremations. In: Brothwell D and Higgs E, eds. *Science in Archaeology,* 2nd edn. London, U.K.: Thames & Hudson. pp. 468–479.

Gilchrist R and Mytum HC. 1986. Experimental archaeology and burnt animal bones from archaeological sites. *Circaea* 4:29–38.

de Gruchy S and Rogers TL. 2002. Identifying chop marks on cremated bone: A preliminary study. *Journal of Forensic Sciences* 47:933–936.

Galloway A. 1999. The biomechanics of fracture production. In Galloway, A. (Ed.), *Broken Bones: Anthropological analysis of blunt force trauma.* Springfield, Il: Thomas, pp. 35–62.

Grevin G, Bailet P, Quartrehomme G, and Ollier A. 1998. Anatomical reconstruction of fragments of burned human bones: A necessary means for forensic identification. *Forensic Science International* 96:129–134.

Grupe G and Hummel S. 1991. Trace-element studies on experimentally cremated bone. 1. Alteration of the chemical-composition at high-temperatures. *Journal of Archaeological Science* 18:177–186.

Guglich EA, Wilson PJ, and White BN. 1994. Forensic application of repetitive DNA markers to the species identification of animal tissues. *Journal of Forensic Sciences* 39:353–361.

Hanson M and Cain CR. 2007. Examining histology to identify burned bone. *Journal of Archaeological Science* 34:1902–1913.

Harsányi L. 1976. Scanning electron microscopic investigation of thermal damage of the teeth. *Acta Morphologica Academiae Scientiarium Hungaricae* 23:271–281.

Herrmann B. 1976. Experimentalle und theoretische beiträge zur leichenbrand unter schung. *Homo* 27:114–118.

Herrmann B. 1977. On histological investigations of cremated human remains. *Journal of Human Evolution* 6:101–103.

Herrmann NP and Bennett JL. 1999. The differentiation of traumatic and heat-related fractures in burned bone. *Journal of Forensic Sciences* 44:461–469.

Hiller JC, Thompson TJU, Evison MP, Chamberlain AT, and Wess TJ. 2003. Bone mineral change during experimental heating: An x-ray scattering investigation. *Biomaterials* 24:5091–5097.

Hiller JC and Wess TJ. 2006. The use of small-angle x-ray scattering to study archaeological and experimentally altered bone. *Journal of Archaeological Science* 33:560–572.

Hillier ML and Bell LS. 2007. Differentiating human bone from animal bone: A review of histological methods. *Journal of Forensic Sciences* 52:249–263.

Huxley AK. 1994. Analysis of ceramic substrate found in cremains. *Journal of Forensic Sciences* 39:287–288.

Huxley KA and Kósa F. 1999. Calculation of percent shrinkage in human fetal diaphyseal lengths from fresh bone to carbonized and calcined bone using Petersohn and Köhler's data. *Journal of Forensic Sciences* 44:577–583.

James SR. 1989. Hominid use of fire in the lower and middle pleistocene. *Current Anthropology* 30:1–26.

Kaczmarek M and Piontik J. 1982. Human cremated remains and the diversity of man. *Homo* 33:230–236.

Kennedy KAR. 1996. The wrong urn: Commingling of cremains in mortuary practices. *Journal of Forensic Sciences* 41:689–692.

Kimmerle EH and Baraybar JP, eds. 2008. *Skeletal Trauma—Identification of Injuries Resulting from Human Rights Abuse and Armed Conflict.* Boca Raton, FL: CRC Press.

Komar DA and Buikstra JE. 2008. *Forensic Anthropology: Contemporary Theory and Practice.* New York: Oxford University Press.

Koon HEC, Nicholson RA, and Collins MJ. 2003. A practical approach to the identification of low temperature heated bone using TEM. *Journal of Archaeological Science* 30:1393–1399.

Kosanke KL, Dujay RC, and Kosanke B. 2003. Characterization of pyrotechnic reaction residue particles by SEM/EDS. *Journal of Forensic Sciences* 48:531–537.

Lain R, Griffiths C, and Hilton JMN. 2003. Forensic dental and medical response to the Bali bombing—A personal perspective. *Medical Journal of Australia* 179:362–365.

Lebon M, Reiche I, Fröhlich F, Bahain JJ, and Falguères C. 2008. Characterization of archaeological burnt bones: Contribution of a new analytical protocol based on derivative FTIR spectroscopy and curve fitting of the $\nu 1\nu 3PO4$ domain. *Analytical and Bioanalytical Chemistry* 392:1479–1488.

Linacre A and Lee JC. 2005. Species determination: The role and use of the cytochrome b gene. *Methods in Molecular Biology: Forensic DNA Typing Protocols* 297:45–52.

Lisowski FP. 1968. The investigation of human cremations. In: Saller K, ed. *Anthropologie und Humangenetik.* Stuttgart, Germany: Gustav Fischer Verlag. pp. 76–83.

Lowenstein J, Reuther J, Hood D, Scheuenstuhl G, Gerlach S, and Ubelaker D. 2005. Identification of animal species by protein radioimmunoassay of bone fragments and bloodstained stone tools. *Forensic Science International* 159:182–188.

Matsuda H, Seo Y, Kakizaki E, Kozawa S, Muraoka E, and Yukawa N. 2005. Identification of DNA of human origin based on amplification of human-specific mitochondrial cytochrome b region. *Forensic Science International* 152:109–114.

Mayne-Correia P and Beattie O. 2002. A critical look at methods for recovering, evaluating and interpreting cremated human remains. In: Haglund WD and Sorg MH, eds. *Advances in Forensic Taphonomy: Method, Theory and Archeological Perspectives.* Boca Raton, FL: CRC Press. pp. 435–450.

McKinley JI. 1989. Cremations: Expectations, methodologies, and reality. In: Roberts CA, Lee F, and Bintliff J, eds. *Burial Archaeology: Current Research, Methods, and Developments.* Oxford, U.K.: BAR British Series 211. pp. 65–76.

McKinley JI. 1994. The Anglo-Saxon cemetery at Spong Hill, North Elmham Part VIII: The cremations. *East Anglian Archaeology Report*, 69, GB.

McKinley JL. 2000. The analysis of cremated bone. In: Cox A and Mays S, eds. *Human Osteology: In Archaeology and Forensic Science*. London, U.K.: Greenwich Medical Media Ltd. pp. 403–421.

Murray KA and Rose JC. 1993. The analysis of cremains—A case-study involving the inappropriate disposal of mortuary remains. *Journal of Forensic Sciences* 38:98–103.

Nelson R. 1992. A microscopic comparison of fresh and burned bones. *Journal of Forensic Sciences* 37:1055–1060.

Owsley DW. 1993. Identification of the fragmentary, burned remains of 2 U.S. journalists 7 years after their disappearance in Guatemala. *Journal of Forensic Sciences* 38:1372–1382.

Owsley DW, Ubelaker DH, Houck MM, Sandness KL, Grant WE, Craig EA, Woltanski TJ, and Peerwani N. 1995. The role of forensic anthropology in the recovery and analysis of Branch Davidian compound victims—Techniques of analysis. *Journal of Forensic Sciences* 40:341–348.

Pai CY, Jein MC, Li LH, Cheng YY, and Yang CH. 2007. Application of forensic entomology to postmortem interval determination of a burned human corpse: A homicide case report from Southern Taiwan. *Journal of the Formosan Medical Association* 106:792–798.

Panaitescu V and Rosu M. 2007. Problems of forensic anthropological identification of carbonized human remains. *Romanian Journal of Legal Medicine* 15:39–44.

Phillips SA. 2001. Pyrotechnic residues analysis—Detection and analysis of characteristic particles by scanning electron microscopy/energy dispersive spectroscopy. *Science & Justice* 41(2):73–80.

Pope EJ and Smith OC. 2004. Identification of traumatic injury in burned cranial bone: An experimental approach. *Journal of Forensic Sciences* 49:431–440.

Randolph-Quinney P. 2010. Towards a standardization of burnt bone analysis: The use of micro-computed tomography and 3-dimensional imaging to assess morphological change. *Proceedings of the American Academy of Forensic Sciences—Annual Scientific Meeting*. Seattle, WA, February 22–27, 2010. Colorado Springs, CO: American Academy of Forensic Sciences. pp. 352–353.

Randolph-Quinney P, Mallett X, and Black SM. 2009. Forensic anthropology. In: Jamieson A and Moenssens A, eds. *Wiley Encyclopedia of Forensic Science*. London, U.K.: John Wiley & Sons Ltd. pp. 152–178.

Rogers KD and Daniels P. 2002. An x-ray diffraction study of the effects of heat treatment on bone mineral microstructure. *Biomaterials* 23:2577–2585.

Rossi DS, De Gruchy and Lovell NC. 2004. A comparative experiment in the consolidation of cremated bone. *International Journal of Osteoarchaeolgy* 14:104–111.

Rothschild MA, Raatschen HJ, and Schneider V. 2001. Suicide by Self-immolation in Berlin from 1990 to 2000. *Forensic Science International* 124:163–166.

Sajantila A, Strom M, Budowle B, Karhunen PJ, and Peltonen L. 1991. The polymerase chain-reaction and postmortem forensic identity testing—Application of amplified D1s80 and Hla-Dq-alpha loci to the identification of fire victims. *Forensic Science International* 51:23–34.

Schmidt CW. 2008. The recovery and study of burned human teeth. In Schmidt, C. W., and Symes, S. A. (Eds.), *The analysis of burned human remains*. London: Academic Press, 55–74.

Schultz JJ, Warren MW, and Krigbaum JS. 2005. Analysis of modern cremated human remains: Gross and chemical methods. In: Schmidt CW and Symes SA, eds. *The Analysis of Burned Human Remains*. London, U.K.: Academic Press. pp. 75–94, 184.

Shahack-Gross R, Bar-Yosef O, and Weiner S. 1997. Black-coloured bones in Hayonim Cave, Israel: Differentiating between burning and oxide staining. *Journal of Archaeological Science* 24:439–446.

Shipman P, Foster G, and Shoeninger M. 1984. Burnt bones and teeth: An experimental study of color, morphology, crystal and shrinkage. *Journal of Archaeological Science* 11:307–325.

Sillen A and Hoering T. 1993. Chemical characterization of burnt bones from Swartkrans. In: Brain CK, ed. *Swartkrans: A Cave's Chronicle of Early Man*. Pretoria, South Africa: Transvaal Museum Monograph 8. pp. 243–250.

Spennemann DHR and Colley SM. 1989. Fire in a pit: The effects of burning on faunal remains. *Archaeozoologia* 3:51–64.

Stauffer E. 2003. Concept of pyrolysis for fire debris analysts. *Science & Justice* 43:29–40.

Stiner MC, Kuhn SL, Weiner S, and Baryosef O. 1995. Differential burning, recrystallization, and fragmentation of archaeological bone. *Journal of Archaeological Science* 22:223–237.

Straus LG. 1989. On early hominid use of fire. *Current Anthropology* 30:488–491.

Symes SA, Rainwater CW, Chapman EM, Gipson DR, and Piper AL. 2008. Patterned thermal destruction of human remains in a forensic setting. In: Schmidt CW and Symes S, eds. *The Analysis of Burned Human Remains*. London, U.K.: Academic Press. pp. 15–54.

Thali MJ, Yen K, Plattner T, Schweitzer W, Vock P, Ozdoba C, and Dirnhofer R. 2002. Charred body: Virtual autopsy with multi-slice computed tomography and magnetic resonance imaging. *Journal of Forensic Sciences* 47:1326–1331.

Thompson T, Gauthier M, and Islam M. 2009. The application of a new method of Fourier transform infrared spectroscopy to the analysis of burned bone. *Journal of Archaeological Science* 36:910–914.

Thompson TJU. 2004. Recent advances in the study of burned bone and their implications for forensic anthropology. *Forensic Science International* 146:S203–S205.

Thompson TJU. 2005. Heat-induced dimensional changes in bone and their consequences for forensic anthropology. *Journal of Forensic Sciences* 50:1008–1015.

Thompson TJU and Chudek JA. 2007. A novel approach to the visualisation of heat-induced structural change in bone. *Science & Justice* 47:99–104.

Trotter M and Hixon BB. 1973. Sequential changes in weight, density, and percentage of ash weight of human skeletons from an early fetal period through old age. *Anatomical Record* 179.

Tsuchimochi T, Iwasa M, Maeno Y, Koyama H, Inoue H, Isobe I, Matoba R, Yokoi M, and Nagao M. 2002. Chelating resin-based extraction of DNA from dental pulp and sex determination from incinerated teeth with Y-chromosomal alphoid repeat and short tandem repeats. *American Journal of Forensic Medicine and Pathology* 23:268–271.

Ubelaker DH. 2009. The forensic evaluation of burned skeletal remains: A synthesis. *Forensic Science International* 183:1 5.

Ubelaker DH, Owsley DW, Houck MM, Craig E, Grant W, Woltanski T, Fram R, Sandness K, and Peerwani N. 1995. The role of forensic anthropology in the recovery and analysis of Branch Davidian compound victims: Recovery procedures and characteristics of the victims. *Journal of Forensic Sciences* 40:335–340.

Valenzuela A, Martin-de las Heras S, Marques T, Exposito N, and Bohoyo JM. 2000. The application of dental methods of identification to human burn victims in a mass disaster. *International Journal of Legal Medicine* 113:236–239.

Walker PL, Miller KWP, and Richman R. 2008. Time, temperature, and oxygen availability: An experimental study of the effects of environmental conditions on the color and organic content of cremated bone. In: Schmidt CW and Symes SA, eds. *The Analysis of Burned Human Remains*. London, U.K.: Academic Press. pp. 129–135.

Warren MW and Maples WR. 1997. The anthropometry of contemporary commercial cremation. *Journal of Forensic Sciences* 42:417–423.

Warren MW, Falsetti AB, Hamilton WF, and Levine LJ. 1999. Evidence of arteriosclerosis in cremated remains. *American Journal of Forensic Medicine and Pathology* 20:277–280.

Warren MW and Schultz JJ. 2002. Post-cremation taphonomy and artifact preservation. *Journal of Forensic Sciences* 47:656–659.

Wells C. 1960. A study of cremation. *Antiquity* 34:29–37.

White TD and Folkens PA. 2005. The Human Bone Manual. California: Elsevier Academic Press.

Whyte TR. 2001. Distinguishing remains of human cremations from burned animal bones. *Journal of Field Archaeology* 28:437–448.

Worley F. 2005. Taphonomic influences on cremation burial deposits: Implications for interpretation. In: O'Connor TP, ed. *Biosphere to Lithosphere: New Studies in Vertebrate Taphonomy*. Oxford, U.K.: Oxbow Books. pp. 64–69.

Xu GC, Ren F, Hou XW, and Yuan LB. 2007. Application of the burned bone morphology and DNA technology in human identification. *Fa Yi Xue Za Zhi* 23:370–372.

Ye J, Ji AQ, Parra EJ, Zheng XF, Jiang CT, Zhao XC, Hu L, and Tu Z. 2004. A simple and efficient method for extracting DNA from old and burned bone. *Journal of Forensic Sciences* 49:754–759.

Zavoi R, Marinescu A, Radu L, and Albita C. 2007. Attempt to camouflage an homicide by burning the cadaver. *Romanian Journal of Legal Medicine* 15:50–54.

Stable Isotopes and Human Provenancing

ERIC BARTELINK, RACHEL BERRY,
AND LESLEY CHESSON

Contents

Introduction

This chapter is intended to showcase the advances in stable isotope analysis (SIA) techniques since the publication of *Forensic Human Identification: An Introduction* (Thompson and Black, 2007). As such, the basic principles of SIA are only briefly described here. Those readers wishing for a more comprehensive review are advised to refer to the previous text, particularly the chapter by Meier-Augenstein (2007).

What Are Stable Isotopes?

The word 'isotope' is derived from the Greek *isos*, meaning equal, and *tópos*, meaning position or place (Fry, 2006). It refers to the periodic table and the fact that all isotopes of the same element occupy an identical site on the table. Chemically speaking, isotopes react in a similar way, as this is largely governed by electronic configuration (Hoefs, 2009). The atomic number is the same for all isotopes of an element due to the same number of protons. However, variation in the number of neutrons means that isotopes of the same element will have different atomic masses (the sum of the number of protons and neutrons). If atoms of elements are present in a variety of isotopic forms during a chemical reaction, then it is likely that there will be an uneven distribution of these isotopes between the products and reactants (Urey, 1947).

Isotopes can be divided into two fundamental kinds—stable and unstable (radioactive species). There are approximately 300 stable isotopes currently identified, and over 1200 unstable isotopes have been discovered. Stable isotopes are those that do not undergo radioactive decay, thus maintaining their nuclear stability and a consistent mass. Although some isotopes are the end products of the decay of radioisotopes, they are considered stable, as they themselves do not undergo further radioactive decay. Examples include an isotope of strontium (^{87}Sr) produced from the decay of rubidium (^{87}Rb) and several lead isotopes (^{206}Pb, ^{207}Pb and ^{208}Pb) that are the stable end accumulations of the decay of uranium (^{238}U, ^{235}U) and thorium (^{232}Th) radioisotopes.

Stable Isotope Natural Abundance and Fractionation

The natural abundance of a stable isotope refers to the abundance of isotopes of a particular chemical element occurring naturally on the planet. The lightest of an element's isotopes (e.g. ^{1}H and ^{14}N) is generally the most abundant in the environment (see Table 8.1).

While the global abundances of elemental isotopes do not vary, abundances at smaller scales do vary and constantly undergo partitioning in a process called 'fractionation', brought about by variation in the mass of the nuclei (Hoefs, 2009). Due to the variation in mass, molecules containing the heavier isotope(s) have reduced mobility and form stronger bonds (Mook and de Vries, 2000). As a consequence of reduced mobility, molecules containing heavier isotopes will have a lower diffusion velocity. Molecules containing heavier isotopes will also have a lower collision frequency, meaning they react more slowly compared to molecules containing the lighter isotope. The ability of heavier isotopes to form stronger bonds with other atoms means that more energy is required to break the

Table 8.1   Stable Isotopes and Natural Abundances of the Elements Hydrogen, Carbon, Nitrogen, Oxygen and Sulphur, as well as International Standards Used for SIA

Element	Isotope	Abundance (%)	International Standards
H	^{1}H	99.98	Standard Mean Ocean
	^{2}H	0.02	Water (SMOW) and VSMOW
C	^{12}C	99.89	PDB and VPDB
	^{13}C	1.11	
N	^{14}N	99.64	Ambient inhalable
	^{15}N	0.46	reservoir (AIR)
O	^{16}O	99.76	SMOW
	^{17}O	0.04	PDB and VPDB
	^{18}O	0.20	
S	^{32}S	95.02	CDT and VCDT
	^{33}S	0.75	
	^{34}S	4.21	
	^{36}S	0.02	

bond between an atom bonded to a heavy isotope of a given element relative to an atom being bonded to the lighter isotope of the same element. If a reaction does not go to completion, the consequences of mass variation result in the product containing more of the light isotope and less of the heavy isotope (Parkes, 1986); if the reaction goes to completion, the cumulative product will have the same isotopic composition as the original substrate (Sulzman, 2008).

Isotopic fractionation occurs constantly and has a major effect on the isotopic content of the food and drink we consume, and hence the isotopic composition of our body tissues. For example, as water passes through the hydrologic cycle, processes such as condensation and evaporation cause mass-dependent fractionation in hydrogen and oxygen isotopes (Dansgaard, 1964). Water molecules containing the lighter isotopes of hydrogen and oxygen evaporate more readily than water molecules containing heavier isotopes. Thus, the resultant vapour formed from a pool of water is isotopically lighter than the pool. As water is transported across continents and precipitation forms, water molecules containing heavier hydrogen and oxygen isotopes condense first, and the isotopic signature of rainfall is thus isotopically heavier relative to the cloud (but lighter relative to the starting pool of water). Serial evaporation and condensation events within a cloud as it moves across the landscape mean rainfall will isotopically vary according to geographic location. Factors such as temperature, humidity, continentality (distance from the sea), and altitude all affect the isotopic composition of precipitation (Craig, 1961; Dansgaard, 1964). The strong relationship between the isotopic ratios of rainfall and geolocation has allowed scientists to construct continent-, country- and even region-specific precipitation maps using geographic information system (GIS) software (Bowen, 2010; Bowen and Wilkinson, 2002). As a result of the fact that the majority of human drinking water is ultimately derived from rainfall, the isotopic signature of local precipitation is incorporated into our body tissues. Figure 8.1 shows

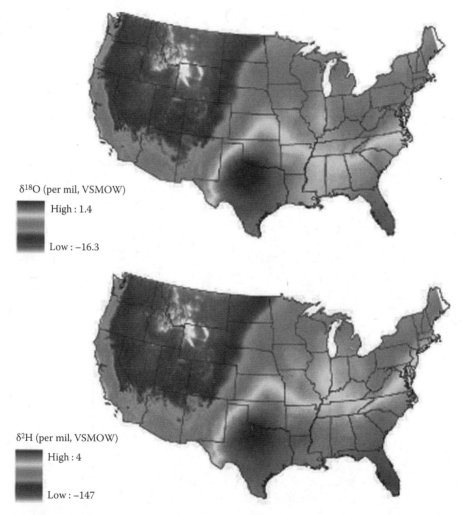

$\delta^{18}O$ (per mil, VSMOW)

High : 1.4

Low : −16.3

$\delta^{2}H$ (per mil, VSMOW)

High : 4

Low : −147

Figure 8.1 (See companion CD for colour figure.) The predicted average oxygen and hydrogen isotope ratios of human body water across the continental United States. (Reprinted with permission from Springer Science + Business Media: *Isoscapes: Understanding Movement, Pattern, and Process on Earth through Isotope Mapping*, A framework for the incorporation of isotopes and isoscapes in geospatial forensic investigations, 2010, Ehleringer, J. R., Thompson, A. H., Podlesak, D., Bowen, G. J., Chesson, L. A., Cerling, T. E., Park, T., Dostie, P., and Schwarcz, H., West, J. B., Bowen, G. J., Dawson, T. E., and Tu, K. P. eds.)

the predicted isotopic composition of human body water across continental United States, which varies geographically because the isotopic composition of the input signal (drinking water) varies based on location. Forensic investigators can use precipitation maps, and more recently tap water maps, in conjunction with the isotopic content of body tissues to make predictions about the provenance and/or recent geographic travels of an individual (Ehleringer et al., 2008a; Podlesak et al., 2012).

Within the body, metabolic processes lead to fractionation and differential retention of molecular components of food and drink (Hedges et al., 2007). The effect of these processes is particularly evident when studying trophic levels, with primary producers having a different isotopic signature from consumers. Nitrogen (N) isotopes demonstrate the most dramatic fractionation, with a consumer's tissues typically being isotopically heavier relative to diet (Ambrose and Norr, 1993; Schoeninger, 1985; Schoeninger and DeNiro, 1984). Similar to water, the isotopic ratios of the foods we consume are incorporated into our body tissues and can be analysed to determine whether an individual was vegetarian (consumed mainly primary producers) or had a significant amount of meat in their diet (ate mainly consumers) (Nakamura et al., 1982; Sponheimer et al., 2003). We note that carbon isotopes in foods are also subject to fractionation, which is ultimately linked to plant photosynthesis, as carbon (C) atoms from CO_2 in the atmosphere are converted to sugars. The fractionation processes associated with plants using different photosynthetic pathways (e.g. C_3, C_4 and CAM) were discussed in detail previously (Meier Augenstein, 2007).

In addition to light stable isotopes, the isotopes of heavy elements, such as strontium (Sr) and lead (Pb), may also provide useful information during investigations of human identification. Considering Sr in particular, the measurement of $^{87}Sr/^{86}Sr$ within a material can reveal geographic location, as Sr from the local bedrock and ecosystem substitutes for Ca in bioapatite (Beard and Johnson, 2000; Schwarcz et al., 2010). Unlike the light elements, there is typically no mass-dependent fractionation of Sr isotopes during incorporation from the environment into tissue (Capo et al., 1998).

Measurement and Instrumentation

Measured isotope data are generally reported as 'delta' values (δ; see the succeeding text for definition) and are ratios that compare the isotopic composition of a sample to that of an internationally accepted standard (Table 8.1). The standard for carbon is Vienna-Pee Dee Belemnite (VPDB), hydrogen and oxygen δ values are reported relative to Vienna Standard Mean Ocean Water (VSMOW), and the standard for sulphur is Vienna Canyon Diablo Troilite (VCDT) (Ambrose and Norr, 1993; Hoefs, 2009; van der Merwe et al., 2003). These international standards are preferred over other standards, as they imply that the measurements have been calibrated in accordance with the International Atomic Energy Agency (IAEA) guidelines. Rather than using international standards during sample measurement, SIA laboratories generally use secondary reference materials that are traceable to IAEA standards, which are cross-checked with other laboratories (Coplen, 2011; Ehleringer and Matheson, 2010).

The delta value is expressed in parts per thousand (‰) difference compared to the appropriate international standard. This is calculated for (as an example) oxygen as follows:

$$\delta^{18}O = \frac{{}^{18}O/{}^{16}O_{sample} - {}^{18}O/{}^{16}O_{standard}}{{}^{18}O/{}^{16}O_{standard}} \times 1000\,(‰)$$

Delta values are reported as either higher (enriched in the heavier isotope) or lower (depleted in the heavier isotope) when compared with a standard (Coplen, 2011; Kendall and Coplen, 2001). For example, if a sample is calculated to have a δ value of +10‰, then it is 10 parts in 1000 enriched in ^{18}O when compared with the standard. If the δ value is −10‰ $\delta^{18}O$, then it is 10 parts in 1000 depleted in ^{18}O compared to the standard. The resulting value is multiplied by 1000 as the difference in abundance of two isotopes is often small, with the measured variation beginning in the second or third decimal digit (Coplen, 2011; Schoeller, 1999).

Isotope analysis is traditionally performed via isotope ratio mass spectrometry (IRMS) using a highly specialised and sensitive type of mass spectrometer (Hoefs, 2009). Isotopic variability can also be measured using infrared isotope ratio spectroscopy (IRIS), which is currently capable of analysing H and O isotopes in water (Lis et al., 2008; Morrison et al., 2001) or C isotopes in carbon dioxide (Murnick and Peer, 1994). Regardless of analytical technique used, samples must first be converted to a gaseous form via combustion or pyrolysis, and the various isotopes within the resultant gas/gases are measured in separate detectors. Instrumentation has developed significantly over recent years, from large machines requiring samples to undergo manual conversion, separation and injection by the operator (Benson et al., 2006) to fully automated and mobile equipment that requires relatively little maintenance or training to operate (Lis et al., 2008). This advancement in technology has eliminated most external manipulation, minimising both expense and instances of contamination (Meier-Augenstein and Liu, 2004).

While the earlier text has focused primarily on the SIA of 'light' elements (e.g. H, C, N, O, S), the analysis of heavy elements (e.g. Sr, Pb) is also becoming more routine. In addition, it is now possible to analyse the isotopic composition of specific compounds contained within an aggregated material rather than conducting a bulk analysis of all atoms of an element present in the sample (Meier Augenstein, 2007). Heavy-element and compound-specific isotope analyses often require additional preparative processes and instrument peripherals. The benefits garnered from the increased time and expense associated with these analytical techniques depend on the question of interest to the investigator. With the application of SIA in forensic casework increasing, it is essential that research designed to develop measurement instrumentation continues.

Forensic Applications of Stable Isotope Analysis

The application of SIA in scientific studies has its roots in biology (Plentl and Schoenheimer, 1944) and geochemistry (Ault and Kulp, 1959) but today is also widely used in hydrology (Gat and Issar, 1974; Worden et al., 2007; Yamanaka et al., 2007) establishing food webs (Michener and Schell, 1994; Schmidt et al., 2007) and determining photosynthetic pathways (Cousins et al., 2007), archaeological research (Hedges et al., 2007; Macko et al., 1999a) and animal migration studies (Hobson, 1999, 2005; Hobson and Wassenaar, 2008). The diversity of applications for SIA has increased substantially over the past 20 years, especially with the development of new analytical techniques and increasingly sophisticated and precise analytical technology.

SIA is a particularly useful tool for forensic investigators, as it is able to provide information suggestive of the geographic, biological and/ or chemical origin of a material under observation and can distinguish between two seemingly 'identical' materials (Meier Augenstein, 2007). In essence, SIA is an invaluable means for providing comparative analysis of materials of interest in forensic casework. These materials have included wooden safety matches (Farmer et al., 2009), architectural paint (Reidy et al., 2005), packaging tape (Carter et al., 2004; Horacek et al., 2008) and other plastic packaging materials (Idoine et al., 2005; Taylor et al., 2008), drug-based samples (Ehleringer et al., 1999; Hurley et al., 2010; West et al., 2009), explosive materials (Ader et al., 2001; Barnette et al., 2011) and adulterated foodstuffs (Padovan et al., 2003; Roßmann et al., 1998).

Applications of Stable Isotope Analysis for Human Identification

SIA may be especially useful during modern forensic investigations involving unidentified human remains, particularly when traditional investigative approaches such as fingerprinting or DNA analysis have been unsuccessful. The vast majority of human-based isotope research has its origin in medicine (Matwiyoff and Ott, 1973), archaeology (Cerling et al., 1997; DeNiro, 1985) and paleoanthropology (Bocherens et al., 2007; Longinelli, 1984). These foundational studies have drawn conclusions by utilising the isotopic content of a number of human tissues including bone, teeth, nails and hair

(DeNiro, 1985; Nakamura et al., 1982; Wright and Schwarcz, 1999), which act as recorders that preserve information about the individual's environmental and health conditions as well as dietary and beverage inputs (West et al., 2006). Essentially 'we are what we eat (and drink)' (Cerling et al., 2003), and the isotopic compositions of food and water consumed are incorporated into the body tissues (Fraser and Meier-Augenstein, 2007; van der Merwe and Vogel, 1978; Sharp et al., 2003; Vogel and van der Merwe, 1977).

The well-documented variation in the growth rate of human tissues means that isotopic analysis of several tissues can allow investigators to construct a chronology of events and document geographic movement (Wilson and Gilbert, 2007). SIA is an important technique for human identification, as it allows an investigator to potentially exploit the relationships between the isotopic content of an individual's diet, the isotopic composition of their body tissues and their provenance and/or recent travels to understand a victim's history prior to death (Cerling et al., 2003; Ehleringer et al., 2008a). Although isotope analysis cannot provide an outright identification, it can provide new leads and narrow search options (e.g. by excluding particular geographic regions from a search) (Meier-Augenstein and Fraser, 2008).

The isotopic compositions of the light elements C, N and S are directly related to dietary inputs (DeNiro and Epstein, 1978, 1981; Minagawa, 1992; Peterson and Fry, 1987) and nutritional stress (Hatch et al., 2006; Mekota et al., 2006; Petzke et al., 2010). They may also indicate lifestyle choices such as a high-protein diet or if an individual was a vegetarian or vegan (O'Connell et al., 2001; O'Connell and Hedges, 1999a; Petzke et al., 2005). For example, the $\delta^{13}C$ value of mineralised tissues such as bone or tooth apatite records the average carbon isotopic composition of all dietary inputs (i.e. carbohydrates, lipids and proteins), while collagen $\delta^{13}C$ values in the protein fraction of bone and tooth dentin are biased toward the protein component of the diet. Because dietary consumption patterns can vary due to cultural and geographic differences (Speedy, 2003), tissue $\delta^{13}C$, $\delta^{15}N$ and $\delta^{34}S$ values may also be useful for estimating geographic origin.

The light elements hydrogen (H) and oxygen (O) record the isotopic composition of drinking water, other water-based beverages, food and inhaled diatomic O_2 (see Ehleringer et al. 2010 and references therein). The δ^2H and $\delta^{18}O$ values of water vary predictably and systematically across the globe, and their covariation can be described by a global meteoric water line (GMWL) (Bowen et al., 2007; Bowen and Revenaugh, 2003; Craig, 1961; Dansgaard, 1964). Thus, H/O isotope analysis is particularly useful for investigating human provenance through the isotopic composition of water recorded by a tissue. Similarly, tissue $^{87}Sr/^{86}Sr$ records information about the local geology of an individual (Åberg, 1995; Beard and Johnson, 2000; Capo et al., 1998; see also Schwarcz et al., 2010 and references therein). As an example, the comparisons of $^{87}Sr/^{86}Sr$ ratios between tooth enamel and bone bioapatite may be able to indicate whether an individual moved from their natal location.

Sample Quality Measures and General Preparation Guidelines

One of the major areas of research in SIA for human identification is the evaluation of sample integrity. There are a number of quality assurance criteria for isotope analyses of bone collagen as well as bone and enamel bioapatite. In most modern forensic cases, chemical alteration of bone and tooth samples (termed diagenesis) is minimal given the short time frame since death. The degree of interaction between groundwater and human remains and the effect of soil pH and microbial activity are major factors influencing diagenesis of bones and teeth (Lee-Thorp, 2002; Lee-Thorp and van der Merwe, 1987; Lee-Thorp and Sponheimer, 2003; Sullivan and Krueger, 1981). Diagenesis of forensic samples is a potential source of error during data interpretation that should be addressed to ensure measured isotope values are recording a biogenic signal, particularly for skeletonised remains recovered from surface or buried contexts. This section discusses the human tissues typically used for SIA in forensic cases, sample quality measures and general sample preparation methods.

Human Tissues Suitable for Stable Isotope Analysis

Stable isotope analyses can be conducted on any human tissue, although studies generally target specific tissues such as the keratin in hair and nails, bone collagen, and bone and tooth bioapatite (Ambrose, 1993; Fry, 2006; Meier-Augenstein, 2010). As mentioned previously, tissues such as hair and nails provide information on recent diet and mobility patterns and represent an incremental growth record (Ehleringer et al., 2008a; Fraser et al., 2006; Meier Augenstein, 2007; Valenzuela et al., 2011). In contrast, bioapatite of tooth enamel provides a permanent record of diet and geographic location at the time of tooth formation (e.g. infancy/childhood through adolescence depending on the specific tooth), and the isotopic content of bone reflects an individual's dietary intake over the past several years of life.

Bone has both an organic (e.g. collagen) and inorganic (e.g. bioapatite) fraction, each of which reflects the isotopic composition of different dietary components. Controlled feeding experiments using rodents and pigs have demonstrated that carbon atoms from dietary protein are preferentially routed to bone collagen, whereas the carbonate in bone bioapatite equilibrates with bicarbonate in the blood (Ambrose and Norr, 1993; Howland et al., 2003;

Passey et al., 2005). Bioapatite therefore reflects the whole diet, including proteins, carbohydrates and lipids (Ambrose and Norr, 1993; Howland et al., 2003; Passey et al., 2005; Tieszen and Fagre, 1993). Building upon this, Kellner and Schoeninger (2007) derived three regression lines for predicting diet type based on the relationship between bioapatite and collagen $\delta^{13}C$ values. These models allow greater discrimination between the relative contributions of different dietary macronutrients (also see revised model in Froehle et al., 2010).

Additionally, it is essential that investigators recognise that bone is constantly being generated and resorbed over an individual's lifetime in a process called 'remodelling'. As a result, the SIA of bones provides a bulk average of diet and mobility history accumulated over several years (e.g. 5 years for adult rib bones and 20–25 years for a femoral midshaft [Hedges et al., 2007; Meier-Augenstein, 2010]). In light of this observation, Meier-Augenstein (2010) recommends sampling both the inner (endosteal) and outer (periosteal) surfaces of a long bone (e.g. femoral midshaft) to provide two time periods of migration history and diet, with the inner surface representing more recently formed bone. Additional research is needed to explore isotopic differences between the endosteal and periosteal surfaces of different long bones based on inter-elemental variation in remodelling rates.

Diagenesis of Organic Materials: Bone Collagen and Hair and Fingernail Keratin

Although in vivo stable isotope values are often preserved in bone collagen exposed to a range of conditions (Ambrose, 1993; Dobberstein et al., 2009; van Klinken, 1999), human hair and nails are less likely to survive after death due to biodegradation in outdoor contexts (Rowe, 1997). Accepted sample quality indicators for hair and nails have not been extensively studied, although atomic C/N ratios for modern hair should fall between 3.0 and 3.8 (O'Connell et al., 2001; O'Connell and Hedges, 1999b). The effects of storage containers and length of storage may have an effect on stable isotope values (Fraser et al., 2008). Glass vials with a secured crimp-sealed lid are recommended as opposed to plastic or paper storage containers, as these may introduce contamination through isotopic exchange with tissue samples.

Atomic C/N bone collagen ratios that fall within 2.9–3.6 (DeNiro, 1985) and percentage collagen yields above 1%–2% are indicative of adequate collagen preservation (Ambrose, 1993; van Klinken, 1999). Bivariate plots showing a correlation between these sample quality indicators and stable isotope values are useful for highlighting potential sample diagenesis. Atomic C/N values less than 2.9 likely reflect non-collagenous material, and values greater than 3.6 indicate probable contamination by humic acids (Ambrose, 1993). In addition to these sample quality indicators, histological analysis of bone can reveal the presence of intact microstructure, and additional measures of protein content (%N) and porosity can shed light on other aspects of bone preservation (Nielsen-Marsh and Hedges, 2000a). For poorly preserved bone samples, a more extensive assessment of diagenesis should be undertaken to ensure a high level of sample quality.

Organic Sample Preparation

Preparation of hair keratin samples generally involves treatment with a methanol/chloroform mixture to remove surficial lipids or residual styling products (O'Connell et al., 2001) and is followed by drying in an oven under a vacuum. To reconstruct changes in location, drinking water and diet, hair samples are sectioned into 1–1.5 cm pieces (1 cm equals approximately 1 month of growth). Sectioned and weighed hair samples are then dried prior to SIA to remove sorbed water (Bowen et al., 2005; Meier-Augenstein, 2010). For stable hydrogen isotope analysis, several days are needed for labile hydrogen to equilibrate with water vapour in the laboratory atmosphere prior to sample sectioning (Bowen et al., 2005; Ehleringer et al., 2008a; Meier-Augenstein, 2010). The fraction of exchangeable hydrogen atoms within a sample can be determined using a conversion equation for the ratio of the difference in δ^2H values for the laboratory hair standard versus the water sources of exchangeable atoms (Bowen et al., 2005; Meier-Augenstein, 2010). Nail keratin samples are subjected to a similar procedure to hair, although additional manual and ultrasonic cleaning may be necessary to remove contaminants (O'Connell et al., 2001), and sectioned pieces may be smaller due to the slower growth rate.

There are several protocols used to extract the 'collagen fraction' from bone, which actually includes both collagenous proteins and a small fraction of non-collagenous proteins (Ambrose, 1990). Cortical bone is typically preferred over trabecular (cancellous) bone, as it is more resistant to diagenesis and easier to clean (Ambrose, 1993), especially when bone has been buried or exposed to environmental contaminants for an extended period of time. For cortical bone, the external and internal surfaces (e.g. periosteal and endosteal) are mechanically cleaned using a Dremel tool with a diamond-studded drill bit. Further removal of contaminants can be achieved using ultrasonic cleaning baths containing distilled–deionised water and ethanol. Bone samples can be demineralised either as intact chunks or as a fine powder (Ambrose, 1990, 1993; Bell et al., 2001) using a dilute solution of hydrochloric acid (HCl) or ethylenediaminetetraacetic acid (EDTA) to remove the mineral fraction (Ambrose, 1993). Sodium hydroxide (NaOH) treatment is usually effective in removing humic acids and other contaminants introduced from the burial environment and can also remove lipids from bone. As lipid $\delta^{13}C$ values are typically 6‰–12‰ lighter than collagen, additional treatment with a methanol/chloroform mixture is recommended for modern bone samples (Ambrose, 1990, 1993; DeNiro and Epstein, 1977). Following treatment, collagen pseudomorphs are solubilised in a weak acid solution and heated to ~95°C. The gelatinised collagen is then centrifuged or filtrated, frozen and lyophilised (Ambrose, 1993).

Diagenesis of Inorganic Materials: Bone and Tooth Bioapatite

In contrast to collagen, bone bioapatite is much more susceptible to diagenetic exchange with the burial environment, especially with groundwater calcium carbonates ($CaCO_3$) (Ambrose, 1993; Koch et al., 1997; Lee-Thorp and van der Merwe, 1987, 1991; Wright and Schwarcz, 1996). Bioapatite of tooth enamel is more resilient to diagenesis due to its smaller pore diameter and more tightly packed crystals, making it ideal for the analysis of fossilised remains. There are several common sample quality indicators for the evaluation of bioapatite, including mineral percentage yield after sodium hypochlorite treatment and the carbonate content (C/P) and bioapatite crystallinity (infrared splitting factor, IRSF) measured with Fourier transform infrared spectroscopy (FTIR). FTIR measures both crystalline structure—including composition, strain, relative size and degree of crystal organisation—and mineralogical properties in bioapatite (Berna et al., 2004; LeGeros, 1981). The C/P ratio and IRSF are often inversely related in diagenetically altered samples (e.g. a low C/P ratio corresponds to a high IRSF ratio), providing parameters for evaluating bioapatite sample quality (Nielsen-Marsh and Hedges, 2000b). FTIR can also be used to detect other diagenetic carbonates present in bioapatite samples (Koch et al., 1997; Lee-Thorp and van der Merwe, 1991). For strontium isotopes in particular, isotope ratios in bone bioapatite may reflect contamination from the local geology instead of a biogenic signal (Price et al., 2002). Other methods for evaluating diagenesis in bioapatite include transmission electron microscopy, x-ray diffraction, small-angle x-ray scattering and the relationship between oxygen isotopes in bioapatite phosphate and carbonate (Pellegrini et al., 2011).

Inorganic Sample Preparation

Mechanical preparation of bioapatite follows the same initial cleaning procedures as for collagen (i.e. Dremel tool with a diamond-studded drill bit, ultrasonic cleaning). Bone or tooth enamel samples are crushed into a fine powder using a mortar and pestle, or alternatively, powder is drilled directly from a cleaned surface. For preparing carbonate from bone bioapatite, the collagen fraction is removed using a sodium hypochlorite (NaOCl) solution. Once thoroughly rinsed, samples are treated with an acetic acid solution to remove diagenetic contaminants from the burial environment.

Different researchers have used a variety of treatment concentrations, including a 1.0 M solution, a 1.0 M acetate-buffered solution and a 0.1 M solution, which have shown negligible differences in some studies of archaeological bone and tooth samples (Garvie-Lok et al., 2004; Koch et al., 1997; Yoder and Bartelink, 2010). Treatment times reported in the literature vary from 4 to 36 h, depending on whether or not bone or tooth samples are fossilised and other preservation factors (Balasse et al., 2002; Bocherens, 2000; Lee-Thorp et al., 1997; Nielsen-Marsh and Hedges, 2000b). Strong treatment concentrations and longer treatment times may result in recrystallisation of bioapatite and may shift stable isotope values (Nielsen-Marsh and Hedges, 2000a,b). Stable oxygen isotope values can also be measured in the phosphate fraction of bioapatite, which is less susceptible to diagenesis than the carbonate fraction due to the stronger P–O (as opposed to C–O) bonds. However, sample preparation is more complex, and this approach is ideally suited for more poorly preserved samples likely affected by diagenesis.

For Sr isotope analysis in particular, tooth enamel (with dentin removed) and bone bioapatite samples are mechanically and ultrasonically cleaned and then digested in an ultrapure nitric acid (HNO_3) solution (Price et al., 2006). Strontium within the digest is collected and purified using resin columns. Purified Sr can be analysed either via thermal-ionisation mass spectrometry (TIMS) or multi-collector inductively coupled plasma mass spectrometry (MC-ICP-MS).

Applications of Stable Isotope Analysis for Human Identification

We next discuss the SIA of both light and heavy elements for human identification and investigating human provenance, focusing on published case studies. Many of the case studies sought to aid investigators in narrowing potential regions of origin for an individual by answering questions related to his or her history: Did the individual move prior to death? Did the individual change diet before death? Do the travel and/or dietary histories suggest that the individual was a resident of a particular region?

Using Multiple Tissues to Reconstruct History

The time period recorded by human tissues commonly collected during forensic investigations varies depending upon tissue type. Consider hard keratinised hair and nail tissues, which grow at a relatively constant—albeit different (1 cm/month vs. 1.5–3 mm/month, respectively [Lehn et al., 2011])—rate and do not isotopically change after growth (Auerwald et al., 2011; Fraser et al., 2008). Due to their constant rates of growth, hair and nails are serial recorders of sequential changes in isotopic composition for many elements, including H and O (O'Brien and Wooller, 2007; Sharp et al., 2003) as well as C and N (Huelsemann et al., 2009; Nardoto et al., 2006). The time periods recorded by these tissues are directly related to (1) the length and (2) the delay between a change in drinking water or diet and the incorporation of isotopes into the tissue. On the other hand, bones are slowly remodelled after formation, and the period of history recorded in skeletal tissues by H and O (Cormie et al., 1994), C (Passey et al., 2005; Schwarcz et al., 2010) and Sr (Beard and Johnson, 2000) can represent several years. Tooth enamel offers a 'snapshot' from an individual's childhood when enamel formed and incorporated isotopes (C, O and Sr) from his or her dietary and drinking water inputs (Daux et al., 2008; Juarez, 2008; Longinelli, 1984; Luz et al., 1984).

The choice to analyse one particular tissue *versus* another is often related to the time period of most interest to the investigator. For example, the SIA of hair from the last year of an individual's life for O can reveal his or her movements just prior to death. This recent record can then be compared to the O SIA of tooth enamel (using the known formation age of the tooth) to determine where the individual might have been born and raised. Detailed descriptions of this type of time period comparison can be found elsewhere (Chesson et al., in press; Ehleringer et al., 2010).

In some instances, however, investigators may choose to analyse one tissue instead of another, such as cases involving incomplete skeletal remains or samples compromised by diagenesis. In these situations, it is important for investigators to understand how each human tissue records the isotopic signals related to diet, drinking water and environment. Research has demonstrated that the isotopic composition of fingernails differs from that of hair from the same individual, even when various growth rates are considered (Fraser et al., 2006; Fraser and Meier-Augenstein, 2007; Lehn et al., 2011; O'Connell et al., 2001). This difference may be related to the more complex and slower formation of nail keratin than hair keratin (Fraser et al., 2006; Lehn et al., 2011), which led Fraser and Meier-Augenstein (2007) to conclude that hair δ^2H values better reflected drinking water isotope composition than nails. Similarly, Lehn et al. (2011) concluded that the $\delta^{13}C$, $\delta^{15}N$ and $\delta^{34}S$ values of hair were more reliable recorders of dietary inputs than nails.

In extreme cases, material for origin investigation via SIA may be highly altered from its original condition, as in the cremation of human bones for burial, due to a disaster, or during the concealment of a homicide. Recent work by Harbeck et al. (2011) focused on understanding the isotopic effect of cremation on bones. At temperatures less than 200°C, the measured $\delta^{13}C$, $\delta^{15}N$ and $\delta^{18}O$ values of heated bones were unchanged but became more negative as higher temperatures were reached. In contrast, Sr isotopes within bone were unaffected by heating, even at a temperature of 1000°C (Harbeck et al., 2011). Another experimental study by Schurr et al. (2008) found no change in bone collagen $\delta^{13}C$ values at temperatures up to 300°C, although $\delta^{15}N$ values were more positive by approximately 6‰.

Investigation of Suspected Migrants

Most investigations into human migration using SIA have focused on pre-historic populations, as evidenced by the publications of multiple archaeological case studies (e.g. Hodell et al., 2004; Price et al., 2002; Schwarcz et al., 2010). The SIA of hair has been used to investigate novel questions such as the sequence of events preceding the ritual killing of four *capacocha* Incan children discovered as mummified bodies located atop mountain peaks. These children were determined to be of highland origin, prepared for sacrifice with a diet of higher-status foods and relocated up to 1420 km prior to sacrifice (Wilson et al., 2007). The C, N and S isotopic composition of hair from the Iceman Ötzi discovered in the Italian Alps in 1991 corroborated tooth wear evidence that suggested he had a primarily vegetarian diet prior to death (Macko et al., 1999a,b), while O and Sr isotope data revealed he may have been a seasonal migrant in areas near his original birthplace (Müller et al., 2003). On a larger scale, Sr isotope analysis has proven useful in understanding the origin of the buried dead at the Trelleborg fortress in Denmark; 32 of 48 investigated individuals likely emigrated from outside Scandinavia to live, work and die under Harald Bluetooth's rule in the tenth century AD (Price et al., 2011).

Despite its rich history in investigations of historic human migrations, there has been relatively little application of SIA in case studies to investigate the origins of modern migrants. Juarez (2008) used $^{87}Sr/^{86}Sr$ to create a model to identify deceased suspected migrants from Mexico to the United States and found three regions within Mexico characterised by significantly different Sr isotope compositions. Bol et al. (2007) measured C, N, O and S in hair collected from recent 'migrants' to a town in England and found that these newly arrived individuals could be discriminated from the local population on the basis of hair isotopic composition. Similarly, the combination of multiple elements (C, O, Sr, Pb) contained within tooth enamel appears useful for categorising individuals as of East Asian or US origin (Regan, 2006). This approach was successfully used in a recent case study from a plane crash site related to the Vietnam War, in which stable carbon isotopes of enamel bioapatite identified a single tooth fragment as being of US origin (Holland et al., 2012).

Investigation of Remains Recovered in a Criminal Case

To the best of our knowledge and based on a review of published literature, there exist only three closed criminal cases involving the discovery of human remains that have used SIA (Chesson et al., in press; Meier-Augenstein and Fraser, 2008; Rauch et al., 2007), though additional open cases have been described (Ehleringer et al., 2010; Kennedy et al., 2011; Meier Augenstein, 2007). For one victim (Mary Alice Wiley; Chesson et al., in press), SIA played a supporting role by identifying potential search regions for law enforcement officers investigating a 'Jane Doe' case (i.e. remains of an unidentified victim). Isotope measurements corroborated details of the case revealed once the victim was identified through DNA matching with a living relative (Chesson et al., in press). For two other victims, however, SIA played a pivotal role in guiding investigations, leading to the eventual identification—and conviction—of those responsible. These cases are summarised here.

In 2007, Rauch et al. described the SIA of both light and heavy elements to investigate the remains of a male found buried near an autobahn in Germany in 2002. Measured hair and nail δ^{15}N values as well as ^{87}Sr/^{86}Sr ratios of bone from the skull were not inconsistent with local Germans from the region. Hair δ^2H values indicated the victim likely lived away from the coast, and hair δ^{13}C values indicated he had eaten relatively more C_4-based foods than would be expected of a typical German citizen. Measured Pb isotope values of the victim's teeth and skull were high and consistent with regions of the United States and Canada; however, an analysis of dental work revealed the victim was likely not a resident of these North American countries. The high Pb values were also consistent with the Balkan countries, specifically areas near a Romanian mine. A search by Romanian investigators located a possible family for the victim. Further investigation led to a confession by a former friend of the man, who admitted he had shot and killed the victim (Rauch et al., 2007).

In 2008, Meier-Augenstein and Fraser presented a combination of H, O, C and N isotope data for the mutilated remains of a male found in 2005 in Dublin, Ireland. The victim's nail and hair δ^{15}N and δ^{13}C values revealed he had consumed a protein-rich diet prior to death, but his diet contained little to no C_4-based foods (Meier-Augenstein and Frasier, 2008). Measured nail and hair δ^2H and δ^{18}O values suggested he had not moved in the 7 months preceding death and had likely lived in or around Dublin (or an area of Ireland with similar water δ^2H and δ^{18}O values). However, the measured δ^{18}O value of bone apatite was high and suggested the victim was not a native of Dublin and may have emigrated from an equatorial environment with a hot climate within the last 10 years. The isotope results were used as justification by investigators for completing DNA analysis of a potential offspring of the victim. The victim was eventually identified as the boyfriend of the child's mother. Originally from Kenya, the man had moved to Ireland 7 years prior to his death and was killed at the hands of his girlfriend's daughters, who were convicted of homicide in 2006 (Meier Augenstein and Fraser, 2008).

Conclusions

Summary

The use of SIA in forensic investigations of human provenance is rapidly expanding, and the technique has the potential to become a regularly employed forensic analytical tool. In this chapter, we have summarised the traditional and emerging novel applications of SIA for reconstructing the geographic and mobility patterns of humans. We have presented details about the elements most often used in human provenance SIA, described the commonly utilised instruments and standards and discussed quality control assessment of samples. Finally, we have summarised a number of case studies demonstrating the power and promise of SIA for investigating human origin in both historic and modern settings.

Limitations

Despite the potential utility of SIA for understanding human provenance, we note that the application of this analytical technique is very limited in comparison to other forensic investigation methods, such as DNA or fingerprint analysis. This is in part because SIA is not yet a routine technique, and many members of the public and the legal system are not familiar with its application. For example, the two forensic case studies cited earlier are the only published accounts where SIA has played a pivotal role in solving a crime (Meier-Augenstein and Fraser, 2008; Rauch et al., 2007).

The fairly limited application of SIA for human identification in the forensic setting is also due in part to challenges related to measurement and data interpretation. Much of the instrumentation required for SIA is large and expensive to purchase and operate. Often the SIA of multiple elements is more useful than the analysis of a single element, increasing costs and making interpretation more complex. The answers to provenance questions provided by SIA are not precise to neighbourhood or even city scale and have the greatest potential for excluding possible source regions. In addition, the interpretation of measured data is often hampered by a lack of verified datasets that can be used for comparison or to generate and test predictions.

Promising Future Research Directions

The publication of several recent reviews of SIA in peer-reviewed scientific journals (Aggarwal et al., 2008; Benson et al., 2006; NicDaeid et al., 2010) and books (Ehleringer et al., 2007, 2008b, 2010; Meier Augenstein, 2007, 2010) is a sign that the application of this technique for human identification is growing. Specifically related to the use of SIA in legal settings, Ehleringer and Matheson Jr. (2010) published a guide for the US courts that describes the due diligence incumbent upon the legal system to certify the appropriateness of stable isotope measurements in criminal cases, especially in regard to meeting the Federal Rules of Evidence and *Daubert* standards. Gentile et al. (2011) also recently published a framework for the methodical application of SIA within forensic settings. Both works are invaluable for members of the court and criminal justice system interested in using SIA.

Related to analytical measurement barriers, a new generation of inexpensive, field-portable instruments using laser spectroscopy (Berden et al., 2000; Crosson, 2008; Lis et al., 2008; O'Keefe and Deacon, 1988) rather than mass spectrometry is poised to revolutionise the way analysts make isotope measurements. Data interpretation is becoming more straightforward, as groups begin to collect datasets of authentic, known-origin samples with which to compare data generated during the investigation of criminal cases (e.g. Ehleringer et al., 2008a; Fraser et al., 2006; Juarez, 2008; Rauch et al., 2007; Regan, 2006; Thompson et al., 2010; Valenzuela et al., 2011, 2012). In addition, there is an increasing number of models that can be used for interpreting measured isotope data from human tissues with some *a priori* assumptions of the relationships between geographic origin and tissue isotopic compositions, including human hair (Ehleringer et al., 2008a), tooth enamel (Ehleringer et al., 2010) and body water (Podlesak et al., 2012). These models are especially relevant when authentic comparison samples are scarce, and the recent development of probabilistic methods to assign likelihood estimates for predicted regions of origin has expanded the application of these models beyond answering simple 'yes or no' questions of provenance (Kennedy et al., 2011; Wunder, 2010).

As forensic applications of SIA continue to expand, the scientific community has formed intensive research collaborations to develop new methods. From 2001 to 2005, the European Union funded the Natural Isotopes and Trace Elements in Criminalistics and Environmental Forensics (NITE-CRIME) project to investigate the utility of isotopes for forensic investigations. The Forensics Isotope Ratio Mass Spectrometry (FIRMS) Network was founded to specifically 'develop the scope of stable isotope techniques in forensic applications' (http://www.forensic-isotopes.org/index.html). Considered in sum, the future of SIA for human provenance appears extremely promising.

Acknowledgments

We would like to acknowledge Melanie Beasley (University of California at San Diego) and Karen Gardner, Amy MacKinnon and Stefanie Kline (California State University, Chico) for reviewing an earlier draft of this chapter and providing invaluable feedback.

References

Åberg, G. (1995). The use of natural strontium isotopes as tracers in environmental studies. *Water, Air and Soil Pollution,* 79, 309–322.

Ader, M., Coleman, M. L., Doyle, S. P., Stroud, M., and Wakelin, D. (2001). Methods for the stable isotopic analysis of chlorine in chlorate and perchlorate compounds. *Analytical Chemistry,* 73, 4946–4950.

Aggarwal, J., Habicht-Mauche, J., and Juarez, C. (2008). Application of heavy stable isotopes in forensic isotope geochemistry: A review. *Applied Geochemistry,* 23, 2658–2666.

Ambrose, S. H. (1990). Preparation and characterization of bone and tooth collagen for isotopic analysis. *Journal of Archaeological Science,* 17, 431–451.

Ambrose, S. H. (1993). Isotopic analysis of paleodiets: Methodological and interpretive considerations. In: Sanford, M. K. (ed.) *Investigations of Ancient Human Tissues: Chemical Analyses in Anthropology.* Langhorne, PA: Gordon and Breach Science Publishers. pp. 59–130.

Ambrose, S. H. and Norr, L. (1993). Experimental evidence for the relationship of the carbon isotopes ratios of whole diet and dietary protein to those of bone collagen and carbonate. In: Lambert, J. B. and Grupe, G. (eds.) *Prehistoric Human Bone: Archaeology at the Molecular Level.* Berlin, Germany: Springer-Verlag. pp. 1–37.

Auerwald, K., Rossmann, A., Schäufele, R., Schwertl, M., Monahan, F. J., and Schnyder, H. (2011). Does natural weathering change the stable isotope composition (^{2}H, ^{13}C, ^{15}N, ^{18}O and ^{34}S) of cattle hair? *Rapid Communications in Mass Spectrometry,* 25, 3741–3748.

Ault, W. U. and Kulp, J. L. (1959). Isotopic geochemistry of sulphur. *Geochimica et Cosmochimica Acta,* 16, 201–235.

Balasse, M., Ambrose, S. H., Smith, A. B., and Price, T. D. (2002). The seasonal mobility model for prehistoric herders in the south-western cape of South Africa assessed by isotopic analysis of sheep tooth enamel. *Journal of Archaeological Science,* 29, 917–932.

Barnette, J. E., Lott, M. J., Howa, J. D., Podlesak, D. W., and Ehleringer, J. R. (2011). Hydrogen and oxygen isotope values in hydrogen peroxide. *Rapid Communications in Mass Spectrometry,* 25, 1422–1428.

Beard, B. L. and Johnson, C. M. (2000). Strontium isotope composition of skeletal material can determine the birth place and geographic mobility of humans and animals. *Journal of Forensic Sciences,* 45, 1049–1061.

Bell, L. S., Cox, G., and Sealy, J. (2001). Determining isotopic life history trajectories using bone density fractionation and stable isotope measurements: A new approach. *American Journal of Physical Anthropology,* 116, 66–79.

Benson, S. J., Lennard, C., Maynard, P., and Roux, C. (2006). Forensic applications of isotope ratio mass spectrometry—A review. *Forensic Science International,* 157, 1–22.

Berden, G., Peeters, R., and Meijer, G. (2000). Cavity ring-down spectroscopy: Experimental schemes and applications. *International Reviews in Physical Chemistry,* 19, 565–607.

Berna, F., Matthews, A., and Weiner, S. (2004). Solubilities of bone mineral from archaeological sites: The recrystallization window. *Journal of Archaeological Science,* 31, 867–882.

Bocherens, H. (2000). Preservation of isotopic signals (^{13}C, ^{15}N) in Pleistocene mammals. In: Ambrose, S. and Katzenberg, M. A. (eds.) *Biogeochemical Approaches to Paleodietary Analysis.* New York: Kluwer Academic/Plenum Publishers. pp. 65–88.

Bocherens, H., Polet, C., and Toussaint, M. (2007). Palaeodiet of Mesolithic and Neolithic populations of Meuse Basin (Belgium): Evidence from stable isotopes. *Journal of Archaeological Science,* 34, 10–27.

Bol, R., Marsh, J., and Heaton, T. (2007). Multiple stable isotope (^{18}O, ^{13}C, ^{15}N and ^{34}S) analysis of human hair to identify the recent migrants to a rural community in SW England. *Rapid Communications in Mass Spectrometry,* 21, 2951–2954.

Bowen, G. J. (2010). Statistical and geostatistical mapping of precipitation water isotope ratios. In: West, J. B., Bowen, G. J., Dawson, T. E., and Tu, K. P. (eds.) *Isoscapes.* Amsterdam, the Netherlands: Springer. pp. 139–160.

Bowen, G. J., Chesson, L., Nielson, K., Cerling, T. E., and Ehleringer, J. R. (2005). Treatment methods for the determination of $\delta^2 H$ and $\delta^{18}O$ of hair keratin by continuous-flow isotope-ratio mass spectrometry. *Rapid Communications in Mass Spectrometry,* 19, 2371–2378.

Bowen, G. J., Ehleringer, J. R., Chesson, L. A., Stange, E., and Cerling, T. E. (2007). Stable isotope ratios of tap water in the contiguous United States. *Water Resources Research,* 43, W03419.

Bowen, G. J. and Revenaugh, J. (2003). Interpolating the isotopic composition of modern meteoric precipitation. *Water Resources Research,* 39, 1299–1311.

Bowen, G. J. and Wilkinson, B. (2002). Spatial distribution of $\delta^{18}O$ in meteoric precipitation. *Geology,* 30, 315–318.

Capo, R. C., Stewart, B. W., and Chadwich, O. A. (1998). Strontium isotopes as tracers of ecosystem processes: Theory and methods. *Geoderma,* 82, 197–225.

Carter, J. F., Grundy, P. L., Hill, J. C., Ronan, N. C., Titterton, E. L., and Sleeman, R. (2004). Forensic isotope ratio mass spectrometry of packaging tapes. *Analyst,* 129, 1206–1210.

Cerling, T. E., Ehleringer, J. R., West, A. G., Stange, E., and Dorigan, J. (2003). Forensic anthropology. *Forensic Science International,* 136, 164–181.

Cerling, T. E., Harris, J. M., Ambrose, S. H., Leakey, M. G., and Solounias, N. (1997). Dietary and environmental reconstruction with stable isotope analyses of herbivore tooth enamel from the Miocene locality of Fort Ternan, Kenya. *Journal of Human Evolution,* 33, 635–650.

Chesson, L. A., Tipple, B. J., Howa, J. D., Bowen, G. J., Barnette, J. E., Cerling, T. E., and Ehleringer, J. R. (in press). 12.24: Stable isotopes in forensic applications. In: Cerling, T. E. (ed.) *Treatise on Geochemistry,* 2nd edn. Oxford, U.K.: Elsevier.

Coplen, T. B. (2011). Guidelines and recommended terms for expression of stable-isotope-ratio and gas-ratio measurement results. *Rapid Communications in Mass Spectrometry,* 25, 2538–2560.

Cormie, A. B., Luz, B., and Schwarcz, H. P. (1994). Relationship between the hydrogen and oxygen isotopes of deer bone and their use in the estimation of relative humidity. *Geochimica et Cosmochimica Acta,* 58, 3439–3449.

Cousins, A. B., Baroli, I., Badger, M. R., Ivakov, A., Lea, P. J., Leegood, R. C., and von Caemmerer, S. (2007). The role of phosphoenolpyruvate carboxylase during C4 photosynthetic isotope exchange and stomatal conductance. *Plant Physiology,* 145, 1006–1017.

Craig, H. (1961). Isotopic variations in meteoric waters. *Science,* 133, 1702–1703.

Crosson, E. R. (2008). A cavity ring-down analyzer for measuring atmospheric levels of methane, carbon dioxide, and water vapor. *Applied Physics B*, 92, 403–408.

Dansgaard, W. (1964). Stable isotopes in precipitation. *Tellus*, 16, 436–468.

Daux, V., Lécuyer, C., Héran, M.-A., Amiot, R., Simon, L., Fourel, F., Martineau, F., Lynnerup, N., Reychler, H., and Escarguel, G. (2008). Oxygen isotope fractionation between human phosphate and water revisited. *Journal of Human Evolution*, 55, 1138–1147.

DeNiro, M. J. (1985). Postmortem preservation and alteration of in vivo bone collagen isotope ratios in relation to palaeodietary reconstruction. *Nature*, 317, 806–809.

DeNiro, M. J. and Epstein, S. (1977). Mechanism of carbon isotope fractionation associated with lipid-synthesis. *Science*, 197, 261–263.

DeNiro, M. J. and Epstein, S. (1978). Influence of diet on the distribution of carbon isotopes in animals. *Geochimica et Cosmochimica Acta*, 42, 495–506.

DeNiro, M. J. and Epstein, S. (1981). Influence of diet on the distribution of nitrogen isotopes in animals. *Geochimica et Cosmochimica Acta*, 45, 341–352.

Dobberstein, R. C., Collins, M. J., Craig, O. E., Taylor, G., Penkman, K. E. H., and Ritz-Timme, S. (2009). Archaeological collagen: Why worry about collagen diagenesis? *Archaeological and Anthropological Sciences*, 1, 31–42.

Ehleringer, J. R., Bowen, G. J., Chesson, L. A., West, A. G., Podlesak, D. W., and Cerling, T. E. (2008a). Hydrogen and oxygen isotope ratios in human hair are related to geography. *Proceedings of the National Academy of Sciences*, 105, 2788–2793.

Ehleringer, J. R., Cerling, T. E., and West, J. B. (2007). Forensic science applications of stable isotope ratio analysis. In: Blackledge, R. D. (ed.) *Forensics Analysis on the Cutting Edge: New Methods for Trace Evidence Analysis*. San Diego, CA: John Wiley & Sons, Inc. pp. 399–422.

Ehleringer, J. R., Cerling, T. E., West, J. B., Podlesak, D. W., Chesson, L. A., and Bowen, G. J. (2008b). Spatial considerations of stable isotope analyses in environmental forensics. In: Hester, R. E. and Harrison, R. M. (eds.) *Environmental Forensics*. Cambridge, U.K.: The Royal Society of Chemistry. pp. 36–53.

Ehleringer, J. R., Cooper, D. A., Lott, M. J., and Cook, C. S. (1999). Geo-location of heroin and cocaine by stable isotope ratios. *Forensic Science International*, 106, 27–35.

Ehleringer, J. R. and Matheson Jr., S. M. (2010). Stable isotopes and the courts. *Utah Law Review*, 2010, 385–442.

Ehleringer, J. R., Thompson, A. H., Podlesak, D., Bowen, G. J., Chesson, L. A., Cerling, T. E., Park, T., Dostie, P., and Schwarcz, H. (2010). A framework for the incorporation of isotopes and isoscapes in geospatial forensic investigations. In: West, J. B., Bowen, G. J., Dawson, T. E., and Tu, K. P. (eds.) *Isoscapes: Understanding Movement, Pattern, and Process on Earth through Isotope Mapping*. Dordrecht, the Netherlands: Springer. pp. 357–387.

Farmer, N., Curran, J., Lucy, N., Nicdaeid, N., and Meier-Augenstein, W. (2009). Stable isotope profiling of burnt wooden safety matches. *Science and Justice*, 49, 107–113.

Fraser, I. and Meier-Augenstein, W. (2007). Stable ^{2}H isotope analysis of modern-day human hair and nails can aid forensic human identification. *Rapid Communications in Mass Spectrometry*, 21, 3279–3285.

Fraser, I., Meier-Augenstein, W., and Kalin, R. M. (2006). The role of stable isotopes in human identification: A longitudinal study into the variability of isotopic signals in human hair and nails. *Rapid Communications in Mass Spectrometry,* 20, 1109–1116.

Fraser, I., Meier-Augenstein, W., and Kalin, R. M. (2008). Stable isotope analysis of human hair and nail samples: The effects of storage on samples. *Journal of Forensic Science,* 53, 95–99.

Froehle, A. W., Kellner, C. M., and Schoeniger, M. J. (2010). Focus: Effect of diet and protein source on carbon stable isotope ratios in collagen: Follow up to Warinner and Tuross (2009). *Journal of Archaeological Science,* 37, 2662–2670.

Fry, B. (2006). *Stable Isotope Ecology.* New York: Springer.

Garvie-Lok, S. J., Varney, T. L., and Katzenberg, M. A. (2004). Preparation of bone carbonate for stable isotope analysis: The effects of treatment time and acid concentration. *Journal of Archaeological Science,* 31, 763–776.

Gat, J. R. and Issar, A. (1974). Desert isotope hydrology: Water sources of the Sinai Desert. *Geochimica et Cosmochimica Acta,* 38, 1117–1131.

Gentile, N., Besson, L., Pazos, D., Delémont, O., and Esseiva, P. (2011). On the use of IRMS in forensic science: Proposals for a methodological approach. *Forensic Science International,* 212, 260–271.

Harbeck, M., Schleuder, R., Schneider, J., Wiechmann, I., Schmahl, W. W., and Grupe, G. (2011). Research potential and limitations of trace analyses of cremated remains. *Forensic Science International,* 204, 191–200.

Hatch, K. A., Crawford, M. A., Kunz, A. W., Thomsen, S. R., Eggett, D. L., Nelson, S. T., and Roeder, B. L. (2006). An objective means of diagnosing anorexia nervosa and bulimia nervosa using $^{15}N/^{14}N$ and $^{13}C/^{12}C$ ratios in hair. *Rapid Communications in Mass Spectrometry,* 20, 3367–3373.

Hedges, R. E. M., Clement, J. G., Thomas, C. D. L., and O'Connell, T. C. (2007). Collagen turnover in the adult femoral mid-shaft: Modeled from anthropogenic radiocarbon tracer measurements. *American Journal of Physical Anthropology,* 133, 808–816.

Hobson, K. A. (1999). Tracing origins and migration of wildlife using stable isotopes: A review. *Oecologia,* 120, 314–326.

Hobson, K. A. (2005). Using stable isotopes to trace long-distance dispersal in birds and other taxa. *Diversity and Distributions,* 11, 157–164.

Hobson, K. A. and Wassenaar, L. I. (2008). *Tracking Animal Migration with Stable Isotopes,* Vol. 2, 1st edn. New York: Elsevier.

Hodell, D. A., Quinn, R. L., Brenner, M., and Kamenov, G. (2004). Spatial variation of strontium isotopes ($^{87}Sr/^{86}Sr$) in the Maya region: A tool for tracking ancient human migration. *Journal of Archaeological Science,* 31, 585–601.

Hoefs, J. (2009). *Stable Isotope Geochemistry,* 6th edn. Berlin, Germany: Springer.

Holland, T. D., Berg, G. E., and Regan, L. A. (2012). Identification of a United States airman using stable isotopes. *Proceedings of the American Academy of Forensic Sciences,* 18, 420–421.

Horacek, M., Min, J., Heo, S., Park, J., and Papesch, W. (2008). The application of isotope ratio mass spectrometry for discrimination and comparison of adhesive tapes. *Rapid Communications in Mass Spectrometry,* 22, 1763–1766.

Howland, M. R., Corr, L. T., Young, S. M. M., Jones, V., Jim, S., van der Merwe, N. J., Mitchell, A. D., and Evershed, R. P. (2003). Expression of the dietary isotope signal in the compound-specific $d^{13}C$ values of pig bone lipids and amino acids. *International Journal of Osteoarchaeology*, 13, 54–65.

Huelsemann, F., Flenker, U., Koehler, K., and Schaenzer, W. (2009). Effect of a controlled dietary change on carbon and nitrogen stable isotope ratios of human hair. *Rapid Communications in Mass Spectrometry*, 23, 2448–2454.

Hurley, J. M., West, J. B., and Ehleringer, J. R. (2010). Stable isotope models to predict geographic origin and cultivation conditions of marijuana. *Science and Justice*, 50, 86–93.

Idoine, F. A., Carter, J. F., and Sleeman, R. (2005). Bulk and compound-specific isotopic characterisation of illicit heroin and cling film. *Rapid Communications in Mass Spectrometry*, 19, 3207–3215.

Juarez, C. A. (2008). Strontium and geolocation, the pathway to identification for deceased undocumented Mexican border-crossers: A preliminary report. *Journal of Forensic Science*, 53, 46–49.

Kellner, C. M. and Schoeninger, M. J. (2007). A simple carbon isotope model for reconstructing prehistoric human diet. *American Journal of Physical Anthropology*, 133, 1112–1127.

Kendall, C. and Coplen, T. B. (2001). Distribution of oxygen-18 and deuterium in river waters across the United States. *Hydrological Processes*, 15, 1363–1393.

Kennedy, C. D., Bowen, G. J., and Ehleringer, J. R. (2011). Temporal variation of oxygen isotope ratios ($\delta^{18}O$) in drinking water: Implications for specifying location of origin with human scalp hair. *Forensic Science International*, 208, 156–166.

van Klinken, G. J. (1999). Bone collagen quality indicators for palaeodietary and radiocarbon measurements. *Journal of Archaeological Science*, 26, 687–695.

Koch, P. L., Tuross, N., and Fogel, M. L. (1997). The effects of sample treatment and diagenesis on the isotopic integrity of carbonate in biogenic hydroxylapatite. *Journal of Archaeological Science*, 24, 417–429.

Lee-Thorp, J. (2002). Two decades of progress towards understanding fossilization processes and isotopic signals in calcified tissue minerals. *Archaeometry*, 44, 435–446.

Lee-Thorp, J., Manning, L., and Sponheimer, M. (1997). Problems and prospects for carbon isotope analysis of very small samples of fossil tooth enamel. *Bulletin De La Societe Geologique De France*, 168, 767–773.

Lee-Thorp, J. and van der Merwe, N. (1987). Carbon isotope analysis of fossil bone apatite. *South African Journal of Science*, 83, 12–15.

Lee-Thorp, J. and Sponheimer, M. (2003). Three case studies used to reassess the reliability of fossil bone and enamel isotope signals for paleodietary studies. *Journal of Anthropological Archaeology*, 22, 208–216.

Lee-Thorp, J. A. and van der Merwe, N. J. (1991). Aspects of the chemistry of modern and fossil biological apatites. *Journal of Archaeological Science*, 18, 343–354.

LeGeros, R. Z. (1981). Apatites in biological systems. *Progress in Crystal Growth Characterization*, 4, 1–45.

Lehn, C., Mutzel, E., and Rossmann, A. (2011). Multi-element stable isotope analysis of H, C, N, and S in hair and nails of contemporary human remains. *International Journal of Legal Medicine*, 125, 695–706.

Lis, G. P., Wassenaar, L. I., and Hendry, M. J. (2008). High-precision laser spectroscopy D/H and $^{18}O/^{16}O$ measurements of microliter natural water samples. *Analytical Chemistry*, 80, 287–293.

Longinelli, A. (1984). Oxygen isotopes in mammal bone phosphate: A new tool for paleohydrological and paleoclimatological research? *Geochimica et Cosmochimica Acta*, 48, 385–390.

Luz, B., Kolodny, Y., and Horowitz, M. (1984). Fractionation of oxygen isotopes between mammalian bone-phosphate and environmental drinking water. *Geochimica et Cosmochimica Acta*, 48, 1689–1693.

Macko, S. A., Engel, M. H., Andrusevich, V., Lubec, G., O'Connell, T. C., and Hedges, R. E. M. (1999a). Documenting the diet in ancient human populations through stable isotope analysis of hair. *Philosophical Transactions of the Royal Society of London Series B—Biological Sciences*, 354, 65–75.

Macko, S. A., Lubec, G., Teschler-Nicola, M., Andrusevich, V., and Engel, M. H. (1999b). The Ice Man's diet as reflected by the stable nitrogen and carbon isotopic composition of his hair. *FASEB Journal*, 13, 559–562.

Matwiyoff, N. A. and Ott, D. G. (1973). Stable isotope tracers in the life sciences and medicine. *Science*, 181, 1125–1133.

Meier-Augenstein, W. (2007). Stable isotope fingerprinting—Chemical element "DNA"? In: Thompson, T. and Black, S. (eds.) *Forensic Human Identification: An Introduction*. Boca Raton, FL: CRC Press. pp. 29–54.

Meier-Augenstein, W. (2010). *Stable Isotope Forensics: An Introduction to the Forensic Applications of Stable Isotope Analysis*. Wiltshire, U.K.: Wiley.

Meier-Augenstein, W. and Fraser, I. (2008). Forensic isotope analysis leads to identification of a mutilated murder victim. *Science and Justice*, 48, 153–159.

Meier-Augenstein, W. and Liu, R. H. (2004). Forensic applications of isotope ratio mass spectrometry. In: Yinon, J. (ed.) *Advances in Forensic Applications of Mass Spectrometry*. Boca Raton, FL: CRC Press. pp. 149–180.

van der Merwe, N. J., Thackeray, J. F., Lee-Thorp, J. A., and Luyt, J. (2003). The carbon isotope ecology and diet of *Australopithecus africanus* at Sterkfontein, South Africa. *Journal of Human Evolution*, 44, 581–597.

van der Merwe, N. J. and Vogel, J. C. (1978). ^{13}C content of human collagen as a measure of prehistoric diet in Woodland North America. *Nature*, 276, 815–816.

Mekota, A., Grupe, G., Ufer, S., and Cuntz, U. (2006). Serial analysis of stable nitrogen and carbon in hair: Monitoring starvation and recovery phases of patients suffering from anorexia nervosa. *Rapid Communications in Mass Spectrometry*, 20, 1604–1610.

Michener, R. H. and Schell, D. M. (1994). Stable isotope ratios as tracers in marine aquatic food webs. In: Lajtha, K. and Michener, R. H. (eds.) *Stable Isotopes in Ecology and Environmental Science*. Oxford, U.K.: Blackwell Scientific Publications. pp. 138–158.

Minagawa, M. (1992). Reconstruction of human diet from $\delta^{13}C$ and $\delta^{15}N$ in contemporary Japanese hair: A stochastic method for estimating multi-source contribution by double isotope tracers. *Applied Geochemistry*, 7, 145–158.

Mook, W. G. (2000). Environmental isotopes in the hydrological cycle: Principles and applications. Volume I: Introduction, theory, methods, review. In: *International Hydrological Programme IHP-V, Technical Documents in Hydrology. UNESCO*, 39, pp. 49–51.

Morrison, J., Brockwell, T., Merren, T., Fourel, F., and Phillips, A. M. (2001). On-line high-precision stable hydrogen isotopic analyses on nanoliter water samples. *Analytical Chemistry*, 73, 3570–3575.

Müller, W., Fricke, H. C., Halliday, A. N., Mcculloch, M. T., and Wartho, J.-A. (2003). Origin and migration of the Alpine Iceman. *Science*, 302, 862–866.

Murnick, D. E. and Peer, B. J. (1994). Laser-based analysis of carbon isotope ratios. *Science*, 263, 945–947.

Nakamura, K., Schoeller, D. A., Winkler, F. J., and Schmidt, H. L. (1982). Geographical variations in the carbon isotope composition of the diet and hair in contemporary man. *Biological Mass Spectrometry*, 9, 390–394.

Nardoto, G., Silva, S., Kendall, C., Ehleringer, J. R., Chesson, L. A., Ferraz, E., Moreira, M., Ometto, J., and Martinelli, L. A. (2006). Geographical patterns of human diet derived from stable-isotope analysis of fingernails. *American Journal of Physical Anthropology*, 131, 137–146.

NicDaeid, N., Buchanan, H. A. S., Savage, K., Fraser, J. G., and Cresswell, S. L. (2010). Recent advances in the application of stable isotope ratio analysis in forensic chemistry. *Australian Journal of Chemistry*, 63, 3–7.

Nielsen-Marsh, C. M. and Hedges, R. E. M. (2000a). Patterns of diagenesis in bone I: The effects of site environments. *Journal of Archaeological Science*, 27, 1139–1150.

Nielsen-Marsh, C. M. and Hedges, R. E. M. (2000b). Patterns of diagenesis in bone II: Effects of acetic acid treatment and the removal of diagenetic CO_3^{2-}. *Journal of Archaeological Science*, 27, 1151–1159.

O'Brien, D. and Wooller, M. (2007). Tracking human travel using stable oxygen and hydrogen isotope analyses of hair and urine. *Rapid Communications in Mass Spectrometry*, 21, 2422–2430.

O'Connell, T. C. and Hedges, R. E. M. (1999a). Investigations into the effect of diet on modern human hair isotopic values. *American Journal of Physical Anthropology*, 108, 409–425.

O'Connell, T. C. and Hedges, R. E. M. (1999b). Isotopic comparison of hair and bone: Archaeological analyses. *Journal of Archaeological Science*, 26, 661–665.

O'Connell, T. C., Hedges, R. E. M., Healey, M. A., and Simpson, A. H. R. (2001). Isotopic comparison of hair, nail and bone: Modern analyses. *Journal of Archaeological Science*, 28, 1247–1255.

O'Keefe, A. and Deacon, D. A. G. (1988). Cavity ring-down spectrometer for absorption measurements using pulsed laser sources. *Review of Scientific Instruments*, 59, 2544–2551.

Padovan, G. J., De Jong, D., Rodrigues, L. P., and Marchini, J. S. (2003). Detection of adulteration of commercial honey samples by the $^{13}C/^{12}C$ isotopic ratio. *Food Chemistry*, 82, 633–636.

Parkes, P. A. (1986). *Current Scientific Techniques in Archaeology*. London, U.K.: Croom Helm.

Passey, B. H., Robinson, T. F., Ayliffe, L. K., Cerling, T. E., Sponheimer, M., Dearing, M. D., Roeder, B. L., and Ehleringer, J. R. (2005). Carbon isotope fractionation between diet, breath CO_2, and bioapatite in different animals. *Journal of Archaeological Science*, 32, 1459–1470.

Pellegrini, M., Lee-Thorp, J. A., and Donahue, R. E. (2011). Exploring the variation of the $\delta^{18}O_p$ and $\delta^{18}O_c$ relationship in enamel increments. *Palaeogeography Palaeoclimatology Palaeoecology*, 310, 71–83.

Peterson, B. J. and Fry, B. (1987). Stable isotopes in ecosystem studies. *Annual Review of Ecology and Systematics,* 18, 293–320.

Petzke, K. J., Boeing, H., Klaus, S., and Metges, C. C. (2005). Carbon and nitrogen stable isotopic composition of hair protein and amino acids can be used as biomarkers for animal-derived dietary protein intake in humans. *Journal of Nutrition,* 135, 1515–1520.

Petzke, K. J., Fuller, B. T., and Metges, C. C. (2010). Advances in natural stable isotope ratio analysis of human hair to determine nutritional and metabolic status. *Current Opinion in Clinical Nutrition and Metabolic Care,* 13, 532–540.

Plentl, A. A. and Schoenheimer, R. (1944). Studies in the metabolism of purines and pyrimidines by means of isotopic nitrogen. *Journal of Biological Chemistry,* 153, 203–217.

Podlesak, D. W., Bowen, G. J., O'grady, S. P., Cerling, T. E., and Ehleringer, J. R. (2012). δ^2H and $\delta^{18}O$ of human body water: A GIS model to distinguish residents from non-residents in the contiguous USA. *Isotopes in Environmental and Health Studies,* 48(2), 259–279, DOI: 10.1080/10256016.2012.644283.

Price, T. D., Burton, J. H., and Bentley, R. A. (2002). The characterization of biologically available strontium isotope ratios for the study of prehistoric migration. *Archaeometry,* 44, 117–135.

Price, T. D., Frei, K. M., Dobat, A. S., Lynnerup, N., and Bennike, P. (2011). Who was in Harold Bluetooth's army? Strontium isotope investigation of the cemetery at the Viking Age fortress at Trelleborg, Denmark. *Antiquity,* 85, 476–489.

Price, T. D., Tiesler, V., and Burton, J. H. (2006). Early African diaspora in colonial Campeche, Mexico: Strontium isotopic evidence. *American Journal of Physical Anthropology,* 130, 485–490.

Rauch, E., Rummel, S., Lehn, C., and Büttner, A. (2007). Origin assignment of unidentified corpses by use of stable isotope ratios of light (bio-) and heavy (geo-) elements—A case report. *Forensic Science International,* 168, 215–218.

Regan, L. A. (2006). Isotopic determination of region of origin in modern peoples: Applications for identification of U.S. war-dead from the Vietnam Conflict. PhD thesis, University of Florida, Gainesville, FL.

Reidy, L. J., Meier-Augenstein, W., and Kalin, R. M. (2005). ^{13}C-Isotope ratio mass spectrometry as a potential tool for the forensic analysis of white architectural paint: A preliminary study. *Rapid Communications in Mass Spectrometry,* 19, 1899–1905.

Roßmann, A., Schmidt, H. L., Hermann, A., and Ristow, R. (1998). Multielement stable isotope ratio analysis of glycerol to determine its origin in wine. *Zeitschrift für Lebensmitteluntersuchung und -Forschung A,* 207, 237–243.

Rowe, W. F. (1997). Biodegradation of hairs and fibers. In: Haglund, W. D. and Sorg, M. H. (eds.) *Forensic Taphonomy: The Postmortem Fate of Human Remains.* Boca Raton, FL: CRC Press. pp. 337–351.

Schmidt, S. N., Olden, J. D., Solomon, C. T., and Zanden, M. J. V. (2007). Quantitative approaches to the analysis of stable isotope food web data. *Ecology,* 88, 2793–2802.

Schoeller, D. A. (1999). Isotope fractionation: Why aren't we what we eat? *Journal of Archaeological Science,* 26, 667–673.

Schoeninger, M. J. (1985). Trophic level effects on $^{15}N/^{14}N$ and $^{13}C/^{12}C$ ratios in bone collagen and strontium levels in bone mineral. *Journal of Human Evolution*, 14, 515–525.

Schoeninger, M. J. and DeNiro, M. J. (1984). Nitrogen and carbon isotopic composition on bone collagen from marine and terrestrial animals. *Geochimica et Cosmochimica Acta*, 48, 624–639.

Schurr, M. R., Hayes, R. G., and Cook, D. C. (2008). Thermally induced changes in the stable carbon and nitrogen isotope ratios of charred bones. In: Schmidt, C. W. and Symes, S. A. (eds.) *The Analysis of Burned Human Remains*. Amsterdam, the Netherlands: Academic Press. pp. 93–108.

Schwarcz, H. P., White, C. D., and Longstaffe, F. J. (2010). Stable and radiogenic isotopes in biological archaeology: Some applications. In: West, J. B., Bowen, G. J., Dawson, T. E., and Tu, K. P. (eds.) *Isoscapes: Understanding Movement, Pattern, and Process on Earth through Isotope Mapping*. Dordrecht, the Netherlands: Springer. pp. 335–356.

Sharp, Z. D., Atudorei, V., Panarello, H. O., Fernández, J., and Douthitt, C. (2003). Hydrogen isotope systematics of hair: Archeological and forensics applications. *Journal of Archaeological Science*, 30, 1709–1716.

Speedy, A. W. (2003). Global production and consumption of animal source foods. *The Journal of Nutrition*, 133, 4048S–4053S.

Sponheimer, M., Robinson, T., Ayliffe, L., Roeder, B., Hammer, J., Passey, B., West, A., Cerling, T. E., Dearing, M. D., and Ehleringer, J. R. (2003). Nitrogen isotopes in mammalian herbivores: Hair $\delta^{15}N$ values from a controlled-feeding study. *International Journal of Osteology*, 13, 80–87.

Sullivan, C. H. and Krueger, H. W. (1981). Carbon isotope analysis of separate chemical phases in modern and fossil bone. *Nature*, 292, 333–335.

Sulzman, E. W. (2008). Stable isotope chemistry and measurement: A primer. In: Lajtha, K. and Michener, R. H. (eds.) *Stable Isotopes in Ecology and Environmental Science*, 2nd edn. Oxford, U.K.: Blackwell Publishing Ltd. pp. 1–21.

Taylor, E., Carter, J. F., Hill, J. C., Morton, C., Nic-Daeid, N., and Sleeman, R. (2008). Stable isotope ratio mass spectrometry and physical comparison for the forensic examination of grip-seal plastic bags. *Forensic Science International*, 177, 214–220.

Thompson, A. H., Chesson, L. A., Podlesak, D. W., Bowen, G. J., Cerling, T. E., and Ehleringer, J. R. (2010). Stable isotope analysis of modern human hair collected from Asia (China, India, Mongolia and Pakistan). *American Journal of Physical Anthropology*, 141(3), 440–451, DOI: 10.1002/ajpa.21162.

Thompson, T. and Black, S. (eds.) (2007). *Forensic Human Identification*. London, U.K.: CRC Press.

Tieszen, L. L. and Fagre, T. (1993). Effect of diet quality and composition on the isotopic composition of respiratory CO_2, bone collagen, bioapatite, and soft tissues. In: Lambert, J. B. and Grupe, G. (eds.) *Prehistoric Human Bone: Archaeology at the Molecular Level*. New York: Springer-Verlag. pp. 121–155.

Urey, H. C. (1947). The thermodynamic properties of isotopic substances. *Journal of the Chemical Society (London)*, 562–581.

Valenzuela, L. O., Chesson, L. A., Bowen, G. J., Cerling, T. E., and Ehleringer, J. R. (2012). Dietary heterogeneity among western industrialized countries reflected in the stable isotope ratios of human hair. *PLoS ONE*, 7, e34234, DOI: 10.1371/journal.pone.0034234.

Valenzuela, L. O., Chesson, L. A., O'grady, S. P., Cerling, T. E., and Ehleringer, J. R. (2011). Spatial distributions of carbon, nitrogen and sulfur isotope ratios in human hair across the central United States. *Rapid Communications in Mass Spectrometry*, 25, 861–868.

Vogel, J. C. and van der Merwe, N. J. (1977). Isotopic evidence for early maize cultivation in New York State. *American Antiquity*, 42, 238–242.

West, J. B., Bowen, G. J., Cerling, T. E., and Ehleringer, J. R. (2006). Stable isotopes as one of nature's ecological recorders. *Trends in Ecology and Evolution*, 21, 408–414.

West, J. B., Hurley, J. M., Dudás, F. O., and Ehleringer, J. R. (2009). The stable isotope ratios of marijuana. II. Strontium isotopes relate to geographic origin. *Journal of Forensic Sciences*, 54, 1261–1269.

Wilson, A. S. and Gilbert, M. T. P. (2007). Hair and nail. In: Thompson, T. and Black, S. (eds.) *Forensic Human Identification*. London, U.K.: CRC Press. pp. 147–174.

Wilson, A. S., Taylor, T., Ceruti, M. C., Chavez, J. A., Reinhard, J., Grimes, V., Meier-Augenstein, W. et al. (2007). Stable isotope and DNA evidence for ritual sequences in Inca child sacrifice. *Proceedings of the National Academy of Sciences*, 104, 16456–16461.

Worden, J., Noone, D., and Bowman, K. (2007). Importance of rain evaporation and continental convection in the tropical water cycle. *Nature*, 445, 528–532.

Wright, L. E. and Schwarcz, H. P. (1996). Infrared and isotopic evidence for diagenesis of bone apatite at Dos Pilas, Guatemala: Palaeodietary implications. *Journal of Archaeological Science*, 23, 933–944.

Wright, L. E. and Schwarcz, H. P. (1999). Correspondence between stable carbon, oxygen and nitrogen isotopes in human tooth enamel and dentine: Infant diets at Kaminaljuyú. *Journal of Archaeological Science*, 26, 1159–1170.

Wunder, M. B. (2010). Using isoscapes to model probability surfaces for determining geographic origins. In: West, J. B., Bowen, G. J., Dawson, T. E., and Tu, K. P. (eds.) *Isoscapes: Understanding Movement, Pattern, and Process on Earth through Isotope Mapping*. Dordrecht, the Netherlands: Springer. pp. 251–270.

Yamanaka, T., Tsujimura, M., Oyunbaatar, D., and Davaa, G. (2007). Isotopic variation of precipitation over Eastern Mongolia and its implication for the atmospheric water cycle. *Journal of Hydrology*, 333, 21–34.

Yoder, C. J. and Bartelink, E. J. (2010). Effects of different sample preparation methods on stable carbon and oxygen isotope values of bone apatite: A comparison of two treatment protocols. *Archaeometry*, 52, 115–130.

Multi-Disciplinary Approach toward the Identification of a Human Skull Found 55 km off the Southeast Coast of Ireland

9

GERARD KEALY, RENÉ GAPERT, LAUREEN BUCKLEY, MARIE CASSIDY, JONATHAN McNULTY, RICHARD WRIGHT, ROBIN FOYLE, WOLFRAM MEIER-AUGENSTEIN, HELEN KEMP, CAROLINE WILKINSON, CHRISTOPHER RYNN AND STEPHEN CLIFFORD

Contents

Introduction

The coast off the southeastern tip of Ireland has been, over the years, the site of many 'finds' involving human remains in various stages of decomposition and disarticulation. There are a number of reasons for this, including the direction of the current and the convergence of two seas, the Irish Sea and the Celtic Sea, via the St. George's Channel. There is a huge volume of shipping traffic, both commercial and passenger, and the area is well known as a graveyard for shipwrecks over the centuries. The area is also heavily fished by commercial trawlers, who themselves have been the victims of many a wreck. The most popular method of fishing is beam trawling, which involves the use of heavy gear trawling the sea floor, and this results in frequent finds by fishermen of remains: In the majority of cases, the finds are quickly excluded as animal in origin; however, on a number of occasions, human remains are recovered.

Figure 9.1 (See companion CD for colour figure.) Map of the United Kingdom and Ireland showing the approximate location of the remains that are thought to have entered the water and location where they were discovered. A distance of approximately 100 km separates both points, movement achieved over a period of 4 months.

One such find involved the recovery of a human skull in the nets of a beam trawler, 'the Willie B', 55 km south of Kilmore Quay, County Wexford (Figure 9.1), on April 3, 2010. The skipper of the trawler, Jim Devlin, placed the skull in a plastic bag and a box of ice in the trawler's cold room and discarded the catch, as is standard practice. He reported the matter via the ship's phone and headed for shore thinking he had recovered the skull of one of his many missing colleagues who had gone down with their trawlers over the years in this region.

On April 4, 2010, upon his return to shore, the captain was met on the pier by Detective Gerard Kealy. On viewing the skull, Detective Kealy made the following observations, comments and notes:

The mandible was missing. Given its gracile appearance, smooth brow ridge, sloping eye orbits, partial metopic suture, narrow nasal opening, small mastoid process, recent dental work, and the presence of tissue and adipocere,

I formed the opinion that I was dealing with a modern adult Caucasian female with a postmortem interval of less than one year. I also noted that although the front teeth were missing postmortem, the sockets indicated that they were uneven and slightly protruding.

This was to prove significant later when he saw a living photograph of the deceased. Detective Kealy immediately reported the details and his observations, both verbally and in writing, to the Coroner and the District Superintendent.

Forensic Analyses

Detective Kealy brought the skull to the mortuary of Wexford General Hospital and secured it. He then contacted the State Pathologist's Office, and after consultation with Professor Cassidy (the State Pathologist), Laureen Buckley (a consultant forensic anthropologist to the State Pathologist's Office) carried out an examination of the skull on April 5, 2010, with Detective Garda Kealy at the mortuary. Buckley reported as follows: 'The skull was heavy indicating a complete brain inside, the base of the skull had some soft tissue and adipocere present, and the first and second cervical vertebrae were still present indicating that the deceased had been in the water for a period of several months but no more than 2 years'. She also found that the mastoid process and external occipital protuberances were not well developed and the orbital rims were narrow indicating female characteristics. The features of the face, narrow nasal opening, nasal sill and retreating zygomatic process indicated that it was a Caucasian skull. Buckley reported that the maxillary sutures are not very accurate when estimating age; however, she noted that the incisive suture was visible although it had started to fuse, indicating the deceased was more than 18 years of age, and she also noted some fusion of the interpalatal suture and that it was not obliterated nor was the intermaxillary suture, indicating that the deceased was less than 50 years of age. Buckley also stated:

> Despite the fact that most of the maxillary dentition had fallen out postmortem, some unusual dental features were observed in that the 2nd molar on the right hand side had developed but had not erupted. In addition the 2nd premolar on the left hand side had been lost antemortem and the gap was not filled. There was also a crown on the 1st molar on the left-hand side, potentially making identification from dental charts relatively straightforward.

In the course of the examination, a perimortem fracture was located adjacent to the squamous part of the temporal bone, part of which was missing, and a secondary fracture from the squamous suture near the anterior edge of the right parietal bone, was also found, running posteriorly almost as far as the lambda. It was decided to discontinue the examination to update the State Pathologist and request her attendance.

Detective Kealy moved the skull to the mortuary at Waterford Regional Hospital where Professor Marie Therese Cassidy carried out an autopsy on the skull in the presence of Detective Kealy who photographed the procedure. Professor Cassidy reported that the remains comprised of a skull with the first and second cervical vertebrae attached and the mandible detached. There was adipocere change to the soft tissue remaining around the cervical spine. The skull features were female. The sutures were not fully closed, and the sagittal suture was offset to the left of the midline. Professor Cassidy also commented on the dentition, in particular a porcelain crown on the sixth upper left with an atypical white metal filling:

> There was a linear fracture running across the right side of the skull, through the parietal and temporal bones, which was partly sprung. The fracture continued across the temporal bone to end at its junction with the greater wing of the sphenoid. The separated fragment of the temporal bone was missing. The fracture line was 17.5 cm long and there was no evidence of trauma to the vertebrae. The skull was opened to reveal dark staining on its outer and inner surface along the line of the fracture. The brain was liquefied but there was an area of dark staining in the right fronto-temporal area. When the brain was removed, this revealed a fracture of the right orbital plate. There was also middle ear congestion.

From a histology point of view, samples of the dura, brain and adipocere were analysed, and they showed complete loss of cellular definition due to decomposition.

In her comments, Professor Cassidy remarked that it was a modern adult female skull and that it was difficult to determine how long she had been in the water, but it was of sufficient time for detachment of the head through the cervical vertebrae:

> This could take anything from several months and up to a few years. The bleeding in the skull was relative to the linear fracture and had occurred perimortem. As there was obvious bleeding into the cranial cavity and possibly into the brain this could have caused at least a period of concussion and it is possible that such an injury could lead to death. As the remains were recovered from the sea, it is possible that the injury was sustained going into the water, i.e. striking her head while falling. There was no way of determining whether or not death was due to drowning however there was evidence of congestion in the middle ears, a finding in some deaths due to drowning or other asphyxial causes of death, but which is not diagnostic of death due to drowning.

Figure 9.2 (See companion CD for colour figure.) The Gully, Manorbier, Wales, where the deceased fell in to the sea. The black dot (see Figure 9.1) denotes approximate location of where the deceased is estimated to have entered the water and asterisk denotes approximate location of deceased's remains when discovered.

She also commented that the deceased's dental work was not typical of that carried out in Ireland. A decay-free premolar was removed for the purpose of DNA analysis and brought to Dr. Stephen Clifford at the State Forensic Science Laboratory Garda Headquarters, Dublin. Although the cause of death was at that time undetermined, Professor Cassidy's findings were consistent with the circumstances of the deceased's death, as it later transpired after identification, in that the deceased fell from a jagged rocky cliff into the sea at Manorbier, off the Southwest Coast of Wales (Figure 9.2).

On May 25, 2010, Detective Kealy brought the skull to Dr. René Gapert at the University College Dublin (UCD) for maceration and further anthropological examination. In the meantime, Detective Kealy had also contacted Professor Wolfram Meier-Augenstein from the University of Dundee regarding stable isotope profiling (SIP). For the purpose of his analysis, Professor Meier-Augenstein required a tooth without decay; therefore, the right second upper molar was removed and transported to the State Forensic Science Laboratory at Garda Headquarters by Detective Kealy, where he switched the premolar for the left second upper molar which had already been submitted to Dr. Stephen Clifford for DNA analysis at the State Forensic Science Laboratory.

Prior to any examination by Dr. Gapert, Jonathan McNulty of the diagnostic imaging section of the UCD School of Medicine and Medical Science carried out a radiographic examination, during which Dr. Gapert wrapped the skull in cling film, to hold the cranium together *in situ* as it has been opened during autopsy. After taking a total of 20 radiographic images of the cranium in various orientations, McNulty reported as follows:

> Radiographic examination revealed agenesis of the left frontal sinus with extension of a lobe from the right frontal sinus across the midline (Figure 9.3A). Unilateral agenesis of the frontal sinus is reported in 14.3% of males and 7.1% of

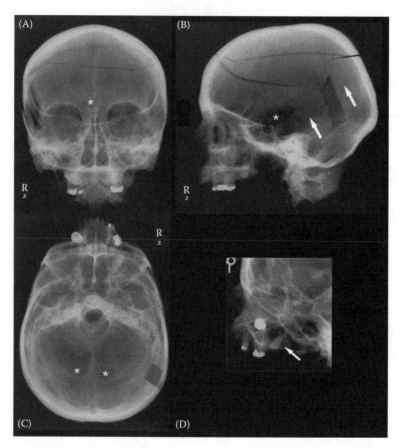

Figure 9.3 Radiographs taken during the examination. (A): Fronto-occipital (anteroposterior) projection demonstrating the agenesis of the left frontal sinus (*), with extension of a lobe from the right frontal sinus across the midline along the right-sided dental amalgam and left-sided crown. (B): Right lateral projection showing the fracture line from the parietal to the temporal, to the sphenoid bone on the right side (arrows) which also indicate the impacted right maxillary second or third molar. (C): Supero-inferior projection highlighting areas of reduced bone density/cortical thinning in the occipital region (*). (D): Right, lateral oblique projection of the maxilla showing the impacted right maxillary second or third molar (arrow), right-sided amalgam restorations of the right maxillary second premolar and right upper second molar, along with a porcelain crown to the left maxillary 1st molar.

females (Quatrehomme et al., 1996; Yoshino et al., 1987) and complete frontal sinus agenesis in approximately 5% of patients which combined with their unique shape facilitate identification. (Schuller, 1943; Yoshino, et al., 1987)

Dr. Jonathan McNulty described the fracture as previously represented (Figure 9.3B) and went on to say:

> radiolucent areas indicating reduced bone density on cortical thinning are evident in the occipital and parietal regions either side of the midline (Figure 9.3C). An anterior-inferiorly impacted right maxillary 2nd or 3rd molar (possible 2nd or 3rd agenesis or early extraction of the 2nd molar) is also evident along with right sided amalgam restorations of the right maxillary 2nd premolar and right upper 2nd molar with a porcelain crown to the left maxillary 1st molar. (Figure 9.3B and D)

Dr. Gapert initiated the maceration process and reported as follows: 'An enzymatic maceration solution was used to break down soft tissues. During the maceration process, three hairs were discovered embedded in soft tissue remnants inside the right eye socket and the cranial base', one of which was a fragment of red head hair (it was found later that the deceased had red hair). Dr. Gapert continued, 'The cranial morphology was deemed to be Caucasian. Craniometric analysis using CRANID strongly suggested European–Caucasian ancestry. All of the observed skull characteristics were female traits'. A further analysis based on discriminate function analyses of cranial base measurements (Gapert et al., 2009a,b) returned results indicating female sex. Moderate dental root transparency was observable. Tooth roots were fully formed, indicating age-related transparency. Fully developed molars and the extent of dental intervention in this case probably indicated an individual above the third decade. The palatal sutures exhibited partial obliteration and suggested middle adulthood of between 35 and 49 years (Bass, 1995; Byers, 2002). Part of the parietal bone separated at the right coronal suture during the maceration process suggested the lower end of middle adulthood. Signs of ageing were evident as arthritic changes in the cervical region (Figure 9.4).
    Dr. Gapert continued as follows:

> A fracture line situated on the right temporal and parietal bones was observed during the morphological examination. The fracture continued into the sphenoid region and also involved the right orbit. No evidence of healing was found at the fracture margins which ruled out the possibility of an ante-mortem traumatic incident. The fracture had the appearance of a peri-mortem injury, the slight curve and raised external edges of the fracture margins are indicative of "green" bone damage. According to Byers (2002) there are five characteristics which would suggest a peri-mortem trauma: sharp edged fracture margins, hinging of bone, formation of fracture lines radiating from the point of impact, shape of broken bone ends, and staining

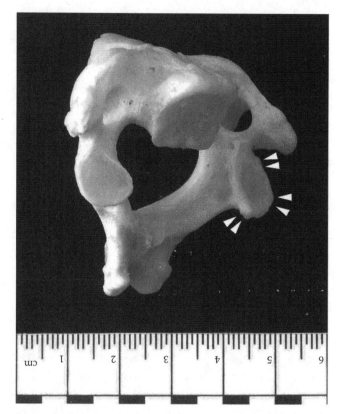

Figure 9.4 Second cervical vertebra (axis)—oblique inferior view. The arrow-heads indicate the arthritic changes on the left inferior articular facet.

from haematomas. Three of these characteristics were present in this case: formation of fracture lines, sharp fracture margins, and a dark staining of the fracture line (noted before maceration). Extensive dental restoration was observed in the remaining teeth. Caries was observed in some of the previously restored teeth. Moderate arthritic changes were found in the cervical region. The articular surfaces of the fovea (atlas) and odontoid process (axis) and the left inferior articular surface of the axis exhibited osteophytic margins (Figure 9.5). Anatomically, this could have led to some stiffness in the neck and, in extreme cases, to a *globus pharyngeus* (lump in the throat) sensation due to musculoskeletal tension in the neck region.

The formation of a left carotico-clinoid foramen was noted in the middle cranial fossa. This is caused by the ossification of the carotico-clinoid ligament or a dural fold extending between the anterior and middle clinoid processes (Özdoğmuş et al., 2003). The carotico-clinoid foramen suggests a developmental anomaly of the chondrocranium rather than an age-related ossification process (Özdoğmuş et al., 2003). The existence of a carotico-clinoid foramen may compress important vascular and neuronal structures. The internal carotid artery may become compressed, tightened or stretched

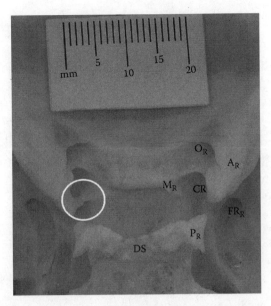

Figure 9.5 Middle cranial fossa—intracranial view. The circled region demonstrates the left carotico-clinoid foramen. Legend (for clarity only the right side of bilateral structures is labelled): A_R, *anterior clinoid process* (right); CR, *carotid sulcus* (right); DS, *dorsum sellae*; FR_R, *foramen rotundum* (right); M_R, *middle clinoid process* (right); O_R, *optic canal* (right); P_R, *posterior clinoid process* (right).

due to the ossification in that region and may lead to insufficient blood supply to the brain (Özdoğmuş et al., 2003). This may cause dizzy spells and/or headaches in some individuals. The apparent presence of soft tissues and of fat suggested a minimum postmortem interval of 5 months to 2 years in the sea. The macerated skull measured 171 mm (length), 141 mm (width), 133 mm (height) and weighed 634 g. The cranial index was calculated at 82.46 (Brachycranic: short, broad skull).

Dr. Gapert sent 29 measurements of the skull to Professor Richard Wright in Australia, for diagnosis of ancestry by CRANID (Wright, 2008). This method compared the shape and size of the skull with 74 samples, which included 3163 crania from around the world. The report by Richard Wright concluded that the morphology of the skull, beyond reasonable doubt, suggested a European ancestry. Less certainly, the deceased was likely to have been female.

Detective Kealy sent the decay-free second molar to Professor Wolfram Meier-Augenstein at the University of Dundee for SIP in an effort to identify the geographic origin of the deceased. Professor Meier-Augenstein reported as follows:

The results of the ^{18}O analysis of tooth enamel (mineral) yielded a $\delta^{18}O$-value of $-6.33 \pm 0.73‰$ for source water consumed by the deceased during formation of late erupting molars, i.e. between 7 to 16 years of age. Using this value as an exclusion criterion, a process of elimination pointed towards the following different geographic regions as potential point of origin where the deceased lived during adolescence (Bell et al., 2009; Henton et al., 2010; Lee-Thorp, 2008; Meier-Augenstein, 2010). These locations included Southern/South Western regions of Ireland, Southern/South Western regions of England, part of central France, near Mediterranean parts of Southern Europe and Eastern parts of the USA. Information gleaned from the ^{13}C analysis of both tooth enamel (mineral) and dentine collagen was used as a further exclusion criterion, which all but excluded the European regions and pointed to the USA as the most likely place (i.e. between 7 to 16 years of age). The pooled averaged value for measured ^{13}C composition of tooth enamel was −12.2 ± 0.40‰. Accounting for the known isotopic shift between pooled ^{13}C composition of an individual's dietary intake and the ^{13}C isotopic composition of carbonate deposited during mineralisation, this value corresponds to a diet with an average ^{13}C composition of −22.70‰ (Lee-Thorpe, 2008; Meier-Augenstein, 2010). A dietary ^{13}C content of on balance −22.70‰ is typical for a diet with a considerable influence of C_4 plant-sourced food products and food ingredients such as sweet corn, corn syrup or cane sugar as it is commonly observed for North Americans and people from most African countries. The pooled averaged value for measured ^{13}C of dentine collagen was −19.31 ± 0.15‰. Accounting for the known isotopic shift between pooled ^{13}C composition of an individual's dietary intake and the ^{13}C isotopic composition of carbonate deposited during mineralisation, this value corresponds to a diet with an average ^{13}C composition of −23.31‰, which is in good agreement with the pooled diet δ^{13} value calculated from the ^{13}C composition of the deceased's tooth enamel.

Dr. Meier-Augenstein continued:

When looking at the ^{15}N isotope data obtained from dentine collagen, an average ^{15}N signature of 11.89 ± 0.37‰ was observed, which is typical for a well nourished omnivore with a higher than average proportion of meat and/or fish derived protein in their staple diet (Meier-Augenstein and Fraser, 2008). However, such a ^{15}N abundance could also found in people suffering from nutritional stress (e.g. brought on by a crash diet) or from long-term illness (Fuller et al., 2005). As it turned out, once the deceased had been positively identified, we learned the deceased had suffered from Addison's disease, a rare chronic disorder that affects the level or balance of corticosteroid hormones (produced in the adrenal cortex). Corticosteroid hormones are well implicated in carbohydrate metabolism (which would affect ^{13}C isotope composition of tissue), protein catabolism (which would affect ^{15}N isotope composition) and blood electrolyte levels, with the latter being of course closely linked to balance and regulation of body water (which would affect ^{18}O isotope composition). In other words, the signal of every one of the stable isotope markers used to gain information on the deceased's life history would have been affected by this chronic disorder. In this particular case, one would even be tempted to say the isotope signatures of ^{13}C, ^{15}N and ^{18}O had been skewed since they were all shifted in the direction of more positive isotope abundance values (i.e. higher abundance levels of ^{13}C, ^{15}N and ^{18}O) than otherwise expected for a healthy person with similar life history.

With the maceration process completed, Detective Kealy took the skull to Professor Caroline Wilkinson and Dr. Chris Rynn at the University of Dundee for facial reconstruction, after obtaining permission from the Coroner to remove the remains from the jurisdiction. They reported as follows:

The skull of an adult female of European ancestry was presented… for craniofacial reconstruction (CFR). CFR is the process by which a face is estimated based upon the morphology of the skull. The technique employed in this case uses averaged facial tissue depth data as a guideline, as the musculature is sculpted with reference to skull morphology, and the features are estimated using various published methods (Rynn et al., 2010; Wilkinson, 2004; Wilkinson et al., 2003; Wilkinson and Mautner, 2003). The accuracy of this technique of CFR had been demonstrated both forensically and in blind accuracy studies (Wilkinson et al., 2006). However, this particular skull, due to extensive maceration at sea, was missing not only the mandible, but also the single-rooted teeth of the maxilla. This meant that the accuracy of the mouth and jaw line was severely compromised. In an effort to get some idea of the dental occlusion, relatively straight-rooted loose teeth were carefully selected from a collection of hundreds, and placed in the sockets of the missing upper incisors and canines. Every tooth is unique to the socket in which it develops, so this process was not expected to provide an accurate depiction of the dentition of this individual, but merely some indication of occlusal type. The angle at which the teeth projected forward suggested a mild type II dental occlusion (i.e. a slight overbite). The skull, with teeth, was laser scanned with the Polhemus Scorpion FastSCAN™ so that all subsequent facial reconstruction could take place virtually, using the SensAble Freeform® Modelling Plus haptic feedback computer sculpture system (http://www.sensable.com/).

The dimensions of the mandible were estimated (Figure 9.6) by way of a method of dental assessment normally used to guide orthodontic intervention (Sassouni, 1957) which has been shown to be satisfactorily accurate at estimating an absent mandible on isolated forensic cases in the white North American population (Krogman and Iscan, 1986) but never thoroughly researched for this purpose. Even at this early stage, a good deal of estimation and extrapolation had taken place, increasing the potential for inaccuracy in the lower face. Furthermore, the absence of any soft tissue evidence meant that the surface textures of the face (skin tone, hair texture, length, style and colour, eye colour, etc.) were unknown and unpredictable. Figure 9.7 shows the CFR process up to the level of what could be estimated from the skull alone.

It was felt necessary to apply some level of texture in order to provide a level of realism and make the facial model easier to recognise as a face

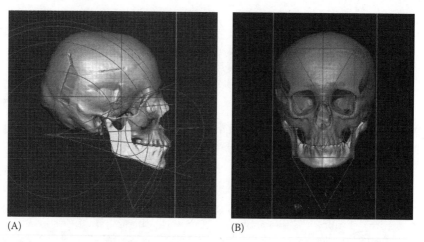

(A)   (B)

Figure 9.6 (See companion CD for colour figure.) Polhemus Scorpion FastSCAN™ of the skull, with teeth (A, B).

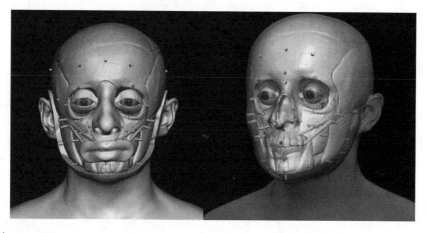

Figure 9.7 (See companion CD for colour figure.) The CFR process up to the skin layer.

Adobe® Photoshop® CS5 was used to add a semi-transparent layer of texture of approximately 15% opacity: small patches of skin and hair texture were sampled from several facial photographs from various sources, layered over the frontal image shown in Figure 9.7, and blended using layer masks. Since, as mentioned, skin tone, eye colour, hair length, texture (curly-straight) and colour were all unknown; monochrome texture was applied to the image, then brightness and contrast altered, and Gaussian blur increased until these details were considered too vague to define (Figure 9.8).

Detective Kealy took the photographs of the skull he had taken to Dr. Robin Foyle, dental surgeon. Dr. Foyle was of the opinion that the porcelain crown

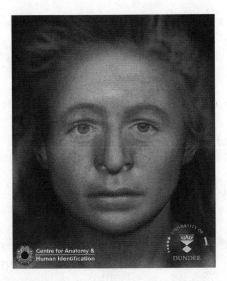

Figure 9.8 (See companion CD for colour figure.) The final textured image presented for press release.

on the sixth upper left was an older-type crown, which he had seen before in Ireland and in the UK National Health Service (NHS). Detective Kealy then obtained a list of females reported missing in the previous 3 years, which exceeded 100. Using the anthropological information accumulated, that is, that the deceased was an adult Caucasian female, allowed the figure to be reduced to 14.

As a tooth without decay was required for stable isotope analysis, Detective Kealy supplied the second-best tooth in the skull (with respect to condition, this was a second premolar with some decay) to Dr. Stephen Clifford of the State Forensic Science Laboratory for the purpose of generating a DNA profile, and as a result he had difficulty generating a profile. Dr. Clifford reported as follows: 'DNA was extracted from the tooth. A partial female DNA profile was generated comprising of 10 elements (out of maximum of 20). The DNA profile was designated "Unknown Female Kilmore Quay"'. This profile was checked against profiles from unsolved cases, including all high-profile cases of missing women believed dead. There were in fact more than 10 elements generated in the profile; however, as a result of the extremely strict quality controls at the State Forensic Laboratory, they were not officially declared.

Using the anthropological, dental and DNA profiles, Detective Kealy was able to eliminate all 14 of the women on the Irish Missing Persons List after acquiring the details of each of these women from the respective investigating officers. At this stage of the investigation, Detective Kealy realised that the deceased was possibly either someone who had not been reported missing (raising the possibility that she was the victim of crime or violence), a recluse or from another jurisdiction.

Detective Kealy collated all the pathological, anthropological and SIP information, the CFR picture and the deceased's dental chart, DNA profile and circumstantial information available and submitted them to Interpol, placing her on the Interpol Blacklist of Unidentified Remains. Bearing in mind that the deceased's disappearance may not have been reported, Detective Kealy wrote to every doctor and dentist in the southeast of Ireland, including the correspondence photos of her teeth, facial reconstruction and a summary of her possible medical symptoms, including neck stiffness or a difficulty turning her head to the left and possibly a history of fainting, dizzy spells or transient ischemic attacks (TIAs), given the narrowing found at the carotico-clinoid foramen of the skull and arthritis found in the cervical vertebrae by Dr. Gapert. The medical practitioners were canvased as to whether the deceased fitted the description of any of their patients, and if so had they seen them since February 1, 2010. Of the doctors who responded, all the possible candidates were accounted for. One dental technician came forward and stated that he was convinced that he had made the porcelain crown sometime in the 1980s or early 1990s. Fortuitously, this particular dental laboratory kept all original dental prescriptions. As a porcelain crown on the sixth upper left was unusual, Detective Kealy reviewed several thousand dental prescriptions confining himself to females. Prescriptions for porcelain crowns on the sixth upper left for seven women were found: however, all of these women were traced and found to be alive.

Media Campaign

Given that the stable isotope analysis results indicated that the deceased may have spent her formative years in the United States, Detective Kealy, through media contacts, mounted a media campaign in the East Coast of America through Mike Fitzpatrick, a journalist with the *Irish Examiner* (a US East Coast newspaper), Marc Cahill (a TV producer), and Barry Cummins of RTE (Ireland's national broadcaster). One woman in particular came to the fore and for a period appeared to be a likely prospect for the deceased: she was a depressed, well-to-do professional middle-aged woman with red hair, born in New York of Irish parents, and known to have visited Ireland following the death of her husband. This woman left her apartment in 2009 telling the building manager that she was going elsewhere in America for 3 months but had actually bought a one-way ticket to Switzerland. She had also hired a car in Switzerland and drove to France, indicating that she could potentially have taken the ferry to Ireland and decided to end her life by jumping off the ferry. The France to Ireland channel passes near where the skull was found, and there have in the past been a number of suicides as a result of passengers jumping from the various ferries and as a consequence suffering fractures by hitting the hull during the fall. However, thanks to a concerted effort by the Irish community in New York as a result of the media campaign, she was traced and found alive, living in New York in poor circumstances with psychiatric issues.

Detective Kealy also mounted a media campaign in Ireland, and the investigation was comprehensively featured on RTE's 'Crimecall' program, again bringing to the public's attention the deceased's facial reconstruction and all associated information, including the fact that she may have spent her childhood in America. Several people came forward to assist, but one caller in particular said he recognised the woman from the reconstruction. He stated that she was born in the United States and returned to Ireland with her parents who had bought and ran a hotel in the Southwest of Ireland. He said he knew her from the hotel in the 1970s, when she would have been a teenager, and was able to supply Detective Kealy with her name. She had a very unusual first name. Detective Kealy made enquiries with the local police and found that such a woman had lived there in the 1970s but had left when her father died and the hotel was closed down. The only information that could be ascertained about her other than her maiden name was that she had had a difficult youth and married a soldier. Detective Kealy carried out exhaustive enquiries throughout Ireland to trace this woman through the police computer system, using her unusual first name as a basis of enquiry. He eventually traced a woman with this name, who was born in the United States and had married a soldier. She had a long history of domestic violence and had not been seen in the area for 2 years after a barring order had been issued against her. Now Detective Kealy had a surname and a date of birth. As this candidate was a person who had a history of dysfunctional behaviour, Detective Kealy carried out enquiries with the Department of Social Protection: he managed to find this woman living in sheltered accommodation at a Dublin address.

Breakthrough in the Case

The breakthrough came in September 2011 when Detective Kealy received the name of a possible candidate from the authorities in the United Kingdom. In a photograph obtained, there were a number of similarities between the deceased and her facial reconstruction, including her red hair, features around the eyes and nose, and in particular uneven, slightly protruding teeth with a broad smile and what appeared to be a visible porcelain crown on her sixth upper left. Her face, however, was very round when compared to the reconstruction. Detective Kealy asked Dr. Chris Rynn, who had carried out the facial reconstruction, to compare by means of superimposition this woman's photograph with the laser scan taken of the skull. Dr. Rynn's response was positive, and he stated that he certainly could not exclude her.

Detective Kealy next contacted the Welsh Police and asked for copies of all available records for the candidate, including her DNA profile (which had been obtained from her glasses). He immediately brought the profile to Dr. Stephen Clifford who reported as follows:

> DNA profile frequencies were calculated using a database of the Irish population. As it is my understanding that the deceased is a UK national a factor has been included in the calculations to ensure that the significance of the evidence is not overstated. All ten elements seen in the partial DNA profile generated from the tooth are also present in the DNA profile of the deceased. I estimate the chance that a person unrelated to the deceased would have this profile would be less than 1 in 340,000.

The circumstances of the deceased's death were that in mid-December 2009, while walking on a cliff path at Manorbier, Wales, in fading light, she fell into the sea at a point known as the Gully (see Figure 9.2). At this stage it was possible to compare the findings of Professor Cassidy with the known facts, which demonstrated that Professor Cassidy's conclusions were consistent with the circumstances of the deceased's death. The anthropological findings of Detective Kealy, Laureen Buckley, and in particular Dr. René Gapert regarding age and medical condition were also consistent in that she was a 45-year-old Caucasian woman with red hair, whose medical records showed that she previously complained of stiffness in her neck and had suffered unexplained incidents of fainting. Her front teeth protruded slightly and were uneven. She was born and spent her formative years in Northern Ireland before moving to the UK mainland.

However, there were also inconsistencies with some of the scientific results when compared to the deceased's profile. For example, SIP has in the past been an invaluable tool in human identification, and the discrepancy in the SIP and facial reconstruction could be accounted for by the fact that the deceased suffered from a rare medical condition called Addison's disease. This condition affects the adrenal cortex and therefore influences nutrient distribution and metabolism and requires treatment with steroids over a protracted period giving rise to a 'full moon' appearance on the face. At the time of her diagnosis, the deceased was only 1 of 18 people with this condition in the United Kingdom that year.

Conclusion

This investigation indicates that a great deal of accurate information can be gathered from the sciences of forensic pathology, forensic anthropology and odontology. However, it also demonstrates the limitations of the normally reliable analytical techniques SIP and craniofacial analysis when exceptional circumstances occur regarding the health of the individual and the effect a protracted period of immersion in seawater may have on samples; as in this case, could the gulfstream current which originates off the US coast have affected the SIP? What effect did saltwater have on the same results? When it comes to DNA recovery from decomposed remains, it is widely accepted that the best source is dental pulp, given the protection it is afforded by dentin and enamel. Saltwater tends to cause rapid cellular degradation, making DNA recovery difficult using standard methods.

In retrospect it would have been wiser to utilise the decay-free tooth for DNA profiling, as the partial profile obtained from the decayed tooth significantly delayed the identification of the deceased. It should also be noted that a number of police officers from Wales who knew the deceased through the investigation into her disappearance could see a resemblance between the deceased and her facial reconstruction, as did Detective Kealy. Another interesting factor from the anthropological and taphonomic point of view, given that the average sea temperature in this area around this period is approximately 10°C, is the short time taken (i.e. 3 months and 3 weeks) for the skull to skeletonise and disarticulate, form extensive adipocere, and cellular destruction of soft tissue to take place. It also emphasises the importance of immediately securing a DNA profile in all cases involving high-risk missing persons in all jurisdictions and the sharing of that information among police forces.

References

Bass, W.M. 1995. *Human Osteology—A Laboratory and Field Manual*, 4th edn. Colombia, MO: Missouri Archaeological Society.

Bell, L.S., Thorp, J.A.L., and Elkerton, A. 2009. The sinking of the Mary Rose warship: A medieval mystery solved? *Journal of Archaeological Science*, 36, 166–173.

Byers, S.N. 2002. *Introduction to Forensic Anthropology—A Textbook*. Boston, MA: Allyn & Bacon.

Fuller, B.T., Fuller, J.L., Sage, N.E., Harris, D.A., O'Connell, T.C., and Hedges, R.E.M. 2005. Nitrogen balance and delta N-15: Why you're not what you eat during nutritional stress, *Rapid Communications in Mass Spectrometry*, 19, 2497–2506.

Gapert, R., Black, S., and Last, J. 2009a. Sex determination from the foramen magnum: Discriminant function analysis in an eighteenth and nineteenth century British sample. *International Journal of Legal Medicine*, 123, 25–33.

Gapert, R., Black, S., and Last, J. 2009b. Sex determination from the occipital condyle: Discriminant function analysis in an eighteenth and nineteenth century British sample. *American Journal of Physical Anthropology*, 138, 384–394.

Henton, E., Meier-Augenstein, W., and Kemp, H.F. 2010. The use of oxygen-18 isotopes in molars of archaeological sheep to investigate herding practices in the Neolithic Settlement of Çatalhöyük, Central Anatolia. *Archaeometry*, 52(3), 429–449, DOI:10.1111/j.1475-4754.2009.00492.x.

Krogman, W.M. and Iscan, Y.M. 1986. *The Human Skeleton in Forensic Medicine*, 2nd edn. Springfield, IL: Thomas Books. pp. 463–468. ISBN 0-398-05224-7.

Lee-Thorp, J.A. 2008. On isotopes and old bones. *Archaeometry*, 50, 925–950.

Meier-Augenstein, W. 2010. *Stable Isotope Forensics: An Introduction to the Forensic Application of Stable Isotope Analysis*. Chichester, U.K.: John Wiley & Sons Ltd. ISBN 978-0-470-51705-5.

Meier-Augenstein, W. and Fraser, I. 2008. Forensic stable isotope analysis leads to identification of a mutilated murder victim. *Science & Justice*, 48, 153–159, DOI:10.1016/j.scijus.2007.10.010.

O'Connell, T.C., Hedges, R.E.M., Healey, M.A., and Simpson, A.H.R. 2001. Isotopic comparison of hair, nail and bone: Modern analyses, *Journal of Archaeological Science*, 28, 1247–1255.

Özdoğmuş, Ö., Saka, E., Tulay, C., Gürdal, E., Üzün, İ., and Çavdar, S. 2003. The anatomy of the carotico-clinoid foramen and its relation with the internal carotid artery. *Surgical and Radiologic Anatomy*, 25, 241–246.

Quatrehomme, G., Fonty, P., Sapanet, M., Grévin, G., Bailet, P., and Ollier, A. 1996. Identification by frontal sinus pattern in forensic anthropology. *Forensic Science International*, 83(2), 147–153.

Rynn, C., Wilkinson, C.M., and Peters, H. 2010. Prediction of nasal morphology from the skull. *Forensic Science Medicine and Pathology*, 6, 20–34, DOI:10.1007/s12024-009-9124-6.

Sassouni, V. 1957. A Syllabus of Roentgenographic Cephalometry. Journal of Forensic Science, 2(4), 434–441. Human Dentition Symposium.

Schuller, A. 1943. A note on the identification of skulls by x-ray pictures of the frontal sinuses. *Medical Journal of Australia*, 1, 554–556.

SensAble. 2012. Products—FreeForm Modeling and Modeling Plus Systems http://www.sensable.com, accessed January 10, 2012.

Wilkinson, C.M. 2004. *Forensic Facial Reconstruction*. Cambridge, U.K.: Cambridge University Press.

Wilkinson, C.M. and Mautner, S.A. 2003. Measurement of eyeball protrusion and its application in facial reconstruction. *Journal of Forensic Science*, 48, 1–5 (technical note).

Wilkinson, C.M., Motwani, M., and Chiang, E. 2003. The relationship between the soft tissues and the skeletal detail of the mouth. *Journal of Forensic Science*, 48, 12–16.

Wilkinson, C.M., Rynn, C., Peters, H., Taister, M., Kau, C.H., and Richmond, S. 2006. A blind accuracy assessment of computer-modelled forensic facial reconstruction using computed tomography data from live subjects. *Journal of Forensic Science, Medicine and Pathology*, 2(3), 179–187.

Wright, R. 2008. Detection of likely ancestry using CRANID. In: Oxenham, Manc (Ed.). Forensic Approaches to Death, Disaster and Abuse. Bowen Hills, Qld.: Australian Academic Press, pp. 111–122.

Yoshino, M., Miiyasaka, S., Sato, H., and Seta, S. 1987. Classification system of frontal sinus patterns by radiography: Its application to identification of unknown remains. *Forensic Science International*, 34, 289–299.

Digital and Biometric Evidence

III

Image Analysis Forensic Facial Comparison: Issues and Misconceptions

10

RAY EVANS

Contents

Introduction

We acknowledge that the face is the most individually recognisable part of the human body, and it is generally accepted that no two faces are the same. Indeed, it has been stated that 'No two faces are alike, not even those of identical twins' (Wilkinson, 2004: p. 5). It may be impossible to verify this statement, having no database of all faces in the world to compare against one another, but neither is it possible to refute it. As a result, on the basis of experience and understanding, the statement is an acceptable truism.

As crime levels have increased, experts are more frequently called upon to express opinions on aspects of human identification in an attempt to identify either victims or criminals. These experts come from disparate fields such as video analysis, medicine, medical art, anthropology and psychology, to name a few. With the increase in the day-to-day use of closed-circuit television (CCTV), the comparison of faces from images for forensic identification has become particularly important in the criminal justice system.

CCTV and Facial Comparison

With the advent of videotape and the associated video recorder in the 1960s, society had a simple, convenient and inexpensive method of capturing moving footage with the added benefit of instantaneous playback (McCahill and Norris, 2002). For those wishing to suppress crime, the significance of these developments was not lost. There is little doubt that the demand for forensic photographic comparisons is fuelled by the proliferation of surveillance camera systems. Britain is often described as having the highest density of surveillance cameras in the world. The number of cameras is routinely cited as being in the region of 4.2± million nationwide (McCahill and Norris, 2003; Norris et al., 2004), or to put this number into context, this constitutes a quarter of the world's surveillance cameras to watch 1% of the world's population (Monahan, 2004). It is cited that in London, 40% of public accessible spaces are monitored by surveillance cameras (Norris et al., 2004). As oft repeated as these statistics are, there is strong evidence that the data and assumptions are somewhat misleading. In a recent study, figures provided by the Association of Chief Police Officers (ACPO) suggest that there are around 1.8 million camera/systems in operation, not including domestic or automated number plate recognition (ANPR) systems (Gerrard and Thompson, 2011). They estimated a more conservative number of CCTV cameras at 2.805 per 100 population, comprising approximately 1,704,773 privately owned cameras, 33,433 publicly owned cameras and 115,000 cameras on public transportation based on data provided by the Transport for London. This is vastly different from the widely reported figures emphasised by politicians 'A CCTV camera for every 14 citizens' (Mail Online, 2008).

While the true numbers are probably fewer than popularly assumed, it is difficult to overstate the fact of high numbers of CCTV systems in England. From the very beginning of the CCTV age, there has been an incredibly high spending on publicly funded CCTV surveillance.

From the first CCTV system being installed in Bournemouth in 1985 (Davies and Thasen, 2000), by 1995 nearly half of all metropolitan and non-metropolitan councils had already installed CCTV within their town centres (Brown, 1995). Available data indicate that between 1996 and 1998, the Home Office made available £34 million to fund CCTV schemes (McCahill and

Norris, 2003). Between 1999 and 2001, they made available a further £170 million under the Crime Reduction Programme CCTV Initiative.

This upward trend in spending on cameras continues today. Requests via the Freedom of Information Act from 428 local authorities revealed that there are now at least 51,600 CCTV cameras operated by local authorities in England and Wales (Big Brother Watch, 2012; Brown, 2012). Between 2007 and 2011, local authorities spent a total of £515m installing, operating and maintaining CCTV systems, with the largest local authority in the country spending over £14 million (Laja, 2012). It is estimated that councils now spend in the region of £250m per year on CCTV systems (Big Brother Watch, 2012; Brown, 2012).

It was reported in Islington in 2008, an area where Visual Images, Identifications and Detections Office (VIIDO) units have been operating, that up to 20% of crimes have resulted in detections of criminals in Tier 1 (serious violence) and Tier 2 (serious acquisitive) crimes; this is the same level or higher of the percentage caught using DNA and fingerprints (*BAPCO Journal*, 2008). The cost benefits for a financially constrained police force are hard to ignore.

While this technology can and does catch criminals in the act, the images caught on camera are of little probative value unless they can be linked to a particular individual with an acceptable degree of confidence. Although it will provide evidence of the action that occurred, it must be realised that general characteristics like age, sex, race and stature can only either suggest or rule out a match, but as we are dealing with imagery, they can seldom be absolutely conclusive in and of themselves (İşcan and Helmer, 1993).

A growing number of images are analysed using facial comparison techniques. A small survey by Evans (2002) considered the increase in deployment and usage of surveillance cameras in the United Kingdom to gauge what, if any, bearing it had on the increased numbers of requests for facial identification reports. The study was based on the names of 11 experts then currently on the National Crime Faculty database and independently advertised experts. It did not consider the qualification or experience of those experts, made no reference to case records, was confined to experts in mainland Britain, and looked at the period from 1992 to 2001. The increase in readily available surveillance material due to the increase in CCTV systems (Armitage, 2002), coupled with increased funding over that period, appeared to coincide with the increase in the use of facial identification known as 'facial mapping'.

Although eight questions were asked, there were five main areas:

1. The numbers of reports performed
2. The increase in numbers (if any) of cases
3. The area of crime most represented

4. The geographic areas covered by experts' services
5. The proportional split between Crown Prosecution Service and defence work undertaken

Of the 11 experts that were sent the questionnaire, 4 could either not respond, could not extract their data in time for inclusion into the survey or felt unable to give the information requested. The final study represented 64% of experts on the registered experts at that time. The responses indicated that overall there had been a twofold increase in the numbers of cases performed over those 9 years, with the largest increase occurring between 1997 and 2001.

In cases of legal identification, be it for purposes of civil or criminal law, it is crucial that transparent, objective and repeatable methods are used to discern one person from another. The comparison of two or more photographs remains a difficult task, open to subjective interpretation. As yet, no mandated procedures have been developed for the analysis of photographs or video images. In most cases, each expert adopts one or more of three 'commonly agreed' techniques to fit the case at hand. The importance, then, of developing a systematic facial comparison methodology, which could give rise to more conclusive identification results, cannot be overstated. The use of these common techniques is not universally endorsed, and any advances in this area would be of immense benefit to the credibility of the field.

A Word about Expert Witnesses

Following a number of wrongful convictions, forensic science as a whole and the role of expert witnesses in particular came under justified scrutiny. In 1999, the UK Government, with full cross-party support, established the Council for the Registration of Forensic Practitioners (CRFP) to give the courts a single point of reference on the competence of forensic practitioners. In the form of a company limited by guarantee, with a memorandum and articles of association, which provided for a governing council, an executive board and sector assessment panels, it looked like the situation regarding 'questionable' forensic experts might be at an end. Despite attracting over 2700 registrants from 26 specialties, the larger numbers projected to join did not materialise, and so, despite being called 'a valuable asset to the criminal justice system' by the then Director of Public Prosecution, Sir Ken MacDonald, the CRFP was closed in 2009 (CRFP, 2008).

There are arguments for and against the use of experts in the field of facial image comparison. Questions have been posed on the effectiveness or otherwise of experts in this area. One study (Wilkinson and Evans, 2009) compared the abilities of a small group of highly experienced facial imagery experts ($n = 2$) with members of the general public, to ascertain whether or not training and experience would affect the ability to identify faces from CCTV footage. The method comprised of the study participants (both experts and non-experts) viewing a number of clips from CCTV footage, after which they were asked to identify the individual in each clip from a face pool of young, white males and females ($n = 61$) and provide a level of confidence in the decision. The experts tested in this study were consistently better at identification than the public, with almost double the identification rates and half the errors. The public volunteers were found to be more likely to make a false match than the experts, suggesting that an average body of people (such as a jury) is more likely to accept an innocent person based on CCTV identification. The results from this study suggest that there is merit in having trained experts perform a comparison and then explain the evidence to a jury, with a view to reducing the number of false identifications and therefore potential miscarriages of justice.

One unpublished study (Davis et al., 2012) used standard techniques to assess the performance of professional identifiers (police officers) and a control sample on a battery of cognitive tests. The results of this research did not reveal any reliable group differences between controls and police officers (so-called superidentifiers), who had previously identified large numbers of offenders from CCTV. None of the superidentifiers or members of the control groups had any special training in image analysis. A separate study, by Lee et al. (2009), assessed the ability of students on a forensic course who had had some exposure to facial comparison techniques, to see if they were any better at identifying poor-quality images than the public. The results indicated that the students were no better at the task than the public at analysing poor-quality material.

Contrasting these results with the previous research suggests that highly specific training, coupled with experience in facial analysis, may be worth exploring in regard to more reliable and accurate facial identification. Further research is required here.

Face: Key to Identification

The face is the most individually recognisable part of the human body. Under normal circumstances, we acquire the ability to recognise faces at an early stage of our development and go on to be able to infer or estimate many characteristics such as age, 'race', and sex with remarkable accuracy. Generally, we all eventually rely upon our 'learnt' knowledge of facial features based on seeing faces daily. We are able to describe the positions of features and become expert at 'reading' faces. That is not to say, however, that we truly look at faces in a way that is prerequisite to accurate facial comparison.

The facial comparison expert must have a sound knowledge of anatomical and common descriptions of the surface anatomy of the face in order to report the results of their comparison. 'Practitioners should be able to demonstrate an ability to compare facial morphology and facial proportions, observing the spatial relationships of features and facial landmarks between images, from more than one source' (NPIA, 2009). Because the face is elastic in the way it moves to alter expression, it is desirable to have a sound knowledge of the underlying anatomy of the face to include all the facial musculature and their mode of action. One basic premise in understanding why facial comparison can be used to identify individuals is the acknowledgment that all skulls are variable between individuals. It follows therefore that all faces are unique to each individual.

Unlike a manufactured device such as a car, an airplane or a gun, which are made from a pattern, the face has an individual shape, dimension and feature detail combination, dictated by genetic combination. It is this unique combination that differentiates one face from another. There is a great deal of evidence to suggest that in recognition, we treat faces not as individual features but as an amalgamation of features and their interrelationships. Bruce and Young (1998) alluded to this in their celebrated book on facial perception *In the Eye of the Beholder* (Bruce and Young, 1998). In it they describe 'how the appearance of an individual face results from a subtle interaction between underlying bone structure, the thickness of the fat layer between bone and skin, and the texture and pigmentation of skin and hair'.

To accurately describe the face, it is not sufficient to use the facial anatomy terms routinely used in medicine. It is, in the author's opinion, better to combine common and anatomical surface naming terms such as those used in plastic surgery (Dunn and Harrison, 1997) with standard photogrammetric terms (Işcan and Helmer, 1993). It must be remembered that the results of a facial comparison for court will most likely be viewed by the general public (the jury) whose knowledge of traditional anatomical or purely photogrammetric terms will be limited (Figure 10.1).

Important Word on Recognition versus Identification

We have a good ability to recognise familiar faces from surprisingly little information but find it difficult to express the differences between similar faces. (Wechsler et al., 1997)

It is important to acknowledge the difference between the acts of recognition and identification, as these are often incorrectly used interchangeably. Face recognition relies on recall of a face seen previously and is imprecise and subject to context, resulting in misinformation being recalled as factual

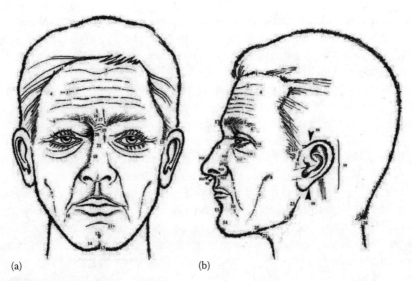

(a)   (b)

Key to Figures 1–2

Key Code		Commonest Name	Alternative Name	Second Alternative
F	1	Hairline		
F	2	Upper forehead crease	Frontalis-galea edge	
F	3	Forehead creases	Forehead lines	Frown line
F	4	Forehead		
F	5	Eyebrow		
F	6	Supra-orbital margin		
F	7	Naso-labial crease	Naso-labial groove	Naso-labial fold
F	8	Buccal pit	Buccal fovea	
F	9	Bucco mandibular groove		
F	10	Marionette line	Down line	Oromental crease
F	11	Mental crease	Labio-mental crease	Mentolabial groove
F	12	Mental pit		
F	13	Median chin crease	Chin crease/cleft	Mental crease/groove
F	14	Chin		
F	15	Sideburn		
F	16	Vertical glabellar lines		
F	17	Glabella		
F	18	External nose		
F	19	Transverse nasal grooves		
F	20	Nasal root		
F	21	Nasal bridge		
F	22	Chin-neck angle	Cervico-submental angle	Cervico-mental angle
F	23	Vertical ramus of mandible	Ascending ramus of mandiable	
F	24	Angle of Mandible		
F	25	Horizontal ramus of mandible	Jawline	
F	26	Nape of neck		

Figure 10.1 Facial nomenclature. (a) Figure 1_Face, full (key code F). (b) Figure 1_Face, side (key codes F+N+E+Y). (Courtesy of Dunn, K.W. and Harrison. R.K., *Br. J. Plast. Surg.*, 50, 584, 1997.)

memory. It is well documented that eyewitness memory and facial recall is fraught with difficulties (Shepherd et al., 1977; Wells, 1993; Henderson et al., 2001; Roebers and Schneider, 2001), and we see many miscarriages of justice based on eyewitness testimony. It is a fact that not all facial features are remembered equally well: it is usual for the gross external features of a face to be the dominant theme in memory. As exposure to that face increases, we become more familiar with the internal features and devote more memory to those elements. We also become more familiar with the relationships in the spacing of those features. It is this fact, that human memory is so fallible, that makes CCTV recording so pertinent to forensic use.

Facial comparison as practiced by an expert witness is distinctly different from the process of face recognition; here, a previously unseen face or photograph is actively compared against a second previously unseen face or photograph. Issues of sameness arise when faces are very similar in shape, gross features and proportions and are further complicated if that face is captured under poor imaging conditions. Many have had the experience of seeing a 'familiar' face only to realise upon closer inspection that it is someone else, albeit similar in some features.

Monozygotic twins are the closest that we can get to 'identicalness'. This can be seen as potentially causing an issue when looking at facial comparison; however, while there are cases of siblings being mistaken or potentially mistaken for each other, in working reality, the likelihood of a pair of identical twins being implicated for the same crime without knowing about it is probably rare. The issue of a non-related lookalike being mistaken for another suspect is, however, a distinct possibility. A fascinating photographic project by François Brunelle demonstrates how closely matched two unrelated strangers can be in facial form (Brunelle, 2006).

As mentioned previously, unlike eyewitness testimony, facial comparison by image comparison does not rely upon memory. It does not suffer from the problems of recalled memory related to encoding (representing of information) and storage of memories. Instead, it is a visual examination of previously unseen imagery, moving or still from a variety of formats, predominantly these days from CCTV.

Unlike other forensic investigations, the original piece of evidence can never actually be examined because we are dealing with a discrete moment in time as opposed to a piece of crime scene material; it is the momentary snapshot of a subject seen through a lens. The image can only ever be an approximation of the subject. Without even including the possibility of deliberate deception, the camera is prone to aberrations and distortions. The resultant image may then have elements that may not have been on the original subject. From these representations of that moment in time, we have to make a visual study and comparison of the differences and similarities. These differences or similarities are then presented to demonstrate their significance in relation to any facial feature or features. The presentation of that result is defined in a scale describing a level of support.

Place in the Evidential Hierarchy

It can be argued that forensic image analysis (including facial comparison) differs from most forensic disciplines. Locard's exchange principle states that 'with contact between two items, there will be an exchange', or, in other words, every contact leaves a trace. Traditional forensic evidence (such as DNA and fingerprints) are collected at a crime scene and used to link a suspect to that crime. Image analysis defies Locard's exchange principle because there is no physical contact between recording and subject. The resultant evidence is variable due to the type of device recording it and the atmospheric conditions. Furthermore, the examined image is susceptible to alteration simply by storing and replaying it. All these details can play a part in how the result is interpreted.

The use of CCTV images for identification purposes in legal cases has divided opinion in courts since its introduction in 1982/1983. One of the first recorded cases of facial identification from video evidence to involve a 'recognised' facial comparison expert occurred at the Old Bailey in 1988, as part of a defence case in which the defendant was found not guilty. After this, other cases rapidly followed.

In the early 1990s, it was observed that evidence of 'facial mapping' was breaking new ground. Such evidence was admitted in court; however, many successful prosecutions were later challenged on appeal (Lord Taylor et al., 1993; Judge Dyson et al., 2001; Lord Justice Waller et al., 2004; Lord Justice Hughes et al., 2009), but the facial comparison evidence in those cases was ruled admissible.

Face mapping was initially advised for use as corroborative evidence. However, from the mid-2000s onward, there were increasing cases coming through where it was presented as the sole evidence in support of identification. There have always been reservations about it being used in this way, both in the industry and within sections of academia and the judiciary. Despite advances, it is inherently an imprecise science, routinely relying on poor-quality material from which precise data cannot be acquired.

Facial Comparison and Issues of Expert Witnesses

It is now an accepted procedure that facial comparison experts be called to give an opinion on the value or otherwise of CCTV material utilised for the purposes of identification. The Attorney General's reference (No. 2 of 2002) established that 'a suitably qualified expert in facial mapping skills could give evidence in relation to photographic images from the scene and a contemporary photograph of the defendant provided that the images and the contemporary photograph were available to the jury' (Rose, 2002). Juries now attach considerable weight to facial recognition reports, so it is essential to establish that just how reliable such a report is.

While not dismissing facial comparison as a valuable tool, and acknowledging there should be future developments in technology, there have been a number of studies that are critical of expert identification evidence based on images as currently practiced. Edmond et al. (2009) note that the term 'facial mapping' is used to cover a wide range of practices and techniques which are not standardised through teaching institutions, formal qualifications and regulatory bodies and have not been evaluated through published experimental studies. They go on to suggest validation studies and briefly outline a simple method of proficiency testing. Further issues are taken with the general acceptance of expert witness evidence and claim to expose the jurisprudence weaknesses of photo comparison and facial mapping evidence in English and Australian courts (Edmond et al., 2010).

Scientific Regulatory Issues

Although the use of facial expert witnesses in court is now common, the use of facial comparison in courts is not universally acknowledged as an acceptable method of comparing individuals from CCTV imagery. The veracity of certain facial identification techniques has come under criticism for their perceived lack of statistical or scientific rigour.

Since the closure of the Forensic Science Service in 2009, experts have had to rely on the office of the Forensic Science Regulator (see Chapter 20), appointed in 2008, to ensure that the provision of forensic science services across the criminal justice system is subject to an appropriate regime of scientific quality standards. As the regulator's recommendations are not yet enforceable, there are still no recognised or mandatory quality standards to which facial comparison experts can sign up.

Methodological, technical and theoretical problems have been cited as reasons for concern with using facial comparison in court cases (Edmond et al., 2010). There are those who, quite properly, question the issue that there is no database of facial characteristics from which to contest the prevalence or otherwise of particular facial features in a given population.

The question of a facial feature database was initially tackled in 1993 with the Home Office Police Systems and Development Working Group looking at the creation of a database of facial features and measurements and to support and develop collaboration between the small number of practitioners operating at that time. In 1994 this culminated with the Home Office awarding a contract to a private consortium to build a facial database of young white males.

Since then, a number of small studies have been undertaken, which created their own databases of faces for this purpose; most used 2D photographic images, but others have adopted 3D scanning of large numbers of faces ($n = 3000+$) (Evison et al., 2010). From this, it might be possible to assess the intended target population's variability, but still not the general population at large. In reality, there are several, if not widely circulated, databases of facial characteristics, but much more work is required to make them a useful tool in general population facial feature statistical occurrence.

Throughout the early history of the use of facial imagery, the descriptions used in expert reports to indicate to the court their strength of feeling about their findings were always somewhat arbitrary and therefore open to error or misinterpretation. To address this, an agreed, though non-binding, scale of terms was devised by the Forensic Image Analysis Group (FIAG), a loose collection of experts involved mainly in image analysis. This scale was adopted in 2006 by most of the then practicing experts in the field, not as a way to negate scientific rigour but simply to enable each expert and the courts to understand the strength of conviction the experts had about a series of approximations. The terms of the scale were prepared to provide guidance on conclusions in cases of facial comparisons. Numerous factors are taken into account for each level, such as

- Image quality
- Number of facial feature similarities/differences observed
- Number of different times the similarities/differences can be observed
- Whether or not a comparison of relative geometry can be made and the closeness of any correlation or difference
- Number of different viewpoints available
- Individual significance attributed to a distinct correlation or difference of a given feature or several features in combination
- The presence/absence of marks, scars and blemishes

The scale is a considered set of words with an explanation of the meaning behind them, but it should be noted that the explanations are not definitive. It is also important to note that the 'levels of support' can be used in order to express the weight of imagery evidence that two persons imaged are not one and the same. Table 10.1 lists some of the agreed meanings for the terms in the scales.

Needless to say, the veracity of the scale has also been questioned on numerous occasions by, in the main, defence lawyers who, rightly, need to test expert findings in court. As things stand, however, facial mapping is almost universally used in UK courts, albeit on a case-by-case basis. The results of an analysis are not always agreed upon by two (or more)

Table 10.1   **Forensic Image Analysis Rating Scale**

	Term	Agreed Meaning
0	Lends no support	There are no significant differences observable from which to eliminate and there may be a number of similarities. The imagery evidence is too poor to permit observation in either direction.
1	Lends limited support	There are a few general characteristics observable. In combination, these provide a low level of facial uniqueness.
2	Lends moderate support	The image quality permits observation of a moderate amount of facial feature detail; that is, for each visible feature, one to a few descriptives can be provided. For example, the nose could be classified as having a narrow bridge and a straight ridge.
3	Lends support	There may or may not be matching geometry, but this is limited to one or two instances. • In combination (or alone), the facial features have an average amount of uniqueness; they are shared by an average number of people.
4	Lends strong support	The image quality permits a good level of individual facial feature detail to be observed. • A high number of facial features are observable.
5	Powerful support	A very high number of facial features are observable. • In combination (or alone), the features provide a high level of facial uniqueness.

experts, and this often leads to the merits of each case being tested in court. At the end of the day, the jury makes the final decision, assisted in their understanding of an expert's particular viewpoint, by the scales (Bromby and Plews, 2006).

Facial Mapping: Manual Techniques

Forensic facial comparison (facial mapping) is now an accepted tool in the armoury of 'identification of the living' techniques. The most widely used practical methods are commonly known and understood and are now referred to consistently.

While there are numerous ways to assess facial features, it is routinely acknowledged that there are three 'standard' techniques of facial comparison, namely, morphological analysis, photo anthropometry and photo/video superimposition. These are well documented in other publications (Catterick, 1992; Porter and Doran, 2000; Oxlee, 2007) to name a few, so these will not be explored in any great detail here. The FIAG has developed and made available guidelines on these techniques. It is worth, however, reviewing their main points, both strengths and weaknesses (FIAG, 2008).

Morphological Analysis

Comparisons of photographic (or video) material are performed systematically using a feature-by-feature approach to guide the expert in making a decision about the viability of a match. This includes an evaluation of characteristics such as facial outline shapes, as well as hairline, and mouth and chin shapes. Although this promotes an apparently objective and consistent approach, appearance of facial features are readily altered by subtle changes in expression and viewpoint and are permanently modified by ageing. Here, the task is to collate a list of suitable features and make comments on their presence or otherwise on the images to be compared. That list of features can run to several dozens. Table 10.2 shows examples of commonly compared features.

As previously mentioned, it is a prerequisite that the practitioner understands facial anatomy and is able to identify key facial anatomical landmarks. Issues which afflict the automatic acceptance of the conclusions in a morphological comparison usually coalesce around differences between experts in relation to an assessment in quality of the material supplied for analysis. The question is usually, 'Is this material of sufficient resolution or quality for specific features to be seen?'

Table 10.2 Commonly Compared Facial Features

	Facial Feature
1	Race skin colour
2	*Face shape, head shape—dolichocephalic—can only be seen from above or profile*
3	Hair and hairline
4	Forehead shape, glabella lines/creases
5	Supraorbital ridge
6	Eyebrows
7	*Eyelids, creases upper and lower (infra and supra)*
8	Nose—dorsal ridge, bridge, alae; tip–septum, columella
9	Nasolabial creases
10	Philtrum—width and depth
11	White roll
12	Upper lip—vermillion, shape, projection
13	Lower lip—vermillion, shape, projection
14	*Teeth*—overbite, overjet, diastema
15	Lip chin (mental region) angle, eversion of lower lip, lip crease–mentolabial creases
16	Buccal creases, Marionette lines, dimples
17	Mental region/chin shape—e.g. square-pointed, receding, orthognathic
18	Ear shape and detail
19	Blemishes—pimples, birthmarks, etc.

Photo-Anthropometric Approach

Various techniques are described in the literature. Catterick (1992), for example, described research into the discrimination power of facial measurements to provide some idea of their value. The method involved measuring the facial dimensions of passport photographs, after which the discrimination power of four facial features was assessed. In this and other techniques, the proportional relationships of the features, rather than their visual similarities, can be compared. This appears to reduce the subjectivity of the comparison, but it also has some obvious problems. For example, in real-world applications, the images may be taken from different angles, which may alter the apparent proportions of the face—as will changes in expression. Care must be taken therefore on the selection of the frames to be compared. There has to be a good understanding of the features of the face and knowledge of where to take the measurements. The task is to identify facial 'landmarks' on each frame; specifically, they must be taken from clearly observed and non-mobile portions of the face such as either canthus of the eyes or the *subnasale* (the point where the nasal septum meets the philtrum or the alar margins). Other less precise points are the commissural crease and the edges of the mouth, but these should only be used when the face is, or appears to be, at rest.

An assessment of relative facial geometry requires that images of the alleged perpetrator and the suspect are selected from the same viewpoints and proportionally scaled to be of comparable size. Alignment of the various, coplanar, facial feature landmarks may reveal differences in the facial proportions or the sizes of the facial features between the two items of comparison. A comparison of facial geometry in this way is an assessment of the relative size, shape and position of the various facial features. Differences are more likely to be evident when the images are aligned on both horizontal and vertical axes rather than on one axis alone. It should also be noted that measurement on its own can, in the main, only be used to eliminate a suspect, since many persons share the same facial proportions. Issues that afflict the automatic acceptance of the conclusions in a photo-anthropometric comparison usually focus around differences between experts in relation to placement of measurement markers or the use of images from viewpoints which may not be congruent.

Photographic/Video Superimposition

The aim of this technique is to determine if facial features and dimensions are directly comparable. Images can be superimposed on top of each other using either computer technology or devices, such as a photo enlarger, to produce two comparatively scaled images. Video fades or 'swipes' can also be used to examine the transition from one image to the other. Again, these

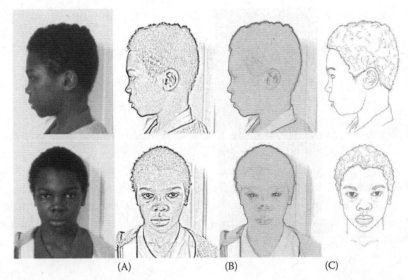

(A)   (B)   (C)

Figure 10.2 Automatic versus manual trace technique over low-resolution image: (A) photocopy filter, (B) find edge filter, (C) manual line drawing.

techniques require images taken under near-identical conditions and so are not methods that can be consistently relied on or utilised in poor-quality CCTV footage or footage that is not from comparable aspect and viewpoint.

With all of these techniques, it is useful to locate the boundary between features to determine the shapes and relationships of the landmarks to each other and the whole. As the human face is not neatly delineated by lines, it is desirable to be able to trace the contour or features of the face. This can be done either manually using appropriate image projection tools and artistic skill or automatically using appropriate computer software applications. As most experts are not trained artists, the automatic method is more usually encountered. However, it is obvious that knowledge of facial anatomy is desirable to understand what is being traced. Figure 10.2 shows the detailed difference between automated 'edge' detection techniques and a manually traced technique.

To these techniques could be added various other video techniques for comparison, such as the viewing of images side by side (or variations of), the viewing of similar consecutive frames (false stereoscopy) or by fading one image into another at various rates (blink comparison). However, these video techniques are susceptible to criticism because they can create an 'illusion' of similarity.

Further Video Issues: Enhancement versus Alteration

It is usually the case that footage proffered for comparison in forensic cases is of poor quality. Using 'analogue' photographic media, it was possible to adjust the tonal range of the image using a variety of photographic enhancement processes. If using videotapes, there were frequently quality issues, as any copying would have a degrading effect. With the advent of digital imagery and bit-for-bit copying, this type of degradation became less of a problem. Today, as a result of the wide use of powerful computer software, the question is 'when does *enhancement* become *alteration*', not a question of semantics, as in forensic casework images can be enhanced but not altered. With digital manipulation of the image, a simple rule of thumb is that no additional information should be added to the image by these processes. It is also imperative that any enhancement process is repeatable by another expert, and the resultant image or images can be compared against the original. The extent to which an enhancement is performed is one for the expert to be comfortable with. In the final analysis, it is he or she who will be in the witness box to explain the transformation, the outcome and reasons for its use.

Issues of Objectivity

It is strongly argued that forensic experts generally underestimate the effect prior knowledge of the details of a case has in potentially influencing them to reach a particular conclusion because of contextual bias. This is no less a problem in facial mapping. Psychological studies demonstrate that contextual bias is a fundamental part of human decision-making. Our 'natural' reaction in assessing a situation is to seek as much information as possible prior to making a decision.

> Having that information may consequently, but subconsciously, influence results; because it is human nature to seize upon evidence that supports the investigator's hypothesis and minimise or discredit evidence to the contrary, the scientist whose results are influenced by prior knowledge is acting naturally rather than immorally.

Understanding that this can happen and knowing the remarkable degree of the extent to which context can influence one's decision shows that it is vital that its root be eliminated.

Another pitfall encountered is 'cognitive dissonance', where persons are loath to disagree with another's view. An example could be a police officer or defence solicitor who may tend to make the facts fit a particular case—emphasising factors that do and minimising those that do not. In this context it is important for expert witnesses to accept fully that their first duty is to the court and not to the client that retained them for the work.

Several suggestions have been made to enable the expert to be as objective as possible. These include the expert receiving only information relevant to his or her role in the case, the expert having no issues of reputation or independence when acting for either party, and assessment of the expert's statement by a peer review system prior to submission to the instructing party.

Current Research and Potential New Developments

Mark Twain is credited with popularising the phrase 'there are three kinds of lies: lies, damn lies, and statistics'. Looking at one of the seemingly intractable problems associated with facial comparison—namely, the accuracy or otherwise of measurement in photogrammetry—it has been suggested that the technique should not be used. Allen (2008) applied a statistical solution to this problem by employing the use of Bayesian networks to the question of identifying faces from CCTV stills. His results suggest that applying Bayesian statistical analysis to the calculation of the error level of measurements could assist with the accuracy of facial landmark measurement. However, the presentation of purely statistical information has historically caused confusion, not only among the jury but also sometimes with the person presenting the statistics. Statistical analysis presented to a court or legal inquisition of lay people is fraught with danger; failure to explain adequately the reasoning behind the analysis runs the risk of the intended audience misunderstanding its inference, or even worse, if statistics are delivered by someone with a misunderstanding of those statistics, the wrong conclusion can be reached. We note this in numerous cases but most prominently in the tragic case of solicitor Sally Clark (R vs. Clark 2003) (R v. Clarke [1995] 2 Cr App R425; [2003] EWCA Crim 1020). Although medical opinion was split, with several leading paediatricians convinced that the children in this case died of natural causes. The prosecution expert witness was certain that it was murder. His evidence was found to have cited faulty statistical analysis. The intention of Professor Meadows was no doubt honourable, wanting to obtain justice for the families of the deceased, but perhaps here we see a case of contextual bias in action, the desire to assist, becoming conflated with the wish to promote a particular view.

Niels Bohr is quoted as describing 'an expert as a man who has made all the mistakes which can be made in a very narrow field'. Working closely with the criminal justice system, one realises that there is a lifetime of learning and therefore a lifetime of mistakes to look forward to. Expert forensic imagery analysts should thus beware. Any effort to reduce the numbers of mistakes or errors made in forensic science is something that experts should embrace, and the push toward accreditation in facial image comparison is seen as one way to do this.

Automated Facial Recognition Technology

It would be desirable to perform reliable, automated identification of faces. It would be preferable to perform one-to-many facial comparisons very quickly (such as in a crowd situation) as this would maximise resources. This goal has been tackled for many years by a variety of researchers.

Face identification techniques can be divided into two main categories: those employing geometric features and those using grey-level information. Our faces display significant variation in appearance when captured in still or moving images. This is due to a multitude of factors, including morphological changes such as in a change in expression, differing hairstyles, as well as external changes such as variable ambient lighting conditions and the orientation of the face in 3D space. There is a requirement for 3D motion tracking, as well as an ability to recognise expressions etc., and these challenges are well described in papers outlining advances in automated expression recognition techniques (Jeni et al., 2012).

To be considered successful, automated systems should be able to suppress these factors to allow any facial image to be rendered expression-free and shown in a standardised 3D orientation with neutral lighting. Systems which can do this exist. Lanitis (1995) described a fully automatic face identification system that tolerates changes in expression, viewpoint and lighting but with very mixed results.

It remains a fact that automated systems, when presented with test subjects in a controlled 'normal' test set, score relatively highly. However, when presented with a difficult test set (images more like those from good surveillance), the scores are unacceptably low, often less than 50% correct classification of faces. These automatic identification system errors may be caused either by failure in locating landmarks accurately or by failure of the classification algorithm. There is little doubt that the goal of a reliable automated identification and recognition system will be perfected, but the question is: Is it here yet?

Summary

While there appear to be fewer disagreements between experts at the 'coal face' on subjects such as the validity of techniques and equipment used, there is still some academic and jurisprudence opposition to the current methods (or apparent lack of them). It seems that a singular and universally accepted method of facial comparison is still a long way off. There is still debate whether facial comparison will continue to be used in its present form, disappear altogether or emerge as a combination of technology and agreed scientific terminology.

There are many areas that still have not been touched in regard to research: areas dealing with understanding the similarities and differences in facial characteristics as a function of age and race and joining and using existing databases to analyse the frequency of occurrence of facial features in a given population to name just two.

It is likely that a foolproof, automated, real-world facial identification system will need a multisensor approach. Individual sensors are always likely to have a false acceptance or rejection rate which would leave them open to question as reliable evidential systems on their own. There will thus be the need for other verification evidence systems such as expert imagery analysis. These latter systems will also have a false alarm inaccuracy, but the overall confidence in the results increases with the number of systems used. The pressure to reduce the costs of criminal trial to the public purse makes it unlikely that two systems would be used to ensure increased accuracy.

The role of the Forensic Science Regulator appears to be the key area where progress can be made. Having a system by which facial comparison evidence is properly presented by expert analysts using properly regulated quality standards is a goal all should aspire to.

References

Allen R. 2008. Exact solutions to Bayesian and maximum likelihood problems in facial identification when population and error distributions are known. *Forensic Science International* 179:211–218.

Armitage R. 2002. To CCTV or not to CCTV?: A review of current research into the effectiveness of CCTV systems in reducing crime. NACRO Community Safety briefing: May 2002. Available from: http://www.nacro.org.uk/data/resources/nacro-2004120299.pdf, accessed January 31, 2013.

BAPCO Journal. 2008. CCTV: Making sense of the bigger picture. British Association of Public Safety Officials. pp. 31–34. Available from: http://www.google.com.au/url?sa=t&rct=j&q=CCTV+in+focus%3A+Making+sense+of+the+bigger+picture.&source=web&cd=2&cad=rja&ved=0CDgQFjAB&url=http%3A%2F%2Fwww.bapcojournal.com%2Fnews%2Fget_file.php3%2Fid%2F6%2Ffile%2FCCTV.pdf&ei=ANgJUfe3LYSWiQf4zICADQ&usg=AFQjCNGtDJRM2c8jTXcuy_b13B17RYbLlw&bvm=bv.41642243,d.aGc, accessed January 31, 2013.

Big Brother Watch. 2012. The price of privacy: How local authorities spent £515m on CCTV in four years. Available from: http://www.bigbrotherwatch.org.uk/files/priceofprivacy/Price_of_privacy_2012.pdf-.T0Olbfl8Cd4, accessed January 31, 2013.

Bromby MC and Plews S. 2006. Guidance for evaluating levels of support Forensic Imagery Analysis Group (FIAG). Available from: http://papers.ssrn.com/sol3/papers.cfm?abstract_id=1550752, accessed January 31, 2013.

Brown B. 1995. CCTV in town centres: Three case studies. Crime Detection and Prevention Series, Paper 68. London, U.K.: Police Research Group.

Brown G. 2012. Birmingham City Council spends more than £14m on CCTV opera-tions. Birmingham Post. Available from: http://www.birminghampost.net/news/west-midlands-news/2012/02/21/birmingham-city-council-spends-14m-on-cctv-operations-65233-30370267/, accessed January 31, 2013.

Bruce V and Young A. 1998. *In the Eye of the Beholder: The Science of Face Perception.* New York: Oxford University Press.

Brunelle F. Lookalike Project 2006. Available from: http://gemssty.com/2006/10/19/francois-brunelle-lookalike-project/, accessed February 08, 2013.

Catterick T. 1992. Facial measurements as an aid to recognition. *Forensic Science International* 56:23–27. Available from: http://www.sciencedirect.com/science/article/pii/037907389290142J, Site accessed January 31, 2013.

CRFP. 2008. CRFP's Submission to the Forensic Science Regulator's Review of the Optimal National Approach to the Registration of Forensic Practitioners. Council for Registration for Forensic Practitioners. Available from: http://www.google.com.au/search?q=http%3A%2F%2Fwww.homeoffice.gov.uk%2Fpublications%2Fpolice%2Foperationalpolicing%2FForensic_Practitiioner_Stan1.pdf%3Fview%3DBinary&ie=utf-8&oe=utf-8&aq=t&rls=org.mozilla:en-US:official&client=firefox-a, accessed January 31, 2013.

Davies G and Thasen S. 2000. Closed-circuit television: How effective an identifica-tion aid? *British Journal of Psychology* 91(Pt 3):411–426.

Davis JP, Lander K, Evans R, and Neville MF. 2012. Facial identification from CCTV: Investigating predictors of exceptional performance amongst police officers. Abstract available from: http://gala.gre.ac.uk/8462/, accessed January 31, 2013.

Dunn KW and Harrison RK. 1997. Naming of parts: A presentation of facial surface anatomical terms. *British Journal of Plastic Surgery* 50:584–589.

Edmond G, Biber K, Kemp R, and Porter G. 2009. Law's looking glass: Expert identification evidence derived from photographic and video images. *Current Issues in Criminal Justice* 20:337–377.

Edmond G, Kemp R, Porter G, Hamer D, Burton M, Bibe K, and Rocque M. 2010. Atkins v The Emperor: The 'cautious' use of unreliable 'expert' opinion. *The International Journal of Evidence and Proof* 14:146–166.

Evans R. 2002. The growth of facial identification use in the United Kingdom— A preliminary review. International Association of Craniofacial Identification (IACI). Bari, Italy.

Evison M, Dryden I, Fieller N, Mallett X, Morecroft L, Schofield D, and Bruegge RV. 2010. Key parameters of face shape variation in 3D in a large sample. *Journal of Forensic Sciences* 55(1):159–162.

FIAG. 2008. Guidance for evaluating levels of support. *Forensic Image Analysis Group Meeting*, Ankara, Turkey, December 02, 2008.

Gerrard G and Thompson R. 2011. Two million cameras in the UK. CCTV Image, No.42. Available from: http://www.securitynewsdesk.com/wp-content/uploads/2011/03/CCTV-Image-42-How-many-cameras-are-there-in-the-UK.pdf, accessed January 31, 2013.

Henderson Z, Bruce V, and Burton AM. 2001. Matching the faces of robbers captured on video. *Applied Cognitive Psychology* 15:445–464.

Işcan MY and Helmer RP. 1993. *Forensic Analysis of the Skull: Craniofacial Analysis, Reconstruction, and Identification.* New York: Wiley-Liss.

Jeni LA, Hashimoto H, and Kubota T. 2012. Robust facial expression recognition using near infrared cameras. *Journal of Advanced Computational Intelligence and Intelligent Informatics* 16:341–348.

Judge Dyson, Judge Steel, and Judge Dyer. 2001. R vs. Briddick [2001] EWCA Crim 984.

Laja S. 2012. Councils spend £515m in four years on CCTV. Avaiable from: http://www.guardian.co.uk/government-computing-network/2012/feb/21/cctv-councils-big-brother-watch, accessed January 31, 2013.

Lanitis A, Taylor CJ, and Cootes TF. 1995. An automatic face identification system using flexible appearance models. *Image and Vision Computing* 13:393–401.

Lee W-J, Wilkinson CM, Memon A, and Houston K. 2009. Matching unfamiliar faces from poor quality closed-circuit television (CCTV) footage: An evaluation of the effect of training on facial identification ability. *Axis* 1:19–28.

Lord Justice Hughes, Justice Rafferty, and Justice Slade. 2009. R vs. Atkins [209] EWCA Crim 1879, [2010] 1 Cr App Rep 117, 173 JP 529, [2010] Crim LR 141, 153 Sol Jo (no 38) 28, [2009] All ER (D) 13 (Oct) Court of Appeal, CA (Crim Div).

Lord Justice Waller, Justice Davis, and Justice David Clark. 2004. R vs. Trevor Elton Gardner [2004] EWCA Crim 1639.

Lord Taylor, Justice Henry, and Justice Blofeld. 1993. R vs. Stockwell [1993] 97 Cr App R 260.

Mail Online. 2008. David Davis's Resignation Statement in Full. Available from: http://www.dailymail.co.uk/news/article-1026066/David-Daviss-resignation-statement-full.html accessed January 31, 2013.

McCahill M and Norris C. 2002. CCTV in Britain: Working Paper No. 3. Available from: http://www.urbaneye.net/results/ue_wp3.pdf, accessed January 31, 2013.

McCahill M and Norris C. 2003. Estimating the extent, sophistication and legality of CCTV in London. In: Gill M (ed.) *CCTV*. Leicester, U.K.: Perpetuity Press. pp. 51–66.

Monahan T. 2004. Counter surveillance as political intervention? *CCTV and Social Control Conference*, Sheffield, U.K.

Norris C, McCahill M, and Wood D. 2004. The growth of CCTV: A global perspective on the international diffusion of video surveillance in publicly accessible space. *Surveillance and Society* 2:110–135.

NPIA. 2009. Facial Identification Guidance 2009. National Policing Improvement Agency. Available from: http://www.npia.police.uk/en/14533.htm accessed January 31, 2013.

Oxlee GJ. 2007. Facial recognition and imagery analysis. In: Thompson T and Black S (eds.) *Forensic Human Identification: An Introduction*. Boca Raton, FL: CRC Press. pp. 257–270.

Porter G and Doran G. 2000. An anatomical and photographic technique for forensic facial identification. *Forensic Science International* 114:97–105.

R v. Clarke [1995] 2 Cr App R 425; [2003] EWCA Crim 1020.

Roebers CM and Schneider W. 2001. Memory of an observed event in the presence of prior misinformation: Developmental patterns of free recall and identification accuracy. *British Journal of Developmental Psychology* 19:507–524.

Rose LJ. 2002. Attorney General's Reference No. 2 of 2002 [2003] EWCA Crim 2373 (October 07, 2002). Available from: http://judgmental.org.uk/judgments/EWCA-Crim/2002/%5B2002%5D_EWCA_Crim_2373.html accessed January 31, 2013.

Shepherd JW, Ellis HD, and Davies GM. 1977. Perceiving and remembering faces. Technical report to the Home Office under contract POL/73/1675/24/1.

Wechsler H, Phillips PJ, Bruce V, Soulié FF, and Huang TS. 1997. Face recognition: From theory to applications. *NATO ASI Series F: Computer and Systems Sciences*, Stirling, Scotland.

Wells GL. 1993. What do we know about eyewitness identification? *American Psychologist* 48:553–571.

Wilkinson C. 2004. *Forensic Facial Reconstruction*. Cambridge, U.K.: Cambridge University Press.

Wilkinson C and Evans R. 2009. Are facial image analysis experts any better than the general public at identifying individuals from CCTV images? *Science & Justice* 51:218–221.

Developments in Forensic Facial Composites

11

CHRIS SOLOMON AND STUART GIBSON

Contents

Introduction

In the event of a crime, a facial composite generated from an eyewitness' memory often constitutes the first and only means available for police forces to identify a criminal suspect. In the most general sense, a facial composite system is a tool designed to allow the expression of the facial appearance retained in the witness' memory in some tangible form, typically digital or a paper, hard copy. The desired outcome is that the generated composite will be of sufficient accuracy that subsequent display to members of the public or selected police officers will result in recognition, and that the name of the suspect will then be revealed. In most cases, the generated composite image will not be accurate enough to result in definitive recognition but may none-theless provoke members of the public who recognise basic similarities to provide the names of possible suspects. Largely, it is the combination of the composite with other basic information such as age, build, domicile, and the type of crime that results in the provision of suspect names.

The basic procedure for construction of composite images in the United Kingdom is loosely governed by the Association of Chief Police Officers (ACPO) guidelines (NPIA, 2009). Assuming that the offender is unknown to the witness, he or she will first be asked to provide a detailed verbal descrip-tion of the offender and to recount the incident in as much detail as possible. When the interview is complete, an attempt is made to produce a likeness under the guidance of a specially trained operator. While sketch artists employing traditional artistic materials are still used reasonably frequently in the United States, this process will most likely (in the United Kingdom at least) use some form of computerised facial composite system.

The process by which a witness and a composite operator arrive at a final facial composite is a complex interplay of computer imaging and human cognitive function, and the final result depends on a number of factors. The overall success of the composite process is, first and foremost, reliant on the witness' ability to retain some memory of the face in question. Operational experience suggests that some people are certainly better equipped to per-form this task than others. There are, however, a large number of uncon-trollable factors that affect the accuracy of the result obtained. These factors include the witness' state of mind (i.e. he or she may be in some degree of shock as a result of the crime), the period of time over which the crime took place, the proximity of the perpetrator to the witness during the crime, and the time elapsed between the crime and the composite construction. From an operational perspective, there are two vital aspects to consider in the design of an effective composite system. It should provide sufficient flexibility of use and image quality to meet the needs of different witnesses and operators and, critically, should be constructed, as far as possible, to match their normal cognitive processes.

Until recently, the facial composite systems used by international police forces were exclusively based on a construction process in which individ-ual facial features (eyes, nose, mouth, eyebrows, face shape, hairstyle) are selected one at a time from a large database and then electronically 'overlaid' to make the composite image. Such systems are often referred to as *feature based*, since they rely on the selection of individual features in isolation.

However, the relative weakness of human beings at the process of recall and description of faces is contrasted with their remarkable capacity for face recognition, which is well documented (for an example, see Tanaka and Farah, 1993). In simple terms, to recall and describe a face accurately (even that of a family member or a close relative) is cognitively difficult for many people.

After a long period of research and development work conducted largely within British universities, systems based on a rather different principle are finding increasing use by police forces (Frowd et al., 2010; Gibson et al., 2009; Solomon et al., 2009). These systems are usually described as holistic or global, as they primarily attempt to create a likeness to the suspect through an evolutionary mechanism in which a witness' response to groups of complete faces (not just individual facial features) converges toward an increasingly accurate image. Although much of this chapter is of broad relevance to holistic systems in general, it will focus on a system that had its origins in research undertaken by the Kent University forensic imaging group and is now commercially established under the name EFIT-V (www.visionmetric. com). In this context, it is worth noting that the most recent commercial incarnation of EFIT-V may best be described as a *hybrid* system, as it exploits not only holistic information processing, but retains some of the feature-based processing employed in most systems of the previous generation, and which operational experience shows are effective under certain conditions.

This chapter is divided into four main sections. In the remainder of this section, the historical background to the development of facial composite techniques is reviewed, and we highlight selected academic research that bears on the development of the new generation of composite systems. In the section entitled Statistical Appearance Model, the central mathematical foundations of the appearance model on which the EFIT-V system is built are outlined, and the conceptual implementation of this approach to composite construction is described. In the section entitled Systematic Operations in the EFIT-V system, we describe both stochastic and systematic means for manipulating the model representation of the face, to achieve convergence toward a satisfactory likeness, along with the empirical adaptations that have proved necessary and effective when working with real witnesses. In the final section, an overview of the operational procedure employed with EFIT-V will be offered, and current and future directions will be outlined.

Background to Facial Composite Systems

Prior to the advent of the personal computer, there were two dominant facial composite systems in the western world—Identikit (developed by Hugh C. McDonald of the Los Angeles Police Department in 1959) and PhotoFIT (developed by Jacques Penry in the United Kingdom, circa 1970). The original Identikit consisted of some 568 drawings of different facial features—specifically, chin/jaws, eyebrows, eyes, mouths, noses, and hairstyles—reproduced on transparent acetate sheets. MacDonald advocated that witnesses be asked to verbally describe each feature in turn, with the operator selecting that acetate foil which best matched the description. The witness could then attempt to refine the initial composite by exchanging and adjusting features until the final composite image was achieved through the superimposition of the selected foils. The foils were number coded, enabling the composite likeness to be rapidly transmitted to distant locations.

In 1970, Jacques Penry introduced the PhotoFIT system to British Police forces. PhotoFIT was based on actual photographs of facial features. In its final form, comparable to Identikit, it contained examples of some 560 facial features, each printed on thin card that could be placed within a special frame to produce the composite face. Like Identikit, PhotoFIT also contained a range of accessories such as hats and spectacles. PhotoFIT was not supplied with any specific instructions as to how it should be used, though Penry published a book illustrating and explaining his approach to physiognomy (Penry, 1971). Most operators, however, were taught to begin by recording a verbal description from the witness who was then directed by the operator to candidate features in the kit. The use of Identikit and PhotoFIT spread to a number of countries around the world, and kits were developed to represent the physiognomy of the native populations of a number of countries. Similar systems were developed in other countries but all were based on the same basic principle of feature selection (Davies et al., 1981).

With the arrival of the PC, the essential approach embodied by Identikit and PhotoFIT was rapidly computerised and rendered more efficient. In the United Kingdom, the Electronic Facial Identification Technique (E-FIT) system came to prominence, and the description and categorisation of features was also improved through the development of the Aberdeen index. For a broad review of the development and effectiveness of both mechanical and electronic feature-based composite systems (see Davies and Valentine, 2007).

It is perhaps surprising that even with the major advances in computers and computer-related technology that have been achieved in the last three decades, all commercially available facial composite systems until 5 years ago operated through this same essential mechanism in which the individual features of the face are described and selected by a witness from databases of examples which have been suitably categorised. The well-known commercial products *E-FIT, Pro-FIT, Identikit, comPHOTOfit*, and *Faces* are electronic facial composite systems that all fall into this broad category (see Figure 11.1). This apparently 'common-sense' approach of selecting features is, however, largely at odds with the psychological evidence on how memory of faces typically works (for an example, see Tanaka and Farah, 1993).

Although not apparently motivated by any considerations of cognitive processing, one of the earliest innovations to move away from the use of

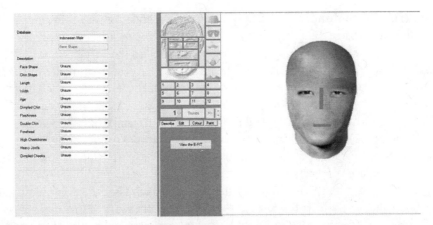

Figure 11.1 (See companion CD for colour figure.) E-FIT is the United Kingdom's most widely used feature-based composite system. The E-FIT interface shown here essentially operates by entering an initial verbal description for each feature which is processed and the database of features organised hierarchically according to the match with the description. The features can be displayed as thumbnail images or loaded directly onto the existing composite, which is built up feature by feature.

feature databases as the basic building blocks was the experimental system developed by Brunelli and Mich (1996) named 'SpotIt!' This system relied on a principal component analysis (PCA) model for each class of feature, achieving a reduction in the dimensionality of the problem and providing a basis from which novel features can be constructed. The 'pre-face' image or starting point in this system was the mean face into which the facial features are set/blended. The appearance of each facial feature is then controlled by seven sliders, where each slider corresponds to a principal component or mode of variation. In reality, the range of composites that can be produced using this technique is fundamentally limited by the finite size of sample used in the PCA. However, Brunelli and Mich (1996) included a tool that allowed the operator to manually distort the shape of a chosen feature. In this limited sense, there was a near-infinite set of feature shapes that could be achieved. One of the major weaknesses was that the sliders incorporated in the interface controlled changes in appearance defined on a mathematical premise and as such did not correspond to a specific perceptual meaning (e.g. 'a turned up nose'). Therefore, any prospective witness/operator found it difficult to locate the optimum slider positions required for a good likeness to the target face.

The first quasi-intelligent search procedure to overcoming the difficulty of selecting the most appropriate features in isolation from an almost unlimited sample was proposed by Caldwell and Johnston (1991) who developed a prototype system called Faceprints, which exploited a genetic algorithm (GA). The GA is initialised with a population of 20 faces that are constructed from individual facial features in a style reminiscent of earlier systems. Faces are displayed to the operator, who is required to assign a fitness score to each face depending on its similarity to the target. Parent faces are chosen from the initial population according to their associated fitness score and bred with each other using the standard principles of crossover and mutation. Faceprints was used in several crimes in the southwest of the United States but was never subsequently commercially developed. Later, DiPaolo (2002), also working in the computer graphics arena, describes such an algorithm for facial appearance, based on an aesthetic selection process in which faces are represented by genotypes comprising 25 parameters.

However, a more elegant and effective approach is both to model facial variation as a whole and *combine this* with genetic search. In this context, we note that the use of whole-face principal components as the elementary building blocks of a face had been explored in the computer vision literature and originated with the seminal work of Sirovich and Kirby (1987) where they were termed 'eigenfaces'. The essential idea here is that any face can be approximated by a suitable linear combination of the eigenfaces. Figure 11.2 shows examples of the first few eigenfaces constructed from a training sample of faces.

To the best of our knowledge, the earliest work to combine PCA modelling with genetic search was that of Hancock (2000) and Hancock et al. (1996) who describes a developmental system that utilises both global PCA face models and a GA. Critically, this design appears to be the first to allow composite images to be created by adjusting global/holistic properties of facial appearance, in a way that is not too demanding of the witness.

In his original prototype system, Hancock et al. (1996) used two separate PCA models, one for face shape and another for pixel intensity values. Using two independent models overcomes problems associated with head pose and blurring which otherwise degrade the composite images. The operator was presented with a selection of 18 faces to which fitness ratings must be assigned on a scale of 0–10. The GA selects faces with a high rating (fitness proportionate selection) as parents. Parameters defining an offspring's appearance were selected at random from the parents (uniform crossover) and a mutation applied to some of the parameter values. This procedure was performed 18 times to form a new generation of faces. Hancock's original PCA model was built on a limited sample of 20 female faces. The system has been subsequently refined and developed by Frowd and Hancock in a series of publications and is now known as EvoFIT (Frowd et al., 2010).

Another experimental system based on an evolutionary/PCA method was proposed by Tredoux et al. (1999) and termed ID, though this system has not seen any subsequent development. The EFIT-V system with which this chapter is primarily concerned was conceived independently of EvoFIT and ID. The research system operated under the name EigenFIT (Gibson et al., 2003)

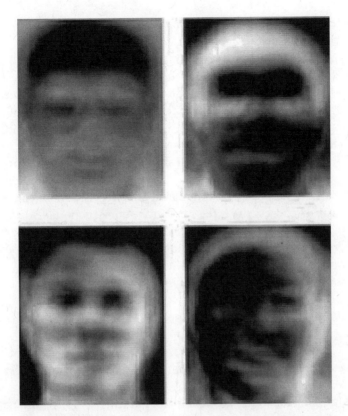

Figure 11.2 An example of the first few 'eigenfaces' calculated from a training sample of photographs. The eigenfaces, calculated through a PCA, can be considered as intensity pattern 'building blocks', suitable combinations of which can approximate any facial appearance within a pattern class.

and assumed commercial form under the name EFIT-V (Gibson et al., 2009; Solomon et al., 2009) in 2007. It is now the most widely used facial composite system in the United Kingdom and currently in use by police forces in 14 other countries. EFIT-V also employs PCA to construct a model of facial appearance but employs a hybrid stochastic–systematic search technique and thus differs somewhat in basic approach and functional details from EvoFIT and ID. However, it can be considered broadly representative of the new direction that has emerged in facial composite construction.

Statistical Appearance Model

Feature-based composite systems such as the commercial systems referred to earlier can, in the most general sense, be considered to employ a model for facial appearance. In this case, the model simply consists of examples of facial features each of which can be scaled and positioned (and in some cases, warped using basic geometric transformations). Textural blending of the components is achieved by ensuring that the intensity at the edges of the components are appropriately matched. From the mathematical perspective, these models are of a relatively crude nature. By contrast, the mathematical model used to represent facial appearance in EFIT-V is that of a shape–texture appearance model (Cootes and Taylor, 2001). The basic aim of such appearance models is to learn the dimensions of the face space by extracting the dominant factors or modes in the shape and texture of a training sample of faces and in this way to achieve a compact parametric representation of facial appearance that can be manipulated and searched more efficiently. We will successively address the three steps in the construction of such a model:

1. *Training*: the generation of the appearance model from a population sample of faces
2. *Decomposition*: of a given face in digital form into its appearance model parameters
3. *Synthesis*: of a face from its appearance model parameters (i.e. the reverse of decomposition)

The three elements of training, decomposition, and synthesis, respectively, enable us to *model* human facial appearance, *reduce* a digital representation of a human face to its most compact (parametric) form, and conversely *reproduce* the facial appearance from its parametric form. The steps in these three stages may be summarised as follows:

Training: The Generation of the Facial Appearance Model

1. The faces in the training set are firsthand marked at a number of control points delineating the main features of the face to form a set of shape model vectors S_i. The Procrustes aligned mean of the shape vectors, $\bar{S}$, is calculated. We refer to this as the *prototype* shape.
2. A PCA is carried out on the ensemble of aligned shape vectors—that is, we find a linear combination of the mean-subtracted shape vectors $P_S = (S - \bar{S})B_S$ which satisfies the required orthogonality relationship $P_S^T P_S = \Lambda_S$ where Λ_S is a diagonal matrix and P_S is the matrix containing the principal components. The required diagonalising matrix B_S can be found by standard eigenvector analysis.
3. The corresponding texture map vectors T_S for each face in the training sample are warped using standard Delaunay triangulation to the prototype shape. The resulting texture values are then referred to as the *shape-free* texture maps.

4. A PCA is carried out on the shape-free texture maps. That is to say, we again find a diagonalising matrix $\mathbf{B}_T$ such that $\mathbf{P}_T = (\mathbf{T} - \overline{\mathbf{T}})\mathbf{B}_T$ with $\mathbf{P}_T^T \mathbf{P}_T = \Lambda_T$.

5. It is important to recognise that the shape and texture in a human face are correlated. In the final stage, we therefore combine the separate linear models by de-correlating the shape and texture. We form a block matrix, $\mathbf{B}$:

$$\mathbf{B} = \begin{bmatrix} \mathbf{WB}_S \\ \mathbf{B}_T \end{bmatrix}$$

where the upper element of the block contains the eigenvectors which diagonalise the shape covariance and the lower element comprises the eigenvectors which diagonalise the texture (shape-normalised) covariance. The matrix $\mathbf{W}$ is a diagonal matrix of weights, which is required to make the shape and texture parameters (which have different units) commensurate (Cootes et al., 1995). This is achieved by scaling the total variance associated with the shape so that it matches the total variance associated with the texture. In this way, equal weighting is ascribed to the shape and texture. This process may be described mathematically as

$$\mathbf{W} = r\mathbf{I} = \begin{bmatrix} r & \cdots & 0 \\ \vdots & \ddots & \vdots \\ 0 & \cdots & r \end{bmatrix}$$

$$r = \frac{\lambda_g}{\lambda_s}, \quad \lambda_g = \sum \lambda_{gi}, \quad \lambda_s = \sum \lambda_{si}$$

where
  λ_{gi} is the variance associated with the ith texture principal component
  λ_{si} is the variance associated with the ith shape principal component

We apply a further PCA on the columns of $\mathbf{B}$, namely, we seek an orthogonal matrix $\mathbf{C}$ such that

$$\mathbf{C} = \mathbf{Q}^T \mathbf{B}$$

where
  the columns of $\mathbf{Q}$ are the eigenvectors
  $\mathbf{C}$ is the matrix of appearance parameters for the training sample

*The key result here is that each column of **C** provides a parametric description of the corresponding face in the training sample that is optimally compact in the linear, least-squares sense.* In Figures 11.3 and 11.4, we show the first few principal components of facial shape and texture according to the procedure outlined earlier.

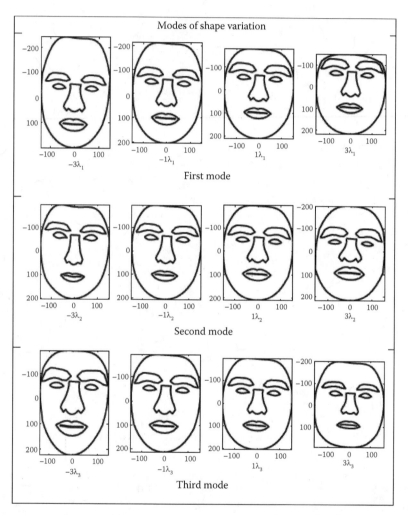

Figure 11.3 Illustration of the shape principal components or shape 'modes' extracted from the training sample of faces. Negative and positive multiples of each of the three modes are added to the average shape to indicate how they affect the face shape. Note how the modes affect multiple aspects of the face simultaneously—for example, the third mode significantly affects head shape ('long and pointed' to 'square'), eyebrows ('thick' to 'thin'), and mouth shape ('full and curved' to 'thin and straight').

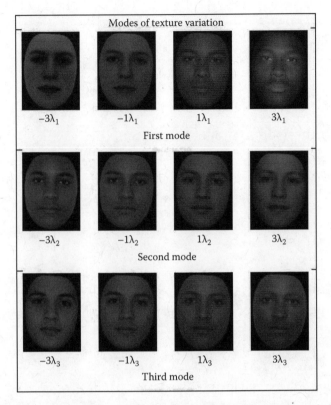

Figure 11.4 (See companion CD for colour figure.) Illustration of the texture principal components or texture 'modes' extracted from the training sample of faces. Negative and positive multiples of each of the three modes are added to the average texture to indicate how they affect the facial appearance. Note that the textures are shape normalised and that the class model in this example is mixed race.

Decomposition into Model Parameters

Decomposition of a given face into its appearance parameters proceeds through the following steps:

1. The facial landmarks are placed and the Procrustes aligned shape vector **S** of the face is calculated.
2. **S** is projected onto the shape principal axes $\mathbf{P}_S$ to yield the *decoupled* shape parameter vector, $\mathbf{b}_S$.
3. The face texture is warped to the prototype or 'shape-free' configuration.
4. The shape-free texture map is projected onto the texture principal axes $\mathbf{P}_T$ to yield the decoupled texture appearance parameters.

5. The appearance parameters are calculated using the eigenvector matrix $\mathbf{Q}$:

$$\mathbf{c} = \mathbf{Q}^T\mathbf{b} = \begin{bmatrix} \mathbf{Q}_S^T & \mathbf{Q}_T^T \end{bmatrix} \begin{bmatrix} \mathbf{Wb}_S \\ \mathbf{b}_T \end{bmatrix}$$

Facial Synthesis from Model Parameters

The reconstruction of the separate shape and (shape-free) texture vectors of a sample face from its appearance parameters $\mathbf{c}$ is calculated through the linearity of the model according to the equations

$$\mathbf{S} = \overline{\mathbf{S}} + \mathbf{P}_S\mathbf{W}_S^{-1}\mathbf{Q}_S\mathbf{c} \quad \mathbf{T} = \overline{\mathbf{T}} + \mathbf{P}_T\mathbf{Q}_T\mathbf{c}$$

where
   $\overline{\mathbf{S}}$ and $\overline{\mathbf{T}}$ are the mean shape and shape-free textures
   $\mathbf{P}_S$ and $\mathbf{P}_T$ are the shape and texture principal components
   $\mathbf{Q}$ is the eigenvector matrix separable into shape and texture block
   form as $\mathbf{Q} = \begin{bmatrix} \mathbf{Q}_S \\ \mathbf{Q}_T \end{bmatrix}$

The decoupled shape and texture appearance parameters are given by

$$\mathbf{b}_S = \mathbf{W}_S^{-1}\mathbf{Q}_S\mathbf{c}; \quad \mathbf{b}_T = \mathbf{Q}_T\mathbf{c}$$

Warping the shape-free texture to the required shape completes the facial synthesis. We refer the reader to the work of Cootes and colleagues (Cootes et al., 1992, 1995, 1998; Cootes and Taylor, 2001) for the comprehensive mathematical details of appearance models.

Relating Model Properties to Facial Appearance

Despite the relative complexity of the appearance model, we can easily summarise the key properties of appearance space:

- Any face can be described as a (parametric) vector of coefficients, $\mathbf{c} = [c_1 \, c_2 \cdots c_{n-1} \, c_n]^T$, providing the extension of the face along each of the appearance space axes.
- Appearance space is a multidimensional vector space, the axes of which correspond to specific shape–texture facial characteristics/features. As such, the appearance parameters control the amount of each global, shape–texture principal component in the face. All dimensions in face space represent *commensurate* quantities that

describe characteristics of the face as a whole. Such a representation is mathematically and intuitively satisfying.

- Appearance space is an optimally compact space. The combined linear PCA on shape and texture ensures that the resulting matrix of appearance parameters is optimally compact in the linear, least-squares sense. Thus, a representative training sample will enable us to reconstruct both in- and out-of-sample images, to within a given least-squares error, using a minimum number of dimensions in appearance space. *The reduction in the dimensionality of the problem is the major advantage of the PCA.*

These properties mean that the appearance space provides a compact, parametric representation of facial appearance, which is inherently *global* or *holistic*. This is so because the alteration of any one of the parameters will in general affect the entire facial appearance. Since the sample distribution of the appearance parameters may be well approximated by a multivariate Gaussian, it is a simple matter to randomly sample the distribution to generate plausible new examples of faces. Figure 11.5 shows examples of such randomly generated faces in EFIT-V for four different class models (White male, Black female, Arab male, Hispanic male).

Uses and Limitations of the Appearance Model

The construction of a statistical appearance model of the human face for a facial composite system requires a sample of facial images that are deemed broadly representative of the faces that one will subsequently wish to synthesise. As such, they should show appropriate variation in age and facial characteristics. Earlier versions of the EFIT-V system constructed a single appearance model over a broad range of ethnicities. While this has

Figure 11.5 (See companion CD for colour figure.) Random generation of faces in EFIT-V through sampling a statistical model of facial appearance. Examples are shown for each of the class models: *Arab male, Black female, Hispanic male, and White male.* Hair and clothing do not form part of the statistical model and have been added separately.

certain advantages in terms of mixed race representations and mixed gender characteristics, more recent versions have employed separate appearance models for each broad ethnic group that are referred to as *class models*. The essential use and significance of the appearance model in our specific context is fourfold:

1. It produces an optimally compact, parametric representation of the face for a selected class model.
2. By manipulation of these parameters, it is possible (at least in the case of a sufficiently large training sample) to accurately approximate any face belonging to the given class even if it was not used as part of the training process.
3. The random generation of examples from the model forms the basic mechanism by which the recognition capacity of the witness is brought to bear on the creation of the composite image.
4. This representation allows us to consider the manipulation of the underlying parameters as a search in a multidimensional face space in which each parameter defines a dimension and has a certain extension within it.

It should also be noted that the appearance model has certain limitations in its capacity to represent facial appearance. The inability to effectively define a point model (i.e. a set of meaningful landmarks that are consistent across a sample of images) for structures such as the hairstyle, facial hair, and a variety of skin-texture effects (wrinkles, eyebags) means that these features must be produced in alternative ways. These are discussed later.

The consideration of how to manipulate the underlying parameters in such a way as to converge toward the solution has been researched in some detail. The method employed in EFIT-V devised by Pallares–Bejarano (2006) is briefly summarised in the following section.

Stochastic Search Algorithm

The appearance model described previously provides the means for synthesising plausible face images, and we find that an adequate approximation to any face can be typically obtained from an appropriate selection of 60 independent appearance model parameters. In principle, the parameter values could be determined using many different approaches. For instance, one approach would be to construct a user interface in which each parameter value is systematically controlled by a slider and the resulting composite face displayed to the witness. This is somewhat naive as a search method, since there is no guarantee that appropriate combinations of the slider values can guide the witness meaningfully toward a result. Another approach would be to implement a purely random search of the parameter space in which a large number of candidate faces are synthesised from which the best likeness to the target face is selected. Although, in theory, both of these methods are capable of achieving a likeness, neither method takes into account 'ease of use' or the time required to achieve a likeness. It is crucial to recognise that the optimum search procedure for this task must be an algorithm that is a suitable compromise between human usability and speed of convergence (i.e. the required number of faces seen and rated by the user before a satisfactory composite is achieved). The stochastic search procedure in EFIT-V is an asexual evolutionary process termed the SCM algorithm (select–clone–mutate) whose steps are as follows:

1. The process is initialised by using a pseudorandom number generator to obtain nine vectors, each containing 60 double-precision random numbers (decision variables) drawn from a standard normal distribution:

$$c \sim N(0,1)$$

   Each of the nine vectors thus constitutes a single genotype, representing an encoded face. Collectively, the nine genotypes are referred to as the initial population. A decoded face image is termed a phenotype. The purpose of the initial population is to seed the evolutionary algorithm, thereby providing a starting point from which a likeness to a target face can be evolved.

2. A transformation is applied to each genotype vector. The transformation maps the standard, normal decision variables to appearance model parameters that follow the multivariate normal distribution relating to the chosen class model.

3. From each of the appearance parameter vectors, a face image is synthesised as described earlier. Figure 11.3 illustrates typical examples of nine such phenotype face images for a given generation.

4. From the array of nine faces, the witness is required to select the single face that most closely resembles the suspect (Figure 11.6) and to (optionally) reject one or more of the weaker examples. The selected face is the fittest phenotype, also referred to here as the stallion. It is the only face in the current generation from which genetic code is propagated into the next generation. The rejected faces can be used to bias the subsequent generation of faces away from regions of the search space occupied by previously rejected faces.

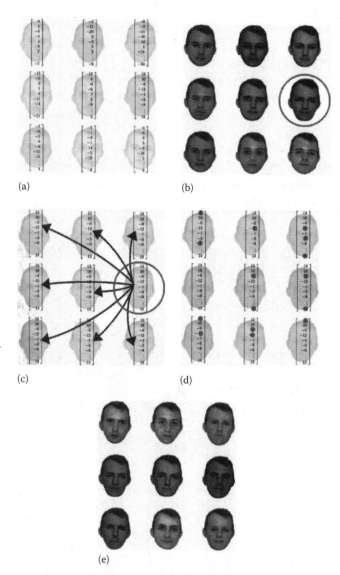

(a)   (b)

(c)   (d)

(e)

Figure 11.6 (See companion CD for colour figure.) The main steps in the SCM search algorithm. (a) Initial population: genotypes generated using PRNG; (b) initial population: phenotypes synthesised from the genotypes—fittest phenotypes (as selected by the witness) circled in red; (c) cloning (multiply): genotype corresponding to fittest phenotype cloned nine times; (d) mutation: random mutations on eight of the nine clones (the stallion remains unaltered, although its position in the new generation is randomised); (e) new generation: based on mutated genetic material from selected face.

5. The genotype corresponding to the stallion is duplicated or cloned nine times, thereby copying the genetic code of the selected face into a new generation of nine faces.
6. Eight of the cloned genotypes are mutated to produce variations on the selected stallion image. The remaining clone is left unaltered and is positioned randomly in the new array of nine faces. From these genotypes, nine new phenotypes are constructed. Thus, a new generation of faces is produced.
7. Steps are repeated until an acceptable likeness to the suspect's face is achieved.

Systematic Search

In the previous section, we described the basic SMM algorithm which is employed in the commercial incarnation of the EFIT-V system. The SMM algorithm has been found empirically to establish a good compromise between simplicity of operation (a human witness can easily make the required decisions) and fast convergence properties.

Here, we now draw explicit attention to the fact that our implementation of the SMM algorithm provides the opportunity for a witness to explicitly *reject* one or more faces in each generation. The ability to reject weak members in each generation appears to have some psychological benefit to witnesses as it is generally easier for the witness to choose the worst examples and thereby simplify the task of selecting the preferred face. However, to date, no explicit reference has been made to the use of rejected faces in the algorithm to speed convergence. It is clear that the rejection of certain faces provides definite information (i.e. 'don't show that face again or one that is close to it') which may, in principle, be harnessed to accelerate convergence to a satisfactory solution. We achieve this by a method we have termed *probability landscaping* in a high-dimensional search space. This section *can easily be skipped by the non-specialist reader* without loss of orientation, but for completeness, we include a brief account of the essence of our approach in the succeeding text.

Candidate solution vectors to our problem are real-valued, N-dimensional genotypes $\mathbf{x} = [x_1, x_2, ..., x_N]$, and there exists a target vector corresponding to the 'ideal' solution denoted by $\mathbf{x}^T = \left[x_1^T, x_2^T, ..., x_N^T \right]$. In each generation, the witness identifies a preferred vector which is *selected* by the witness $\mathbf{x}^S = \left[x_1^S, x_2^S, ..., x_N^S \right]$ and a least preferred or *rejected* vector $\mathbf{x}^R = \left[x_1^R, x_2^R, ..., x_N^R \right]$.

Consider a point P lying on the line $\mathbf{w} = \mathbf{x}^S - \mathbf{x}^R$ at a distance $\alpha|\mathbf{w}|$ from point $\mathbf{x}^R$. We construct an N-dimensional hyperplane which passes through point P and which is orthogonal to the line w. The hyperplane defines a discriminant function $g(\mathbf{x})$ which has the form

$$g(\mathbf{x}) = \mathbf{W} \cdot \mathbf{x} + \omega_0 = 0$$

$$\mathbf{W} = \mathbf{x}_S - \mathbf{x}_R, \quad \omega_0 = -\left(\mathbf{W} \cdot \mathbf{x}_R + \alpha |\mathbf{W}|^2\right)$$

The discriminant function divides the space into two mutually exclusive regions—$\mathbb{R}_S$ the region in which $\mathbf{x}^S$ is located and $\mathbb{R}_R$ the region in which $\mathbf{x}^R$ is located. In general, for an arbitrary genotype x, we have

$$g(\mathbf{x}) > 0 \Rightarrow \qquad \mathbf{x} \in \mathbb{R}_S$$

$$g(\mathbf{x}) \leq 0 \Rightarrow \qquad \mathbf{x} \in \mathbb{R}_R$$

After we have constructed the discriminant function, any subsequent genotype produced by the SMM procedure which satisfies $g(\mathbf{x}) \leq 0$ has its phenotype conversion probability *correspondingly reduced* through multiplication by factor p_R, $0 \leq p_R \leq 1$. In this way, the probability landscape is successively modified to favour generation from within those regions of the search space lying closer to $\mathbf{x}^S$. By the kth generation, K discriminant functions $\{g_1(\mathbf{x}'), g_2(\mathbf{x}') \cdots g_K(\mathbf{x}')\}$ have been produced such that an arbitrary genotype $\mathbf{x}$ has a conversion probability given by

$$\beta(\mathbf{x}) = (p_R)^m \quad \text{where } m = \sum_{k=1}^{K} \text{logical}\{g_k(\mathbf{x}) > 0\}$$

The fundamental assumption in our approach is that the preferred face in the generation (genotype $\mathbf{x}^S$) *will lie closer to the target vector* $\mathbf{x}^T$ than the rejected vector $\mathbf{x}^R$. If this assumption were strictly valid, it would guarantee that the target face $\mathbf{x}^T$ *always lies* within $\mathbb{R}_S$. Under these circumstances, we would be justified in setting $\alpha = 1/2$ and $p_R = 0$ and thereby maximally reducing the volume of the search space at each step. However, we assert this only in the average, statistical sense and not absolutely. This is because the relationship between the perceptual similarity of two different faces to a given target and the Euclidean distance to that target in the model space is nonlinear, and it is possible that a face whose Euclidean distance is further from a target face than another may nonetheless be perceived as more similar.

Intuitively, it is reasonable to assume that progressively small (or even negative) values for α, which move the hyperplane closer to $\mathbf{x}^R$, will progressively increase the likelihood that $g(\mathbf{x}^T) > 0$ and thus that $\mathbf{x}^T \in \mathbb{R}_S$. However, increasing α will generally reduce the volume of the search space which is partially suppressed. Accordingly, empirical optimisation takes place over the 2-D parameter space defined by α, which controls the position of the hyperplane, and p_R, which controls the 'strength' at which the probability landscape is altered.

Finally, we note that in practice, witnesses make three types of decision in the evolutionary process. These are *selection*, *explicit* rejection (in which a face is positively identified as a poor likeness and removed from view), and *implicit* rejection (in which the face is simply not chosen as the preferred likeness). In principle, we may also construct hyperplanes for *implicitly* rejected faces in which the probability landscape on the negative side of the hyperplane is weighted by some factor p_R^{imp} (in general, $p_R^{imp} < p_R$), but this method is not currently implemented in the commercial EFIT-V system.

Systematic Operations in the EFIT-V System

Although strong evidence has been marshalled to support the notion that observers achieve face recognition tasks through holistic and configurational cues, it is nonetheless common for a witness to remember particular, distinctive features and to sometimes encounter profound difficulty in progressing to the composite until the desired feature is incorporated. Under such circumstances, it is clearly less than ideal to request that a witness 'wait until a suitable feature is evolved'—a situation that is forced upon us by using an exclusively stochastic search method. Feedback from police forces using early versions of the system and subsequent operational feedback strongly support the notion that witnesses should have the freedom to alter the appearance deterministically at any time.

Further, many important aspects of facial appearance which appear to be closely related to identity *cannot be modelled* effectively using the statistical approach outlined previously. These aspects include hairstyle, effects bearing on the complexion of the skin (such as wrinkles, freckles, acne, and pockmarks). Also, some distinctive features, such as dimpled chins, are not well captured by the model.

In this section, we therefore outline some of the means provided in EFIT-V for exploiting this kind of witness information. The integration of feature-based (a large, hooked nose) and semantic information (he looked really sleazy) with a holistic–evolutionary mode of operation thus results in a hybrid system, providing maximum flexibility to the witness and operator.

Locking Facial Features

A relatively common occurrence for a witness operating in the evolutionary mode is to identify a specific facial feature within a face that is deemed satisfactory and which they do not wish to change. EFIT-V allows the operator to lock a facial feature by selecting the corresponding region on a schematic face image. Once the feature has been locked, it appears highlighted in the schematic image to inform the user that no further shape deformation of the selected feature will occur during subsequent generations. In terms of our underlying mathematical model, the process is expressed by a vector addition comprising the current stallion shape S_t and a snapshot of a previous stallion S_{t_0} captured at time t_0. Here, we use *time* to refer to a particular generation number, with $t > t_0$:

$$s'_t = s_t[\mathbf{I} - \mathbf{W}_f] + s_{t_0}\mathbf{W}_f$$

where
  $\mathbf{I}$ is the identity matrix
  $\mathbf{W}_f$ is a diagonal matrix with elements equal to one or zero

$\mathbf{W}_f$ is referred to as the feature selector since it effectively extracts all of the coordinates from S_{t_0} corresponding to the fixed feature. We can extend the equation earlier to include multiple features, locked at different instances (generations):

$$s'_t = s_t[\mathbf{I} - \mathbf{W}_{f1} - \mathbf{W}_{f2} - \mathbf{W}_{f3} \cdots - \mathbf{W}_{fN}] + s_{t_1}\mathbf{W}_{f1} + s_{t_2}\mathbf{W}_{f2} + \cdots s_{t_N}\mathbf{W}_{fN}$$

where
  $\mathbf{W}_{f1}, \mathbf{W}_{f2}, \ldots, \mathbf{W}_{fN}$ are the feature selectors for the first, second, …, and nth features, respectively (i.e. nose, mouth)
  $\mathbf{S}_{t1}, \mathbf{S}_{t2}, \ldots, \mathbf{S}_{tN}$ are snapshots of the stallion taken at times $t_1, t_2 \ldots, t_n$

Hence, one or more features may be locked at once. If the user wishes to evolve a single feature in isolation, all other features can be locked.

Feature Clone Tool

A closely related function to feature locking, and one that was developed as a result of feedback from police operators, is the *feature clone* function. This function allows a witness to identify an individual feature within one of the faces in the given generation and then copy that feature across the whole generation. This functionality is particularly useful when a witness is able to accurately recognise a feature but does not deem the face in which it is found to be the most accurate. Feature cloning copies the shape only to avoid problems with blending the texture between features. Rather than attempt to impose the feature in terms of the global appearance model that may not span the vector space, we adopt a simpler *ad hoc* approach. This is essentially similar to that used in the manipulation of individual feature shapes.

Blend Tool

The simplicity of the SCM algorithm employed in EFIT-V excludes the option of carrying over facial characteristics from more than one phenotype to the next set of nine faces. This can be accomplished in some measure through systematic blending of one or more faces in the current generation. This is achieved by forming a weighted combination of the genotypes (appearance model parameter vectors $\{c_i\}$) comprising the current generation. Faces for which $c_i = 0$ do not contribute to the blended face. If the blended face is considered to bear a better likeness to the target than the current stallion, the current stallion is replaced by the blended face. The updated stallion is reconstructed from the appearance model parameter vector in the usual way.

Facial Attribute Manipulation

Descriptive semantic labels are often used to describe facial appearance. For instance, a witness may describe a perpetrator as 'more masculine', less 'healthy looking', or 'older' with respect to the current composite image. Traditional methods for producing composite imagery are incapable of allowing direct control of such perceived attributes. Conversely, this is relatively easy to implement in the EFIT-V system framework and is achieved by identifying directions in the parameter space that can be directly related through statistical methods to a perceived increase or decrease in a specific attribute.

We outline here a simple procedure for defining such a direction through the appearance model parameter space, corresponding to maximum variation in a specified facial attribute. A similar approach to modifying facial appearance has previously been described by Benson and Perrett (1993) and Burt and Perrett (1995), in which shape and texture were treated separately. An appearance model offers a more elegant solution, in which facial appearance can be modified by perturbing a single vector of parameters that simultaneously control both shape and texture.

Training Process

To manipulate a chosen facial attribute, a prior training procedure is required in which a relationship is sought between the feature of interest and each appearance parameter. For attributes in which a dichotomy exists, such as the sex characteristic, the simplest approach is to separate the training examples into two classes A and B (e.g. males and females). Prototypes (constructed from class means) can then be formed by determining the mean vector of appearance model parameters for each class, $\bar{c}_A$ and $\bar{c}_B$.

Having formed two prototypes, a direction in appearance space is simply calculated as the difference vector between them:

$$\Delta c = c_{att} = \overline{c}_A - \overline{c}_B$$

We refer to the vector of appearance model parameters c_{att} as the attribute vector. For attributes that vary continuously (albeit on a discrete scale, e.g. age) with respect to variations in appearance model parameter values, an alternative approach is required. One such approach is to perform a multiple regression analysis, relating the attribute to the parameter values using a regression equation. Regression methods are closely related to the techniques and procedures employed in classification problems. Ramanathan and Chellappa (2005) used probabilistic eigenspaces and a Bayesian classifier to determine the age difference indicated by two images of the same subject's face, where the time interval between the first and second image was in the range 1–9 years. Details of alternative approaches to manipulating age (a subtly different problem from classification) can be found in Lanitis et al. (2002) and Scandrett et al. (2006). However, a simpler approach that has been found to produce visually acceptable results in our application is to arrange the attribute values (scores) in ascending order and perform a median cut, thereby forcing a dichotomy. In this case, each sample face is decomposed into its appearance model parameters and assigned to either class A or B as follows:

$$c_i = \begin{cases} \text{class } A \text{ if rank}(i) \leq \text{Median} \\ \text{class } B \text{ if rank}(i) > \text{Median} \end{cases}$$

Prototypes and the attribute vector can then be constructed exactly as previously described. The current commercial version of EFIT-V allows the transformation of age and distinctiveness, and it is likely that other attributes on which there is a high level of agreement among observers will be included in the near future.

A face is aged or rejuvenated by adding or subtracting a scalar multiple of the ageing attribute vector to the appearance model parameters representing the composite face and then reconstructing the image. In EFIT-V, the attribute manipulation is always performed on the current stallion. The attribute transformation process can be represented using vector notation as

$$c_i' = c_i + \alpha c_{att}$$

where the scalar α controls the degree of ageing or, for negative values of α, the rejuvenation of the face. An example of facial ageing of an EFIT-V image using this method is shown in Figure 11.7.

Figure 11.7 (See companion CD for colour figure.) Automatic aging in EFIT-V using the learned ageing direction in appearance space.

Local Feature Manipulation

Although one of the main strengths of the PCA model is its capacity to generate complete and plausible face images, with facial features properly related in the context of the whole face, there are instances when this holistic approach can be a disadvantage. One important case in which the global manipulation method proves inadequate is when the witness has remembered something distinctive about a particular facial feature and wishes to make a change to a localised region of the composite image. Localised modifications of this nature cannot be accommodated by the appearance model because in the global PCA framework, alterations to individual features are always accompanied by uncontrollable changes to the face as a whole.

EFIT-V allows the operator to manipulate the aspect ratio, position, and overall size of the individual facial features, as well as to effect a trapezoidal transform on the coordinates. The procedure involves shape modifications only, thereby avoiding any potential problems associated with blending of texture patches. This straightforward method provides a powerful tool for making adjustments to the ongoing composite image that is not too onerous for the witness. Statements regarding the width, height, and position of facial features are easily interpreted and do not require any complex vocabulary that could be misconstrued. As with any user-defined change in facial appearance, the operators themselves may also place implicit constraints on the deformation. With these constraints in place, face shapes that are modified using this local feature tool retain a realistic appearance despite the fact that in general they lie outside the span of the shape principal components. This implies that the local feature tool provides a means for introducing new plausible shape variation.

Managing Feature Manipulation in Appearance Space

The construction of the statistical appearance model means that the core elements of the face are represented by a vector $\mathbf{c} = (c_1, c_2, ..., c_n)$ of global appearance parameters. These parameters are global in the sense that altering a single parameter alters both the shape and texture of the entire facial appearance. Distinct parameter vectors $\mathbf{b}_s$ for the shape and $\mathbf{b}_T$ for the texture can be obtained directly from the appearance model via the following equations:

$$\mathbf{b}_s = \mathbf{Q}_s \mathbf{c} \mathbf{W}^{-1}$$

$$\mathbf{b}_T = \mathbf{Q}_T \mathbf{c}$$

In turn, the actual global shape vector $\mathbf{x}$ of the face and the shape-normalised texture map $\mathbf{g}$ of the face can be generated as

$$\mathbf{x} = \overline{\mathbf{x}} + \mathbf{P}_s \mathbf{b}_s$$

$$\mathbf{g} = \overline{\mathbf{g}} + \mathbf{P}_T \mathbf{b}_T$$

Consider now some arbitrary change introduced into the coordinates of $\mathbf{x}$ by a local manipulation of a feature shape such as the nose or mouth so that

$$\mathbf{x} \longmapsto \mathbf{x}' = \mathbf{x} + \Delta\mathbf{x}$$

To represent this vector in the global shape space, spanned by the principal components, we must project the vector onto the shape principal components contained in the columns of matrix $\mathbf{P}_s$ as

$$\mathbf{b}_s' = \mathbf{P}_s^T (\mathbf{x}' - \overline{\mathbf{x}})$$

In general, the localised manipulation of coordinates can result in a new shape vector, which *does not lie* within the span of the shape space, and the new shape vector $\mathbf{b}_s'$ will not, in general, enable exact reconstruction of the shape vector. Rather, we have

$$\mathbf{x}' = \overline{\mathbf{x}} + \mathbf{P}_s \mathbf{b}_s' + \vec{\varepsilon}_s$$

where $\vec{\varepsilon}_s$ defines a residual component of the modified shape that cannot be constructed using a linear combination of the shape principal components $\mathbf{P}_s$, since it is orthogonal to the vector space spanned by the columns of $\mathbf{P}_s$. It is clear that to maintain an accurate parametric representation of the generated composite, it is necessary to keep a record of both the global appearance vector $\mathbf{c}$ and the component of the shape deformation that is perpendicular to the shape principal components. The dimensionality of $\vec{\varepsilon}_s$ is high compared to the very compact representation provided by the appearance vector (or indeed its associated shape and texture parameters). One approach to the bookkeeping of composite production is to incorporate any local deterministic changes introduced by the operator and witness through repeated projection of the shape and texture vectors onto their respective principal components, thus obtaining the nearest global representation together with the component $\vec{\varepsilon}_s$. In this work, a simpler but equally effective approach was taken, which is summarised as follows:

1. Allow the core evolutionary procedure to continue as in the standard mode of operation, resulting in instances of whole-face variations on the current stallion.
2. Any deterministic changes to the shape and texture introduced by the witness are recorded and treated independently of the global model as offset vectors. In effect, the net deviation of the shape and texture from that predicted by the global model is updated on each occasion that deterministic changes are made.

The major advantage of this approach is that it removes the computational overhead, which is associated with recalculation of the global model and simplifies the implementation. The approach is schematically summarised in Figure 11.8.

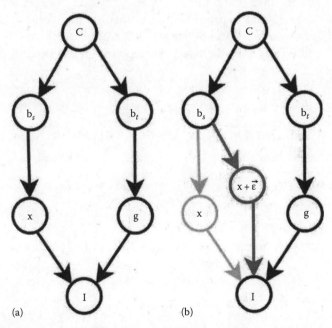

(a)   (b)

Figure 11.8 (See companion CD for colour figure.) (a) Construction of a composite image within the confines of the learned appearance space (left). The appearance model parameters $\mathbf{c} = (c_1, c_2, ..., c_n)$ are decoupled into shape and texture parameters $\mathbf{b}_s$ and $\mathbf{b}_T$. These in turn are used to generate the shape-free texture $\mathbf{g}$ and shape $\mathbf{x}$ before the final image $\mathbf{I}$ is created. (b) The same sequence but systematic offsets which lie outside the span of the appearance space are added to the shape vector before the final image is created.

Textural Effects in Composite Images

In general, given an appropriate training sample, the AM is capable of capturing *most* of the natural variation in facial appearance. However, finer textural aspects such as wrinkles, freckles, and pockmarks that often occur in real faces are not well modelled. This shortfall is particularly apparent when generating faces of old subjects since fine facial detail becomes more prevalent with an increase in age. The problem is intrinsic to the process by which new examples of faces are synthesised, whereby a new example of a face is constructed by a weighted average of existing face images. Inevitably, this averaging procedure results in a certain degree of smoothing in the synthesised face. Fine details that exhibit low spatial correlation between observations (sample faces) tend to be 'averaged out' by this process. Although wrinkles are often more common in specific regions of the face (e.g. 'crow's feet' appear at the outer corners of the eyes), their prominence, exact position, and frequency of occurrence vary from subject to subject. Landmarking these delicate features is not practicable; therefore, a different approach is required. The issue of enhancing fine detail in averaged face images has been investigated in previous work. In Tiddeman et al. (2001), a prototype face, formed by averaging a sample of face images, was decomposed using a wavelet analysis and the high-order details boosted to compensate for the inherent loss of high spatial frequency information.

EFIT-V employs an empirical but effective method for applying fine facial detail to a target face. A detailed mathematical description is a little lengthy, and so we restrict the explanation here to the essential idea, namely, to extract the fine facial details from a sample face A with the intention of applying these details directly to some target face B in a plausible fashion. The procedure breaks down into five basic steps:

1. First, identify a face image containing the detailed structures (e.g. wrinkles).
2. Perform a piecewise affine warp on the landmark coordinates to transform the shape to a reference (typically, the average shape).
3. Perform a high-pass Fourier filtering of the image to extract only the detailed structure.
4. Add some (adjustable) fraction of the high-pass filtered image to the Fourier domain version of the shape-normalised target image.
5. Inverse the Fourier transform and reverse the affine warp.

An example image is shown in Figure 11.9.

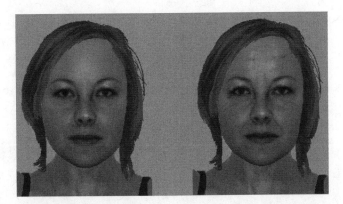

Figure 11.9 **(See companion CD for colour figure.)** Application of high-frequency image structure to a composite face image.

Application of EFIT-V

EFIT-V Construction Procedure

In this chapter so far, we have reviewed the methodology of facial composite systems and described the elements of the *EFIT*-V system in some detail. As we have shown, this system uses an approach that is fundamentally different from feature-based composite systems. EFIT-V has been in regular use for nearly 5 years, undergoing continuous and significant developments during this time. It is in routine operational use by approximately 70 police forces in 14 countries, and it seems highly likely that this fundamentally new approach, supported by increasing evidence from research (Solomon et al., 2009, 2012), will have a lasting influence on the way that composites are produced in the future. In the United Kingdom, the use of cognitive interview (CI) techniques (Fisher and Geiselman, 1992) has formed an integral part of the training of composite operators for two decades. The use of the CI has undergone some modification in recent years to reflect the now dominant use of the evolutionary approach embodied in EFIT-V and EvoFIT, but remains a standard in the current ACPO guidelines. The premium that is placed in the CI on facilitating recall and description by the witness is arguably much less appropriate for evolutionary systems. A system such as EFIT-V primarily relies on jogging the memory through repeated exposure to groups of faces broadly matching a basic description—that is, to an increasingly refined, direct stimulus–response method, rather than starting by extensively filtering the facial memory through the verbal medium. Academic research in the last few years has begun to acknowledge and explore alternative interview methods (see Frowd et al., 2008, for an example), which are better adapted to the cognitive processes of witnesses and more time-efficient. These techniques are now incorporated into the training programmes of the main UK composite system providers.

The most recent version of EFIT-V is designed to be flexible, allowing a witness to provide information through both holistic and feature-based channels so that the face construction can be adapted to the individual witness and his or her natural abilities and preferences. For this reason, no rigid operational procedure is recommended, and effective use of the system will respect those abilities and preferences. However, the following sequence of events may be considered typical of the EFIT-V interview and composite construction process:

1. An initial interview is first conducted. Given the finite time and financial resources of police officers, some criterion for whether composite construction should even sensibly be attempted is important. In the past, this decision was often made based on the quality of the facial description provided by the witness in a preliminary telephone interview. Given the decidedly weak correlation between actual facial memory and verbal description (i.e. the pronounced inability of many to offer coherent facial descriptions of well-known faces and even close relatives), the deficiencies of that approach are clear. In the use of EFIT-V, one simple question to the witness has evolved as a fairly standard indicator of whether an interview may yield useful intelligence, namely, *'If you saw the offender again, do you think you would recognise him or her?'*

2. In practice, the elementary principles of the CI continue to be respected in the EFIT-V interview—in particular, good rapport building and allowing free recall of the incident and facial appearance without interruption. In passing, we note that there is arguably nothing unique to the CI in this—rather they are common-sense principles followed by any good and experienced interviewer. Witnesses volunteer information about the incident and the facial appearance of the suspect in any way that is natural to them, with the operator taking note to raise specific details for the attention of the witness at the appropriate point in the construction procedure. Crucial differences, however, are that the witness is not forcibly prompted to describe the individual features of the face or encouraged to repeat information already volunteered. Typical EFIT-V interviews also do not employ methods such as reversal of the time sequence of events or viewing the scenario from the perspective of another person in a different situation at the scene—techniques sometimes employed in the CI.

3. A short holistic cognitive interview (HCI) along the lines outlined by Frowd et al. (2008) completes the interview process.

4. On system start-up, a Police and Criminal Evidence Act (PACE), UK complaint form is displayed into which details that identify the composite are entered. Fields are provided for the witness' forenames, surname, date of birth, and also the operator's rank and number. This information is combined with the current date to generate a unique reference number that can be used to identify the composite in the future.

5. Armed with the salient points from the initial interview stages, the operator may initiate the construction stages through one of two routes, which are termed the *direct* and *guided* modes. As the basic process in EFIT-V is to view screens of faces, make selections and rejections, and thereby progress toward an increasingly good likeness, it will clearly be more efficient if the initial generation of faces to which the witness is exposed bear a closer resemblance to the target face (insofar as this is possible). The guided mode achieves this by allowing the witness the option of choosing any of the individual features from a collection of feature prototypes as the basic starting point. An option to 'skip' exists in which case the initial generation of faces only varies about the average of the skipped feature. In this way, any relevant information on the individual appearance of features can be incorporated at the start of the evolutionary procedure.

6. If the witness has volunteered no information whatsoever on the appearance of the individual facial features, the operator may choose to proceed through the direct mode in which the first generation of faces are given by perturbations about the average. In practice, this is quite rare.

7. The witness then proceeds to select the hairstyle or, in the event that this was not visible, the headwear worn by the suspect. From a perceptual point of view, it is sensible to ask the witness to select an appropriate hairstyle first as the external features are more salient in unfamiliar faces and there is evidence to suggest that facial features should be selected in order of decreasing significance. The user can scroll through the available hairstyles using a slider, with each increment in slider position displaying nine more hairstyles in the familiar three-by-three configuration. Hairstyles are mapped onto a blank head shape so that the witness may view the hair in some context. A filter is provided to sort the hairstyles into categories describing the length and colour. Thus, the number of candidate hairstyles that the witness must examine can be greatly reduced by marking the appropriate checkboxes provided in the filter.

8. At this point, the stochastic search begins, and the first generation of nine faces is presented. The witness is probed (but not compelled) to select a single face from the nine which best resembles the suspect.

If none is deemed to bear sufficient resemblance, the witness may request to see another group until a face appears that constitutes a satisfactory starting point. The witness also has the option of rejecting one or more of the faces in each generation that are deemed to exhibit a poor likeness to the target, and these are automatically removed from view. The rejection serves two purposes. Firstly, it declutters the field of view making it easier for the witness to form an opinion on the suitability of the remaining visible faces. Secondly, the designation of some faces as poorer is used to guide the search and bias it away from regions of the search space populated by rejected faces.

9. Once the witness has made an initial choice, the current population is then replaced by nine more faces comprising the next generation, and the process of selecting a face is repeated. In this mode, the user has the option to lock the shape of a particular facial feature that exhibits a good likeness to the corresponding feature in the target face. This is achieved by choosing a region in an iconic face located on the right-hand side of the interface and then selecting one of the nine virtual faces. Placing the cursor over a feature in the iconic face and using a single click of the left mouse button turns that region from grey to blue, indicating that the shape of the chosen feature will be fixed through subsequent generations. Deselecting a region of the iconic face reintroduces shape variation in the previously locked feature. If required, more than one feature may be fixed at any given instant. The available choices of features that can be locked are the eyebrows (left/right pair), eyes (left/right pair), nose, mouth, and face shape, or any combination of these.

10. Typically, after a witness has selected the preferred face from five or six generations, he or she will be prompted to provide feedback on the composite image so far and whether there are any definite characteristics or features that they would like to alter. The operator will then respond using the array of systematic tools at their disposition in an attempt to 'progress' the composite toward a better likeness. This step is an important and characteristic one in the use of EFIT-V since the operator should resist (in general) any attempt to create a final product at this stage but only to use the information provided by the witness to progress the composite likeness and confirm whether (or not) the modified composite now represents a *better likeness*.

11. If the witness indeed confirms an improved likeness, the system immediately reverts to the evolutionary mode and takes this likeness as the starting point for the subsequent stochastic variations. Again, the witness is then asked to select the best example from a sequence of generations, three to six being typical.

12. Further systematic changes may be requested at this stage, including the use of paintwork using an associated graphics package such as Adobe Photoshop or Corel PaintShop. Paintwork can be added to EFIT-V images at any time and the system used subsequently in the normal way, but it is generally advisable to defer certain forms of artistic enhancement to late in the process due to the inherent problems of image registration. In effect, the EFIT-V image is constantly changing through the generations, and there is no simple automatic way to adapt the static paint layers to keep track.

13. An *undo* function (1 step back at a time) and a *load* function (back to an arbitrary step in the construction) are available. Typically, these are used when the witness feels that a poor choice of face has been made or a face has been selected unintentionally and another image is preferred.

14. Once an acceptable likeness has been obtained, the current stallion image (best likeness) is saved both as a graphics file and as a file internal to EFIT-V, which can be loaded into the programme at any point in the future. A complete audit trail is kept by EFIT-V so that the time, date, personnel involved, and all steps in the construction process are saved to the hard disk of the computer. The entire contents can also be burned directly to CD from within EFIT-V as an exhibit for subsequent evidential procedures.

Effective Composite Systems and Future Development

A meaningful evaluation of the effectiveness of any facial composite system is surprisingly complex. From a policing perspective, the primary goal is very simple, namely, the provision of a correct name for the suspect. Secondary goals also exist, that is, speed and ease of use, which can have direct financial implications for police forces. In reality, the attempt to achieve the primary goal is affected by many factors:

- The inherent capability of the composite system to create good likenesses (i.e. its *imaging* capability).
- Its inherent methodology (i.e. the degree to which the system matches the cognitive processes and needs of the witness and operator).
- The capability and skills of the police operator. Although standardised training courses exist, operator skill and experience vary widely.
- The capability, willingness, and emotional state of the witness.
- The nature of the crime or offence. There is, for example, some provisional but compelling evidence to suggest that offences in which

the witness has time or presence of mind to consciously attempt to commit the face to memory (e.g. an abduction) generally *result in a different encoding of the face* compared to offences in which no conscious attempt is made (e.g. a distraction burglary during which the victim will have no reason to consciously attempt to remember the face of the perpetrator *at the time of the incident*).

- The effective use of the composite once it has been created. In simple terms, a composite image may represent a good likeness to the target subject, but if the subsequent procedures followed by the police do not result in a sufficient or appropriate cross section of the police or public seeing the image, it will fail in its basic objective. This crucial operational aspect and its impact on success rates are often strangely overlooked.

- The supply of relevant supplementary information along with the composite image can affect the ability and willingness of someone to offer a name. For example, an image supplied with supplementary information such as 'a white male aged 30–35 years, with a strong northern accent and scruffily dressed' is likely to have better chances of success than the image alone.

The EFIT-V is currently in routine use by 33 of the United Kingdom's 51 police forces and in 14 other countries. As a commercial system, the evaluation of its effectiveness to date has largely been gauged by feedback from police forces using the system routinely rather than through academic studies. At the E-FIT user conference in 2009, West Yorkshire police reported a 40% naming rate over an 18-month period from May 2008 to November 2009 that encompassed more than 1000 interviews. In 2010, the same force reported a naming rate of over 50% from a consecutive sample of nearly 400 monitored interviews. This indicates that when all the factors mentioned earlier are properly considered, performance can be excellent.* Technical and functional developments of the system are continuing, driven by the real-life requirements of operators and witnesses but also informed by advances in our understanding of facial processing and image processing.

Figure 11.10 shows an array of famous faces, all of which were created by trainees on various training courses delivered in 2010. These images were not produced under conditions of strict forensic validity, but were produced from memory and indicate EFIT-V's inherent capacity to produce accurate likenesses of the subject.

---

* It is worth noting in this context that a novice user at Wiltshire police with less than 1 year's experience and no formal training reported a naming rate of 30% in 2011.

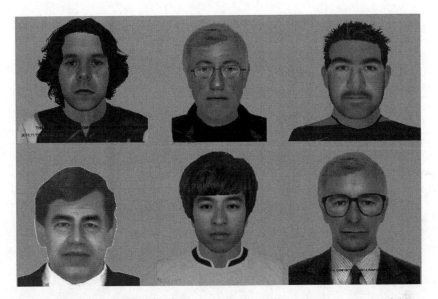

Figure 11.10 (See companion CD for colour figure.) Construction of famous faces from memory using the EFIT-V system. The images earlier were created during training of police operators. Proceeding from the top row, left to right, the target subjects are Carlos Tevez (footballer), Alex Ferguson (football manager), Eric Cantona (former footballer and now actor), Gordon Brown (former Prime Minister, United Kingdom), Bruce Lee (martial artist), and John Major (former Prime Minister, United Kingdom).

Summary

The major innovations in forensic facial composites over the last 15 years have resulted in a gradual shift in the centre of gravity. From a position in which the face was exclusively represented and constructed in terms of the constituent features and their relative geometric placement, we have now moved toward a global or holistic model in which the memory of the witness is probed by displaying whole faces, and their response guides a stochastic or evolutionary search toward a facial likeness. Many papers exist that address various aspects of this work, but the overall trend is documented in the important contributions made by Caldwell and Johnston (1991), Frowd (2002), Frowd et al. (2010), Gibson et al. (2003), Hancock et al. (1996), Hancock (2000), Solomon et al. (2009), Solomon et al. (2012), and Tredoux et al. (1999).

On the global scale, despite the intensive research conducted within largely British universities and the increasing evidence for the superiority of the guided–stochastic approach described in this chapter, forensic facial composites largely continue for the moment to be constructed by sketch artists or by software programmes employing the feature-based methodology. However, the documented academic and operational success in Britain, which in 2011 saw formal introduction into a number of US police forces, seems likely to have an enduring influence.

References

Benson, P. J. and Perrett, D. I. 1993. Extracting prototypical facial images from exemplars. *Perception*, 22, 257–262.

Brunelli, R. and Mich, O. 1996. SpotIt! an interactive identikit system. *Graphical Models and Image Processing: GMIP*, 58, 399–404.

Burt, D. M. and Perrett, D. I. 1995. Perception of age in adult Caucasian male faces: Computer graphic manipulation of shape and colour information. *Royal Society Proceedings B*, 259, 137–143.

Caldwell, C. and Johnston, V. S. 1991. Tracking a criminal suspect through face-space with a genetic algorithm. *In:* Belew, R. K. and Booker, L. B. (eds.) *Proceedings of the Fourth International Conference on Genetic Algorithms*, San Diego, CA; San Mateo, CA: Morgan Kauffman Publications, pp. 416–421.

Cootes, T. F., Edwards, G. J., and Taylor, C. J. 1998. Active appearance models. *In:* Burkhardt, H. and Neumann, B. (eds.) *Proceedings of the Fifth European Conference on Computer Vision*, Vol. 2, Freiburg, Germany; Berlin, Germany: Springer, pp. 484–498.

Cootes, T. F. and Taylor, C. J. 2001. Statistical models of appearance for computer vision. Manchester, U.K.: University of Manchester.

Cootes, T. F., Taylor, C. J., Cooper, D. H., and Graham, J. 1992. Training models of shape from sets of examples. *Proceedings of the British Machine Vision Conference*, Leeds, U.K., pp. 9–18.

Cootes, T. F., Taylor, C. J., Cooper, D. H., and Graham, J. 1995. Active shape models—Their training and application. *Computer Vision and Image Understanding*, 61, 38–59.

Davies, G., Ellis, H., and Shepherd, J. 1981. *Perceiving and Remembering Faces*, New York: Academic Press.

Davies, G. M. and Valentine, T. 2007. Facial composites: Forensic utility and psychological research. *In:* Lindsay, R. C. L., Ross, D. F., Read, J. D., and Toglia, M. P. (eds.) *Handbook of Eyewitness Psychology, Vol. 2: Memory for People*. Mahwah, NJ: Lawrence Erlbaum Associates, pp. 59–83.

Dipaolo, S. 2002. Investigating face space. *Proceedings of the SIGGRAPH 2002 Conference*, San Antonio, TX; New York: ACM, pp. 207.

Fisher, R. P. and Geiselman, R. E. 1992. *Memory-Enhancing Techniques for Investigative Interviewing: The Cognitive Interview*. Springfield, IL: Charles C. Thomas.

Frowd, C. D. 2002. EvoFIT: A holistic, evolutionary facial imaging system. PhD thesis, University of Stirling, Stirling, Scotland.

Frowd, C. D., Bruce, V., Smith, A. J., and Hancock, P. J. B. 2008. Improving the quality of facial composites using a holistic cognitive interview. *Journal of Experimental Psychology: Applied*, 14, 276–287.

Frowd, C. D., Hancock, P. J. B., Bruce, V., Mcintyre, A. H., Pitchford, M., Atkins, R., Webster, A. et al. 2010. Giving crime the 'evo': Catching criminals using EvoFIT facial composites. *In:* Howells, G., Sirlantzis, K., Stoica, A., Huntsberger, T., and Arslan, A. T. (eds.) *IEEE International Conference on Emerging Security Technologies*, Canterbury, U.K., pp. 36–43.

Gibson, S. J., Solomon, C. J., Maylin, M. I. S., and Clark, C. 2009. New methodology in facial composite construction: From theory to practice. *International Journal of Electronic Security and Digital Forensics*, 2, 156–168.

Gibson, S. J., Solomon, C. J., and Pallares Bejarano, A. 2003. Synthesis of photographic quality facial composites using evolutionary algorithms. *In:* Harvey, R. and Bangham, J. A. (eds.) *British Machine Vision Conference 2003*, Vol. 1, Norwich, U.K., pp. 221–230.

Hancock, P. J. B. 2000. Evolving faces from principal components. *Behavior Research Methods, Instruments and Computers*, 32, 327–333.

Hancock, P. J. B., Burton, A. M., and Bruce, V. 1996. Face processing: Human perception and principal components analysis. *Memory and Cognition*, 24(1), 26–40.

Lanitis, A., Taylor, C. J., and Cootes, T. F. 2002. Toward automatic simulation of aging effects on face images. *IEEE Transactions on Pattern Analysis and Machine Intelligence*, 24, 442–455.

NPIA. 2009. Facial identification guidance. National Policing Improvement Agency. Available from: http://www.npia.police.uk/en/14533.htm accessed January 31, 2013.

Pallares-Bejarano, A. 2006. Evolutionary algorithms for facial composite synthesis. PhD thesis, University of Kent, Kent, U.K.

Penry, J. 1971. *Looking at Faces and Remembering Them: A Guide to Facial Identification*. London, U.K.: Elek Books.

Ramanathan, N. and Chellappa, R. 2005. Face verification across age progression. *IEEE Computer Vision and Pattern Recognition*, 2, 462–469.

Scandrett, C. M., Solomon, C. J., and Gibson, S. J. 2006. A person specific, rigorous aging model of the human face. *Pattern Recognition Letters: Vision for Crime Detection and Prevention*, 27, 1776–1787.

Sirovich, L. and Kirby, M. 1987. Low dimensional procedure for the characterization of human faces. *Journal of the Optical Society of America*, 4, 519–524.

Solomon, C., Gibson, S., and Maylin, M. 2009. A new computational methodology for the construction of forensic, facial composites. *Computational Forensics*, 5718, 67–77.

Solomon, C., Gibson, S., and Maylin, M. 2012. Evolutionary algorithms and computer composites. *In:* Wilkinson, C. and Rynn, C. (eds.) *Craniofacial Identification*. Cambridge, U.K.: Cambridge University Press.

Tanaka, J. W. and Farah, M. J. 1993. Parts and wholes in face recognition. *Quarterly Journal of Experimental Psychology*, 46A, 225–245.

Tiddeman, B., Burt, M., and Perrett, D. 2001. Prototyping and transforming facial textures for perception research. *IEEE Computer Graphics and Applications*, 21, 42–50.

Tredoux, C., Rosenthal, J., Da Costa, L., and Nunez, D. 1999. *Reconstructing Faces with an Eigenface Composite System*. Boulder, CO: SARMAC III.

Virtual Anthropology and Virtopsy in Human Identification

12

STEPHANIE L. DAVY-JOW AND SUMMER J. DECKER

Contents

Introduction

The essential questions facing forensic anthropologists have not changed remarkably over the last few decades. When presented with remains, practitioners must determine whether they are human and if they are of archaeological or forensic significance. A biological profile must be generated including age at death, sex, ancestry, living stature, indications of interpersonal violence or trauma, illness, injury, or other unique characteristics, as well as determination of any taphonomic factors that have acted on the remains since the death of the individual, in order to aid in identification and explain the circumstances surrounding the death and postmortem interval (PMI). Although these basic duties have changed very little, the science underpinning the way forensic anthropologists embark upon them has changed immensely.

In recent decades, there has been a paradigm shift in the field. It has grown from a small group of experienced physical anthropologists/ osteoarchaeologists primarily tasked with examining bones, to a vibrant field of practitioners and researchers working to validate and improve existing techniques or to discover new ones. As forensic science and expert testimony in general has come under scrutiny and new legislation (Daubert v. Merrell Dow Pharmaceuticals Inc., 1993; Kumho Tire Co. Ltd. v. Carmichael, 1999; National Academies, 2009; U.S. Federal Government, 2000), the discipline has had to face the challenges of meeting stringent scientific scrutiny where little quantitative information previously existed. Due to the mercurial nature of the casework undertaken by anthropologists, obtaining such data can be very difficult. It is practically impossible to undertake a rigorous scientific study of the techniques that rely mainly on qualitative, experiential, and pattern recognition skills. Activities such as estimation of the postmortem interval (time since death) and recognition of bone modification activities can be difficult to quantify, despite being a regular part of an anthropologist's duties (Grivas and Komar, 2008). A scientific working group, known as the Scientific Working Group for Forensic Anthropology (SWGANTH), was established in 2008 to address these types of issues (Christensen and Crowder, 2009) in the United States, as have organisations such as the fledgling British Association of Forensic Anthropology (BAFA) (established 2011) in the United Kingdom.

In the interim, however, efforts have been made to standardise the ways in which data are collected. Buikstra and Ubelaker (1994) produced an edited volume outlining standard data collection procedures for dealing with human remains. The United Kingdom published similar guidelines in 2004, mainly for osteoarchaeologists (Brickley and McKinley, 2005). The University of Tennessee at Knoxville has also developed FORDISC 3.0 (Ousley and Jantz, 2005), a software package which uses discriminant function analysis to classify the sex and ancestry of unknown remains using information of known individuals in the Forensic Data Bank. This software is widely used and, by extension, dictates the type of metric measurements that are taken during anthropological assessments of skeletal remains. In addition to more rigorous standards for day-to-day practice, the field is also beginning to welcome technologies that have, until recently, been utilised by only a few researchers.

3D Surface Scanning

3D surface scanning has a wide variety of applications from special effects in films to the digital preservation of artefacts. Photogrammetric scanners utilise multiple cameras that register images together to generate a 3D representation of an object. The more accurate laser scanners pass (an) infrared beam(s) over the surface of an object, generating a dense cloud of coordinate points. From these points, a wireframe mesh and solid representation can be generated. The data can be viewed and manipulated in 3D and exported to external packages for editing, modelling, and measurement. Depending upon the scanner and software capabilities, laser scanners can be accurate to the micron level. Some capture both shape and texture information (colour is stored as a 2D photographic image), and all are noncontact and nondestructive.

The scanners range in price, size, and accuracy. Like most technology, over time laser scanner quality has increased and the price has decreased. It is now possible to purchase scanners suitable for scanning bones from as little as £5,000 and plug-and-play portable scanners from £12,000. Larger systems can be used to quickly scan entire crime scenes or individuals.

Medical Imaging Technologies

'3D volumetric data' are the type of data that are the standard output of current 3D image acquisition devices and are used in medical imaging modalities like magnetic resonance imaging (MRI) and computed tomography (CT). Commonly referred to as DICOM images, these volumetric data are embedded with an abundant amount of information that is often not fully utilised by modern medical practitioners (Udupa and Herman, 2000). From x-ray to CT, each imaging method has provided an insight into the internal structure and function of the human body.

Imaging of anatomical structures for medicine began with the discovery of x-radiation by Wilhelm Roentgen in 1895 and W.D. Coolidge's x-ray tube in 1903. For the first time, images of the internal body could be taken of living individuals (Nobelprize.org, 2008; Röntgen, 1967). X-ray imaging involves taking a piece of film in a cassette and placing it between the object being imaged (body part) and the x-ray emission device or source. The film (or image capture receptor) detects the x-ray's waves and creates an image of the anatomy that it passed through. X-ray images are known to be effective in capturing bone and other dense structures but are less useful in distinguishing soft tissue (Enderle et al., 2005). X-rays (Figure 12.1) were the gold standard for 2D imagery until 1973 when the first 2D magnetic resonance imager was released.

With the introduction of MRI, medical imagery was finally able to capture much of the soft tissue that had been elusive in x-ray imagery. In MRI, the nuclei of the hydrogen atoms in the body are polarised via an extremely strong magnet that creates a gradient or magnetic field over the body. The stronger the magnetic field is, the higher the resolution of the image will be. Proportions in voltage between the nuclei's polarised and relaxed states are sensed (Enderle et al., 2005), and a grayscale image is created using reconstruction algorithms (Figure 12.2). MRI is seen as one of the safest medical imaging techniques because it does not emit any ionising radiation like x-ray.

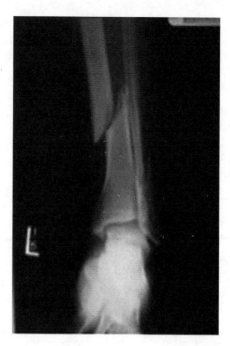

Figure 12.1 X-ray image showing a break of the tibial shaft.

In 1967, Sir Godfrey Hounsfield developed the first computed axial tomography (CAT) imaging device, based on the concept that large series of x-ray images could be grouped at angles around an axis and reconstructed with an algorithm to create a more in-depth image than the standard x-ray. CT images are based on algorithms (mostly Fourier transforms) (Enderle et al., 2005) that depend on the speed and accuracy of the scanner itself for the quality of the image. In a CT scan, x-rays are absorbed by the body so that overall 'mean attenuation' images result along the directed path. CT differs from MRI in that it captures the scatter from tissues in the body from the x-ray rather than the wavelength. Radioactive agents, like contrast, can enhance this scatter, resulting in higher-quality images and definition. CTs are best at capturing bone, lungs, and more dense organs, as well as foreign bodies like surgical implants. Each CT scanner has a series of convolution kernels that are included by the manufacturer which assist in maximising specific types of tissue like bone and the lungs (Butler et al., 1999; Schaller et al., 2003) (Figure 12.3). Due to the use of large series x-ray, CT scans have more ionising radiation than any of the other medical imaging modalities. This is low-dose radiation that poses little health danger without repeated exposure (Fazel et al., 2009).

3D images from MRI and CT are created from tiny cubes called voxels (voxel $= \Delta x\ \Delta y\ \Delta z$), which are reconstructed to create 3D models of the

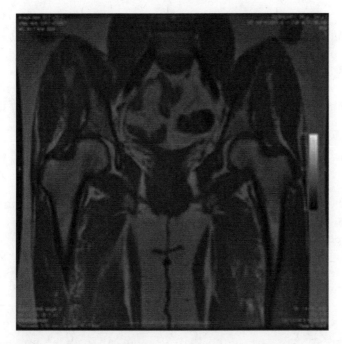

Figure 12.2 MRI image of a pelvis.

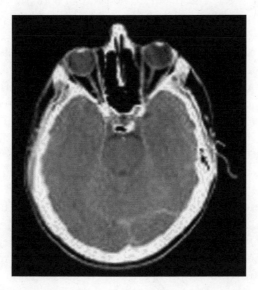

Figure 12.3 CT scan of a skull.

2D and 3D images taken from the scanner (Enderle et al., 2005). However, until recently, technological restrictions such as computer processor speed and scanner resolution have limited the 3D applications of the data. With advances in computer and imaging technologies, higher-resolution images and models are now possible, and a trend toward using the extracted 3D volumetric data and models to create more quantitative 3D anatomy is emerging (Swennen et al., 2006; Vaidyanath and Temkin, 2006).

Virtopsy

The methods employed for forensic autopsy have changed little in the past 100 years, while the demands of modern forensic investigations have changed tremendously in the wake of the *Daubert* standard (Daubert v. Merrell Dow Pharmaceuticals Inc., 1993) and high-profile cases such as the OJ Simpson/ Nicole Brown and Stephen Lawrence murder trials. High crime rates and growing attention focused on the field have created pressures on the forensic community nationally and internationally to develop alternative methods to assist with standardising techniques and processing caseloads.

Recent studies have found that CT and MRI can be useful tools in visualising the internal body for the 3D documentation of disease, injury, and forensic issues (Bolliger et al., 2008; Yen et al., 2007). Several forensic researchers have begun to apply these medical imaging modalities to traditional autopsy. Virtopsy (Thali et al., 2003) is a recent application from Swiss researchers that uses CT, MRI, laser scanning, and focused biopsy for a 'minimally invasive autopsy'. The Victorian Institute of Forensic Medicine (VIFM) in Melbourne, Australia, has been a leader in this field. In 2005, a CT scanner was installed in the mortuary at VIFM. Since that time, most biological material admitted to the institute has been scanned. This is still one of the few mortuaries in the world to have access to such technology and provides an opportunity for accurate visualisations of postmortem (PM) evidence to begin to be introduced into Australian courtrooms (O'Donnell et al., 2007).

The virtopsy procedure (Thali et al., 2003) involves a full-body CT scan of the remains. CT is used initially because it is the best medical image modality at quickly displaying bone for the documentation of any traumatic injury or metallic implants or fragments (bullets) and overall gross anatomical features. These images are diagnostically reviewed and a list of regions of interest developed for further study. MRI scans are used more sparingly due to the scan time and the potential of interfering with any metallic objects. MRI, however, is better at examining specific regions of interest shown on CT because it is best for viewing soft tissues and organs. Next, the body is captured in 3D using a laser scanner for the documentation of external pathologies and trauma. Unlike the invasive approach of traditional autopsy's full-body dissection, only select punch biopsies and fluids are taken for histology and biochemical profiles.

Using imaging techniques (CT and MRI), photographic documentation, laser surface scans, and 3D measurements, all forensic findings can be examined in an accurate virtual model of both internal and external anatomy. These models can then be used for biomechanical studies to test causes of death scenarios. Additionally, postmortem biochemical profiles developed from the remains are extremely helpful in the estimation of time of death.

The techniques pioneered by the virtopsy group are steadily becoming part of routine PM procedures around the world. In addition to the Swiss group, Shimofusa et al. (2009) have reported using postmortem images to assist autopsy in Japan and Denmark (Jacobsen and Lynnerup, 2010), among others (Shimofusa et al., 2009).

There are some limitations to the virtopsy approach. In ideal circumstances, it serves as a supplement to traditional autopsy rather than a replacement for it. In a study of over 150 autopsies, Leth and Christoffersen (2008) showed that CT was a valuable resource alongside traditional autopsy to examine injuries *in situ*, especially in violent death and traffic cases. However, they did note that in approximately half of the cases, CT missed some findings from autopsy. However, in 9% of cases, traditional autopsy overlooked important findings that were picked up by CT. Filograna et al. (2010) report a case in which ballistic trauma went undetected due to a radiologist's error.

One of the most significant benefits of the virtual autopsy method is that it allows for long-term documentation and archiving of virtual physical evidence. This is extremely important for use in court, biomechanical studies, the repatriation and timely burial of remains, and simulations or crime scene reconstructions. Further benefits include limited handling of potentially infectious or high-risk cadavers, as well as being considerate and observant of concerns held by different cultures and religions. There is momentum within the forensic community in support of virtual autopsies, at the very least to augment the traditional exam. As medical imaging costs decline and the technique is further validated, virtopsy will likely become a regular, essential part of the forensic death investigation.

Virtual Anthropology in Human Identification

Traditional Anthropological Techniques

Biological profile components, such as determination of sex or ancestry, utilise observational techniques in which a set of unknown remains is compared morphologically to type specimens that fall along a continuum or via metric comparison to a known dataset. For example, sex traits are generally classified using a scoring system based on the morphology of various parts of the pelvis (ischiopubic ramus, greater sciatic notch, ventral portion of the pubis) and presence or absence of sex indicators (preauricular sulcus and subpubic concavity) (Buikstra and Ubelaker, 1994) with accuracy exceeding 90% for experienced observers. Sex of the skull can be similarly evaluated using a scoring system based on a suite of sex traits with an accuracy of above 90% (Williams and Rogers, 2006). To a lesser degree, one may also use bone dimensions to discriminate between males and females (France, 1998); within a given population, males tend to be larger than females. Similar techniques are used to estimate the age at death from the pelvis, using the auricular surface of the ischium (Osborne et al., 2004) and the pubic symphysis (Brooks and Suchey, 1990), as well as from the sternal end of the fourth rib (İşcan and Loth, 1986). To a lesser extent, age at death can also be estimated from scoring dental wear and fusion of the epiphyses and cranial sutures. However, such classifications are often inherently subjective. Buikstra and Komar (2008) provide a thorough overview of these techniques and their associated error rates.

Over the past two decades, there has been a transition toward computerised analyses in forensic anthropology. Software packages such as FORDISC and CRANID (Wright, 2009) have provided methods of computerised analysis; however, they are based on the input of traditional metric osteological measurements conducted on the actual specimen into the package. Geometric morphometric analyses, or the study of the size and shape of the biological form, have also been applied to forensic cases. Using this technique, 3D coordinate data (in X, Y, and Z planes) are collected from the bone and recorded for analysis. The coordinate data are compared to a repository of measurements from other specimens in order to classify the unknown specimen into a similar group. While traditional distance measurements can be generated from these data, geometric morphometric methods allow the researcher to better visualise the data in 3D space (Bookstein, 1991; Lestrel, 2000). Two limitations to these methods loom large. The first is that in order to reproduce a study or re-examine a case, one must have access to the specimen, which makes it difficult if investigators are not in the same geographic location or if the remains have been repatriated. This is especially pertinent when dealing with law enforcement and the associated concerns on maintaining the chain of custody for physical evidence (Decker et al., 2009). The second limitation is that because the original specimens are not available for additional study, any repository of comparative measurements operates under the assumption that previous observers have correctly obtained and recorded the measurements, and further studies are limited to the subset of measurements recorded.

As practitioners we may be confident that our techniques are reliable and robust; however, it is imperative that the discipline can refer to an appropriate catalogue of scientific research to ensure that the wider forensic and legal communities can be as confident in our techniques. The impact of experience on the observations and interpretations made by practitioners must be quantified for two reasons. Any method, no matter how widely used, is of little value if only a small subset of those using it can carry it out successfully. Also, to be considered an expert in using such methods, a practitioner should be able to consistently demonstrate proficiency within parameters appropriate to each method. The efficacy of many of the traditional methods described earlier has been proven to be correlated with experience (İşcan and Loth, 1986; MacLaughlin and Bruce, 1990; Rogers and Saunders, 1997; Ubelaker and Volk, 2002). Large-scale quantification of error rates is needed for commonly used methods and the impact of experience. Another important consideration is the internal and external validity of anthropological standards to ensure that unknown remains can be compared to relevant and representative samples. The biological profile can only contribute toward a positive identification if it is calculated from an appropriate data source. For example, Komar (2003) describes the inadequacies of traditional methods for the estimation of age and stature in a Bosnian mass grave because the standards used were based on North American populations. Population-specific standards are being researched for groups all over the world, but there is still far more work to be done.

Benefits of Virtual Technology

Virtual technology provides supplemental capabilities to traditional techniques and can offer new methods for data interpretation, examination, and collaboration. As a supplement to traditional data collection/documentation techniques, 3D data can be used as an additional method of recording evidence and observations. For example, 3D records of pelvic or cranial anatomy can be scanned. These copies of skeletal remains can be re-examined or facial approximations performed long after the return of remains. Fleshed and fragile remains can be examined via CT and MRI without defleshing or disruption of the surface. Fragmented remains can be reassembled without the risk of further damage from handling or adhesives. The noninvasive nature of the scans are also well suited for examining the inside and surface of mummies without need for unwrapping or even removal from the cartonnage. In some cases, noninvasive imaging techniques provide an alternative to PM, for instance, in circumstances where cultural restrictions are placed on damage to the body.

Prior to autopsy, surface laser scans can be photomapped to document injuries or other markings on a cadaver. The method is noncontact and can provide a resource for presentations to juries or investigation teams. Internal structures can be examined via medical imaging before they are irreversibly disturbed by more invasive examinations during postmortem. The 3D image can be sanitised to prevent emotive influence of graphic images while still accurately illustrating important evidences such as bruising or weapon trajectories.

Another benefit of virtual models is that they can be shared electronically for collaboration or remote consultation, in addition to which 3D data can provide information which is not always best expressed via photography. By sharing accurate models of bones electronically, the risk of damage to the specimen during transport is negated, and geographic barriers to choosing the right expert are erased. However, care must be exercised to maintain electronic security and chain of custody, where appropriate.

The benefits of using anthropological techniques in virtual space extend beyond the autopsy suite and into teaching and research. Collection and analysis of measurement data are no longer constrained to simple linear relationships and angles traditionally collected for craniometric studies or studies of sexual dimorphism. Shape relationships can be examined over thousands of points, which is impossible when collecting measurements by hand. Differences in surface area and volume can be quantitatively illustrated between two scans of two objects/individuals (such as faces or bones) or changes over time between the same object/individual examined in ways that conventional measurement techniques cannot achieve. This wealth of data can be explored in new ways that may not yet have even been conceived. Virtual repositories of human skeletal and soft-tissue data will allow for international collaborations and comparisons of population data that were unthinkable even a decade ago.

Current Applications

Since the mid-1990s, laser scanners have been used in the United Kingdom to capture skull data for use in forensic facial reconstruction (Evison and Green, 1999), and 3D computer modelling software has been used to reconstruct faces for forensic and archaeological cases (Davy, 2007; Davy et al., 2005; Wilkinson, 2005). Faces can be reconstructed from the same skull multiple times by multiple practitioners and rendered in any orientation to match antemortem (AM) reference photos.

More recently, it has become possible to investigate the relationship between the skull and overlying soft tissues in vivo. Soft-tissue depth measurements of the face are traditionally used to assist forensic practitioners in understanding the relationship between the skull and the facial soft tissue that overlays it. These depths are utilised by forensic researchers, such as facial approximation specialists, to recreate a face of an unknown individual on a skull. The measurements themselves are taken by needle or pin puncture at specific craniofacial landmarks on the cadaver (Domaracki and Stephan, 2006). Commonly, the tip of a pin is covered in soot and placed in the face at a desired landmark. Once the pin reaches bone, it is removed, and the amount of soot that has been wiped off is measured. This measurement is recorded as the depth from the skin to the bone. Numerous studies have attempted to examine alternative methods of depth analyses (Stephan and Simpson, 2008a,b) such as ultrasound, x-ray, CT, and MRI, but it is commonly accepted that the pin method is the most cost-efficient. CT and MRI are useful tools in visualising the relationship between bone and facial geometry and have recently become viable both economically and practically for large studies (Shaw et al., 2010). Some researchers have expressed some concerns about the limitations of embalmed and fixed cadaveric material in facial studies (Domaracki and Stephan, 2006). Virtual scan data (Figure 12.4) provide an opportunity to study living tissues without the distortion that sometimes occurs in the cadaver embalming process. CT also allows for the tissue depths to be taken free of distortion from PM change or transducer depression/angle. A small degree of posterolateral tissue displacement may occur due to patients being scanned in the reclined position, but the technique still offers the best visualisation of the entire head and its structures of any technique. Advances in CT imaging technologies, such as cone beam computerised tomography (CBCT) and upright CT, are emerging, that will be able to address the limitation resulting from supine scanning.

In addition to tissue depths, one can also examine shape relationships. Recent novel relationships between the morphology of the external nose and

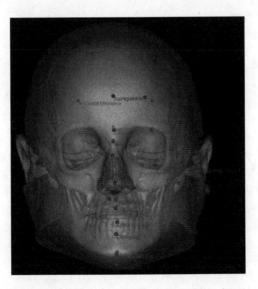

Figure 12.4 Virtual scan data showing the soft and hard tissues of the face.

splanchnocranium using CT have been discovered that would likely not have been possible before the advent of virtual techniques (Davy-Jow et al., 2011; Wilkinson et al., 2006).

Evidence of trauma can be investigated *in situ* using MRI and CT. The authors and others (Grassberger et al., 2011) have used the technologies to match weapons to blunt force trauma impressions in three dimensions without the need for defleshing. These techniques have applications in fatal cases as well as in assault/attempted homicide cases in which the victim has survived, but evidence linking a suspected weapon to an injury is required.

The need for testing traditional anthropological techniques for establishing the biological profile on a variety of populations is widely accepted. Without standards for individual populations, not only is it impossible to ensure accurate ageing and sexing within a population, it is also impossible to understand the full range of global individual variation. However, the same arguments are not often acknowledged and applied temporally. As populations, and indeed humans as a species, change and adapt over time in response to different lifestyles, migration patterns, and simple evolution, we must also consider how this affects our datasets. The individuals that are on the mortuary examination tables of today are not necessarily the same as those from decades or centuries ago in the skeletal collections from which the standards for ageing and sexing have been established. It has been shown that in at least one population, traditional morphological and metric techniques based on skeletal collections from similar regions but earlier time periods are not accurate on a contemporary, living dataset derived from clinical scans (Decker et al., 2011).

Future Applications

Laser scanning of skeletal remains has been successfully and routinely employed by a small number of UK forensic anthropology researchers and practitioners since before the millennium (Davy et al., 2005; Evison and Green, 1999; Wilkinson et al., 2006), and these researchers have also expanded into small-scale medical imaging studies. A few research groups such as those based at the universities of Bern, South Florida, and Copenhagen have been working at the forefront of virtual anatomy and its applications to forensic anthropology for at least a decade, but the discipline as a whole has been relatively slow to take on new technology during routine practice. Thus far, strides that have been made and potential future ones have not been given the attention that they deserve. This may be due, in part, to the cost-prohibitive nature of medical imaging equipment or the requisite hardware and software required by researchers in traditionally underfunded departments of anthropology. Anthropologists working in medicolegal settings such as city/county medical examiners' or coroners' offices are often too overwhelmed by casework to make use of CT or MRI equipment when available, and those in more rural locales may not have access to the technology at all.

Despite its limited availability, this very technology could enable the cross-comparative population research and large-scale validation studies of anthropological techniques on modern populations that the field urgently needs, in order to reach a higher standard for courtroom admissibility. A recent study by Decker et al. (2011) demonstrated that some of the traditional pelvic sex discriminators such as subpubic angle misclassified an unacceptably high proportion (100% of females or 57% of the overall sample) of cases from a modern, living population in the United States. However, updated calculations based on the population produced accurate (100%) sex estimation. Although many forensic anthropologists would not be able to scan and measure pelves in virtual space during the course of a normal case, the data demonstrate that modernised methods derived from imaging studies can be applied to traditional measurements on dry bone. Well-constructed virtual studies can produce repeatable methods that can be applied to traditional mortuary-based casework.

Virtual anatomy, coupled with anthropological techniques, can produce what are essentially modern skeletal collections from populations from around the globe. The number of individuals will increase daily as patients are scanned and will not be limited by traditional barriers such as body donation or excavation of centuries-old cemeteries. The information available for each individual can include age, sex, ancestry, body mass, stature, occupation, and even medical history. This wealth of information allows for studies (both population-specific and global) on a previously unimaginable scale. We can quantifiably test the reliability of our current practices on new population sets as well as potentially discover more effective ones.

Further research is needed in a number of areas in order for forensic anthropology to meet the higher legal standards outlined by the National Academy of Sciences report (National Research Council, 2009). Quantifiable error ranges for sex and age estimates from a variety of cranial and postcranial skeletal elements have yet to be standardised for courtroom purposes. Additional research must still be conducted to ease identification issues such as estimation of ancestry in closely related or admixed groups, including craniometric investigations, wider studies investigating the prevalence of nonmetric traits, or other geographically relevant identifiers. Other necessary studies include investigations of secular change as a means to establish the speed at which population standards change. Forensic anthropologists on the witness stand must be able to cite large-scale, independently verified studies. We also need techniques and measurements that can be employed in the coroner's office or autopsy suite. Virtual anthropology can provide information normally unattainable using traditional skeletal collections.

An ongoing debate in the United States and in various parts of Europe including the United Kingdom is that of practitioner standards and accreditation. One potential solution to the ever-present issues of establishing a fair method of expert validation or testing for accreditation across large geographical areas is to use 3D printed specimens as standards for at least some portions of the testing process. This does not solve the myriad of logistical and internal political problems associated with administering such exams but could at least provide an opportunity for examinees to be tested using comparable specimens.

Ethics

As this chapter illustrates, the use of virtual human remains in forensic anthropology has been steadily increasing, as the technology to capture and view them becomes more affordable and accessible. In the future, medical imaging tools such as CT and MRI scanners and software along with other data capture capabilities including laser scanning will become as much of a routine component of the anthropologist's toolkit as radiographs and photographs are today. This digital human data can be explored in a multitude of unprecedented and heretofore unimagined ways, both for investigative and research purposes. It has not yet been decided whether these new types of medical images will be considered as a simple increase in sophistication from existing tools or if the differences are so marked that they will be subject to a new set of rules that has yet to be defined. As a discipline, practitioners must consider the potential contentious aspects surrounding the retention and future use of virtual skeletal remains. There is potential for a vast amount of knowledge to emerge from such specimens, but public attitude toward virtual human remains is largely unexplored.

In the clinical setting, patient image data rights are retained by the institution or facility in which the patient was scanned. In 1996, the United States passed the Health Insurance Portability and Accountability Act (HIPAA), which changed the way patient medical records and privacy are controlled. Patients often sign a release for the physician and facility to store their data for a set number of years. While the patients retain ownership of the data that appear in their medical records, it is the facility that stores the information that owns the medical record itself. According to federal guidelines, institutional review board (IRB) approval along with patient informed consent is needed for use of any medical information or biomaterials that can be identified. Often in medical research, the use of biological tissue must be approved by the patient or designated surrogate and regulated through an IRB if the information could lead to identification of the individual. However, if the tissue or patient data can be stripped of any potentially individuating information, it can be used for general research without patient consent. Physicians often conduct clinical review studies using patient scans for education or training purposes. It is unclear at the time of writing if the current policy will be extended to virtual remains or 3D models of virtual tissue, and whether medicolegal professionals will continue to have the right to retain them for future reference without consent.

It is important to consider not just how the virtual remains can be used in the future (Davy-Jow et al., 2011) but also who actually 'owns' them. Currently, after human remains are positively identified, all attempts are made to return the remains to the decedent's family. However, virtual copies of the individual are not returned. Current legal guidelines have recommended that 3D images and virtual remains be treated no different from other case information, such as case photos and notes, in that anonymised information can be used and shared for research and teaching purposes.

Conclusions

Cutting-edge computer technologies and imaging methods, such as medical imaging and laser scanning, are providing forensic anthropologists and pathologists with new tools for human identification and the documentation of forensic evidence. As technology becomes more accessible to researchers and practitioners, these novel tools have the potential to increase the accuracy of analyses and to readdress field standards. These advances come at a pivotal time in which forensic anthropology must rise to the challenge posed by increased legal scrutiny for expert witness testimony. Virtual anthropology is providing the pathway to more rigorous scientific support for anthropological techniques used in forensic contexts. While there are numerous benefits to these new virtual data, practitioners also need to be aware of the potential ethical concerns. These emerging methods will advance the fields of forensic anthropology and pathology and change the future of forensic human identification.

References

Bolliger, S., Thali, M., Ross, S., Buck, U., Naether, S., and Vock, P. 2008. Virtual autopsy using imaging: Bridging radiologic and forensic sciences. A review of the virtopsy and similar projects. *European Radiology*, 18, 273–282.

Bookstein, F. L. 1991. *Morphometric Tools for Landmark Data: Geometry and Biology*. Cambridge, U.K.: Cambridge University Press.

Brickley, M. and McKinley, J. 2005. Association news: Guidelines to the standards for recording human remains. *In:* Clegg, M., Steele, J., and Zakrzewski, S. (eds.) *British Association of Biological Anthropology and Osteoarchaeology Annual Review*. Southampton, U.K.: BABAO, University of Southampton.

Brooks, S. and Suchey, J. M. 1990. Skeletal age determination based on the Os pubis: Comparison of the Acsádi–Nemeskéri and Suchey–Brooks methods. *Human Evolution*, 5, 227–238.

Buikstra, J. and Komar, D. A. 2008. *Forensic Anthropology: Contemporary Theory and Practice*, Oxford, U.K.: Oxford University Press.

Buikstra, J. E. and Ubelaker, D. H. 1994. *Standards for Data Collection from Human Skeletal Remains*. Fayetteville, AR: Arkansas Archeological Survey.

Butler, P., Mitchell, A. W., and Ellis, H. (eds.) 1999. *Applied Radiological Anatomy*. Cambridge, U.K.: Cambridge University Press.

Christensen, A. M. and Crowder, C. M. 2009. Evidentiary standards for forensic anthropology. *Journal of Forensic Sciences*, 54, 1211–1216.

Daubert v. Merrell Dow Pharmaceuticals Inc. 1993. 509 US 579.

Davy, S. L. 2007. Forensic facial reconstruction using three-dimensional computer modelling techniques. PhD thesis, University of Sheffield, Sheffield, U.K.

Davy, S. L., Gilbert, T., Schofield, D., and Evison, M. P. 2005. Forensic facial reconstruction using computer modeling software. *In:* Clement, J. G. and Marks, M. K. (eds.) *Computer-Graphic Facial Reconstruction*. Burlington, MA: Elsevier Academic Press.

Davy-Jow, S. L., Decker, S. J., and Schofield, D. 2011. Virtual forensic anthropology applications of advanced computer graphics technology to the identification of human remains. *In:* Yang, H. H. and Uen, S. C. (eds.) *Handbook of Research on Practices and Outcomes in Virtual Worlds and Environments*. Hershey, PA: IGI Global. pp. 217–235.

Decker, S. J., Davy-Jow, S. L., Ford, J. M., and Hilbelink, D. R. 2011. Virtual determination of sex: Phenice and metrics of the pelvis from 3D Computed Tomography (CT) models. *Journal of Forensic Sciences*, 56, 1107–1114.

Decker, S. J., Ford, J. M., and Hilbelink, D. R. 2009. Maintaining custody: A virtual method of creating accurate reproductions of skeletal remains for facial approximation. *Proceedings of the American Academy of Forensic Sciences 61st Annual Scientific Meeting*, Denver, CO.

Domaracki, M. and Stephan, C. N. 2006. Facial soft tissue thicknesses in Australian adult cadavers. *Journal of Forensic Sciences*, 51, 5–10.

Enderle, J. D., Blanchard, S. M., and Brozino, J. D. 2005. *Introduction to Biomedical Engineering*, 2nd edn. London, U.K.: Elsevier Academic Press.

Evison, M. P. and Green, M. A. 1999. Presenting three-dimensional forensic facial simulations on the Internet using VRML. *Journal of Forensic Sciences*, 44, 1216–1220.

Fazel, R., Krumholz, H. M., Wang, Y., Ross, J. S., Chen, J., Ting, H. H., Shah, N. D., Nasir, K., Einstein, A. J., and Nallamothu, B. K. 2009. Exposure to low-dose ionizing radiation from medical imaging procedures. *New England Journal of Medicine*, 361, 849–857.

Filograna, L., Tartaglione, T., Filograna, E., Cittadini, F., Oliva, A., and Pascali, V. L. 2010. Computed tomography (CT) virtual autopsy and classical autopsy discrepancies: Radiologist's error or a demonstration of post-mortem multi-detector computed tomography (MDCT) limitation? *Forensic Science International*, 195, e13–e17.

France, D. L. 1998. Observational and metric analysis of sex in the skeleton. *In:* Reichs, K. J. (ed.) *Forensic Osteology: Advances in the Identification of Human Remains*. Springfield, IL: Charles C. Thomas. pp. 163–186.

Grassberger, M., Gehl, A., Püschel, K., and Turk, E. E. 2011. 3D reconstruction of emergency cranial computed tomography scans as a tool in clinical forensic radiology after survived blunt head trauma—Report of two cases. *Forensic Science International*, 207, e19–e23.

Grivas, C. R. and Komar, D. A. 2008. Kumho, Daubert, and the nature of scientific inquiry: Implications for forensic anthropology. *Journal of Forensic Sciences*, 53, 771–776.

İşcan, M. Y. and Loth, S. R. 1986. Determination of age from the sternal rib in white males: A test of the phase method. *Journal of Forensic Sciences*, 31, 122–132.

Jacobsen, C. and Lynnerup, N. 2010. Craniocerebral trauma—Congruence between postmortem computed tomography diagnoses and autopsy results: A 2-year retrospective study. *Forensic Science International*, 194, 9–14.

Komar, D. 2003. Lessons from Srebrenica: The contributions and limitations of physical anthropology in identifying victims of war crimes. *Journal of Forensic Sciences*, 48, 713–716.

Kumho Tire Co. Ltd. v. Carmichael. 1999. 526 US 137.

Lestrel, P. E. 2000. *Morphometrics for the Life Sciences*. Singapore: World Scientific Publishing Company.

Leth, P. M. and Christoffersen, C. 2008. Computertomografi Anvendt ved Restsmedicininske Obduktioner. *Ugeskr Læger*, 170, 444–447.

Maclaughlin, S. M. and Bruce, M. F. 1990. The accuracy of sex identification in European skeletal remains using the Phenice characters. *Journal of Forensic Sciences*, 35, 1384–1392.

National Academies. 2009. 'Badly Fragmented' forensic science system needs overhaul; Evidence to support reliability of many techniques is lacking. Available from: http://www8.nationalacademies.org/onpinews/newsitem. aspx?recordid=12589, accessed February 26, 2013.

National Research Council 2009. *Strengthening Forensic Science in the United States: A path forward*. Washington, DC: National Academies Press.

Nobelprize.org. 2008. Biography—Wilhelm Conrad Röntgen. Available from: http://www.nobelprize.org/nobel_prizes/physics/laureates/1901/rontgen-bio.html accessed February 26, 2013.

O'Donnell, C., Rotman, A., Collett, S., and Woodford, N. 2007. Current status of routine postmortem CT in Melbourne, Australia. *Forensic Science, Medicine, and Pathology*, 3, 226–232.

Osborne, D. L., Simmons, T. L., and Nawrocki, S. P. 2004. Reconsidering the auricular surface as an indicator of age at death. *Journal of Forensic Sciences*, 49, 1–7.

Ousley, S. D. and Jantz, R. L. 2005. *FORDISC 3.0* edn., Knoxville, TN: University of Tennessee.

Rogers, T. and Saunders, S. R. 1997. Accuracy of sex determination using morphological traits of the human pelvis. *Journal of Forensic Sciences*, 39, 1047–1056.

Röntgen, W. C. 1967. *Wilhelm Conrad Röntgen. Nobel Lectures, Physics 1901–1921*. Amsterdam, the Netherlands: Elsevier.

Schaller, S., Wildberger, J. E., Raupach, R., Niethammer, M., Klingenbeck-Regn, K., and Flohr, T. 2003. Spatial domain filtering for fast modification of the tradeoff between image sharpness and pixel noise in computed tomography. *IEEE Transactions on Medical Imaging*, 22, 846–853.

Shaw, R. B. J., Katzel, E. B., Koltz, P. F., Kahn, D. M., Girotto, J. A., and Langstein, H. N. 2010. Aging of the mandible and its aesthetic implications. *Plastic and Reconstructive Surgery*, 125, 332–342.

Shimofusa, R., Yamamoto, S., Horikoshi, T., and Iwase, H. 2009. Applicability of facial soft tissue thickness measurements in 3-dimensionally. *Legal Medicine*, 11, S256–S259.

Stephan, C. N. and Simpson, E. K. 2008a. Facial soft tissue depths in craniofacial identification (Part 1): An analytical review of the published adult data. *Journal of Forensic Sciences*, 53, 1257–1272.

Stephan, C. N. and Simpson, E. K. 2008b. Facial soft tissue depths in craniofacial identification (Part 2): An analytical review of the published sub-adult data. *Journal of Forensic Sciences*, 53, 1273–1279.

Swennen, G. R., Schutyser, F., Barth, E. L., De Groeve, P., and De Mey, A. 2006. A new method of 3-D cephalometry part I: The anatomic cartesian 3-D reference system. *Journal of Craniofacial Surgery*, 17, 314–325.

Thali, M. J., Yen, K., Schweitzer, W., Vock, P., Boesch, C., Ozdoba, C., Schroth, G. et al. 2003. Virtopsy, a new imaging horizon in forensic pathology: Virtual autopsy by postmortem multislice computed tomography (MSCT) and magnetic resonance imaging (MRI)—A feasibility study. *Journal of Forensic Sciences*, 48, 386–403.

Ubelaker, D. H. and Volk, C. G. 2002. A test of the phenice method for estimation of sex. *Journal of Forensic Sciences*, 47, 19–24.

Udupa, J. K. and Herman, G. T. (eds.) 2000. *3D Imaging in Medicine*, 2nd edn. Boca Raton, FL: CRC Press.

U.S. Federal Government. 2000. FRE 702: Testimony by experts. Federal rules of evidence. As amended 04/17/2000, effective 12/01/2000. Available from: http://federalevidence.com/pdf/FRE_Amendments/2000Amendments/Amendment_Transmit_2000.pdf, accessed May 16, 2012.

Vaidyanath, S. and Temkin, B. 2006. Registration and segmentation for the high resolution visible human male images. *Studies in Health Technology and Informatics*, 119, 556–558.

Wilkinson, C. M. 2005. Computerized forensic facial reconstruction. *Forensic Science, Medicine, and Pathology*, 1, 173–177.

Wilkinson, C., Rynn, C., Peters, H., Taister, M., Kau, C. H., and Richmond, S. 2006. A blind accuracy assessment of computer-modeled forensic facial reconstruction using computed tomography data from live subjects. *Journal of Forensic Science, Medicine, and Pathology*, 2, 179–187.

Williams, B. A. and Rogers, T. L. 2006. Evaluating the accuracy and precision of cranial morphological traits for sex determination. *Journal of Forensic Sciences*, 51, 729–735.

Wright, R. 2009. Guide to using the CRANID Programs CR6aInd: For linear and nearest neighbours discriminant analysis. Available from: http://www.box.net/shared/h0674knjzl, accessed February 26, 2013.

Yen, K., Lövblad, K.-O., Scheurer, E., Ozdoba, C., Thali, M. J., Aghayev, E., Jackowski, C. et al. 2007. Post-mortem forensic neuroimaging: Correlation of MSCT and MRI findings with autopsy results. *Forensic Science International*, 173, 21–35.

RNA Profiling
A New Tool in Forensic Science

13

MARIELLE VENNEMANN AND ANTJE HUTH

Contents

Introduction

Human identification often begins with the initial examination of human remains. In an archeological context, this might be bones or other preserved tissues. In forensic casework, however, the 'remains' often occur in the form of body fluid stains, such as blood, semen or saliva stains. Identification in these cases is usually performed via analysis of specific markers or polymorphisms in the human genetic material, the deoxyribonucleic acid (DNA). The DNA profile of the stain is then compared to the DNA profile of a person, and if the profiles match, the statistical likelihood of the match will require calculation.

The success of DNA-based identification procedures often relies on the correct identification of the type of body fluid present in a biological stain. Knowledge of the type of body fluid or the composition of a mixed stain is important for correct subsequent processing of such samples in the laboratory. In some forensic cases, knowledge of the type of body fluid directly aids police investigations, for example, in cases of alleged sexual assault, the presence or absence of body fluids related to sexual activity bears important information for the case (Allard, 2009).

Forensic investigations also include the determination of the cause and the circumstances of death in humans. In some cases, however, the technical possibilities of conventional postmortem (PM) examination are not sufficient to explain why a person has died. For example, distinguishing between a sudden cardiac death without any macroscopically visible signs of infarction or coronary thrombosis and a (potentially violent) death by suffocation can be difficult to determine without the use of further molecular diagnostics (Jardine et al., 2011).

In this chapter, we will demonstrate how ribonucleic acid (RNA) profiling may be used in human identification and forensic investigations of death. To understand the potential use of RNA, we need to understand the biology and characteristics of this class of molecules.

Ribonucleic Acid

When the 3D structure of DNA was first discovered by Watson and Crick in 1953, they had a basic preconception of how genetic information was encoded and transferred from one generation to the next. Essentially, DNA contains the information needed for protein synthesis. When genes are active, their DNA sequence is first transcribed into messenger ribonucleic acid (mRNA), the intermediate template of gene expression, and then translated into proteins. Proteins will then fulfil the function needed in a cell at a specific time point. Other classes of RNA, such as microRNA (miRNA) and transfer RNA, fulfil functions connected with the regulation of protein synthesis but are not necessarily translated into proteins themselves. The composition of all RNAs in a cell or a cellular compound is called the transcriptome. Analysis of the relative amounts of certain RNAs, and particularly mRNAs, can reveal which genes are active and which proteins are currently built within the cell. So we can regard DNA as the molecule that 'stores' genetic information. A high-stability, long half-life and suitable quality control mechanism of DNA as the carrier molecule is an important prerequisite for successful transfer of genetic information from one cell to its daughter cells, as well as from one generation to the next (Wilusz et al., 2001).

One of the main functions of RNA, on the other hand, is to regulate and perform the transfer of genetic information into proteins. mRNA is synthesised by enzymes known collectively as RNA polymerases. It is synthesised as single-stranded, complementary copies of the coding DNA strands, with many mRNAs subsequently serving as templates for protein synthesis. Uncontrolled accumulation of such a template needs to be avoided to facilitate the regulation of the rather complex process of gene expression and protein synthesis. Thus, as soon as its function as template for proteins is fulfilled, mRNA molecules are destroyed by omnipresent, highly reactive ribonucleases (RNases) (Phang et al., 1994). This is an essential part of post-transcriptional regulation and assists in controlling the amount of synthesised gene product (Bauer and Patzelt, 2003a). Thus, gene transcripts, and mainly mRNAs, are built when needed and destroyed when they have served their purpose. This means that the composition of mRNA pools within a cell depends on the specific needs and functions of that cell. Since the needs and functions of cells and tissues can change, the RNA pool is both tissue specific and variable, while DNA remains the same in different tissues as well as under varying conditions (Vennemann and Koppelkamm, 2010a).

Potential Applications of RNA Profiling in Forensic Science

Many basic cellular decisions, including those of growth and differentiation as well as survival or death of the cell, are represented by varying gene expression patterns within cells and tissues. Thus, the absolute and quantitative analysis of transcript abundances has gained increasing interest in life science research and diagnostics. Detection of mRNA as the intermediate template of protein synthesis provides the possibility to reflect gene activity within a certain cell type at a specific point in time (Bustin, 2000). The composition of mRNA pools is tissue specific and variable. These two characteristics explain the new interest in RNA typing within the forensic field. If RNA pools are indeed tissue specific, it should be possible to use 'RNA fingerprints' for the identification of unknown tissue types, for example, human body fluids found in biological traces. Furthermore, since RNA degrades faster than DNA, it was proposed that degradation patterns of gene transcript might be useful for the determination of the age of a biological trace (Bauer et al., 2003).

RNA pools have been identified as variable; that is, the composition and relative abundances of certain gene transcripts change in response to internal and/or external stimuli. Essentially this means that there is a link between gene expression patterns and their stimuli that could be exploited by investigators. In forensic pathology, this relationship could assist in establishing a molecular tool for the determination of the cause and/or circumstances of death based on specific gene expression patterns revealed in tissue samples collected postmortem (Ikematsu et al., 2005; Vennemann and Koppelkamm, 2010a).

Identification of Body Fluids

Blood and saliva are the most commonly encountered types of body fluid in biological stains found at crime scenes. Other types of fluid that may be collected include semen and vaginal secretions, tears, sweat and urine. Identification of the type of body fluid by macroscopic inspection is often impossible, but knowledge of the cell type present in a trace sample can be essential. It is important for police investigations; for example, in an alleged sexual assault case, the presence or absence of semen on a vaginal swab (with or without spermatozoa present) forms an important piece of evidence. Also, in such a case, a bloodstain on clothes or other fabric could give rise to the question of whether it is formed by menstrual fluid or blood resultant from injury.

Conventional forensic tests for identification of body fluid type are often based on chemical reactions or the detection of tissue-specific proteins (Hedman et al., 2011; Laffan et al., 2011; Tobe and Linacre, 2008). The advantages of such tests are that they are rapid, cost-effective and simple to perform and that data are easy to interpret. However, the disadvantages for many tests, such as the commonly used Kastle–Meyer test for blood (a presumptive blood test, where a chemical indicator is applied to detect possible traces of haemoglobin), include cross-reactivity with conventional household chemicals, such as hypochlorite (bleach), and reaction with animal body fluids (i.e. not human specific) (Tobe and Linacre, 2008). Thus, the nature of these tests is presumptive rather than confirmatory, meaning that when a positive result is achieved, the presence of a certain body fluid is presumed, but cannot be proven. Furthermore, the range of tests currently used in forensic laboratories is limited to certain body fluids. For example, there is no conventional test available for the detection of menstrual blood, vaginal fluid, sweat, tears, urine or skin cells.

Recent studies evaluated the use of tissue-specific RNAs as biomarkers for the identification of body fluids. Initial research demonstrated that mRNA of sufficient quantity and quality can be obtained from biological traces, thus allowing analysis of tissue-specific gene transcripts (Juusola and Ballantyne, 2003). Subsequently, several studies illustrated the potential for extracting both (co-extracting) RNA and DNA from the same sample. This is particularly useful when limited sample is available, as it means two extraction procedures can be performed using the same material with little loss (Alvarez et al., 2004; Bauer et al., 2003; Haas et al., 2012a).

Fleming and Harbison (2010) first described a multiplex reverse transcription polymerase chain reaction (RT-PCR) technique that is able to detect several body fluids in one reaction. More recently, a large multiplex RT-PCR analysis was published (Lindenbergh et al., 2012), which contains two markers for each, saliva, semen, menstrual secretion, vaginal mucosa and skin cells. Furthermore, it contains three markers for blood and general mucosa, as well as three reference genes as a proof of the presence of sufficiently intact mRNA in the sample. The results demonstrated a surprisingly high sensitivity for this multiplex reaction and excellent stability of the markers. For example, they were able to positively identify blood and semen stains from samples stored for 28 years.

In addition, Zubakov et al. (2008) analysed the whole transcriptome, that is, the entire entity of mRNAs in a certain tissue by a method known as microarray analysis. By this they identified 14 stable mRNA markers for the identification of blood and saliva. The microarray platform was also applied to screen for suitable candidate miRNA markers for the detection of body fluids (Zubakov et al., 2010). Using RT-PCR, they were able to confirm the specific expression of several miRNAs for the detection of semen and saliva, but no suitable miRNA markers for other body fluids were found. Despite the expectation for miRNA to be less prone to degradation (as a result of their small size, secondary structure and long half-life), the most successful data and most promising techniques were obtained with the use of mRNA markers.

The high stability of the mRNA transcripts, the potential for co-extraction with DNA and the ability to test all relevant body fluids in one single reaction demonstrate the strength of recently published data. As a result, it is expected that mRNA profiling will become a regularly applied technique in forensic laboratories in the near future. Table 13.1 gives a brief overview of recently published RNA markers for the identification of body fluids.

Following reverse transcription of RNA into complementary DNA (cDNA), many studies are based on end point PCR followed by capillary electrophoresis. This procedure comprises a qualitative analysis, that is, it provides information about presence or absence of a transcript, but not its relative abundance in a specific tissue type. The advantage of this technique is that it is well established and data are easily interpreted by the presence or absence of the respective peak in an electrophoretogram. However, this technique requires very careful validation of the biomarkers to ensure that their expression is indeed limited to one specific body fluid and there is no cross-reactivity with other body fluids (Vennemann and Koppelkamm, 2010b). Many mRNAs previously thought to be tissue specific may be present in low abundances in other tissue types when a suitably sensitive detection method is applied. For example, Nussbaumer et al. (2006) demonstrated that transcripts of haemoglobin alpha (HBA) locus 1 and mucein (MUC) are expressed in large amounts in semen but also in lower abundances in saliva and vaginal secretions. The same researchers also illustrated that kallikrein 3 (KLK) is expressed only in semen and will not be detectable in blood, saliva or vaginal secretions. In conclusion, KLK appears a promising marker for the detection of semen, while for HBA and MUC, the purely qualitative assay of end point PCR is not an adequate detection technique, because the differences between tissue types are more quantitative in nature. Thus, it is essential to evaluate the tissue-specific nature of any potential biomarkers intended for use in mRNA profiling of body fluids.

Another challenge is the relatively low stability of mRNA compared to DNA. Despite several groups reporting successful mRNA typing from

Table 13.1 Overview of Specific RNA Markers for the Identification of Human Body Fluids

Body Fluid	RNA Markers	References
Blood	Delta-aminolevulinate synthase (ALAS2)	Haas et al. (2011a,b, 2012a), Juusola and Ballantyne (2007) and Richard et al. (2012)
	Haemoglobin alpha (HBA)	Haas et al. (2011b, 2012a) and Nussbaumer et al. (2006)
	Haemoglobin beta (HBB)	Haas et al. (2009a, 2011b, 2012a) and Noreault-Conti and Buel (2007)
	Beta-spectrin (SPTB)	Alvarez et al. (2004), Haas et al. (2009a, 2011a,b, 2012a), Juusola and Ballantyne (2005), Juusola and Ballantyne (2007), Noreault-Conti and Buel (2007) and Setzer et al. (2008)
	Porphobilinogen deaminase (PBGD)	Haas et al. (2009a, 2011a,b, 2012a), Juusola and Ballantyne (2005) and Setzer et al. (2008)
	CD3 γ molecule (CD3G)	Haas et al. (2011b, 2012a) and Noreault-Conti and Buel (2007)
	Ankyrin 1 (ANK1)	Fang et al. (2006) and Haas et al. (2011b, 2012a)
Menstrual blood	Matrix metalloproteinase 7 (MMP7)	Bauer and Patzelt (2002, 2008), Haas et al. (2009a), Juusola and Ballantyne (2005, 2007), and Richard et al. (2012)
	Matrix metalloproteinase 10 (MMP10)	Bauer and Patzelt (2002), Fang et al. (2006) and Juusola and Ballantyne (2007)
	Matrix metalloproteinase 11 (MMP11)	Bauer and Patzelt (2002, 2008), Ferri et al. (2004), Fleming and Harbison (2010) and Haas et al. (2009a)
	Glycophorin A (GlycoA)	Fleming and Harbison (2010)
Saliva	Statherin (STATH)	Fleming and Harbison (2010), Haas et al. (2009a), Juusola and Ballantyne (2003, 2005, 2007), Richard et al. (2012) and Setzer et al. (2008)
	Histatin 3 (HTN3)	Alvarez et al. (2004), Fleming and Harbison (2010), Haas et al. (2009a), Juusola and Ballantyne (2003, 2005, 2007), Richard et al. (2012) and Setzer et al. (2008)
Semen	Protamine 1 (PRM1)	Alvarez et al. (2004), Bauer and Patzelt (2003b), Haas et al. (2009a,b), Juusola and Ballantyne (2005, 2007) and Setzer et al. (2008)
	Protamine 2 (PRM2)	Bauer and Patzelt (2003b), Fleming and Harbison (2010), Haas et al. (2009a,b), Juusola and Ballantyne (2005, 2007), Noreault-Conti and Buel (2007), Richard et al. (2012) and Setzer et al. (2008)
	KLK/prostate-specific antigen (PSA)	Haas et al. (2009b), Noreault-Conti and Buel (2007) and Nussbaumer et al. (2006)
	Transglutaminase 4 (TGM4)	Fang et al. (2006), Fleming and Harbison (2010) and Richard et al. (2012)
	Semenolegin 1 (SEMG1)	Fang et al. (2006), Haas et al. (2009b) and Noreault-Conti and Buel (2007)

Table 13.1 (continued)   Overview of Specific RNA Markers for the Identification of Human Body Fluids

Body Fluid	RNA Markers	References
Vaginal secretions	Human β-defensin 1 (HBD1)	Juusola and Ballantyne (2005)
	Mucin 4 (MUC4)	Alvarez et al. (2004), Haas et al. (2009a), Juusola and Ballantyne (2005), Nussbaumer et al. (2006), Richard et al. (2012) and Setzer et al. (2008)
	16S rRNA	Akutsu et al. (2012)
	Human β-defensin 1 (HBD1)	Haas et al. (2009a) and Juusola and Ballantyne (2005)
Skin	Corneodesmosin (CDSN)	Visser et al. (2011)
	Loricrin (LOR)	Visser et al. (2011)
	Cytokeratin 9 (KRT9)	Visser et al. (2011)
	Late cornified envelope protein 1C (LCE1C)	Hanson et al. (2012)

Source: Adapted from Haas, C. et al., *Meth. Mol. Biol.,* 830, 169, 2012b.

In addition to the markers mentioned here, Zubakov et al. (2008) described 14 specific markers for blood and saliva, and Haas et al. (2011a) evaluated the specificity of 9 mRNA markers for the detection of human blood.

biological traces (even after several months of storage under various conditions) (Lindenbergh et al., 2012; Setzer et al., 2008), the risk of obtaining false-negative results due to RNA degradation is still high. The absence of a marker for a certain body fluid may be the result either of an absence of the body fluid itself or of a failed analysis of the transcript due to degradation of RNA. Juusola and Ballantyne (2007) presented a possible solution by using a set of two specific biomarkers and a reference gene as positive control for each body fluid tested. Subsequent studies adopted this method so that currently, the use of multiplexes with several markers for each body fluid is standard (Fleming and Harbison, 2010; Lindenbergh et al., 2012).

In essence, reference genes are genes whose transcript (=mRNA) abundances remain stable between tissues as well as during the storage of the samples. In the context of body fluid identification, they are used as a proof for the presence of cDNA as a copy of RNA. This is important for the interpretation of RNA profiles because RNA is a molecule that easily degrades. Thus, the use of reference genes can assist in highlighting false-negative outcomes resulting from RNA degradation. However, the use of such reference genes is only applicable if the transcripts of interest are equally or more stable than those of the reference genes. This means that not only the biomarkers of interest but also the transcripts of the reference genes need to be validated carefully.

Determination of the Age (Time Since Deposition) of Biological Traces

Forensic investigators are often interested not only in the type of body fluid present in a biological stain and the identification of the person who placed that stain, but also in the time of its deposition. For example, when a cigarette butt is discovered at a crime scene, it would be useful for investigators to know whether it was deposited at the time the crime was committed (and potentially by the offender himself) or whether it was there before the crime was committed and has no immediate connection to the case.

Several attempts have been made to determine the true age (and therefore time since deposition) of bloodstains based on the degradation state of RNA molecules. Bauer et al. (2003) published an initial study demonstrating that successful RNA extraction and quantification were possible even after 15 years of sample storage. Furthermore, they noticed a relationship between the abundance of RNA in a sample and its time in storage. Thus, they concluded that the age of a sample could be estimated based on the decrease in the amount of certain transcripts. However, this approach needs several years of storage time between samples; for forensic purposes, a much higher resolution would be required to aid investigations.

A second study performed by Anderson et al. (2005) exploited the varying stabilities of RNA families and introduced a ratio of abundance between two transcripts from different RNA classes, namely, β-actin and 18S rRNA. In theory β-actin, as an mRNA molecule, is expected to degrade faster, resulting partly from its lack of protective protein complex shielding it from degradation through environmental impact. In contrast, the ribosomal RNA molecule is expected to have greater stability and protection from the environment as it is usually combined with proteins to form the ribosomal structure. The ratio between β-actin and 18S rRNA transcript abundances was found to be able to predict the age of bloodstains (Anderson et al., 2005). The resolution of this technique is considered slightly better compared to Bauer et al. (2003) approach, as it is able to determine the age of samples in terms of months rather than years, but still provides a rather crude estimate. However, the method was successfully applied to determine the age of a hair sample (Hampson et al., 2011), demonstrating that this approach requires further investigation.

Anderson et al. (2011) presented further research in this area in which they used various sizes of PCR products from the same transcript and subjected the abundances of the amplicons to a multivariate analysis to predict the age of a bloodstain. In contrast, Setzer et al. (2008) could not find a significant relationship between storage time of bloodstains and the total abundance of several blood-specific mRNA markers.

Molecular Analysis of Cause of Death

The specific composition of mRNAs within a cell or tissue is not fixed but varies in accordance with the specific needs and functions of the cell, with these needs and functions being influenced by internal and external stimuli. Such events can sometimes cause dramatic changes in the activities of certain genes and thus the relative abundance of transcripts within the mRNA pool. Death can be seen as an extreme event that is likely to cause dramatic changes in gene activity. However, death of an organism does not necessarily mean that all cells within the organism cease their metabolic activities. It is more likely that variation in gene expression patterns still occurs after death. Ikematsu et al. (2005) used rats to demonstrate the continued gene expression changes for up to 30 min postmortem. This study also included an approach to determining the cause of death using genetic biomarkers. They analysed the transcript abundance of several genes expressed in the skin of rats after slow strangulation and compared them with a group that was executed by rapid decapitation using a guillotine. They discovered four genes showing different expression patterns, allowing investigators to distinguish the two study groups based on the cause of death. Such markers could potentially serve as biomarkers indicating asphyxia as the cause of death and could complement existing autopsy techniques (Ikematsu et al., 2005).

Ikematsu et al. (2008) also illustrated that after strangulation, immediate early gene (IEG) expression (namely, c-fos and fos-B) in the brain of mice was increased compared to the control group. This demonstrates that oxygen stress prior to death elicits a response in the form of varied gene activity. Furthermore, a change in the expression of IEG c-fos, fos-B, c-jun and dusp-1 was described in the heart tissue of mice after premortem medication with methamphetamines (Matsuo et al., 2009).

Takahashi (2008) analysed gene expression patterns after blunt force injury of the hind limb of rats and found that expression of tyrosine hydroxylase (TH) was upregulated in the adrenal gland compared to the control group. Furthermore, Takahashi et al. (2009) discovered an increase in the expression of five mRNAs in the lung tissue of mice after mechanical asphyxiation.

Heinrich et al. (2007b) used human tissue samples obtained during postmortem examination to demonstrate that successful extraction of RNA in suitable quality and quantity for RT-PCR is possible even after prolonged postmortem intervals (PMIs). They showed successful amplification of long fragments of the glyceraldehyde-3-phosphate dehydrogenase (GAPDH) gene even after more than 4 days of PMI. The same group also considered the impact of partial RNA degradation on the reliability of future gene expression studies (Koppelkamm et al., 2011) and found significant correlations between the RNA integrity numbers (RINs) (Schroeder et al., 2006) and cycle of quantification (Cq) values obtained by quantification experiments. Careful normalisation against a validated set of four endogenous control genes (Koppelkamm et al., 2010) could partially compensate this effect.

RNA quality and integrity can be measured by miniature electrophoresis using a lab-on-a-chip technique resulting in an electrophoretogram (Bioanalyzer, Agilent Technologies) (Schroeder et al., 2006). Based on the peak heights of the fragments representing the ribosomal RNAs compared to the background noise representing degraded RNA fragments, the RIN is calculated ranging from 10 (very high-quality, intact RNA) to 1 (completely degraded RNA). Koppelkamm et al. (2011) demonstrated that highly variable RIN values could be obtained from human postmortem tissue samples but that these did not correlate with the PMI. They analysed the influence of different parameters on the RNA integrity, such as cause of death and storage conditions of the body. In addition, they studied individual parameters such as age, sex and body mass index. Despite a significant correlation between obesity and low RIN values in skeletal muscle tissue, none of these parameters were able to explain all variations found between tissue donors. Thus, further investigations of the mechanisms of postmortem RNA degradation are urgently needed.

However, even though at least a partial degradation of RNA in PM human tissue samples needs to be considered, many studies demonstrated that RNA of surprisingly high quality can be obtained from postmortem samples of various species (see, e.g., Fitzpatrick et al., 2002; Heinrich et al., 2007b; Inoue et al., 2002; Preece, 2003). Thus, RNA quantification could be used to complement current techniques for the determination of the cause of death in forensic pathology. The first studies that identified possible biomarkers for the determination of the cause of death in human material were presented by the group of Hitoshi Maeda (Zhao et al., 2006, 2008). They analysed the expression patterns of hypoxia-related genes in postmortem human tissue and found significant changes of expression in various tissue types as a response to pre- and perimortem oxygen stress. Also, Huth et al. (2013) showed that the transcript abundance of the vascular endothelial growth factor (VEGF) gene in cardiac muscle tissue shows statistically significant differences between cases of cardiac death versus asphyxia.

Quantitative Real-Time PCR for Postmortem Gene Expression Analysis

In contrast to mRNA profiling for body fluid identification, where a qualitative detection of transcripts is sufficient and end point PCR can be applied (see previous text and Table 13.1), the detection of changes in gene expression and thus transcript abundances are of quantitative nature and require a different analytical approach. After reverse transcription, cDNA is subjected to quantitative real-time PCR. Using fluorescent dyes, which are either incorporated into the newly synthesised double strand during each PCR cycle or attached to specific probes which detect the newly synthesised strands, it is possible to track the increase in abundance of the PCR product in real time. With the use of a standard curve and a linear regression analysis, the absolute or relative amount of starting material can be calculated from the real-time PCR raw data, the Cq values. Therefore, the amount of a certain transcript within the RNA extract from a tissue sample can be determined (Huggett et al., 2005). This method of RNA profiling is very sensitive and can reveal even slight changes in the amount of a certain gene transcript. However, the highly sensitive nature of this technique also requires powerful measures to ensure that true changes in expression activities are quantified rather than apparent differences in the abundance of transcripts, which may be influenced by many parameters such as the amount of starting tissue material and the efficiency of extraction, reverse transcription and PCR. Furthermore, interindividual differences in health, lifestyle or nutrition and medication before death may also influence gene expression (Vennemann and Koppelkamm, 2010b). To ensure that true expression activities are recorded, it is recommended that biological and technical replicates are used as well as normalisation of the raw data against a validated set of reference genes (Bustin, 2000; Huggett et al., 2005).

Endogenous control genes should ideally be expressed ubiquitously in all tissue types and at a stable rate of expression that is not influenced by internal or external stimuli. In early gene expression studies, a single control gene was used to normalise data. Commonly used control genes were GAPDH, β-actin and 18S rRNA (Watson et al., 1987). In recent years, however, it was revealed that many of these endogenous control genes showed varying expression under different experimental conditions and are thus not suitable as normalisers (Heinrich et al., 2007a).

Vandesompele et al. (2002) introduced a technique to overcome this problem by using not one but a set of at least three endogenous control genes. These genes show stability as a group but not necessarily unchanging transcript abundances of each of its members. This requires careful validation to identify powerful normaliser sets for the particular collection of samples investigated in each gene expression study. Several software applications are now available for the validation of endogenous control genes (Andersen et al., 2004; Vandesompele et al., 2002). These software packages assist in identifying the most stable control genes among a larger set and the minimum number of genes required for reliable normalisation of quantitative gene expression data.

For gene expression analysis in human PM tissue, the use of at least four endogenous controls seems to be appropriate (Koppelkamm et al., 2010). This author identified HMBS, ubiquitin C (UBC), TATA-box-binding protein (TBP) and SDHA as a suitable set for reliable data normalisation in PM human brain, cardiac muscle and skeletal muscle tissue.

Data normalisation can assist in controlling some of the parameters that may influence transcript abundance observed in human postmortem tissue. However, other parameters, such as an individual's lifestyle and health characteristics, cannot be controlled. Careful moderation of these parameters is therefore important in future gene expression studies for the determination of cause and circumstances of human death (Vennemann and Koppelkamm, 2010b).

Conclusion

The most widely studied application of RNA in human identification and forensic science is the identification of human body fluids found in biological traces. The use of large reverse transcription multiplex reactions enables scientists to test for the presence of several body fluids in one reaction. The main advantages of RNA-based body fluid identification compared to conventional presumptive testing is the possibility of co-extracting RNA alongside with DNA and the human specific nature of the markers. Another advantage of using RNA profiling is the possibility of identification of body fluids for which we currently have no commonly used presumptive tests, such as menstrual blood, vaginal secretion and skin cells.

Another field in which RNA profiling can be of future interest is the determination of the age of a biological trace, that is, the time since it was deposited at a crime scene. If the time of deposition does not correlate with the time of the committed crime, the trace might not be of significant interest to investigators.

Finally, RNA profiling may be useful when attempting to determine the cause and circumstances of death. Postmortem gene expression studies could be a valuable tool able to complement current methods of PM examination and medicolegal autopsies, particularly in cases in which the cause of death cannot be determined due to a lack of macroscopic evidence of disease or injury. In such cases, mRNA profiling could be used as a tool of molecular diagnostics in addition to conventional histological or microbial analyses of tissue samples.

References

Akutsu, T., Motani, H., Watanabe, K., Iwase, H., and Sakurada, K. 2012. Detection of bacterial 16S ribosomal RNA genes for forensic identification of vaginal fluid. *Legal Medicine (Tokyo),* 14, 160–162.

Allard, J. 2009. Body fluids in sexual offences. In: Fraser, J. and Williams, R. (eds.) *Handbook of Forensic Science.* Cullompton, U.K.: William Publishing. pp. 142–165.

Alvarez, M., Juusola, J., and Ballantyne, J. 2004. An mRNA and DNA co-isolation method for forensic casework samples. *Analytical Biochemistry*, 335, 289–298.

Anderson, S., Howard, B., Hobbs, G. R., and Bishop, C. P. 2005. A method for determining the age of a bloodstain. *Forensic Science International*, 148, 37–45.

Anderson, S. E., Hobbs, G. R., and Bishop, C. P. 2011. Multivariate analysis for estimating the age of a bloodstain. *Journal of Forensic Sciences*, 56, 186–193.

Andersen, C. L., Ledet-Jensen, J., and Ørntoft, T. 2004. Normalization of real-time quantitative RT-PCR data: A model based variance estimation approach to identify genes suited for normalization—Applied to bladder- and colon-cancer data-sets. *Cancer Research*, 64, 5245–5250.

Bauer, M. and Patzelt, D. 2002. Evaluation of mRNA markers for the identification of menstrual blood. *Journal of Forensic Sciences*, 47, 1278–1282.

Bauer, M. and Patzelt, D. 2003a. A method for simultaneous RNA and DNA isolation from dried blood and semen stains. *Forensic Science International*, 136, 76–78.

Bauer, M. and Patzelt, D. 2003b. Protamine mRNA as molecular marker for spermatozoa in semen stains. *International Journal of Legal Medicine*, 117, 175–179.

Bauer, M. and Patzelt, D. 2008. Identification of menstrual blood by real time RT-PCR: Technical improvements and the practical value of negative results. *Forensic Science International*, 174, 54–58.

Bauer, M., Polzin, S., and Patzelt, D. 2003. Quantification of RNA degradation by semi-quantitative duplex and competitive RT-PCR: A possible indicator of the age of bloodstains? *Forensic Science International*, 138, 94–103.

Bustin, S. 2000. Absolute quantification of mRNA using real-time reverse transcription polymerase chain reaction assays. *Journal of Molecular Endocrinology*, 25, 169–193.

Fang, R., Manohar, C. F., Shulse, C., Brevnov, M., Wong, A., Petrauskene, O. V., Brzoska, P., and Furtado, M. R. 2006. Real-time PCR assays for the detection of tissue and body fluid specific mRNAs. *International Congress Series*, 1288, 685–687.

Ferri, G., Bini, C., Ceccardi, S., and Pelotti, S. 2004. Successful identification of two years old menstrual bloodstain by using MMP-11 shorter amplicons. *Forensic Science International*, 49, 1387.

Fitzpatrick, R., Casey, O. M., Morris, D., Smith, T., Powell, R., and Sreenan, J. M. 2002. Postmortem stability of RNA isolated from bovine reproductive tissue. *Biochimica et Biophysica Acta*, 1574, 10–14.

Fleming, R. I. and Harbison, S.-A. 2010. The development of a mRNA multiplex RT-PCR assay for the definitive identification of body fluids. *Forensic Science International*, 4, 244–256.

Haas, C., Hanson, E., Anjos, M. J., Bär, W., Banemann, R., Berti, A., Borges, E. et al. 2012a. RNA/DNA co-analysis from blood stains—Results of a second collaborative EDNAP exercise. *Forensic Science International: Genetics*, 6, 70–80.

Haas, C., Hanson, E., and Ballantyne, J. 2012b. Capillary electrophoresis of a multiplex reverse transcription-polymerase chain reaction to target messenger RNA markers for body fluid identification. *Methods in Molecular Biology*, 830, 169–183.

Haas, C., Hanson, E., Bära, W., Banemanni, R., Bentom, A. M., Bertig, A., Borgesp, E. et al. 2011a. mRNA profiling for the identification of blood—Results of a collaborative EDNAP exercise. *Forensic Science International: Genetics*, 5, 21–26.

Haas, C., Hanson, E., Kratzer, A., Bär, W., and Ballantyne, J. 2011b. Selection of highly specific and sensitive mRNA biomarkers for the identification of blood. *Forensic Science International: Genetics,* 5, 449–458.

Haas, C., Klesser, B., Maake, C., Bär, W., and Kratzer, A. 2009a. mRNA profiling for body fluid identification by reverse transcription endpoint PCR and real-time PCR. *Forensic Science, Medicine, and Pathology,* 3, 80–88.

Haas, C., Muheim, C., Kratzer, A., Bär, W., and Maake, C. 2009b. mRNA profiling for the identification of sperm and seminal plasma. *Forensic Science International: Genetics Supplement Series,* 2, 534–535.

Hampson, C., Louhelainen, J., and Mccoll, S. 2011. An RNA expression method for aging forensic hair samples. *Journal of Forensic Sciences,* 56, 359–369.

Hanson, E., Haas, C., Jucker, R., and Ballantyne, J. 2012. Specific and sensitive mRNA biomarkers for the identification of skin in 'Touch DNA' evidence. *Forensic Science International,* 6, 548–558.

Hedman, J., Dalin, E., Rasmusson, B., and Ansell, R. 2011. Evaluation of amylase testing as a tool for saliva screening of crime scene trace swabs. *Forensic Science International: Genetics,* 5, 194–198.

Heinrich, M., Lutz-Bonengel, S., Matt, K., and Schmidt, U. 2007a. Real-time PCR detection of five different "Endogenous Control Gene" transcripts in forensic autopsy material. *Forensic Science International,* 27, 163–169.

Heinrich, M., Matt, K., and Lutz-Bonengel, S. 2007b. Successful RNA extraction from various human postmortem tissue. *International Journal of Legal Medicine,* 121, 136–142.

Huggett, J., Dheda, K., Bustin, S., and Zumla, A. 2005. Real-time RT-PCR normalization; strategies and considerations. *Genes & Immunity,* 6, 279–284.

Huth, A., Vennemann, B., Fracasso, T., Lutz-Bonengel, S., and Vennemann, M. 2013. Apparent versus true gene expression changes of three hypoxia related genes in autopsy derived tissues and the importance of normalisation. *International Journal of Legal Medicine,* 127, 335–344.

Ikematsu, K., Takahashi, H., Kondo, T., Tsuda, R., and Nakasono, I. 2008. Temporal expression of immediate early gene mRNA during the supravital reaction in mouse brain and lung after mechanical asphyxiation. *Forensic Science International,* 179, 152–156.

Ikematsu, K., Tsuda, R., and Nakasono, I. 2005. Gene response of mouse skin to pressure injury in the neck region. *Legal Medicine,* 8, 128–131.

Inoue, H., Kimura, A., and Tuji, T. 2002. Degradation profile of mRNA in a dead rat body: Basic semi-quantification study. *Forensic Science International,* 130, 127–132.

Jardine, D., Cornel, L., and Emond, M. 2011. Gene expression analysis characterizes antemortem stress and has implications for establishing cause of death. *Physiological Genomics,* 43, 974–980.

Juusola, J. and Ballantyne, J. 2003. Messenger RNA profiling: A proper method to supplant conventional methods for body fluid identification. *Forensic Science International,* 135, 85–96.

Juusola, J. and Ballantyne, J. 2005. Multiplex mRNA profiling for the identification of body fluids. *Forensic Science International,* 152, 1–12.

Juusola, J. and Ballantyne, J. 2007. mRNA profiling for body fluid identification by multiplex quantitative RT PCR. *Journal of Forensic Sciences,* 52, 1252–1262.

Koppelkamm, A., Vennemann, B., Fracasso, T., Lutz-Bonengel, S., Schmidt, U., and Heinrich, M. 2010. Validation of adequate endogenous reference genes for the normalisation of qPCR gene expression data in human post mortem tissue. *International Journal of Legal Medicine*, 124, 371–380.

Koppelkamm, A., Vennemann, B., Lutz-Bonengel, S., Fracasso, T., and Vennemann, M. 2011. RNA integrity in post mortem samples: Influencing parameters and implications on RT-qPCR assays. *International Journal of Legal Medicine*, 125, 573–580.

Laffan, Á., Sawyer, I., Quinones, I., and Daniel, B. 2011. Evaluation of semen presumptive tests for use at crime scenes. *Medicine, Science and the Law*, 51, 11–17.

Lindenbergh, A., De Pagter, M., Ramdayal, G., Visser, M., Zubakov, D., Kayser, M., and Sijen, T. 2012. A multiplex (m)RNA-profiling system for the forensic identification of body fluids and contact traces. *Forensic Science International: Genetics*, 5, 565–577.

Matsuo, A., Ikematsu, K., and Nakasono, I. 2009. C-fos, fos-B, c-jun and dusp-1 expression in the mouse heart after single and repeated methamphetamine administration. *Legal Medicine*, 11, 285–290.

Noreault-Conti, T. L. and Buel, E. 2007. The use of real-time PCR for forensic stain identification. *Promega Profiles in DNA*, 10, 3–5.

Nussbaumer, C., Gharehbaghi-Schnell, E., and Korschineck, I. 2006. Messenger RNA profiling: A novel method for body fluid identification by real-time PCR. *Forensic Science International*, 157, 181–186.

Phang, T. W., Shi, C. Y., Chia, J. N., and Ong, C. N. 1994. Amplification of cDNA via RT-PCR using RNA extracted from post-mortem tissue. *Journal of Forensic Sciences*, 39, 1275–1279.

Preece, P. 2003. An optimistic view for quantifying mRNA in post-mortem human brain. *Molecular Brain Research*, 116, 7–16.

Richard, M. L., Harper, K. A., Craig, R. L., Onorato, A. J., Robertson, J. M., and Donfack, J. 2012. Evaluation of mRNA marker specificity for the identification of five human body fluids by capillary electrophoresis. *Forensic Science International: Genetics*, 6, 452–460.

Schroeder, A., Mueller, O., Stocker, S., Salowsky, R., Leiber, M., Gassmann, M., Lightfoot, S., Menzel, W., Granzow, M., and Ragg, T. 2006. The RIN: An RNA integrity number for assigning integrity values to RNA measurements. *BMC Molecular Biology*, 7, 3.

Setzer, M., Juusola, J., and Ballantyne, J. 2008. Recovery and stability of RNA in vaginal swabs and blood, semen and saliva stains. *Journal of Forensic Sciences*, 53, 296–305.

Takahashi, S. 2008. Expression levels of mRNAs for catecholamine biosynthetic enzymes as markers of acute response to contusion stress during the early postmortem period. *Tohoku Journal of Experimental Medicine*, 216, 239–248.

Takahashi, H., Ikematsu, K., Tsuda, R., and Nakasono, I. 2009. Increase in dual specificity phosphatase 1, TGF-beta stimulated gene 22, domain family protein 3 and Luc7 homolog (S. cerevisiae)-like messenger RNA after mechanical asphyxiation in the mouse lung. *Legal Medicine (Tokyo)*, 11, 181–185.

Tobe, S. S. and Linacre, A. M. 2008. A technique for the quantification of human and non-human mammalian mitochondrial DNA copy number in forensic and other mixtures. *Forensic Science International: Genetics*, 2, 249–256.

Vandesompele, J., Depreter, K., Pattyn, F., Poppe, B., Vanroy, N., Depappe, A., and Speleman, F. 2002. Accurate normalization of real-time quantitative RT-PCR data by geometric averaging of multiple internal control genes. *Genome Biology,* 3, RESEARCH0034.

Vennemann, M. and Koppelkamm, A. 2010a. mRNA profiling in forensic genetics I: Possibilities and limitations. *Forensic Science International,* 203, 71–75.

Vennemann, M. and Koppelkamm, A. 2010b. Postmortem mRNA profiling II: Practical considerations. *Forensic Science International,* 203, 76–78.

Visser, M., Zubakov, D., Ballantyne, K. N., and Kayser, M. 2011. mRNA-based skin identification for forensic applications. *International Journal of Legal Medicine,* 125, 253–263.

Watson, J. D., Hopkins, N. H., Roberts, J. W., Steitz, J. A., and Weiner, A. M. 1987. *Molecular Biology of the Gene,* 4th edn. Menlo Park, CA: Benjamin-Cummings Publishing Company.

Wilusz, C. J., Wang, W., and Peltz, S. W. 2001. Curbing the nonsense: The activation and regulation of mRNA surveillance. *Genes & Development,* 15, 2781–2785.

Zhao, D., Ishikawa, T., Quan, L., Li, D. R., Michiue, T., Yoshida, C., Komatu, A., Chen, J. H., Zhu, B. L., and Maeda, H. 2008. Tissue-specific differences in mRNA quantification of glucose transporter 1 and vascular endothelial growth factor with special regard to death investigations of fatal injuries. *Forensic Science International,* 177, 176–183.

Zhao, D., Zhu, B., Ishikawa, T., Li, D., Michiue, T., and Maeda, H. 2006. Quantitative RT-PCR assays of hypoxia-inducible factor-1α, erythropoietin and vascular endothelial growth factor mRNA transcripts in the kidneys with regard to the cause of death in medicolegal autopsy. *Legal Medicine,* 8, 258–263.

Zubakov, D., Boersma, A. W., Choi, Y., Van Kuijk, P. F., Wiemer, E. A., and Kayser, M. 2010. MicroRNA markers for forensic body fluid identification obtained from microarray screening and quantitative RT-PCR confirmation. *International Journal of Legal Medicine,* 124, 217–226.

Zubakov, D., Hanekamp, E., Kokshoorn, M., Van Ijcken, W., and Kayser, M. 2008. Stable RNA markers for identification of blood and saliva stains revealed from whole genome expression analysis of time-wise degraded samples. *International Journal of Legal Medicine,* 122, 135–142.

Advances in Fingerprint Techniques

14

MELANIE HARGREAVES-O'KANE AND JOHN DIXON

Contents

Introduction

In recent years, UK police fingerprinting services have undergone significant changes, in both their structure and training processes. In 2007 Centrex (the National Police Training Center) was replaced by the National Policing Improvements Agency (NPIA) in an attempt to standardise the delivery of fingerprint training to all UK police forces. With the disbanding of the National Fingerprint Board in 2008, the fingerprint service turned to the newly appointed Forensic Science Regulator for guidance. The Forensic Science Regulator (see Chapter 20) (sponsored by the Home Office) was established to ensure that the provision of forensic science services across the criminal justice system is subject to an appropriate regime of scientific quality standards (Home Office n.d.). The year 2012 saw the introduction of Police and Crime Commissioners as well as proposals for regionalisation of some police forces. The impact of these changes has yet to be fully revealed, but they have the potential to affect the provision of scientific support within UK police forces. Further change in 2012 saw the operational functions of the NPIA being transferred to the College of Policing, a new professional body designed to increase professionalism in policing. These revisions, as well as the ongoing review of the fingerprint service by the Fingerprint Quality Standards Specialist Group (FQSSG), mean that further changes to the operation of the UK fingerprint service are highly likely.

The use of friction ridge detail for human identification has been extensively researched and well documented. From the formation of the first British Fingerprint Bureau at New Scotland Yard in 1901 and the first prosecution in Britain of an individual based on fingerprint evidence in 1902 (Lambourne, 1978), the use of fingerprint-based evidence spread rapidly across the United Kingdom. One of the first forces to establish a regional bureau was West Riding (Yorkshire) in 1906, and with divergences in practices and levels of evidence, a national standard for fingerprint evidence was introduced in 1953 (Leadbetter, 2005).

The science of fingerprint recovery and comparison has steadily evolved over the last century, with progression particularly evident over the past 20 years (Galloway and Charlton, 2007). Much of this development can be attributed to the computerisation and digitisation of many of the processes. With the advent of digital photography and the increased use of large databases has come a certain level of sophistication; however, final comparison and identification of friction ridge detail is still performed by the human eye. Today, friction ridge analysis encompasses collection of prints from various regions of the body, including fingers, thumbs and the palmar and plantar surfaces of the hand and foot, respectively.

This chapter will discuss the progression of fingerprint retrieval and analytical techniques developed since the previous publication of *Forensic Human Identification: An Introduction* (Galloway and Charlton, 2007). Since this text, there have been many advances in this field, with legislative and technological changes impacting the collection, retention and processing of fingerprints. Furthermore, as a result of mass disasters such as the 2004 Boxing Day tsunami, progression is particularly evident within the disaster victim identification (DVI) context and the collection of friction ridge detail from deceased individuals. Thus, the latter part of this chapter will focus on techniques developed for the collection of fingerprint impressions from friction ridge skin of decomposing human remains.

Recovery of Fingerprints from the Living

The recovery techniques applied to living individuals have become increasingly sophisticated, with ink and paper being replaced by digital capture. The introduction of Livescan (a computerised method of digitally recording fingerprints) to some UK police custody suites in 2001 revolutionised the collection and comparison of friction ridge detail. Livescan allows officers to capture fingerprints and perform an immediate and rapid search of millions of potential matches on the national automated fingerprint identification system (NAFIS, presently IDENT1) (Komarinski, 2005). This means officers can easily check if individuals in custody are 'wanted', pose a security risk to officers or themselves or are operating under an alias.

With the implementation of 'Operation Lantern' (a trial of mobile fingerprint scanners) in 2006 came the introduction of mobile fingerprint scanners to several police forces in England and Wales (Elliott, 2009). This enabled officers on the ground to identify unknown individuals rapidly, without the requirement to report to the custody suite. Although the capture of palm prints had been common practice for many years, some fingerprint bureaux purchased a separate palm scanner unit in 2004/2005, permitting the comparison of crime scene palm prints against those in the computer database (Figure 14.1). However, it was not until this facility

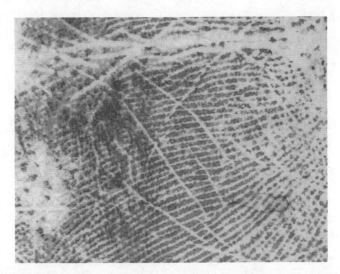

Figure 14.1 Photograph of an impression of the hypothenar area of a palm which (when scaled correctly to actual size) would be orientated, cropped and uploaded onto IDENT1, to allow officers to make a rapid comparison with palm prints of those held on the database. The quality of this impression is significantly better than the average crime scene mark. (Copyright: West Yorkshire Police, U.K.)

was incorporated into the IDENT1 database in 2006 that the comparison of palm prints against crime scene marks in England, Scotland and Wales became routine. The addition of this palm print database to IDENT1 has led to many police forces reinvestigating cold cases involving recovered palm prints. Currently, the technology of both Livescan and IDENT1 has been introduced to police forces throughout England, Wales, Scotland and Northern Ireland, as well as some partner agencies. The contract for IDENT1 expires in 2015, along with the contracts for Livescan and Mobile ID services, and therefore, collaboration to find their replacements is ongoing (Denison, 2013, personal communication).

In addition to the collection of fingerprints from detainees, procedures have been introduced which permit potential victims of crime to volunteer their fingerprints, also authorising their storage and use with IDENT1. The Forced Marriage Civil Protection Act of 2007 led to the Association of Chief Police Officers (ACPO) producing a guidance document in 2008 designed to direct officers in the collection of fingerprints, DNA and photographs from victims or potential victims of forced marriage (U.K. Government, 2007). This means that if the at-risk individual *does* fall victim to honour-based violence (HBV),* their samples may prove invaluable when attempting to identify them. The Forced Marriage Civil Protection Act of 2007 (U.K. Government, 2007) specifies best practice by police forces for the retrieval and storage of samples from those considered at risk from HBV while also protecting their identity. During the first 5 years of operation, this scheme has prompted around 375 individuals in the West Yorkshire Police area alone to request collection and storage of their fingerprints (Swaine 2013, personal communication).

Recovery of Fingerprints from Items

The examinations conducted by crime scene personnel have remained fairly constant in recent years, while the procedures involved in processing the associated friction ridge detail have advanced significantly. 'Lifting' fingerprint impressions using fingerprint powder and adhesive tape is still the primary technique for fingerprint recovery from crime scenes throughout the United Kingdom, with the lifts being photographed once they arrive at the bureau. Some police forces even employ digital technology to send images (referred to as 'remote transmission') of these lifts directly to the Identification Bureau from the crime scene (Allinson et al., 2007). The main advantage of using this method is the rapid processing of fingerprints.

---

* ACPO defines HBV as '...a crime or incident, which has or may have been committed to protect or defend the honour of the family and/or community' (ACPO 2008).

By transmitting a high-quality digital image of the lift, fingerprint officers have often examined, compared and identified impressions by the time the lifts themselves arrive at the bureau. Lincolnshire Police were one of the first forces to use remote transmission, which (since 2004) has been adopted by 75% of UK police forces (Police Oracle, 2011).

The majority of fingerprint examinations can be performed on scene, but there are some items that require further processing in a laboratory environment. A complete list of recommended techniques for scene and laboratory examination is published by the Home Office's Centre for Applied Science and Technology (formerly the Home Office Scientific Development Branch [HOSDB]) in a comprehensive manual detailing current fingerprint enhancement methods (HOSDB, 2012).

Those police forces able to afford laser technology have replaced Quaser as a primary fluorescence examination method for recovering latent prints from items (O'Hara, 2011, personal communication). The application of powder suspensions (e.g. white wet powder or black wet powder) as a fingerprint development technique has also increased in popularity. This is partly due to the reduction in use of gentian violet for adhesive surfaces resulting from health and safety restrictions. First applied to adhesive surfaces, powder suspension techniques are now being used on nonadhesive porous surfaces (HOSDB, 2007). The development of fingerprints using cyanoacrylate fumes is a proven technique on nonporous, nonadhesive items (Figure 14.2). The cyanoacrylate bonds to the salt/moisture in sweat, which means that wetted items where the salts may have been dissolved are difficult to obtain fingerprints from. In contrast, powder suspension can be applied to both wetted and dry items and to adhesive and nonadhesive surfaces. As a result of this obvious advantage, many UK police forces are increasingly applying powder suspension techniques to examine non-wetted substrates that would normally have been subject to the cyanoacrylate (superglue) method. An inadvertent discovery at Loughborough University found that the fumes of disulfur dinitride (S_2N_2) turn exposed fingerprints on glassware items a blue-black colour (Kelly et al., 2008). The disulfur dinitride polymerises on latent fingerprints on a range of surfaces (even if the item has been thoroughly washed), and ongoing research is focused on why the vapour polymerises along the ridges of fingerprints (Hadlington, 2012).

The vacuum metal deposition (VMD) technique is recognised as a sensitive and effective method for recovering fingerprints from nonporous items such as plastic carrier bags (Jones et al., 2012). The main advantage of VMD is that it can be used to detect fingerprints from items that have been immersed in water. The process involves depositing a thin layer of gold followed by a thin layer of zinc on nonporous items within a vacuum. The fingerprints are revealed as a positive or negative image in a grey film

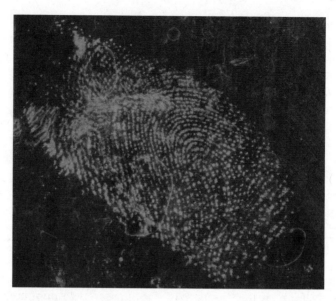

Figure 14.2 (See companion CD for colour figure.) Photograph showing an area of friction ridge detail that has been processed using cyanoacrylate (superglue) and then dyed with BY40. The BY40 makes the recovered fingerprint glow against the background when the item is examined using a crime light. This photograph was taken with a filter of the desired wavelength over the camera lens. (Copyright: West Yorkshire Police, U.K.)

of metallic zinc. Unfortunately, the recent increase in plastic carrier bag recycling has led to a rise in the levels of regrind added to the thermoplastic compound used to manufacture plastic bags. This in turn has affected the physical properties of plastic bags, leading to a reduced effectiveness of the VMD technique (O'Hara, 2011, personal communication). As a direct result of this, many forces have increased the use of the superglue/ethanol BY40 technique on non-wetted items. In some circumstances, the VMD method may be used afterwards to reveal additional friction ridge detail. A study by the (as was) HOSDB investigated alternatives to the VMD and other conventional techniques on surfaces where they had been deemed ineffective (HOSDB, 2010). Their research suggests that the use of silver instead of gold followed by zinc (as is done with VMD) may overcome some of the issues, and this amended method has already been adopted by some police forces (HOSDB, 2010). A new technique for visualising fingerprints on paper has been developed by chemists at the Hebrew University of Jerusalem. Jaber et al., (2012) used nanotechnology to produce a negative image of a fingerprint that was deposited on paper. The technique uses gold nanoparticles (Au-NPs) and then a silver physical developer (Ag-PD) or single-metal deposition (SMD), and the reaction with the fatty acids creates the negative fingerprint image (Jaber et al., 2012). Although research is ongoing, it may have implications for the processing of porous items that have been wet.

The technique by which bullets are examined for fingerprints is currently under review, with revolutionary techniques under development that may improve not only the quality of their processing but also the associated photography of curved surfaces. One method, developed by John Bond and the University of Leicester, has been listed as one of Time Magazine's top inventions of 2008 (Time, 2008). The technique exploits the principle that minute corrosion occurs on some metals when sweat is deposited. By coating the piece of metal in a metallic powder and applying a current, the corroded metal may be visualised as a fingerprint (Sauser, 2008). Although this method has yet to be adopted by many UK police forces, there has been worldwide interest in the technique and some success in recovering new fingerprint evidence in US cold case reviews (University of Leicester n.d.).* Another method for processing friction ridge detail on bullets and other metals is currently under development at Swansea University. Researchers are attempting to use the conductivity of metals to visualise fingerprints from their surface. The method involves the use of a scanning Kelvin probe (SKP) and works by measuring the volta (outer) potential difference between a metallic probe and the electrically conductive surface (Williams, 2010). Visualisation of friction ridge detail is derived from an interaction between the fingerprint itself and the surface on which it has been deposited. It is important to be able to exploit both fingerprint and DNA evidence on one object if possible (Raymond et al., 2004), while also being aware of the risk of possible contamination or destruction of DNA evidence when using certain fingerprint processing techniques prior to DNA extraction (van Oorschot et al., 2005). An advantage of SKP is its ability to reveal fingerprints when they have been deposited on irregular or highly nonplanar surfaces by mapping the volta potential patterns of small 3D metallic items (Williams and McMurray, 2007). This means that it may be useful in the recovery of fingerprints from cylindrical surfaces, for example, coins and cartridge casings postfiring (Williams and McMurray, 2007) and exposure to high temperatures (Williams et al., 2001). In addition the Bond technique can reveal friction ridge detail even when an item has been 'wiped clean' (University of Leicester n.d.), which can equally be said of the SKP technique. Despite both methods demonstrating an ability to reveal fingerprints from small

---

* Two cases of note are both unsolved murder investigations (University of Leicester 2012); the 2007 murder of Marianne Wilkinson (68) near Texas and a 1999 double murder investigation in Kingsland, Georgia. In both cases Bond was requested by investigating officers to examine the evidence, and in both cases, his technique recovered fingerprint evidence from the shell casings (Gray, 2009).

metal items after many years, they are still under development, and time and experience will show whether they are more effective than current standard techniques. The high cost of these methods, in addition to their limited availability, may mean that they are only applied to the most serious casework.

Research Using the Constituents of the Fingerprint Impression

Latent fingerprints, deposited by the friction ridges of the finger, palm or sole of the foot, are a complex mixture of natural secretions and contaminants from the environment (Singh et al., 2012). Croxton et al. (2010) advise us that these secretions are predominantly from the eccrine and sebaceous glands, which secrete sweat predominantly consisting of water, a highly complex mixture of organic and inorganic material (in the case of eccrine sweat), and fatty acids, glycerides, cholesterol, squalene and a variety of lipids (in the case of sebaceous secretions) (Croxton et al., 2010). As well as these constituents, there are also possible environmental contaminants such as bacteria spores, dust (Ramotowski, 2001), cosmetics, food residue or drugs and their metabolites (Girod et al., 2012), which may contribute to the chemical constituents of a fingerprint impression. Recent studies have examined contaminants left in fingerprint residue with a view to utilising the information for various purposes. Studies have included those looking at the detection of drug metabolites present within the fingerprint impression, which could potentially provide an insight into the lifestyle of the particular individual (Hazarika et al., 2008; Leggett et al., 2007; Szynkowska et al., 2009). One particular study involved the application of Raman spectroscopy to the analysis of drugs of abuse* in latent fingerprints that had been treated with powders and subsequently lifted with adhesive tapes (West and Went, 2008). The powdering and adhesive lifting of fingerprint impressions is the same method used throughout the majority of UK crime scenes and is therefore very similar to the forensic conditions in which this test could potentially be used. It is also important to note that the fingerprint lifts did not require removal from the evidence bags to be examined nor for the drug of abuse to be correctly identified, thus minimising the risk of evidential contamination. Research by Leggett et al. (2007) describes a method called 'intelligent fingerprinting', which enables both identification of an individual and simultaneous recognition of any drugs of abuse (and nicotine) within their sweat. Their research uses the functionalisation of nanoparticles with other antibodies, thus enabling the specific detection of numerous antigens within a fingerprint.

---

* Handled rather than ingested drugs.

Sample kits have been developed to analyse samples taken directly from an individual and also for the analysis of latent fingerprints recovered from touched surfaces (Intelligent Fingerprinting n.d.). Being able to detect the presence of drugs by taking individuals' fingerprints could have implications for not only roadside drug testing but also in testing athletes for banned substances (Hadlington, 2012).

Researchers at Sheffield Hallam University have been using matrix-assisted laser desorption ionisation mass spectrometry imaging (MALDI MSI) to reveal important areas of intelligence that may be gathered from latent fingerprint impressions. This is done by allowing the kind of evidence produced currently in a court of law to be generated prior to subsequent MALDI MSI analysis which, by providing chemical information, potentially adds intelligence to the case under investigation (Ferguson et al., 2011). Bradshaw et al., (2012) used MALDI MSI to separate overlapping fingerprints made by different individuals by looking at the different constituents that make up each of the impressions. This allowed them to produce two separate images of the originally overlapping fingerprints* (Bradshaw et al., 2012). Their research has also shown the feasibility of using MALDI MSI in fingerprint aging studies as well as being integrated within routine forensic analysis (Wolstenholme et al., 2009). MALDI MSI has also been used to simultaneously obtain images of the fingerprint ridge pattern and detect the presence of specific condom lubricants within a latent fingerprint impression (Bradshaw et al., 2011). This has been successful on fingerprints for up to 3 months after deposition (Francese and Wolstenholme, 2011). This research may appear to be highly specific to a certain set of circumstances (individual handles condom; condom lubricant transfers onto individual's fingers and is then inadvertently transferred to a surface and becomes a contaminant within the fingerprint impression) but could prove to be absolutely invaluable intelligence to investigating officers of sexual assaults. As the attacker is known to the victim in a high percentage of cases, there is often an argument of legitimate access to the crime scene. If condom lubricant can be detected in fingerprints, it would improve the evidence for the prosecution by establishing the assailant's presence at the scene and, crucially, having had contact with a condom, thus reducing the defence of legitimate access (Bradshaw et al., 2011). The most recent research by the university group using MALDI MSI has enabled the determination of sex of the fingerprint donor with 85% accuracy (Ferguson et al., 2012). They also suggest within their research the ability to provide information on traits such as nutritional habits, drug use or hormonal status. This ongoing research

---

* The method is only applicable to overlapping fingerprints from different individuals, rather than from the same person.

by Sheffield Hallam University highlights the potential of MALDI MSI to fingerprint services worldwide.

Other studies involving the analysis of fingerprint constituents include Day et al. (2004) who tried to detect the presence of caffeine and Benton et al. (2010) who assessed the presence of nicotine residue within latent impressions (Benton et al., 2010; Day et al., 2004). In addition, research has also been conducted investigating the detection of explosives *directly* deposited on the fingers after handling (Cotte-Rodriguez et al., 2006; Ifa et al., 2008; Justes et al., 2007). Rowell et al. (2012) have found a method for successfully detecting nitro-organic and peroxide explosives in *latent fingerprints* using mass spectrometry. They studied fingerprints deposited on a multitude of surfaces (laminated wood, plastic tape, paper, plastic bag, metal can and ceramic tile), which were then dusted with black powder and lifted using adhesive lifting tape. Although only currently successful under certain circumstances, the future development of these applications might have relevance in terrorism investigations as well as other investigations in relation to alternative chemicals (Girod et al., 2012; Rowell et al., 2012). A study by Antoine et al. (2010) suggests a way of estimating the age of the individual that deposited the fingerprint impression. Infrared microscopy revealed that differences in the sebum composition (the oily secretion from the sebaceous glands) of fingerprints could be used to distinguish between adult and child donors for up to 4 weeks post-deposition. Antoine et al. also reported that fingerprint composition changes with time differently in children versus adults, making it a sensitive metric to estimate the age of an individual, especially when the age of the print is known (Antoine et al., 2010). Several recent studies have attempted to age a fingerprint impression by analysing the change over time of the constituents left behind on the surface (Archer et al., 2005, De Paoli et al., 2010, Weyermann et al., 2011) or by using nanotechnology. This new method, developed by Spindler, uses nanoparticles and antibodies designed to target amino acids within a latent fingerprint and can detect aged, dry and weak fingerprints (University of Technology, Sydney 2011). Further research is ongoing as the technique has only been tested up to a fingerprint age of 1 year. Several other studies have explored the possibility of being able to sex the donor who left the fingerprint impression either by looking at the density of friction ridges within an impression (Nayak et al., 2010) by chemical composition alone (Asano et al., 2002) or by the aforementioned MALDI MSI technique (Ferguson et al., 2012). A recent study investigated the issue of overlapping electronically captured fingerprints and used an algorithm to separate them (Chen et al., 2011). Although it is not yet known if any of the previously mentioned techniques have been (or could be) successfully applied within a forensic context, they are discussed here with reference to possible future applications.

Presentation of Fingerprint Evidence in Court

In recent years there has been a rise in the number of television series portraying criminal investigations and the role forensic evidence plays in these. Although it is considered more of an issue in the United States than the United Kingdom, crime show viewing is thought to have the potential to affect a juror's trial decision—known as the 'CSI effect' (Hayes-Smith and Levett, 2011). This so-called CSI effect includes the increased and unrealistic expectation that crime scenes will yield plentiful forensic samples that can be analysed by near-infallible forensic science techniques and will be presented as such in court (Holmgren and Fordham, 2011). Overall, the CSI effect is reported to cause jurors to believe that they are experts on forensic evidence (Hayes-Smith and Levett, 2011). There are several studies which look at the considered effect that the increased level and popularity of criminal investigative shows has on forensic evidence in court by analysing information on viewing habits of jury members, as well as their response to the forensic evidence within a case. Tyler (2006) found that jurors who watched crime dramas were more likely to convict a defendant regardless of whether there was a presence or absence of forensic evidence (Tyler, 2006). As a direct contrast, however, in one study Shelton et al. (2007) questioned over 1000 jurors and found no direct correlation between their tendency to convict and their crime show viewing habits (Shelton et al., 2007). A study by Holmgren and Fordham (2011) suggested that Canadian jurors were clearly influenced in their treatment of some forensic evidence by their television viewing habits but found no support suggesting that the CSI effect was detrimental. However, they also noted that the Australian jury data they studied found that jurors assessed forensic evidence in a balanced and thoughtful manner (Holmgren and Fordham, 2011). The popularity of these television shows has also been blamed for offenders having a more sophisticated understanding of forensic processes (Greenwood, 2006; Pace, 2006). The CSI effect can also be argued to have led to members of the public having a greater expectation of forensic science than can be delivered (Schweitzer and Saks, 2007).

In a similar fashion, the 'tech effect' has contributed to society's overconfidence in forensic technology (Shelton et al., 2009). Shelton et al. (2009) provides an example of the expectations of one juror who expressed their disappointment that a lawn had not been dusted for fingerprints. As the public (and therefore jurors) view technologically advanced presentations of forensic processes on the aforementioned television shows, they have come to expect the same from their own courtroom experiences (Ley et al., 2012). A study by Weaver et al., (2012) looked at the suggested CSI effect at University and examined the perceptions of forensic science students regarding the forensic-related television programmes they watched. The results indicated that the students had mixed impressions of how the programmes portrayed forensic science professionalism and ethics, and believed they gave an unrealistic representation of the profession to the public (Weaver et al., 2012).

With an ever-increasing reliance on forensic evidence to prove a case and establish the facts, there is a tendency for this evidence to become ever more complex. With this in mind, some imaging units in UK police forces are becoming renowned for their ability to present evidence (including fingerprints) to the court in a clear and concise manner. A common query relates to the location and orientation of the recovered friction ridge detail. It is essential that a clear and thorough explanation is provided to the jurors as this often forms part of the suspected offender's defence. West Yorkshire Police have provided visual presentations of the precise location and orientation of recovered fingerprints in several high-profile cases. This not only assists the jury in understanding the processes fingerprints are subjected to in a forensic laboratory but can also save valuable court time during such cases. Examples of the graphical depiction of the orientation of fingerprints on a crime scene lift is in Figures 14.3 and 14.4, and when shown in conjunction with a Scene of Crime Officer's (SOCOs) scene diagram (Figure 14.5), it can paint a rather vivid picture to the jury. However, it is always worth stressing (when being questioned as to the orientation of marks) that identification experts are only ever able to offer a *possible* scenario of how the marks were left. Without actually being present when the friction ridge skin impressions were made, it is

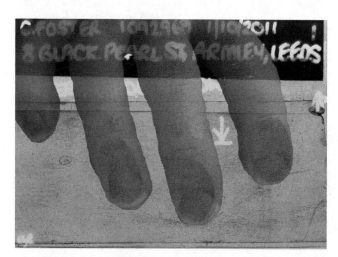

Figure 14.3 (See companion CD for colour figure.) A photograph of a crime scene lift with an overlaid photograph showing identified corresponding digits of a right hand—the sequence of impressions could have been considered to be 'climbing in marks' at the 'point of entry' window. (Copyright: West Yorkshire Police, U.K.)

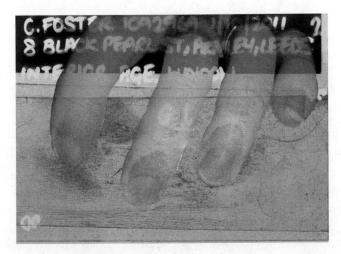

Figure 14.4 (See companion CD for colour figure.) A photograph of a crime scene lift with an overlaid photograph showing identified corresponding digits of a left hand—the sequence of impressions could have been considered to be 'climbing in marks' at the 'point of entry' window. (Copyright: West Yorkshire Police, U.K.)

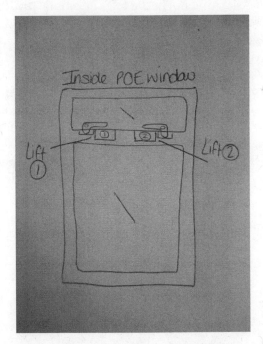

Figure 14.5 An example of a scene diagram drawn by a SOCO visiting the crime scene and showing where the fingerprint lifts were recovered from. (Copyright: West Yorkshire Police, U.K.)

not possible to say with absolute certainty how the impressions came to be there, only suggesting (in some cases) possible circumstances which may have led to deposition.

Friction Ridge Recovery from Damaged or Decomposing Remains

Performing friction ridge recovery on the deceased can seem like a simple process; however, there are many factors affecting the success of various fingerprinting techniques. It is emphasised that a bodyprinting expert be consulted prior to any attempt to recover friction ridge detail.

The majority of prints are collected for human identification purposes and for application in crime scene mark elimination or identification. There are many methods of recovery and processing used across the fingerprint service. Some techniques do not yield sufficient quality of results, while others may take a substantial amount of time to perform (delaying the repatriation of remains or potential prosecution of serious crimes) and/or require the use of substances hazardous to health. In the past harsh chemical treatments have been used to soften the hands of victims prior to the fingerprinting process, but following the Asian tsunami in 2004, DVI teams in Thailand often applied formalin to decomposing bodies to act as a preservative prior to the bodies being assessed and processed by the fingerprint experts. It was quickly realised that this could have serious implications for the health of the DVI teams. The authors emphasise the requirement to follow all health and safety protocols, as well as personal protective equipment (PPE) directives; as there is the potential to contract serious infections from handling human tissue without due care.

Current fingerprint manuals still advocate techniques such as inking and printing or using casting agents, which are in the authors' opinion obsolete. Personal experiences and preferences are often favoured, but there are four crucial stages to friction ridge recovery that must be performed to ensure best practice:

1. Assessment
2. Cleanup (though not in certain cases—e.g. Figure 14.6 where blood can be seen to improve friction ridge clarity)
3. Development/treatment
4. Capture

Assessment

The assessment process can be relatively simple when prints have been recovered from fresh, intact bodies, as the skin is often resistant to further

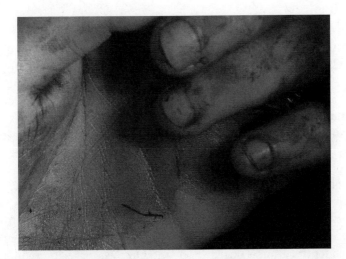

Figure 14.6 (See companion CD for colour figure.) The cleanup stage of the fingerprinting process is not always required—the clarity of the friction ridges photographed here is a direct result of the contrast provided by blood. (Copyright: West Yorkshire Police, U.K.)

damage when touched or manipulated. The surface is also able to withstand an intense cleanup stage, and it is sufficiently easy to capture excellent definition of ridge detail unless age, injury or medical conditions have affected the robusticity of the skin. For damaged or decomposed remains, the assessment should take into consideration the layer to be printed (dermal or epidermal) and whether the skin is *in situ* (i.e. attached to the body). In addition, the condition of the skin (softness and/or flexibility) will decide which method of recovery will be used, and the robusticity of the surface will determine which cleanup and development/treatment procedures can be applied. If after the initial assessment the case is deemed sufficiently complex, then the available detail and scale photographs of the relevant skin areas should be taken and passed to a bodyprinting specialist. If ridge detail is not immediately obvious, as long as the dermis (see Case 1) or epidermis (see Case 5) is available, then development may be possible. It must be noted that the skin of juveniles is less resistant to treatment processes, consequently the skin of adults may withstand direct contact with chemicals or waterborne heat, that of juveniles may not. It is essential to determine whether the epidermis is detached prior to examination or removed for the purposes of print recovery, as in mass fatality incidents (MFIs), as the detached epidermis may originate from a different individual from that which it was recovered from. It is essential that all such observations are recorded, as this evidence will be used in the human identification process.

Cleanup

The cleanup stage is particularly important, as in the majority of cases contaminants such as body fluids and dirt can interfere with the lifting process. They may have a detrimental effect on the quality and ease of lifting a fingerprint, as well as resulting in the loss of photographic definition. Heavy contamination can be removed with surgical spirit or wet wipes (if the skin is deemed sufficiently robust), and spirit gel may be applied for a deeper clean and/or to inhibit the leakage of body fluid through the skin. Drying of skin is more important when a powder and printing method is utilised as opposed to scale photography, when a moist or wet surface may improve contrast quality of the photograph (Lennard, 2007). There may be some instances where the cleanup stage cannot be performed; for example, when the hands of the deceased cannot be touched as a forensic examination is pending, but a positive identification is urgently sought. On these occasions contaminants such as blood may act to improve photographic contrast (Figure 14.6). It is important to note that PPE and Control of Substances Hazardous to Health (COSHH) protocols should be followed at all times.

Development/Treatment

The skin located on the palms of the hands, the digits and the soles of the feet is much thicker and more robust than elsewhere on the body (Kusuma et al., 2010). It is for this reason that the skin in these areas may still be apparent even when the rest of the remains are virtually skeletal (see Case 1).

The principles of development are generally quite simple; the skin of recently deceased individuals is subjected to the cleanup process and dried. A uniform coating of aluminium or black powder is then applied, and prints are recovered using clear lifting tape. To speed up the identification process, it is good practice to have a preprinted clear acetate cadaver print form ready to mount the recovered lifts. These are placed on the reverse side of the form in the format of a 10-print set, which is used on the computer searching system, and can be scanned in with minimal effort.

The task of developing a print becomes more challenging when the skin is damaged or decomposed. If the dermis and/or epidermis is overly soft or macerated (due to putrefaction or prolonged immersion in water), then it requires drying (Kahana et al., 2001) and stiffening to develop ridge detail. If the skin is desiccated, mummified, hard or leathery, then it requires softening through rehydration before fingerprints can be taken. There have been various techniques of rehydration suggested over previous decades (Haglund, 1988; Zugibe and Costello, 1986), some based on archaeological techniques (Schmidt et al., 2000) and some within the forensic literature (Fields and Molina, 2008). If the hard skin is smooth to the touch, then it may need to be stripped away. It is suggested to proceed with caution when using destructive methods (e.g. caustic soda, potassium hydroxide), as when applied incorrectly, they may damage the print irreparably. The techniques described here are those most utilised, based on many years of personal experience within an Identification Bureau, and are considered to provide the best results.

Heat Treatments

Heat treatments can be used to tighten overly soft skin and emphasise friction ridge detail. This can be either through direct contact with the skin using hot or boiling water (Case 1) or from a strong light source. If, for example, the dermis of a largely intact macerated hand requires development, then it can be placed into boiling water for up to 10 s (depending upon an assessment by the fingerprint expert as to the tissue's durability). After the hand has been dried, the friction ridge detail will appear more pronounced but smaller in size.* This process may be repeated in stages in order to develop the prints further, but it is advised to proceed with caution as it is possible to overdevelop the tissue. It is important to record the results at each stage as overdevelopment can cause the skin to lose integrity when overtreated. If there are open wounds, it is best to bind these areas first and use shorter heat bursts so as not to increase their size and destroy the prints further.

If the tissue is severely damaged or there are only isolated areas of friction ridge skin on the body, then either dabbing boiling water on these regions using a sponge or pouring the water in short bursts (spotting) will cause skin shrinkage and development of friction ridge detail (see Case 1). If the epidermis is too damaged to use for print recovery but is still firmly attached to the dermis, then immersing the hand in a jug of boiling water for 10 s (or more stages if required) will allow the two layers to be separated. A longer immersion time may be required to develop friction ridge detail of the dermis (Case 2). Very delicate skin (e.g. that of juveniles or the elderly) requires the application of a noncontact strong heat source such as a 500 W halogen lamp, which acts to dry and thus tighten the tissue for print capture. This particular method was used to great effect on victims of the 2004 Asian tsunami. Once the epidermis has been detached, it should be cleaned appropriately, taking into consideration its quality and strength. The majority of tissues will be able to withstand gentle washing in warm soapy water, which is performed on both surfaces to avoid slippage during the mounting process.

---

* The size difference however is within the margin of error for comparisons with fingerprints on the computer database (currently IDENT1) and is negligible enough to still enable visual comparisons between the fingerprint and other fingerprint records without resizing being necessary.

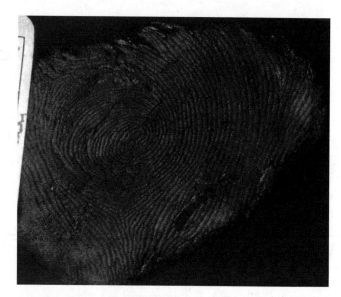

Figure 14.7 (See companion CD for colour figure.) Dried out, reconstructed, macerated skin mounted with shaped putty to enable optimum recovery of friction ridge detail. (Copyright: West Yorkshire Police, U.K.)

It is essential to differentiate between the inner and outer surfaces of the skin, with partial pieces of palmar or plantar tissue more challenging to assess, as it is possible to develop friction ridge detail on both sides of a surface. If the detached epidermis is removed intact, it can be used to perform the 'glove method' in which the skin of the deceased is placed over a volunteer's hand (in a similar fashion to a glove) and then developed accordingly (Cutro, 2011; Knobel, 2005; Pounder, 1992). For more intricate reconstructions (in particular for a delicate or waterlogged epidermis), a mounting surface made of shaped putty is required (Figure 14.7). Imaging of a robust epidermis can be performed by trapping the tissue between two glass plates and using backlighting to highlight friction ridge detail (Figure 14.8).

Chemical Treatments

If hard skin requires softening, it is best to apply a chemical soak. This method entails the prolonged soaking of the area of skin (e.g. hand or finger) in potassium hydroxide or similar caustic solution. Most chemical techniques require days to achieve the desired effect (time that may not be available), or the risk of significant damage is too great. These methods require controlled conditions and thus permission from the coroner is required to remove the hand or digit under investigation for transportation

Figure 14.8 Left palm epidermis held between glass plates and backlit. (Copyright: West Yorkshire Police, U.K.)

to the laboratory. For many years, removal of areas of the body to aid friction ridge recovery was considered routine. However, following the Marchioness riverboat disaster in 1989, where the removal of macerated hands to aid the identification process was not undertaken in a controlled manner, changes were implemented regarding the rules for the removal and retention of body parts for scientific evaluation (Walker and Mallett, 2011). More recent technical developments have reduced the need to remove human body parts, and this is now only performed if absolutely essential. The treatment of desiccated skin (smooth and without friction ridge detail) can now be performed in the mortuary with a high concentration of hot caustic, which rapidly softens the damaged outer layer. This can then be removed to reveal the intact lower layer for printing (Case 4).

Capture

Once ridge detail has developed sufficiently, it is possible to capture the print using fingerprint powder and lifting tape. Although there is low strength lifting tape available for delicate skin, the use of scale photography is favoured. This can prevent the need for further processing if print recovery is solely for identification of the individual as opposed to capturing a full set of finger-prints for comparisons against crime scene marks). If additional stages are required to develop ridge detail, then it is important to photograph the tissue and record any observations before proceeding with potentially destructive recovery methods.

Case Studies

Case 1

Figure 14.9 is an example of a near-skeletal, decomposed body with a small area of smooth dermal skin available for print recovery. After assessing scene photographs, it was decided that the right palmar surface (Figure 14.10) was likely to provide the best opportunity for print capture. This region was cleared of maggot infestation and cleaned with wet wipes and spirit gel. After removal of contaminants, friction ridge development was carried out by firstly sponging and then spotting boiling water on to the palm.

Figure 14.9 (See companion CD for colour figure.) An overview of the extent of decomposition. (Copyright: West Yorkshire Police, U.K.)

Figure 14.10 (See companion CD for colour figure.) A pre-cleanup view of the dermal area of the palm. (Copyright: West Yorkshire Police, U.K.)

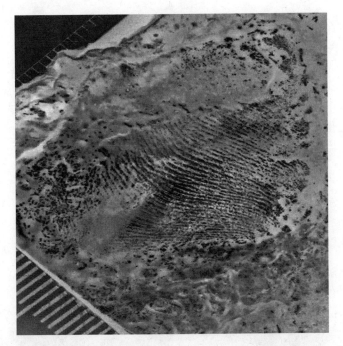

Figure 14.11 The resultant scale photograph of the treated friction ridge detail. (Copyright: West Yorkshire Police, U.K.)

This technique caused the skin to contract to nearly half its original size and led to pronounced ridge detail, as can be seen in Figure 14.11. The above photograph of the palm was used to positively identify the individual.

Case 2

Case 2 demonstrates the techniques used to develop and capture fingerprints from a macerated hand with badly damaged epidermis, which was still firmly adhered to the dermis (Figure 14.12). The hand was immersed in boiling water for 10 s, after which the epidermis could be easily removed from the dermis (Figure 14.13). To develop the dermis, the hand was placed in boiling water for a further 5 s. It was then dried and powdered, and tape was applied to lift the print (Figure 14.14). The deceased was positively identified when a comparison was made with antemortem fingerprints.

Case 3

Case 3 shows a desiccated, badly decomposed and insect-infested body that had lain undiscovered for several months (Figure 14.15). The joints were fused, and the flesh was very hard and heavily creased; therefore, a request

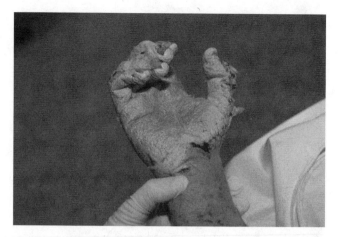

Figure 14.12 (**See companion CD for colour figure.**) The macerated hand with damaged epidermis still attached to the dermis. (Copyright: West Yorkshire Police, U.K.)

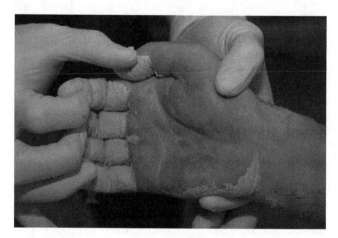

Figure 14.13 (**See companion CD for colour figure.**) The same hand with epidermis peeled away and dried. (Copyright: West Yorkshire Police, U.K.)

was made to the coroner for removal of the fourth digit to permit easier handling and decrease the likelihood of damaging friction ridge patterns. After receiving approval, the ring finger was removed at the middle interphalangeal joint and soaked in potassium hydroxide solution by means of a suspension (or 'tea bag') method. This particular technique is designed to minimise damage caused by surfaces touching the skin. The now softened skin favoured removal of the contaminated, decomposed outer layers, revealing sufficient ridge detail for identification purposes (Figure 14.16). Ideally immersing the finger for longer would be recommended, resulting in a more pliable digit and greater definition of friction ridge detail. Unfortunately, due

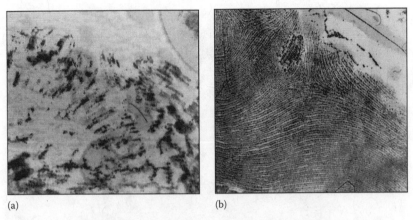

(a)   (b)

Figure 14.14 The contrast between epidermal (a) and dermal (b) layers is apparent. (Copyright: West Yorkshire Police, U.K.)

Figure 14.15 (See companion CD for colour figure.) An image demonstrating the extent of decomposition of the hand. (Copyright: West Yorkshire Police, U.K.)

to time constraints on the case, this was not possible. Following capture, the tissue was returned for storage with the rest of the remains.

Case 4

In this case, an electronic image of a hard piece of epidermal skin located at a murder scene was passed to the Identification Bureau (Figure 14.17). The tissue was thought to originate from the victim, but the SOCO was unsure as to whether print capture was possible. After reviewing the photograph, it was requested that the skin be brought to the fingerprint laboratory for analysis. Upon arrival the tissue was softened in a hot caustic solution

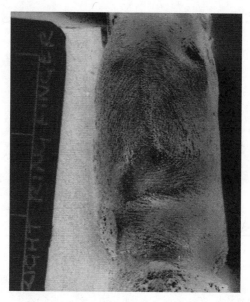

Figure 14.16 The treated finger illustrating a whorl pattern. (Copyright: West Yorkshire Police, U.K.)

Figure 14.17 (See companion CD for colour figure.) The hard, desiccated, epidermal skin prior to treatment. (Copyright: West Yorkshire Police, U.K.)

(only a few seconds were required), rinsed and then dried. It was then coated in black powder, stuck to clear adhesive tape and mounted on a transparent plastic cup. A backlight was applied to improve photographic contrast, and an image was captured (Figure 14.18). A comparison was performed with existing fingerprint records, and the tissue was identified as originating from

Figure 14.18 (See companion CD for colour figure.) The mounted and developed skin showing clear and identifiable ridge detail. (Copyright: West Yorkshire Police, U.K.)

the left forefinger of the murder victim. Following treatment and capture, the skin was returned to the body.

Conclusion

As is evident from the examples given, the process of enhancing, capturing and comparing friction ridge detail in forensic contexts has progressed significantly. Continued development is important as fingerprint evidence remains a key component of the criminal justice system, and it is safe to assume that advancements in the techniques used to prepare and analyse this type of evidence will persist. In instances where friction ridge recovery appears difficult, it is advised to consult a bodyprint expert, as attempts to treat and develop tissue by untrained individuals can result in irreparable damage and destruction of crucial evidence. It is therefore essential to discuss the potential courses of action with a professional before proceeding with any treatments or development techniques. This cannot be more serious than in forensic scenarios, as there is the potential for the release of an offender, prosecution of an innocent individual or misidentification of human remains. Consequently, for those working within the forensic field, this chapter has attempted to bring these advances to the fore and made suggestions for best practice.

References

ACPO. 2008. Honour based violence strategy. Association of Chief Police Officers. Available from: http://www.acpo.police.uk/documents/crime/2008/200810CRIHBV01.pdf, Site accessed January 21, 2013.

Allinson NM, Sivarajah J, Gledhill I, Carling M, and Allinson LJ. 2007. Robust wireless transmission of compressed latent fingerprint images. *IEEE Transactions on Information Forensics and Security—Part 1* 2(3):331–340.

Antoine KM, Mortazavi S, Miller AD, and Miller LM. 2010. Chemical differences are observed in children's versus adults' latent fingerprints as a function of time. *Journal of Forensic Sciences* 55(2):513–518.

Archer NE, Charles Y, Elliott JA, and Jickells S. 2005. Changes in the lipid composition of latent fingerprint residue with time after deposition on a surface. *Forensic Science International* 154(2–3):224–239.

Asano KG, Bayne CK, Horsman KM, and Buchanan MV. 2002. Chemical composition of fingerprints for gender determination. *Journal of Forensic Science* 47(4):805–807.

Benton M, Chua MJ, Gu F, Rowell F, and Ma J. 2010. Environmental nicotine contamination in latent fingermarks from smoker contacts and passive smoking. *Forensic Science International* 200(1–3):28–34.

Bradshaw R, Rao W, Wolstenholme R, Clench MR, Bleay S, and Francese S. 2012. Separation of overlapping fingermarks by matrix assisted laser desorption ionisation mass spectrometry imaging. *Forensic Science International* 222(1–3):318–326.

Bradshaw R, Wolstenholme R, Blackledge RD, Clench MR, Ferguson LS, and Francese S. 2011. A novel matrix-assisted laser desorption/ionisation mass spectrometry imaging based methodology for the identification of sexual assault suspects. *Rapid Communications in Mass Spectrometry* 25(3):415–422.

Chen F, Feng J, Jain AK, Zhou J, and Zhang J. 2011. Separating overlapped fingerprints. *IEEE Transactions on Information Forensics and Security* 6(2):346–359.

Cotte-Rodriguez I, Chen H, and Cooks RG. 2006. Rapid trace detection of triacetone triperoxide (TATP) by complexation reactions during desorption electrospray ionization. *Chemical Communications* (9):953–955.

Croxton RS, Baron MG, Butler D, Kent T, and Sears VG. 2010. Variation in amino acid and lipid composition of latent fingerprints. *Forensic Science International* 199(1–3):93–102.

Cutro BT. 2011. Recording living and postmortem friction ridge skin exemplars. In: McRoberts A, ed. *The Fingerprint Sourcebook*. Washington, DC: U.S. Department of Justice.

Day JS, Edwards HGM, Dobrowski SA, and Voice AM. 2004. The detection of drugs of abuse in fingerprints using Raman spectroscopy I: Latent fingerprints. *Spectrochimica Acta Part A: Molecular and Biomolecular Spectroscopy* 60(3):563–568.

De Paoli G, Lewis Sr SA, Schuette EL, Lewis LA, Connatser RM, and Farkas T. 2010. Photo- and thermal-degradation studies of select eccrine fingerprint constituents. *Journal of Forensic Sciences* 55(4):962–969.

Denison N. 2013. Personal communication. Discussion with Head of Regional Identification Services (for Yorkshire and the Humber). In: Hargreaves-O'Kane JDaM, ed. West Yorkshire Police Identification Bureau.

Elliott J. 2009. Going mobile. *Biometric Technology Today* 17(4):7–9.

Ferguson L, Bradshaw R, Wolstenholme R, Clench M, and Francese S. 2011. Two-step matrix application for the enhancement and imaging of latent fingermarks. *Analytical Chemistry* 83(14):5585–5591.

Ferguson LS, Wulfert F, Wolstenholme R, Fonville JM, Clench MR, Carolan VA, and Francese S. 2012. Direct detection of peptides and small proteins in fingermarks and determination of sex by MALDI mass spectrometry profiling. *Analyst* 137(20):4686–4692.

Fields R and Molina DK. 2008. A novel approach for fingerprinting mummified hands. *Journal of Forensic Sciences* 53(4):952–955.

Francese S and Wolstenholme R. 2011. A novel MALDI-MSI based analytical tool to process fingermarks recovered at a sexual assault crime scene. The Forensic Technological Review.

Galloway V and Charlton D. 2007. Fingerprints. In: Thompson T and Black S, eds. *Forensic Human Identification: An Introduction*. Boca Raton, FL: CRC Press.

Girod A, Ramotowski R, and Weyermann C. 2012. Composition of fingermark residue: A qualitative and quantitative review. *Forensic Science International* 223(1–3):10–24.

Greenwood JK. 2006. Criminals get tips from forensic television shows. http://wwwpittsburghlivecom/x/pittsburghtrib/news/pittsburgh/s_481326html Pittsburgh Tribune Review.

Hadlington S. 2012. Another brick in the whorl. http://wwwrscorg/chemistryworld/Issues/2012/March/another-brick-in-the-whorlasp (Accessed January 6, 2013).

Haglund WD. 1988. A technique to enhance fingerprinting of mummified fingers. *Journal of Forensic Science* 33(5):1244–1248.

Hayes-Smith RM and Levett LM. 2011. Jury's still out: How television and crime show viewing influences Jurors' evaluations of evidence. *Applied Psychology in Criminal Justice* 7(1):29–46.

Hazarika P, Jickells SM, Wolff K, and Russell DA. 2008. Imaging of latent fingerprints through the detection of drugs and metabolites. *Angewandte Chemie International Edition* 47(52):10167–10170.

Holmgren JA and Fordham J. 2011. The CSI effect and the Canadian and the Australian Jury. *Journal of Forensic Sciences* 56:S63–S71.

Home Office. 2011. Forensic science regulator. Available from: http://www.homeoffice.gov.uk/agencies-public-bodies/fsr/, accessed January 18, 2013.

HOSDB. 2007. *Powder Suspensions and use with Adhesive and Non-Adhesive Items*. Fingerprint and Footwear Forensics Publication No 59/07.

HOSDB. 2010. Fingerprints and footwear forensics. http://tnaeuroparchiveorg/20100413151426/http://scienceandresearchhomeofficegovuk/hosdb/fingerprints-footwear-marks/fingerprinting-methods/indexhtml

HOSDB. 2012. *Fingerprint Source Book*. Home Office Scientific Development Branch. Available from: http://www.homeoffice.gov.uk/publications/science/cast/crime-investigation/fingerprint-source-book-2012/

Ifa DR, Manicke NE, Dill AL, and Cooks RG. 2008. Latent fingerprint chemical imaging by mass spectrometry. *Science* 321(5890):805.

Intelligent Fingerprinting. 2008. Homepage. University of East Anglia. Available from: http://www.intelligentfingerprinting.com/, accessed January 18, 2013.

Jaber N, Lesniewski A, Gabizon H, Shenawi S, Mandler D, and Almog J. 2012. Visualization of latent fingermarks by nanotechnology: Reversed development on paper—A remedy to the variation in sweat composition. *Angewandte Chemie International Edition* 51(49):12224–12227.

Jones BJ, Downham R, and Sears VG. 2012. Nanoscale analysis of the interaction between cyanoacrylate and vacuum metal deposition in the development of latent fingermarks on low-density polyethylene. *Journal of Forensic Sciences* 57(1):196–200.

Justes DR, Talaty N, Cotte-Rodriguez I, and Cooks RG. 2007. Detection of explosives on skin using ambient ionization mass spectrometry. *Chemical Communications* (21):2142–2144.

Kahana T, Grande A, Tancredi DM, Penalver J, and Hiss J. 2001. Fingerprinting the deceased: Traditional and new techniques. *Journal of Forensic Science* 46(4):908–912.

Kelly PF, King RSP, and Mortimer RJ. 2008. Fingerprint and inkjet-trace imaging using disulfur dinitride. *Chemical Communications* (46):6111–6113.

Knobel GJ. 2005. Taking fingerprints from a decomposed body using the "Indirect Cadaver Hand Skin-Glove Method". *South African Medical Journal* 95(9):665–666.

Komarinski P. 2005. *Automated Fingerprint Identification Systems (AFIS)*. Boston, MA: Elsevier.

Kusuma S, Vuthoori RK, Piliand M, and Zins JE. 2010. Skin anatomy and physiology. In: Siemionow MZ and Eisenmann-Klein M, eds. *Plastic and Reconstructive Surgery*. London, U.K.: Springer-Verlag.

Lambourne G. 1978. A brief history of fingerprints. *Journal of Forensic Science* 17(2–3):95–98.

Leadbetter MJ. 2005. Fingerprint evidence in England and Wales—The revised standard. *Medicine, Science and The Law* 45(1):1–6.

Leggett R, Lee-Smith EE, Jickells SM, and Russell DA. 2007. "Intelligent" fingerprinting: Simultaneous identification of drug metabolites and individuals by using antibody-functionalized nanoparticles. *Angewandte Chemie International Edition* 46(22):4100–4103.

Lennard C. 2007. Fingerprint detection: Current capabilities. *Australian Journal of Forensic Sciences* 39(2):55–71.

Ley BL, Jankowski N, and Brewer PR. 2012. Investigating *CSI*: Portrayals of DNA testing on a forensic crime show and their potential effects. *Public Understanding of Science* 21(1):57–67.

Nayak VC, Rastogi P, Kanchan T, Lobo SW, Yoganarasimha K, Nayak S, Rao NG, Pradeep Kumar G, Suresh Kumar Shetty B, and Menezes RG. 2010. Sex differences from fingerprint ridge density in the Indian population. *Journal of Forensic and Legal Medicine* 17(2):84–86.

van Oorschot RA, Treadwell S, Beaurepaire J, Holding NL, and Mitchell RJ. 2005. Beware the possibility of fingerprinting techniques transferring DNA. *Journal of Forensic Science* 50(6):1417–1422.

O'Hara, J. 2013. Pers. Comm. Head of West Yorkshire Police Fingerprint Enhancement Laboratory, Discussion regarding use of quaser and fluorescence examinations. Feb 2013.

Pace G. 2006. CSI: Crime Scene Instructions? http://wwwcbsnewscom/stories/2006/01/30/entertainment/main1259502shtml

Police Oracle. 2011. Fingerprint tech on the move. Available from: http://www.policeoracle.com/news/Fingerprint-Tech-On-The-Move-_33925.html accessed January 21, 2013.

Pounder D. 1992. Bodies from water. http://wwwdundeeacuk/forensicmedicine/notes/waterpdf

Ramotowski R. 2001. Composition of latent print residue. In: Henry C, Lee R, and Gaensslen RE, eds. *Advances in Fingerprint Technology*, 2nd edn. Boca Raton, FL: CRC Press. pp. 63–104.

Raymond JJ, Roux C, Du-Pasquier E, Sutton J, and Lennard C. 2004. The effect of common fingerprint detection techniques on the DNA typing of fingerprints deposited on different surfaces. *Journal of Forensic Identification* 54:22–37.

Rowell F, Seviour J, Lim AY, Elumbaring-Salazar CG, Loke J, and Ma J. 2012. Detection of nitro-organic and peroxide explosives in latent fingermarks by DART- and SALDI-TOF-mass spectrometry. *Forensic Science International* 221(1–3):84–91.

Sauser B. 2008. A way to find hidden fingerprints. http://wwwtechnologyreviewcom/communications/21331/, MIT Technology Review.

Schmidt CW, Nawrocki SP, Williamson MA, and Marlin DC. 2000. Obtaining fingerprints from mummified fingers: A method for tissue rehydration adapted from the archaeological literature. *Journal of Forensic Science* 45(4):874–875.

Schweitzer NJ and Saks MJ. 2007. The CSI effect: Popular fiction about forensic science affects public expectations about real forensic science. *Jurimetrics* 47:357.

Shelton DE, Barak G, and Kim YS. 2007. A study of juror expectations and demands concerning scientific evidence: Does the "CSI Effect" exist? *Vanderbilt Journal of Entertainment and Technology Law* 9(2):331–368.

Shelton DE, Kim YS, and Barak G. 2009. An indirect-effects model of mediated adjudication: The CSI myth, the tech effect, and metropolitan jurors' expectations for scientific evidence. *Vanderbilt Journal of Entertainment and Technology Law* 12(1):9.

Singh K, Sharma S, and Garg RK. 2013. Visualization of latent fingerprints using silica gel G: A new technique. *Egyptian Journal of Forensic Sciences* 3(1):20–25.

Swaine G. 2013. Personal communication. Individual in charge of HBV sets of fingerprints within West Yorkshire police. In: Hargreaves-O'Kane JDaM, ed. West Yorkshire Police Identification Bureau.

Szynkowska MI, Czerski K, Rogowski J, Paryjczak T, and Parczewski A. 2009. ToF-SIMS application in the visualization and analysis of fingerprints after contact with amphetamine drugs. *Forensic Science International* 184(1–3):e24–e26.

Time. 2008. Best Inventions of 2008: 39. Enhanced fingerprints. Available from: http://www.time.com/time/specials/packages/article/0,28804,1852747_1854195_1854178,00.html accessed January 18, 2013.

Tyler TR. 2006. Viewing *CSI* and the threshold of guilt: Managing truth and justice in reality and fiction. *The Yale Law Journal* 115:1050–1085.

U.K. Government. 2007. Forced Marriage (Civil Protection Act). Available from: http://www.justice.gov.uk/downloads/protecting-the-vulnerable/forced-marriage/forced-marriage.pdf, accessed January 18, 2013.

University of Leicester. 2012. Reopening 'Cold Cases'. Available from: http://www2.le.ac.uk/study/why-us/discoveries/reopening-cold-cases?searchterm=rutty, accessed January 18, 2013.

University of Technology Sydney. 2011. A step towards a revolution in law enforcement. Available from: http://newsroom.uts.edu.au/news/2011/06/a-step-towards-a-revolution-in-law-enforcement, accessed January 18, 2013.

Walker G and Mallett X. 2011. The Marchioness river boat disaster, August 20, 1989. In: Black S, Sunderland G, Hackman L, and Mallett X, eds. *The DVI Casebook: Experience and Practice*. Boca Raton, FL: CRC Press. pp. 127–141.

Weaver R, Salamonson Y, Koch J, and Porter G. 2012. The CSI effect at university: Forensic science students' television viewing and perceptions of ethical issues. *Australian Journal of Forensic Sciences* 44(4):381–391.

West MJ and Went MJ. 2008. The spectroscopic detection of exogenous material in fingerprints after development with powders and recovery with adhesive lifters. *Forensic Science International* 174(1):1–5.

Weyermann C, Roux C, and Champod C. 2011. Initial results on the composition of fingerprints and its evolution as a function of time by GC/MS analysis. *Journal of Forensic Sciences* 56(1):102–108.

Williams G. 2010. Visualisation of fingerprints on metal surfaces using a scanning Kelvin probe. *Fingerprint Whorld* 36(139):51–60.

Williams G and McMurray N. 2007. Latent fingermark visualisation using a scanning Kelvin probe. *Forensic Science International* 167(2):102–109.

Williams G, Murray HN, and Worsley DA. 2001. Latent fingerprint detection using a scanning Kelvin microprobe. *Journal of Forensic Science* 46(5):1085–1092.

Wolstenholme R, Bradshaw R, Clench MR, and Francese S. 2009. Study of latent fingermarks by matrix-assisted laser desorption/ionisation mass spectrometry imaging of endogenous lipids. *Rapid Communications in Mass Spectrometry* 23(19):3031–3039.

Zugibe FT and Costello JT. 1986. A new method for softening mummified fingers. *Journal of Forensic Science* 31(2):726–731.

Legal Issues: An International Perspective IV

Admissibility of Expert Evidence

15

XANTHÉ MALLETT

Contents

Introduction

The significance of the concept of reliability cannot be overestimated in a criminal trial, particularly in relation to the presentation of evidence, and this is even more pressing when scientific methods and the evidence produced are of a highly technical or specialised nature, to help a jury reach a decision on the guilt of a defendant/s. All courts are governed by rules that detail what types of evidence are admissible. One key aspect for the admission of evidence is whether it proves, or helps prove, a fact or issue in that case. Here we will consider the current approaches to courtroom admissibility of expert evidence in the United States and England and Wales, in light of recent reports that have aimed to highlight and offer solutions to some of the ongoing problems.

There are two types of witnesses who proffer evidence in a trial: lay witnesses, who speak only of their own experiences, and experts, who are called upon to assist the jury understand the evidence being presented to them. Expert witnesses are permitted to speak on aspects of the case within their own immediate experience and offer opinion evidence as to the likelihood of an event having happened; what is the likelihood that a hair sample originated from the suspect? In reference to opinion evidence, Federal Rules of Evidence (FREs) 716.01(c) (Probative Value of

Objective Evidence [R-2]—700 Examination of Applications) (U.S. Federal Government, n.d.-a) state that

> In assessing the probative value of an expert opinion, the examiner must consider the nature of the matter sought to be established, the strength of any opposing evidence, the interest of the expert in the outcome of the case, and the presence or absence of factual support for the expert's opinion.

Expert witnesses are a recognised and accepted part of the criminal justice system and often make significant and valuable contributions to cases. However, the reliability of the expert evidence can be difficult to determine. Legal theory is guided by the principles of the authority of the expert and the authority of the knowledge. Consequently, there are two sides to this evaluation: the evidence (the method used, the conclusions drawn, etc.) and the expert (their qualifications, training, etc.). In short, all evidence heard by the jury must be more 'probative'* than prejudicial.[†] Evidence can, of course, be both probative *and* prejudicial, and the FREs (which, although only enacted in the United States, are highly influential in the United Kingdom and elsewhere) have delegated the task of regulating prejudicial evidence to trial judges (Tanford, 1989; U.S. Federal Government, n.d.-b).

What constitutes 'authority' can be difficult to define, but in a legal setting the authority of knowledge is based on validity, currency and relevance. The authority of an expert is centred on a number of factors, including their competency to evaluate the knowledge—through education and experience—and their currency in doing so, whether it is specific rather than general knowledge, and whether the expert is to be used to clarify information that it is necessary for the jury to understand. Ideally, each expert should be assessed with a view to examining the justification, relevance and currency of each premise in the opinion. Furthermore, the degree to which an expert uses the expertise of others as a premise for their own opinion, their ability to understand and assimilate it and the authority of these other experts upon which they rely are all components which must be considered when assessing the authority of the opinion. In addition, the expert's opinion must be appropriate and comprehensible and the sources of conclusions explicit. Finally, continuing research that contributes to the advancement of the science is expected, and the research agenda must also enable criminal justice practitioners to understand the uses and limitations of the technique (Roberts, 2009; Taylor, 2000; Uglow, 1997).

---

* Probative evidence establishes or contributes to proof.
† 'The danger of unfair prejudice is typically shown where the evidence may lead a jury to adopt an illegitimate form of reasoning or give the evidence undue weight (NSW Government 1995)'.

The evaluation of an expert's potential contribution to any particular case occurs at various stages of the process. Initially, during a case, an investigating agency may seek the services of an individual experienced in that area to advise them on an aspect of the investigation. This investigation can be either civil in nature, for example, being undertaken by social services in relation to alleged or suspect familial child abuse, or criminal cases prosecuted by the Crown Presecution Service (CPS), for example, murder. A suitably qualified expert may be sought as a result of word of mouth—having acted as an expert for that group in the past—or may be on a list of registered experts. However that expert is obtained, even if they are well recognised as an expert in that field and have been used many times as a witness in court, it does not mean that their evidence will be reliable.

The next stage at which that expert's evidence is evaluated is, in criminal trials, a pre-trial hearing. At this stage, the judge acts as a 'gatekeeper', reviewing both the expert's qualifications and experience against the evidence they are proposing to give—the aim being to prevent unsound or potentially prejudicial evidence from reaching the jury, as research indicates that once prejudicial evidence is heard, it is not possible to remove the prejudicial impact from the case (Jackson, 2012; Reedy, 2011).

Judges have significant latitude in the evidence they admit and, however knowledgeable, will sometimes make the wrong decision—to either include prejudicial or exclude probative evidence—under the time pressure of an ongoing trial (Gibbs, 1958; Mengler, 1989). This has unfortunately been demonstrated countless times in high-profile miscarriages of justice.*

The jury undertakes the final stage in the evaluation of the expert and the evidence they offer, although the judge may provide direction. The jury, comprising members of the community, are guided through the evidence by counsel, whose role is to elicit information from the expert. The expert is then cross-examined, a feature of the adversarial process, the aim of which, among other things, is to allow opposing counsel to test the veracity of the evidence being presented by confronting and attempting to undermine the opposition's case by exposing deficiencies in witness testimony (Australian Law Reform Commission, 2010). This gives the jury the opportunity to recognise these limitations and consider these in their deliberations. However, the complexity of the evidence, together with lack of clear legal directive aimed at ensuring reliability of expert testimony, means that the process of cross-examination may not always reveal potential flaws and limitations of the evidence being presented.

The inclusion of expert evidence in both civil and criminal proceedings is beyond question, as jurors lack the skills to interpret the reliability

---

* For example, the Birmingham 6, or Shirley McKie (discussed in relation to the Scottish Fingerprint Inquiry in a later section).

of what is often complex material, particularly in the case of scientific evidence. This can lead to jurors simply deferring to the opinion of the expert, without a sound basis for their conclusion. Where opposing experts are presented, the jurors' decisions can be made more on the grounds of the expert's skills in presenting their evidence (Cutler and Kovera, 2011; Kovera et al., 1997) and the counsel's proficiency in directing their witness and cross-examining the opposing witness (Gibbs, 1958) than in the strength of the evidence.

Background to Evidential Admissibility

United States

As may be seen from the previous discussion, the admissibility of expert evidence into the courtroom is complex. More than that, the situation is constantly in a state of flux, as judicial precedent continues to influence case outcomes. This multifaceted arena is further complicated by the fact that a comparison of the evidence evaluation systems in England (and Wales) and United States reveals two distinctively different methods: England bases the appraisal on common law, with case law (and judicial precedent) having a large impact on future trials, and in the United States, the foundation for evidence assessment is the FREs, as interpreted by the courts, a more formal structure. This being said, the FREs in the United States have been extremely influential on other countries, such as the United Kingdom and Australia, as can be evidenced by the outcomes of cases in these countries. For example, in Australia, rules of evidence are typically set forth on a state-by-state basis; however, since the FREs were established, nearly 40 states abide by these regulations (LawFirms.com, n.d.).

Standards for courtroom admissibility of evidence vary by jurisdiction, from country to country and even within countries from state to state. However, prior to the enactment of the FREs, an early and broad precedent for the admissibility of expert evidence was established in the U.S. Court of Appeals in *Frye v. United States 293 F. 1013 (CADC)* [1923] (Frye v. United States, 1923), which provided the standard that governed the introduction of expert evidence for over half a century. The *Frye* court held that expert evidence is admissible as long as it is 'generally accepted' within the relevant scientific community.

This 'general acceptance' standard was the primary precedent in federal courts until 1975, when, following Supreme Court initiatives, Congress enacted the FREs (United States Congress House Committee on the Judiciary, 1975). The aim was to govern the admission of expert testimony in the federal court system. Rule 702 established a requirement for the expert to have specialist 'knowledge, skill, training, or education'

(U.S. Federal Government, 2000). While Rule 702 did not specify a general acceptance requirement, federal courts continued to apply *Frye*, until 1993 during *Daubert v. Merrell Dow Pharmaceuticals Inc.* [1993] 509 US 57 (Daubert v. Merrell Dow Pharmaceuticals Inc., 1993) when the Supreme Court held that Rule 702 superseded *Frye*. The Supreme Court ruled that it is the judge's responsibility to ensure expert evidence is reliable and relevant to the case—to act as gatekeepers—and, where relevant, scientifically valid (Gebauer, 2002). The Supreme Court directed that the trial judge must rule on scientific validity and further identified a number of factors of relevance when making this determination: The evidence must be based on a testable theory or technique; peer review should have taken place; there exists a known or potential associated error rate of the theory or technique when applied; and there are controls and standards in existence for the application of the theory or technique; and general acceptance within the scientific community. It was made clear, however, that this list was not exhaustive, and the ruling makes clear that judges should be open to employing their own criteria.

Following *Daubert*, the Supreme Court issued two further opinions that, when taken together with *Daubert*, are referred to as the *Daubert* trilogy. The first, in 1997, was *General Electric Company v. Joiner 522 US 136* [1997] (General Electric Co. v. Joiner, 1997), during which the court broadened the gatekeeping role when it ruled that the judge should assess all evidence described as scientific, technical or of other specialised knowledge. Further, *Joiner* stated that the trial judge should review experts' reasoning process (something rarely done under *Frye*) (Bernstein and Jackson, 2004), stating that Rule 702 'requires a valid scientific connection to the pertinent inquiry as a precondition to admissibility' (Daubert v. Merrell Dow Pharmaceuticals Inc., 1993).

As a result of the *Daubert* and *Joiner* rulings, a number of questions arose regarding what evidence was affected by the *Daubert* standard. The Supreme Court addressed these in 1999 during *Kumho Tire Company v. Carmichael 526 US 137* [1999], a product case that stipulated that the trial judge's gatekeeping role should be extended to include all expert testimony (Mallett, 2010; Mallett and Evison, 2013). It established that the trial judge has the authority to determine whether and to what extent the enumerated Daubert factors are applicable to a case.

Together, the Supreme Court's *Daubert* trilogy tightened the rules for the admissibility of expert evidence, and consequently the admission of potentially damaging, prejudicial or inappropriate expert evidence was reduced (Bernstein and Jackson, 2004). In 2000, elements embodied in the *Daubert* trilogy were codified into the Federal Rules, with FRE 702 altered to explicitly require that the testimony is the product of reliable principles and methods, the testimony is based upon sufficient data or facts and the witness has applied the methods and principles reliably to the facts of the case (U.S. Federal Government, 2000). Any step that renders the testimony unreliable renders the evidence inadmissible.

The situation in state courts remains unsettled, however. Policy variations in different US state jurisdictions have led to a mixed application of *Frye* or the FREs, or a hybrid of the two, with a small minority of states continuing to apply *Frye* (Frye v. United States, 1923). Regardless, 94% of state court judges note that they have found *Daubert* of value during decision-making (Bernstein and Jackson, 2004; Moreno, 2003).

England and Wales

The United Kingdom, Australia, Canada and the United States share a history based on the English common-law system. Approaches taken to expert evidence admissibility in other jurisdictions (Gold, 2003; Roberts, 2009; Taylor, 2000; Uglow, 1997) are similar to that taken in the United States—reflecting the importance of comparable concepts or relevance, reliability and probative significance. Consequently, US legal precedents can be seen to be influential to these countries' courts, and vice versa.

Civil case law provides clear precedent regarding the duties and responsibilities of expert witnesses (National Justice Compania Naviera S.A. v Prudential Assurance Co. Ltd., 1993), directing that expert evidence should be and should be seen to be (1) independent; (2) relevant and unbiased; (3) based on a balanced review of the facts; (4) within the witnesses' field of expertise; (5) qualified as being provisional or incomplete, as required; (6) based on an open disclosure of change of view; and (7) supported by free exchange of reports and data (Mallett and Evison, 2013).

Despite the evident similarities between the United Kingdom and the United States regarding the admissibility of expert evidence, there are a number of notable differences. Firstly, under the FRE 704, an expert in the United States may (under most circumstances) give opinion on ultimate issues of fact (guilt of the defendant)—other than the psychological state as an element of the crime (U.S. Federal Government, 1984). Secondly, admissibility requirements may be considered more relaxed in England and Wales, compared to the United States where they tend to be interpreted more narrowly. Thirdly, while most US courts, including the federal courts, allow experts to give an opinion without having to state the facts or data 'reasonably relied upon by experts in the particular field', experts in England and Wales must state the facts on which an opinion is based (National Justice Compania Naviera S.A. v Prudential Assurance Co. Ltd., 1993). US courts rely on cross-examination to offset bias, while English and Welsh courts, in addition, direct that evidence must be independent and unbiased (National Justice Compania Naviera S.A. v Prudential Assurance Co. Ltd., 1993; Toth v. Jarman, 2006).

Courts in England (and Wales) have all but adopted the criteria as laid out by FRE 702; however, the question remains as to how successfully and consistently these doctrines have been applied, considering a number of recent publications (National Research Council, 2009; Scottish Parliament, 2011a,b; The Law Commission, 2011b), and indeed how suitable their application is to real-world scenarios. Consequently, the confusion regarding how to suitably assess experts and the evidence they present in court remains. This lack of clear legal direction has impacted even the most widely accepted evidence types (National Research Council, 2009; Scottish Parliament, 2011a; The Forensic Regulator, 2009), as well as novel methods which are yet to gain 'general acceptance', as required within the relevant scientific community: The resultant evidence produced is therefore vulnerable to being found inadmissible, even if the conclusions drawn can be demonstrated to be founded upon reliable and valid scientific method and theory.

Recent Publications Seeking to Improve the Use of Expert Evidence

Many groups have made recommendations with a view to improving the consistency of judges' evaluation of expert evidence. In 2005, a paper appeared in *Science* announcing a 'coming paradigm shift in forensic identification science' (Saks and Koehler, 2005). The authors hypothesised that claims of the ability to individualise in forensic science are often exaggerated—an argument supported by the observation that even forensic DNA profiling makes no claim to individual identification in the event of a correspondence between two profiles but relies instead on a statistical random match probability derived from the frequency of the DNA profile in the wider population (Butler, 2009). This was followed in 2008 by the publication of proposals for the accreditation of experts and expert knowledge by the U.K. Forensic Science Regulator (Rennison, 2008) which stated that

> Each method (product or service) should be based on sound science supported by both sufficient data to justify its use within the CJS [Criminal Justice System] and a robust, transparent, balanced and logical interpretation model, and where possible validated according to accepted scientific procedures.

U.S. National Academy of Sciences Report 2009

In 2009, the U.S. National Research Council of the National Academy of Sciences (NAS) (National Research Council, 2009) produced a report that called for a fundamental reassessment of the scientific basis of a number of forensic science sub-disciplines. In respect to admissibility, the NAS report states:

> Two very important questions should underlie the law's admission of and reliance upon forensic evidence in criminal trials: (1) the extent to which a particular forensic discipline is founded on a reliable scientific methodology that gives it the capacity to accurately analyze evidence and report findings and (2) the extent to which practitioners in a particular forensic discipline rely on human interpretation that could be tainted by error, the threat of bias, or the absence of sound operational procedures and robust performance standards.

The report concluded that the forensic science disciplines are currently an assortment of practices and methods, used in both public and private arenas, with forensic facilities undertaking them varying widely in capacity. Furthermore, the report indicated that the providers lack mandatory and enforceable standards, grounded on rigorous research and testing, accreditation programmes and certification requirements. The system was described as 'fragmented', with the concern raised that this may lead to the quality of evidence presented in court, and its associated interpretation, varying unpredictably according to jurisdiction (National Research Council, 2009).

The report's primary recommendation was the establishment of the National Institute of Forensic Science (NIFS), which the report suggests should be led by personnel experienced in developing and executing national strategies and plans for setting standards across the broad range of forensic disciplines. The NIFS would also manage accreditation and testing procedures, as well as develop and implement rule-making, oversight and sanctioning processes (National Research Council, 2009).

Scottish Fingerprint Inquiry 2011

In 2008 the Cabinet Secretary for Justice, Kenny MacAskill, announced in the Scottish Parliament that the Scottish Government was establishing an independent public inquiry under the Inquiries Act (2005) to inquire into the case of Shirley McKie (*HM Advocate v McKie*), which he said had 'cast a cloud over the individuals involved and has been a source of serious concern for the criminal justice system for the past decade' (MacAskill, 2011).

The publication in 2011 of the resultant Scottish Fingerprint Inquiry report caused a significant shift in the assessment of expert evidence, which will not be limited to the application of fingerprint evidence. The report made a total of 86 suggestions for future action as a result of the inquiry, with 10 of those recognised as key recommendations. Among the most notable is Recommendation 1: 'Fingerprint evidence should be recognized as opinion evidence, not fact, and those involved in the criminal justice system need to assess it as such on its merits' (Scottish Parliament, 2011a). This will have significant repercussions for all forensic evidence and could see the downgrading of all identification methods to opinion, rather than fact-based, evidence.

English Law Commission Report 2011

Admissibility of expert evidence in England and Wales has not, until recently, received the same regulatory attention as it has from the Supreme Court and Congress of the United States. The Law Commission publication titled *Expert Evidence in Criminal Proceedings in England and Wales (No 325)* (The Law Commission, 2011b) is an acknowledgment of the continuing problems with the admissibility of expert evidence. The report considers all types of forensic evidence. The aim of the report and its proceeding consultation paper *The Admissibility of Expert Evidence in Criminal Proceedings in England and Wales* was to evaluate the feeling within the scientific community regarding the Law Commission's recommendations for reforming the law relating to expert evidence in criminal cases.

The report states that the current judicial approach to the admissibility of expert evidence in England and Wales is unrestrictive, and as a result, too much expert opinion evidence is admitted without adequate scrutiny because no clear test is being applied to determine whether the evidence is sufficiently reliable to be admitted. Ultimately, the Law Commission hopes to reduce miscarriages of justice and increase confidence in the criminal justice system. To achieve this, the report recommends that there should be a new reliability-based admissibility test to be applied to expert evidence in criminal cases, the purpose of which would be to exclude defective expert evidence; consequently only evidence determined as suitably reliable would be heard by the jury (The Law Commission, 2011b). The Law Commission's provisional proposals suggest tests for (1) reliability based on sound principles, (2) relevance, (3) appropriate application, (4) specialist knowledge and (5) impartiality (The Law Commission, 2011b).

The report includes a draft Criminal Evidence (Experts) Bill (as Appendix A to the report) (The Law Commission, 2011c) which sets out the proposed admissibility test that judges would apply. The Bill states that

Admissibility: 1 Basic rules

1. Expert evidence is admissible in criminal proceedings only if:
   a. the court is satisfied that it would provide information which is likely to be outside a judge or jury's experience and knowledge, and which would give them help they need in arriving at their conclusions;

    b. the person who gives it is qualified to do so (see section 2), and

    c. the evidence is not made inadmissible as a result of section 3 (impartiality).

2. In addition, expert opinion evidence is admissible in criminal proceedings only if it is sufficiently reliable to be admitted (see section 4).

3. If there is a doubt about whether an expert's evidence is evidence of fact or is opinion evidence, it is to be taken to be opinion evidence.

"Qualified to do so"

1. For the purposes of section 1(1)(b), a person may be qualified to give expert evidence by virtue of study, training, experience or any other appropriate means.

2. The court must be satisfied on the balance of probabilities that the person is so qualified."

(The Law Commission, 2011c, p. 146)

Importantly, the Bill provides guidance notes that judges would need if applying the test, including reasons why an expert's evidence might be unreliable, as well as a diagram to guide trial judges as to whether expert evidence should be admitted, and what aspects render the opinion inadmissible at various stages of the legal process (The Law Commission, 2011c). The Bill also includes procedural rules and provisions that would give the Criminal Procedure Rule Committee (U.K. Government, n.d.) the power to create further procedural rules, to supplement the provisions in the Bill. The Commission suggests that the recommendations made in the report, and the provisions in the associated Bill, would establish an appropriate framework in criminal proceedings for screening expert evidence at the admissibility stage, prior to being heard by the jury. The Commission states that a further result may be to encourage generally higher standards among expert witnesses, resulting in expert evidence of greater reliability being tendered for admission (The Law Commission, 2011b).

Conclusion

Admissibility criteria in the United States and England (and Wales) can be summarised as relating to reliability and relevance. Whether the evidence, and the subsequent conclusions drawn from it, is reliable ostensibly rests on a number of accepted and proposed tests, including general acceptance: it must be based on specialised knowledge, skill, experience, training or education; it must have been published and peer reviewed; the application must be appropriate leading to justifiable conclusions; and the evidence should be based on sufficient data and the concept of scientific validity (Mallett and Evison, 2013). The degree of certainty and weight that is afforded to scientific evidence is particularly relevant when a truly novel technique is being developed, and there is an expectation that it must be sufficiently evaluated and tested for forensic application. Considering the diversity of forensic methods, practitioners may (as a result of novel science or novel crimes) be working on a case-led basis, resulting in analyses that cannot be verified using standardised methods. They, and the judge acting in their role as gatekeeper, may, nevertheless, be obliged to consider what the results mean in a particular case. At such times it is simply not possible to apply strict admissibility standards without the risk of disadvantaging the justice system.

Edmond (2011a,b) (Edmond et al., 2009) provides a comprehensive review of admissibility issues facing various human identification methods, particularly from the perspective of Australian jurisdictions, from where *R v. Bonython* 38 SASR 45 [1984] (R v. Bonython, 1984) arises as equivalent to the *Frye* test in the United States. Procedural scrutiny is available via the courtroom process of cross-examination but, as with all evidence, it remains for the judge to decide when identification evidence is unreliable and, therefore, to withdraw it from the proceedings (Heydon and Ockelton, 1996). However, Edmond et al. (2009) argue that admissibility practices are too inclusive and therefore potentially prejudicial.

Evidence suggests that judges continue to struggle with the appropriate assessment of scientific testimony. One study demonstrated that 48% of US state judges, when speaking candidly, indicated that they were not adequately prepared to deal with the range of scientific evidence given in court (Gatowski, 2001). Furthermore, 96% could not demonstrate a basic understanding of two of the four *Daubert* criteria (*ibid.*). Additional research is necessary to understand the apparent dissonance between the criteria for admissibility expressed in rulings, regulations and scientific reports and case-by-case decisions made by trial judges in the courts—who are required to make prompt decisions under pressure resting on 'real-life' circumstances.

The publication of the plethora of reports relating to the admissibility of expert evidence demonstrates that there is a will to improve the current situation, and communication and collaboration between the domains of science and law is desirable if admissibility rulings on scientific testimony are to be meaningful to both disciplines. However, with the reports largely limiting themselves to discussion of procedure and practice within national boundaries, it is difficult to see how the complex nature of forensic evidence will be addressed—when criminal activity is unrestricted by jurisdictional or geographic limitations. The only way in which crimes can be investigated efficiently is through a global response, with common rules and standards applied on a transnational basis.

References

Australian Law Reform Commission. 2010. Family violence—A national legal response, Report 114. Part 28. Other trial processes: cross-examination. Australian Government. Available from: http://www.alrc.gov.au/publications/28. OtherTrialProcesses/cross-examination, accessed July 21, 2012.

Bernstein, D. E. and Jackson, J. D. 2004. The Daubert trilogy in the States. *Jurimetrics,* 44, 351–366.

Butler, J. M. 2009. *Fundamentals of Forensic DNA Typing.* San Diego, CA: Elsevier.

Cutler, B. L. and Kovera, M. B. 2011. Expert psychological testimony. *Current Directions in Psychological Science,* 20, 53–57.

Daubert v. Merrell Dow Pharmaceuticals Inc. [1993] 509 US 579.

Edmond, G. 2011a. Actual innocents? Legal limitations and their implications for forensic science and medicine. *Australian Journal of Forensic Sciences,* 43, 177–212.

Edmond, G. 2011b. The building blocks of forensic science and law: Recent work on DNA profiling (and photo comparison). *Social Studies of Science,* 41, 127–152.

Edmond, G., Biber, K., Kemp, R., and Porter, G. 2009. Law's looking glass: Expert identification evidence derived from photographic and video images. *Current Issues in Criminal Justice,* 20, 337–377.

Frye v. United States 293 F. 1013 (CADC [1923]).

Gatowski, S. I. 2001. Asking the gatekeepers: A national survey of judges on judging expert evidence in a post-*Daubert* world. *Law and Human Behavior,* 25, 433–442.

Gebauer, M. E. 2002. The "what" and the "how" of Daubert challenges to expert testimony under the New Federal Rule of Evidence 702. *Pennsylvania Bar Association Quarterly,* 73, 76–83.

General Electric Co. v. Joiner 522 US 136 [1997].

Gibbs, R. W. 1958. Prejudicial error: Admissions and exclusions of evidence in the federal courts. *Villanova Law Review,* 48, 48–70.

Gold, A. D. 2003. *Expert Evidence in Criminal Law the Scientific Approach.* Toronto, Ontario, Canada: Irwin Law Inc.

Heydon, J. D. and Ockelton, M. 1996. *Evidence, Cases and Materials.* London, U.K.: Butterworths.

Jackson, M. M. 2012. Timely death of the show-up procedure: Why the supreme court should adopt a per se exclusionary rule. *Howard Law Journal,* 56, 329–358.

Kovera, M. B., Gresham, A. W., Borgida, E., Gray, E., and Regan, P. C. 1997. Does expert testimony inform or influence juror decision-making? A social cognitive analysis. *Journal of Applied Psychology,* 82, 178–191.

LawFirms.com n.d. Evidence in criminal trials. Available from: http://www.lawfirms.com/resources/criminal-defense/criminal-defense-case/evidence-at-trial.htm accessed March 01, 2013.

MacAskill, K. 2011. The fingerprint inquiry: Scotland. Preface. Scottish Parliament. Available from: http://www.thefingerprintinquiryscotland.org.uk/inquiry/3141.406. html accessed July 22, 2012.

Mallett, X. 2010. Admissibility. In: Evison, M. P. and Vorder Bruegge, R. W. (eds.) *Computer-Aided Forensic Facial Comparison.* New York: Taylor & Francis Group. pp. 139–144.

Mallett, X. D. G. and Evison, M. P. 2013. Forensic facial comparison: Issues of admissibility in the development of novel analytical techniques. *Journal of Forensic Sciences*, (Available online in open access from March 2013).

Mengler, T. M. 1989. The theory of discretion in the federal rules of evidence. *Iowa Law Review*, 74, 413–466.

Moreno, J. A. 2003. Einstein on the bench? Exposing what judges do not know about science and using child abuse cases to improve how courts evaluate scientific evidence. *Ohio State Law Journal*, 64, 531–544.

National Justice Compania Naviera S.A. v Prudential Assurance Co. Ltd. [1993] 2 Lloyd's Rep 68.

National Research Council. 2009. *Strengthening Forensic Science in the United States: A Path Forward*. Washington, DC: National Academies Press.

NSW Government. 1995. Evidence Act [1995]. [4-1630] Exclusion of prejudicial evidence in criminal proceedings—s 137. New South Wales Government, Australia. Available from: http://www.judcom.nsw.gov.au/publications/benchbks/civil/discretions_to_exclude_evidence.html-p4-1630 accessed July 21, 2012.

R v. Bonython 38 SASR 45 [1984].

Reedy, M. J. 2011. Witnessing the witness: The case for exclusion of eyewitness expert testimony. *Notre Dame Law Review*, 86, 905–938.

Rennison, A. 2008. *Manual of Forensic Science Regulation*. Available from the Home Office, Office of the Forensic Science Regulator: http://www.homeoffice.gov.uk/publications/police/operational-policing/Manual_of_Regulation_22.9.08.pdf, accessed July 22, 2012.

Roberts, P. 2009. The science of proof: Forensic evidence in English criminal trials. In: Fraser, J. and Williams, R. (eds.) *Handbook of Forensic Science*. Cullompton, U.K.: Willan.

Saks, M. and Koehler, J. 2005. The coming paradigm shift in forensic identification science. *Science*, 309, 892–895.

Scottish Parliament. 2011a. *The Fingerprint Inquiry: Scotland*. Edinburgh, U.K.: APS Group Scotland. Available from: http://www.thefingerprintinquiry scotland.org.uk/inquiry/files/TheFingerprintInquiryReport_Low_res.pdf, July 22, 2012.

Scottish Parliament. 2011b. Chapter 43: Recommendations. In: *The Fingerprint Inquiry: Scotland. Part 8: Key Findings and Recommendations*. Edinburgh, U.K.: APS Group Scotland. Available from: http://www.thefingerprintinquiryscotland.org.uk/inquiry/files/TheFingerprintInquiryReport_Low_res.pdf, accessed July 22, 2012.

Tanford, J. A. 1989. A political-choice approach to limiting prejudicial evidence. *Indiana Law Journal*, 64, 831–872.

Taylor, A. 2000. *Principles of Evidence*. London, U.K.: Cavendish.

The Forensic Regulator. 2009. Report for the Scottish Fingerprint Inquiry. Available from: http://www.thefingerprintinquiryscotland.org.uk/inquiry/files/EB_0001.pdf, accessed July 22, 2012.

The Law Commission. 2011a. The admissibility of expert evidence in criminal proceedings in England and Wales: A new approach to the determination of evidentiary reliability. A consultation paper (No 190). Available from: http://lawcommission.justice.gov.uk/docs/cp190_Expert_Evidence_Consultation.pdf, accessed July 22, 2012.

The Law Commission. 2011b. Expert evidence in criminal proceedings in England and Wales. Law Commission Report No 325. Available from: http://www. official-documents.gov.uk/document/hc1011/hc08/0829/0829.pdf, accessed July 22, 2012.

The Law Commission. 2011c. Expert evidence in criminal proceedings in England and Wales. Law Commission Report No 325: Appendix A—Draft of a Bill to make provision about expert evidence in criminal proceedings. Available from: http://www.justice.gov.uk/lawcommission/docs/lc325_Expert_Evidence_ Report.pdf, accessed December 08, 2011.

Toth v. Jarman Ewca Civ 1028 [2006].

Uglow, S. 1997. *Evidence, Text and Materials.* London, U.K.: Sweet and Maxwell Limited.

U.K. Government. n.d. Criminal Procedure Rules Committee. Available from: http:// www.justice.gov.uk/about/moj/advisory-groups/criminal-procedure-rule-committee, accessed July 22, 2012.

United States Congress House Committee on the Judiciary. 1975. An Act to Establish Rules of Evidence for Certain Courts and Proceedings... H R. 93–595, 88 Stat. 1926. Washington, DC: U.S. Government Print Office.

U.S. Federal Government. 1984. FRE 704: Opinion on ultimate issue. Federal Rules of Evidence. As amended 10/121984. Available from: http://federalevidence. com/rules-of-evidence, accessed July 14, 2011.

U.S. Federal Government. 2000. FRE 702: Testimony by experts. Federal Rules of Evidence. As amended 04/17/2000, effective 12/01/2000. Available from: http:// federalevidence.com/pdf/FRE_Amendments/2000Amendments/Amendment_ Transmit_2000.pdf, accessed May 16, 2012.

U.S. Federal Government. n.d.-a. 716.01(c) Probative value of objective evidence [R-2]— 700 examination of applications. Federal Rules of Evidence. Available from: http://www.uspto.gov/web/offices/pac/mpep/documents/0700_716_01_c.htm accessed July 21, 2012.

U.S. Federal Government. n.d.-b. Rule 403. Excluding relevant evidence for prejudice, confusion, waste of time, or other reasons. Federal Rules of Evidence/ Available from: http://federalevidence.com/rules-of-evidence-Rule403, accessed July 21, 2012.

Expert Scientific Evidence in the Investigation and Prosecution of Child Sexual Abuse in Adversarial Jurisdictions

16

FIONA E. RAITT

Contents

Introduction

This chapter explores some problematic areas for expert scientific evidence in the investigation and prosecution of cases of child sexual abuse (CSA), an area of increased social importance. In particular, it focuses on the difficulties of gathering sufficient evidence to justify a prosecution and the challenges concerning trustworthiness presented by emerging science. Each of these areas exemplifies the close dependency between the two disciplines while also revealing the tensions that shape their interactions more generally (Jasinoff, 1995; Redmayne, 2001). The chapter draws on examples from the common-law countries, that is, English-speaking jurisdictions with an adversarial background: Australia, Canada, England and Wales, Ireland, New Zealand, North America and Scotland. The disciplines of law and science have a unique and enduring relationship. They perform a distinctive role within the adversarial criminal justice system. The rules for admissibility of expert evidence in adversarial jurisdictions share a common heritage

351

and a broad set of principles, values and anticipated outcomes. Although the law in these jurisdictions is subject to regional variation, the science has universal application. As such, the practices in all countries following an adversarial approach have relevance for one another.

Science, Certainty and Miscarriages of Justice

The relationship between law and science in the courtroom has never been more important, nor has it ever been scrutinised, as thoroughly as it is today. This is due in part to the relationship's inevitable inter-dependency in finding solutions to new forms of criminal activity and in exploring the potential of emerging science to identify perpetrators of crime.

Scientific evidence frequently plays a crucial role in achieving criminal convictions. Generally this works to the mutual benefit of law and science. However, on occasion, the confidence accorded to scientific evidence is seriously misplaced. In the 1980s, the so-called Irish terrorist cases led to a series of miscarriages of justice when scientific evidence vital to conviction was improperly produced and presented in court. The realisation that a large number of convictions had been obtained through reliance upon fabricated scientific evidence severely shook the legal and scientific establishments. It resulted in a major re-organisation of the way in which the police and government scientists operated (Schurr, 1993; U.K. Government, 1993). More recently, the misuse in court of evidence of statistical probabilities in prosecutions concerning sudden unexplained death in infants caused a number of mothers to be wrongly accused, and in some cases convicted, of the murder of their children (RCP and RCPCH, 2004). Despite the inevitable anxieties over the role of science in court, there is growing recognition that proof of innocence or guilt in matters such as the identification of perpetrators, and the causes of injury and death, increasingly requires answers from cutting-edge medical and forensic science (National Research Council, 2009). Although reliance upon novel science carries inherent risks, those have to be set against the need for mechanisms to combat contemporary methods of offending and the sophistication of serious and organised crime. The focus of legal vigilance has therefore switched to the rules and procedures required to monitor the quality and reliability of the scientific evidence admitted into court (Cromwell, 2011; National Research Council, 2009). Accordingly, as discussed in more detail elsewhere in this book, some jurisdictions have developed sophisticated criteria to govern the admissibility of scientific evidence in the courtroom and encourage judges to act as gatekeepers of reliable and trustworthy science. However, the complexity associated with these criteria can create uncertainty in litigators and scientists, which may explain why other jurisdictions have been reluctant to go very far down that road (Edmond, 2012; Law Commission, 2011). Nonetheless, even if countries differ in their conclusion as to the best test for ensuring reliability of expertise, they still all agree that *a* test is necessary and that the bar for admissibility of trustworthy evidence should be rigorous.

Against an imperative for admissibility of reliable scientific evidence, tackling contemporary forms of crime may only be possible through contemporary scientific discoveries. Scientific theories and techniques, even in their infancy, can of course still deliver reliable evidence. However, in order to retain public confidence in emerging science that has yet to be accepted as sufficiently established to be considered trustworthy, the legal system requires mechanisms to ensure that only 'safe' science is admitted into the courtroom (Auld, 2001; RCP and RCPCH, 2004; U.K. Government, 2005).

While this is not a new tension for law and science, it is fair to say that the pace of scientific discovery and the temptation to deploy it at the earliest to combat offending is an increasing pressure. The desire not to repeat the mistakes of the past is also an understandable constant anxiety. Both law and science seek levels of certainty and consistency in their pursuit of the 'truth', and rightly so. However, the pursuit of 'certainty' in the science or in its application to the evidence is an unrealistic goal. It raises false expectations to give the impression that if we only redouble our efforts at accuracy, clarity and due diligence, we will eradicate wrongful convictions. The criminal standard of proof is proof beyond reasonable doubt. That concept conveys the impression that we expect near certainty in decision making from the fact finders in trials. Faced with jury verdicts of guilt, judges sometimes make declarations that are unqualified in their certainty—but are later proven to be incorrect. For example, Angela Cannings was wrongfully convicted in 2004 of the murder of two of her children, both of whom had died suddenly in unexplained circumstances. A third child also died in infancy but no charges were brought in respect of her. In sentencing Cannings to imprisonment, the trial judge, Justice Hallet, reinforced a sense that the evidence led at the trial was infallible. She noted:

> I have no doubt that for a woman like you to have committed the terrible acts of suffocating your own babies there must have been something seriously wrong with you. All the evidence indicates you wanted the children, apart from these terrible incidents you cherished them, so in my layman's view, it is no coincidence that these events took place within weeks of your giving birth. It can, in my view, *be the only explanation* (emphasis added) for why someone like you could have committed these acts when you have such a loving and supportive family. (Cannings v. R. 2004. 1 EWCA CRIM. 01: paragraph 5)

The judge's compassionate inference that Cannings suffered from post-natal depression was however not the 'only explanation'. On appeal the court found there was another plausible reason for the death of these children: they may have died of natural causes. The experts who gave evidence at the trial disagreed about crucial issues and were unable to agree on the cause of death. After the trial it also transpired that a distant relative of Cannings had a baby who had also died an unexplained death, from which it was concluded that the children from the two families very probably shared a genetic defect. Certainty in the evidence led in court is elusive, but the need for law to generate public confidence in legal decision making gives the impression that legal processes are capable of producing unassailable certainty. There is always scope for human error, mendacity, incompetence and new discoveries. Of course, there has to be a judicial conclusion in all trials, but that does not equate to certainty that the conclusion is correct. Every set of 'facts' must be approached with an open mind and alive to the possibility that there may be alternative plausible interpretations. The challenge we face is to acknowledge that our inability to achieve certainty is not a failure, but a normal outcome of the joint legal and scientific enterprise. With that in mind, I turn to one class of cases where certainty is often in short supply.

Role of Expert Evidence in Child Sexual Abuse Prosecutions

The phenomenon of CSA as it is understood in its modern guise has been part of public awareness since the 1960s through the combined efforts of enlightened paediatricians and the feminist movement. The former uncovered empirical evidence of the levels of the incidence and prevalence of child abuse (Helfer and Kempe, 1987), while the latter exposed the sexist and patriarchal context within which abuse occurred and was then concealed (Kelly, 1988). More recent abuse scandals have been discovered in the United Kingdom in state institutions charged with the care of children (BBC News), as well as the historically endemic abuse of children in the Catholic Church (Henley, 2010; Irish Government, 2009), confirming that this phenomenon continues to thrive. Although CSA is not confined to the home, the home remains one of the places where children are most likely to encounter sexual abuse from a family member or a family friend (Hoyano and Keenan, 2010). Beyond the home, the scope for the commission of abuse has fundamentally transformed due to developments in digital technology and global geo-politics. Civil war, poverty and diminishing economic options have led to mass migration and refugees, which affords opportunities for criminal child exploitation on an unchecked scale (UNICEF, 2010). Where countries are willing and able to respond, science plays a vital role in the process of gathering and interpreting the evidence to establish whether a crime has been committed and the identity of the perpetrator(s). The effective investigation of child abuse requires substantial resources and an integrated multidisciplinary approach to provide appropriate protection, care and support of child victims. Even if those are in place, there are significant evidential barriers to a successful prosecution. Understanding these barriers is the first step towards harnessing science to assist us to overcome them.

Barriers to Prosecution

Numerous international treaties recognise the rights of the child and their specific right to be protected from exploitation (United Nations, 1948, 1989, 2001). To a greater or lesser degree, these international rights are translated into domestic legal protections for abused children when they encounter the criminal justice system (Doak, 2008). They are classed as vulnerable witnesses with entitlements to specific support and protection. Adversarial jurisdictions pose particular stress for children due to the twin emphasis on live oral testimony in court and on cross-examination (Ellison, 2001). These two central features of the trial process are indisputably traumatic experiences for children and are known to constitute secondary victimisation (Spencer and Lamb, 2012). Status in law as a vulnerable witness therefore brings some relief for children as it opens the door to various special measures to help them produce the best evidence of which they are capable (Spencer and Lamb, 2012). For children who are able and willing to give oral evidence, the best practice at the stage of reporting abuse is for a 'forensic interview' to be conducted. This is a video-recorded interview conducted jointly by specially trained police officers and social workers. It conforms to recognised protocols to minimise the strain on children and maximise the evidential value of the interview (Almerigogna et al., 2007; Lamb and Spencer, 2012). Effective interviewing is designed to reduce the need for further interviews with the child victim, an important consideration, as repetitive questioning can be very damaging. Not only might it delay or disrupt a child's recovery, it can lead to subsequent suggestions by defence counsel of 'coaching' or confusing the witness, or even of contaminating their evidence (Ellison, 2001).

If cases go to trial, in adversarial proceedings children with adequate language skills will have to undergo cross-examination to test their evidence. Of all adversarial practices, cross-examination attracts the most condemnation from critics (Spencer and Lamb, 2012). Empirical studies consistently report that cross-examination is the element of the trial that children fear most in prospect and that causes them most distress in retrospect (Yamamoto et al., 1987). Its ability to distort testimony and become a test of memory causes children gratuitous distress of a sort that is readily portrayed as a symptom of unreliability. The video-recorded forensic interview removes a great deal of the distress associated with live oral testimony, but it only substitutes for evidence in chief. Live cross-examination remains the norm. Other special measures typically used include giving evidence from behind a screen, or by CCTV, to avoid eye contact with the defendant, having a supporter with the child in court, and clearing the courtroom of unnecessary personnel. However, even with the benefit of special measures, it is widely accepted that children find the trial process intimidating and deeply unpleasant. A particular challenge for law and science lies in how best to ensure that every legal system implements measures to support those children who have the resilience and courage to appear as witnesses.

Overcoming Barriers to Prosecution: Obtaining Evidence

If it is available, scientific evidence from a scene of crime, or from a child's body, will be powerful evidence of the commission of a crime and, depending on the circumstances, the identity of the perpetrator. Unfortunately, such evidence may be rare. If children make a disclosure within a time frame close to the period of offending, it may be possible to recover forensic evidence through a medical examination. However, this is unlikely for two reasons: delay in reporting sexual abuse is common (Kelly, 1988), and there is often no physical evidence to attribute to the abusive behaviour (Newman, 1994). Despite an absence of forensic evidence, as Myers (2010) has observed, one must not rush to conclusions:

> The lack of physical evidence alone should not lead to the conclusion that inappropriate sexual contact did not occur.... If the child incurred an injury that was superficial, and the time interval since the last contact is more than 72 hours, it is unlikely that any residua will be identified.... Healed diagnostic genital and anal findings that can stand alone to confirm sexual contact are present in approximately 5% of cases. (Myers, 2010: pp. 5)

The legal evidential requirements for obtaining evidence from medical examinations to a standard that will be admissible in court are tightly proscribed (Newman, 1994; Royal College of Physicians, 1997, 2012). Any departure from the protocols of a forensic investigation may invalidate the evidence recovered and prevent a subsequent prosecution. The time frame is also tight. Some studies indicate a limit of 24 h after an assault of a type that would leave traces (Young et al., 2006). In reality, children may report weeks or months after the event, waiting for the 'right' moment to confide in a safe person. A great deal of what we know about CSA (and there is much we are still learning) confirms that the conditions in which it occurs rarely lend themselves to the production of incriminatory scientific evidence. It is likely to take place in secret, with no witnesses, with no obvious physical injury or with injuries that are capable of benign explanations (e.g. AJE v.HM Advocate. 2002. J.C. 215). In the absence of forensic evidence or testimony from the victim, the prosecutor's options are limited. In addition, for the purposes of proof, there are some cases where the child victim cannot provide oral evidence. This could occur in cases where the child has been abused and then murdered, or is preverbal, is too traumatised by their experience to recount it or is too frightened of retaliation to describe what has happened to them, let alone be willing to say who did it.

If there is no forensic evidence to prove a criminal offence, the focus will often turn to behavioural science to supply explanations. Evidence from the social and behavioural sciences (often referred to as psychosocial sciences) can perform an educational role, operating as social framework evidence, to set certain kinds of knowledge in context for the fact find-ers in criminal trials. Typically, this could be evidence of the reliability of eyewitness testimony or the reliability of confession evidence (Monahan and Walker, 2004). Those who advocate the admissibility of such evidence defend its value and claim that, if appropriately controlled, it is capable of providing broad general conclusions from social science research to deter-mine factual issues in specific cases. In situations where 'experts seek to link social science principles to particular cases', appropriate controls have been described as 'methodologically rigorous social fact studies' (Mitchell et al., 2010: pp. 4).

For court purposes, the suitability and reliability of social framework evidence in court remains controversial and has generated a vast literature. The rules of admissibility of evidence tend to exclude much behavioural sci-ence from the criminal courts, less so the family courts, and the basis of exclusion relates to its usefulness for the trier of fact. Courts are more likely to reject evidence of human behaviour because it is perceived in law to be 'common sense', or 'within the knowledge of the fact finder'. This renders it inadmissible evidence, as it is unnecessary and unhelpful to permit evidence into court that will not contribute to the fact-finding exercise. The legal prin-ciple applied in all adversarial jurisdictions is that laid down in the English case of R v. Turner. 1975. QB 834, namely, that an expert witness may not testify as to matters that are well within the knowledge and experience of the trier of fact. *Turner* was charged with the murder of his girlfriend, appar-ently carried out while he was in a blind rage induced by her sexual taunts and admissions of infidelity. His defence counsel sought to lead psychiatric evidence to show that although *Turner* was not suffering from a recognised mental illness, the sort of experience to which he had been subjected by his girlfriend would result in intense provocation even to a normal person. The trial judge excluded the psychiatric opinion evidence as irrelevant, a ruling upheld by the Court of Appeal, where Lord Justice Lawton reminded the parties of the purpose and parameters of opinion evidence:

> An expert's opinion is admissible to furnish the court with scientific information which is likely to be outside the experience and knowledge of a judge or jury. If on the proven facts a judge or jury can form their own conclusions without help, then the opinion of an expert is unnecessary. In such a case if it is given dressed up in scientific jargon it may make judgment more difficult. The fact that an expert witness has impressive scientific qualifications does not by that fact alone make his opinion on matters of human nature and behaviour within the limits of normality any more helpful than that of the jurors themselves; but there is a danger that they may think it does at *Turner*. (R v. Turner. 1975. QB 834: pp. 841)

The Court of Appeal stated that once the psychiatrist had determined that the defendant was mentally normal, there was no further role for expert evidence, because 'Jurors do not need psychiatrists to tell them how ordinary folk who are not suffering from any mental illness are likely to react to the stresses and strains of life' (R v. Turner. 1975. QB 834: pp. 841). Some clinicians and academics take exception to this portrayal of their work as 'common sense', pointing out that so-called universal knowledge is often contrary to expectations, and human behaviour is regularly counterintuitive (Colman and Mackay, 1993).

Compared with psychosocial science, judges are more willing to admit science derived from the physical and live sciences or grounded in medical science. These categories of science more easily satisfy the test of being beyond the knowledge of the judge or jury. Nonetheless, proponents of psychosocial expertise argue that few fact finders have any appreciation of the multilayered complexities that constitute a phenomenon such as CSA (Warner, 2009). In such complex cases, it is claimed that psychosocial evidence can have a relevant contribution to make to the diagnostic process and to the proof of guilt (Raitt and Zeedyk, 2000). Given the polarised approaches to admissibility of evidence in this area, psychosocial experts who are permitted to give evidence face exacting standards. The testimony of mental health experts may be admitted if it is accepted that they are capable of providing evidence that is reliable and beyond the knowledge of the fact finder. This might include testimony concerning the behavioural reactions and mental health impact arising from the sexual abuse of a child. The problematic nature of admitting this type of expertise in court is summarised by Newman (1994: pp. 183):

> [M]ental health experts [will] be held to a high standard of quality when presenting opinions and recommendations in court. This in turn requires informed cross-examination by lawyers (something not always done well in

these cases) and judicial awareness of the virtues and pitfalls of this type of testimony. Legal professionals must avoid the conclusion that what the expert offers is purely scientific. Clinical opinion – the form of expertise most often heard in family cases – is a blend of many things: expert knowledge, theoretical preferences, beliefs derived from the expert's unique set of past clinical cases, inferences and interpretations drawn from interviews with and observations of the principal actors in the case, predictions of future behavior, and individual character, values, intuition and judgment. It is subject to many limitations, both professional and personal ...

Prosecutors who wish to lead expert evidence that a child victim's behaviour is commensurate with having suffered a sexual assault will have to persuade the judge that such evidence is beyond the knowledge of the jury. Ironically, as the prevalence of CSA becomes more widely known in society, it is sometimes assumed that jury members as fact finders have adequate knowledge to understand the behaviour of children who have been exposed to abuse. Thus, in the Scottish case of *HM Advocate* v. *Grimmond* (HM Advocate v. Grimmond. 2001. SCCR 708), the court refused to allow the prosecutor to lead expert opinion evidence as to the commonality of partial, then full, disclosure of revelations in CSA cases. In *Grimmond*, two boys, aged 7 and 8 years, respectively, and from different families, reported relatively low-level abuse that resulted in a conviction. Some months later, the boys made the more serious allegation that they were in fact raped by the convicted perpetrator. The prosecutor applied to the court to lead expert evidence to explain to the jury that it was not unusual for children to disclose abuse in stages—testing out the reactions of adults before giving a full account. The prosecutor argued that without such expert evidence the jury might assume that fragmented disclosure pointed to a false allegation. In ruling that the expert evidence was unnecessary and inadmissible, the trial judge reasoned that in the absence of evidence that either child was suffering from any sort of mental illness, the assessment of their credibility was entirely a matter for the jury 'taking into account their experience and knowledge of human nature and affairs' (HM Advocate v. Grimmond. 2001. SCCR 708: 713D). The decision was heavily criticised and led to the Scottish Parliament introducing legislation to permit such evidence in future cases of this type (Vulnerable Witnesses (Scotland) Act) (Scottish Parliament, 2004: Section 5).

For older children, who have the language and confidence to disclose abuse and to give evidence in court, the principal evidential obstacle facing them is the focus by the defence lawyer on their credibility as a witness and the reliability of their account. At the reporting stage, professionals with responsibility for diagnosing CSA are today trained to adopt a child-centred perspective, which acknowledges the difficulty children have in disclosing and provides a supportive environment for disclosure. This is intended to counter the historical distrust of children who made allegations of abuse but whose motivation was often dismissed as fantasy, attention seeking or malicious (Raitt, 2004). These perceptions have been robustly challenged (Kelly, 1988), and it is fair to say that the previous culture of systemic disbelief has today largely been replaced by a more informed and painstaking inquiry by trained investigators. However, no matter how well conducted the investigation is, if cases go to trial, older children must still deal with the embarrassment and anxiety of giving evidence and the process of cross-examination. Unfortunately, many of the myths surrounding CSA continue to shape legal tactics in the courtroom (Ellison, 2001). It is not difficult today for lawyers to use delay in reporting abuse to discredit the child's account as it is such an easy platform from which to suggest that the allegations are fabricated, exaggerated or a misunderstanding (Spencer and Lamb, 2012). Indeed, defence lawyers could point out that they are obliged to exploit all available avenues in the interests of their client. Provided the evidence is capable of a particular interpretation, the defence lawyer may be at fault if they do not explore possible malign explanations for delay. They may otherwise face a complaint of presenting an inadequate defence at trial. This occurred in the Scottish case *AJE v. HM Advocate* (AJE v. HM Advocate. 2002. J.C. 215) where, following AJE's conviction for the rape of his two daughters, both aged under 5 years at the time of the alleged offending, *AJE* accused his defence lawyer of failing to follow instructions to attack the credibility of the children. The appeal was upheld, though the Court of Appeal also considered that there were additional reasons to challenge the verdict.

A further consequence of delay and reluctance to report is the loss of opportunity to collect forensic evidence such as DNA that could prove penetration, internal damage or other indicators of sexual assault. As already mentioned, gathering forensic evidence in CSA cases is not straightforward. Many factors conspire to block early disclosure by children. Aside from the child who is silenced due to age or trauma, children are prone to believe that they are to blame for the abuse that occurred and thus reluctant to complain. The grooming process, which is often integral to CSA, deploys tactics designed to deter disclosure. For example, abusers may convince victims that a sibling or pet will be harmed if the abuse is disclosed. In Internet-based criminality, or where children have been trafficked, they will almost certainly not even be aware of the identity of the perpetrators. Given the difficulties in obtaining forensic evidence from children and of introducing expert evidence from the behavioural sciences, it is not surprising that the police and the prosecuting authorities are keen to consider the potential of emerging science to contribute to the proof process in appropriate cases.

Potential of Emerging Science

The growth of Internet pornography, where vulnerable children are subjected to sophisticated methods of abuse, poses yet further challenges for the effective investigation and prosecution of the crimes committed. In addition to the familiar problems of delay, preverbal victims and the silencing effect, we have to add the invisibility of those who create and distribute digital images of abuse online. In one of the largest-scale investigations in Scotland concerning a paedophile ring, known as Operation Algebra (BBC News, 2009), two of the children involved were 3 months old and 18 months old, respectively.

The convictions of eight men relied upon emerging human identification techniques developed by a team of forensic anthropologists, led by Professor Sue Black at the Centre for Anatomy and Human Identification at the University of Dundee, Scotland. New anatomical comparison techniques permit analysis of photographic images or other digital images held on computers. For example, the appearance of a scar on a digital image of abuse may be matched by the team with a digital image of a scar on a suspect's hands, as may be burns, freckles, age spots and many other characteristics. Aside from fingerprints, hands display features that have discriminatory capacity and include the pattern of the superficial veins, the pattern of knuckle skin creases and even the shape of fingernails and cuticles that may be distinctive. At present, anthropologists are not able to state the statistical likelihood that a suspect *is* the perpetrator, but extensive research is ongoing to investigate the robustness of such statistical application. Called as an expert witness for the prosecution at the suspect's trial, their testimony does not currently include statistical data on the likelihood that the suspect's and perpetrator's hands are one and the same—no such statistics are as yet available—but can point out the many areas of similarity or difference between the two. According to Black, such comparisons can be powerful statements of evidence especially when the features examined cross different aetiologies of origin (Black et al., 2009). Black's expert testimony was a core element of the prosecution case in Operation Algebra. Without the evidence Black was able to provide, it is uncertain whether the prosecutions would have been attainable.

Emerging science therefore presents major opportunities to progress and support a criminal investigation, but this is accompanied by many challenges. All science, but more so science in its infancy, must satisfy a test of admissibility before it can be introduced into court. Although jurisdictions share a common motivation to develop rules to weed out untrustworthy experts and untrustworthy science, in practice these give rise to numerous difficulties. These have been well documented and suffice to say that no single set of rules is a guarantee against the admissibility of unreliable evidence (Hartsthorne and Miola, 2010). Unreliable evidence is not necessarily driven by bad faith. World-renowned experts can make astonishing errors in their evidence simply by stepping outside their area of expertise (General Medical Council v. Meadow. 2006. EWCA CIV 1390) or by the pressure of the occasion (McCreight, v. HMA. 2009. HCJAC 69). In these circumstances the optimum approach to securing the reliability of what is admitted in court needs a twin-track approach—the judiciary to be trained to act as gatekeepers and the jury to be educated to discharge their duties from a more informed position. Gatekeeping is discussed elsewhere in Chapters 15 and 19 (see Mallett this volume and Shelton this volume). Concerns about juries include how well equipped they are to determine the reliability and quality of the expert evidence put before them and to withstand being unduly influenced by articulate experts who 'blind them with science', one of the points made in *Turner* (R v. Turner. 1975. QB 834), discussed earlier. Assuming that there are appropriate rules in place to govern the quality of the science admitted, juries ought to be able to rely upon directions from the trial judge to guide their deliberations at the conclusion of the trial. However, in complex cases, which typically include CSA trials, it can be very difficult for judges to capture accurately the essence of the factual issues that the jury must deliberate upon to reach a verdict. This can be compounded if the case involves a significant number of expert scientific witnesses offering dense and contradictory evidence. The Scottish case of *Walker v. HMA* (Walker v. HMA. 2011. HCJAC 51) concerned the murder of a baby. Expert evidence was led from 15 witnesses from the fields of haematology, radiology, paediatric respiratory medicine, endocrinology, pathology, statistics and microbiology. There was no consensus on the cause of the death. After the evidence had been led, neither the prosecutor nor the defence counsel opted to address the jury on how to interpret the expertise they had heard on the basis that it was so complicated there was a risk that they, the lawyers, would 'get it wrong' (Walker v. HMA. 2011. HCJAC 51: paragraph 32). The defence counsel colourfully described the quantity of expert evidence as 'a mountain, maybe a swamp of professional opinion to assess'. Although the trial judge directed the jury on how to approach the assessment of expert evidence, he declined to 'rehearse the evidence' (Walker v. HMA. 2011. HCJAC 51: paragraph 34). The Court of Appeal acknowledged that trial judges had considerable discretion in the directions they give juries. However, the court also considered that it was essential for juries to have the tools to enable them to reach a decision through a reasoned process. This was particularly important where medical science was disputed, and the cause of death may not even have been ascertainable. The trial judge's failure to address the position of each of the principal experts amounted to a material misdirection, and the verdict was therefore quashed.

Conclusion

This chapter has considered some of the challenges facing the law-and-science relationship, especially the use of expert scientific evidence in court. It is an area of fruitful and strengthening collaboration towards the objective of establishing proof of innocence and guilt in criminal trials. At the same time, it can be a risky activity. Law is keen to invoke science as part of the forensic proof process, but there may be a temptation to expect too much of science or to demand a definitive analysis of data and evidence in circumstances where there is not yet, and may never be, the degree of definition and certainty that lawyers seek. Finding a satisfactory way to educate jurors as key fact finders appears an essential step. So too does requiring judges to adopt a gatekeeping role in the task of excluding unreliable evidence from creeping into court. Errors occur because of the unpredictable human factor. The best safeguard against error and potential miscarriages of justice is to encourage a deepening critical understanding across the disciplines so that individual academics and practitioners remain vigilant caretakers of their own discipline as well as that of the others. None of us are exempt from making errors. The more aware we remain to the threat of error, the more likely we will be to avert its painful consequences. To that end, engaging with the law and science debates is unavoidable for anyone in either camp committed to the health of their discipline.

References

AJE v. and HM Advocate. 2002. J.C. 215.

Almerigogna, J., Ost, J., Bull, R., and Akehurst, L. 2007. A state of high anxiety: How non-supportive interviews can increase the suggestibility of child witnesses. *Applied Cognitive Psychology*, 21, 963–974.

Auld, R. 2001. A review of the criminal courts of England and Wales. Available from: http://webarchive.nationalarchives.gov.uk/+/http://www.criminal-courts-review.org.uk/, accessed March 04, 2013.

BBC News. 2009. Rochdale Grooming Trial: Nine found guilty of child sex charges. Available from: http://www.bbc.co.uk/news/uk-england-17989463, accessed March 04, 2013.

BBC News. 2009. Eight guilty in child abuse case. Available from: http://news.bbc.co.uk/1/hi/scotland/edinburgh_and_east/8035680.stm, accessed March 04, 2013.

Black, S. M., Mallett, X., Rynn, C., and Duffield, N. 2009. Case history: Forensic hand image comparison as an aide for paedophile investigations. *Police Professional*, 184, 21–24.

Cannings v. R. 2004. 1 EWCA CRIM. 01.

Colman, A. M. and Mackay, R. D. 1993. Legal issues surrounding the admissibility of expert psychological and psychiatric testimony. *Issues in Criminological and Legal Psychology*, 20, 46–50.

Cromwell, T. A. 2011. *The Challenges of Scientific Evidence*, Edinburgh, U.K.: Royal Society of Edinburgh, Available from: http://www.scottishlawreports.org.uk/publications/macfadyen-2011.html accessed March 04, 2013.

Doak, J. 2008. *Victims' Rights, Human Rights, and Criminal Justice*, Oxford, U.K.: Hart Publishing.

Edmond, G. 2012. Is reliability sufficient? The law commission and expert evidence in international and interdisciplinary perspective. *International Journal of Evidence & Proof,* 16, 30–65.

Ellison, L. 2001. *The Adversarial Process and the Vulnerable Witness*, Oxford, U.K.: Oxford University Press.

General Medical Council v. Meadow. 2006. EWCA CIV 1390.

Hartsthorne, J. and Miola, J. 2010. Expert evidence: Difficulties and solutions in prosecutions for infant harm. *Legal Studies,* 20, 279–300.

Helfer, R. E. and Kempe, R. S. (eds.) 1987. *The Battered Child,* 4th Edn., Chicago, IL: University of Chicago Press.

Henley, J. 2010. How the Boston Globe exposed the abuse scandal that rocked the catholic church. The guardian newspaper. Available from: http://www.guardian.co.uk/world/2010/apr/21/boston-globe-abuse-scandal-catholic, accessed March 04, 2013.

HM Advocate v. Grimmond. 2001. SCCR 708.

Hoyano, L. and Keenan, C. 2010. *Child Abuse: Law and Policy Across Boundaries,* Oxford, U.K.: Oxford University Press.

Irish Government. 2009. Report by commission of investigation into catholic diocese of cloyne. Available from: http://www.justice.ie/en/JELR/Cloyne_Rpt.pdf/Files/Cloyne_Rpt.pdf, accessed March 02, 2013.

Jasinoff, S. 1995. *Science at the Bar: Law, Science, and Technology in America,* Cambridge, MA: Harvard University Press.

Kelly, L. 1988. *Surviving Sexual Violence,* Cambridge, U.K.: Polity Press.

Law Commission. 2011. Expert evidence in criminal proceedings in England and Wales. Law Commission Report No 325. Available from: http://www.official-documents.gov.uk/document/hc1011/hc08/0829/0829.pdf, accessed July 22, 2012.

Mccreight, v. HMA. 2009. HCJAC 69.

Mitchell, G., Walker, L., and Monahan, J. 2010. Beyond context: Social facts as case-specific evidence. University of Virginia School of Law Public Law and Legal Research Paper Series. Available from: http://ssrn.com/abstract=1564724, accessed March 02, 2013.

Myers, J. 2010. Expert testimony in child sexual abuse litigation: Consensus and confusion. *U.C. Davis Journal of Juvenile Law and Policy,* 14, 1–57.

National Research Council. 2009. *Strengthening Forensic Science in the United States: A Path Forward,* Washington, DC: National Academies Press.

Newman, S. A. 1994. Assessing the quality of expert testimony in cases involving children. *The Journal of Psychiatry & Law,* 22, 181–234.

R v. Turner. 1975. QB 834.

Raitt, F. E. 2004. Expert evidence as context: Historical patterns and contemporary attitudes in the prosecution of sexual offences. *Feminist Legal Studies,* 12, 233–244.

Raitt, F. and Zeedyk, S. 2000. *The Implicit Relation of Psychology and Law: Women and Syndrome Evidence*. London, U.K.: Routledge.

RCP & RCPCH. 2004. *Sudden Unexpected Death in Infancy: A Multi-Agency Protocol for Care and Investigation*. London, U.K.: Royal College of Pathologists (RCP) and the Royal College of Paediatrics and Child Health (RCPCH). Available from: http://www.rcpath.org/publications.../sudden-unexpected-death-in-infancy, accessed March 04, 2013.

Redmayne, M. 2001. *Expert Evidence and Criminal Justice*. New York: Oxford University Press Inc.

Schurr, B. 1993. *Expert Witnesses and the Duties of Disclosure & Impartiality: The Lessons of the IRA Cases in England*. Sydney, Australia: NSW Legal Aid Commission. Available from: http://www.aic.gov.au/media_library/conferences/medicine/schurr.pdf, accessed March 04, 2013.

Scottish Parliament. 2004. Vulnerable Witnesses (Scotland) Act 2004. Available from: http://www.legislation.gov.uk/asp/2004/3/contents, accessed March 04, 2013.

Spencer, J. R. and Lamb, M. E. (eds.) 2012. *Children and Cross-examination: Time to Change the Rules?* Oxford, U.K.: Hart Publishing.

U.K. Government. 1993. *Royal Commission on Criminal Justice (Runciman Commission)*. London, U.K.: Stationery Office. Available from: http://discovery.nationalarchives.gov.uk/SearchUI/details?Uri=C3042, accessed March 04, 2013.

U.K. Government. 2005. Home Office. Forensic science on trial. House of commons science and technology committee seventh report of session 2004–2005. London, U.K.: The Stationary Office Limited. Available from: http://www.publications.parliament.uk/pa/cm200405/cmselect/cmsctech/96/96i.pdf, accessed January 20, 2012.

UNICEF. 2010. Progress for children. Available from: http://www.unicef.org/protection/Progress_for_Children-No.9_EN_081710.pdf, accessed March 04, 2013.

United Nations. 1948. Universal declaration on Human Rights. Office of the High Commissioner for Human Rights. Available from: http://www.ohchr.org/EN/UDHR/Documents/UDHR_Translations/eng.pdf, accessed November 04, 2011.

United Nations. 1989. Convention on the rights of the child. Available from: http://www2.ohchr.org/english/law/crc.htm accessed October 29, 2012.

United Nations. 2001. Optional protocol to the UN convention on the rights of the child on the sale of children, Child prostitution and child pornography. Available from: http://www.undemocracy.com/A-RES-54-263.pdf, accessed April 30, 2012.

Walker v. HMA. 2011. HCJAC 51.

Yamamoto, K., Somina, A., Parsons, J., and Davies. 1987. Voices in unison: Stressful events in the lives of children in six countries. *Journal of Child Psychology and Psychiatry*, 28, 855.

Young, K. L., Jones, J. G., Worthington, T., Simpson, P., and Casey, P. H. 2006. Forensic laboratory evidence in sexually abused children and adolescents. *Archives of Pediatrics and Adolescent Medicine*, 160, 585–588.

Child Sex Tourism at the US–Mexico Border

17

JIM WALTERS AND PATRICIA H. DAVIS

Contents

> Municipal police in Nogales, Sonora say they have arrested a 53-year-old US citizen after he allegedly paid a 15-year-old girl for sex. Kenneth Jerome Turner was stopped Friday night after city police spotted him coming out of a hotel at Internacional and Campillo streets with the girl. The police said Turner protested his arrest, saying that he didn't know the girl was a minor. He also allegedly accused the police of singling him out among the many men who patronize the city's prostitutes. The police said they also confiscated a cell phone from Turner that contained photos of the girl in her underwear.
>
> **Nogales International, January 10, 2012**

Introduction

Nogales, San Diego, Tijuana, Matamoras, Brownsville, Juarez and El Paso—all are US–Mexico border towns that conjure up romantic images of the old southwest: dusty streets, cantinas and the 'Wild West'. Or, perhaps more recently, these towns bring to mind images of the violence and chaos associated with the Mexican drug cartels fighting over drug routes to feed the insatiable demand for marijuana, heroin, cocaine and methamphetamines in the north.

Whatever images these cities bring to mind, most people do not associate the border with a much darker enterprise. For over 200 years, border cities have supplied another commodity—human lives and human bodies. Although it is seldom acknowledged, the exploitation of women and children is as much a part of the border region as Pancho Villa or the Texas Rangers.

This chapter will discuss child sex tourism (CST) on the US–Mexico border. Parts two through four include the historical context of the border, the global sex tourism industry and the expanding problem of CST on the border and worldwide. Section 5 is a case study of one young Mexican woman's experience of being lured into, groomed for and forced into the CST industry near Tijuana, Mexico. Part six discusses the connection of CST with Mexican cartels, followed by an outline of international and US law concerning CST. The final aspect describes global and local efforts to combat the problem.

History of the Borderlands

The US–Mexico border has always been a place of shifting and contested boundaries, legal and illegal immigration, cross-border trade and illegal smuggling and military, cultural, economic and legal struggles. Long before there was even the concept of a border, indigenous communities had created highly developed cultures and civilisations between the Gulf of Mexico and the Pacific Ocean. These cultures and their territorial boundaries were largely obliterated however, in the early sixteenth century by invaders from Spain. The *conquistadors* took ownership of the land until the Mexican War of Independence in 1810. During the 300 years of Spanish domination of the region, the indigenous population was largely decimated by war and disease, but a deep intermingling of the indigenous and European cultures also took place.

In 1846, conflicts relating to the border between Texas and Mexico resulted in the Mexican–American War. At the end of this conflict in 1848, with the signing of the Guadalupe Hidalgo Treaty, Mexico had lost half of its territory to the United States (including what is currently California, Arizona, New Mexico, Utah, Nevada Texas and parts of Colorado, Oklahoma, Wyoming and Kansas). The Gadsden Purchase in 1853 finally settled the legal boundaries between the United States and Mexico.

For political and economic reasons, the population of the new northern border of Mexico increased significantly during the Mexican Revolution, which began in 1910. The Revolution was a conflict between the overwhelmingly poor general population and a very few wealthy landowners; it was marked by a time of devastating hardship for most Mexican citizens. During this period, migration patterns from communities in the south to towns in the north became established; populations from certain areas in the south became accustomed to migrating north to established destinations on the northern Mexican border and also into the United States. These migration patterns have largely remained the same for close to a century.

More recently, especially since the 1980s, economic and political refugees from the Central American civil wars have also contributed to migratory influx to and across the border. Individuals and groups of Mexicans (mostly from southern Mexico) and Central Americans were attracted to the border in search of safety, economic betterment and the inevitable legal and illegal opportunities created by the border itself. Most current research about the border regions suggests that the flow of migrants north across the border may have reversed itself in the past few years—with as many or more people currently returning (or being deported) south as coming into the United States. This is due to decreasing economic opportunities in the United States, increasing legal and cultural hostility to immigrants in the US and improving economic circumstances in Mexico. It is also due to increasing dangers of kidnapping, violence and murder by drug trafficking organisations (DTOs) or cartels which are in the midst of battles over trafficking and migration means and routes (personal communication with shelter directors in Nogales, Sonora, Matamoros, Tamaulipas, fall 2011; Aguilera, 2011).

This history of shifting boundaries, changing faces and military and organised crime warfare is the foundation for today's border context, which tolerates and even promotes corruption of officials; the smuggling of drugs, weapons and money; and widespread sexual exploitation, including abuse of children. In a region that identifies itself with rapid change and adaptability, but also lawlessness, those in Mexico who seek profit by any means see the border region as an opportunity rather than an obstacle. Similarly, those from the north see the region as a destination and source for cheap goods and medicine, contraband, narcotics and easily exploitable human beings—including children.

Industry of Sex Tourism and Its Victims

CST is a complex, multifaceted phenomenon that exists due to multiple intertwined legal, economic, political and cultural forces. One primary cultural force is the tragic belief that children are without human rights and are therefore suitable objects for exploitation by families, commercial interests and 'tourist' perpetrators. This belief is held by many, despite national and international laws, international covenants and nearly universal moral and ethical systems that mandate the special protection of children because of their vulnerability.

According to UNICEF (2007), nearly 1 million children globally are enslaved by prostitution every year. The International Labour Organization (ILO) estimates that in the year 2000 there were as many as 1.8 million children exploited by prostitution or pornography. Both organisations caution, however, that any statistics relating to the global number of children subjected to prostitution are broad estimates, because of the shadowy nature of the crime.

An international study by the nongovernmental organisation (NGO), Save the Children (2003), suggests that child sexual exploitation (CSE) is increasing, with evidence of growing criminal activities relating to trafficking of children for sexual purposes—including exploitation by tourists and travellers, and pornography and Internet-related crimes. These are all supported by 'corrupt judicial systems, incomplete or complex laws and lack of a child protection system [which make] children extremely vulnerable' (Save the Children, 2003: pp. 3).

CST is one part of this multibillion dollar CSE industry. CST is defined as 'the commercial sexual exploitation of children by men or women who travel from one place to another, usually from a richer country to one that is less developed, and there engage in sexual acts with children, defined as anyone aged under 18' (ECPAT International, n.d.). Many sectors of tourist destination nations' economies benefit from the sex industry, including in the travel and tourism business sectors and individuals such as taxi drivers and airline, hotel and restaurant employees. With few exceptions, the sexually exploited are the most vulnerable in society and suffer from poverty, marginalisation, violence, disease and (often compelled) substance abuse (Hannum, 2002). Sexual exploitation of children in tourist destinations is often tightly controlled by criminal networks and linked to drug and human trafficking (O'Briain et al., 2008).

CST includes abuse by both business travellers and tourists—including people who visit countries initially as tourists and extend their stays—and by people who work abroad, such as teachers, NGO workers, emergency assistance or social service workers and military personnel. According to the United Nations World Tourism Organization (UNWTO, n.d.), anyone who lives and/or works in a country for longer than a year does not qualify as a 'tourist' under this definition. Most NGOs, however, consider these people to be child sex tourists regardless of the time spent in the country where they exploit children (O'Briain et al., 2008; World Vision International, n.d.).

In the 1970s and 1980s, the enterprise of sex tourism was largely managed and organised by the formal tourism industry through tour operators and hotel chains. Currently, the market has shifted to individuals who arrange their own travel via the Internet and mobile phones (O'Briain et al., 2008). The Internet provides sex tourists with accounts of sexual encounters with children written by other such tourists and details on sex establishments, prices and how to procure children (Department of Justice, n.d.). Predators also obtain information about children being sold for sex (through brothels or by other means) from local taxi drivers, hotel concierges, restaurant wait staff and local newspaper advertisements (US Department of Justice, 2010).

Understandings about who sex tourists are have also changed. Where sex tourists were formerly thought to be primarily older male paedophiles, the current profile includes more 'opportunistic' or 'situational' abusers— young, mostly male, not primarily attracted to children as sex objects, and from all social classes (O'Briain et al., 2008). These opportunistic abusers would not normally exploit children in their home cities but often excuse their behaviour on the basis of 'cultural difference', pretending that a child is older than he or she appears, or rationalising that they are actually assisting the child and his or her family to survive through the money paid for sexual services (O'Briain et al., 2008; Figure 17.1). Perpetrators usually are citizens of Western European countries and the United States (Department of Justice, n.d.).

Factors that make children vulnerable to exploitation such as CST are severe poverty and family dysfunction—including violence and drug abuse, low educational levels of the parents and perceived cultural obligations to assist in supporting the family (International Labour Office, 2003). Children who run away from (or are forced out of) their homes are vulnerable to exploitation simply to survive (*ibid.*). In addition, countries with turbulent politics and unstable economies, high illiteracy rates and otherwise bleak financial circumstances for families have the highest rates of CSE. Children in very poor families are seen as easy targets for 'recruiters' who offer them jobs in cities and then force them into prostitution (Department of Justice, 2012).

Figure 17.1 (See companion CD for colour figure.) Photograph of a prostituted girl standing on a corner in a mostly deserted part of Ciudad, Juarez—taken in 2009 when Ciudad Juarez was a virtual war zone.

Children in prostitution experience both long- and short-term problems including physical and psychological trauma, disease (including HIV–AIDS, tuberculosis and sexually transmitted infections), drug addiction, pregnancies, premature childbirth, violence, malnutrition, social ostracism and possibly death (Department of Justice, 2012: pp. 10). This is all compounded by the fact that the children's 'usefulness' to traffickers and pimps is short lived—due to the ravages of the work to which they are exposed and their decreasing attractiveness to clients as they age (Azaola, 2002).

Child Sex Tourism on the US–Mexico Border

It wasn't something I decided to do…. It can be very… very scary. A lot of times those guys are American.

Najeri, a 16-year-old female prostituted in Tijuana

Many of the poorest men, women and children who live near the US–Mexico border find themselves in demand by industries—legal and illegal—needing cheap labour on both sides. Because these people live in poverty, they are extremely vulnerable to financial and labour exploitation by unscrupulous commercial interests and traffickers from both south and north. The women and children (including both boys and girls) are also vulnerable to sexual exploitation.

According to the US Department of State's *2011 Trafficking in Persons (TIP) Report*, Mexico remains a large source, transit and destination country for men, women and children subjected to forced labour and sex trafficking (Department of Justice, 2012). Women and girls who are victimised by forced or bonded labour are often sexually exploited as well. CST continues to grow in Mexico, especially in tourist areas such as Acapulco, Cancun and on the northern border in cities such as Tijuana and Juarez (*ibid.*). Sex with a child in Tijuana can be obtained for as little as $40 (Castelan, 2011; Figure 17.2).

According to the Mexico City Human Rights Commission (MCHRC), there are at least 20 locations in Mexico where CSE 'flourishes' under the protection of corrupt elements of local police forces—including tourist resorts on the border (Godoy, 2007). The MCHRC reports that 95% of Mexico City's 13,000 street children have had at least one sexual encounter with an adult (*ibid.*). In addition, Mexican authorities estimate that up to 16,000 children and adolescents in Mexico have been victims of sexual exploitation including prostitution, pornography, sex tourism and trafficking (United Nations, 2011).

The Human Rights Commission of Baja California estimates that the commercial sexual exploitation of children on the border creates profits

Figure 17.2 (See companion CD for colour figure.) Showing street girls of Mexico City.

close to $32 million a year, much of that from Americans crossing into Mexico (Castelan, 2011). The Female Association of Tourist Enterprise Executive estimates that 250,000 children between 10 and 16 years of age have been the victims of 'sexual tourism' in cities like Guadalajara, Cancun, Acapulco, Puerto Vallarta and Tijuana (La Botz, 1999). Tijuana is estimated to be home to 5000 children 'at risk' of being forced into the sex trade (UPI. com, 2005).

Pornography involving children is frequently a crime committed in areas where children are sold for sex, and the US–Mexico border region is also a major destination for child pornographers from the United States (Department of Justice, 2009, 2010). Internet monitoring carried out by the Mexican Federal Preventive Police, through the Child Predator Cybercrime Unit, has identified over 1300 sites displaying child pornography of which over 300 are Mexican sites (United Nations, 2011). In her 2005 book, *Demons of Eden,* journalist Lydia Cacho exposed a child sex and pornography ring in the tourist destination, Cancun, associated with highly respected government and business officials. She has been arrested and has received multiple death threats related to that book and her subsequent investigations of the child sex trade (Amnesty International, 2012; Gehlert, 2007).

Recent personal interviews with migrant shelter directors, former child protection workers and directors of shelters for abused girls and young women from Mexican border towns confirm that despite the dangers of violence for Americans crossing the border, 'border brothels' that cater to men who are seeking child victims are thriving. One former DIF (Mexican child protection agency) investigator estimates that over 50 houses of prostitution are currently operating in one border city alone—with as many as 10–20 underage girls in each. Others say they hear stories of kidnappings of young girls who are then drugged and forced into prostitution. One shelter director told of receiving calls from distraught mothers whose daughters had been drugged, seduced or otherwise tricked into leaving with 'boyfriends' or suitors and have not been seen or heard from since.

Mexican doctors and psychologists who treat girls who have been ejected from the brothels or who have escaped talk about the severe traumas the girls have sustained—emotionally, physically and spiritually—and about being themselves threatened (sometimes at gunpoint) because of their work. They tell of trying to make reports to local police only to be rebuked and told that the issue was 'none of their business'.

In this context of corruption, economic distress, neglect and disregard of the problem, it is especially difficult for Mexican children or witnesses to report CST. They fear reporting their cases because judicial systems are rife with potential for further victimisation, and justice is often not accomplished where burdens of proof are difficult and the impact of crime on the child victims is rarely properly considered. Where reporting could result in an investigation by a social service agency, removal of the child or abuser from the home or the child being expelled from school if reporting on teachers' abuse, few victims will take those risks. Reporting may also result in anger and blame toward the child in the family and the community—including the stigma attached to the perception that the child victims have violated sociocultural values.

In addition, it is not uncommon that the victims of sexual abuse are themselves treated as the criminals (Save the Children, 2003). All too often, young victims have simply been labelled 'child prostitutes'—an unacceptable term, as no child can consent to being prostituted or exploited.

Tragically, the demand from sex tourists creates an endless need for child victims who are prostituted by pimps and even their own families. These children are only financially 'useful' to pimps for relatively short periods of time. As stated earlier, when the victims are no longer attractive or young enough to earn requisite profits, or if they become seriously ill, they may be abandoned, further victimised in other ways or even allowed to die or be killed to prevent discovery of the operations. This perpetuates a cycle of abuse, degradation, destruction, shame, death, exploitation and constant demand for more victims.

Case Study: Claudia

Claudia, currently aged 19 years, is from a small coastal town in the state of Sinaloa, a region famous for the export of drugs and humans. Nestled between the Pacific Ocean and the Sierra Madre mountains in Mexico's northwest, Sinaloa is just a 2 day drive from the US border. This state, says former Mexican Federal Police Commander Guillermo Gonzalez Calderoni, 'is the cradle of the biggest traffickers Mexico has ever known' (Bergman, n.d.).

For decades Sinaloa has produced vast amounts of marijuana and heroin destined for US markets. Sinaloa's formerly poor farmers have made huge profits—growing and selling these narcotics and becoming major players in Mexico's drug cartels. Culiacan, Sinaloa is (or has been) home to some of Mexico's most powerful, rich and notorious drug traffickers, including Ernesto 'Don Neto' Fonseca Carillo, Miguel Angel Felix Gallardo and Rafael Caro Quintero (former leaders of the Guadalajara Cartel); Amado Carillo Fuentes (former leader of the Juarez Cartel); Héctor Luis Palma Salazar ('El Güero Palma'), Ismael 'El Mayo' Zambada and Joaquin 'El Chapo' Guzman (former and current leaders of the Sinaloa Cartel); Manuel Salcido Uzeta ('El Cochiloco') (deceased folk hero and assassin of the Guadalajara Cartel); and the Arellano-Félix family (leaders of the Arellano-Félix Cartel) (Jake Bergman, n.d.). While many Americans know too well the connection between Sinaloa and the drug cartels, fewer are aware of the history of that region for supplying women to the sex industry of the border region and north into the United States.

Claudia was like a lot of young women from Sinaloa—at age 15, her prospects were dim. The constant battles between gunmen from the Sinaloa and Zeta cartels made life dangerous, jobs were scarce, and her mother had too many mouths to feed. The one ray of hope for Claudia was her older sister, Martha. Martha, 4 years older than her younger sister, had escaped the poverty of their Sinaloa home and had moved to the border city of Tijuana.

Martha boasted to Claudia of shopping across the border in San Diego and talked of the many opportunities to be found along the border. It did not take long for Claudia to agree to travel to Tijuana to live and work with her sister. A 2 day bus ride brought her to the bustling border city, which for decades has been the calling place of young sailors and marines on leave and college students seeking liberal drinking laws and to take advantage of the devalued peso.

Claudia probably did not know about the darker side of Tijuana. She did not know about 'La Zona Norte', the red light district along Tijuana's Coahuila Street, long known as a hub of sex tourism. This is a place where a person with enough money could find anything they were looking for.

When Claudia arrived in Tijuana, she found that her sister lived in a two-room apartment on the edge of 'La Zona Norte' and that life was not quite as glamorous as she had been led to believe. However, she was away from home and ready for the challenge. Claudia's first days were spent babysitting her sister's children. She was essentially a live-in nanny, cook and house cleaner. As the weeks passed, her sister increasingly pressed her to do her part to add to the household budget. Claudia found several jobs in the city. What she brought home, however, never seemed to be enough.

Claudia recalled the evening that her sister first brought up the idea of sex and money. She told Claudia that she could make more money in 1 day than in an entire month working as a house cleaner in Tijuana. Claudia, the product of a Catholic home in Sinaloa, was repulsed by the idea. Her sister dropped the subject, although she became increasingly demanding of her sister and seemed 'angry all the time'.

What Claudia had not realised was that she was slowly being groomed for sexual exploitation. Whether it is the promises of marriage by a 'boy-friend' who later turns out to be a pimp or the increasingly ugly act of family members pushing their children and siblings into the sex trade, most cases of CSE initially involve false promises, fabricated crises, guilt, shame and coercion—the same techniques have been used on thousands of boys and girls in Claudia's position.

It took Martha about 3 weeks to overcome Claudia's resistance. The particular evening started with alcohol and marijuana. When Claudia refused, her sister hit her repeatedly with a broom handle, pulled her hair and told her that she would leave her in the streets.

Claudia, afraid and isolated, gave in to her sister's demands. She was introduced to an older man from the neighbourhood, a man she had seen with her sister many times. What she remembered most was that he was as old as her father and that he smelled bad. Claudia lost her virginity on a mattress on the floor of her sister's apartment while Martha waited outside. The man paid Martha 200 pesos when he left, the approximate equivalent of $18.00 US dollars.

For almost 2 years, Claudia was exploited by four to eight men a night. She says that while most of the men were Mexicans, there were many from the United States as well. These ones from the United States were special to her sister, because they paid better. When Claudia was bought by a local, her sister would receive from 100 to 250 pesos. A 'Norte Americano' would bring $100, more than four times what the locals paid.

There were also the men who did not pay. They often came wearing the uniform of local prevention police. In a time when cartel members are known to pose as police officers, it is not certain that these men were real police officers, but in Claudia's mind it proved that she had nobody to turn to for help.

Claudia is a small, quiet girl. She is not quite five feet tall, with deep, expressive brown eyes and the features of a child. She looks younger than her actual age, which puts her into a special category for sexual exploitation. She did not have to be told why the older men were attracted to her. She recalled her sister telling the men that 'she has never been with a man before' and the eager looks on their faces. Her sister once convinced a man who said he was from Los Angeles to pay $150 US dollars for her 'virgin' sister.

Claudia's ordeal ended when she became so ill that her sister was forced to take her to a local hospital. She was admitted with a fever and seizures that resulted from a *Staphylococcus* infection. While she was being admitted, the hospital staff observed that Claudia suffered from more than one sexually transmitted diseases and noticed signs of physical abuse. Unfortunately, this was not a new sight for healthcare workers in Baja California's largest city.

Claudia told investigators from the Mexican Human Trafficking Commission that she could not recall the number of times she had been sold. She did know that for the 3 months preceding her hospitalisation she had not left her sister's apartment. She had been sick much of that time, often in a fever-induced haze. She still has images of men entering the room, having sex with her while she lay motionless on the mattress. When asked if these men had used condoms or protection when they raped her, her response was: 'Some did, some did not'. Proof of this was soon to come. The hospital discovered that Claudia not only suffered from a number of infections and diseases, she was also two months pregnant.

As tragic as her story is, Claudia can—in some small sense—be considered a 'lucky' victim: she and her baby lived to tell her story. She is home today, living with her mother and sisters in Sinaloa. Her baby is well, and although she has received little counselling or aftercare, she says the memories of that time in Tijuana fade each day.

Her sister and the man who raped her that first time in her sister's apartment are in jail. Investigators learned that Claudia was not the first girl the pair had used in this way. The two had as many as five girls working out of two apartments at any given time. None of the other girls would testify against the two, so prosecutors had only Claudia's case to work with. In the end, the two each received sentences of only 2 years in prison.

Claudia's case is a perfect example of how traffickers lure, entrap and exploit their victims. Martha lured her to Tijuana with the promise of a better life. She took control of Claudia's life, isolating her from the rest of her family, her friends and the outside world. Claudia became financially and emotionally dependent on Martha. Drugs and alcohol were introduced to lessen her resistance and to complete the dependence on her sister. Martha convinced her that providing sex to men was the only way to help the family, then resorted to physical assault and finally rape to complete the process.

Claudia's story is like many on the US–Mexico border. In his 2010 research study, San Diego State University researcher, Sheldon Zhang, and his team were able to interview 26 subjects who had been forced into prostitution, at least initially, by their 'boyfriends', 'husbands' or pimps. These men employed a wide range of techniques to manipulate or physically force the women into the sex trade. Nine of the subjects indicated that they were unable to go places without permission from or without being accompanied by their pimps. These women were socially isolated and deprived of support from and connections with their families. They distrusted the authorities and felt too ashamed to call for help (Zhang, 2010).

When she was asked why she never fled the situation, Claudia looked confused. 'How could I? I was ashamed, nobody would help me. I knew nobody in this place. Could I tell my mother what I had been doing for money? I was trapped'.

Cartel Involvement in Child Sex Tourism

Authorities in Ciudad Juarez arrested more than 1,000 people over the weekend in an operation aimed at cracking down on human trafficking, police said. Federal police said raids in two dozen bars, hotels and boarding houses netted arrests of 500 men and 530 women they suspect are connected with human trafficking and sexual exploitation. In addition, 20 female minors were rescued, police said. (CNN World, July 25, 2011)

Mexican drug cartels' businesses on the US–Mexico border have increasingly evolved from mainly trafficking drugs, weapons and money to also include procuring and providing children and prostitutes for sex tourism, pornography and associated sex trades in the United States (Gutman, 2004). The State Human Rights Commission of Baja California estimates that sex trafficking of children in Tijuana is the cartels' third highest revenue generator after the drug trade and gun smuggling (Castelan, 2011). The women and children who have become cartel victims are border natives or immigrants from South and Central America and southern Mexico.

Cartels hold controlling interests in the sex tourism industry on the border and also create the dangerous conditions that make it almost impossible to protect children and prosecute exploiters. One contributing factor to cartel involvement in sex tourism is the heightened Mexican federal law enforcement and military attention to drug and weapon smuggling since President Felipe Calderón declared war on the cartels in 2006. Human trafficking and sexual exploitation has been made easier and more profitable for the cartels by the lack of strong penalties and enforcement for these crimes. As Mexican Congresswoman Rosi Orozco told the Washington Post recently, 'If narcotics traffickers are caught [in Mexico] they go to high-security prisons, but with the trafficking of women, they have found absolute impunity' (O'Connor, 2011). US diplomats report that the larger cartels are all involved in sex trafficking, including CST. Los Zetas—one of the largest and most violent of the cartels—in particular, have begun their own prostitution ventures, rather than merely acting as suppliers of women and children for other traffickers. The leadership of Los Zetas is former Mexican Army Special Forces who originally worked as security and enforcers for the Gulf Cartel and then became their own gang. Los Zetas are in continuous battle with the Gulf and Beltran Leyvá cartels to control all organised crime enterprises in areas contiguous with Neuvo Laredo (Laredo, Texas) and Monterrey, while they are also at war with the Sinaloa and Beltran Leyvá cartels for the US–Mexico border area contiguous with the Mexican States of Sonora and Chihuahua (which includes Tijuana (Baja California), Arizona, New Mexico and parts of Texas on the US side). In January 2012, the Mexican government reported that over 47,000 people have been killed in violence due to these cartel battles—a figure that many believe is much too conservative (Cave, 2012).

David Aguilar, Deputy Commissioner of US Customs and Border Protection, has recently reported that Mexican cartels control important sections of the US–Mexico border. '[The cartels are] Mafia-like organization[s] that are specializing not just in any one crime, not in the singular fashion ... [They are becoming] involved in ... the exploitation of young men, young women, children for human trafficking, slavery, forced labor, and things of this nature' (Mora, 2011). Individuals or smaller criminal organisations are either put out of business or must pay for protection for their businesses in areas controlled by cartels. In Neuvo Laredo, for example, Los Zetas now control most organised crime activities, including sex trafficking, in the area known as 'Boys Town' or 'Zona Rosa'. 'Boys Town' has, for generations, been a 'rite-of-passage' destination for Texas boys who are 'coming of age'; before Los Zetas took over, sex trafficking there had been controlled by a combination of small local enterprises and individual traffickers.

For the cartels, human trafficking and CST are additional forms of income that do not require much adjustment to their business strategies; they already have established routes and means of drug trafficking from South and Central America across Mexico and to the US–Mexico border. The process of bringing humans north for exploitation is less dangerous than moving drugs, and if they are caught trafficking young women, the 'contraband' is not confiscated as it would be if they were caught with drugs. The cartel leaders (or 'lieutenants') are not at personal risk when smuggling women and children, and the 'mules' (carriers or guides) are seen as expendable. In addition, the Mexican government's current ability to investigate organised crime relating to CST is nonexistent, due to the more urgent problems of the cartels' internecine and intra-gang violence, the generally poor economic status of most citizens and official corruption.

A few Mexican federal government officials have been diligent in the fight against the cartels and child trafficking including, most notably, President Calderón, Congresswoman Orozco and Attorney General Marisela Morales. Morales was appointed in April 2011 and within months announced her intention to fight corruption in government by charging over 100 people in her department with fraud and embezzlement and by firing almost 200 more for incompetent criminal investigations (*The New York Times*, 2011). However, even these efforts at the highest levels seem inconsequential, given the massive amount of corruption and cartel violence at the local level.

Municipal police are often implicated in cartel violence and crime; they are known to be corrupted by cartels, including being involved in protection rackets for them. US government officials unofficially report that it is common for 'shelters' for children who have been rescued from sexual exploitation to actually function as brothels—for which local police act as protectors in return for sexual 'favours' from the children. One young girl who was rescued from a 'shelter'/brothel reported that she was forced to have sex with up to 50 men/day, including the police.

Those law enforcement officials who attempt to work against the corruption and CSE place themselves in grave danger of violence or death. In February 2009, a US Department of Justice programme—the Southern Border Initiative (SBI)—brought 26 Mexican municipal officials to El Paso, Texas, for an initial meeting to work toward developing trainings on CSE and abductions. The group from Mexico primarily consisted of chiefs of police, prosecutors and investigators. When the SBI attempted to reconvene the group in 2011, only 12 of the original group were still alive and able to be located; the rest had been assassinated or 'disappeared'.

One very discouraging recent phenomenon for the Mexican government's war against the cartels is the announcement of several Mexican entertainment celebrities that they have more faith in the honesty and power of the drug lords (such as 'El Chapo' Guzman, the reported head of the Sinaloa cartel) than the government (Shoichet, 2012). Thus, unhappily for the government, it may soon find itself not only in the midst of an escalating war against cartel violence and exploitation but increasingly defending its own honour and entitlement to use force to control its own citizens.

US and International Law Prohibiting Child Sex Tourism

CSE (including CST) is recognised to be among the worst forms of human rights abuse and is universally outlawed. It has been prohibited through international covenants and protocols and is criminalised in both US and Mexican law.

The first legally binding international agreement to protect children from sexual exploitation was the United Nations Convention of the Rights of the Child (CRC) that became effective in 1990 (United Nations, 1989). Article 34 of this Convention articulates that children are to be protected from 'inducement to engage in any unlawful sexual activity', exploitation through 'prostitution or other unlawful sexual activity', and their 'exploitative use...in pornographic performances or materials'. This Convention has been ratified by 140 nations: the United States and Somalia are two exceptions (United Nations, 1989).

The only express reference to CST in international law is found in Article 10 of the Optional Protocol to the CRC on the Sale of Children, Child Prostitution and Child Pornography (United Nations, 2001). Article 10 requires State Parties to strengthen international co-operation for the 'prevention, detection, investigation, prosecution and punishment of those responsible for acts involving the sale of children, child prostitution, child pornography and child sex tourism' (United Nations, 2001). It also requires collaboration with the State Parties in the assistance of child victims and in addressing root causes 'such as poverty and underdevelopment' (ibid.). As of December 2011, this Optional Protocol has 119 signatories including Mexico (March 2002) and the United States (December 2002) (United Nations, 2001).

Although the CRC and the Optional Protocol have been recognised as being important international statements about the necessity of protecting vulnerable children from all forms of exploitation, including CST, they have also been criticised as being of limited usefulness to child victims. Policing and prosecution remain the responsibilities of individual State Parties: failure to comply results in negative publicity (largely generated by NGOs who monitor various States) but nothing further. The unfortunate reality for many underdeveloped nations which are destination countries for CST is that compliance is often made extremely difficult by corrupt governments, inadequate and corrupt law enforcement and judicial systems and cultural patterns that facilitate the abuse of poor children (Hall, 2011).

In 2003, in response to a growing awareness and concern about the sexual abuse of children by US citizens within the United States and abroad, the US Congress passed what has become known as the 'PROTECT Act' (Prosecutorial Remedies and Other Tools to End the Exploitation of Children Today Act of 2003) (Department of State, 2003). Among other provisions of the Act (which include stricter mandatory sentences for repeat child sex offenders, the elimination of the statute of limitations for prosecution for child abductions and the creation of a nationwide AMBER Alert programme), the Congress strengthened laws prohibiting CST (18 USC § 2423 [c]–[g]). These changes include increasing the maximum potential imprisonment time from 15 to 30 years and establishing extraterritorial jurisdiction over those who violate the statute.

Under 18 USC §§ 2423 (b) and (c) (Department of State, 2003), it is a federal offence for US citizens or permanent residents to engage in 'illicit sexual conduct' (defined as an illegal sex act with a person under 18 years of age or any commercial sex act with a person under 18 years of age) while outside of the country (or while travelling in interstate commerce). This is true whether or not the person *intended* to travel for the purposes of engaging in sexual activity with a child. The statute also prohibits arranging or facilitating (for commercial or personal financial gain) any other person's travel to engage in sexual activity with a child. Conviction for arranging or facilitating travel also carries a maximum of 30 years of incarceration (18 USC § 2423 [d]). In addition, it is a violation of federal law to attempt or conspire to violate the earlier subsections (18 USC §§ 2423 [e]). Finally, it is a federal offence to transport a child in interstate or foreign commerce with the intent that the child either engage in prostitution or any sexual activity for which a person can be charged with a criminal offence (18 USC §§ 2423 [a]). The penalty for conviction of subsection (a) [transporting a child] is a minimum of 10 years imprisonment (Department of State, 2003).

There is no centralised federal reporting system for arrests, prosecutions or convictions for CST, so it is difficult to estimate how many suspected perpetrators have been arrested or tried since passage of the PROTECT Act (Department of State, 2003). Nevertheless, there are several indicators that the public is becoming more aware of CST, including the National Center for Missing & Exploited Children's (NCMEC) CyberTipline (NCMEC, n.d.), which has reported almost 4000 calls relating to CST incidents since it began operating in 1998 and 244 reports of CST in the first 11 months of 2011 (NCMEC, n.d.; PRI News wire, 2011).

An audit of FBI investigations into CST in 2009 found that the United States had, at that time, only one proactive investigatory unit for CST, which was based in Miami, Florida. This unit is recognised for creating a fictitious travel agency that purported to arrange trips to Latin America for individuals who expressed interest in travelling for the purpose of engaging in sexual activity with minors. As of summer 2008, 15 individuals had been convicted for arranging CST trips through the undercover travel agency. Of these 15, 14 were men; half were between 40 and 60 years of age; most were divorced or separated; all of the males were employed, most in lucrative jobs; most admitted they were travelling internationally because of fear of arrest for child exploitation in the United States; and most were not primarily oriented toward children as sex objects (Patterson, 2007).

Efforts to Eliminate Child Sex Tourism

With the exception of the work of journalist Lydia Cacho (which has exposed child pornography and child trafficking and prostitution rings in Cancun and elsewhere in Mexico), efforts to combat CST on the US–Mexico border have largely been focused on individual perpetrators (traffickers and 'tourists') and not on the larger criminal enterprises or the cartels. Unfortunately, this is largely in accord with the strategies and methods employed by those who are part of the global fight against CST.

The fight against CST (and all forms of exploitation) has been undertaken internationally—since the 1980s—by national governments; the tourism industry; journalists; international, national and local law enforcement agencies; NGOs; and religious organisations, from various perspectives and on different fronts. Four of the most significant ongoing efforts include: the UNWTO's promulgation and promotion of *The Global Code of Ethics for Tourism*; the ILO's *Convention Concerning the Prohibition and Immediate Action for the Elimination of the Worst Forms of Child Labour* (International Labour Organization, 1999); the United Nations' *Optional Protocol to the Convention on the Rights of the Child on the Sale of Children, Child Prostitution and Child Pornography* (United Nations, 2001); ECPAT International's work—which began in southeast Asia—including research, promoting public awareness and worldwide lobbying to combat commercial CSE in all forms; and the tourism industry's own *Code of Conduct for the Protection of Children from Sexual Exploitation in Travel and Tourism* ('The Code') which is supported by the UNWTO, ECPAT, UNICEF and other NGOs (The Code.org, n.d.-b).

The Code is of particular significance as it involves the private business sector. Its membership includes over 1000 companies in 42 countries including such well-respected travel and tourism companies as Accor, Kuoni, Carlson and Delta airlines (The Code.org, n.d.-b). Tourism businesses that sign The Code pledge to adopt six criteria (The Code.org, n.d.-a):

1. Establish an ethical policy against sexual exploitation of children.
2. Train personnel and staff members.
3. Introduce a clause about being a member of The Code in contracts with suppliers.
4. Provide information to travellers in the form of brochures, web pages or other materials.
5. Provide information to 'key persons' at the destination.
6. Report annually on the implementation of actions associated with these six criteria.

The Code received widespread publicity when it was adopted and promoted preceding the World Cup in Johannesburg in 2010 by Fair Trade and Tourism South Africa, along with businesses such as Avis, Hertz, Budget, Sun International and Radisson Hotels in conjunction with a UNICEF-led campaign, 'Let's Give a Red Card to Child Exploitation' (UNICEF, 2010).

One recent example of law enforcement's engagement with this crime is INTERPOL's Victim Identification programme—in which investigators analyse photographs and films depicting the sexual abuse of a child, a frequent product of CST, with the objective of identifying the victim and perpetrator depicted. INTERPOL points out that photographs and films portraying child sexual abuse which are disseminated on the Internet are not 'merely online crime'—they are 'representations of a real crime involving real people and real suffering'. The purpose of the programme is 'to alleviate the suffering of the child by identifying and locating him or her, and to bring that child's abuser to justice' (Interpol, n.d.-a).

INTERPOL also manages the International Child Sexual Exploitation image database (ICSE DB) (Interpol, n.d.-b) launched in March 2009 that uses image recognition software to make connections between victims and locations. Certified investigators from any member country can connect to INTERPOL's secure 1-24/7 network, upload material into the database and compare it with images seised worldwide. In addition to the ICSE DB, INTERPOL also issues Green Notices internationally to provide warnings and criminal intelligence to worldwide law enforcement agencies about persons who have committed criminal offences and are likely to repeat these crimes in other countries. One of the major aims of this programme is preventing offenders from crossing international borders (Interpol, n.d.-b).

In the United States, the Department of Homeland Security's (DHS) Cyber Crimes Center, Child Exploitation Section (CES) manages Operation Predator, designed to identify, investigate and prosecute international and transborder child predators in partnership with other national, international and local law enforcement agencies. The Child Sex Tourism Program, which is part of the CES, investigates US citizens and US permanent residents who are arrested in and/or travel to foreign countries for engaging in sexual acts with children.

In the first 5 years of Operation Predator, ICE (US Immigration and Customs Enforcement) made 99 arrests under the travelling child sex offender provisions of the 2003 PROTECT Act (Department of State, 2003; ICE, 2012). The investigative branch of DHS, ICE's Office of Intelligence includes Operation Angel Watch, which works to end CST by identifying registered sex offenders travelling internationally 'who demonstrate behavior indicative of travel to gain access to children for sexual exploitation' (Department of Justice, 2010: pp. 83–85).

On the US–Mexico border, the Department of Justice and Operation Predator have formed alliances with state law enforcement agencies and with the Mexican government to protect children from CST and other forms of CSE. Two recent examples of successful operations involve prosecution of an intended child sex tourist in 2010 (Figure 17.3) and the recovery (through a newly adopted AMBER Alert system) of a 16-year-old disabled boy. The boy, who had run away from home, was found at a bus station attempting to meet a predator who had found him on the Internet (Department of Justice, 2012).

Despite increasing public awareness, however, and the efforts of law enforcement, NGOs, governments and important sectors of the tourism

Office of the United States Attorney
District of Arizona

FOR IMMEDIATE RELEASE
Thursday, August 5, 2010

Public Affairs
WYN HORNBUCKLE
Telephone: (602) 514-7573
Cell: (602) 740-2422

FORMER TUCSON SCHOOL SUPERINTENDENT SENTENCED TO OVER EIGHT YEARS IN PRISON FOR CHILD SEX TOURISM AND CHILD PORNOGRAPHY CHARGES

PHOENIX – Albert Thomas Rogers, 52, of Tucson, Ariz., was sentenced today by U.S. District Judge Roslyn O. Silver to 100 months in federal prison followed by lifetime supervised release for Attempted Travel with Intent to Engage in Sex with a Minor and Possession of Child Pornography. These offenses occurred in the District of Arizona. Rogers, a former Tucson area school official, pled guilty in November 2009 to charges he attempted to travel to Mexico in order to have sex with a 13 to 14 year old boy, and that he knowingly possessed child pornography.

Rogers admitted to booking a sex tourism visit to Mexico through Yuma, Ariz., where on June 19, 2009 he traveled and met someone whom he believed was the driver for the business (but in reality was an undercover ICE Agent). Rogers paid the "driver" $260 to cover the costs of his travel to Mexico, hotel, and sex with a young boy. Rogers admitted to being collector of child pornography which included a video of a child as young as five years old engaged in sexually explicit conduct.

"It is disturbing that someone, having held such a trusted position with children, could have acted with such depravity and committed these illegal acts targeting child victims," said U.S. Attorney Dennis K. Burke. "Now Rogers will pay a price for predatory behavior."

On June 24, 2009, federal agents obtained a warrant and searched the defendant's residence in Tucson and found approximately 974 images and 98 video files containing child pornography. Rogers was a school superintendent with the Tanque Verde Unified School District at the time of his arrest.

The investigation in this case was conducted by the Department of Homeland Security, Immigrations and Customs Enforcement. The prosecution was handled by Dimitra H. Sampson, Assistant U.S. Attorney, District of Arizona, Phoenix.

CASE NUMBER: CR-09-0748-PHX-ROS
RELEASE NUMBER: 2010-166(Rogers)

# # #

For more information on the U.S. Attorney's Office, District of Arizona, visit
http://www.usdoj.gov/usao/az/

Figure 17.3 Recent examples of a successful operation involving the prosecution of an intended child sex tourist in 2010.

industry, global CST continues nearly unabated and under prosecuted for various reasons. Victim advocates have long pointed to the fact that trafficking victims tend to be perceived and treated more as criminals than as victims by law enforcement. This perception and treatment is based in part on how law enforcement routinely handles traditional types of crimes. Well-established investigative procedures which are used to investigate human-trafficking-related crimes (such as local vice crimes, assault, rape, immigration offences, threats, health and fire code violations) are often so narrowly defined that they actually assist traffickers by overlooking their methods of inducement and control used. When investigating CST, law enforcement officials should apply internal policies and procedures that would rule out human trafficking before proceeding with traditional investigative techniques and prosecution for other related crimes (Department of Home land Security, 2008).

In addition to investigative policies and procedures that tend to render crimes of trafficking invisible, law enforcement and prosecutors often conduct only 'reactive' CST investigations—those carried out in response to a complaint. 'Reactive' investigations, however, are usually costly and complex and involve large amounts of time and highly trained personnel resources. In addition, even when individual perpetrators are identified and located in these kinds of cases, it remains difficult to prosecute them for a variety of reasons, including difficulty in maintaining contact with victims, difficulty in establishing victims' ages, perpetrators who successfully bribe children and their families to remain silent and cultural and language barriers (Newman et al., 2011). Further, much of the evidence needed for prosecution of these cases remains in the country where the exploitation occurred—forcing investigators and prosecutors to deal with different laws, different societal expectations and possibly unco-operative or even corrupt local authorities (Patterson, 2007).

The current situation, therefore, remains discouraging. Although there have been significant efforts to reduce the tourist sex trade globally and on the US–Mexico border and to break its ties with the travel industry, these have generally been unsuccessful in stemming an ever-increasing phenomenon. While much of the practice may have gone 'underground', the Internet abounds with forums and chat rooms which openly discuss the best places to find sex for sale (O'Briain et al., 2008). In addition, cartels and other large criminal enterprises increasingly compete for the lucrative profits CST can realise with very small risk to them. Women and children, unfortunately, continue to fill the demand created in this increasingly more complicated market (Castelan, 2011).

Conclusion

CST on the US–Mexico border is a multifaceted, highly profitable and currently low-risk, criminal enterprise. It is engaged in by individual traffickers, families, unscrupulous individuals and businesses in the tourist industry and largely controlled by criminal organisations, including cartels. It is fuelled by demand from (mostly) men from the north who rationalise their own exploitive behaviours with children—rarely accepting responsibility for the devastating harm they are causing. Further, it is run in the context of corrupt law enforcement and government officials who are understaffed and/or underresourced to devote the efforts needed to ameliorate the problem in the context of the larger trafficking and violence issues on the border and who (in the worst cases) participate in and profit from child exploitation themselves.

There are no quick fixes to the problem of CST or other forms of child exploitation. As long as there is a demand, there will be those who supply children to satisfy that need. Authorities and policy makers in both the United States and Mexico need to recognise that human trafficking, child exploitation and CST are problems for both countries and that (except for a possible deterrent affect) attacking the problem only on the level of the individual trafficker or 'tourist'/exploiter cannot hope to solve it.

As the Optional Protocol to the Convention on the Rights of the Child makes clear, nations—such as the United States and Mexico—must deal with the root problems of poverty, underdevelopment and corruption alongside efforts to prosecute individual criminals and protect individual victims. As long as there are impoverished people in Mexico and Central and South America, there are people who will be exploited.

Ultimately, the solution to child sex trafficking may need to be developed by economists, because in addition to being a horrendous human rights violation, CST is an extremely profitable industry. Furthermore, as long as it remains relatively risk-free and reward-intensive, CST will continue. Cartels, individual traffickers and 'tourist'/exploiters must face greater risks and higher costs of doing business—in terms of higher rates of apprehension and greater penalties (cultural, civil and criminal) if CST is to be eliminated.

Opinions or points of view expressed are those of the author and do not necessarily reflect the official position or policies of the US Department of Justice.

'Claudia's' name has been changed for her protection. Unless otherwise noted, observations and conclusions are based on inquiry, investigation, interviews and personal experiences of the authors.

References

Aguilera E. 2011. Illegal immigration from Mexico continues decline. San Diego Union Tribune. Available from: http://www.utsandiego.com/news/2011/jul/07/illegal-immigration-mexico-continues-decline/, accessed February 28, 2013.

Amnesty International. 2012. Document—Mexico: Journalist and human rights defender at risk: Lydia Cacho. Available from: http://195.234.175.160/en/library/asset/AMR41/045/2011/en/d737ad45-bae7-4e48-9c8b-f25042160116/amr410452011en.html accessed February 28, 2013.

Azaola E. 2002. Boy and girl victims of sexual exploitation in Mexico. UNICEF-DIF. Available from: http://www.sp2.upenn.edu/restes/Mexico_Final_Report_001015.pdf, accessed February 28, 2013.

Bergman J. N. D. The place Mexican drug kingpins call home. Available from: http://www.pbs.org/wgbh/pages/frontline/shows/drugs/business/place.html accessed February 28, 2013.

Castelan A. 2011. Riverside girl trapped in Tijuana child sex trade. Available from: http://www.nbcsandiego.com/news/local/riverside-girl-tijuana-child-sex-slave-133106238.html accessed February 28, 2013.

Cave D. 2012. Mexico updates death toll in drug war to 47,515, but critics dispute the data. The New York Times. Available from: http://www.nytimes.com/2012/01/12/world/americas/mexico-updates-drug-war-death-toll-but-critics-dispute-data.html?_r=0 accessed February 28, 2013.

CNN World. 2011. Mexican police arrest more than 1,000 in human trafficking raids. Available from: http://articles.cnn.com/2011-07-25/world/mexico.human.trafficking_1_human-trafficking-mexican-police-arrest-trafficking-and-sexual-exploitation?_s=PM:WORLD, accessed February 28, 2013.

Department of Homeland Security. 2008. Domestic human trafficking—An internal issue. Human Smuggling and Trafficking Center, U.S. Government. Available from: http://www.state.gov/documents/organization/113612.pdf, February 28, 2013.

Department of Justice. 2009. The Federal Bureau of Investigation's efforts to combat crimes against children. U.S. Government. Available from http://www.justice.gov/oig/reports/FBI/a0908/final.pdf—United States, accessed February 28, 2013.

Department of Justice. 2010. The national strategy of child exploitation prevention and interdiction. U.S. Government. Available from: http://www.justice.gov/psc/docs/natstrategyreport.pdf—United States, accessed February 28, 2013.

Department of Justice. 2012. Trafficking in persons report. U.S. Government. Available from: http://www.state.gov/j/tip/rls/tiprpt/, accessed February 28, 2013.

Department of Justice. n.d. Child exploitation and obscenity section—Extraterritorial sexual exploitation of children. U.S. Government. Available from: http://www.justice.gov/criminal/ceos/subjectareas/trafficking.html accessed February 28, 2013.

Department of State. 2003. Prosecutorial remedies and other tools to end the exploitation of children today act of 2003 (PROTECT Act). U.S. Government. Available from: http://www.state.gov/j/tip/laws/120170.htm accessed February 28, 2013.

ECPAT International. n.d. CSEC Terminology. Available from: http://www.ecpat.net/ei/Csec_terminology.asp, accessed February 28, 2013.

Gehlert H. 2007. Child pornography and human trafficking: Cancun's dark side. Alternet.org. Available from: http://www.alternet.org/story/51326/child_pornography_and_human_trafficking%3A_cancun%27s_dark_side, accessed February 28, 2013.

Godoy E. 2007. Rights-Mexico: 16,000 victims of child sexual exploitation. Available from: http://www.ipsnews.net/2007/08/rights-mexico-16000-victims-of-child-sexual-exploitation/, accessed February 28, 2013.

Gutman W. E. 2004. Child prostitution: A growing scourge. Available from: http://www.thepanamanews.com/pn/v_10/issue_07/travel_01.html accessed February 28, 2013.

Hall J. A. 2011. Sex offenders and child sex tourism: The case for passport revocation. Virginia journal of social policy and the law 18: Available from: http://papers.ssrn.com/sol3/papers.cfm?abstract_id=1930625, accessed 1930628/1930602/1932013.

Hannum A. B. 2002. Sex tourism in latin America. ReVista, Harvard REview of Latin America. Available from: http://www.drclas.harvard.edu/publications/revistaonline/winter-2002/sex-tourism-latin-america, accessed February 28, 2013.

ICE. 2012. Fact sheet: Operation predator—Targeting child exploitation and sexual crimes. US immigration and customs enforcement (ICE). Available from: http://www.ice.gov/news/library/factsheets/predator.htm accessed February 28, 2013.

International Labour Office. 2003. Facts on commercial sexual exploitation of children. www.oete.de/dokumente/docs%20zukunft-reisen/ilo_facts.pdf, accessed August 18, 2013.

International Labour Organization. 1999. Convention 182. Convention concerning the prohibition and immediate action for the elimination of the world's worst forms of child labour. Available from: http://www.ilo.org/public/english/standards/relm/ilc/ilc87/com-chic.htm February 28, 2013.

Interpol. n.d.-a. Crimes against children. Available from: http://www.interpol.int/Crime-areas/Crimes-against-children/Crimes-against-children, accessed January 18, /2013.

Interpol. n.d.-b. Victim identification. Available from: http://www.interpol.int/Crime-areas/Crimes-against-children/Victim-identification, accessed February 28, 2013.

La Botz D. 1999. Women and children—Labor base of Mexican, North American economy. Corp watch. Available from: http://www.corpwatch.org/article.php?id=799, accessed February 28, 2013.

Mora E. 2011. Border patrol official: Drug cartels 'have taken control' of 'several areas along our border'. cnsnews.com. Available from: http://cnsnews.com/news/article/border-patrol-official-drug-cartels-have-taken-control-several-areas-along-our-border, accessed February 28, 2013.

NCMEC. n.d. CyberTipline. National center for missing and exploited children. Available from http://www.missingkids.com/CybertipLine, accessed February 28, 2013.

Newman W. J., Holt B. W., Rabun J. S., Phillips G., and Scott C. L. 2011. Child sex tourism: Extending the borders of sexual offender legislation. *International Journal of Law and Psychiatry* 34, 116–121.

O'Briain M, Grillo M, and Barbosa H. 2008. Sexual exploitation of children and adolescents in tourism. ECPAT international to the world congress III against sexual exploitation of children and adolescents. Brazil: ECPAT international. Available from: http://www.ecpat.net/worldcongressIII/.../Thematic_Paper_CST_ENG.pdf, accessed February 28, 2013.

O'Connor A-M. 2011. Mexican cartels move into human trafficking. The Washington post. Available from: http://articles.washingtonpost.com/2011-07-27/world/35267252_1_sexual-exploitation-marisela-morales-cartels, accessed February 28, 2013.

Patterson T. 2007. Child sex tourism: A dark journey. The FBI law enforcement bulletin. Available from: http://www.questia.com/library/1G1-158959083/child-sex-tourism-a-dark-journey, accessed February 28, 2013.

PRI Newswire. 2011. Google technology makes reporting child sexual exploitation easier. Available from: http://www.prnewswire.com/news-releases/google-technology-makes-reporting-child-sexual-exploitation-easier-136318218.html accessed February 28, 2013.

Save the children. 2003. Save the children's policy on protecting children from sexual abuse and exploitation. Available from: http://resourcecentre.savethechildren.se/content/library/documents/save-childrens-policy-protecting-children-sexual-abuse-and-exploitation, accessed February 28, 2013.

Shoichet C. E. 2012. Mexican actress: Drug lord could be 'hero of heroes'. CNN entertainment. Available from: http://articles.cnn.com/2012-01-11/entertainment/showbiz_mexico-actress-drug-lord_1_drug-trafficker-drug-lord-mexico-drug-violence?_s=PM:SHOWBIZ, accessed February 28, 2013.

The Code.org. n.d.-a. About the code. Available from: http://www.thecode.org/about/, accessed February 28, 2013.

The Code.org. n.d.-b. Homepage: We protect children from sex tourism. Available from: http://cp32.stablehost.com/~thecode1/about/, accessed February 28, 2013.

The New York Times. 2011. Mexican prosecutors face charges. Available from: http://www.nytimes.com/2011/07/22/world/americas/22mexico.html?_r=0 accessed February 28, 2013.

UNICEF. 2007. Implementation handbook for the convention on the rights of the child: Fully revised third edition. Available form: http://www.unicef.org/publications/index_43110.html accessed February 28, 2013.

UNICEF. 2010. UNICEF applauds tourism industry's commitment to stop child sex tourism. Available from: http://www.unicef.org/media/media_53882.html accessed February 28, 2013.

United Nations. 1989. Convention on the rights of the child. Available from: http://www.ohchr.org/EN/ProfessionalInterest/Pages/CRC.aspx, accessed February 28, 2013.

United Nations. 2001. Optional protocol to the UN convention on the rights of the child on the sale of children. Child prostitution and child pornography. Available from: http://www.undemocracy.com/A-RES-54-263.pdf, accessed April 30, 2012.

United Nations. 2011. Committee examines reports of Mexico on optional protocols to convention on rights of child. United nations human rights. Available from: http://www.ohchr.org/en/NewsEvents/Pages/DisplayNews.aspx?NewsID=10694&LangID=E, accessed February 28, 2013.

UNWTO. n.d. Homepage. World tourism organization. Available from: http://www2.unwto.org/en/content/who-we-are-0, accessed February 28, 2013.

UPI.com. 2005. Child prostitution on rise in border town. Available from: http://www.upi.com/Top_News/2005/04/04/Child-prostitution-on-rise-in-border-town/UPI-68091112646689/, accessed February 28, 2013.

World vision international. n.d. What is sex tourism?: Available from: http://www.worldvision.org/content.nsf/learn/globalissues-stp, accessed February 28, 2013.

Zhang S. 2010. Sex trafficking in a border community: A field study of sex trafficking in Tijuana, Mexico—Final Report. Available from: http://www.ncjrs.gov/pdffiles1/nij/grants/234472.pdf, accessed February 28, 2013.

Forensic Identification and Miscarriages of Justice in England and Wales

18

CAROLE McCARTNEY AND CLIVE WALKER

Contents

Introduction

Any fair and effective criminal justice system must ensure that evidence of guilt will be decisively more convincing than the defendant's claim to innocence. This burden on the prosecution, to satisfy the judge or jury of proof beyond a reasonable doubt, promotes an acceptance in law (if not in the popular press) that 'It is better that ten guilty persons escape than that one innocent suffer' (Blackstone, 1769: Vol. ivp.27). Despite such fundamental tenets, and despite even the sophistication of contemporary forensic science, the criminal process does still convict the innocent.

While forensic science is acclaimed in the media, it has a blemished history in reality. Many infamous miscarriages of justice suffered from scientific evidence that was flawed, misrepresented, or suppressed (Walker and Starmer, 1999). 'Scientific' methods of identifying criminal perpetrators have certainly advanced dramatically but are not infallible.

In this chapter, we shall outline the meanings and prime causes of 'miscarriage of justice', providing examples of cases where forensic identification methods have been at the heart of miscarriages of justice. We then examine the mechanisms in England and Wales for remedying miscarriages of justice and assess their success.

Faulty Criminal Process in England and Wales

Miscarriages of Justice

A 'miscarriage' means literally a failure to reach an intended destination or goal. A miscarriage of justice is therefore a failure to attain the desired end result of 'justice', Justice is about distributions—according persons their fair shares and treatment. The primacy of individual autonomy and rights is central to the 'due process model' of criminal justice (Packer, 1969), which recognises that the possibility of human fallibility and error can thereby yield grave injustice, as when the system convicts the innocent or even convicts without respecting procedural rights. Thus, a possible definition of 'miscarriage' is that it occurs whenever suspects or defendants or convicts are treated by the state in breach of their rights, because of the following: first, the deficient processes; second, the laws which are applied to them; third, because there is no factual justification for the applied treatment or punishment; fourth, whenever suspects or defendants or convicts are treated adversely by the state to a disproportionate extent in comparison with the need to protect the rights of others; fifth, whenever the rights of others are not effectively or proportionately protected or vindicated by state action against wrongdoers; or sixth, by state law itself.

The third category of miscarriage—where there is no factual justification for the treatment or punishment—can result in a conviction even when the defendant in reality has committed the offence. This broader definition has caused some debate over the proper focus of researchers, with some claiming that an exclusive focus on the 'innocent' is vital. They prefer the term 'wrongful conviction' (although this too can have wider meaning, to include the factually and legally innocent as well as those convicted through unjust procedures [Risinger, 2007]), to distinguish those convicted but innocent, from those unjustly convicted. The House of Lords (now called the Supreme Court) considered such nomenclature in the case of *R v. Secretary of State for the Home Department, ex parte Mullen*:

> 'Miscarriage of justice' is an expression, which, although very familiar, is not a legal term of art and has no settled meaning. Like 'wrongful conviction' it can be used to describe the conviction of the demonstrably innocent... But, again, like 'wrongful conviction', it can be and has been used to describe cases in which defendants, guilty or not, certainly should not have been convicted. (R v. Secretary of State for the Home Department ex parte Mullen [2004] UKHL 18: paragraph 9)

The debate over taxonomy continues (Naughton, 2010), but we use the term 'miscarriage of justice' throughout the chapter to refer to those unjustly convicted rather than seeking to assert 'innocence', a status which is not officially bestowed, even if it is knowable.

The most important catalogue of contemporary miscarriages in England and Wales concerned Irish 'terrorist' cases of the 1970s. Most of these and other miscarriages arise from a multiplicity of causes. For instance, the Criminal Cases Review Commission (CCRC) (2000) specified the following causes in the 80 cases it had by then referred to the Court of Appeal (some with multiple causes per case): police/prosecution failings = 27; scientific evidence = 26; nondisclosure = 23; new evidence = 23; defective summing up = 11; defective legal arguments = 10; false confessions = 6; and defence lawyer failings = 6.

The most grievous danger is the falsification of evidence. For example, informers who are co-accused may have self-serving reasons for exaggerating the role of the defendant. The police are also in a powerful position to manipulate evidence, for example, by pressuring an accused or falsely recording statements. Both the police and lay witnesses may be unreliable when attempting to identify a suspect, especially if the sighting was momentary and in a situation of stress (R v. Turnbull [1977] QB 224 (CA)). The evidential value of expert testimony has also been overestimated because the tests being used were inherently unreliable, because the scientists conducting them were incompetent or both. A further issue may be the nondisclosure to the defence of relevant evidence by the police, prosecution or their experts.

The conduct of the trial may also produce miscarriages. For example, judges are sometimes prone to favour the prosecution evidence rather than acting as impartial umpires. Equally, defence lawyers may not always be as competent or assertive as they should be. There can also be problems concerning the presentation of defendants in a prejudicial manner. An insidious way of achieving this effect is the pejorative labelling of them by the media as 'terrorists' or 'bad mothers'. Similarly, heavy-handed security arrangements accompanying trips to court and a defendant's quarantined appearance in the dock inevitably convey an impression of guilt and menace.

Forensic Identification and Criminal Investigations

The identification of perpetrators is central to any criminal investigation, though most crimes are easily resolved since the perpetrators are identified red-handed at the scene or swiftly traced, usually by the agency of the public rather than of the police or forensic experts. Where public assistance is not enough, forensic identification techniques, such as fingerprints and DNA profiles, can discern the true perpetrators, even years after the crime. However, the perception (perhaps propagated by television series such as 'CSI') that reliance upon expert witnesses and forensic evidence predominates in investigations and trials is misguided. While it has grown over 30 years, it probably still features in a minority of criminal cases (U.K. Government, 2005). Furthermore, the increased availability and affordability of a plethora of forensic techniques incurs the risk of undue trust in this type of evidence. A few examples of flawed forensic identifications will serve to illustrate these misgivings.

Fingerprints and the Case of Shirley McKie

For over a century, investigators have been collating the fingerprints of suspects and criminals. Indeed, fingerprints, with their notion of 'uniqueness', have become perhaps the most trusted identification method and continue to be used daily in identifications across the world, with the support of large databases and, latterly, Automatic Fingerprint Identification System (AFIS) technology. However, problematic identifications and questions over the expertise and techniques of fingerprint examiners have arisen.

In 1997, Marion Ross was murdered in her home in Kilmarnock, Scotland. The investigation led to David Asbury, who became a suspect when a fingerprint found on a biscuit tin containing money at his home was identified as belonging to the victim (Scottish Parliament, 2011). Shirley McKie, a uniformed police officer, was called to guard the crime scene while investigators worked inside. They claimed to find McKie's fingerprint inside the Ross house, but McKie denied ever having ventured inside the house, calling into question the accuracy of the fingerprint 'match'. During testimony at the trial of David Asbury, she confirmed that she had not been into the house, leading to a charge of perjury for lying about her movements. She was acquitted in 1999 after the court heard the testimony of two American fingerprint experts that the Scottish Criminal Records Office (SCRO) had wrongly found a match. David Asbury was freed in 2002 after the conclusion was reached that other crucial fingerprints were also erroneous. Eventually, the Scottish government set up a comprehensive inquiry under Sir Anthony Campbell (a retired senior judge). His *Fingerprint Inquiry Report* (Scottish Parliament, 2011) reaches many conclusions concerning not only errors in McKie's case but also about fingerprint comparison as a 'science'. It concluded that

> Fingerprint examiners are presently ill-equipped to reason their conclusions as they are accustomed to regarding their conclusions as a matter of certainty and seldom challenged... There is no reason to suggest that fingerprint comparison in general is an inherently unreliable form of evidence but practitioners and fact-finders alike require to give due consideration to the limits of the discipline. (Scottish Parliament, 2011: pp. 739)

The report then recommends that 'Fingerprint evidence should be recognised as opinion evidence, not fact...' and that 'Examiners should discontinue reporting conclusions on identification or exclusion with a claim to 100% certainty or on any other basis suggesting that fingerprint evidence is infallible' (Scottish Parliament, 2011: pp. 740).

Fingerprints are facing a challenging time. Their 'scientific' basis has now been called into question, and there are growing numbers of inquiries and cases in England too (such as R v. Smith [2011] EWCA CRIM. 1296) where fingerprint evidence has been challenged, something unheard of in previous decades. Issues around the 'science' of fingerprinting, and the 'expertise' of examiners, now require concerted effort on behalf of the fingerprint expert community, if fingerprints are to retain their validity as a reliable identification technique.

'Old' v. 'New' Forensic Technology: The Case of Stefan Kiszko

Stefan Kiszko was convicted of the murder of 11-year-old Lesley Molseed in 1975 (R v. Kiszko [1979] 68 CR.APP. R 62). Lesley's killer had ejaculated on her underclothes. In the 1970s, a semen sample taken from Kiszko during the investigation did not contain sperm because he suffered from hypogonadism.* The killer's ejaculate did contain sperm. These results were kept from the defence. It was not until 1992, after 16 years in prison, that the Court of Appeal was to hear the convincing scientific evidence that Stefan Kiszko could not have been Lesley's killer. The killer of Lesley Molseed had apparently evaded justice, until evidence from her murder featured in a 'cold case' review. This time, DNA techniques were able to obtain a profile from

---

* In men, failure of the testes to produce sperm, androgen or in some cases both.

the semen sample. Ronald Castree had earlier been arrested in 2005 in connection with another sex attack but was not then charged. However, his DNA had been taken and placed on the National DNA Database (NDNAD). The profile from the NDNAD then matched the new profile obtained from Lesley Molseed's underclothes. It took over 30 years to convict the true killer of Lesley Molseed, using DNA techniques unavailable when Kiszko was convicted, but Ronald Castree was found guilty (R v. Castree [2008] EWCA Crim. 1866). Kiszko had died shortly after his release and never saw the real perpetrator of the crime imprisoned.

'Ear Prints' and the Case of Mark Dallagher

In 1998, Mark Dallagher was found guilty of the murder of 94-year-old Dorothy Woods. He was identified by a new 'ear-printing' technique developed in the Netherlands. The technique was primarily used to identify burglars who habitually 'listen' at walls or windows to detect occupiers before entering an abode. While listening, burglars would press their ears against a surface, and based upon the same principles of fingerprinting, an 'ear print' would be left. This 'print' could then be compared to that of a suspect using computer technology. Two experts, Van Der Lugt, a Dutch police officer, and Regius Professor of Forensic Medicine and Science Peter Vanezis of Glasgow University, testified in court that they had 'matched' Dallagher's ear prints to those on Dorothy Wood's window. Dallagher continued to maintain his innocence throughout his six-year imprisonment, before DNA testing on exhibits at the crime scene pointed to a different perpetrator. At his appeal, the Crown claimed to have 'anxieties' about the case and offered no contest, leaving Dallagher to walk free (R v. Dallagher [2002] EWCA CRIM. 1903).

The Dallagher case highlights the dangers of reliance upon new identification techniques. Expertise in the courtroom can be highly persuasive, but its scientific base should be rigorously tested before being applied in criminal cases. In this instance, DNA testing demonstrated the fallacy of the ear print 'science', whereas neither the scientific community nor the courts had been effective at testing the 'science'.

DNA 'Gold Standard'?

The advent of forensic DNA testing has been revolutionary, leading to the accurate detection and conviction of many criminals and the exoneration of hundreds of those wrongly convicted. However, while DNA is lauded as the 'gold standard' of forensic identification technology, there is sometimes confusion as to the extent of its proof, including a need to distinguish identity match from matters such as *when* or *why* a person came to be identified.

A recent illustration of the disputes concerns the investigation into the murder of two British soldiers at Massereene Barracks, Northern Ireland, in 2009 (R v. Duffy and Shivers [2011] NICC 37). Much of the evidence was based on identifications at the scene, testimony of the defendants and materials found in the burned-out getaway car. DNA tests had linked one defendant, Duffy, to the tip of a latex glove and seat-belt buckle in the abandoned car. The DNA of Shivers was linked to matches and a mobile phone. The judge, sitting without a jury, decided that while he was satisfied that the DNA link to the car was soundly established, the prosecution had failed to demonstrate that the DNA alone linked Duffy to the murder plot, whereas stronger evidence was adduced against Shivers, including lies about his whereabouts. A further crucial issue in the case was also whether the novel statistical process used could be regarded as having achieved sufficient recognition as valid and reliable.

This controversy had earlier received publicity in another Northern Ireland case, in the prosecution of Sean Hoey for the Omagh bombing (R v. Hoey [2007] NICC 49). In that case, the judge ruled that the 'novel' technique of testing ever-smaller samples of DNA known as 'low template number DNA' (LTDNA) had not yet reached the level of 'general acceptance' within the scientific community. For that, among other reasons, the judge ordered an acquittal. In 2010, LTDNA was further considered in *R v. Reed and Reed* (R v. Reed and Reed [2010] 1 CR. APP. R. 23) and this time admitted as evidence by the English Court of Appeal.

Features of Flawed Forensic Science Cases

There are common features to many of the cases involving flawed forensic evidence.

Contamination and Errors

The collection of materials, which will eventually be tested in forensic laboratories, is primarily at the discretion of the police. Thus, the obvious dangers arise that nonscientists will accidentally contaminate evidence or that they will fail to appreciate the value of available evidence and will fail to forward it to the laboratory (perhaps because of budgetary constraints). The deployment of professional Scenes of Crime Officers (SOCOs) or Scenes of Crime Examiners (SCEs) by no means solves all the problems, since they attend only a minority of crime scenes, often only after other police officers have visited. The *Disclosure Manual* (CPS, 2005), issued under the Criminal Procedure and Investigations Act 1996, requires police investigators to 'ensure that all reasonable steps are taken for the purposes of the investigation and, in particular, that all reasonable lines of enquiry are pursued' (CPS, 2005: paragraph 3.5). However, there are no specified means of enforcement, and defence teams are not given resources to check for themselves. As well as the contamination of exhibits and samples at the scene of the crime, the samples placed in the hands of police and scientists are also at risk if not handled properly. For example, in Germany, police forces expended thousands of hours in chasing the 'Phantom of Heilbronn' (CPS, 2005: paragraph 3.5). The basis of this was the DNA profile of an unknown woman that was turning up at crime scenes for several years. The 'Phantom' was considered a criminal mastermind, evading capture despite large rewards for her identification. However, investigators finally realised that contamination was the more likely answer, and cotton swabs used in the DNA process were eventually shown to be the cause.

Recent high-profile errors have also arisen in the United Kingdom in 2012. A young man in Exeter, Adam Scott, was charged with a rape in Manchester, on the basis of a DNA 'match'. He denied ever having traveled to Manchester, and his lawyer pressed for further testing of the results. It transpired that the DNA from the rape case had been contaminated with the laboratories of LGC Forensics by a sample taken from Scott when arrested for a minor affray offence (BBC, 2009).

During the lengthy and perplexing police investigation into the death of MI6 employee, Gareth Williams, LGC Forensics provided police with a DNA profile from the scene. The police spent a year attempting to trace the individual responsible for leaving the DNA, to no avail. It was later discovered that an LGC employee, manually entering the DNA profile into a computer, had transposed the numbers '3' and '5', rendering the DNA profile incorrect. This typographical error led to a costly pursuit of a nonexistent individual (Dodd and Malik, 2012).

Quality and Competency

Concerns arise about all the professions that come into contact with potential evidence and an investigation, but the particular focus here is about the quality and competency of forensic science personnel. The attempt to foster quality and efficiency in forensic science by market competition has yet to prove that it is immune to the other 'problems' of markets including the creation of 'bargain basement' forensic science. An ambitious forensic regulation scheme rose and fell with the demise (in 2009) of the Council for the Registration of Forensic Practitioners, which had registered 'competent' forensic experts and was praised by the courts (Schlesinger and Hamilton, 2012). The Home Office's Forensic Science Regulator (see Chapter 20) has authority to accredit for government contracting purposes, but only scrutinises laboratories and companies, the assumption being that their employees will be monitored and checked as part of their quality assurance measures.

Translation into Proof

The competency of lawyers to spot and explore problematic scientific issues is by no means unblemished, and their deficiencies will in turn hamper the comprehension levels of juries (General Medical Council v. Meadow [2006] EWCA Civ 1390: paragraph 226).

In many international jurisdictions, judges have been given the role of 'gatekeeper' to ensure that 'junk science' remains inadmissible at trial. However, they have also been criticised (Cassella and McCartney, 2011; Garrett and Neufeld, 2009). It has been concluded that 'Scientific illiteracy on the part of the legal profession, when coupled with the flaws in forensic science, forms a "toxic combination"' (Cassella and McCartney, 2011: pp. 82). Proposals to alleviate the situation in a lengthy and complex Law Commission Report (Edmond, 2011) await implementation.

Funding for Forensic Work

Budgetary constraints are restricting the extent to which police employ forensic scientists. In this way, an ability to pay impacts strongly the ways in which criminal justice is delivered. A further consequence is a trend towards in-house police scientists or less qualified or less experienced independent forensic scientists. Disquiet arises about the quality and independence of small or isolated scientific units. Access by the defence to properly qualified, experienced forensic scientists is even more hampered by inadequate funding. In the worst cases, legal aid authorities may withhold funds altogether on the grounds that, for example, the scientific evidence is, in their (lay) view, unassailable. Even when funds are forthcoming, the defence may be required to instruct a 'local expert' who is not viewed as suitable.

Biases

During the appeal of Judith Ward (2011), who was exonerated from involvement in an IRA coach bombing, Lord Justice Glidewell explained (R v. Ward [1992] 96 CR.APP. R. 1):

> For lawyers and judges a forensic scientist conjures up the image of a man in a white coat working in a laboratory, approaching his task with cold neutrality, dedicated only to the pursuit of scientific truth. It is a sombre thought that the reality is sometimes different... Forensic scientists employed by the government may come to see their function as helping the police. They may lose their objectivity.

Recent scholarly examination of the processes involved in forensic evidence 'generation' has focused on the possible biases of scientists, in particular the impact of cognitive bias. The National Research Council of the National Academy of Science's Report on forensic science in the United States (ibid.: pp. 51) condemned the infiltration of prosecution biases into the work of laboratories that operated within and overseen by police agencies. In England and Wales, such concerns led to the absorption into the independent Forensic Science Service (FSS) of police laboratories such as, in 1996, the Metropolitan Police Laboratory. Yet, the FSS closed on cost grounds in 2012 (2009), and forensic science in England and Wales is now provided by private companies and in-house police facilities.

Developments/Improvements in Science

Several forensic techniques relied upon in the past have been shown through later scientific developments to be flawed or imprecise. One example is serology, while polygraphs are also considered unacceptable in English trials (U.K. Government, 2011). Arson investigation has had to be radically overhauled in the United States since common assumptions were based on experiences which, when tested under experimental conditions, were proven wrong (R v. Chapman [2006] EWCA CRIM. 2545).

Mechanisms to Redress Residual Error

Many of the safeguards against wrongful convictions must reside within fair and rational legal rules and the professional working cultures fostered by appropriate training and management and assured by accreditation, quality assurance and validation processes, within the police, prosecution, forensic science, judiciary and advocates. Nevertheless, whatever care is expended, mistakes are inevitable, and so effective processes for remedying error remain essential even after conviction.

The Court of Appeal, originally established in 1907 after several high-profile wrongful convictions, can overturn convictions if it considers the conviction to be 'unsafe' under section 2(1) of the Criminal Appeal Act 1995 (National Fire Protection Association, 1992). There may be two interpretations of unsafe: that a factually innocent person has been wrongly convicted or a factually guilty person has been convicted but there has been a serious procedural or legal error or illegality (U.K. Government, 1995). The Court's own approach is summed up in *R v. Hickey* (Roberts, 2003):

> This court is not concerned with the guilt or innocence of the appellants; but only with the safety of their convictions... the integrity of the criminal process is the most important consideration for courts which have to hear appeals against conviction. Both the innocent and the guilty are entitled to fair trials.

Difficulties have especially occurred when appeals arise on factual error grounds, necessarily forcing the Court of Appeal to trespass on the role of the jury but confined to a 'review' and not rehearing the case. The Court of Appeal only hears fresh evidence when 'necessary or expedient in the interests of justice' under section 23(1) of the Criminal Appeal Act 1968 (Rv. Hickey [1997]. Unreported) and must have regard under section 23(2) to the following: (1) whether the evidence appears to be 'capable of belief', (2) whether the evidence may afford any ground for allowing the appeal, (3) whether the evidence would have been admissible at trial and (4) whether there is a reasonable explanation for the failure to adduce the evidence at trial.

Three main complaints are levelled at the Court: that too much deference is shown to the jury verdict, that there is undue reverence to the principle of finality and that the court is motivated by the fear of 'opening the floodgates' to a deluge of appellants beyond its resources (U.K. Government, 1968).

Major high-profile miscarriages of justice in England and Wales have been seminal in prompting changes to the appellate system. The ultimate, successful appeal of the Birmingham Six (Spencer, 2006; U.K. Government, 1993) wrongly convicted of mass murders in Irish Republican Army (IRA) pub bombings was swiftly followed by the announcement of a Royal Commission into Criminal Justice. Its subsequent report (R v. McIlkenny and others [1992] 2 ALL E.R. 417) called for the establishment of a new independent body to investigate alleged miscarriages of justice, replacing the politically tainted and under-resourced process of petitioning the Home Office. The idea was implemented in the shape of the CCRC by Part II of the Criminal Appeal Act 1995 (U.K. Government, 1993).

The role of the CCRC resembles its Home Office forerunner in that it cannot determine the outcome of cases, but if certain criteria are established, it can refer a case back to the Court of Appeal. However, there are critical differences between the old and new systems:

1. *Preparation of the application*: The establishment of the CCRC has removed some initial practical obstacles from the petitioner. Though the CCRC is not proactive, the application process is user-friendly, though the availability of legal advice remains a distinct advantage (Smith, 1995; U.K. Government, 1995).
2. *Structures*: In addition to the 11 commissioners, the CCRC employs dozens of caseworkers. Its annual budget of around £6 million represents a substantial increase in resources compared to the Home Office. However, the CCRC has faced financial and staffing cutbacks, beginning in 2004 with a reduction of 30 percent in caseworking staff since then (Hodgson and Horne, 2009).
3. *Consideration of the application*: The reluctance of the Home Office to refer cases because of 'political embarrassment' could only be

overcome by a body independent of the executive. The independence of the CCRC is provided for in section 8(2), whereby it 'shall not be regarded as the servant or agent of the Crown...'. At least one-third of the CCRC's membership must be legally qualified, and under section 8(6), at least two-thirds 'shall be persons who appear to the Prime Minister to have knowledge or experience of any aspect of the criminal justice system...'. However, the selection of commissioners over the years could be criticised as deriving too heavily from prosecution interests and also reflecting too much the white, male, middle class background so redolent of British judicial institutions.

4. *Reinvestigations*: It is vital to the success of the CCRC that it is seen to have thorough and transparent investigative processes. However, the government has stood fast against resourcing CCRC in-house investigative staff. Instead, investigations are mainly carried out by the police under CCRC supervision, a relationship which demands a more 'trusting attitude to the police' than perhaps is warranted (Criminal Cases Review Commission, 2009: paragraph 7).

5. *Disclosure of evidence*: The CCRC has a wide power to obtain documents from public bodies under section 17 of the 1995 Act, but these powers do not extend to private bodies (which may include forensic laboratories). As regards disclosure of information to the applicant, the Court in *R v. Secretary of State for the Home Department* (Malet, 1995) insisted that when the Home Secretary was minded to reject an applicant's petition on the basis of evidence gathered in any further inquiries, the applicant should be given an opportunity to make representations upon such material before a final decision is made. However, there is no general duty to disclose all the information gathered during any investigation or reinvestigation (Rv. Secretary of State for the Home Department ex parte Hickey (no. 2) [1995] 1ALL ER 490).

6. *Referral to the Court of Appeal*: To trigger a referral to the Court of Appeal, the CCRC under section 13(1) must 'consider that there is a real possibility that the conviction... would not be upheld were a reference to be made...'. This 'real possibility' can be realised through 'an argument, or evidence, not raised in the proceedings...'. Yet, the Act left much to be determined through the interpretations of the CCRC and also the receptivity of the Court of Appeal, which has to be second-guessed by the CCRC. More radical solutions would have been to give the commission the power to determine applications or at least to make recommendations to the Court of Appeal either to acquit or to order a retrial, placing the onus on the judges to find reasons to disagree. However, such ideas would arguably have interfered too much with judicial independence and the finality of verdicts.

Performance of the CCRC

In terms of design, the CCRC is an important and innovative reform, which recognises the possibility of residual errors and works to facilitate their correction. The CCRC has been widely accepted, in theory and in practice, to be a great improvement in terms of independence, resources, expertise and performance on the predecessor C3 Department of the Home Office and the equivalent unit in the Northern Ireland Office (including four times the rate of referrals). However, increasing criticisms are levelled at the decision-making processes, the resources and ultimately the remit.

The CCRC began work on April 1, 1997, with 279 cases transferred to it from the Home Office and 12 from the Northern Ireland Office. By March 31, 2012, the commission had received 14,506 applications, of which 13,969 have been completed. Of these applications, 498 referrals have been made to the Court of Appeal, of which 460 have been heard, resulting in 321 quashed convictions or sentence variations.

Evidenced by the foregoing low rate of referrals, the CCRC adopts an inherently cautious approach, reflected by its internal decision-making protocols. While just a single commissioner can refuse referral, it requires three to refer (Nunn V. Chief Constable of the Suffolk Constabulary [2012] EWHC 1186 (Admin)). In practice, Case Review Managers (CRMs), who have the main responsibility for investigating cases, have internalised this 'one CM to refuse, three CMs to refer' system with the result that they have transformed the working practice of the 'real possibility test' into 'a real possibility of a real possibility test' when deciding whether or not to recommend a referral. In this way, the single CRM must decide whether there is a 'real possibility' that three commission members will refer before making their own recommendation (Criminal Cases Review Commission, 2004).

It could be contended that in looking for a 'real possibility' that a conviction would be reversed by the Court of Appeal, the CCRC is second-guessing the Court of Appeal and only refers those cases which are sure to be overturned—the high success rate in the Court of Appeal combined with the low rate of referrals is indicative of this tendency. However, a greater propensity to refer might reduce the engagement in investigative work, thereby weakening the chances in court. The Court of Appeal can in turn direct the CCRC to carry out investigations under the Criminal Appeal Act 1995 (Elks, 2008), sections 5 and 15, but rarely exercises the power. If the quality of preliminary investigation is reduced, the CCRC will quickly become discredited. In the view of the CCRC itself (U.K. Government, 1995), it might 'perpetuate the very miscarriages of justice that the Commission was set up to review...'. There is also the danger of hampering the ability of the Court of Appeal to scrutinise effectively if a sizable proportion of weak referrals fail.

Moving from its handling of individual cases, a wider performance defect of the CCRC is that it has concentrated too much on individual cases and has failed to undertake a broader analysis and audit of systemic failures and necessary reforms. This aspect of inquiry would be 'value-added' work that the CCRC is well placed to carry out or facilitate (Criminal Cases Review Commission, 2001: pp. 26) but which is currently neglected by the criminal justice system.

Performance of the Court of Appeal

Crucial to the success of the scheme must be the receptivity to CCRC referrals on the part of the Court of Appeal. The Court has generally shown respect for the CCRC but the meaning of the statutory test for referral remains a key problem.

As stated, the 1995 Act provides that there must be a 'real possibility' that the original conviction, finding or sentence would not be upheld as 'safe' were the conviction to be referred back to the Court of Appeal. In the case of a conviction, the 'real possibility' must be as a result of an argument or evidence not raised in the original proceedings or of 'exceptional circumstances' such as wholly inadequate defence representation. The leading case on the interpretation of section 13 has been *R v. Criminal Cases Review Commission* (Elks, 2008: pp. 348). It was held that the meaning of 'real possibility' 'plainly denotes a contingency which in the Commission's judgment is more than an outside chance or a bare possibility but which may be less than a probability or likelihood or a racing certainty'. Those standards were applied both to the admission of fresh evidence (if relevant) and also to the assessment of the evidence by the court. Whether this provides a sufficiently clear signal of society's determination to avoid miscarriages is questionable. It still leaves much discretion—some defendants might be lucky to be heard by receptive judges, others might not.

Conclusions

Miscarriages of justice involving forensic evidence have provided plentiful opportunity for the legal and scientific communities to reflect upon failings of both science and law. While a recent U.S. National Research Council of the National Academy of Sciences Report (R v. Criminal Cases Review Commission ex parte Pearson [2000] 1Cr.App.R141: pp. 149) was scathing about the lack of 'science' underlying some prominent forensic techniques, the report also contained 'the somewhat hushed admonition that lawyers and judges often have insufficient training and background in scientific methodology and they often fail to fully comprehend the approaches employed by different forensic science disciplines and the reliability of the forensic science evidence that is offered at trial' (National Research Council, 2009). Not only must the forensic disciplines attend to the scientific bases for their processes and conclusions, but equally legal professions and agencies must more soundly incorporate forensic evidence within investigation and trial processes. Decision-making by all scientists and legal professionals alike must also be informed by the apprehension that forensic science has never been, and will never be, infallible.

References

BBC. 2009. "DNA Bungle" haunts German police. Available from: http://news.bbc.co.uk/1/hi/world/europe/7966641.stm, accessed March 03, 2013.

Blackstone, W. 1769. Commentaries on the Law of England, 1765-9. Available from: http://www.lonang.com/exlibris/blackstone/, accessed March 05, 2013.

Cassella, J. and Mccartney, C. 2011. Lowering the drawbridges: Legal and forensic science education for the 21st Century. *Forensic Science Policy & Management*, 2, 81–93.

CPS. 2005. Disclosure Manual. Crown prosecution service. Available from: http://www.cps.gov.uk/legal/d_to_g/disclosure_manual/, accessed March 03, 2013.

Criminal Cases Review Commission. 2000. Third Annual Report 1999-00.

Criminal Cases Review Commission. 2001. Fourth Annual Report 2000-01.

Criminal Cases Review Commission. 2004. Seventh Annual Report 2003-04 (2003-04 HC 9).

Criminal Cases Review Commission. 2009. Memorandum submitted to the house of commons justice select committee, The work of the criminal cases review commission (HC 343-i).

Dodd, V. and Malik, S. 2012. Forensics blunder "May Endanger Convictions". The Guardian. Available from: http://www.guardian.co.uk/law/2012/mar/08/forensics-blunder-convictions, accessed March 05, 2013.

Edmond, G. 2011. Actual innocents? Legal limitations and their implications for forensic science and medicine. *Australian Journal of Forensic Sciences*, 43, 177–212.

Elks, L. 2008. *Righting Miscarriages of Justice*, London, U.K., Justice.

Garrett, B. L. and Neufeld, P. J. 2009. Invalid forensic science testimony and wrongful convictions. University of Virginia law school: Public law and legal theory working paper series, 1–95.

General Medical Council v. Meadow [2006] EWCA CIV 1390.

Hodgson, J. and Horne, J. 2009. *The Extent and Impact of Legal Representation on Applications to the Criminal Cases Review Commission*, London, U.K., Legal Services Commission.

Malet, D. 1995. The new regime for the correction of miscarriages of Justice. *Justice of the Peace*, 159, 716–735.

National Fire Protection Association, 1992. NFPA 921: Guide for fire and explosion investigations. Available from: http://www.nfpa.org/aboutthecodes/AboutTheCodes.asp?DocNum=921&EditionID=3006, accessed March 05, 2013.

National Research Council. 2009. *Strengthening Forensic Science in the United States: A path forward*, Washington, DC, National Academies Press.

Naughton, M. 2010. *The Criminal Cases Review Commission: Hope for the innocent?*, London, U.K., Palgrave Macmillan.

Nunn V. Chief Constable of the Suffolk Constabulary [2012] EWHC 1186 (ADMIN).

Packer, H. L. 1969. *Limits of the Criminal Sanction*, Stanford, CA, Stanford University Press.

R v. Castree [2008] EWCA CRIM. 1866.

R v. Chapman [2006] EWCA CRIM. 2545.

R v. Criminal Cases Review Commission EX Parte Pearson [2000] 1 CR. APP. R 141.

R v. Dallagher [2002] EWCA CRIM. 1903.

R v. Duffy and Shivers [2011] NICC 37.

R v. Hickey [1997]. Unreported.

R v. Hoey [2007] NICC 49.

R v. Kiszko [1979] 68 CR. APP. R 62.

R v. Mcilkenny and Others [1992] 2 ALL E.R. 417.

R v. Reed and Reed [2010] 1 CR. APP. R 23.

R v. Secretary of State for the Home Department EX Parte Hickey (NO. 2) [1995] 1ALL ER 490.

R v. Secretary of State for the Home Department EX Parte Mullen [2004] UKHL 18.

R v. Smith [2011] EWCA CRIM. 1296.

R v. Turnbull [1977] QB 224 (CA).

R v. Ward [1992] 96 CR. APP. R. 1.

Risinger, D. M. 2007. Innocents convicted. *Journal of Criminal Law & Criminology*, 97, 761–806.

Roberts, S. 2003. Unsafe convictions: Defining and compensating miscarriages of justice. *Modern Law Review*, 66, 441–451.

Schlesinger, F. and Hamilton, F. 2012. Someone knows how spy ended up dead in that bag, coroner declares. The Times. Available from: http://www.thetimes.co.uk/tto/news/uk/crime/article3402508.ece, accessed March 05, 2013.

Scottish Parliament. 2011. *The Fingerprint Inquiry: Scotland*. Edinburgh, U.K., APS Group Scotland. Available from: http://www.thefingerprintinquiryscotland.org.uk/inquiry/files/TheFingerprintInquiryReport_Low_res.pdf, accessed July 22, 2012.

Smith, J. C. 1995. The Criminal Appeal Act 1995: Appeals against conviction. *Criminal Law Review*, 920.

Spencer, J. R. 2006. Does our Present Criminal Appeal System Make Sense. *Criminal Law Review*, 677–694.

The Law Commission. 2011. Expert evidence in criminal proceedings in England and Wales. Law Commission Report No 325. Available from: http://www.official-documents.gov.uk/document/hc1011/hc08/0829/0829.pdf, accessed July 22, 2012.

U.K. Government. 1968. Criminal appeal act [1968]. Available from: http://www.legislation.gov.uk/ukpga/1968/19/contents, accessed March 05, 2013.

U.K. Government. 1993. The royal commission on criminal justice: Report. Available from: http://www.official-documents.gov.uk/document/cm22/2263/2263.pdf, accessed March 05, 2013.

U.K. Government. 1995. Criminal appeal act [1995]. Available from: http://www.legislation.gov.uk/ukpga/1995/35/contents, accessed March 05, 2013.

U.K. Government. 2005. Home office. Forensic science on trial. House of commons science and technology committee seventh report of session 2004-5. The Stationary Office Limited, London, U.K. Available from: http://www.publications.parliament.uk/pa/cm200405/cmselect/cmsctech/96/96i.pdf, accessed January 20, 2012.

U.K. Government. 2011. House of commons science and technology committee: The forensic science service. Available from: http://www.publications.parliament.uk/pa/cm201012/cmselect/cmsctech/855/85502.htm accessed March 05, 2013.

Walker, C. P. and Starmer, K. (eds.) 1999. *Miscarriages of Justice,* London, U.K., Blackstone Press.

Forensic Science Evidence and Miscarriages of Justice

19

DONALD E. SHELTON

Contents

> The reliability of forensic pathology opinions matters a great deal to the criminal justice system. [W]hether the flawed pathology plays a part in a wrongful conviction or in allowing a criminal to escape detection, justice is not served and public confidence in the legal system is diminished.
>
> **Justice Stephen T. Goudge**

Introduction

In a 20 year span, a government paediatric pathologist in Canada conducted autopsies in over 45 child death cases in Ontario. A later review of his opinions by five world experts found that he was wrong in at least 20 of those cases. In the meantime, 12 people had been convicted and sent to prison based on his reports. Several other parents and caregivers had been accused of murdering their children. A formal government inquiry concluded that the doctor 'lacked basic knowledge about forensic pathology' and 'failed to understand that his role as an expert in the criminal justice system required independence and objectivity' (Goudge, 2008).

Over a similar two decades, an American police laboratory chemist in Oklahoma gave evidence about blood, hair, semen and fibres that sent two dozen people to death row and several thousand to prison. She was considered so adept at finding incriminating scientific evidence that she was nicknamed 'black magic' by the police. An FBI investigation initially looked at eight of those cases and found that her testimony was 'beyond the acceptable limits of forensic science' and that she 'overstated the importance of hair and fiber evidence'. Subsequent investigations led to the release of several people who had been wrongfully convicted by her testimony, including some who had served over 15 years in prison. In convicting one innocent defendant, she testified that she excluded a different suspect, who was later found to be the actual perpetrator (Garrett, 2011; Kohn, 2009; Yardley, 2001).

In Boston, Massachusetts, in a trial of a man accused of killing a police officer, a government fingerprint examiner testified that a thumbprint on a glass mug handled by the assailant was a match of the defendant's print. The defendant was convicted, but after serving over 5 years of a 30–45 year sentence, he was exonerated by DNA testing. Re-examination of the thumbprint by state police and an independent auditor showed that the defendant was actually excluded by the print comparison (Garrett, 2011; The Innocence Project, n.d.-b). How do these and many, many other miscarriages of justice result from flawed forensic science testimony?

DNA Exonerations and Forensic Science Testimony

In recent decades, DNA has become the 'gold standard' of human identification forensic scientific evidence and DNA typing is now universally recognised as the standard against which many other forensic individualisation techniques are judged. For the same reasons, however, DNA testing has the remarkable ability, in the right circumstances, to provide conclusive *exculpatory* evidence after conviction when specimens were not tested at the time of trial. The highly publicised Innocence Project reports that, as of 2011, there have been 284 post-conviction exonerations by DNA testing in the United States, including 17 people who had been sentenced to death before DNA proved their innocence and led to their release (The Innocence Project, n.d.-a). The increasing incidence of exoneration is shown by the project's chronological graph (*ibid.*) (Figure 19.1).

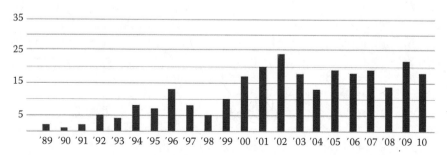

Figure 19.1 (See companion CD for colour figure.) DNA exonerations by year in the United States.

These exonerations reveal disturbing truths about some of the more traditional types of forensic science evidence that trial judges have long treated as reliable and generally accepted. Post-conviction DNA testing has resulted in proof of wrongful convictions that were based on seemingly reliable non-DNA forensic scientific evidence (Findley, 2008). For example, 22% of the first 200 post-conviction DNA exonerations had been based on false hair or fibre comparisons, and almost 40% had been based on serology evidence (Garrett, 2008). These exonerations are undisputable proof of the unreliability of other forms of scientific evidence, including perhaps such traditionally admitted forms of evidence such as fingerprints. In an analysis of trial records of exonerees, a recent study found that forensic science testimony had been used to wrongfully convict 74% of them (Garrett, 2011). The exonerations, and the apparent association of their underlying convictions with many forms of routinely admitted prosecution forensic science evidence, are clear factors in causing the public, defence lawyers and the courts to doubt or at least re-examine the scientific validity of such evidence. As one observer optimistically put it:

> The issues raised by DNA exonerations have led to an overhaul of the criminal justice system. Some states now require that evidence be preserved; others require mandatory videotaping of interrogations. Several states, including Illinois, New Jersey, and New York, abolished the death penalty largely because of concerns about executing an innocent person. North Carolina, meanwhile, has created an independent commission to review innocence claims. And some prosecutors' offices, including those in New York and Dallas, have created conviction integrity units (Martin, 2011).

On the other hand, many prosecutors simply refuse to accept any notion that DNA evidence actually exonerates persons against whom they have 'won' a conviction. They seek to explain away newly discovered DNA evidence in any manner that is consistent with the defendant's guilt. For example, where a post-conviction DNA test reveals sperm of someone else in a sexual assault murder case, prosecutors will then claim that the victim must have had intercourse with a different unknown person before the defendant killed them (Martin, 2011). In the highly publicised case of *People v. Rivera* (People v. Rivera [2011] Ill. App. 2d No. 091060), the Illinois Court of Appeals recently overturned a murder conviction after a retrial where the prosecution claimed that the sperm found in the victim, which was admittedly not that of the defendant, must have been from prior intercourse. The prosecution claim was based solely on 'anecdotal testimony from the victim's sister recounting a masturbation experience and an alleged sexual molestation three years prior by a neighborhood friend's brother' (People v. Rivera [2011] Ill. App. 2d No. 091060: paragraph 32). The Court of Appeals found that the 'State's theories distort to an absurd degree the real and undisputed testimony that the sperm was deposited shortly before the victim died' (People v. Rivera [2011]

Ill. App. 2d No. 091060: paragraph 17). However, as one prosecutor revealingly explained, 'The taxpayers don't pay us for intellectual curiosity. They pay us to get convictions' (Mills and Black, 2010).

In the United States, wrongful convictions based on forensic science testimony led the Congress to commission an exhaustive study by the National Research Council of the National Academy of Sciences (NAS) (National Research Council, 2009). The Council conducted a lengthy 2-year study of the use of forensic science in criminal cases and made specific findings both generally and as to several specific areas of commonly admitted evidence. Those findings were relayed to the Congress in 2009 in a report of over 300 pages. The summary included this caustic analysis of the use of forensic science in criminal cases:

> The bottom line is simple: In a number of forensic science disciplines, forensic science professionals have yet to establish either the validity of their approach or the accuracy of their conclusions, and the courts have been utterly ineffective in addressing this problem. For a variety of reasons–including the rules governing the admissibility of forensic evidence, the applicable standards governing appellate review of trial court decisions, the limitations of the adversary process, and the common lack of scientific expertise among judges and lawyers who must try to comprehend and evaluate forensic evidence–the legal system is ill-equipped to correct the problems of the forensic science community. (National Research Council, 2009: p. 53)

The specific analyses of each of the separate areas of forensic evidence were, for the most part, damning. The Council researched the alleged scientific basis for each specialty, the training requirements for persons holding themselves out as experts in that field and the nature of the substantive testimony proffered in court by those persons. With the exception of nuclear DNA typing and testing, in most areas of forensic science the NAS report (National Research Council, 2009) found a distinct failure to provide the type of reliability criteria mandated in federal courts.

In Canada, exonerations led to the creation of several formal inquiries, including the Goudge inquiry (2008), condemning much of the practice of forensic paediatric pathology (Goudge, 2008). In 2002, the federal Heads of Prosecutions Committee established a Working Group on the Prevention of Miscarriages of Justice and made an initial report in 2005. In a follow-up report in 2011, the group stated:

> We need to rethink our approach to expert witnesses and expert testimony. The very reason that courts rely on expert witnesses—for their specialized knowledge—makes it difficult to challenge their expertise and opinions. Checks and balances are required to overcome this frailty and the danger of creating "battles of the experts." The recommendations from the *Inquiry*

Pediatric Forensic Pathology highlight the need for all participants in the criminal justice system to exercise vigilance and caution in assessing expert opinion evidence to ensure that it meets the standards of excellence required to guard against wrongful convictions. (Public Prosecution Service of Canada, 2011)

In Britain, the legal system was slow to utilise DNA in post-conviction testing. Nevertheless, it has focused on wrongful convictions in an orderly manner through the 1997 creation of the Criminal Cases Review Commission to investigate possible miscarriages of justice and, where appropriate, to refer cases back to the appeal courts. Alleged miscarriages of justice resulting from forensic science testimony have become one aspect of the Commission's role, leading it to remark in its most recent report:

> There is no doubt that the way in which expert evidence is presented to juries, and the weight that is attached to it, will become an increasingly important feature in appeals. (Criminal Cases Review Commission, 2011: p. 19)

High-profile cases of wrongful conviction based on forensic expert testimony led the Law Commission to recommend tightening of the reliability standards for the admissibility of such testimony in a 2011 report to Parliament:

> The current judicial approach to the admissibility of expert evidence in England and Wales is one of laissez-faire. Too much expert opinion evidence is admitted without adequate scrutiny because no clear test is being applied to determine whether the evidence is sufficiently reliable to be admitted. This problem is exacerbated in two ways. First, because expert evidence (particularly scientific evidence) will often be technical and complex, jurors will understandably lack the experience to be able to assess the reliability of such evidence. There is a danger that they may simply defer to the opinion of the specialist who has been called to provide expert evidence. Secondly, in the absence of a clear legal test to ensure the reliability of expert evidence, advocates do not always cross-examine experts effectively to reveal potential flaws in the experts' methodology, data and reasoning. Juries may therefore be reaching conclusions on the basis of unreliable evidence. This conclusion is confirmed by a number of miscarriages of justice in recent years. (Law Commission, 2011)

Inherent Dangers of Expert Testimony

In criminal cases, jurors are the finders of fact. To determine those facts, they are presented with evidence from witness testimony about what the witness observed or heard. It is for the jury to decide whether that testimony proves, either directly or circumstantially, beyond a reasonable doubt, that the defendant committed the crime with which he or she is charged.

Additionally, however, the jury is allowed to hear conclusion or opinion testimony from persons who are regarded as 'experts'. They may only give opinion testimony when those opinions would assist the jury in reaching the decision regarding the ultimate issue. The testimony is limited to areas that are beyond the normal or common experience of jurors and where an expert's special knowledge will help the jury understand the importance of the factual evidence it hears. Testimony from scientific experts is the classic form of such expert testimony. The expert may testify as to whether a particular event occurred, who the person was who caused the event to occur, or how the event occurred. These basic questions of 'whether', 'who' and 'how' are the subjects of the variety of scientific evidence seen in courtrooms today.

Before an expert can testify, they must be accepted by the judge as a qualified expert. The announcement to a jury that the judge has allowed the witness to testify as an expert carries weight into the jury box beyond its words. The jury already perceives the judge as the only impartial lawyer in the room and when he or she tells them that they have accepted the witness as an 'expert', the jury gives whatever the witness says added credibility. The judge, presumably acting only as the 'gatekeeper' of admissible evidence, in effect vouches for the expertise of the witness in the jurors' eyes.

Decisions about the admissibility of forensic science evidence assume even larger importance to the extent that jurors consider such evidence to be especially critical to their ultimate decision about guilt. It is widely perceived, especially by prosecutors and other law enforcement agencies, that modern juries give a great deal of weight to scientific evidence. They even complain that jurors today demand more from the prosecution in the way of scientific evidence and that they will 'wrongfully' acquit defendants when such evidence is not presented. Empirical studies of American jurors were conducted in 2006 and 2009 to determine whether current juries do expect and demand scientific evidence (Shelton et al., 2007, 2009a; Shelton, 2010b; for a further analysis of the 2006 study data see Shelton et al., 2009b). The studies found that jurors do indeed expect prosecutors to present scientific evidence and that, especially in cases in which the rest of the evidence is circumstantial, they will demand scientific evidence before they will return a verdict of guilty (Shelton et al., 2009b). In light of those documented expectations and demands, jurors are clearly going to rely upon the forensic science expert testimony that the judge has already told them is reliable enough for them to hear. If that testimony is indeed flawed or biased, it poses a significant danger of leading to a miscarriage of justice. It may even lead to the execution of an innocent man.

Todd Willingham was executed in Texas for the alleged murder of his three children by setting fire to his own home. He was convicted based on testimony from a Texas fire marshal investigator who stated that the fire in Willingham's home had burned 'fast and hot' and had been started using a liquid accelerant. On appeal, the Texas Court of Criminal Appeals summarised the fire origin expert testimony in simple terms:

> An expert witness for the State testified that the floors, front threshold, and front concrete porch were burned, which only occurs when an accelerant has been used to purposely burn these areas. This witness further testified that this igniting of the floors and thresholds is typically employed to impede firemen in their rescue attempts. (Willingham v. State 897S. W. 2d351 (Tex. Ct. Crim. App [1995]))

Prior to Willingham's execution, a fire origin expert working *pro bono* for the defence made a detailed report finding that the conclusions of arson made by the fire investigators were invalid (Hurst, 2004). Nevertheless, the Texas Board of Pardons and Paroles voted unanimously to recommend denial of clemency, which Governor Rick Perry did, and Willingham was executed on February 17, 2004. Willingham's execution in spite of the report quickly generated press coverage detailing the controversy over the validity of the fire origin expert testimony in his case, including a statement by the defence expert that '[t]here's nothing to suggest to any reasonable arson investigator that this was an arson fire' (Mills and Possley, 2004). Three other independent experts also reached a similar conclusion (*ibid.*). The governor and other politicians claim that the scientific reports are part of a conspiracy to oppose the death penalty, and the political controversy continues. Todd Willingham can no longer be heard on the issue of his innocence.

Assumptions of Uniqueness

Most identification testimony is based on the premise that the identifying characteristic of the evidence being examined is unique to an individual, whether that be fingerprints, hair, dentition, handwriting or whatever. What we have learned from DNA exonerations and renewed studies of those fields is that there appears to be little if any scientific evidence to support what is in many cases simply an assumption of uniqueness.

The forensic science community has long regarded fingerprinting, or friction ridge analysis, as a primary method for assessing 'individualisation', the conclusion that a suspect fingerprint impression comes, unambiguously, from a single person. The technique used to examine fingerprints goes by the acronym ACE-V, for 'analysis, comparison, evaluation and verification'. In spite of the seeming formality of the fingerprint analysis process adopted by qualified examiners, the reality is that the assessment of fingerprint identification is nevertheless a subjective human interpretation. As the NAS report stated:

Although some Automated Fingerprint Identification Systems (AFIS) permit fully automated identification of fingerprint records related to criminal history (e.g., for screening job applicants), the assessment of latent prints from crime scenes is based largely on human interpretation. Note that the ACE-V method does not specify particular measurements or a standard test protocol, and examiners must make subjective assessments throughout. In the United States, the threshold for making a source identification is deliberately kept subjective, so that the examiner can take into account both the quantity and quality of comparable details. As a result, the outcome of a friction ridge analysis is not necessarily repeatable from examiner to examiner...

This subjectivity is intrinsic to friction ridge analysis, as can be seen when comparing it with DNA analysis... For these reasons, population statistics for fingerprints have not been developed, and friction ridge analysis relies on subjective judgments by the examiner. Little research has been directed toward developing population statistics, although more would be feasible. (National Research Council, 2009: pp. 139–140; see also Haber and Haber, 2008)

In fact, many of the most basic tenets of fingerprint identification have never been subjected to empirical analysis. Most modern researchers who have examined fingerprinting comparison have concluded that the broad claims of fingerprint identification accuracy cannot be substantiated (Benedict, 2004; Cole, 2004, 2005, 2006; Epstein, 2002; Faigman et al., 2010; Saks and Koehler, 2005). As one commentator put it, the 'gold standard' of fingerprinting identification may be more akin to 'fool's gold' (Malcom, 2008).

In handwriting, determining whether each person's handwriting is truly unique would necessitate a study of a large number of randomly chosen persons and the categorisation and measurement of the multitude of possible variations (Lissitzyn, 2007). There are no standardised measurements, and there is not even a public record of handwriting samples that can be scientifically used to develop such measurements or to test the basic underlying theories of handwriting analysis (Saks and VanderHaar, 2005). No formal empirical testing has been completed (Risinger, 2010). The scant studies which have been undertaken do not provide statistical support for uniqueness (Cha et al., 2001; Muehlberger et al., 1977).

As to bite marks, despite its acceptance in various cases, there is significant disagreement among odontologists and other scientists about the basic premise of dental uniqueness. The American Society of Forensic Odontology asserts that the uniqueness premise has been established by at least two studies (Rawson et al., Sognnaes et al., 1982; 1984; Sweet, 1997), and odontologists are convinced that human dentition is unique to each living person (Bowers, 2006; Giannelli, 2007; Pretty and Turnbull, 2001; Moriarty and Saks, 2005; Wilkinson and Gerughty, 1985). However, the NAS report concluded after 2 years of study that 'the uniqueness of the human dentition has not been scientifically established' (National Research Council, 2009: p. 175).

That conclusion is supported by the studies of several other scholars (Bowers, 2013; Pretty, 2003).

The reality is that even in DNA profiling, where there could be some scientific claims for uniqueness, expert witnesses refuse to adopt the 'match' testimony used by these other witnesses and testify as to the scientifically established statistical probability of another person in the relevant population with a similar profile. The insistence by other experts on telling lay jurors that they have 'matched' the evidence to the defendant, and only the defendant, when they have no scientific basis to do so, increases the likelihood of a miscarriage of justice.

Pro-Prosecution Bias and Forensic Evidence

Almost all forensic science examiners in criminal cases are employed by the government as part of the law enforcement hierarchy. They report to the police or prosecutor and come to see themselves as part of the prosecution of criminal defendants. Sometimes that leads to a conscious bias toward finding the incriminating evidence that the police or prosecutor are looking for and ignoring any potentially exculpatory findings. For example, the pathologist in the Goudge inquiry in Canada testified that he believed that his role was to act as an advocate for the Crown and to 'make a case look good' (Goudge, 2008). Regardless of conscious intent, their law enforcement position can lead to a cognitive bias. That bias can be exaggerated when combined with other allegedly incriminating information they have been given by police about the case, even though it is unrelated to the evidence the expert is examining. As a recent report explained:

> Cognitive biases may be thought of as systematic distortions in thinking that occur when information passes through the subjective filters of human beliefs, attitudes, and experiences. For example, expectation bias is a particular form of cognitive bias in which one's expectations about what he or she should see or find affect what one actually does see or find. Confirmation bias is another form of cognitive bias in which people test hypotheses by looking for confirming evidence rather than potentially disconfirming evidence. Contextual bias is a form of cognitive bias that is of particular concern in the forensic realm. Contextual bias occurs when information that an examiner has aside from the forensic evidence itself influences (consciously or unconsciously) the examiner's judgments about that evidence. For example, examiners may learn that the case against a particular suspect is strong or that a particular suspect has committed similar crimes in the past. Such extraneous or contextual information, though perhaps diagnostic of whether the suspect is guilty and/ or the source of the trace evidence in question, can bias the examiner's judgment about the forensic evidence that he or she must analyze. Examiners who

began an exam believing that the suspect is the source may therefore be more inclined to call close or ambiguous matches a match than they would if they did not hold this belief. Like most people, examiners may feel that they are not subject to such biases or that they can eliminate them merely by trying to be objective. But the psychological research... clearly indicates otherwise. (Kohler and Meixner, 2011)

An example of extraneous evidence influencing an expert opinion occurred in the recent highly publicised Casey Anthony trial in Florida. The medical examiner there assessed the remains of the child's body that had been exposed to the elements in a wooded area for over 2 months. She testified that she concluded the cause of death was a homicide, based not on anything she found in the remains during the autopsy but rather on the 'circumstantial evidence' and 'observational data' that no one had called 911 to report the child missing (Garavaglia, 2011).

The question remains: How does unreliable evidence get before the jury? How does it so often get the blessing of the 'gatekeeper' judge?

First, the defence does not often challenge the admissibility of prosecution forensic science evidence. Second, when the defence does make such a challenge, they usually lose. What accounts for the relative lack of defence challenges to government expert testimony in criminal cases and the overwhelming court rejection of those challenges that are made? As to the lack of challenges, some have suggested that it is 'poorly funded, unskilled counsel' and an 'inadequate pool of experts' available to the defence, especially when compared to resources available to civil plaintiffs (Neufeld, 2005). As to the overwhelming judicial rejection of criminal defence challenges that are made, there are several possibilities.

One possibility is that the science being proffered by the government in criminal cases is simply of higher quality than that being offered by civil plaintiffs. The findings in the NAS report indicate that many non-DNA is forms of expert testimony used by prosecutors is of questionable validity and should dispel that notion. Moreover, judicial decisions for the most part do not indicate that the judges, trial or appellate, weighed the scientific validity of the proffered evidence in any meaningful way (see Faigman et al., 2010). Rather, most of the decisions simply rationalised admissibility based on the prior admission of such evidence by other judges.

More likely is the suggestion that there is also a systemic pro-prosecution bias on the part of judges and that such a bias is reflected in admissibility decisions, regardless of the 'gatekeeping' admissibility standard (Shelton, 2010a). As Groscup et al. (2002) found in the United States, 'the *Daubert* decision did not impact on the admission rates of expert testimony at either the trial or the appellate court levels' (Groscup et al., 2002: p. 364). To put the bias question another way, 'as a general proposition, judges disfavor civil plaintiffs and criminal defendants and are more likely to rule against them than against their opposites even when presenting equivalent evidence or arguments' (Faigman et al., 2010: p. 112).

Systemic pro-prosecution bias is also a function of fairly obvious psychological concepts. Guthrie (2007) described judicial bias as a reflection of an 'attitudinal blinder', relying on significant empirical studies of judicial attitudes and actions:

> Whether elected or appointed, judges come to the bench with political views. This is not to say that they have pre-committed to positions in particular cases, but it strains credulity to claim, as, for example, Justice Alito claimed during his Supreme Court confirmation hearings, that a judge 'can't have any preferred outcome in any particular case.' Rather, judges do have opinions, and these opinions or attitudes can predispose them to rule in ways that are consistent with those opinions or attitudes.
>
> To establish the presence of attitudinal blinders among judges, political scientists have developed, and provided empirical evidence to support, the so-called attitudinal theory or model. Most of this work has focused on the Supreme Court, but political scientists and legal scholars have also explored whether judicial attitudes influence judges on the courts of appeals and on the trial bench. The evidence suggests that attitudinal blinders are an issue not only at the highest court in the land but also in these lower courts. (The Guthrie, 2007; Washington Post, 2006)

These attitudinal blinders are especially prevalent in criminal cases and especially in the state courts where most criminal cases are tried. As Uphoff remarked,

> In the end, state court judges are, for the most part, rational actors whose attitudinal biases reflect their self-interest and their backgrounds. Most are answerable to a tough-on-crime electorate and are often reluctant, therefore, to make risky political decisions upholding the constitutional rights of criminal defendants (Uphoff, 2007: p. 532, and see Tulsky, 2007, claiming that 'in a fourth of all jury cases, are view finds, members of the bench apply their tremendous powers in ways that hurt defendants').

Specifically, Uphoff comments on how this attitudinal bias manifests itself in criminal cases:

> Most judges, especially those with prosecutorial experience, presume that most defendants are, in fact, guilty, even though some are, in fact, innocent. This presumption of guilt, pro-prosecution perspective not only affects the manner in which many judges rule on motions, evaluate witnesses, and exercise their discretion, but it also adversely affects the willingness of many judges to police law enforcement agents and prosecutors. Judges tolerate sloppy police work

because they do not want to be viewed as micro-managing the police. Judicial reluctance to let the guilty go free has meant a decreased use of the exclusionary rule. Similarly, courts are hesitant to dismiss cases because of Brady violations or take other steps to reign in prosecutorial misconduct. Finally, even when courts find error, too many errors are deemed harmless. The expanded use of harmless error not only allows questionable verdicts to stand, it does little to discourage misconduct and sloppy practices in the administration of justice. (Uphoff, 2007: pp. 543–544)

As the result of what appears to be a distinct pro-prosecution bias in trial and appellate judges, the current legal state of forensic science evidence in criminal cases is somewhat schizophrenic. While many scientists and scholars, and even national studies, seriously question whether there is validity to non-DNA forensic evidence, trial judges simply continue to admit such evidence and appellate judges continue to affirm those decisions.

The Casey Anthony case also presented an example of pro-prosecution judicial bias. The prosecution theorised that the defendant had killed her daughter, placed the body in the trunk of her car and then dumped the body where the remains were later found. To support that theory, the prosecution offered the testimony of a forensic anthropologist who claimed that he had perfected a process of 'human decomposition odour analysis' by which he could identify whether the scent of a decomposing human body was in the air. The police had gathered air from the trunk in metal cans, and the expert used gas chromatography to identify the gases present in the sample. He claimed that 79.2% of the gases were consistent with those of a decomposing human body (State of Florida v. Casey Marie Anthony Case No. 48-2008-CF-015606-O, 2011).

Florida is a state that required that scientific evidence be generally accepted in the scientific community to be admissible. The expert did not testify that his theory was generally accepted but insisted that it was 'scientifically valid' and cited his two published articles describing his research (Vass et al., 2004, 2008). Defence experts in chemistry and biochemistry told the judge that the concept 'odor signatures of human composition' is not generally accepted in the scientific community and that 'there are no scientifically validated methods capable of identifying the presence of human remains based on the presence or absence of specific chemical residues' (State of Florida v. Casey Marie Anthony Case No. 48-2008-CF-015606-O, 2011). Ultimately, the judge admitted the prosecution testimony, using an unusual interpretation of the law to say that while the technique used by the expert must be generally accepted, the expert's opinion need not be. Thus, the judge reasoned, since the gas chromatography and mass spectrometry equipment used to detect the gases was generally accepted, the expert's claimed ability to analyse the data from those instruments need not be (State of Florida v. Casey Marie Anthony Case No. 48-2008-CF-015606-O, 2011: p. 21).

The judge's opinion, however, amazingly went further than allowing the anthropologist to give his database conclusions and also included some comments that would later be a factor in what the jury heard. The judge held:

> As pointed out in [a prosecution] article, the odor of putrefaction is characteristic and familiar to the front line criminal experts such as police investigators, forensic pathologists, anthropologists, entomologists, crime scene technicians and other medical and non-medical professionals. *It is simply common sense* that, to some extent, all of us have organoleptic expertise. Generally, we exercise the powers of sight, smell, and feel in our daily lives to detect odors and smells... Thus, [the prosecution expert], based upon his background and experience could offer testimony concerning the odor he smelled emanating from the sealed container (emphasis added). (State of Florida v. Casey Marie Anthony Case No. 48-2008-CF-015606-O, 2011: pp. 19–20)

The judge in effect ruled that the anthropologists, and apparently others, were lay experts whose noses can detect the odour of a dead human body as distinguished from any other odours, including that of other dead mammals. When the case went before the jury, the anthropologist not only testified to his conclusions from the organic compound testing but also was allowed to state that his olfactory senses were so attuned that he immediately knew the captured air was from a place where there had been a decomposing human:

> [The expert] recalled jumping back after opening the can of air. He said he could not believe such a tiny can could contain such a strong odor. He went on to say the odor was consistent with what he knows to be the smell of human decomposition, and went as far as to say he could not think of anything other than a dead and decomposing body that would explain the results he got from the samples he analyzed. (as reported by local news media in Fell et al., 2011b)

Following the judge's lead in the opinion, the prosecution was also even allowed to present the testimony of a tow truck driver that when he was towing the defendant's car, he could 'smell a dead body in the closed trunk' (as reported by local news media in Fell et al., 2011a).

Ultimately, the jury saw through it all and acquitted Anthony. The trial judge's opinions and rulings will never be subjected to appellate review.

Conclusion

Making a decision that can either deprive one person of liberty, even life, or endanger a whole community by releasing a guilty person is a daunting task. It is therefore an odd twist that the scientific evidence that we thought would give us more certainty in that determining an individual's guilt or innocence, has turned out in some cases to be the source itself of horrendous mistakes and miscarriages of justice.

The development of DNA that has shown the flaws in such evidence should lead true scientists to re-examine the premises of those forms of evidence and to attempt to prove or disprove their validity. It should also lead judges to re-examine the routine admissibility of such evidence in criminal trials. Indeed, notwithstanding the adversarial nature of our justice system, it should lead prosecutors to insulate forensic examiners from pro-prosecution influences and to be self-critical in their decisions to offer such evidence.

Unfortunately, we have seen little inclination by any of these professionals to follow that lead. Flawed forensic science continues to be offered and admitted in criminal trials. As long as it does so, the significant risk of miscarriages of justice will continue. Like other humans, these judicial participants develop an irrational loyalty to their beliefs and struggle to find evidence that supports their opinions and discredits or avoids information that does not. Let us hope that Max Planck was not right when he said:

> A new scientific truth does not triumph by convincing its opponents and making them see the light, but rather because its opponents eventually die, and a new generation grows up that is familiar with it.

References

Benedict, N. 2004. Fingerprints and the Daubert standard for admission of scientific evidence: Why fingerprints fail and a proposed remedy. *Arizona Law Review*, 46, 519–549.

Bowers, C. M. 2006. Problem-based analysis in bite mark misidentifications: The role of DNA. *Forensic Science International (Supp. 1)*, 159, S104–S109.

Bowers, C. M. 2013. Identification from bitemarks: Scientific issues. In: Faigman, D. L., Blumenthal, J. A., Cheng, E. K., Moonkin, J. L., Murphy, E. E., and Sanders, J. (eds.) *Modern Scientific Evidence: The Law and Science of Expert Testimony*, 2012–2013 edn. Eagan, MN: Thomson Reuters/West, vol. 5, pp. 30–85.

Cha, S.-H., Hina, A., Arora, H., and Klee, S. 2001. Individuality of handwriting: A validation study. *Proceedings of the 6th International Conference on Document Analysis and Recognition*, Seattle, WA, pp. 106–109. Available from: http://www.cedar.buffalo.edu/papers/articles/Individuality_Handwriting_2001.pdf, accessed March 05, 2013.

Cole, S. A. 2004. Grandfathering evidence: Fingerprint admissibility rulings from Jennings to Llera Plaza and back again. *American Criminal Law Review*, 1189, 1196–1197.

Cole, S. A. 2005. More than zero: Accounting for error in latent fingerprint identification. *The Journal of Criminal Law & Criminology*, 95, 985–1078.

Cole, S. A. 2006. The prevalence and potential causes of wrongful conviction by fingerprint evidence. *Golden Gate University Law Review*, 37, 39–105.

Criminal Cases Review Commission. 2011. Annual Report and Accounts 2010–2011. U.K. Government. Available from: http://www.ccrc.gov.uk/CCRC_Uploads/CCRCAnnualReportandAccounts2010-11.pdf, accessed March 02, 2013.

Epstein, R. 2002. Fingerprints meet Daubert: The myth of fingerprint "science". *Southern California Law Review*, 75, 605–658.

Faigman, D. L., Saks, M. J., Sanders, J., and Cheng, E. K. 2010. *Modern Scientific Evidence: The Law and Science of Expert Testimony*, 2009–2010 edn. Eagan, MN: Thomson Reuters/West.

Fell, J., Longo, A., and Cook, K. 2011a. Day 4: George Anthony questioned about smell in Casey's car. Central Florida News. Available from: http://www.baynews9. com/content/news/baynews9/news/article.html/content/news/articles/ot/ both/2011/05/27/Day_4_George_Anthony_questioned_about_smell_in_ Casey_s_car.html accessed March 03, 2013.

Fell, J., Longon, A., and Cook, K. 2011b. Expert smelled death in air samples from Casey Anthony's car. Central Florida News. Available from: http://www. cfnews13.com/article/news/2011/june/257538/, accessed March 03, 2013.

Findley, K. A. 2008. Innocents at risk: Adversary imbalance, forensic science, and the search for truth. *Seton Hall Law Review*, 38, 893–973.

Garavaglia, J. C. 2011. Testimony of Jan C. Garavaglia, M.D. State v. Anthony Ninth Judicial Circuit of Florida Case No. 48-2008-CF-015606-O. Available from: http://www.youtube.com/watch?feature=endscreen&NR=1&v=0a7W4IE6dJI, accessed March 03, 2013.

Garrett, B. L. 2008. Judging innocence. *108 Columbia Law Review*, 108, 55–142.

Garrett, B. L. 2011. *Convicting the Innocent: Where Criminal Prosecutions Go Wrong*. Cambridge, MA: Harvard University Press.

Giannelli, P. C. 2007. Bite mark analysis. *Criminal Law Bulletin*, 43, 930–936.

Goudge, S. T. 2008. Inquiry into forensic pediatric pathology in Ontario. Available from: http://www.attorneygeneral.jus.gov.on.ca/inquiries/goudge/index.html accessed January 24, 2012.

Groscup, J. L., Penrod, S. D., Studebaker, C. A., Huss, M. T., and O'neil, K. M. 2002. The effects of Daubert on the admissibility of expert testimony in state and federal criminal cases. *Psychology Public Policy and Law*, 8, 339.

Guthrie, C. 2007. Misjudging. *Nevada Law Journal*, 420, 438–440.

Haber, L. and Haber, R. N. 2008. Scientific validation of fingerprint evidence under Daubert. *Law, Probability and Risk*, 7, 87.

Hurst, G. 2004. Cameron Todd Willingham report of D. Gerald Hurst. Available from: http://www.scribd.com/doc/37712737/Gerald-Hurst-s-Report-on-Todd-Willingham-Arson-Investigation, accessed March 02, 2013.

Kohler, J. J. and Meixner, J. 2011. *Workshop on Cognitive Bias and Forensic Science*. Northwestern University School of Law, Chicago, IL. Available from: http:// www.law.northwestern.edu/faculty/conferences/workshops/cognitivebias/ documents/NSFWorkshopReportFinal.pdf, accessed March 03, 2013.

Kohn, D. 2009. Under the Microscope, CBS News 60 Minutes. Available from: http:// www.cbsnews.com/stories/2001/05/08/60II/main290046.shtml accessed January 24, 2012.

Law Commission. 2011. Expert evidence in criminal proceedings in England and Wales. Law Commission Report No. 325. Available from: http://www.official-documents.gov.uk/document/hc1011/hc08/0829/0829.pdf, accessed July 22, 2012.

Lissitzyn, C. B. 2007. *Forensic Evidence in Court: A Case Study Approach*. Durham, NC: Carolina Academic Press.

Malcom, B. G. 2008. Convictions predicated on DNA evidence alone: How reliable evidence became infallible. *Cumberland Law Review,* 38, 313–338.

Martin, A. 2011. The prosecution's case against DNA. New York Times Magazine. Available from: http://www.nytimes.com/2011/11/27/magazine/dna-evidence-lake-county.html?ref=magazine accessed March 02, 2013.

Mills, S. and Black, L. 2010. Learning victim's name not enough for new trial: Man convicted of 1999 murder recants confession prosecutors say case sound. Chicago Tribune. Available from: http://articles.chicagotribune.com/2010-10-11/news/ct-met-confession-conviction-new-vers20101011_1_murder-conviction-mary-kate-sunderlin-dna-evidence, accessed March 02, 2013.

Mills, S. and Possley, M. M. 2004. Man executed on disproved forensics. Chicago Tribune. Available from: http://www.chicagotribune.com/news/nationworld/chi-0412090169dec09,0,1173806.story, accessed March 02, 2013.

Moriarty, J. C. and Saks, M. J. 2005. Forensic science: Grand goals, tragic flaws, and judicial gatekeeping. *Judges' Journal,* 44, 16–33.

Muehlberger, R. J., Newman, K. W., Regent, J., and Wichmann, J. G. 1977. A statistical examination of selected handwriting characteristics. *Journal of Forensic Sciences,* 22, 206–215.

National Research Council. 2009. *Strengthening Forensic Science in the United States: A Path Forward.* Washington, DC: National Academies Press.

Neufeld, P. J. 2005. Irrelevance of Daubert to criminal justice and some suggestions for reform. *American Journal of Public Health,* 95, 107.

People v. Rivera [2011] Ill. App. 2d No. 091060. Available from: http://www.state.il.us/court/Opinions/AppellateCourt/2011/2ndDistrict/December/2091060.pdf, accessed March 02, 2013.

Pretty, I. A. 2003. A web-based survey of odontologist's opinions concerning bite-mark analyses. *Journal of Forensic Sciences,* 48, 1117–1120.

Pretty, I. and Turnbull, M. D. 2001. Lack of dental uniqueness between two bite mark suspects. *Journal of Forensic Sciences,* 46, 1487–1491.

Public Prosecution Service of Canada. 2011. *The Path to Justice: Preventing Wrongful Convictions.* Forensic evidence and expert testimony, Chapter 9. Available from: http://www.ppsc-sppc.gc.ca/eng/pub/ptj-spj/ch9.html accessed March 02, 2013.

Rawson, R. D., Ommen, R. K., Kinard, G., Johnson, J., and Yfantis, A. 1984. Statistical evidence for the individuality of the human dentition. *Journal of Forensic Sciences,* 29, 245–253.

Risinger, D. M. 2010. Handwriting identification. In: Faigman, D. L., Saks, M. J., Sanders, J., and Cheng, E. K. (eds.) *Modern Scientific Evidence: The Law and Science of Expert Testimony,* 2009–2010 edn. Eagan, MN: Thomson Reuters/West, pp. 451–643.

Saks, M. and Koehler, J. 2005. The coming paradigm shift in forensic identification science. *Science,* 309, 892–895.

Saks, M. J. and Vanderhaar, H. 2005. On the "General Acceptance" of handwriting identification principles. *Journal of the Forensic Sciences,* 50, 119–126.

Shelton, D. E. 2010a. Forensic science evidence and judicial bias in criminal cases. *Judges' Journal,* 49, 18.

Shelton, D. E. 2010b. Juror expectations for scientific evidence in criminal cases: Perceptions and reality about the "CSI effect" myth. *Thomas M. Cooley Law Review,* 27, 1–35.

Shelton, D. E., Barak, G., and Kim, Y. S. 2007. A study of juror expectations and demands concerning scientific evidence: Does the "CSI effect" exist? *Vanderbilt Journal of Entertainment and Technology Law*, 9, 331–368.

Shelton, D. E., Kim, Y. S., and Barak, G. 2009a. An indirect-effects model of mediated adjudication: The CSI myth, the tech effect, and Metropolitan jurors' expectations for scientific evidence. *Vanderbilt Journal of Entertainment and Technology Law*, 12, 9.

Shelton, D. E., Young, K. S., and Barak, G. 2009b. Examining the "CSI-effect" in the cases of circumstantial evidence and eyewitness testimony: Multivariate and path analyses. *Journal of Criminal Justice*, 37, 452–460.

Sognnaes, R. F., Rawson, R. D., Gratt, B. M., and Nguyen, N. B. 1982. Computer comparison of bitemark patterns in identical twins. *Journal of the American Dental Association*, 105, 449.

State of Florida v. Casey Marie Anthony Case No. 48-2008-CF-015606-O. 2011. Motion to exclude unreliable evidence. Ninth Judicial Circuit of Florida. Available from: http://www.ninthcircuit.org/news/High-Profile-Cases/Anthony/orders&motions.shtml accessed July 17, 2013.

Sweet, D. J. 1997. Human bitemarks: Examination, recovery, and analysis. In: Bowers, M. C. and Bell, G. L. (eds.) *Manual of Forensic Odontology*, 3rd edn. Colorado Springs, CO: American Society of Forensic Odontology, pp. 148–170.

The Innocence Project. n.d.-a. Homepage. Available from: http://www.innocenceproject.org/, accessed July 17, 2013.

The Innocence Project. n.d.-b. The Innocence Project: Stephen Cowans. Available from: http://www.innocenceproject.org/Content/Stephan_Cowans.php, accessed July 17, 2013.

The Washington Post. 2006. U.S. Senate Judiciary Committee Hearing on Judge Samuel Alito's Nomination to the Supreme Court—Transcript. Available from: http://www.washingtonpost.com/wp-dyn/content/article/2006/01/09/AR2006010901016.html accessed July 17, 2013.

Tulsky, F. N. 2007. How judges favor the prosecution. Mercury News.com. Available from: http://www.mercurynews.com/search/ci_5128172?IADID=Search-www.mercurynews.com-www.mercurynews.com, accessed March 03, 2013.

Uphoff, R. J. 2007. On misjudging and its implications for criminal defendants, their lawyers and the criminal justice system. *Nevada Law Journal*, 7, 521–547.

Vass, A. A., Smith, R. R., Thompson, C. V., Burnett, M. N., Dulgerian, N., and Eckenrode, B. A. 2008. Odor analysis of decomposing buried human remains. *Journal of Forensic Sciences*, 53, 384–391.

Vass, A. A., Smith, R. R., Thompson, C. V., Burnett, M. N., Wolf, D. A., Synstelien, J. A., Dulgerian, N., and Eckenrode, B. A. 2004. Decompositional odor analysis database. *Journal of Forensic Sciences*, 49, 1–10.

Wilkinson, A. P. and Gerughty, R. M. 1985. Bite mark evidence: Its admissibility is hard to swallow. *W. St. U. L. Rev.*, 12, 519.

Willingham v. State 897 S.W.2D 351 (Tex. Ct. Crim. App [1995]).

Yardley, J. 2001. Flaws in chemist's findings free man at Center of Inquiry. *New York Times*. Available from: http://www.nytimes.com/2001/05/08/us/flaws-in-chemist-s-findings-free-man-at-center-of-inquiry.html accessed January 16, 2012.

Future
Considerations
and Conclusions

V

Future of Forensic Science in the United Kingdom

20

ANDREW RENNISON

Contents

Introduction

The turbulence of the last 2 years has left many in the forensic science community feeling unsure and even worried about the future prospects of forensic science and forensic scientists in England and Wales. This is mirrored to a much lesser extent in Scotland and Northern Ireland; across the United Kingdom, forensic science is feeling the weight of change driven largely by financial pressures. However, whatever changes do occur, forensic science will continue to sit at the heart of criminal investigations by the police and other law enforcement bodies. The government sees it as '... vital for the smooth running of the criminal justice system, for fighting crime and combating terrorism' (U.K. Government, n.d.-b). How does this view of forensic science balance against the significant changes we have witnessed, for example, the closure of the Forensic Science Service (FSS)? What can we distil from recent events as indicators of the future of science in the criminal justice system? This chapter will explore recent events and the pressures for change as the context within which to assess the future of forensic science.

What Is Forensic Science?

The term 'forensic' is used as an adjective for the application of scientific methods and techniques to the investigation of crime or as a noun (forensics) for the tests and techniques used in support of such investigations (Oxford Dictionaries, n.d.). Forensic science as a generic label encompasses a broad range of science-based activities and even some that are not underpinned by any science. From a regulatory perspective, forensic science is broken down into identifiable facets of activity by forensic practitioners: crime scene investigations, the examination of victims and suspects, screening of exhibits, sampling, presumptive testing, laboratory analyses and interpretation and presentation of evidence. Occasional experts, such as forensic anthropologists, who generally work outside forensics but are brought in as and when needed, sometimes support these activities. It might seem odd to include nonscience methods, which flies in the face of the dictionary definition, but the earliest and still one of the most commonly used forensic methods for human identification, fingerprint comparison evidence, is not a science in that it is derived from a theory or coherent set of principles (U.K. Government, 2011a), but it does benefit from the disciplines and quality assurance that science methods routinely operate on.

Government Strategy

Political and government involvement in forensic science, as in every aspect of policing and criminal justice, is certainly not a new phenomenon and to be expected. Modern forensic science operates routinely a cross the United Kingdom at all levels of crime investigations and is the product of government investment and radical strategies, including the DNA expansion programme and the creation of a commercial market (in England and Wales) to provide forensic science laboratory services to the police and other law enforcement agencies (Cooper and Mason, 2009). These radical strategies have not always sat comfortably with practitioners or Parliament and have been the subject of two critical reports by the House of Commons Science and Technology Committee (U.K. Government, 2005b, 2011d), the latter exploring the government's decision to close, through a managed wind down, the FSS (U.K. Government, 2010). Who could have predicted such a fundamental change to the United Kingdom and global forensic science landscape? Such was the reach and reputation of the FSS that the announcement of the closure made in December 2010 sent shockwaves through the worldwide forensic science community. The decision to close the FSS will be debated and argued for years to come. Ministers decided on a managed wind down involving government support and funding as the best and only alternative to the FSS entering administration in early 2011, which would have seriously damaged the forensic capability to the criminal justice system (U.K. Government, 2011c). The closure was a consequence of the privatisation of forensic laboratory services which left the FSS unable to compete in a shrinking market shaped by reduced spending, as police forces managed cuts to their budgets.

At a different level, the political mix was evident in the Coalition Agreement (U.K. Government, n.d.-a) under the heading of 'Freedom, Fairness and Responsibility' as the government sought to introduce protections around the National DNA Database. This translated into the Protection of Freedoms Act (2012), which includes new rules for the retention and destruction of fingerprints, DNA samples and footwear impressions, as well as the creation of a new post of Commissioner for the Retention and Use of Biometric Material (U.K. Government, 2012a).

Add to these changes the government's planned reforms to the criminal justice system (U.K. Government, 2012b), which includes specific focus on forensic science with the plans for streamlined forensic reporting as a subset of the swift justice agenda.

There is no doubt that political and government strategies shape forensic science, no more so than through investment (such as the DNA expansion programme) or latterly the cuts in police budgets.

Police Budgets

It is difficult to assess the reductions in police spending on forensic science services since the announcement of the comprehensive spending review in October 2010 and to predict the shape and size of the market in the future. In evidence to the Science and Technology Committee, a Home Office Minister stated:

> The forensics market has drastically shrunk in recent years, from around £170 million in 2009 towards a projected figure of around £110 million by 2015. This reflects a range of factors including increased efficiency; closer work with prosecutors, and the completion of the previous Government's DNA Expansion Programme.

These figures represent the spending by police forces to purchase forensic laboratory services, but do not include the amounts spent internally by forces on activities such as crime scene investigations and fingerprint comparisons. Police spending in the commercial market that provides forensic science laboratory services is shrinking and is predicted to continue doing so. Equally, as police budgets continue to come under pressure to achieve savings, we can expect police forces to reduce their internal spending on forensic services and to seek new ways of working, for example, through regional collaboration programmes; an example is the joint project between Derbyshire, Nottinghamshire and Lincolnshire police forces who aim to save £9.5 million on forensic spending over a 4 year period (Derbyshire Police, 2012; East Midlands Police, 2009). This reshaping of police in-house forensic services will lead to the regionalisation of services, the insourcing of some services such as evidence recovery, and drugs and footwear analysis, but may yet in turn lead to outsourcing of other services to the private sector and challenge, for example, the traditional police in-house provision of fingerprint services.

Commercial Market

The strengths and weaknesses of the commercial model combined with police in-house activities will continue to be debated with a broad range of views (see the written evidence to the Science and Technology Committee). The model, through police contracts with the commercial providers, expects and measures laboratory turnaround times (from submission of sample to the laboratories to the return of results) in days rather than weeks and months; backlogs are not tolerated, and high quality is expected through regulated standards with processes in place to explore and repair quality failings. It puts decisions about forensic strategies in the hands of the police, who control the spending in each case; this works well where there are good lines of communication with the scientists at the laboratories, the police and Crown Prosecution Service (CPS) lawyers to give and receive advice. Communication expectations are set out in the CPS protocol for the supply of forensic science services to the police and the CPS (2005). It works less well where police decision making lacks scientific input or communications are poor.

Coalface Forensics

Forensic science is no longer the preserve of serious cases but is routinely called upon in support of the investigation of all levels of crime; it is an increasingly significant factor in both exceptional and routine investigations (Cooper and Mason, 2009) and produces quick, reliable results that provide early intelligence and evidence to identify offenders and link crimes, and drive effective decision making by investigators. This routine use of forensic sciences at the coalface of policing is the result of forensic science being transformed in every aspect (Barclay, 2009), with improvements in organisation supported by government funding, central support to police forces, investigative aids and the introduction of additional services such as the National Ballistics Intelligence Service (NABIS, n.d.).

Regulation

Where in this sea of change and modernisation does the role of the Forensic Science Regulator fit? The Regulator was brought in by the previous government as a safety valve to the commercialisation of the provision of forensic science services, to the police (Rennison, 2008; U.K. Government, 2006). The privatisation of forensic science services brought new risks to the quality of those services, as procurement programmes tested prices and challenged the relationships between quality, timeliness and price. The fear was that price reductions would have a negative impact on the quality or timeliness (through delayed results) of forensic analysis. The commercial market for forensic laboratory service provision is only part of the overall picture; the police manage a larger proportion of the activities that collectively make up the full spread of forensic science: crime scene investigations, fingerprint comparisons and some police in-house laboratory functions. The Regulator was given the task of managing the quality standards that apply to all aspects of forensic science, not just the commercially provided laboratory services. This has led to the police and the commercial laboratories working with the Regulator to drive standards through all aspects of forensic science provision and a move from the ad hoc approaches, to a single quality standards framework built on a code of practice (Rennison, 2011). The Regulator fills a position that is not underpinned by any legislation and has no powers. His functions were set out by the Secretary of State for the Home Department in a written ministerial statement in July 2007:

> ...to advise Government and the Criminal Justice System on quality standards in the provision of forensic science. This will involve identifying the requirement for new or improved quality standards; leading on the development of new standards where necessary; providing advice and guidance so that providers will be able to demonstrate compliance with common standards, for example, in procurement and the courts; ensuring that satisfactory arrangements exist to provide assurance and monitoring of the standards and reporting on quality standards generally.

Quality standards are also a European concern. In November 2009 the Council of the European Union agreed on measures to regulate the accreditation of fingerprint and DNA laboratory activities (Council of the European Union, 2009). This was followed in 2011 by plans to create a European forensic science area in which forensic science operates to common standards and good practice (Council of the European Union, 2011). The former requires that DNA laboratory activities be accredited against the BS/EN ISO 17025 laboratory standard by the end of November 2013 and fingerprint laboratory activities by the end of November 2015. The latter is still in the formative stages but has led to the formation of a European standards committee for forensic science services through CEN, the European Committee for Standardization (CEN/TC 419).

Expert Witnesses

Expert witnesses hold a unique status in the criminal courts; many forensic scientists and specialists provide evidence as expert witnesses. The use of expert witnesses is regulated by the Criminal Procedure Rules (U.K. Government, 2005a). In March 2011 the Law Commission entered the arena with the publication of its report on expert evidence in criminal proceedings (The Law Commission, 2011), which included a draft Criminal Evidence (Experts) Bill to give effect to its principal recommendations. The report sought to address concerns that expert opinion evidence was being admitted in criminal proceedings too readily, with insufficient scrutiny. The report is currently with the Ministry of Justice for a government response to the recommendations. The rules, case law and expectations that surround expert witnesses and the evidence they provide are confusing and place onerous duties on each expert. In an effort to support forensic science experts with these onerous duties, the Regulator has published guidance to experts in order that they can meet their obligations to the criminal justice system (Rennison, 2012).

Legal and Other Pressures

Since 2009 the Court of Appeal has issued a series of judgements that comment on forensic science (R v. Reed and Reed and Garmson [2009] EWCA Crim 2698, R v. T [2010] EWCA Crim 2439, R v. Smith [2011] EWCA Crim 1296), all of which make the Court's expectations of forensic science validity and quality abundantly clear. These cases sit alongside the Scottish public judicial inquiry into fingerprint evidence (Scottish Parliament, 2011) that asked searching and fundamental questions about fingerprint evidence while remaining comfortable with the basic tenet that fingerprint evidence is reliable.

The courts and others are asking correct questions about the reliability and validity of evidence that is provided by forensic scientists and other experts. In the United States, these questions were gathered into a single comprehensive review and report by the U.S. National Academies of Sciences

(National Research Council, 2009) and repeated in lectures by the U.S. judge who sat as the co-chair to the committee that produced the report (National Academy of Sciences, 2010).

Research

Science by its very nature is built on a solid bedrock of research. The closure of the FSS raised many questions about the future of forensic science research and development; the FSS was by no means the epicentre of forensic science research, but it did play a leading role through the years in the development of new methods and improvements to established techniques, of which the leading example is DNA profiling. Following the closure of the FSS, the United Kingdom's standing in the field of forensic science research has, in the eyes of the international forensic science community, been dented (U.K. Government, 2011b: see Q263).

Forensic science research and development was the subject of a review by the Home Office Chief Scientific Adviser, Professor Bernard Silverman (U.K. Government, 2011e), whose recommendations seek to build a more integrated research and development environment.

Conclusions

It is against this backdrop of government, judicial, financial, operational, research and quality pressures that the future of forensic science has to be assessed. An assessment undertaken 2 years ago would never have predicted the closure of the FSS; such is the scale, speed and extent of change that sets the context for forensic science now and in the future. Funding sits at the heart of these changes; the biggest single impact on forensic science now and in the immediate future is the level of funding that is available to police forces. In this aspect forensic science is no different from all areas of government spending and is not singled out for special treatment. That is not to say that funding will cease, but that the budgets will be reduced, probably by as much as a quarter. This is driving new ways of operating, particularly in the absence of the FSS as the dominant provider of laboratory services.

The judicial system is increasingly policing the Criminal Procedure Rules that set clear expectations and requirements for forensic experts. The disclosure rules and CPS guidance to experts set equally demanding requirements. The courts are making justifiable demands about the reliability and quality of science and expert evidence. In response to some of these pressures, a single and accessible quality standards framework is being established, a framework that is built on the cornerstones of organisational competence (forensic science is delivered by organisations that must have established quality management systems with accountability resting with those at the top), individual practitioner competence, validity of methods and evidence of impartiality (objective analysis and reporting of evidence and opinions).

Within this context of unmatched change built on a stable foundation of rules, quality standards and guidance, what does the future hold for forensic science? Investigators, prosecutors, defendants and their advisors and the courts will continue to look to science, technology and expertise to assist with their work in seeking justice at all levels of crime and criminality; the demand for forensic science will not diminish, and users will continue to expect fast and reliable results. In order to meet that demand for services aligned to swift justice within a difficult economic environment, we will continue to see reshaping of the models used to supply forensic science services as waste is cut from the system and efficiencies achieved through procurement strategies, economies of scale, better use of technology and generally better ways of working. For all its strengths, a system that relies on competition and market forces to deliver core laboratory analytical services leaves difficult questions regarding the risks inherent in a commercial market with shrinking revenues. We have already seen one provider close for business. What guarantees are there that others will not leave a diminishing market?

References

Barclay, D. 2009. Using forensic science in major inquiries. In: Fraser, J. and Williams, R. (eds.), *Handbook of Forensic Science*. Cullumpton, U.K.: Willan Publishing Ltd, pp. 337–358.

Cooper, A. and Mason, L. 2009. Forensic resources and criminal investigations. In: Fraser, J. and Williams, R. (eds.) *Handbook of Forensic Science*. Cullumpton, U.K.: Willan Publishing Ltd, pp. 285–308.

Council of the European Union. 2009. Council framework decision. Available from: http://eur-lex.europa.eu/LexUriServ/LexUriServ.do?uri=OJ:L:2009:322:0014:0016:EN:PDF, accessed March 06, 2013.

Council of the European Union. 2011. Council Conclusions on the Vision for European Forensic Science 2020 including the Creation of a European Forensic Science Area and the Development of Forensic Science Infrastructure in Europe. Available from: http://www.consilium.europa.eu/uedocs/cms_data/docs/pressdata/en/jha/126875.pdf, accessed March 06, 2013.

Crown Prosecution Service. 2005. Protocol for the supply of forensic science services to the Police and the Crown Prosecution Service. Available from: http://www.cps.gov.uk/publications/agencies/forensic.html accessed March 06, 2013.

Derbyshire Police. 2012. Three forces collaborate on forensic science. Available from: http://policeauthority.derbyshire.police.uk/Latest-News/Articles/2012/19Jun-EMPCForensic.aspx, accessed March 06, 2013.

East Midlands Police. 2009. East Midlands Police Collaboration for Policing 2009–2010. Available from: http://www.nottinghamshire.police.uk/uploads/library/476/Collaboration_Plan_2009–12.pdf, accessed March 06, 2013.

Nabis. n.d. Homepage. National Ballistics Intelligence Service. Available from: http://www.nabis.police.uk/, accessed March 06, 2013.

National Academy of Sciences. 2010. The National Academy of Sciences report on forensic sciences: What it means for the bench and bar. Available from: http://www.cadc.uscourts.gov/internet/home.nsf/AttachmentsByTitle/NAS+Report+on+Forensic+Science/$FILE/Edwards,+The+NAS+Report+on+Forensic+Science.pdf, accessed March 06, 2013.

National Research Council. 2009. *Strengthening Forensic Science in the United States: A Path Forward.* Washington, DC: National Academies Press.

Oxford Dictionaries. n.d. Forensic. Available from: http://oxforddictionaries.com/definition/english/forensic, accessed March 06, 2013.

R v. Reed and Reed and Garmson [2009] EWCA Crim 2698.

R v. Smith [2011] EWCA Crim 1296.

R v. T [2010] EWCA Crim 2439.

Rennison, A. 2008. Manual of regulation—Part 1: Policy and principles. *Forensic Science Regulator.* Available from: 1http://www.publications.parliament.uk/pa/cm200607/cmhansrd/cm070712/wmstext/70712m0002.htm-07071262000011 accessed March 06, 2011.

Rennison, A. 2012. Legal obligations. The Forensic Regulator. Available from: http://www.homeoffice.gov.uk/publications/agencies-public-bodies/fsr/legal-obligations/legal-obligations-issue-1?view=Binary, accessed March 06, 2013.

Rennison, A. 2011. Codes of practice and manual of regulation: Quality standards for forensic science service providers. The Forensic Regulator. Available from: http://www.homeoffice.gov.uk/agencies-public-bodies/fsr/codes-practice/, accessed March 06, 2013.

Scottish Parliament. 2011. *The Fingerprint Inquiry: Scotland.* Edinburgh, U.K.: APS Group Scotland. Available from: http://www.thefingerprintinquiryscotland.org.uk/inquiry/files/TheFingerprintInquiryReport_Low_res.pdf, accessed July 22, 2012.

The Law Commission. 2011. Expert evidence in criminal proceedings in England and Wales. Law Commission Report No 325. Available from: http://lawcommission.justice.gov.uk/docs/lc325_Expert_Evidence_Report.pdf, accessed July 22, 2012.

U.K. Government. 2005a. Criminal Procedure Rules [2005]: Part 33—Expert evidence. Available from: http://webarchive.nationalarchives.gov.uk/20091009065536/http://www.justice.gov.uk/criminal/procrules_fin/contents/rules/part_33.htm accessed March 06, 2013.

U.K. Government. 2005b. House of Commons Science and Technology Committee: Forensic science on trial—Seventh report of session 2004–05. The Stationary Office Limited, London, U.K. Available from: http://www.publications.parliament.uk/pa/cm200405/cmselect/cmsctech/96/96i.pdf, accessed March 04, 2013.

U.K. Government. 2006. Forensic Regulator: Consultation paper. Available from: http://webarchive.nationalarchives.gov.uk/+//http://www.homeoffice.gov.uk/documents/cons-2006-forensic-regulator/consultation-paper2835.pdf?view=Binary, accessed December 12, 2012.

U.K. Government. 2010a. Written ministerial statements: Home Department—Forensic Science. Available from: http://www.publications.parliament.uk/pa/cm201011/cmhansrd/cm101214/wmstext/101214m0001.htm-column_94WS accessed March 18, 2013.

U.K. Government. 2011a. Developing a quality standard for fingerprint examination. Home Office. Available from: http://www.homeoffice.gov.uk/publications/agencies-public-bodies/fsr/dev-quality-std-fingerprint-exam?view=Standard&pubID=969840, accessed March 06, 2013.

U.K. Government. 2011b. Examination of witnesses (Question Numbers 229–294). Available from: http://www.publications.parliament.uk/pa/cm201012/cmselect/cmsctech/855/11042702.htm accessed March 06, 2013.

U.K. Government. 2011c. The government response to the seventh report from the House of Commons Science and Technology Committee session 2010–12 HC 855: The Forensic Science Service. Home Department. Available from: http://www.official-documents.gov.uk/document/cm82/8215/8215.pdf, accessed March 18, 2013.

U.K. Government. 2011d. House of Commons Science and Technology Committee: The Forensic Science Service: Seventh report of session 2010–12. Available from: http://www.publications.parliament.uk/pa/cm201012/cmselect/cmsctech/855/85502.htm accessed March 05, 2013.

U.K. Government. 2011e. Research and development in forensic science: A review. Home Office. Available from: http://www.homeoffice.gov.uk/publications/agencies-public-bodies/fsr/forensic-science-review/, accessed March 18, 2013.

U.K. Government. 2012a. Protection of Freedoms Act [2012]. Available from: http://www.legislation.gov.uk/ukpga/2012/9/contents/enacted, accessed March 06, 2013.

U.K. Government. 2012b. Swift and Sure Justice: The Government's plans for reform of the criminal justice system. Ministry of Justice. Available from: http://www.justice.gov.uk/downloads/publications/policy/moj/swift-and-sure-justice.pdf, accessed March 18, 2010.

U.K. Government. 2010b. The Coalition Documentation. Available from: https://http://www.gov.uk/government/publications/the-coalition-documentation, accessed March 06, 2010.

U.K. Government. 2011f. Forensic Science. Home Office. Available from: http://www.homeoffice.gov.uk/science-research/research-statistics/science/forensic-science/, accessed March 06, 2011.

Index

I